THE
SUNDAY
2023

PEOPLE'S EDITION

Sundays Year A

From First Sunday of Advent 2022
to Christ the King 2023

Texts approved for use
in England and Wales, Scotland, and Ireland.

CATHOLIC
TRUTH
SOCIETY

Catholic Truth Society
42-46 Harleyford Road, London, SE11 5AY
First Published 2022

ISBN

The CTS Sunday Missal 2023 (RM41): 978 1 78469 743 3

Cover design, compilation and typographical design and layout
© 2022 Catholic Truth Society

Concordat cum originali: Paul Moynihan.

Nihil Obstat: The Reverend Monsignor Timothy Galligan.

Imprimatur: The Reverend Monsignor Matthew J Dickens VG.
12th July 2022, Feast of St John Jones, priest and martyr.

Acknowledgements:

The CTS is grateful for the help of the Association for Latin in the Liturgy in the preparation of this volume.

Extracts from scripture (excepting Psalm texts) from the Jerusalem Bible © 1966 Darton Longman and Todd and Doubleday & Company Inc.

The English translation of the Gospel Readings for the Palm Sunday Procession from the Catholic Edition of the Revised Standard Version of the Bible © 1965, 1966 by the Division of Christian Education of the National Council of the Churches of Christ in the United States of America. Used by permission. All rights reserved.

Psalm texts from the Grail Psalms © 1963 The Grail (England).

New English Translation 2010, granted recognitio by the Congregation for Divine Worship and the Discipline of the Sacraments, for the dioceses of the Bishops' Conferences of England and Wales (Prot. N. 915/06/L, 28 March 2010), and Scotland, (Prot. N. 1021/07/L, 23 June 2010), and Ireland (Prot. N. 516/05/L, 18 June 2010).

The English translation and chants of The Roman Missal © 2010, International Commission on English in the Liturgy Corporation. All rights reserved.

Latin text of Missale Romanum, Libreria Editrice Vaticana omnia sibi vindicat iura. Sine eiusdem licentia scripto data nemini liceat hunc Missale denuo imprimere aut in aliam linguam vertere © 2008, Libreria Editrice Vaticana.

Papal Magisterium used for introductions to feasts and seasons © Libreria Editrice Vaticana, Vatican City State.

Rite of Eucharistic Exposition and Benediction taken from *Holy Communion and Worship of the Eucharist Outside Mass* (The Roman Ritual) Vol. 1, Approved by the Bishops' Conference of England and Wales, Ireland and Scotland and confirmed by decree of the Sacred Congregation for the Sacraments and Divine Worship 29th May 1976.

Rosary Meditations and material for Preparation for Mass and Thanksgiving after Mass taken from *Eucharistic Adoration* D667 first published CTS, 2004.

TABLE OF CONTENTS

Preparation for Mass 5

The Order of Mass 9

Thanksgiving After Mass 152

27 November	First Sunday of Advent	161
30 November	Saint Andrew (Scotland)	165
4 December	Second Sunday of Advent	169
8 December	Immaculate Conception of the Blessed Virgin Mary	174
11 December	Third Sunday of Advent	180
18 December	Fourth Sunday of Advent	184
25 December	The Nativity of the Lord	188
30 December	The Holy Family of Jesus, Mary and Joseph	207
1 January	Solemnity of Mary, the Holy Mother of God	211
6 January	The Epiphany of the Lord (England, Wales & Ireland)	216
8 January	The Epiphany of the Lord (Scotland)	216
8 January	The Baptism of the Lord (England, Wales & Ireland)	224
9 January	The Baptism of the Lord (Scotland)	224
15 January	Second Sunday in Ordinary Time	230
22 January	Third Sunday in Ordinary Time	234
29 January	Fourth Sunday in Ordinary Time	238
2 February	The Presentation of the Lord (Candlemas)	242
5 February	Fifth Sunday in Ordinary Time	251
12 February	Sixth Sunday in Ordinary Time	254
19 February	Seventh Sunday in Ordinary Time	259
22 February	Ash Wednesday	263
26 February	First Sunday of Lent	271
1 March	Saint David (Wales)	277
5 March	Second Sunday of Lent	281
12 March	Third Sunday of Lent	286
17 March	Saint Patrick (Ireland)	292
19 March	Fourth Sunday of Lent	297
20 March	Saint Joseph	304
25 March	The Annunciation of the Lord	309
26 March	Fifth Sunday of Lent	314
2 April	Palm Sunday of the Passion of the Lord	320
	The Sacred Paschal Triduum	341
6 April	Thursday of the Lord's Supper	342
7 April	Friday of the Passion of the Lord	352
8 April	Easter Vigil	380
9 April	Easter Sunday Mass during the day	423
16 April	Second Sunday of Easter (Divine Mercy Sunday)	428

23 April	Third Sunday of Easter	433
24 April	Saint George (England)	438
30 April	Fourth Sunday of Easter	443
7 May	Fifth Sunday of Easter	447
14 May	Sixth Sunday of Easter	451
18 May	The Ascension of the Lord (England, Wales & Scotland)	455
21 May	The Ascension of the Lord (Ireland)	455
21 May	Seventh Sunday of Easter (England, Wales & Scotland)	464
28 May	Pentecost Sunday	468
4 June	The Most Holy Trinity	487
11 June	The Most Holy Body and Blood of Christ	492
16 June	The Most Sacred Heart of Jesus	499
18 June	Eleventh Sunday in Ordinary Time	505
24 June	The Nativity of Saint John the Baptist	509
25 June	Twelfth Sunday in Ordinary Time	518
29 June	Saints Peter and Paul	522
2 July	Thirteenth Sunday in Ordinary Time	532
9 July	Fourteenth Sunday in Ordinary Time	535
16 July	Fifteenth Sunday in Ordinary Time	538
23 July	Sixteenth Sunday in Ordinary Time	543
30 July	Seventeenth Sunday in Ordinary Time	547
6 August	The Transfiguration of the Lord	551
13 August	Nineteenth Sunday in Ordinary Time	556
15 August	The Assumption of the Blessed Virgin Mary	560
20 August	Twentieth Sunday in Ordinary Time	568
27 August	Twenty-First Sunday in Ordinary Time	572
3 September	Twenty-Second Sunday in Ordinary Time	575
10 September	Twenty-Third Sunday in Ordinary Time	579
17 September	Twenty-Fourth Sunday in Ordinary Time	583
24 September	Twenty-Fifth Sunday in Ordinary Time	586
1 October	Twenty-Sixth Sunday in Ordinary Time	590
8 October	Twenty-Seventh Sunday in Ordinary Time	594
15 October	Twenty-Eighth Sunday in Ordinary Time	598
22 October	Twenty-Ninth Sunday in Ordinary Time	602
29 October	Thirtieth Sunday in Ordinary Time	606
1 November	All Saints	609
2 November	The Commemoration of all the Faithful Departed	614
5 November	Thirty-First Sunday in Ordinary Time	621
12 November	Thirty-Second Sunday in Ordinary Time	624
19 November	Thirty-Third Sunday in Ordinary Time	627
26 November	Our Lord Jesus Christ, King of the Universe	632
Rite of Eucharistic Exposition and Benediction		637

PREPARATION FOR MASS

Prayer of Saint Ambrose

I draw near, loving Lord Jesus Christ,
to the table of your most
    delightful banquet
in fear and trembling,
a sinner, presuming not
    upon my own merits,
but trusting rather in your
    goodness and mercy.
I have a heart and body
    defiled by my many offences,
a mind and tongue
over which I have kept no good watch.
Therefore, O loving God,
    O awesome Majesty,
I turn in my misery, caught in snares,
to you the fountain of mercy,
hastening to you for healing,
flying to you for protection;
and while I do not look forward
    to having you as Judge,
I long to have you as Saviour.
To you, O Lord, I display my wounds,
to you I uncover my shame.
I am aware of my many and great sins,
for which I fear,
but I hope in your mercies,
which are without number.
Look upon me, then,
    with eyes of mercy,
Lord Jesus Christ, eternal King,
God and Man, crucified for mankind.
Listen to me,
    as I place my hope in you,
have pity on me, full of miseries
    and sins,
you, who will never cease
to let the fountain of compassion flow.
Hail, O Saving Victim,

Oratio S. Ambrosii

Ad mensam dulcissimi convivii tui,
    pie Domine Iesu Christe,
ego peccator de propriis meis
    meritis nihil præsumens,
sed de tua confidens misericordia
    et bonitate,
accedere vereor et contremisco.
Nam cor et corpus habeo multis
    criminibus maculatum,
mentem et linguam non
    caute custoditam.

Ergo, o pia Deitas,
    o tremenda maiestas,
ego miser,
    inter angustias deprehensus,
ad te fontem misericordiæ recurro,
ad te festino sanandus,
sub tuam protectionem fugio;
et, quem Iudicem sustinere nequeo,
Salvatorem habere suspiro.
Tibi, Domine, plagas meas ostendo,
tibi verecundiam meam detego.
Scio peccata mea multa
    et magna, pro quibus timeo:
spero in misericordias tuas,
    quarum non est numerus.
Respice ergo in me oculis
    misericordiæ tuæ,
Domine Iesu Christe, Rex æterne,
    Deus et homo,
crucifixus propter hominem.
Exaudi me sperantem in te:
miserere mei pleni miseriis
    et peccatis,
tu qui fontem miserationis
numquam manare cessabis.
Salve, salutaris victima,

offered for me and
    for the whole human race
on the wood of the Cross.

Hail, O noble and precious Blood,
flowing from the wounds
of Jesus Christ, my crucified Lord,
and washing away the sins
    of all the world.

Remember, Lord, your creature,
whom you redeemed by your Blood.
I am repentant of my sins,
I desire to put right what I have done.
Take from me, therefore, most
    merciful Father,
all my iniquities and sins,
so that, purified in mind and body,
I may worthily taste the Holy of Holies.
And grant that this sacred foretaste
of your Body and Blood
which I, though unworthy,
    intend to receive,
may be the remission of my sins,
the perfect cleansing of my faults,
the banishment of shameful thoughts,
and the rebirth of right sentiments;
and may it encourage
a wholesome and
    effective performance
of deeds pleasing to you
and be a most firm defence
    of body and soul
against the snares of my enemies.
Amen.

pro me et omni humano genere
    in patibulo Crucis oblata.

Salve, nobilis et pretiose Sanguis,
de vulneribus crucifixi Domini mei
    Iesu Christi profluens,
et peccata totius mundi abluens.

Recordare, Domine, creaturæ tuæ,
quam tuo Sanguine redemisti.
Pænitet me peccasse,
cupio emendare quod feci.
Aufer ergo a me, clementissime Pater,
omnes iniquitates et peccata mea,
ut, purificatus mente et corpore,
digne degustare merear
    Sancta sanctorum.
Et concede, ut hæc sancta
    prælibatio Corporis
    et Sanguinis tui,
quam ego indignus
    sumere intendo,
sit peccatorum meorum remissio,
sit delictorum perfecta purgatio,
sit turpium cogitationum effugatio
ac bonorum sensuum regeneratio,
operumque tibi placentium
    salubris efficacia,
animæ quoque et corporis
contra inimicorum meorum
    insidias firmissima tuitio.
Amen.

Prayer of Saint Thomas Aquinas

Almighty eternal God,
behold, I come to the Sacrament
of your Only Begotten Son,
our Lord Jesus Christ,
as one sick to the physician of life,
as one unclean to

Oratio S. Thomæ Aquinatis

Omnipotens sempiterne Deus,
ecce accedo ad sacramentum
    Unigeniti Filii tui,
Domini nostri Iesu Christi,
accedo tamquam infirmus
    ad medicum vitæ

the fountain of mercy,
as one blind to the light
of eternal brightness,
as one poor and needy to
the Lord of heaven and earth.
I ask, therefore, for the abundance
of your immense generosity,
that you may graciously cure
my sickness,
wash away my defilement,
give light to my blindness,
enrich my poverty,
clothe my nakedness,
so that I may receive
the bread of Angels,
the King of kings and Lord of lords,
with such reverence and humility,
such contrition and devotion,
such purity and faith,
such purpose and intention
as are conducive to the salvation of
my soul.
Grant, I pray, that I may receive
not only the Sacrament
of the Lord's Body and Blood,
but also the reality and power
of that Sacrament.
O most gentle God,
grant that I may so receive
the Body of your Only Begotten
Son our Lord Jesus Christ,
which he took from
the Virgin Mary,
that I may be made worthy
to be incorporated into his
Mystical Body
and to be counted among
its members.
O most loving Father,
grant that I may at last gaze for ever
upon the unveiled face

immundus ad
fontem misericordiæ,
cæcus ad lumen claritatis æternæ,
pauper et egenus ad
Dominum cæli et terræ.
Rogo ergo immensæ largitatis
tuæ abundantiam,
quatenus meam curare
digneris infirmitatem,
lavare fœditatem,
illuminare cæcitatem,
ditare paupertatem,
vestire nuditatem,
ut panem Angelorum,
Regem regum
et Dominum dominantium,
tanta suscipiam reverentia
et humilitate,
tanta contritione et devotione,
tanta puritate et fide,
tali proposito et intentione,
sicut expedit saluti animæ meæ.
Da mihi, quæso,
dominici Corporis et Sanguinis
non solum suscipere sacramentum,
sed etiam rem
et virtutem sacramenti.
O mitissime Deus,
da mihi Corpus Unigeniti Filii tui,
Domini nostri Iesu Christi,
quod traxit de Virgine Maria,
sic suscipere,
ut corpori suo mystico
merear incorporari
et inter eius membra connumerari.

O amantissime Pater,
concede mihi dilectum
Filium tuum,

of your beloved Son,
whom I, a wayfarer,
propose to receive now veiled
    under these species:
Who lives and reigns with you
    for ever and ever.
Amen.

quem nunc velatum
    in via suscipere propono,
revelata tandem facie
    perpetuo contemplari:
Qui tecum vivit et regnat
in sæcula sæculorum.
Amen.

PRAYER BEFORE MASS

O God, to whom every heart is open, every desire known and from whom
no secrets are hidden; purify the thoughts of our hearts by the inspiration
of your Holy Spirit, that we may perfectly love you, and worthily praise
your holy name. Amen.

Before Holy Communion

Prayer for Help

O God, help me to make a good Communion. Mary, my dearest mother,
pray to Jesus for me. My dear Angel Guardian, lead me to the Altar of God.

Act of Faith

O God, because you have said it, I believe that I shall receive the Sacred
Body of Jesus Christ to eat, and his Precious Blood to drink. My God, I
believe this with all my heart.

Act of Humility

My God, I confess that I am a poor sinner; I am not worthy to receive the
Body and Blood of Jesus, on account of my sins. Lord, I am not worthy
to receive you under my roof; but only say the word, and my soul will
be healed.

Act of Sorrow

My God, I detest all the sins of my life. I am sorry for them, because they
have offended you, my God, you who are so good. I resolve never to commit
sin any more. My good God, pity me, have mercy on me, forgive me.

Act of Adoration

O Jesus, great God, present on the Altar, I bow down before you.
I adore you.

Act of Love and Desire

Jesus, I love you. I desire with all my heart to receive you. Jesus, come into
my poor soul, and give me your Flesh to eat and your Blood to drink.

Give me your whole Self, Body, Blood, Soul and Divinity, that I may live
for ever with you.

THE ORDER OF MASS

ORDO MISSÆ CUM POPULO

THE INTRODUCTORY RITES

Before Mass begins, the people gather in a spirit of recollection, preparing for their participation in the Mass.

All stand during the entrance procession.

SIGN OF THE CROSS

After the Entrance Chant, the Priest and the faithful sign themselves with the Sign of the Cross:

Priest: In nómine Patris, et Fílii, et Spíritus Sancti.

A-men.

Response: **Amen.**

GREETING

The Priest greets the people, with one of the following:

1. Pr. Grátia Dómini nostri Iesu Christi,
   et cáritas Dei,
   et communicátio Sancti Spíritus
   sit cum ómnibus vobis.

Et cum spí-ri-tu tu-o.

   R. **Et cum spíritu tuo.**

2. Pr. Grátia vobis et pax a Deo Patre nostro
   et Dómino Iesu Christo.
   R. **Et cum spíritu tuo.**

3. Pr. Dóminus vobíscum.
   R. **Et cum spíritu tuo.**

The Priest, or a Deacon, or another minister, may very briefly introduce the faithful to the Mass of the day.

THE ORDER OF MASS WITH A CONGREGATION

THE INTRODUCTORY RITES

Before Mass begins, the people gather in a spirit of recollection, preparing for their participation in the Mass.

All stand during the entrance procession.

SIGN OF THE CROSS

After the Entrance Chant, the Priest and the faithful sign themselves with the Sign of the Cross:

Priest: In the name of the Father, and of the Son, and of the Holy Spirit.

A-men.

Response: Amen.

GREETING

The Priest greets the people, with one of the following:

1. **Pr.** **The grace of our Lord Jesus Christ,**
   and the love of God,
   and the communion of the Holy Spirit
   be with you all.

And with your spir-it.

   R. And with your spirit.

2. **Pr.** **Grace to you and peace from God our Father**
   and the Lord Jesus Christ.
   R. And with your spirit.

3. **Pr.** **The Lord be with you.**
   R. And with your spirit.

The Priest, or a Deacon, or another minister, may very briefly introduce the faithful to the Mass of the day.

PENITENTIAL ACT*

There are three forms of the Penitential Act which may be chosen from as appropriate.
Each Penitential Act begins with the invitation to the faithful by the Priest:

Pr. Fratres, agnoscámus peccáta nostra,
    ut apti simus ad sacra mystéria celebránda.

A brief pause for silence follows.

Then one of the following forms is used:

**1. Confíteor Deo omnipoténti et vobis, fratres,
quia peccávi nimis
cogitatióne, verbo, ópere et omissióne:**

(and, striking their breast, they say:)

**mea culpa, mea culpa, mea máxima culpa.
Ideo precor beátam Mariám semper Vírginem,
omnes Angelos et Sanctos,
et vos, fratres, oráre pro me
ad Dóminum Deum nostrum.**

---

2. Pr. Miserére nostri, Dómine.

Qui- a peccá- vi- mus ti- bi.

R. **Quia peccávimus tibi.**

Pr. Osténde nobis, Dómine, misericórdiam tuam.

Et sa- lu- tá- re tu- um da no- bis.

R. **Et salutáre tuum da nobis.**

---

* From time to time on Sundays, especially in Easter Time, instead of the customary Penitential
Act, the blessing and sprinkling of water may take place (as in pp.16-21) as a reminder of Baptism.

PENITENTIAL ACT*

There are three forms of the Penitential Act which may be chosen from as appropriate. Each Penitential Act begins with the invitation to the faithful by the Priest:

Pr. **Brethren (brothers and sisters),**
let us acknowledge our sins,
and so prepare ourselves to celebrate the sacred mysteries.

A brief pause for silence follows.

Then one of the following forms is used:

---

1. I confess to almighty God
and to you, my brothers and sisters,
that I have greatly sinned,
in my thoughts and in my words,
in what I have done and in what I have failed to do,

(and, striking their breast, they say:)

through my fault, through my fault,
through my most grievous fault;
therefore I ask blessed Mary ever-Virgin,
all the Angels and Saints,
and you, my brothers and sisters,
to pray for me to the Lord our God.

---

2. **Pr.** Have mercy on us, O Lord.

For we have sinned a-gainst you.

R. **For we have sinned against you.**

Pr. Show us, O Lord, your mercy.

And grant us your sal-va-tion.

R. **And grant us your salvation.**

---

* From time to time on Sundays, especially in Easter Time, instead of the customary Penitential Act, the blessing and sprinkling of water may take place (as in pp.16-21) as a reminder of Baptism.

Invocations naming the gracious works of the Lord may be made, as in the example below:

3. Pr. Qui missus es sanáre contrítos corde:
    Kýrie, eléison.

Ký- ri- e,   e- lé- i- son.

R. **Kýrie, eléison.**

Pr. Qui peccatóres vocáre venísti:
    Christe, eléison.

Chri- ste,   e- lé- i- son.

R. **Christe, eléison.**

Pr. Qui ad déxteram Patris sedes, ad interpellándum pro nobis:
    Kýrie, eléison.

Ký- ri- e,   e- lé- i- son.

R. **Kýrie, eléison.**

The absolution by the Priest follows:

Pr. Misereátur nostri omnípotens Deus
    et, dimíssis peccátis nostris,
    perdúcat nos ad vitam ætérnam.

A-men.

R. **Amen.**

The **Kýrie, eléison** (Lord, have mercy) invocations follow, unless they have just occurred.

Pr. Kýrie, eléison.

y-ri-e,   e-lé- i-son.

Invocations naming the gracious works of the Lord may be made, as in the example below:

3. Pr. You were sent to heal the contrite of heart:
Lord, have mercy. Or: Kýrie, eléison.

 Or: repeat music/words from Latin, p.14.

Lord, have mer-cy.

R. **Lord, have mercy.**

Pr. You came to call sinners:
Christ, have mercy. Or: Christe, eléison.

 Or: repeat music/words from Latin, p.14.

Christ, have mer-cy.

R. **Christ, have mercy.**

Pr. You are seated at the right hand of the Father to intercede for us:
Lord, have mercy. Or: Kýrie, eléison.

 Or: repeat music/words from Latin, p.14.

Lord, have mer-cy.

R. **Lord, have mercy.**

The absolution by the Priest follows:

Pr. May almighty God have mercy on us,
forgive us our sins,
and bring us to everlasting life.

A-men.

R. **Amen.**

The **Kýrie, eléison** (**Lord, have mercy**) invocations follow, unless they have just occurred.

Pr. Lord, have mercy.

R. Lord, have mer-cy.

Pr. Christe, eléison.

R.   Chris-te, e-lé-i-son.

Pr. Kýrie eléison.

R.   Ky-ri-e,   e-lé-i-son.   Vel: R.   Ky-ri-e,   e- lé- i-son.

RITE FOR THE BLESSING AND SPRINKLING OF WATER

If this rite is celebrated during Mass, it takes the place of the usual Penitential Act at the beginning of Mass. After the greeting, the Priest calls upon the people to pray in these or similar words:

Dominum Deum nostrum, fratres carissimi,
suppliciter deprecemur,
ut hanc creaturam aquæ benedicere dignetur,
super nos aspergendam in nostri memoriam baptismi.
Ipse autem nos adiuvare dignetur,
ut fideles Spiritui, quem accepimus, maneamus.

And after a brief pause for silence, he continues with hands joined:

Omnipotens sempiterne Deus, qui voluisti ut per aquam,
fontem vitæ ac purificationis principium,
etiam animæ mundarentur
æternæque vitæ munus exciperent,
dignare, quæsumus, hanc aquam ✠ benedicere,
qua volumus hac die tua, Domine, communiri.
Fontem vivum in nobis tuæ gratiæ renovari
et ab omni malo spiritus et corporis
per ipsam nos defendi concedas,
ut mundis tibi cordibus propinquare
tuamque digne salutem valeamus accipere.
Per Christum Dominum nostrum.
R. Amen.

Pr. Christ, have mercy.

R. Christ, have mer-cy.

Pr. Lord, have mercy.

R. Lord, have mer-cy.

RITE FOR THE BLESSING AND SPRINKLING OF WATER

If this rite is celebrated during Mass, it takes the place of the usual Penitential Act at the beginning of Mass. After the greeting, the Priest calls upon the people to pray in these or similar words:

Dear brethren (brothers and sisters),
let us humbly beseech the Lord our God
to bless this water he has created,
which will be sprinkled on us
as a memorial of our Baptism.
May he help us by his grace
to remain faithful to the Spirit we have received.

And after a brief pause for silence, he continues with hands joined:

Almighty ever-living God,
who willed that through water,
the fountain of life and the source of purification,
even souls should be cleansed
and receive the gift of eternal life;
be pleased, we pray, to ✠ bless this water,
by which we seek protection on this your day, O Lord.
Renew the living spring of your grace within us
and grant that by this water we may be defended
from all ills of spirit and body,
and so approach you with hearts made clean
and worthily receive your salvation.
Through Christ our Lord.
R. Amen.

Or:

Domine Deus omnipotens,
qui es totius vitæ corporis et animæ fons et origo,
hanc aquam, te quæsumus, ✠ benedicas,
qua fidenter utimur
ad nostrorum implorandam veniam peccatorum
et adversus omnes morbos inimicique insidias
tuæ defensionem gratiæ consequendam.
Præsta, Domine, ut, misericordia tua interveniente,
aquæ vivæ semper nobis saliant in salutem,
ut mundo tibi corde appropinquare possimus,
et omnia corporis animæque pericula devitemus.
Per Christum Dominum nostrum.
℟. Amen.

Or, during Easter Time:

Domine Deus omnipotens,
precibus populi tui adesto propitius;
et nobis, mirabile nostræ creationis opus,
sed et redemptionis nostræ mirabilius, memorantibus,
hanc aquam ✠ benedicere tu dignare.
Ipsam enim tu fecisti,
ut et arva fecunditate donaret,
et levamen corporibus nostris munditiamque præberet.
Aquam etiam tuæ ministram misericordiæ condidisti;
nam per ipsam solvisti tui populi servitutem,
illiusque sitim in deserto sedasti;
per ipsam novum foedus nuntiaverunt prophetæ,
quod eras cum hominibus initurus;
per ipsam denique, quam Christus in Iordane sacravit,
corruptam naturæ nostræ substantiam
in regenerationis lavacro renovasti.
Sit igitur hæc aqua nobis suscepti baptismatis memoria,
et cum fratribus nostris, qui sunt in Paschate baptizati,
gaudia nos tribuas sociare.
Per Christum Dominum nostrum.
℟. Amen.

Or:

Almighty Lord and God,
who are the source and origin of all life,
whether of body or soul,
we ask you to ✠ bless this water,
which we use in confidence
to implore forgiveness for our sins
and to obtain the protection of your grace
against all illness and every snare of the enemy.
Grant, O Lord, in your mercy,
that living waters may always spring up for our salvation,
and so may we approach you with a pure heart
and avoid all danger to body and soul.
Through Christ our Lord.
R. Amen.

Or, during Easter Time:

Lord our God,
in your mercy be present to your people's prayers,
and, for us who recall the wondrous work of our creation
and the still greater work of our redemption,
graciously ✠ bless this water.
For you created water to make the fields fruitful
and to refresh and cleanse our bodies.
You also made water the instrument of your mercy:
for through water you freed your people from slavery
and quenched their thirst in the desert;
through water the Prophets proclaimed the new covenant
you were to enter upon with the human race;
and last of all,
through water, which Christ made holy in the Jordan,
you have renewed our corrupted nature
in the bath of regeneration.
Therefore, may this water be for us
a memorial of the Baptism we have received,
and grant that we may share
in the gladness of our brothers and sisters
who at Easter have received their Baptism.
Through Christ our Lord.
R. Amen.

Where the circumstances of the place or the custom of the people suggest that the mixing of salt be preserved in the blessing of water, the Priest may bless salt, saying:

Supplices te rogamus, omnipotens Deus,
ut hanc creaturam salis
benedicere ✠ tua pietate digneris,
qui per Eliseum prophetam in aquam mitti eam iussisti,
ut sanaretur sterilitas aquæ.
Præsta, Domine, quæsumus,
ut, ubicumque hæc salis et aquæ commixtio
fuerit aspersa,
omni impugnatione inimici depulsa,
præsentia Sancti tui Spiritus nos iugiter custodiat.
Per Christum Dominum nostrum.
R. Amen.

Then he pours the salt into the water, without saying anything.
Afterward, taking the aspergillum, the Priest sprinkles himself and the ministers, then the clergy and people, moving through the church, if appropriate.
Meanwhile, one of the following chants, or another appropriate chant is sung.

Outside Easter Time

Antiphon   Ps 50:9
Asperges me, Domine, hyssopo et mundabor:
lavabis me, et super nivem dealbabor.

During Easter Time

Antiphon   Cf. Ez 47:1-2,9
Vidi aquam egredientem de templo,
a latere dextro, alleluia;
et omnes, ad quos pervenit aqua ista, salvi facti sunt,
et dicent: alleluia, alleluia.

When he returns to his chair and the singing is over, the Priest stands facing the people and, with hands joined, says:

Deus omnipotens nos a peccatis purificet,
et per huius Eucharistiæ celebrationem dignos nos reddat,
qui mensæ regni sui participes efficiamur.
R. Amen.

Then, when it is prescribed, the hymn Gloria in excelsis (Glory to God in the highest) is sung or said.

Where the circumstances of the place or the custom of the people suggest that the mixing of salt be preserved in the blessing of water, the Priest may bless salt, saying:

We humbly ask you, almighty God:
be pleased in your faithful love to bless ✠ this salt
you have created,
for it was you who commanded the prophet Elisha
to cast salt into water,
that impure water might be purified.
Grant, O Lord, we pray,
that, wherever this mixture of salt and water is sprinkled,
every attack of the enemy may be repulsed
and your Holy Spirit may be present
to keep us safe at all times.
Through Christ our Lord.
R. **Amen.**

Then he pours the salt into the water, without saying anything.

Afterward, taking the aspergillum, the Priest sprinkles himself and the ministers, then the clergy and people, moving through the church, if appropriate.

Meanwhile, one of the following chants, or another appropriate chant is sung.

Outside Easter Time

Antiphon   Ps 50:9

Sprinkle me with hyssop, O Lord, and I shall be cleansed;
wash me and I shall be whiter than snow.

During Easter Time

Antiphon   Cf. Ez 47:1-2,9

I saw water flowing from the Temple,
from its right-hand side, alleluia:
and all to whom this water came
were saved and shall say: alleluia, alleluia.

When he returns to his chair and the singing is over, the Priest stands facing the people and, with hands joined, says:

May almighty God cleanse us of our sins,
and through the celebration of this Eucharist
make us worthy to share at the table of his Kingdom.
R. **Amen.**

Then, when it is prescribed, the hymn **Gloria in excelsis** (**Glory to God in the highest**) is sung or said.

THE GLORIA

On Sundays (outside Advent and Lent), Solemnities and Feast Days, this hymn is
either sung or said:

Gló-ri-a in ex-cél-sis De- o. Et in ter-ra pax ho-mí-ni-bus bo-næ

vol-un-tá-tis. Lau-dá- mus te. Be-ne-dí-ci-mus te   Ado-rá-

mus te. Glo-ri-fi-cámus te.   Grá-ti- as á-gi-mus ti-bi   prop-ter

mag-nam gló-ri-am tu-am. Dó-mi-ne De- us, Rex cæ-léstis,   De-us

Pa-ter om-ní-po-tens. Dómi-ne Fi-li uni-gé-ni-te,   Ie-su Christe.

Dómi-ne De-us, Agnus De-i,   Fí-li-us Pa-tris, Qui tollis peccáta

mun- di,   mi-se-ré- re nobis. Qui tollis peccáta mundi,   súscipe de-

pre-ca-ti-ó-nem no- stram. Qui sedes ad déxteram Patris,   mi-seré-

THE GLORIA

On Sundays (outside Advent and Lent), Solemnities and Feast Days, this hymn is either sung or said:

Glo-ry to God in the high-est,

and on earth peace to peo-ple of good will.

We praise you, we bless you, we a-dore you, we glo-ri-fy you,

we give you thanks for your great glo-ry,

Lord God, heav-en-ly King, O God, al-might-y Fa-ther.

Lord Je-sus Christ, On-ly Be-got-ten Son,

Lord God, Lamb of God, Son of the Fa-ther,

you take a-way the sins of the world, have mer-cy on us;

you take a-way the sins of the world, re-ceive our prayer;

you are seat-ed at the right hand of the Fa-ther, have mer-cy on us.

re nobis. Quóni-am tu solus Sanctus. Tu solus Dó-mi-nus Tu so-

lus Al-tíssimus, Ie-su Christe. Cum Sancto Spí-ri-tu, in gló-ri-a

De- i Pa- tris. A- men.

**Glória in excélsis Deo
et in terra pax homínibus bonæ voluntátis.**

**Laudámus te,
benedícimus te,
adorámus te,
glorificámus te,
grátias ágimus tibi propter magnam glóriam tuam,
Dómine Deus, Rex cæléstis,
Deus Pater omnípotens.**

**Dómine Fili Unigénite, Iesu Christe,
Dómine Deus, Agnus Dei, Fílius Patris,
qui tollis peccáta mundi, miserére nobis;
qui tollis peccáta mundi, súscipe deprecatiónem nostram.
Qui sedes ad déxteram Patris, miserére nobis.**

**Quóniam tu solus Sanctus, tu solus Dóminus, tu solus Altíssimus,
Iesu Christe, cum Sancto Spíritu: in glória Dei Patris.
Amen.**

When this hymn is concluded, the Priest, says: **Pr. Orémus.**
And all pray in silence. Then the Priest says the Collect prayer, which ends:
R. Amen.

For you a-lone are the Ho-ly One, you a-lone are the Lord, you a-lone are the Most High, Je-sus Christ, with the Ho-ly Spir-it, in the glo-ry of God the Fa - ther. A - men.

Glory to God in the highest,
and on earth peace to people of good will.

We praise you,
we bless you,
we adore you,
we glorify you,
we give you thanks for your great glory,
Lord God, heavenly King,
O God, almighty Father.

Lord Jesus Christ, Only Begotten Son,
Lord God, Lamb of God, Son of the Father,
you take away the sins of the world, have mercy on us;
you take away the sins of the world, receive our prayer;
you are seated at the right hand of the Father,
have mercy on us.

For you alone are the Holy One,
you alone are the Lord,
you alone are the Most High,
Jesus Christ,
with the Holy Spirit,
in the glory of God the Father.
Amen.

When this hymn is concluded, the Priest, says: **Pr.** **Let us pray.**
And all pray in silence. Then the Priest says the Collect prayer, which ends:
R. **Amen.**

THE LITURGY OF THE WORD

By hearing the word proclaimed in worship, the faithful again enter into the unending dialogue between God and the covenant people.

FIRST READING

The reader goes to the ambo and proclaims the First Reading, while all sit and listen. The reader ends:

Verbum Dómini.

De- o grá- ti- as

R. **Deo grátias.**

It is appropriate to have a brief time of quiet between readings as those present take the word of God to heart.

PSALM

The psalmist or cantor sings or says the Psalm, with the people making the response.

SECOND READING

On Sundays and certain other days there is a second reading. The reader ends:

Verbum Dómini.

De- o grá- ti- as

R. **Deo grátias.**

GOSPEL

The assembly stands for the Gospel Acclamation. Except during Lent the Acclamation is:

R. **Allelúia!**

During Lent the following forms may be used or another similar phrase:

R. **Laus tibi, Christe, Rex ætérnæ glóriæ!** Or:

R. **Laus et honor tibi, Dómine Iesu!** Or:

R. **Glória et laus tibi, Christe!** Or:

R. **Glória tibi, Christe, Verbo Dei!**

THE LITURGY OF THE WORD

By hearing the word proclaimed in worship, the faithful again enter into the unending dialogue between God and the covenant people.

FIRST READING

The reader goes to the ambo and proclaims the First Reading, while all sit and listen. The reader ends:

The word of the Lord.

Thanks be to God.

R. **Thanks be to God.**

It is appropriate to have a brief time of quiet between readings as those present take the word of God to heart.

PSALM

The psalmist or cantor sings or says the Psalm, with the people making the response.

SECOND READING

On Sundays and certain other days there is a second reading. The reader ends:

The word of the Lord.

Thanks be to God.

R. **Thanks be to God.**

GOSPEL

The assembly stands for the Gospel Acclamation. Except during Lent the Acclamation is:

R. **Alleluia!**

During Lent the following forms may be used or another similar phrase:

R. **Praise to you, O Christ, king of eternal glory!** Or:

R. **Praise and honour to you, Lord Jesus!** Or:

R. **Glory and praise to you, O Christ!** Or:

R. **Glory to you, O Christ, you are the Word of God!**

At the ambo the Deacon, or the Priest says:

Pr. **Dóminus vobíscum.**

   Et cum spíritu tuo.

R. **Et cum spíritu tuo.**

Pr. **Léctio sancti Evangélii secúndum N.**

He makes the Sign of the Cross on the book and, together with the people, on his forehead, lips, and breast.

   Glória tibi Dómine.

R. **Glória tibi, Dómine.**

At the end of the Gospel:

Pr. **Verbum Dómini.**

   Laus ti-bi, Christe.

R. **Laus tibi, Christe.**

THE HOMILY

Then follows the Homily, which is preached by a Priest or Deacon on all Sundays and Holydays of Obligation. After a brief silence all stand.

THE CREED

On Sundays and Solemnities, the Profession of Faith will follow. Especially during Lent and Easter Time, the Apostles' Creed may be used.

THE NICENO-CONSTANTINOPOLITAN CREED

Credo in unum De- um, Patrem omni-poténtem factó-rem cæli et terræ, vi-sibili-um óm-nium et invi-si-bí- lium. Et in unum Dó-

At the ambo the Deacon, or the Priest says:

Pr. **The Lord be with you.**

And with your spir-it.

R. **And with your spirit.**

Pr. A reading from the holy Gospel according to N.

He makes the Sign of the Cross on the book and, together with the people, on his forehead, lips, and breast.

Glory to you, O Lord.

R. **Glory to you, O Lord.**

At the end of the Gospel:

Pr. **The Gospel of the Lord.**

Praise to you, Lord Je-sus Christ.

R. **Praise to you, Lord Jesus Christ.**

THE HOMILY

Then follows the Homily, which is preached by a Priest or Deacon on all Sundays and Holydays of Obligation. After a brief silence all stand.

THE CREED

On Sundays and Solemnities, the Profession of Faith will follow. Especially during Lent and Easter Time, the Apostles' Creed may be used.

THE NICENO-CONSTANTINOPOLITAN CREED

I be-lieve in one God,   the Fa-ther al-might-y,   mak-er of heav-en and earth,   of all things   vis-i-ble and in-vis-i-ble.

minum Iesum Christum, Fí-lium De-i uni-gé-ni-tum. Et ex Pa-

tre na- tum ante ómni-a sæ- cu-la. De-um de De-o, lumen de

lumine, De-um verum de De-o vero. Géni-tum, non fac-tum, con-

substanti-á-lem Patri: per quem ómni-a facta sunt. Qui propter nos

homines et propter nostram sa-lútem descéndit de cæ-lis. Et in-

At the words that follow, up to and including **et homo factus est**, all bow.

carná-tus est de Spí-ri-tu Sancto ex Ma-rí-a Vírgi-ne, et homo

factus est. Cru-ci-fí- xus é-ti-am pro nobis sub Pónti-o Pi-lá-to,

passus et sepúl- tus est. Et resurré-xit térti-a di-e, secúndum Scrip-

turas, Et ascéndit in cæ- lum, sedet ad déxteram Patris. Et í-terum

I be-lieve in one Lord Je-sus Christ, the Only Be-got-ten Son of God, born of the Father be-fore all a-ges. God from God, Light from Light, true God from true God, be-got-ten, not made, con-sub-stan-tial with the Fa-ther; through him all things were made. For us men and for our sal-va-tion he came down from heav-en,

At the words that follow, up to and including **and became man**, all bow.

and by the Ho-ly Spir-it was in-car-nate of the Vir-gin Mar-y, and be-came man.

For our sake he was cru-ci-fied un-der Pon-tius Pi-late, he suffered death and was bur-ied, and rose a-gain on the third day in accordance with the Scrip-tures. He as-cend-ed in-to heav-en ventúrus est cum gló-ri-a,   iudicá-re vivos et mórtu-os, cu-ius reg-

ni non e-rit fi-nis.   Et in Spí-ri-tum Sanctum, Dóminum   et vi-vi-

fi-cántem: qui ex Patre Fi-li-óque pro-cédit.   Qui cum Patre et Fí-

li-o   simul adorá-tur   et conglo-ri-ficá-tur: qui locú-tus est per

prophé-tas.   Et unam, sanctam, cathó-li-cam et apostó-li-cam Ec-

clé-si-am. Confí-te-or unum baptísma   in remissi - ónem pec-ca

tó-rum. Et exspécto resurrecti-ó-nem mortu-ó-rum. Et vi-tam ven-

túri sæ-cu-li.   A-   men

and is seated at the right hand of the Fa-ther.   He will come a-gain
in glo-ry   to judge the living and the dead   and his kingdom will
have no end.

I be-lieve in the Ho-ly Spir-it,   the Lord, the giv-er of life,   who
pro-ceeds from the Father and the Son,   who with the Fa-ther and
the Son   is   adored and glo-ri-fied,   who has spoken through the
proph-ets.   I be-lieve in one, ho-ly, ca-tho-lic   and a-pos-tol-ic
Church.   I con-fess one Bap-tism   for the for - give-ness of sins
and I look for-ward to the res-ur-rec-tion of the dead   and the life
of the world to come.   A - men.

Credo in unum Deum,
Patrem omnipoténtem,
factórem cæli et terræ,
visibílium ómnium et invisibílium.

Et in unum Dóminum Iesum Christum,
Fílium Dei Unigénitum,
et ex Patre natum ante ómnia sǽcula.
Deum de Deo, lumen de lúmine,
    Deum verum de Deo vero,
génitum, non factum, consubstantiálem Patri:
per quem ómnia facta sunt.
Qui propter nos hómines et propter nostram salútem
descéndit de cælis.

(all bow)

Et incarnátus est de Spíritu Sancto
ex María Vírgine, et homo factus est.

Crucifíxus étiam pro nobis sub Póntio Piláto;
passus et sepúltus est,
et resurréxit tértia die, secúndum Scriptúras,
et ascéndit in cælum, sedet ad déxteram Patris.

Et íterum ventúrus est cum glória,
    iudicáre vivos et mórtuos,
cuius regni non erit finis.

Et in Spíritum Sanctum, Dóminum et vivificántem:
qui ex Patre Filióque procédit.
Qui cum Patre et Fílio simul adorátur et conglorificátur:
qui locútus est per prophétas.

Et unam, sanctam, cathólicam et apostólicam Ecclésiam.
Confíteor unum baptísma in remissiónem peccatórum.
Et exspécto resurrectiónem mortuórum,
et vitam ventúri sǽculi. Amen.

I believe in one God,
the Father almighty,
maker of heaven and earth,
of all things visible and invisible.

I believe in one Lord Jesus Christ,
the Only Begotten Son of God,
born of the Father before all ages.
God from God, Light from Light,
true God from true God,
begotten, not made, consubstantial with the Father;
through him all things were made.
For us men and for our salvation
he came down from heaven,

(all bow)

and by the Holy Spirit was incarnate of the Virgin Mary,
and became man.

For our sake he was crucified under Pontius Pilate,
he suffered death and was buried,
and rose again on the third day
in accordance with the Scriptures.
He ascended into heaven
and is seated at the right hand of the Father.
He will come again in glory
to judge the living and the dead
and his kingdom will have no end.

I believe in the Holy Spirit, the Lord, the giver of life,
who proceeds from the Father and the Son,
who with the Father and the Son is adored and glorified,
who has spoken through the prophets.

I believe in one, holy, catholic and apostolic Church.
I confess one Baptism for the forgiveness of sins
and I look forward to the resurrection of the dead
and the life of the world to come. Amen.

THE APOSTLES' CREED

Credo in Deum, Patrem omnipoténtem,
Creatórem cæli et terræ,
et in Iesum Christum, Fílium eius únicum,
Dóminum nostrum,

at the words that follow up to and including **Maria Virgine**, all bow.

qui concéptus est de Spíritu Sancto,
natus ex María Vírgine,
passus sub Póntio Piláto,
crucifíxus, mórtuus, et sepúltus,
descéndit ad ínferos,
tértia die resurréxit a mórtuis,
ascéndit ad cælos,
sedet ad déxteram Dei Patris omnipoténtis,
inde ventúrus est iudicáre vivos et mórtuos.

Credo in Spíritum Sanctum,
sanctam Ecclésiam cathólicam,
Sanctórum communiónem,
remissiónem peccatórum,
carnis resurrectiónem,
vitam ætérnam. Amen.

THE PRAYER OF THE FAITHFUL (BIDDING PRAYERS)

Intentions will normally be for the Church; for the world; for those in particular need; and for the local community. After each there is time for silent prayer, followed by the next intention, or concluded with a sung phrase such as Christe audi nos, or Christe exaudi nos, or by a responsory such as:

R.   **Præsta, ætérne omnípotens Deus.** Or:

R.   **Te rogámus audi nos.** Or:

R.   **Kýrie, eléison.**

The Priest concludes the Prayer with a collect.

THE APOSTLES' CREED

I believe in God,
the Father almighty
Creator of heaven and earth,
and in Jesus Christ, his only Son, our Lord,

at the words that follow up to and including **the Virgin Mary**, all bow.

who was conceived by the Holy Spirit,
born of the Virgin Mary,
suffered under Pontius Pilate,
was crucified, died and was buried;
he descended into hell;
on the third day he rose again from the dead;
he ascended into heaven,
and is seated at the right hand of God
    the Father almighty;
from there he will come to judge the living and the dead.

I believe in the Holy Spirit,
the holy catholic Church,
the communion of saints,
the forgiveness of sins,
the resurrection of the body,
and life everlasting. Amen.

THE PRAYER OF THE FAITHFUL (BIDDING PRAYERS)

Intentions will normally be for the Church; for the world; for those in particular need; and for the local community. After each there is time for silent prayer, followed by the next intention, or concluded with a sung phrase such as Christ, hear us, or Christ graciously hear us, or by a responsory such as:

Let us pray to the Lord.

R. **Grant this, almighty God.** Or:

R. **Lord, have mercy.** Or:

R. **Kýrie, eléison.**

The Priest concludes the Prayer with a collect.

THE LITURGY OF THE EUCHARIST

For Catholics, the Eucharist is the source and summit of the whole
Christian life.

After the Liturgy of the Word, the people sit and the Offertory Chant begins. The
faithful express their participation by making an offering, bringing forward bread
and wine for the celebration of the Eucharist and perhaps other gifts to relieve the
needs of the Church and of the poor.

PREPARATORY PRAYERS

Standing at the altar, the Priest takes the paten with the bread and holds it slightly
raised above the altar with both hands, saying:

Pr. Benedíctus es, Dómine, Deus univérsi,
    quia de tua largitáte accépimus panem,
    quem tibi offérimus,
    fructum terræ et óperis mánuum hóminum:
    ex quo nobis fiet panis vitæ.

R. **Benedíctus Deus in sǽcula.**

The Priest then takes the chalice and holds it slightly raised above the altar with
both hands, saying:

Pr. Benedíctus es, Dómine, Deus univérsi,
    quia de tua largitáte accépimus vinum,
    quod tibi offérimus,
    fructum vitis et óperis mánuum hóminum,
    ex quo nobis fiet potus spiritális.

R. **Benedíctus Deus in sǽcula.**

The Priest completes additional personal preparatory rites, and the people rise as
he says:

Pr. Oráte, fratres:
    ut meum ac vestrum sacrifícium
    acceptábile fiat apud Deum Patrem omnipoténtem.

R. **Suscípiat Dóminus sacrifícium de mánibus tuis**
   ad laudem et glóriam nóminis sui,
   ad utilitátem quoque nostram
   totiúsque Ecclésiæ suæ sanctæ.

PRAYER OVER THE OFFERINGS

The Priest says the Prayer over the Offerings, at the end of which the people acclaim:

R. **Amen.**

THE LITURGY OF THE EUCHARIST

For Catholics, the Eucharist is the source and summit of the whole Christian life.

After the Liturgy of the Word, the people sit and the Offertory Chant begins. The faithful express their participation by making an offering, bringing forward bread and wine for the celebration of the Eucharist and perhaps other gifts to relieve the needs of the Church and of the poor.

PREPARATORY PRAYERS

Standing at the altar, the Priest takes the paten with the bread and holds it slightly raised above the altar with both hands, saying:

Pr. Blessed are you, Lord God of all creation,
for through your goodness we have received
the bread we offer you:
fruit of the earth and work of human hands,
it will become for us the bread of life.

R. **Blessed be God for ever.**

The Priest then takes the chalice and holds it slightly raised above the altar with both hands, saying:

Pr. Blessed are you, Lord God of all creation,
for through your goodness we have received
the wine we offer you:
fruit of the vine and work of human hands,
it will become our spiritual drink.

R. **Blessed be God for ever.**

The Priest completes additional personal preparatory rites, and the people rise as he says:

Pr. Pray, brethren (brothers and sisters),
that my sacrifice and yours
may be acceptable to God,
the almighty Father.

R. **May the Lord accept the sacrifice at your hands
for the praise and glory of his name,
for our good
and the good of all his holy Church.**

PRAYER OVER THE OFFERINGS

The Priest says the Prayer over the Offerings, at the end of which the people acclaim:

R. **Amen.**

THE EUCHARISTIC PRAYER

Extending his hands, the Priest says:

Pr. Dóminus vobíscum.

Et cum spí-ri-tu tu-o.

R. **Et cum spíritu tuo.**

Pr. Sursum corda.

Habémus ad Dóminum.

R. **Habémus ad Dóminum.**

Pr. Grátias agámus Dómino Deo nostro.

Dignum et iustum est.

R. **Dignum et iustum est.**

The Priest continues with the Preface appropriate to the Season or Feast at the end of which all sing or say:

anc-tus, * Sanc-tus, Sanc-tus Dó-mi-nus De-us Sá-ba-oth. Plé-ni
sunt cæ-li et ter-ra gló-ri-a tu-a. Ho-sán-na in ex-cél-sis. Be-ne-díc-
tus qui ve-nit in nómine Dómini.   Ho-sán-na in excél-sis.

THE EUCHARISTIC PRAYER

Extending his hands, the Priest says:

Pr. **The Lord be with you.**

R. And with your spir-it.

R. **And with your spirit.**

Pr. Lift up your hearts.

R. We lift them up to the Lord.

R. **We lift them up to the Lord.**

Pr. Let us give thanks to the Lord our God.

R. It is right and just.

R. **It is right and just.**

The Priest continues with the Preface appropriate to the Season or Feast at the end of which all sing or say:

Ho-ly, Ho-ly, Ho-ly Lord God of hosts. Heav-en and earth are full of your glo-ry. Ho-san-na in the high-est. Bless-ed is he who comes in the name of the Lord. Ho-san-na in the high-est.

Sanctus, Sanctus, Sanctus Dóminus Deus Sábaoth.
Pleni sunt cæli et terra glória tua.
Hosánna in excélsis.
Benedíctus qui venit in nómine Dómini.
Hosánna in excélsis.

After the Sanctus the congregation kneels for the remainder of the Eucharistic Prayer. (Texts for the four principal Eucharistic Prayers follow: Eucharistic Prayer I at p.80, II at p.92, III at p.100, IV at p.110.)

PREFACES

ADVENT

PRÆFATIO I DE ADVENTU

De duobus adventibus Christi

In Missis de tempore a prima dominica Adventus usque ad diem 16 decembris

Vere dignum et iustum est, æquum et salutare,
nos tibi semper et ubique gratias agere:
Domine, sancte Pater, omnipotens æterne Deus:
per Christum Dominum nostrum.

Qui, primo adventu in humilitate carnis assumptæ,
dispositionis antiquæ munus implevit,
nobisque salutis perpetuæ tramitem reseravit:
ut, cum secundo venerit in suæ gloria maiestatis,
manifesto demum munere capiamus,
quod vigilantes nunc audemus exspectare promissum.

Et ideo cum Angelis et Archangelis,
cum Thronis et Dominationibus,
cumque omni militia cælestis exercitus,
hymnum gloriæ tuæ canimus,
sine fine dicentes:

Sanctus, Sanctus, Sanctus Dominus Deus Sabaoth. . .

Holy, Holy, Holy Lord God of hosts.
Heaven and earth are full of your glory.
Hosanna in the highest.
Blessed is he who comes in the name of the Lord.
Hosanna in the highest.

After the Sanctus the congregation kneels for the remainder of the Eucharistic Prayer. (Texts for the four principal Eucharistic Prayers follow: Eucharistic Prayer I at p. 81, II at p. 93, III at p. 101, IV at p. 111.)

PREFACES

ADVENT

PREFACE I OF ADVENT

The two comings of Christ

From the First Sunday of Advent until 16 December

It is truly right and just, our duty and our salvation,
always and everywhere to give you thanks,
Lord, holy Father, almighty and eternal God,
through Christ our Lord.

For he assumed at his first coming
the lowliness of human flesh,
and so fulfilled the design you formed long ago,
and opened for us the way to eternal salvation,
that, when he comes again in glory and majesty
and all is at last made manifest,
we who watch for that day
may inherit the great promise
in which now we dare to hope.

And so, with Angels and Archangels,
with Thrones and Dominions,
and with all the hosts and Powers of heaven,
we sing the hymn of your glory,
as without end we acclaim:

Holy, Holy, Holy Lord God of hosts. . .

PRÆFATIO II DE ADVENTU

De duplici exspectatione Christi

17 decembris-24 decembris

Vere dignum et iustum est, æquum et salutare,
nos tibi semper et ubique gratias agere:
Domine, sancte Pater, omnipotens æterne Deus:
per Christum Dominum nostrum.

Quem prædixerunt cunctorum præconia prophetarum,
Virgo Mater ineffabili dilectione sustinuit,
Ioannes cecinit affuturum et adesse monstravit.
Qui suæ nativitatis mysterium
tribuit nos prævenire gaudentes,
ut et in oratione pervigiles
et in suis inveniat laudibus exsultantes.

Et ideo cum Angelis et Archangelis,
cum Thronis et Dominationibus,
cumque omni militia cælestis exercitus,
hymnum gloriæ tuæ canimus,
sine fine dicentes:
Sanctus, Sanctus, Sanctus Dominus Deus Sabaoth. . .

CHRISTMAS

PRÆFATIO I DE NATIVITATE DOMINI

De Christo luce

Vere dignum et iustum est, æquum et salutare,
nos tibi semper et ubique gratias agere:
Domine, sancte Pater, omnipotens æterne Deus:

Quia per incarnati Verbi mysterium
nova mentis nostræ oculis lux tuæ claritatis infulsit:
ut, dum visibiliter Deum cognoscimus,
per hunc in invisibilium amorem rapiamur.

Et ideo cum Angelis et Archangelis,
cum Thronis et Dominationibus,
cumque omni militia cælestis exercitus,
hymnum gloriæ tuæ canimus, sine fine dicentes:
Sanctus, Sanctus, Sanctus Dominus Deus Sabaoth. . .

PREFACE II OF ADVENT

The twofold expectation of Christ

17 December-24 December

It is truly right and just, our duty and our salvation,
always and everywhere to give you thanks,
Lord, holy Father, almighty and eternal God,
through Christ our Lord.

For all the oracles of the prophets foretold him,
the Virgin Mother longed for him
with love beyond all telling,
John the Baptist sang of his coming
and proclaimed his presence when he came.

It is by his gift that already we rejoice
at the mystery of his Nativity,
so that he may find us watchful in prayer
and exultant in his praise.

And so, with Angels and Archangels,
with Thrones and Dominions,
and with all the hosts and Powers of heaven,
we sing the hymn of your glory,
as without end we acclaim:

Holy, Holy, Holy Lord God of hosts. . .

CHRISTMAS

PREFACE I OF THE NATIVITY OF THE LORD

Christ the Light

It is truly right and just, our duty and our salvation,
always and everywhere to give you thanks,
Lord, holy Father, almighty and eternal God.

For in the mystery of the Word made flesh
a new light of your glory has shone upon the eyes of our mind,
so that, as we recognise in him God made visible,
we may be caught up through him in love of things invisible.

And so, with Angels and Archangels,
with Thrones and Dominions,
and with all the hosts and Powers of heaven,
we sing the hymn of your glory,
as without end we acclaim:

Holy, Holy, Holy Lord God of hosts. . .

PRÆFATIO II DE NATIVITATE DOMINI

De restauratione universa in Incarnatione

Vere dignum et iustum est, æquum et salutare,
nos tibi semper et ubique gratias agere:
Domine, sancte Pater, omnipotens æterne Deus:
per Christum Dominum nostrum.

Qui, in huius venerandi festivitate mysterii,
invisibilis in suis, visibilis in nostris apparuit,
et ante tempora genitus esse cœpit in tempore;
ut, in se erigens cuncta deiecta,
in integrum restitueret universa,
et hominem perditum ad cælestia regna revocaret.

Unde et nos, cum omnibus Angelis te laudamus,
iucunda celebratione clamantes:

Sanctus, Sanctus, Sanctus Dominus Deus Sabaoth. . .

PRÆFATIO III DE NATIVITATE DOMINI

De commercio in Incarnatione Verbi

Vere dignum et iustum est, æquum et salutare,
nos tibi semper et ubique gratias agere:
Domine, sancte Pater, omnipotens æterne Deus:
per Christum Dominum nostrum.

Per quem hodie commercium nostræ reparationis effulsit,
quia, dum nostra fragilitas a tuo Verbo suscipitur,
humana mortalitas non solum
in perpetuum transit honorem,
sed nos quoque, mirando consortio, reddit æternos.

Et ideo, choris angelicis sociati,
te laudamus in gaudio confitentes:

Sanctus, Sanctus, Sanctus Dominus Deus Sabaoth. . .

PREFACE II OF THE NATIVITY OF THE LORD

The restoration of all things in the Incarnation

It is truly right and just, our duty and our salvation,
always and everywhere to give you thanks,
Lord, holy Father, almighty and eternal God,
through Christ our Lord.

For on the feast of this awe-filled mystery,
though invisible in his own divine nature,
he has appeared visibly in ours;
and begotten before all ages,
he has begun to exist in time;
so that, raising up in himself all that was cast down,
he might restore unity to all creation
and call straying humanity back to the heavenly Kingdom.

And so, with all the Angels, we praise you,
as in joyful celebration we acclaim:

Holy, Holy, Holy Lord God of hosts. . .

PREFACE III OF THE NATIVITY OF THE LORD

The exchange in the Incarnation of the Word

It is truly right and just, our duty and our salvation,
always and everywhere to give you thanks,
Lord, holy Father, almighty and eternal God,
through Christ our Lord.

For through him the holy exchange that restores our life
has shone forth today in splendour:
when our frailty is assumed by your Word
not only does human mortality receive unending honour
but by this wondrous union we, too, are made eternal.

And so, in company with the choirs of Angels,
we praise you, and with joy we proclaim:

Holy, Holy, Holy Lord God of hosts. . .

PRÆFATIO DE EPIPHANIA DOMINI

De Christo lumine gentium

Vere dignum et iustum est, æquum et salutare,
nos tibi semper et ubique gratias agere:
Domine, sancte Pater, omnipotens æterne Deus:

Quia ipsum in Christo salutis nostræ mysterium
hodie ad lumen gentium revelasti,
et, cum in substantia nostræ mortalitatis apparuit,
nova nos immortalitatis eius gloria reparasti.

Et ideo cum Angelis et Archangelis,
cum Thronis et Dominationibus,
cumque omni militia cælestis exercitus,
hymnum gloriæ tuæ canimus,
sine fine dicentes:

Sanctus, Sanctus, Sanctus Dominus Deus Sabaoth. . .

LENT
PRÆFATIO I DE QUADRAGESIMA

De spiritali significatione Quadregesimæ

Vere dignum et iustum est, æquum et salutare,
nos tibi semper et ubique gratias agere:
Domine, sancte Pater, omnipotens æterne Deus:
per Christum Dominum nostrum.

Quia fidelibus tuis dignanter concedis
quotannis paschalia sacramenta
in gaudio purificatis mentibus exspectare:
ut, pietatis officia et opera caritatis propensius exsequentes,
frequentatione mysteriorum, quibus renati sunt,
ad gratiæ filiorum plenitudinem perducantur.

Et ideo cum Angelis et Archangelis,
cum Thronis et Dominationibus,
cumque omni militia cælestis exercitus,
hymnum gloriæ tuæ canimus,
sine fine dicentes:

Sanctus, Sanctus, Sanctus Dominus Deus Sabaoth. . .

PREFACE OF THE EPIPHANY OF THE LORD
Christ the light of the nations

It is truly right and just, our duty and our salvation,
always and everywhere to give you thanks,
Lord, holy Father, almighty and eternal God.

For today you have revealed the mystery
of our salvation in Christ
as a light for the nations,
and, when he appeared in our mortal nature,
you made us new by the glory of his immortal nature.

And so, with Angels and Archangels,
with Thrones and Dominions,
and with all the hosts and Powers of heaven,
we sing the hymn of your glory,
as without end we acclaim:

Holy, Holy, Holy Lord God of hosts. . .

LENT
PREFACE I OF LENT
The spiritual meaning of Lent

It is truly right and just, our duty and our salvation,
always and everywhere to give you thanks,
Lord, holy Father, almighty and eternal God,
through Christ our Lord.

For by your gracious gift each year
your faithful await the sacred paschal feasts
with the joy of minds made pure,
so that, more eagerly intent on prayer
and on the works of charity,
and participating in the mysteries
by which they have been reborn,
they may be led to the fullness of grace
that you bestow on your sons and daughters.

And so, with Angels and Archangels,
with Thrones and Dominions,
and with all the hosts and Powers of heaven,
we sing the hymn of your glory,
as without end we acclaim:

Holy, Holy, Holy Lord God of hosts. . .

PRÆFATIO II DE QUADRAGESIMA
De spiritali pænitentia

Vere dignum et iustum est, æquum et salutare,
nos tibi semper et ubique gratias agere:
Domine, sancte Pater, omnipotens æterne Deus:

Qui filiis tuis ad reparandam mentium puritatem,
tempus præcipuum salubriter statuisti,
quo, mente ab inordinatis affectibus expedita,
sic incumberent transituris
ut rebus potius perpetuis inhærerent.

Et ideo, cum Sanctis et Angelis universis,
te collaudamus, sine fine dicentes:
Sanctus, Sanctus, Sanctus Dominus Deus Sabaoth. . .

PRÆFATIO III DE QUADRAGESIMA
De fructibus abstinentiæ

Vere dignum et iustum est, æquum et salutare,
nos tibi semper et ubique gratias agere:
Domine, sancte Pater, omnipotens æterne Deus:

Qui nos per abstinentiam tibi gratias referre voluisti,
ut ipsa et nos peccatores ab insolentia mitigaret,
et, egentium proficiens alimento,
imitatores tuæ benignitatis efficeret.

Et ideo, cum innumeris Angelis,
una te magnificamus laudis voce dicentes:
Sanctus, Sanctus, Sanctus Dominus Deus Sabaoth. . .

PRÆFATIO IV DE QUADRAGESIMA
De fructibus ieiunii

Vere dignum et iustum est, æquum et salutare,
nos tibi semper et ubique gratias agere:
Domine, sancte Pater, omnipotens æterne Deus:

Qui corporali ieiunio vitia comprimis, mentem elevas,
virtutem largiris et præmia:
per Christum Dominum nostrum.

PREFACE II OF LENT

Spiritual penance

It is truly right and just, our duty and our salvation,
always and everywhere to give you thanks,
Lord, holy Father, almighty and eternal God.

For you have given your children a sacred time
for the renewing and purifying of their hearts,
that, freed from disordered affections,
they may so deal with the things of this passing world
as to hold rather to the things that eternally endure.

And so, with all the Angels and Saints,
we praise you, as without end we acclaim:

Holy, Holy, Holy Lord God of hosts. . .

PREFACE III OF LENT

The fruits of abstinence

It is truly right and just, our duty and our salvation,
always and everywhere to give you thanks,
Lord, holy Father, almighty and eternal God.

For you will that our self-denial should give you thanks,
humble our sinful pride,
contribute to the feeding of the poor,
and so help us imitate you in your kindness.

And so we glorify you with countless Angels,
as with one voice of praise we acclaim:

Holy, Holy, Holy Lord God of hosts. . .

PREFACE IV OF LENT

The fruits of fasting

It is truly right and just, our duty and our salvation,
always and everywhere to give you thanks,
Lord, holy Father, almighty and eternal God.

For through bodily fasting you restrain our faults,
raise up our minds,
and bestow both virtue and its rewards,
through Christ our Lord.

Per quem maiestatem tuam laudant Angeli,
adorant Dominationes, tremunt Potestates.
Cæli cælorumque Virtutes, ac beata Seraphim,
socia exsultatione concelebrant.

Cum quibus et nostras voces ut admitti iubeas, deprecamur,
supplici confessione dicentes:

Sanctus, Sanctus, Sanctus Dominus Deus Sabaoth. . .

PRÆFATIO I DE PASSIONE DOMINI

De virtute Crucis

Vere dignum et iustum est, æquum et salutare,
nos tibi semper et ubique gratias agere:
Domine, sancte Pater, omnipotens æterne Deus:

Quia per Filii tui salutiferam passionem
sensum confitendæ tuæ maiestatis totus mundus accepit,
dum ineffabili crucis potentia
iudicium mundi et potestas emicat Crucifixi.

Unde et nos, Domine, cum Angelis et Sanctis universis,
tibi confitemur, in exsultatione dicentes:

Sanctus, Sanctus, Sanctus Dominus Deus Sabaoth. . .

EASTER

PRÆFATIO PASCHALIS I

De mysterio paschali

Vere dignum et iustum est, æquum et salutare:
Te quidem, Domine, omni tempore confiteri,
sed in hac potissimum nocte (die) gloriosius prædicare,
(sed in hoc potissimum gloriosius prædicare,)
cum Pascha nostrum immolatus est Christus.

Ipse enim verus est Agnus
qui abstulit peccata mundi.
Qui mortem nostram moriendo destruxit,
et vitam resurgendo reparavit.

Quapropter, profusis paschalibus gaudiis,
totus in orbe terrarum mundus exsultat.

Through him the Angels praise your majesty,
Dominions adore and Powers tremble before you.
Heaven and the Virtues of heaven and the blessed Seraphim
worship together with exultation.
May our voices, we pray, join with theirs
in humble praise, as we acclaim:

Holy, Holy, Holy Lord God of hosts. . .

PREFACE I OF THE PASSION OF THE LORD

The power of the Cross

It is truly right and just, our duty and our salvation,
always and everywhere to give you thanks,
Lord, holy Father, almighty and eternal God.

For through the saving Passion of your Son
the whole world has received a heart
to confess the infinite power of your majesty,
since by the wondrous power of the Cross
your judgement on the world is now revealed
and the authority of Christ crucified.

And so, Lord, with all the Angels and Saints,
we, too, give you thanks, as in exultation we acclaim:

Holy, Holy, Holy Lord God of hosts. . .

EASTER

PREFACE I OF EASTER

The Paschal Mystery

It is truly right and just, our duty and our salvation,
at all times to acclaim you, O Lord,
but (on this night / on this day / in this time) above all
to laud you yet more gloriously,
when Christ our Passover has been sacrificed.

For he is the true Lamb
who has taken away the sins of the world;
by dying he has destroyed our death,
and by rising, restored our life.

Therefore, overcome with paschal joy,
every land, every people exults in your praise

Sed et supernæ virtutes atque angelicæ potestates
hymnum gloriæ tuæ concinunt, sine fine dicentes:

Sanctus, Sanctus, Sanctus Dominus Deus Sabaoth. . .

PRÆFATIO PASCHALIS II

De vita nova in Christo

Vere dignum et iustum est, æquum et salutare:
Te quidem, Domine, omni tempore confiteri,
sed in hoc potissimum gloriosius prædicare,
cum Pascha nostrum immolatus est Christus.

Per quem in æternam vitam filii lucis oriuntur,
et regni cælestis atria fidelibus reserantur.
Quia mors nostra est eius morte redempta,
et in eius resurrectione vita omnium resurrexit.

Quapropter, profusis paschalibus gaudiis,
totus in orbe terrarum mundus exsultat.
Sed et supernæ virtutes atque angelicæ potestates
hymnum gloriæ tuæ concinunt, sine fine dicentes:

Sanctus, Sanctus, Sanctus Dominus Deus Sabaoth. . .

PRÆFATIO PASCHALIS III

De Christo vivente et semper interpellante pro nobis

Vere dignum et iustum est, æquum et salutare:
Te quidem, Domine, omni tempore confiteri,
sed in hoc potissimum gloriosius prædicare,
cum Pascha nostrum immolatus est Christus.

Qui se pro nobis offerre non desinit,
nosque apud te perenni advocatione defendit;
qui immolatus iam non moritur,
sed semper vivit occisus.

Quapropter, profusis paschalibus gaudiis,
totus in orbe terrarum mundus exsultat.
Sed et supernæ virtutes atque angelicæ potestates
hymnum gloriæ tuæ concinunt, sine fine dicentes:

Sanctus, Sanctus, Sanctus Dominus Deus Sabaoth. . .

and even the heavenly Powers, with the angelic hosts,
sing together the unending hymn of your glory,
as they acclaim:

Holy, Holy, Holy Lord God of hosts. . .

PREFACE II OF EASTER

New life in Christ

It is truly right and just, our duty and our salvation,
at all times to acclaim you, O Lord,
but in this time above all to laud you yet more gloriously,
when Christ our Passover has been sacrificed.

Through him the children of light rise to eternal life
and the halls of the heavenly Kingdom
are thrown open to the faithful;
for his Death is our ransom from death,
and in his rising the life of all has risen.

Therefore, overcome with paschal joy,
every land, every people exults in your praise
and even the heavenly Powers, with the angelic hosts,
sing together the unending hymn of your glory,
as they acclaim:

Holy, Holy, Holy Lord God of hosts. . .

PREFACE III OF EASTER

Christ living and always interceding for us

It is truly right and just, our duty and our salvation,
at all times to acclaim you, O Lord,
but in this time above all to laud you yet more gloriously,
when Christ our Passover has been sacrificed.

He never ceases to offer himself for us
but defends us and ever pleads our cause before you:
he is the sacrificial Victim who dies no more,
the Lamb, once slain, who lives for ever.

Therefore, overcome with paschal joy,
every land, every people exults in your praise
and even the heavenly Powers, with the angelic hosts,
sing together the unending hymn of your glory,
as they acclaim:

Holy, Holy, Holy Lord God of hosts. . .

PRÆFATIO PASCHALIS IV

De restauratione universi per mysterium paschale

Vere dignum et iustum est, æquum et salutare:
Te quidem, Domine, omni tempore confiteri,
sed in hoc potissimum gloriosius prædicare,
cum Pascha nostrum immolatus est Christus.

Quia, vetustate destructa, renovantur universa deiecta,
et vitæ nobis in Christo reparatur integritas.

Quapropter, profusis paschalibus gaudiis,
totus in orbe terrarum mundus exsultat.
Sed et supernæ virtutes atque angelicæ potestates
hymnum gloriæ tuæ concinunt, sine fine dicentes:

Sanctus, Sanctus, Sanctus Dominus Deus Sabaoth. . .

PRÆFATIO PASCHALIS V

De Christo sacerdote et victima

Vere dignum et iustum est, æquum et salutare:
Te quidem, Domine, omni tempore confiteri,
sed in hoc potissimum gloriosius prædicare,
cum Pascha nostrum immolatus est Christus.

Qui, oblatione corporis sui,
antiqua sacrificia in crucis veritate perfecit,
et, seipsum tibi pro nostra salute commendans,
idem sacerdos, altare et agnus exhibuit.

Quapropter, profusis paschalibus gaudiis,
totus in orbe terrarum mundus exsultat.
Sed et supernæ virtutes atque angelicæ potestates
hymnum gloriæ tuæ concinunt, sine fine dicentes:

Sanctus, Sanctus, Sanctus Dominus Deus Sabaoth. . .

PREFACE IV OF EASTER

The restoration of the universe through the Paschal Mystery

It is truly right and just, our duty and our salvation,
at all times to acclaim you, O Lord,
but in this time above all to laud you yet more gloriously,
when Christ our Passover has been sacrificed.

For, with the old order destroyed,
a universe cast down is renewed,
and integrity of life is restored to us in Christ.

Therefore, overcome with paschal joy,
every land, every people exults in your praise
and even the heavenly Powers, with the angelic hosts,
sing together the unending hymn of your glory,
as they acclaim:

Holy, Holy, Holy Lord God of hosts. . .

PREFACE V OF EASTER

Christ, Priest and Victim

It is truly right and just, our duty and our salvation,
at all times to acclaim you, O Lord,
but in this time above all to laud you yet more gloriously,
when Christ our Passover has been sacrificed.

By the oblation of his Body,
he brought the sacrifices of old to fulfilment
in the reality of the Cross
and, by commending himself to you for our salvation,
showed himself the Priest, the Altar, and the Lamb of sacrifice.

Therefore, overcome with paschal joy,
every land, every people exults in your praise
and even the heavenly Powers, with the angelic hosts,
sing together the unending hymn of your glory,
as they acclaim:

Holy, Holy, Holy Lord God of hosts. . .

PRÆFATIO I DE ASCENSIONE DOMINI

De mysterio Ascensionis

Vere dignum et iustum est, æquum et salutare,
nos tibi semper et ubique gratias agere:
Domine, sancte Pater, omnipotens æterne Deus:

Quia Dominus Iesus, Rex gloriæ,
peccati triumphator et mortis,
mirantibus Angelis, ascendit (hodie) summa cælorum,
Mediator Dei et hominum,
Iudex mundi Dominusque virtutum;
non ut a nostra humilitate discederet,
sed ut illuc confideremus, sua membra, nos subsequi
quo ipse, caput nostrum principiumque, præcessit.

Quapropter, profusis paschalibus gaudiis,
totus in orbe terrarum mundus exsultat.
Sed et supernæ virtutes atque angelicæ potestates
hymnum gloriæ tuæ concinunt, sine fine dicentes:
Sanctus, Sanctus, Sanctus Dominus Deus Sabaoth. . .

PRÆFATIO II DE ASCENSIONE DOMINI

De mysterio Ascensionis

Vere dignum et iustum est, æquum et salutare,
nos tibi semper et ubique gratias agere:
Domine, sancte Pater, omnipotens æterne Deus:
per Christum Dominum nostrum.

Qui post resurrectionem suam
omnibus discipulis suis manifestus apparuit,
et ipsis cernentibus est elevatus in cælum,
ut nos divinitatis suæ tribueret esse participes.

Quapropter, profusis paschalibus gaudiis,
totus in orbe terrarum mundus exsultat.
Sed et supernæ virtutes atque angelicæ potestates
hymnum gloriæ tuæ concinunt, sine fine dicentes:

Sanctus, Sanctus, Sanctus Dominus Deus Sabaoth. . .

PREFACE I OF THE ASCENSION OF THE LORD

The mystery of the Ascension

It is truly right and just, our duty and our salvation,
always and everywhere to give you thanks,
Lord, holy Father, almighty and eternal God.

For the Lord Jesus, the King of glory,
conqueror of sin and death,
ascended (today) to the highest heavens,
as the Angels gazed in wonder.

Mediator between God and man,
judge of the world and Lord of hosts,
he ascended, not to distance himself from our lowly state
but that we, his members, might be confident of following
where he, our Head and Founder, has gone before.

Therefore, overcome with paschal joy,
every land, every people exults in your praise
and even the heavenly Powers, with the angelic hosts,
sing together the unending hymn of your glory,
as they acclaim:

Holy, Holy, Holy Lord God of hosts. . .

PREFACE II OF THE ASCENSION OF THE LORD

The mystery of the Ascension

It is truly right and just, our duty and our salvation,
always and everywhere to give you thanks,
Lord, holy Father, almighty and eternal God,
through Christ our Lord.

For after his Resurrection
he plainly appeared to all his disciples
and was taken up to heaven in their sight,
that he might make us sharers in his divinity.

Therefore, overcome with paschal joy,
every land, every people exults in your praise
and even the heavenly Powers, with the angelic hosts,
sing together the unending hymn of your glory,
as they acclaim:

Holy, Holy, Holy Lord God of hosts. . .

PRÆFATIO I DE DOMINICIS « PER ANNUM »

De mysterio paschali et de populo Dei

Vere dignum et iustum est, æquum et salutare,
nos tibi semper et ubique gratias agere:
Domine, sancte Pater, omnipotens æterne Deus:
per Christum Dominum nostrum.

Cuius hoc mirificum fuit opus per paschale mysterium,
ut de peccato et mortis iugo ad hanc gloriam vocaremur,
qua nunc genus electum, regale sacerdotium,
gens sancta et acquisitionis populus diceremur,
et tuas annuntiaremus ubique virtutes,
qui nos de tenebris ad tuum admirabile lumen vocasti.

Et ideo cum Angelis et Archangelis,
cum Thronis et Dominationibus,
cumque omni militia cælestis exercitus,
hymnum gloriæ tuæ canimus,
sine fine dicentes:

Sanctus, Sanctus, Sanctus Dominus Deus Sabaoth. . .

PRÆFATIO II DE DOMINICIS « PER ANNUM »

De mysterio salutis

Vere dignum et iustum est, æquum et salutare,
nos tibi semper et ubique gratias agere:
Domine, sancte Pater, omnipotens æterne Deus:
per Christum Dominum nostrum.

Qui, humanis miseratus erroribus,
de Virgine nasci dignatus est.
Qui, crucem passus, a perpetua morte nos liberavit
et, a mortuis resurgens, vitam nobis donavit æternam.

Et ideo cum Angelis et Archangelis,
cum Thronis et Dominationibus,
cumque omni militia cælestis exercitus,
hymnum gloriæ tuæ canimus,
sine fine dicentes:

Sanctus, Sanctus, Sanctus Dominus Deus Sabaoth. . .

PREFACE I OF THE SUNDAYS IN ORDINARY TIME

The Paschal Mystery and the People of God

It is truly right and just, our duty and our salvation,
always and everywhere to give you thanks,
Lord, holy Father, almighty and eternal God,
through Christ our Lord.

For through his Paschal Mystery,
he accomplished the marvellous deed,
by which he has freed us from the yoke of sin and death,
summoning us to the glory of being now called
a chosen race, a royal priesthood,
a holy nation, a people for your own possession,
to proclaim everywhere your mighty works,
for you have called us out of darkness
into your own wonderful light.

And so, with Angels and Archangels,
with Thrones and Dominions,
and with all the hosts and Powers of heaven,
we sing the hymn of your glory,
as without end we acclaim:

Holy, Holy, Holy Lord God of hosts. . .

PREFACE II OF THE SUNDAYS IN ORDINARY TIME

The mystery of salvation

It is truly right and just, our duty and our salvation,
always and everywhere to give you thanks,
Lord, holy Father, almighty and eternal God,
through Christ our Lord.

For out of compassion for the waywardness that is ours,
he humbled himself and was born of the Virgin;
by the passion of the Cross he freed us from unending death,
and by rising from the dead he gave us life eternal.

And so, with Angels and Archangels,
with Thrones and Dominions,
and with all the hosts and Powers of heaven,
we sing the hymn of your glory,
as without end we acclaim:

Holy, Holy, Holy Lord God of hosts. . .

PRÆFATIO III DE DOMINICIS « PER ANNUM »
De salvatione hominis per hominem

Vere dignum et iustum est, æquum et salutare,
nos tibi semper et ubique gratias agere:
Domine, sancte Pater, omnipotens æterne Deus:

Ad cuius immensam gloriam pertinere cognoscimus
ut mortalibus tua deitate succurreres;
sed et nobis provideres de ipsa
mortalitate nostra remedium,
et perditos quosque unde perierant, inde salvares,
per Christum Dominum nostrum.

Per quem maiestatem tuam adorat exercitus Angelorum,
ante conspectum tuum in æternitate lætantium.

Cum quibus et nostras voces ut admitti iubeas, deprecamur,
socia exsultatione dicentes:

Sanctus, Sanctus, Sanctus Dominus Deus Sabaoth. . .

PRÆFATIO IV DE DOMINICIS « PER ANNUM »
De historia salutis

Vere dignum et iustum est, æquum et salutare,
nos tibi semper et ubique gratias agere:
Domine, sancte Pater, omnipotens æterne Deus:
per Christum Dominum nostrum.

Ipse enim nascendo vetustatem hominum renovavit,
patiendo delevit nostra peccata,
æternæ vitæ aditum præstitit a mortuis resurgendo,
ad te Patrem ascendendo cælestes ianuas reseravit.

Et ideo, cum Angelorum atque Sanctorum turba,
hymnum laudis tibi canimus, sine fine dicentes:
Sanctus, Sanctus, Sanctus Dominus Deus Sabaoth. . .

PREFACE III OF THE SUNDAYS IN ORDINARY TIME

The salvation of man by a man

It is truly right and just, our duty and our salvation,
always and everywhere to give you thanks,
Lord, holy Father, almighty and eternal God.

For we know it belongs to your boundless glory,
that you came to the aid of mortal beings with your divinity
and even fashioned for us a remedy out of mortality itself,
that the cause of our downfall
might become the means of our salvation,
through Christ our Lord.

Through him the host of Angels adores your majesty
and rejoices in your presence for ever.
May our voices, we pray, join with theirs
in one chorus of exultant praise, as we acclaim:

Holy, Holy, Holy Lord God of hosts. . .

PREFACE IV OF THE SUNDAYS IN ORDINARY TIME

The history of salvation

It is truly right and just, our duty and our salvation,
always and everywhere to give you thanks,
Lord, holy Father, almighty and eternal God,
through Christ our Lord.

For by his birth he brought renewal
to humanity's fallen state,
and by his suffering cancelled out our sins;
by his rising from the dead
he has opened the way to eternal life,
and by ascending to you, O Father,
he has unlocked the gates of heaven.

And so, with the company of Angels and Saints,
we sing the hymn of your praise,
as without end we acclaim:

Holy, Holy, Holy Lord God of hosts. . .

PRÆFATIO V DE DOMINICIS « PER ANNUM »

De creatione

Vere dignum et iustum est, æquum et salutare,
nos tibi semper et ubique gratias agere:
Domine, sancte Pater, omnipotens æterne Deus:

Qui omnia mundi elementa fecisti,
et vices disposuisti temporum variari;
hominem vero formasti ad imaginem tuam,
et rerum ei subiecisti universa miracula,
ut vicario munere dominaretur omnibus quæ creasti,
et in operum tuorum magnalibus iugiter te laudaret,
per Christum Dominum nostrum.

Unde et nos cum omnibus Angelis te laudamus,
iucunda celebratione clamantes:

Sanctus, Sanctus, Sanctus Dominus Deus Sabaoth. . .

PRÆFATIO VI DE DOMINICIS « PER ANNUM »

De pignore æterni Paschatis

Vere dignum et iustum est, æquum et salutare,
nos tibi semper et ubique gratias agere:
Domine, sancte Pater, omnipotens æterne Deus:

In quo vivimus, movemur et sumus,
atque in hoc corpore constituti
non solum pietatis tuæ cotidianos experimur effectus,
sed æternitatis etiam pignora iam tenemus.
Primitias enim Spiritus habentes,
per quem suscitasti Iesum a mortuis,
paschale mysterium speramus nobis esse perpetuum.

Unde et nos cum omnibus Angelis te laudamus,
iucunda celebratione clamantes:

Sanctus, Sanctus, Sanctus Dominus Deus Sabaoth. . .

PREFACE V OF THE SUNDAYS IN ORDINARY TIME

Creation

It is truly right and just, our duty and our salvation,
always and everywhere to give you thanks,
Lord, holy Father, almighty and eternal God.

For you laid the foundations of the world
and have arranged the changing of times and seasons;
you formed man in your own image
and set humanity over the whole world in all its wonder,
to rule in your name over all you have made
and for ever praise you in your mighty works,
through Christ our Lord.

And so, with all the Angels, we praise you,
as in joyful celebration we acclaim:

Holy, Holy, Holy Lord God of hosts. . .

PREFACE VI OF THE SUNDAYS IN ORDINARY TIME

The pledge of the eternal Passover

It is truly right and just, our duty and our salvation,
always and everywhere to give you thanks,
Lord, holy Father, almighty and eternal God.

For in you we live and move and have our being,
and while in this body
we not only experience the daily effects of your care,
but even now possess the pledge of life eternal.

For, having received the first fruits of the Spirit,
through whom you raised up Jesus from the dead,
we hope for an everlasting share in the Paschal Mystery.

And so, with all the Angels, we praise you,
as in joyful celebration we acclaim:

Holy, Holy, Holy Lord God of hosts. . .

PRÆFATIO VII DE DOMINICIS « PER ANNUM »

De salute per obœdientiam Christi

Vere dignum et iustum est, æquum et salutare,
nos tibi semper et ubique gratias agere:
Domine, sancte Pater, omnipotens æterne Deus:

Quia sic mundum misericorditer dilexisti,
ut ipsum nobis mitteres Redemptorem,
quem absque peccato
in nostra voluisti similitudine conversari,
ut amares in nobis quod diligebas in Filio,
cuius obœdientia sumus ad tua dona reparati,
quæ per inobœdientiam amiseramus peccando.

Unde et nos, Domine, cum Angelis et Sanctis universis
tibi confitemur, in exsultatione dicentes:

Sanctus, Sanctus, Sanctus Dominus Deus Sabaoth. . .

PRÆFATIO VIII DE DOMINICIS « PER ANNUM »

De Ecclesia adunata ex unitate Trinitatis

Vere dignum et iustum est, æquum et salutare,
nos tibi semper et ubique gratias agere:
Domine, sancte Pater, omnipotens æterne Deus:

Quia filios, quos longe peccati crimen abstulerat,
per sanguinem Filii tui Spiritusque virtute,
in unum ad te denuo congregare voluisti:
ut plebs, de unitate Trinitatis adunata,
in tuæ laudem sapientiæ multiformis
Christi corpus templumque Spiritus nosceretur Ecclesia.

Et ideo, choris angelicis sociati,
te laudamus in gaudio confitentes:

Sanctus, Sanctus, Sanctus Dominus Deus Sabaoth. . .

PREFACE VII OF THE SUNDAYS IN ORDINARY TIME

Salvation through the obedience of Christ

It is truly right and just, our duty and our salvation,
always and everywhere to give you thanks,
Lord, holy Father, almighty and eternal God.

For you so loved the world
that in your mercy you sent us the Redeemer,
to live like us in all things but sin,
so that you might love in us what you loved in your Son,
by whose obedience we have been restored to those gifts of yours
that, by sinning, we had lost in disobedience.

And so, Lord, with all the Angels and Saints,
we, too, give you thanks, as in exultation we acclaim:

Holy, Holy, Holy Lord God of hosts. . .

PREFACE VIII OF THE SUNDAYS IN ORDINARY TIME

The Church united by the unity of the Trinity

It is truly right and just, our duty and our salvation,
always and everywhere to give you thanks,
Lord, holy Father, almighty and eternal God.

For, when your children were scattered afar by sin,
through the Blood of your Son and the power of the Spirit,
you gathered them again to yourself,
that a people, formed as one by the unity of the Trinity,
made the body of Christ and the temple of the Holy Spirit,
might, to the praise of your manifold wisdom,
be manifest as the Church.

And so, in company with the choirs of Angels,
we praise you, and with joy we proclaim:

Holy, Holy, Holy Lord God of hosts. . .

PRÆFATIO I DE SS.MA EUCHARISTIA

De sacrificia ex de sacramento Christi

Vere dignum et iustum est, æquum et salutare,
nos tibi semper et ubique gratias agere:
Domine, sancte Pater, omnipotens æterne Deus:
per Christum Dominum nostrum.

Qui, verus æternusque Sacerdos,
formam sacrificii perennis instituens,
hostiam tibi se primus obtulit salutarem,
et nos, in sui memoriam, præcepit offerre.
Cuius carnem pro nobis immolatam
dum sumimus, roboramur,
et fusum pro nobis sanguinem dum potamus, abluimur.

Et ideo cum Angelis et Archangelis,
cum Thronis et Dominationibus,
cumque omni militia cælestis exercitus,
hymnum gloriæ tuæ canimus,
sine fine dicentes:

Sanctus, Sanctus, Sanctus Dominus Deus Sabaoth. . .

PRÆFATIO II DE SS.MA EUCHARISTIA

De fructibus Sanctissimæ Eucharistiæ

Vere dignum et iustum est, æquum et salutare,
nos tibi semper et ubique gratias agere:
Domine, sancte Pater, omnipotens æterne Deus:
per Christum Dominum nostrum.

Qui cum Apostolis suis in novissima cena convescens,
salutiferam crucis memoriam prosecuturus in sæcula,
Agnum sine macula se tibi obtulit,
perfectæ laudis munus acceptum.

Quo venerabili mysterio fideles tuos alendo sanctificas,
ut humanum genus, quod continet unus orbis,
una fides illuminet, caritas una coniungat.

Ad mensam igitur accedimus tam mirabilis sacramenti,
ut, gratiæ tuæ suavitate perfusi,
ad cælestis formæ imaginem transeamus.

PREFACE I OF THE MOST HOLY EUCHARIST

The Sacrifice and the Sacrament of Christ

It is truly right and just, our duty and our salvation,
always and everywhere to give you thanks,
Lord, holy Father, almighty and eternal God,
through Christ our Lord.

For he is the true and eternal Priest,
who instituted the pattern of an everlasting sacrifice,
and was the first to offer himself as the saving Victim,
commanding us to make this offering as his memorial.
As we eat his flesh that was sacrificed for us,
we are made strong,
and, as we drink his Blood that was poured out for us,
we are washed clean.

And so, with Angels and Archangels,
with Thrones and Dominions,
and with all the hosts and Powers of heaven,
we sing the hymn of your glory,
as without end we acclaim:

Holy, Holy, Holy Lord God of hosts. . .

PREFACE II OF THE MOST HOLY EUCHARIST

The fruits of the Most Holy Eucharist

It is truly right and just, our duty and our salvation,
always and everywhere to give you thanks,
Lord, holy Father, almighty and eternal God,
through Christ our Lord.

For at the Last Supper with his Apostles,
establishing for the ages to come the saving memorial of the Cross,
he offered himself to you as the unblemished Lamb,
the acceptable gift of perfect praise.

Nourishing your faithful by this sacred mystery,
you make them holy, so that the human race,
bounded by one world,
may be enlightened by one faith
and united by one bond of charity.

And so, we approach the table of this wondrous Sacrament,
so that, bathed in the sweetness of your grace,
we may pass over to the heavenly realities here foreshadowed.

Propter quod cælestia tibi atque terrestria
canticum novum concinunt adorando,
et nos cum omni exercitu Angelorum proclamamus,
sine fine dicentes:

Sanctus, Sanctus, Sanctus Dominus Deus Sabaoth. . .

PRÆFATIO I DE APOSTOLIS

De Apostolis pastoribus populi Dei

Vere dignum et iustum est, æquum et salutare,
nos tibi semper et ubique gratias agere:
Domine, sancte Pater, omnipotens æterne Deus:

Qui gregem tuum, Pastor æterne, non deseris,
sed per beatos Apostolos continua protectione custodis,
ut iisdem rectoribus gubernetur,
quos Filii tui vicarios eidem contulisti præesse pastores.

Et ideo cum Angelis et Archangelis,
cum Thronis et Dominationibus,
cumque omni militia cælestis exercitus,
hymnum gloriæ tuæ canimus,
sine fine dicentes:

Sanctus, Sanctus, Sanctus Dominus Deus Sabaoth. . .

PRÆFATIO II DE APOSTOLIS

De apostolico fundamento et testimonio

Vere dignum et iustum est, æquum et salutare,
nos tibi semper et ubique gratias agere:
Domine, sancte Pater, omnipotens æterne Deus:
per Christum Dominum nostrum.

Quoniam Ecclesiam tuam
in apostolicis tribuisti consistere fundamentis,
ut signum sanctitatis tuæ in terris maneret ipsa perpetuum,
et cælestia præberet cunctis hominibus documenta.

Quapropter nunc et usque in sæculum
cum omni militia Angelorum
devota tibi mente concinimus,
clamantes atque dicentes:

Sanctus, Sanctus, Sanctus Dominus Deus Sabaoth. . .

Therefore, all creatures of heaven and earth
sing a new song in adoration,
and we, with all the host of Angels,
cry out, and without end we acclaim:

Holy, Holy, Holy Lord God of hosts. . .

PREFACE I OF APOSTLES

The Apostles, shepherds of God's people

It is truly right and just, our duty and our salvation,
always and everywhere to give you thanks,
Lord, holy Father, almighty and eternal God.

For you, eternal Shepherd, do not desert your flock,
but through the blessed Apostles
watch over it and protect it always,
so that it may be governed
by those you have appointed shepherds
to lead it in the name of your Son.

And so, with Angels and Archangels,
with Thrones and Dominions,
and with all the hosts and Powers of heaven,
we sing the hymn of your glory,
as without end we acclaim:

Holy, Holy, Holy Lord God of hosts. . .

PREFACE II OF APOSTLES

The apostolic foundation and witness

It is truly right and just, our duty and our salvation,
always and everywhere to give you thanks,
Lord, holy Father, almighty and eternal God,
through Christ our Lord.

For you have built your Church
to stand firm on apostolic foundations,
to be a lasting sign of your holiness on earth
and offer all humanity your heavenly teaching.

Therefore, now and for ages unending,
with all the host of Angels,
we sing to you with all our hearts,
crying out as we acclaim:

Holy, Holy, Holy Lord God of hosts. . .

PRÆFATIO I DE SANCTIS MARTYRIBUS
De signo et exemplo martyrii

Vere dignum et iustum est, æquum et salutare,
nos tibi semper et ubique gratias agere:
Domine, sancte Pater, omnipotens æterne Deus:

Quoniam beati martyris N. pro confessione nominis tui,
ad imitationem Christi,
sanguis effusus tua mirabilia manifestat,
quibus perficis in fragilitate virtutem,
et vires infirmas ad testimonium roboras,
per Christum Dominum nostrum.

Et ideo, cum cælorum Virtutibus,
in terris te iugiter celebramus,
maiestati tuæ sine fine clamantes:

Sanctus, Sanctus, Sanctus Dominus Deus Sabaoth. . .

PRÆFATIO II DE SANCTIS MARTYRIBUS
De mirabilibus Dei in martyrum victoria

Vere dignum et iustum est, æquum et salutare,
nos tibi semper et ubique gratias agere:
Domine, sancte Pater, omnipotens æterne Deus:

Quoniam tu magnificaris in tuorum laude Sanctorum,
et quidquid ad eorum pertinet passionem,
tuæ sunt opera miranda potentiæ:
qui huius fidei tribuis clementer ardorem,
qui suggeris perseverantiæ firmitatem,
qui largiris in agone victoriam,
per Christum Dominum nostrum.

Propter quod cælestia tibi atque terrestria
canticum novum concinunt adorando,
et nos cum omni exercitu Angelorum
proclamamus, sine fine dicentes:

Sanctus, Sanctus, Sanctus Dominus Deus Sabaoth. . .

PREFACE I OF HOLY MARTYRS

The sign and example of martyrdom

It is truly right and just, our duty and our salvation,
always and everywhere to give you thanks,
Lord, holy Father, almighty and eternal God.

For the blood of your blessed Martyr N.,
poured out like Christ's to glorify your name,
shows forth your marvellous works,
by which in our weakness you perfect your power
and on the feeble bestow strength to bear you witness,
through Christ our Lord.

And so, with the Powers of heaven,
we worship you constantly on earth,
and before your majesty
without end we acclaim:

Holy, Holy, Holy Lord God of hosts. . .

PREFACE II OF HOLY MARTYRS

The wonders of God in the victory of the Martyrs

It is truly right and just, our duty and our salvation,
always and everywhere to give you thanks,
Lord, holy Father, almighty and eternal God.

For you are glorified when your Saints are praised;
their very sufferings are but wonders of your might:
in your mercy you give ardour to their faith,
to their endurance you grant firm resolve,
and in their struggle the victory is yours,
through Christ our Lord.

Therefore, all creatures of heaven and earth
sing a new song in adoration,
and we, with all the host of Angels,
cry out, and without end we acclaim:

Holy, Holy, Holy Lord God of hosts. . .

PRÆFATIO I DE DEFUNCTIS

De spe resurrectionis in Christo

Vere dignum et iustum est, æquum et salutare,
nos tibi semper et ubique gratias agere:
Domine, sancte Pater, omnipotens æterne Deus:
per Christum Dominum nostrum.

In quo nobis spes beatæ resurrectionis effulsit,
ut, quos contristat certa moriendi condicio,
eosdem consoletur futuræ immortalitatis promissio.
Tuis enim fidelibus, Domine, vita mutatur, non tollitur,
et, dissoluta terrestris huius incolatus domo,
æterna in cælis habitatio comparatur.

Et ideo cum Angelis et Archangelis,
cum Thronis et Dominationibus,
cumque omni militia cælestis exercitus,
hymnum gloriæ tuæ canimus,
sine fine dicentes:

Sanctus, Sanctus, Sanctus Dominus Deus Sabaoth. . .

PRÆFATIO II DE DEFUNCTIS

Christus mortuus est pro vita nostra

Vere dignum et iustum est, æquum et salutare,
nos tibi semper et ubique gratias agere:
Domine, sancte Pater, omnipotens æterne Deus:
per Christum Dominum nostrum.

Ipse enim mortem unus accepit,
ne omnes nos moreremur;
immo unus mori dignatus est,
ut omnes tibi perpetuo viveremus.

Et ideo, choris angelicis sociati,
te laudamus in gaudio confitentes:

Sanctus, Sanctus, Sanctus Dominus Deus Sabaoth. . .

PREFACE I FOR THE DEAD

The hope of resurrection in Christ

It is truly right and just, our duty and our salvation,
always and everywhere to give you thanks,
Lord, holy Father, almighty and eternal God,
through Christ our Lord.

In him the hope of blessed resurrection has dawned,
that those saddened by the certainty of dying
might be consoled by the promise of immortality to come.
Indeed for your faithful, Lord,
life is changed not ended,
and, when this earthly dwelling turns to dust,
an eternal dwelling is made ready for them in heaven.

And so, with Angels and Archangels,
with Thrones and Dominions,
and with all the hosts and Powers of heaven,
we sing the hymn of your glory,
as without end we acclaim:

Holy, Holy, Holy Lord God of hosts. . .

PREFACE II FOR THE DEAD

Christ died so that we might live

It is truly right and just, our duty and our salvation,
always and everywhere to give you thanks,
Lord, holy Father, almighty and eternal God,
through Christ our Lord.

For as one alone he accepted death,
so that we might all escape from dying;
as one man he chose to die,
so that in your sight we all might live for ever.

And so, in company with the choirs of Angels,
we praise you, and with joy we proclaim:

Holy, Holy, Holy Lord God of hosts. . .

PRÆFATIO III DE DEFUNCTIS

Christus, salus et vita

Vere dignum et iustum est, æquum et salutare,
nos tibi semper et ubique gratias agere:
Domine, sancte Pater, omnipotens æterne Deus:
per Christum Dominum nostrum:

Qui est salus mundi, vita hominum, resurrectio mortuorum.

Per quem maiestatem tuam adorat exercitus Angelorum,
ante conspectum tuum in æternitate lætantium.
Cum quibus et nostras voces ut admitti iubeas, deprecamur,
socia exsultatione dicentes:

Sanctus, Sanctus, Sanctus Dominus Deus Sabaoth. . .

PRÆFATIO IV DE DEFUNCTIS

De vita terrena ad gloriam cælestem

Vere dignum et iustum est, æquum et salutare,
nos tibi semper et ubique gratias agere:
Domine, sancte Pater, omnipotens æterne Deus:

Cuius imperio nascimur, cuius arbitrio regimur,
cuius præcepto in terra, de qua sumpti sumus,
peccati lege absolvimur.
Et, qui per mortem Filii tui redempti sumus,
ad ipsius resurrectionis gloriam
tuo nutu excitamur.

Et ideo, cum Angelorum atque Sanctorum turba,
hymnum laudis tibi canimus, sine fine dicentes:

Sanctus, Sanctus, Sanctus Dominus Deus Sabaoth. . .

PREFACE III FOR THE DEAD

Christ, the salvation and the life

It is truly right and just, our duty and our salvation,
always and everywhere to give you thanks,
Lord, holy Father, almighty and eternal God,
through Christ our Lord.

For he is the salvation of the world,
the life of the human race,
the resurrection of the dead.

Through him the host of Angels adores your majesty
and rejoices in your presence for ever.
May our voices, we pray, join with theirs
in one chorus of exultant praise, as we acclaim:

Holy, Holy, Holy Lord God of hosts. . .

PREFACE IV FOR THE DEAD

From earthly life to heavenly glory

It is truly right and just, our duty and our salvation,
always and everywhere to give you thanks,
Lord, holy Father, almighty and eternal God.

For it is at your summons that we come to birth,
by your will that we are governed,
and at your command that we return,
on account of sin,
to that earth from which we came.

And when you give the sign,
we who have been redeemed by the Death of your Son,
shall be raised up to the glory of his Resurrection.

And so, with the company of Angels and Saints,
we sing the hymn of your praise,
as without end we acclaim:

Holy, Holy, Holy Lord God of hosts. . .

PRÆFATIO V DE DEFUNCTIS

De resurrectione nostra per victoriam Christi

Vere dignum et iustum est, æquum et salutare,
nos tibi semper et ubique gratias agere:
Domine, sancte Pater, omnipotens æterne Deus:

Quia, etsi nostri est meriti quod perimus,
tuæ tamen est pietatis et gratiæ
quod, pro peccato morte consumpti,
per Christi victoriam redempti,
cum ipso revocamur ad vitam.

Et ideo, cum cælorum Virtutibus,
in terris te iugiter celebramus,
maiestati tuæ sine fine clamantes:

Sanctus, Sanctus, Sanctus Dominus Deus Sabaoth. . .

PREFACE V FOR THE DEAD

Our resurrection through the victory of Christ

It is truly right and just, our duty and our salvation,
always and everywhere to give you thanks,
Lord, holy Father, almighty and eternal God.

For even though by our own fault we perish,
yet by your compassion and your grace,
when seized by death according to our sins,
we are redeemed through Christ's great victory,
and with him called back into life.

And so, with the Powers of heaven,
we worship you constantly on earth,
and before your majesty
without end we acclaim:

Holy, Holy, Holy Lord God of hosts. . .

EUCHARISTIC PRAYER I
(THE ROMAN CANON)

Pr. Te ígitur, clementíssime Pater,
per Iesum Christum, Fílium tuum,
Dóminum nostrum,
súpplices rogámus ac pétimus,
uti accépta hábeas
et benedícas ✠ hæc dona, hæc múnera,
hæc sancta sacrifícia illibáta,
in primis, quæ tibi offérimus
pro Ecclésia tua sancta cathólica:
quam pacificáre, custodíre, adunáre
et régere dignéris toto orbe terrárum:
una cum fámulo tuo Papa nostro N.
et Antístite nostro N.*
et ómnibus orthodóxis atque cathólicæ
et apostólicæ fídei cultóribus.

Commemoration of the Living.

Meménto, Dómine,
famulórum famularúmque tuárum N. et N.
et ómnium circumstántium,
quorum tibi fides cógnita est et nota devótio,
pro quibus tibi offérimus:
vel qui tibi ófferunt hoc sacrifícium laudis,
pro se suísque ómnibus:
pro redemptióne animárum suárum,
pro spe salútis et incolumitátis suæ:
tibíque reddunt vota sua
ætérno Deo, vivo et vero.

Within the Action

Communicántes,
et memóriam venerántes,
in primis gloriósæ semper Vírginis Maríæ,
Genetrícis Dei et Dómini nostri Iesu Christi:
† sed et beáti Ioseph, eiúsdem Vírginis Sponsi,
et beatórum Apostolórum ac Mártyrum tuórum,
Petri et Pauli, Andréæ,
(Iacóbi, Ioánnis,
Thomæ, Iacóbi, Philíppi,

---

*Mention may be made here of the Coadjutor Bishop or Auxiliary Bishops.

EUCHARISTIC PRAYER I
(THE ROMAN CANON)

Pr. To you, therefore, most merciful Father,
we make humble prayer and petition
through Jesus Christ, your Son, our Lord:
that you accept
and bless ✠ these gifts, these offerings,
these holy and unblemished sacrifices,
which we offer you firstly
for your holy catholic Church.
Be pleased to grant her peace,
to guard, unite and govern her
throughout the whole world,
together with your servant N. our Pope
and N. our Bishop,[*]
and all those who, holding to the truth,
hand on the catholic and apostolic faith.

Commemoration of the Living.
Remember, Lord, your servants N. and N.
and all gathered here,
whose faith and devotion are known to you.
For them, we offer you this sacrifice of praise
or they offer it for themselves
and all who are dear to them:
for the redemption of their souls,
in hope of health and well-being,
and paying their homage to you,
the eternal God, living and true.

Within the Action
In communion with those whose memory we venerate,
especially the glorious ever-Virgin Mary,
Mother of our God and Lord, Jesus Christ,
† and blessed Joseph, her Spouse,
your blessed Apostles and Martyrs,
Peter and Paul, Andrew,
(James, John,
Thomas, James, Philip,

---

[*] Mention may be made here of the Coadjutor Bishop or Auxiliary Bishops.

Bartholomǽi, Matthǽi,
Simónis et Thaddǽi:
Lini, Cleti, Cleméntis, Xysti,
Cornélii, Cypriáni,
Lauréntii, Chrysógoni,
Ioánnis et Pauli,
Cosmæ et Damiáni)
et ómnium Sanctórum tuórum;
quorum méritis precibúsque concédas,
ut in ómnibus protectiónis tuæ muniámur auxílio.
(Per Christum Dóminum nostrum. Amen.)

PROPER FORMS OF THE COMMUNICANTES

On the Nativity of the Lord and throughout the Octave

> Communicántes,
> et (noctem sacratíssimam) diem sacratíssimum celebrántes,
> (qua) quo beátæ Maríæ intemeráta virgínitas
> huic mundo édidit Salvatórem:
> sed et memóriam venerántes,
> in primis eiúsdem gloriósæ semper Vírginis Maríæ,
> Genetrícis eiúsdem Dei et Dómini nostri Iesu Christi: †

On the Epiphany of the Lord

> Communicántes,
> et diem sacratíssimum celebrántes,
> quo Unigénitus tuus, in tua tecum glória coætérnus,
> in veritáte carnis nostræ visibíliter corporális appáruit:
> sed et memóriam venerántes,
> in primis gloriósæ semper Vírginis Maríæ,
> Genetrícis eiúsdem Dei et Dómini nostri Iesu Christi: †

From the Mass of the Easter Vigil until the Second Sunday of Easter

> Communicántes,
> et (noctem sacratíssimam) diem sacratíssimum celebrántes
> Resurrectiónis Dómini nostri Iesu Christi secúndum carnem:
> sed et memóriam venerántes,
> in primis gloriósæ semper Vírginis Maríæ,
> Genetrícis eiúsdem Dei et Dómini nostri Iesu Christi: †

Bartholomew, Matthew,
Simon and Jude;
Linus, Cletus, Clement, Sixtus,
Cornelius, Cyprian,
Lawrence, Chrysogonus,
John and Paul,
Cosmas and Damian)
and all your Saints;
we ask that through their merits and prayers,
in all things we may be defended
by your protecting help.
(Through Christ our Lord. Amen.)

PROPER FORMS OF THE COMMUNICANTES

On the Nativity of the Lord and throughout the Octave

Celebrating the most sacred night (day)
on which blessed Mary the immaculate Virgin
brought forth the Saviour for this world,
and in communion with those whose memory we venerate,
especially the glorious ever-Virgin Mary,
Mother of our God and Lord, Jesus Christ, †

On the Epiphany of the Lord

Celebrating the most sacred day
on which your Only Begotten Son,
eternal with you in your glory,
appeared in a human body, truly sharing our flesh,
and in communion with those whose memory we venerate,
especially the glorious ever-Virgin Mary,
Mother of our God and Lord, Jesus Christ, †

From the Mass of the Easter Vigil until the Second Sunday of Easter

Celebrating the most sacred night (day)
of the Resurrection of our Lord Jesus Christ in the flesh,
and in communion with those whose memory we venerate,
especially the glorious ever-Virgin Mary,
Mother of our God and Lord, Jesus Christ, †

On the Ascension of the Lord

> Communicántes,
> et diem sacratíssimum celebrántes,
> quo Dóminus noster, Unigénitus Fílius tuus,
> unítam sibi fragilitátis nostræ substántiam
> in glóriæ tuæ déxtera collocávit:
> sed et memóriam venerántes,
> in primis gloriósæ semper Vírginis Maríæ,
> Genetrícis eiúsdem Dei et Dómini nostri Iesu Christi: †

On Pentecost Sunday

> Communicántes,
> et diem sacratíssimum Pentecóstes celebrántes,
> quo Spíritus Sanctus
> Apóstolis in ígneis linguis appáruit:
> sed et memóriam venerántes,
> in primis gloriósæ semper Vírginis Maríæ,
> Genetrícis Dei et Dómini nostri Iesu Christi: †

Hanc ígitur oblatiónem servitútis nostræ,
sed et cunctæ famíliæ tuæ,
quǽsumus, Dómine, ut placátus accípias:
diésque nostros in tua pace dispónas,
atque ab ætérna damnatióne nos éripi
et in electórum tuórum iúbeas grege numerári.
(Per Christum Dóminum nostrum. Amen.)

From the Mass of the Easter Vigil until the Second Sunday of Easter

> Hanc ígitur oblatiónem servitútis nostræ,
> sed et cunctæ famíliæ tuæ,
> quam tibi offérimus
> pro his quoque, quos regeneráre dignátus es ex aqua et Spíritu Sancto,
> tríbuens eis remissiónem ómnium peccatórum,
> quǽsumus, Dómine, ut placátus accípias:
> diésque nostros in tua pace dispónas,
> atque ab ætérna damnatióne nos éripi
> et in electórum tuórum iúbeas grege numerári.
> (Per Christum Dóminum nostrum. Amen.)

On the Ascension of the Lord

> Celebrating the most sacred day
> on which your Only Begotten Son, our Lord,
> placed at the right hand of your glory
> our weak human nature,
> which he had united to himself,
> and in communion with those whose memory we venerate,
> especially the glorious ever-Virgin Mary,
> Mother of our God and Lord, Jesus Christ, †

On Pentecost Sunday

> Celebrating the most sacred day of Pentecost,
> on which the Holy Spirit
> appeared to the Apostles in tongues of fire,
> and in communion with those whose memory we venerate,
> especially the glorious ever-Virgin Mary,
> Mother of our God and Lord, Jesus Christ, †

Therefore, Lord, we pray:
graciously accept this oblation of our service,
that of your whole family;
order our days in your peace,
and command that we be delivered from eternal damnation
and counted among the flock of those you have chosen.
(Through Christ Our Lord. Amen.)

From the Mass of the Easter Vigil until the Second Sunday of Easter

> Therefore, Lord, we pray:
> graciously accept this oblation of our service,
> that of your whole family,
> which we make to you
> also for those to whom you have been pleased to give
> the new birth of water and the Holy Spirit,
> granting them forgiveness of all their sins;
> order our days in your peace,
> and command that we be delivered from eternal damnation
> and counted among the flock of those you have chosen.
> (Through Christ our Lord. Amen.)

Quam oblatiónem tu, Deus, in ómnibus, quǽsumus,
benedíctam, adscríptam, ratam,
rationábilem, acceptabilémque fácere dignéris:
ut nobis Corpus et Sanguis fiat dilectíssimi Fílii tui,
Dómini nostri Iesu Christi.

Qui, prídie quam paterétur,
accépit panem in sanctas ac venerábiles manus suas,
et elevátis óculis in cælum
ad te Deum Patrem suum omnipoténtem,
tibi grátias agens benedíxit,
fregit,
dedítque discípulis suis, dicens:

ACCÍPITE ET MANDUCÁTE EX HOC OMNES:
HOC EST ENIM CORPUS MEUM,
QUOD PRO VOBIS TRADÉTUR.

Símili modo, postquam cenátum est,
accípiens et hunc præclárum cálicem
in sanctas ac venerábiles manus suas,
item tibi grátias agens benedíxit,
dedítque discípulis suis dicens:

ACCÍPITE ET BÍBITE EX EO OMNES:
HIC EST ENIM CALIX SÁNGUINIS MEI
NOVI ET ÆTÉRNI TESTAMÉNTI,
QUI PRO VOBIS ET PRO MULTIS EFFUNDÉTUR
IN REMISSIÓNEM PECCATÓRUM.
HOC FÁCITE IN MEAM COMMEMORATIÓNEM.

Be pleased, O God, we pray,
to bless, acknowledge,
and approve this offering in every respect;
make it spiritual and acceptable,
so that it may become for us
the Body and Blood of your most beloved Son,
our Lord Jesus Christ.

On the day before he was to suffer,
he took bread in his holy and venerable hands,
and with eyes raised to heaven
to you, O God, his almighty Father,
giving you thanks, he said the blessing,
broke the bread
and gave it to his disciples, saying:

TAKE THIS, ALL OF YOU, AND EAT OF IT,
FOR THIS IS MY BODY,
WHICH WILL BE GIVEN UP FOR YOU.

In a similar way, when supper was ended,
he took this precious chalice
in his holy and venerable hands,
and once more giving you thanks, he said the blessing
and gave the chalice to his disciples, saying:

TAKE THIS, ALL OF YOU, AND DRINK FROM IT,
FOR THIS IS THE CHALICE OF MY BLOOD,
THE BLOOD OF THE NEW AND ETERNAL COVENANT,
WHICH WILL BE POURED OUT FOR YOU AND FOR MANY
FOR THE FORGIVENESS OF SINS.
DO THIS IN MEMORY OF ME.

Pr. Mystérium fídei.

The people continue, acclaiming one of the following:

Mortem tu-am annunti-ámus, Dómi-ne,   et tu-am resurrecti-ó-

nem confi-témur, do-nec vé-ni-as.

**1. Mortem tuam annuntiámus, Dómine,
et tuam resurrectiónem confitémur, donec vénias.**

Quoti-escúmque manducámus panem hunc   et cálicem bíbimus,

mortem tu-am annunti-ámus, Dómine, donec vé- ni-as.

**2. Quotiescúmque manducámus panem hunc
et cálicem bíbimus,
mortem tuam annuntiámus, Dómine, donec vénias.**

Salvátor mundi, salva nos, qui per crucem et resurrecti-ónem tu-am

li-be-rá- sti nos.

**3. Salvátor mundi, salva nos,
qui per crucem et resurrectiónem tuam liberásti nos.**

Pr. The mystery of faith.

The people continue, acclaiming one of the following:

We pro-claim your Death, O Lord, and pro-fess your Res-ur-rec-tion un-til you come a-gain.

1. **We proclaim your Death, O Lord,**
and profess your Resurrection
until you come again.

When we eat this Bread and drink this Cup, we pro-claim your Death, O Lord, un-til you come a-gain.

2. **When we eat this Bread and drink this Cup,**
we proclaim your Death, O Lord,
until you come again.

Save us, Sav-iour of the world, for by your Cross and Res-ur-rec-tion you have set us free.

3. **Save us, Saviour of the world,**
for by your Cross and Resurrection
you have set us free.

Only in Ireland: 4. **My Lord and my God.**

Pr. Unde et mémores, Dómine,
nos servi tui,
sed et plebs tua sancta,
eiúsdem Christi, Fílii tui, Dómini nostri,
tam beátæ passiónis,
necnon et ab ínferis resurrectiónis,
sed et in cælos gloriósæ ascensiónis:
offérimus præcláræ maiestáti tuæ
de tuis donis ac datis
hóstiam puram,
hóstiam sanctam,
hóstiam immaculátam,
Panem sanctum vitæ ætérnæ
et Cálicem salútis perpétuæ.

Supra quæ propítio ac seréno vultu
respícere dignéris:
et accépta habére,
sícuti accépta habére dignátus es
múnera púeri tui iusti Abel,
et sacrifícium Patriárchæ nostri Abrahæ,
et quod tibi óbtulit summus sacérdos tuus Melchísedech,
sanctum sacrifícium, immaculátam hóstiam.

Súpplices te rogámus, omnípotens Deus:
iube hæc perférri per manus sancti Angeli tui
in sublíme altáre tuum,
in conspéctu divínæ maiestátis tuæ;
ut, quotquot ex hac altáris participatióne
sacrosánctum Fílii tui Corpus et Sánguinem sumpsérimus,
omni benedictióne cælésti et grátia repleámur
(Per Christum Dóminum nostrum. Amen.)

Commemoration of the Dead.

Meménto étiam, Dómine, famulórum famularúmque tuárum N. et N.,
qui nos præcessérunt cum signo fídei,
et dórmiunt in somno pacis.
Ipsis, Dómine, et ómnibus in Christo quiescéntibus,
locum refrigérii, lucis et pacis,
ut indúlgeas, deprecámur.
(Per Christum Dóminum nostrum. Amen.)

Nobis quoque peccatóribus fámulis tuis,
de multitúdine miseratiónum tuárum sperántibus,

Pr. Therefore, O Lord,
as we celebrate the memorial of the blessed Passion,
the Resurrection from the dead,
and the glorious Ascension into heaven
of Christ, your Son, our Lord,
we, your servants and your holy people,
offer to your glorious majesty
from the gifts that you have given us,
this pure victim,
this holy victim,
this spotless victim,
the holy Bread of eternal life
and the Chalice of everlasting salvation.

Be pleased to look upon these offerings
with a serene and kindly countenance,
and to accept them,
as once you were pleased to accept
the gifts of your servant Abel the just,
the sacrifice of Abraham, our father in faith,
and the offering of your high priest Melchizedek,
a holy sacrifice, a spotless victim.

In humble prayer we ask you, almighty God:
command that these gifts be borne
by the hands of your holy Angel
to your altar on high
in the sight of your divine majesty,
so that all of us, who through this participation at the altar
receive the most holy Body and Blood of your Son,
may be filled with every grace and heavenly blessing.
(Through Christ our Lord. Amen.)

Commemoration of the Dead.

Remember also, Lord, your servants N. and N.,
who have gone before us with the sign of faith
and rest in the sleep of peace.
Grant them, O Lord, we pray,
and all who sleep in Christ,
a place of refreshment, light and peace.
(Through Christ our Lord. Amen.)

To us, also, your servants, who, though sinners,
hope in your abundant mercies,

partem áliquam et societátem donáre dignéris
cum tuis sanctis Apóstolis et Martýribus:
cum Ioánne, Stéphano,
Matthía, Bárnaba,
(Ignátio, Alexándro,
Marcellíno, Petro,
Felicitáte, Perpétua,
Agatha, Lúcia,
Agnéte, Cæcília, Anastásia)
et ómnibus Sanctis tuis:
intra quorum nos consórtium,
non æstimátor mériti,
sed véniæ, quǽsumus, largítor admítte.
Per Christum Dóminum nostrum.

Per quem hæc ómnia, Dómine,
semper bona creas, sanctíficas, vivíficas, benedícis,
et præstas nobis.

Pr. Per ipsum, et cum ipso, et in ipso,
est tibi Deo Patri omnipoténti,
in unitáte Spíritus Sancti,
omnis honor et glória
per ómnia sǽcula sæculórum.

   A-men.
R.   **Amen.**

Then follows the Communion Rite, p.120.

EUCHARISTIC PRAYER II

Pr. Dóminus vóbiscum.
R.   **Et cum spíritu tuo.**
Pr. Sursum corda.
R.   **Habémus ad Dóminum.**
Pr. Grátias agámus Dómino Deo nostro.
R.   **Dignum et iustum est.**
Pr. Vere dignum et iustum est, æquum et salutáre, nos tibi, sancte Pater,

graciously grant some share
and fellowship with your holy Apostles and Martyrs:
with John the Baptist, Stephen,
Matthias, Barnabas,
(Ignatius, Alexander,
Marcellinus, Peter,
Felicity, Perpetua,
Agatha, Lucy,
Agnes, Cecilia, Anastasia)
and all your Saints;
admit us, we beseech you,
into their company,
not weighing our merits,
but granting us your pardon,
through Christ our Lord.
Through whom
you continue to make all these good things, O Lord;
you sanctify them, fill them with life,
bless them, and bestow them upon us.

Pr. Through him, and with him, and in him,
O God, almighty Father,
in the unity of the Holy Spirit,
all glory and honour is yours,
for ever and ever.

A-men.

R. **Amen.**

Then follows the Communion Rite, p.121.

EUCHARISTIC PRAYER II

Pr. The Lord be with you.
R. **And with your spirit.**
Pr. Lift up your hearts.
R. **We lift them up to the Lord.**
Pr. Let us give thanks to the Lord our God.
R. **It is right and just.**
Pr. It is truly right and just, our duty and our salvation,

semper et ubíque grátias ágere
per Fílium dilectiónis tuæ Iesum Christum,
Verbum tuum per quod cuncta fecísti:
quem misísti nobis Salvatórem et Redemptórem,
incarnátum de Spíritu Sancto et ex Vírgine natum.

Qui voluntátem tuam adímplens
et pópulum tibi sanctum acquírens
exténdit manus cum paterétur,
ut mortem sólveret et resurrectiónem manifestáret.

Et ídeo cum Angelis et ómnibus Sanctis
glóriam tuam prædicámus, una voce dicéntes:

The people sing or say aloud the Sanctus.

Sanc-tus, * Sanc-tus, Sanc-tus Dó-mi-nus De-us Sá-ba-oth. Ple-ni

sunt cæ-li et ter-ra gló-ri-a tu-a. Ho-sán-na in ex-cél-sis. Be-ne-díc-

tus qui ve-nit in nómine Dómini.   Ho-sán-na in excél-sis.

Sanctus, Sanctus, Sanctus Dóminus Deus Sábaoth.
Pleni sunt cæli et terra glória tua.
Hosánna in excélsis.
Benedíctus qui venit in nómine Dómini.
Hosánna in excélsis.

Pr. Vere Sanctus es, Dómine, fons omnis sanctitátis.

Hæc ergo dona, quǽsumus,
Spíritus tui rore sanctífica,
ut nobis Corpus et ✠ Sanguis fiant
Dómini nostri Iesu Christi.

always and everywhere to give you thanks, Father most holy,
through your beloved Son, Jesus Christ,
your Word through whom you made all things,
whom you sent as our Saviour and Redeemer,
incarnate by the Holy Spirit and born of the Virgin.

Fulfilling your will and gaining for you a holy people,
he stretched out his hands as he endured his Passion,
so as to break the bonds of death and manifest the resurrection.

And so, with the Angels and all the Saints
we declare your glory,
as with one voice we acclaim:

The people sing or say aloud the Sanctus.

Ho-ly, Ho-ly, Ho-ly Lord God of hosts. Heav-en and earth are full of your glo-ry. Ho-san-na in the high-est. Bless-ed is he who comes in the name of the Lord. Ho-san-na in the high-est.

Holy, Holy, Holy Lord God of hosts.
Heaven and earth are full of your glory.
Hosanna in the highest.
Blessed is he who comes in the name of the Lord.
Hosanna in the highest.

Pr. You are indeed Holy, O Lord,
the fount of all holiness.

Make holy, therefore, these gifts, we pray,
by sending down your Spirit upon them like the dewfall,
so that they may become for us
the Body and ✠ Blood of our Lord Jesus Christ.

Qui cum Passióni voluntárie traderétur,
accépit panem et grátias agens fregit,
dedítque discípulis suis, dicens:

Accípite et manducáte ex hoc omnes:
hoc est enim Corpus meum,
quod pro vobis tradétur.

Símili modo, postquam cenátum est,
accípiens et cálicem,
íterum grátias agens dedit discípulis suis, dicens:

Accípite et bíbite ex eo omnes:
hic est enim calix Sánguinis mei
novi et ætérni testaménti,
qui pro vobis et pro multis effundétur
in remissiónem peccatórum.
Hoc fácite in meam commemoratiónem.

Pr. Mystérium fídei.

The people continue, acclaiming one of the following:

Mortem tu-am annunti-ámus, Dómi-ne,　et tu-am resurrecti-ó-

nem confi-témur, do-nec vé-ni-as.

1. **Mortem tuam annuntiámus, Dómine,
et tuam resurrectiónem confitémur, donec vénias.**

At the time he was betrayed
and entered willingly into his Passion,
he took bread and, giving thanks, broke it,
and gave it to his disciples, saying:

TAKE THIS, ALL OF YOU, AND EAT OF IT,
FOR THIS IS MY BODY,
WHICH WILL BE GIVEN UP FOR YOU.

In a similar way, when supper was ended,
he took the chalice
and, once more giving thanks,
he gave it to his disciples, saying:

TAKE THIS, ALL OF YOU, AND DRINK FROM IT,
FOR THIS IS THE CHALICE OF MY BLOOD,
THE BLOOD OF THE NEW AND ETERNAL COVENANT,
WHICH WILL BE POURED OUT FOR YOU AND FOR MANY
FOR THE FORGIVENESS OF SINS.
DO THIS IN MEMORY OF ME.

Pr. The mystery of faith.

The people continue, acclaiming one of the following:

We pro-claim your Death, O Lord, and pro-fess your Res-ur-rec-tion un-til you come a-gain.

1. We proclaim your Death, O Lord,
and profess your Resurrection
until you come again.

Quoti-escúmque manducámus panem hunc   et cálicem bíbimus,

mortem tu-am annunti-ámus, Dómine, donec vé- ni-as.

**2. Quotiescúmque manducámus panem hunc
et cálicem bíbimus,
mortem tuam annuntiámus, Dómine, donec vénias.**

Salvátor mundi, salva nos, qui per crucem et resurrecti-ónem tu-am

li-be-rá- sti nos.

**3. Salvátor mundi, salva nos,
qui per crucem et resurrectiónem tuam liberásti nos.**

Pr. Mémores ígitur mortis et resurrectiónis eius,
tibi, Dómine, panem vitæ
et cálicem salútis offérimus,
grátias agéntes quia nos dignos habuísti
astáre coram te et tibi ministráre.

Et súpplices deprecámur
ut Córporis et Sánguinis Christi partícipes
a Spíritu Sancto congregémur in unum.

Recordáre, Dómine, Ecclésiæ tuæ toto orbe diffúsæ,
ut eam in caritáte perfícias
una cum Papa nostro N. et Epíscopo nostro N.*
et univérso clero.

---

* Mention may be made here of the Coadjutor Bishop or Auxiliary Bishops.

When we eat this Bread and drink this Cup, we pro-claim your Death, O Lord, un-til you come a-gain.

**2. When we eat this Bread and drink this Cup,
we proclaim your Death, O Lord,
until you come again.**

Save us, Sav-iour of the world, for by your Cross and Res-ur-rec-tion you have set us free.

**3. Save us, Saviour of the world,
for by your Cross and Resurrection
you have set us free.**

Only in Ireland: **4. My Lord and my God.**

Pr. Therefore, as we celebrate
the memorial of his Death and Resurrection,
we offer you, Lord,
the Bread of life and the Chalice of salvation,
giving thanks that you have held us worthy
to be in your presence and minister to you.

Humbly we pray
that, partaking of the Body and Blood of Christ,
we may be gathered into one by the Holy Spirit.

Remember, Lord, your Church,
spread throughout the world,
and bring her to the fullness of charity,
together with N. our Pope and N. our Bishop*
and all the clergy.

* Mention may be made here of the Coadjutor Bishop or Auxiliary Bishops.

In Masses for the Dead, the following may be added:

Meménto fámuli tui (fámulæ tuæ) N.,
quem (quam) (hódie) ad te ex hoc mundo vocásti.
Concéde, ut, qui (quæ) complantátus (complantáta) fuit
    similitúdini mortis Fílii tui,
simul fiat et resurrectiónis ipsíus.

Meménto étiam fratrum nostrórum,
qui in spe resurrectiónis dormiérunt,
omniúmque in tua miseratióne defunctórum,
et eos in lumen vultus tui admítte.
Omnium nostrum, quǽsumus, miserére,
ut cum beáta Dei Genetríce Vírgine María,
beáto Ioseph, eius Sponso,
beátis Apostólis et ómnibus Sanctis,
qui tibi a sǽculo placuérunt,
ætérnæ vitæ mereámur esse consórtes,
et te laudémus et glorificémus
per Fílium tuum Iesum Christum.

Per ipsum, et cum ipso, et in ipso,
est tibi Deo Patri omnipoténti,
in unitáte Spíritus Sancti,
omnis honor et glória
per ómnia sǽcula sæculórum.

A-men.
R. Amen.

Then follows the Communion Rite, p.120.

EUCHARISTIC PRAYER III

Pr. Vere Sanctus es, Dómine,
et mérito te laudat omnis a te cóndita creatúra,
quia per Fílium tuum,
Dóminum nostrum Iesum Christum,
Spíritus Sancti operánte virtúte,
vivíficas et sanctíficas univérsa,
et pópulum tibi congregáre non désinis,

In Masses for the Dead, the following may be added:

Remember your servant N.,
whom you have called (today)
from this world to yourself.
Grant that he (she) who was united with your Son in a death like his,
may also be one with him in his Resurrection.

Remember also our brothers and sisters
who have fallen asleep in the hope of the resurrection,
and all who have died in your mercy:
welcome them into the light of your face.
Have mercy on us all, we pray,
that with the Blessed Virgin Mary, Mother of God,
with blessed Joseph, her Spouse,
with the blessed Apostles,
and all the Saints who have pleased you throughout the ages,
we may merit to be coheirs to eternal life,
and may praise and glorify you
through your Son, Jesus Christ.

Through him, and with him, and in him,
O God, almighty Father,
in the unity of the Holy Spirit,
all glory and honour is yours,
for ever and ever.

A-men.

R. Amen.

Then follows the Communion Rite, p.121.

EUCHARISTIC PRAYER III

Pr. You are indeed Holy, O Lord,
and all you have created
rightly gives you praise,
for through your Son our Lord Jesus Christ,
by the power and working of the Holy Spirit,
you give life to all things and make them holy,
and you never cease to gather a people to yourself,

ut a solis ortu usque ad occásum
oblátio munda offerátur nómini tuo.

Súpplices ergo te, Dómine, deprecámur,
ut hæc múnera, quæ tibi sacránda detúlimus,
eódem Spíritu sanctificáre dignéris,
ut Corpus et ✠ Sanguis fiant
Fílii tui Dómini nostri Iesu Christi,
cuius mandáto hæc mystéria celebrámus.

Ipse enim in qua nocte tradebátur
accépit panem
et tibi grátias agens benedíxit,
fregit, dedítque discípulis suis, dicens:

ACCÍPITE ET MANDUCÁTE EX HOC OMNES:
HOC EST ENIM CORPUS MEUM,
QUOD PRO VOBIS TRADÉTUR.

Símili modo, postquam cenátum est,
accípiens cálicem,
et tibi grátias agens benedíxit,
dedítque discípulis suis, dicens:

ACCÍPITE ET BÍBITE EX EO OMNES:
HIC EST ENIM CALIX SÁNGUINIS MEI
NOVI ET ÆTÉRNI TESTAMÉNTI,
QUI PRO VOBIS ET PRO MULTIS EFFUNDÉTUR
IN REMISSIÓNEM PECCATÓRUM.
HOC FÁCITE IN MEAM COMMEMORATIÓNEM.

so that from the rising of the sun to its setting
a pure sacrifice may be offered to your name.

Therefore, O Lord, we humbly implore you:
by the same Spirit graciously make holy
these gifts we have brought to you for consecration,
that they may become the Body and ✠ Blood
of your Son our Lord Jesus Christ,
at whose command we celebrate these mysteries.

For on the night he was betrayed
he himself took bread,
and, giving you thanks, he said the blessing,
broke the bread and gave it to his disciples, saying:

TAKE THIS, ALL OF YOU, AND EAT OF IT,
FOR THIS IS MY BODY,
WHICH WILL BE GIVEN UP FOR YOU.

In a similar way, when supper was ended,
he took the chalice,
and, giving you thanks, he said the blessing,
and gave the chalice to his disciples, saying:

TAKE THIS, ALL OF YOU, AND DRINK FROM IT,
FOR THIS IS THE CHALICE OF MY BLOOD,
THE BLOOD OF THE NEW AND ETERNAL COVENANT,
WHICH WILL BE POURED OUT FOR YOU AND FOR MANY
FOR THE FORGIVENESS OF SINS.
DO THIS IN MEMORY OF ME.

Pr. Mystérium fídei.

The people continue, acclaiming one of the following:

Mortem tu-am annunti-ámus, Dómi-ne, et tu-am resurrecti-ó-

nem confi-témur, do-nec vé-ni-as.

1. **Mortem tuam annuntiámus, Dómine,
et tuam resurrectiónem confitémur, donec vénias.**

Quoti-escúmque manducámus panem hunc et cálicem bíbimus,

mortem tu-am annunti-ámus, Dómine, donec vé- ni-as.

2. **Quotiescúmque manducámus panem hunc
et cálicem bíbimus,
mortem tuam annuntiámus, Dómine, donec vénias.**

Salvátor mundi, salva nos, qui per crucem et resurrecti-ónem tu-am

li-be-rá- sti nos.

3. **Salvátor mundi, salva nos,
qui per crucem et resurrectiónem tuam liberásti nos.**

Pr. The mystery of faith.

The people continue, acclaiming one of the following:

We pro-claim your Death, O Lord, and pro-fess your Res-ur-rec-tion un-til you come a-gain.

**1. We proclaim your Death, O Lord,
and profess your Resurrection
until you come again.**

When we eat this Bread and drink this Cup, we pro-claim your Death, O Lord, un-til you come a-gain.

**2. When we eat this Bread and drink this Cup,
we proclaim your Death, O Lord,
until you come again.**

Save us, Sav-iour of the world, for by your Cross and Res-ur-rec-tion you have set us free.

**3. Save us, Saviour of the world,
for by your Cross and Resurrection
you have set us free.**

Only in Ireland: **4. My Lord and my God.**

Pr. Mémores ígitur, Dómine,
eiúsdem Fílii tui salutíferæ passiónis
necnon mirábilis resurrectiónis
et ascensiónis in cælum,
sed et præstolántes álterum eius advéntum,
offérimus tibi, grátias reveréntes,
hoc sacrifícium vivum et sanctum.

Réspice, quǽsumus, in oblatiónem Ecclésiæ tuæ
et, agnóscens Hóstiam,
cuius voluísti immolatióne placári,
concéde, ut qui Córpore et Sánguine Fílii tui refícimur,
Spíritu eius Sancto repléti,
unum corpus et unus spíritus inveniámur in Christo.

Ipse nos tibi perfíciat munus ætérnum,
ut cum eléctis tuis hereditátem cónsequi valeámus,
in primis cum beátissima Vírgine, Dei Genetríce, María,
cum beáto Ioseph, eius Sponso,
cum beátis Apóstolis tuis et gloriósis Martýribus
(cum Sancto N.: the saint of the day or Patron Saint)
et ómnibus Sanctis, ·
quorum intercessióne
perpétuo apud te confídimus adiuvári.

Hæc Hóstia nostræ reconciliatiónis profíciat,
quǽsumus, Dómine,
ad totíus mundi pacem atque salútem.
Ecclésiam tuam, peregrinántem in terra,
in fide et caritáte firmáre dignéris
cum fámulo tuo Papa nostro N. et Epíscopo nostro N.*,
cum episcopáli órdine et univérso clero
et omni pópulo acquisitiónis tuæ.

Votis huius famíliæ, quam tibi astáre voluísti,
adésto propítius.
Omnes fílios tuos ubíque dispérsos
tibi, clemens Pater, miserátus coniúnge.

---

*Mention may be made here of the Coadjutor Bishop or Auxiliary Bishops.

Pr. Therefore, O Lord, as we celebrate the memorial
of the saving Passion of your Son,
his wondrous Resurrection
and Ascension into heaven,
and as we look forward to his second coming,
we offer you in thanksgiving
this holy and living sacrifice.

Look, we pray, upon the oblation of your Church
and, recognising the sacrificial Victim by whose death
you willed to reconcile us to yourself,
grant that we, who are nourished
by the Body and Blood of your Son
and filled with his Holy Spirit,
may become one body, one spirit in Christ.

May he make of us
an eternal offering to you,
so that we may obtain an inheritance with your elect,
especially with the most Blessed Virgin Mary, Mother of God,
with blessed Joseph, her Spouse,
with your blessed Apostles and glorious Martyrs
(with Saint N.: the Saint of the day or Patron Saint)
and with all the Saints,
on whose constant intercession in your presence
we rely for unfailing help.

May this Sacrifice of our reconciliation,
we pray, O Lord,
advance the peace and salvation of all the world.
Be pleased to confirm in faith and charity
your pilgrim Church on earth,
with your servant N. our Pope and N. our Bishop*,
the Order of Bishops, all the clergy,
and the entire people you have gained for your own.

Listen graciously to the prayers of this family,
whom you have summoned before you:
in your compassion, O merciful Father,
gather to yourself all your children
scattered throughout the world.

---

* Mention may be made here of the Coadjutor Bishop or Auxiliary Bishops.

† Fratres nostros defúnctos
et omnes qui, tibi placéntes, ex hoc sǽculo transiérunt,
in regnum tuum benígnus admítte,
ubi fore sperámus,
ut simul glória tua perénniter satiémur,
per Christum Dóminum nostrum,
per quem mundo bona cuncta largíris. †

Per ipsum, et cum ipso, et in ipso,
est tibi Deo Patri omnipoténti,
in unitáte Spíritus Sancti,
omnis honor et glória
per ómnia sǽcula sæculórum.

A-men.

R.   **Amen.**

Then follows the Communion Rite, p.120.

When this Eucharistic Prayer is used in Masses for the Dead, the following may be said:

† Meménto fámuli tui (fámulæ tuæ) N.,
quem (quam) (hódie) ad te ex hoc mundo vocásti.
Concéde, ut, qui (quæ) complantátus (complantáta)
      fuit similitúdini mortis Fílii tui,
simul fiat et resurrectiónis ipsíus,
quando mórtuos suscitábit in carne de terra
et corpus humilitátis nostræ
configurábit córpori claritátis suæ.
Sed et fratres nostros defúnctos,
et omnes qui, tibi placéntes, ex hoc sǽculo transiérunt,
in regnum tuum benígnus admítte,
ubi fore sperámus,
ut simul glória tua perénniter satiémur,
quando omnem lácrimam abstérges ab óculis nostris,
quia te, sícuti es, Deum nostrum vidéntes,
tibi símiles érimus cuncta per sǽcula,
et te sine fine laudábimus,
per Christum Dóminum nostrum,
per quem mundo bona cuncta largíris. †

† To our departed brothers and sisters
and to all who were pleasing to you
at their passing from this life,
give kind admittance to your kingdom.
There we hope to enjoy for ever the fullness of your glory
through Christ our Lord,
through whom you bestow on the world all that is good. †

Through him, and with him, and in him,
O God, almighty Father,
in the unity of the Holy Spirit,
all glory and honour is yours,
for ever and ever.

A-men.

R. **Amen.**

Then follows the Communion Rite, p.121.

When this Eucharistic Prayer is used in Masses for the Dead, the following may be said:

† Remember your servant N.
whom you have called (today)
from this world to yourself.
Grant that he (she) who was united with your Son in a death like his,
may also be one with him in his Resurrection,
when from the earth
he will raise up in the flesh those who have died,
and transform our lowly body
after the pattern of his own glorious body.
To our departed brothers and sisters, too,
and to all who were pleasing to you
at their passing from this life,
give kind admittance to your kingdom.
There we hope to enjoy for ever the fullness of your glory,
when you will wipe away every tear from our eyes.
For seeing you, our God, as you are,
we shall be like you for all the ages
and praise you without end,
through Christ our Lord,
through whom you bestow on the world all that is good. †

EUCHARISTIC PRAYER IV

Pr. Dóminus vóbiscum.
R. **Et cum spíritu tuo.**
Pr. Sursum corda.
R. **Habémus ad Dóminum.**
Pr. Grátias agámus Dómino Deo nostro.
R. **Dignum et iustum est.**

Pr. Vere dignum est tibi grátias ágere,
vere iustum est te glorificáre, Pater sancte,
quia unus es Deus vivus et verus,
qui es ante sǽcula et pérmanes in ætérnum,
inaccessíbilem lucem inhábitans;
sed et qui unus bonus atque fons vitæ cuncta fecísti,
ut creatúras tuas benedictiónibus adimpléres
multásque lætificáres tui lúminis claritáte.

Et ídeo coram te innúmeræ astant turbæ Angelórum,
qui die ac nocte sérviunt tibi
et, vultus tui glóriam contemplántes,
te incessánter gloríficant.

Cum quibus et nos et, per nostram vocem,
omnis quæ sub cælo est creatúra
nomen tuum in exsultatióne confitémur, canéntes:

The people sing or say aloud the Sanctus.

S anc-tus, * Sanc-tus, Sanc-tus Dó-mi-nus De-us Sá-ba-oth. Ple-ni

sunt cæ-li et ter-ra gló-ri-a tu-a. Ho-sán-na in ex-cél-sis. Be-ne-díc-

tus qui ve-nit in nómine Dómini.   Ho-sán-na in excél-sis.

EUCHARISTIC PRAYER IV

Pr. The Lord be with you.

R. And with your spirit.

Pr. Lift up your hearts.

R. We lift them up to the Lord.

Pr. Let us give thanks to the Lord our God.

R. It is right and just.

Pr. It is truly right to give you thanks,
truly just to give you glory, Father most holy,
for you are the one God living and true,
existing before all ages and abiding for all eternity,
dwelling in unapproachable light;
yet you, who alone are good, the source of life,
have made all that is,
so that you might fill your creatures with blessings
and bring joy to many of them by the glory of your light.

And so, in your presence are countless hosts of Angels,
who serve you day and night
and, gazing upon the glory of your face,
glorify you without ceasing.

With them we, too, confess your name in exultation,
giving voice to every creature under heaven,
as we acclaim:

The people sing or say aloud the Sanctus.

Ho-ly, Ho-ly, Ho-ly Lord God of hosts. Heav-en and earth are full of your glo-ry. Ho-san-na in the high-est. Bless-ed is he who comes in the name of the Lord. Ho-san-na in the high-est.

Sanctus, Sanctus, Sanctus Dóminus Deus Sábaoth.
Pleni sunt cæli et terra glória tua.
Hosánna in excélsis.
Benedíctus qui venit in nómine Dómini.
Hosánna in excélsis.

Pr. Confitémur tibi, Pater sancte,
quia magnus es et ómnia ópera tua
in sapiéntia et caritáte fecísti.
Hóminem ad tuam imáginem condidísti,
eíque commisísti mundi curam univérsi,
ut, tibi soli Creatóri sérviens,
creatúris ómnibus imperáret.
Et cum amicítiam tuam, non obœdiens, amisísset,
non eum dereliquísti in mortis império.
Omnibus enim misericórditer subvenísti,
ut te quæréntes invenírent.
Sed et fœdera plúries homínibus obtulísti
eósque per prophétas erudísti in exspectatióne salútis.

Et sic, Pater sancte, mundum dilexísti,
ut, compléta plenitúdine témporum,
Unigénitum tuum nobis mítteres Salvatórem.
Qui, incarnátus de Spíritu Sancto
et natus ex María Vírgine,
in nostra condiciónis forma est conversátus
per ómnia absque peccáto;
salútem evangelizávit paupéribus,
redemptiónem captívis,
mæstis corde lætítiam.
Ut tuam vero dispensatiónem impléret,
in mortem trádidit semetípsum
ac, resúrgens a mórtuis,
mortem destrúxit vitámque renovávit.

Et, ut non ámplius nobismetípsis viverémus,
sed sibi qui pro nobis mórtuus est atque surréxit,
a te, Pater, misit Spíritum Sanctum
primítias credéntibus,

Holy, Holy, Holy Lord God of hosts.
Heaven and earth are full of your glory.
Hosanna in the highest.
Blessed is he who comes in the name of the Lord.
Hosanna in the highest.

Pr. We give you praise, Father most holy,
for you are great
and you have fashioned all your works
in wisdom and in love.
You formed man in your own image
and entrusted the whole world to his care,
so that in serving you alone, the Creator,
he might have dominion over all creatures.
And when through disobedience he had lost your friendship,
you did not abandon him to the domain of death.
For you came in mercy to the aid of all,
so that those who seek might find you.
Time and again you offered them covenants
and through the prophets
taught them to look forward to salvation.

And you so loved the world, Father most holy,
that in the fullness of time
you sent your Only Begotten Son to be our Saviour.
Made incarnate by the Holy Spirit
and born of the Virgin Mary,
he shared our human nature
in all things but sin.
To the poor he proclaimed the good news of salvation,
to prisoners, freedom,
and to the sorrowful of heart, joy.
To accomplish your plan,
he gave himself up to death,
and, rising from the dead,
he destroyed death and restored life.

And that we might live no longer for ourselves
but for him who died and rose again for us,
he sent the Holy Spirit from you, Father,

qui, opus suum in mundo perfíciens,
omnem sanctificatiónem compléret.

Quǽsumus ígitur, Dómine,
ut idem Spíritus Sanctus
hæc múnera sanctificáre dignétur,
ut Corpus et ✠ Sanguis fiant
Dómini nostri Iesu Christi
ad hoc magnum mystérium celebrándum,
quod ipse nobis relíquit in fœdus ætérnum.

Ipse enim, cum hora venísset
ut glorificarétur a te, Pater sancte,
ac dilexísset suos qui erant in mundo,
in finem diléxit eos:
et cenántibus illis
accépit panem, benedíxit ac fregit,
dedítque discípulis suis, dicens:

Accípite et manducáte ex hoc omnes:
hoc est enim Corpus meum,
quod pro vobis tradétur.

Símili modo
accípiens cálicem, ex genímine vitis replétum,
grátias egit, dedítque discípulis suis, dicens:

Accípite et bíbite ex eo omnes:
hic est enim calix Sánguinis mei
novi et ætérni testaménti,
qui pro vobis et pro multis effundétur
in remissiónem peccatórum.
Hoc fácite in meam commemoratiónem.

Pr. Mystérium fídei.

The people continue, acclaiming one of the following:

as the first fruits for those who believe,
so that, bringing to perfection his work in the world,
he might sanctify creation to the full.

Therefore, O Lord, we pray:
may this same Holy Spirit
graciously sanctify these offerings,
that they may become
the Body and ✠ Blood of our Lord Jesus Christ
for the celebration of this great mystery,
which he himself left us
as an eternal covenant.

For when the hour had come
for him to be glorified by you, Father most holy,
having loved his own who were in the world,
he loved them to the end:
and while they were at supper,
he took bread, blessed and broke it,
and gave it to his disciples, saying:

TAKE THIS, ALL OF YOU, AND EAT OF IT,
FOR THIS IS MY BODY,
WHICH WILL BE GIVEN UP FOR YOU.

In a similar way,
taking the chalice filled with the fruit of the vine,
he gave thanks,
and gave the chalice to his disciples, saying:

TAKE THIS, ALL OF YOU, AND DRINK FROM IT,
FOR THIS IS THE CHALICE OF MY BLOOD,
THE BLOOD OF THE NEW AND ETERNAL COVENANT,
WHICH WILL BE POURED OUT FOR YOU AND FOR MANY
FOR THE FORGIVENESS OF SINS.
DO THIS IN MEMORY OF ME.

Pr. The mystery of faith.

The people continue, acclaiming one of the following:

Mortem tu-am annunti-ámus, Dómi-ne,   et tu-am resurrecti-ó-

nem confi-témur, do-nec vé-ni-as.

**1. Mortem tuam annuntiámus, Dómine,
et tuam resurrectiónem confitémur, donec vénias.**

Quoti-escúmque manducámus panem hunc   et cálicem bíbimus,

mortem tu-am annunti-ámus, Dómine, donec vé- ni-as.

**2. Quotiescúmque manducámus panem hunc
et cálicem bíbimus,
mortem tuam annuntiámus, Dómine, donec vénias.**

Salvátor mundi, salva nos, qui per crucem et resurrecti-ónem tu-am

li-be-rá- sti nos.

**3. Salvátor mundi, salva nos,
qui per crucem et resurrectiónem tuam liberásti nos.**

Pr. Unde et nos, Dómine, redemptiónis nostræ memoriále nunc celebrántes, mortem Christi
eiúsque descénsum ad ínferos recólimus,
eius resurrectiónem
et ascensiónem ad tuam déxteram profitémur,

We pro-claim your Death, O Lord, and pro-fess your Res-ur-rec-tion un-til you come a-gain.

1. **We proclaim your Death, O Lord,
and profess your Resurrection
until you come again.**

When we eat this Bread and drink this Cup, we pro-claim your Death, O Lord, un-til you come a-gain.

2. **When we eat this Bread and drink this Cup,
we proclaim your Death, O Lord,
until you come again.**

Save us, Sav-iour of the world, for by your Cross and Res-ur-rec-tion you have set us free.

3. **Save us, Saviour of the world,
for by your Cross and Resurrection
you have set us free.**

Only in Ireland: 4. **My Lord and my God.**

Pr. Therefore, O Lord,
as we now celebrate the memorial of our redemption,
we remember Christ's Death
and his descent to the realm of the dead,
we proclaim his Resurrection
and his Ascension to your right hand,

et, exspectántes ipsíus advéntum in glória,
offérimus tibi eius Corpus et Sánguinem,
sacrifícium tibi acceptábile et toti mundo salutáre.

Réspice, Dómine, in Hóstiam,
quam Ecclésiæ tuæ ipse parásti,
et concéde benígnus ómnibus
qui ex hoc uno pane participábunt et cálice,
ut, in unum corpus a Sancto Spíritu congregáti,
in Christo hóstia viva perficiántur,
ad laudem glóriæ tuæ.

Nunc ergo, Dómine, ómnium recordáre,
pro quibus tibi hanc oblatiónem offérimus:
in primis fámuli tui, Papæ nostri N.,
Epíscopi nostri N.*, et Episcopórum órdinis univérsi,
sed et totíus cleri, et offeréntium,
et circumstántium,
et cuncti pópuli tui,
et ómnium, qui te quærunt corde sincéro.

Meménto étiam illórum,
qui obiérunt in pace Christi tui,
et ómnium defunctórum,
quorum fidem tu solus cognovísti.

Nobis ómnibus, fíliis tuis, clemens Pater, concéde,
ut cæléstem hereditátem cónsequi valeámus
cum beáta Vírgine, Dei Genetríce, María,
cum beáto Ioseph, eius Sponso,
cum Apóstolis et Sanctis tuis
in regno tuo, ubi cum univérsa creatúra,
a corruptióne peccáti et mortis liberáta,
te glorificémus per Christum Dóminum nostrum,
per quem mundo bona cuncta largíris.

Per ipsum, et cum ipso, et in ipso,
est tibi Deo Patri omnipoténti,
in unitáte Spíritus Sancti,
omnis honor et glória
per ómnia sǽcula sæculórum.

---

* Mention may be made here of the Coadjutor Bishop or Auxiliary Bishops.

and, as we await his coming in glory,
we offer you his Body and Blood,
the sacrifice acceptable to you
which brings salvation to the whole world.

Look, O Lord, upon the Sacrifice
which you yourself have provided for your Church,
and grant in your loving kindness
to all who partake of this one Bread and one Chalice
that, gathered into one body by the Holy Spirit,
they may truly become a living sacrifice in Christ
to the praise of your glory.

Therefore, Lord, remember now
all for whom we offer this sacrifice:
especially your servant N. our Pope,
N. our Bishop,* and the whole Order of Bishops,
all the clergy,
those who take part in this offering,
those gathered here before you,
your entire people,
and all who seek you with a sincere heart.

Remember also
those who have died in the peace of your Christ
and all the dead,
whose faith you alone have known.

To all of us, your children,
grant, O merciful Father,
that we may enter into a heavenly inheritance
with the Blessed Virgin Mary, Mother of God,
with blessed Joseph, her Spouse,
and with your Apostles and Saints in your kingdom.
There, with the whole of creation,
freed from the corruption of sin and death,
may we glorify you through Christ our Lord,
through whom you bestow on the world all that is good.

Through him, and with him, and in him,
O God, almighty Father,
in the unity of the Holy Spirit,
all glory and honour is yours,
for ever and ever.

---

* Mention may be made here of the Coadjutor Bishop or Auxiliary Bishops.

A-men.

R. **Amen.**

Then follows the Communion Rite.

THE COMMUNION RITE

The eating and drinking together of the Lord's Body and Blood in a Paschal meal is the culmination of the Eucharist

THE LORD'S PRAYER

After the chalice and paten have been set down, the congregation stands and the Priest says:

Pr. **Præcéptis salutáribus móniti,
et divína institutióne formáti,
audémus dícere:**

Together with the people, he continues:

Pa-ter noster, qui es in cæ-lis: sancti-fi-cé-tur nomen tu-um; advéni-at regnum tu-um; fi-at volúntas tu-a, sic-ut in cæ-lo, et in terra. Pa-nem nostrum coti-di-ánum da nobis hódi-e; et dimítte nobis débi-ta nostra, sicut et nos dimíttimus de-bi-tó-ribus nostris; et ne nos indúcas in tenta-ti-ó-nem; sed líbera nos a ma-lo.

A-men.

R. **Amen.**

Then follows the Communion Rite.

THE COMMUNION RITE

The eating and drinking together of the Lord's Body and Blood in a Paschal meal is the culmination of the Eucharist

THE LORD'S PRAYER

After the chalice and paten have been set down, the congregation stands and the Priest says:

Pr. At the Saviour's command
and formed by divine teaching,
we dare to say:

Together with the people, he continues:

Our Fa-ther, who art in heav-en, hal-lowed be thy name; thy
king-dom come, thy will be done on earth as it is in heav-en.
Give us this day our dai-ly bread, and for-give us our tres-pass-es,
as we for-give those who tres-pass a-gainst us; and lead us not
in-to temp-ta-tion, but de-liv-er us from e-vil.

R.   Pater noster, qui es in cælis:
sanctificétur nomen tuum;
advéniat regnum tuum;
fiat volúntas tua, sicut in cælo, et in terra.
Panem nostrum cotidiánum da nobis hódie;
et dimítte nobis debíta nostra,
sicut et nos dimíttimus debitóribus nostris;
et ne nos indúcas in tentatiónem;
sed líbera nos a malo.

Pr. Líbera nos, quæsumus, Dómine, ab ómnibus malis,
da propítius pacem in diébus nostris,
ut, ope misericórdiæ tuæ adiúti,
et a peccáto simus semper líberi
et ab omni perturbatióne secúri:
exspectántes beátam spem
et advéntum Salvatóris nostri Iesu Christi.

Qui-a tu-um est regnum, et po-téstas,

et gló- ri- a in saecu-la.

R.   Quia tuum est regnum,
et potéstas, et glória
in sǽcula.

THE PEACE

Pr. Dómine Iesu Christe, qui dixísti Apostólis tuis:
Pacem relínquo vobis, pacem meam do vobis:
ne respícias peccáta nostra,
sed fidem Ecclésiæ tuæ;
eámque secúndum voluntátem tuam
pacificáre et coadunáre dignéris.
Qui vivis et regnas in sǽcula sæculórum.

R.   Amen.

R. Our Father, who art in heaven,
hallowed be thy name;
thy kingdom come,
thy will be done
on earth as it is in heaven.
Give us this day our daily bread,
and forgive us our trespasses,
as we forgive those who trespass against us;
and lead us not into temptation,
but deliver us from evil.

Pr. Deliver us, Lord, we pray, from every evil,
graciously grant peace in our days,
that, by the help of your mercy,
we may be always free from sin
and safe from all distress,
as we await the blessed hope
and the coming of our Saviour, Jesus Christ.

For the king-dom, the power and the glo-ry are yours   now and for

ev-er.

R. For the kingdom,
the power and the glory are yours
now and for ever.

THE PEACE

Pr. Lord Jesus Christ,
who said to your Apostles:
Peace I leave you, my peace I give you;
look not on our sins,
but on the faith of your Church,
and graciously grant her peace and unity
in accordance with your will.
Who live and reign for ever and ever.
R. Amen.

Pr. Pax Dómini sit semper vobíscum.

Et cum spí-ri- tu tu- o.

R. **Et cum spíritu tuo.**

Then, if appropriate, the Deacon, or the Priest, adds:

Pr. Offérte vobis pacem.

And all offer one another the customary sign of peace.

BREAKING OF THE BREAD

Then the Priest takes the host, breaks it over the paten, and places a small piece in the chalice. Meanwhile the following is sung or said:

A g-nus De-i, * qui tol-lis pec-cá-ta mundi:

mi-se-ré-re no-bis.

Ag-nus De-i, * qui tol-lis pec-cá-ta mundi:

mi-se-ré-re no-bis.

Ag-nus De-i, * qui tol-lis pec-cá-ta mun-di:

do-na no-bis pa-cem.

Pr. The peace of the Lord be with you always.

And with your spir-it.

R. **And with your spirit.**

Then, if appropriate, the Deacon, or the Priest, adds:

Pr. Let us offer each other the sign of peace.

And all offer one another the customary sign of peace.

BREAKING OF THE BREAD

Then the Priest takes the host, breaks it over the paten, and places a small piece in the chalice. Meanwhile the following is sung or said:

Lamb of God, * you take a-way the sins of the world,

have mer-cy on us.

Lamb of God, * you take a-way the sins of the world,

have mer-cy on us.

Lamb of God, * you take a-way the sins of the world,

grant us peace.

The invocation may even be repeated several times if the fraction is prolonged. Only the final time, however, is **grant us peace** said.

Agnus Dei, qui tollis peccáta mundi: miserére nobis.
Agnus Dei, qui tollis peccáta mundi: miserére nobis.
Agnus Dei, qui tollis peccáta mundi: dona nobis pacem.

Then the Priest, with hands joined, says quietly:

Domine Iesu Christe, Fili Dei vivi,
qui ex voluntate Patris,
cooperante Spiritu Sancto,
per mortem tuam mundum vivificasti:
libera me per hoc sacrosanctum Corpus et Sanguinem tuum
ab omnibus iniquitatibus meis et universis malis:
et fac me tuis semper inhærere mandatis,
et a te numquam separari permittas.

Or:

Perceptio Corporis et Sanguinis tui, Domine Iesu Christe,
non mihi proveniat in iudicium et condemnationem:
sed pro tua pietate prosit mihi
ad tutamentum mentis et corporis,
et ad medelam percipiendam.

INVITATION TO COMMUNION

All kneel. The Priest genuflects, takes the host and, holding it slightly raised above
the paten or above the chalice says aloud:

Pr. Ecce Agnus Dei, ecce qui tollit peccáta mundi.
Beáti qui ad cenam Agni vocáti sunt.

R. **Dómine, non sum dignus, ut intres sub tectum meum,**
sed tantum dic verbo, et sanábitur ánima mea.

While the Priest is receiving the Body of Christ, the Communion Chant begins.

COMMUNION PROCESSION

After the priest has reverently consumed the Body and Blood of Christ he takes the
paten or ciborium and approaches the communicants.

The Priest raises the host slightly and shows it to each of the communicants, saying:

Pr. Corpus Christi.

R. **Amen.**

Lamb of God, you take away the sins of the world, have mercy on us.
Lamb of God, you take away the sins of the world, have mercy on us.
Lamb of God, you take away the sins of the world, grant us peace.

Then the Priest, with hands joined, says quietly:

Lord Jesus Christ, Son of the living God,
who, by the will of the Father
and the work of the Holy Spirit,
through your Death gave life to the world,
free me by this, your most holy Body and Blood,
from all my sins and from every evil;
keep me always faithful to your commandments,
and never let me be parted from you.

Or:

May the receiving of your Body and Blood,
Lord Jesus Christ,
not bring me to judgement and condemnation,
but through your loving mercy
be for me protection in mind and body
and a healing remedy.

INVITATION TO COMMUNION

All kneel. The Priest genuflects, takes the host and, holding it slightly raised above the paten or above the chalice says aloud:

Pr. Behold the Lamb of God,
     behold him who takes away the sins of the world.
     Blessed are those called to the supper of the Lamb.

R. **Lord, I am not worthy**
    that you should enter under my roof,
    but only say the word
    and my soul shall be healed.

While the Priest is receiving the Body of Christ, the Communion Chant begins.

COMMUNION PROCESSION

After the priest has reverently consumed the Body and Blood of Christ he takes the paten or ciborium and approaches the communicants.

The Priest raises the host slightly and shows it to each of the communicants, saying:

Pr. The Body of Christ.

R. **Amen.**

When Communion is ministered from the chalice:

Pr. Sanguis Christi.

R. Amen.

After the distribution of Communion, if appropriate, a sacred silence may be observed for a while, or a psalm or other canticle of praise or a hymn may be sung.

PRAYER AFTER COMMUNION

Then, the Priest says:

Pr. Orémus.

All stand and pray in silence for a while, unless silence has just been observed. Then the Priest says the Prayer after Communion, at the end of which the people acclaim:

R. Amen.

THE CONCLUDING RITES

The Mass closes, sending the people forth to put what they have celebrated into effect in their daily lives.

Any brief announcements follow here. Then the dismissal takes place.

Pr. Dóminus vóbiscum.

Et cum spí-ri-tu tu-o.

R. Et cum spíritu tuo.

The Priest blesses the people, saying:

Pr. Benedícat vos omnípotens Deus,
   Pater, et Fílius, ✠ et Spíritus Sanctus.

A-men.

R. Amen.

When Communion is ministered from the chalice:

Pr. **The Blood of Christ.**

R. **Amen.**

After the distribution of Communion, if appropriate, a sacred silence may be observed for a while, or a psalm or other canticle of praise or a hymn may be sung.

PRAYER AFTER COMMUNION

Then, the Priest says:

Pr. **Let us pray.**

All stand and pray in silence for a while, unless silence has just been observed. Then the Priest says the Prayer after Communion, at the end of which the people acclaim:

R. **Amen.**

THE CONCLUDING RITES

The Mass closes, sending the people forth to put what they have celebrated into effect in their daily lives.

Any brief announcements follow here. Then the dismissal takes place.

Pr. **The Lord be with you.**

And with your spir-it.

R. **And with your spirit.**

The Priest blesses the people, saying:

Pr. **May almighty God bless you,
the Father, and the Son, ✠ and the Holy Spirit.**

A-men.

R. **Amen.**

Then the Deacon, or the Priest himself says the Dismissal:

Pr. Ite, missa est.

Or:

Pr. Ite, ad Evangélium Dómini annuntiándum.

Or:

Pr. Ite in pace, glorificándo vita vestra Dóminum.

De- o grá- ti-as.

R. Deo grátias.

Or:

Pr. Ite in pace.

De- o grá- ti- as.

R. Deo grátias.

Then the Priest venerates the altar as at the beginning. After making a profound bow with the ministers, he withdraws.

Then the Deacon, or the Priest himself says the Dismissal:

Pr. **Go forth, the Mass is ended.**

Or:

Pr. **Go and announce the Gospel of the Lord.**

Or:

Pr. **Go in peace, glorifying the Lord by your life.**

R. Thanks be to God.

R. **Thanks be to God.**

Or:

Pr. **Go in peace.**

R. Thanks be to God.

R. **Thanks be to God.**

Then the Priest venerates the altar as at the beginning. After making a profound bow with the ministers, he withdraws.

SOLEMN BLESSINGS

The following blessings may be used, at the discretion of the Priest, at the end of the celebration of Mass, or of a Liturgy of the Word, or of the Office, or of the Sacraments.

The Deacon or, in his absence, the Priest himself, says the invitation: **Inclinate vos ad benedictionem**. Then the Priest, with hands extended over the people, says the blessing, with all responding: Amen.

I. For Celebrations in the Different Liturgical Times

1. In Adventu

Omnipotens et misericors Deus, cuius Unigeniti adventum
et præteritum creditis, et futurum exspectatis,
eiusdem adventus vos illustratione sanctificet
et sua benedictione locupletet.
R. Amen.

In præsentis vitæ stadio reddat vos in fide stabiles,
spe gaudentes, et in caritate efficaces.
R. Amen.

Ut, qui de adventu Redemptoris nostri
secundum carnem devota mente lætamini,
in secundo, cum in maiestate sua venerit,
præmiis æternæ vitæ ditemini.
R. Amen.

Et benedictio Dei omnipotentis,
Patris, et Filii, ✠ et Spiritus Sancti,
descendat super vos et maneat semper.
R. Amen.

2. In Nativitate Domini

Deus infinitæ bonitatis,
qui incarnatione Filii sui mundi tenebras effugavit,
et eius gloriosa nativitate
hanc noctem (diem) sacratissimam irradiavit,
effuget a vobis tenebras vitiorum,
et irradiet corda vestra luce virtutum.
R. Amen.

Quique eius salutiferæ nativitatis gaudium magnum
pastoribus ab Angelo voluit nuntiari,
ipse mentes vestras suo gaudio impleat,
et vos Evangelii sui nuntios efficiat.
R. Amen.

SOLEMN BLESSINGS

The following blessings may be used, at the discretion of the Priest, at the end of the celebration of Mass, or of a Liturgy of the Word, or of the Office, or of the Sacraments. The Deacon or, in his absence, the Priest himself, says the invitation: **Bow down for the blessing**. Then the Priest, with hands extended over the people, says the blessing, with all responding: **Amen**.

I. For Celebrations in the Different Liturgical Times

1. Advent

May the almighty and merciful God,
by whose grace you have placed your faith
in the First Coming of his Only Begotten Son
and yearn for his coming again,
sanctify you by the radiance of Christ's Advent
and enrich you with his blessing.
R. Amen.

As you run the race of this present life,
may he make you firm in faith,
joyful in hope and active in charity.
R. Amen.

So that, rejoicing now with devotion
at the Redeemer's coming in the flesh,
you may be endowed with the rich reward of eternal life
when he comes again in majesty.
R. Amen.

And may the blessing of almighty God,
the Father, and the Son, ✠ and the Holy Spirit,
come down on you and remain with you for ever.
R. Amen.

2. The Nativity of the Lord

May the God of infinite goodness,
who by the Incarnation of his Son has driven darkness from the world
and by that glorious Birth has illumined this most holy night (day),
drive far from you the darkness of vice
and illumine your hearts with the light of virtue.
R. Amen.

May God, who willed that the great joy
of his Son's saving Birth
be announced to shepherds by the Angel,
fill your minds with the gladness he gives
and make you heralds of his Gospel.
R. Amen.

Et, qui per eius incarnationem terrena cælestibus sociavit,
dono vos suæ pacis et bonæ repleat voluntatis,
et vos faciat Ecclesiæ consortes esse cælestis.
R. Amen.

Et benedictio Dei omnipotentis,
Patris, et Filii, ✠ et Spiritus Sancti,
descendat super vos et maneat semper.
R. Amen.

3. Initio anni

Deus, fons et origo totius benedictionis,
gratiam vobis concedat,
benedictionis suæ largitatem infundat,
atque per totum annum vos salvos et incolumes protegat.
R. Amen.

Custodiat fidei vobis integritatem,
tribuat spei longanimitatem,
perseverantem usque ad finem
cum sancta patientia caritatem.
R. Amen.

Dies et actus vestros in sua pace disponat,
preces hic et ubique exaudiat,
et ad vitam æternam feliciter vos perducat.
R. Amen.

Et benedictio Dei omnipotentis,
Patris, et Filii, ✠ et Spiritus Sancti,
descendat super vos et maneat semper.
R. Amen.

4. In Epiphania Domini

Deus, qui vos de tenebris vocavit in admirabile lumen suum,
suam vobis benedictionem benignus infundat,
et corda vestra fide, spe et caritate stabiliat.
R. Amen.

Et quia Christum sequimini confidenter,
qui hodie mundo apparuit lux relucens in tenebris,
faciat et vos lucem esse fratribus vestris.
R. Amen.

And may God, who by the Incarnation
brought together the earthly and heavenly realm,
fill you with the gift of his peace and favour
and make you sharers with the Church in heaven.
R. Amen.

And may the blessing of almighty God,
the Father, and the Son, ✠ and the Holy Spirit,
come down on you and remain with you for ever.
R. Amen.

3. The Beginning of the Year

May God, the source and origin of all blessing,
grant you grace,
pour out his blessing in abundance,
and keep you safe from harm throughout the year.
R. Amen.

May he give you integrity in the faith,
endurance in hope,
and perseverance in charity
with holy patience to the end.
R. Amen.

May he order your days and your deeds in his peace,
grant your prayers in this and in every place,
and lead you happily to eternal life.
R. Amen.

And may the blessing of almighty God,
the Father, and the Son, ✠ and the Holy Spirit,
come down on you and remain with you for ever.
R. Amen.

4. The Epiphany of the Lord

May God, who has called you
out of darkness into his wonderful light,
pour out in kindness his blessing upon you
and make your hearts firm
in faith, hope and charity.
R. Amen.

And since in all confidence you follow Christ,
who today appeared in the world
as a light shining in darkness,
may God make you, too,
a light for your brothers and sisters.
R. Amen.

Quatenus, peregrinatione peracta,
perveniatis ad eum, quem magi stella prævia quæsierunt,
et gaudio magno, lucem de luce,
Christum Dominum invenerunt.
R. Amen.

Et benedictio Dei omnipotentis,
Patris, et Filii, ✠ et Spiritus Sancti,
descendat super vos et maneat semper.
R. Amen.

5. De Passione Domini

Deus, Pater misericordiarum, qui Unigeniti sui passione
tribuit vobis caritatis exemplum,
præstet ut, per servitium Dei et hominum,
percipiatis suæ benedictionis ineffabile donum.
R. Amen.

Ut ab eo sempiternæ vitæ munus obtineatis,
per cuius temporalem mortem, æternam vos evadere creditis.
R. Amen.

Quatenus, cuius humilitatis sequimini documenta,
eius resurrectionis possideatis consortia.
R. Amen.

Et benedictio Dei omnipotentis,
Patris, et Filii, ✠ et Spiritus Sancti,
descendat super vos et maneat semper.
R. Amen.

6. Tempore paschali

Deus, qui per resurrectionem Unigeniti sui
dignatus est vobis bonum redemptionis
adoptionisque conferre,
sua benedictione vos tribuat congaudere.
R. Amen.

And so when your pilgrimage is ended,
may you come to him
whom the Magi sought as they followed the star
and whom they found with great joy, the Light from Light,
who is Christ the Lord.
R. Amen.

And may the blessing of almighty God,
the Father, and the Son, ✠ and the Holy Spirit,
come down on you and remain with you for ever.
R. Amen.

5. The Passion of the Lord

May God, the Father of mercies,
who has given you an example of love
in the Passion of his Only Begotten Son,
grant that, by serving God and your neighbour,
you may lay hold of the wondrous gift of his blessing.
R. Amen.

So that you may receive the reward of everlasting life from him,
through whose earthly Death
you believe that you escape eternal death.
R. Amen.

And by following the example of his self-abasement,
may you possess a share in his Resurrection.
R. Amen.

And may the blessing of almighty God,
the Father, and the Son, ✠ and the Holy Spirit,
come down on you and remain with you for ever.
R. Amen.

6. Easter Time

May God, who by the Resurrection of his Only Begotten Son
was pleased to confer on you
the gift of redemption and of adoption,
give you gladness by his blessing.
R. Amen.

Et quo redimente percepistis donum perpetuæ libertatis,
eo largiente hereditatis æternæ consortes effici valeatis.
R. Amen.

Et cui resurrexistis in baptismate iam credendo,
adiungi mereamini in patria cælesti nunc recte vivendo.
R. Amen.

Et benedictio Dei omnipotentis,
Patris, et Filii, ✠ et Spiritus Sancti,
descendat super vos et maneat semper.
R. Amen.

7. In Ascensione Domini
Benedicat vos omnipotens Deus,
cuius Unigenitus hodierna die cælorum alta penetravit,
et vobis, ubi est ipse, ascendendi aditum reseravit.
R. Amen.

Concedat ut, sicut Christus post resurrectionem suam
visus est discipulis manifestus,
ita vobis in iudicium veniens
appareat pro æternitate placatus.
R. Amen.

Et qui eum consedere Patri in sua creditis maiestate,
ipsum usque in finem sæculi vobiscum permanere
secundum eius promissionem læti valeatis experire.
R. Amen.

Et benedictio Dei omnipotentis,
Patris, et Filii, ✠ et Spiritus Sancti,
descendat super vos et maneat semper.
R. Amen.

8. De Spiritu Sancto
Deus, Pater luminum, qui discipulorum mentes
Spiritus Paracliti infusione dignatus est illustrare,
sua vos faciat benedictione gaudere,
et perpetuo donis eiusdem Spiritus abundare.
R. Amen.

May he, by whose redeeming work
you have received the gift of everlasting freedom,
make you heirs to an eternal inheritance.
R. Amen.

And may you, who have already risen with Christ
in Baptism through faith,
by living in a right manner on this earth,
be united with him in the homeland of heaven.
R. Amen.

And may the blessing of almighty God,
the Father, and the Son, ✠ and the Holy Spirit,
come down on you and remain with you for ever.
R. Amen.

7. The Ascension of the Lord

May almighty God bless you,
for on this very day his Only Begotten Son
pierced the heights of heaven
and unlocked for you the way
to ascend to where he is.
R. Amen.

May he grant that,
as Christ after his Resurrection
was seen plainly by his disciples,
so when he comes as Judge
he may show himself merciful to you for all eternity.
R. Amen.

And may you, who believe he is seated
with the Father in his majesty,
know with joy the fulfilment of his promise
to stay with you until the end of time.
R. Amen.

And may the blessing of almighty God,
the Father, and the Son, ✠ and the Holy Spirit,
come down on you and remain with you for ever.
R. Amen.

8. The Holy Spirit

May God, the Father of lights,
who was pleased to enlighten the disciples' minds
by the outpouring of the Spirit, the Paraclete,
grant you gladness by his blessing
and make you always abound with the gifts of the same Spirit.
R. Amen.

Ignis ille, qui super discipulos mirandus apparuit,
corda vestra ab omni malo potenter expurget,
et sui luminis infusione perlustret.
R. Amen.

Quique dignatus est in unius fidei confessione
diversitatem adunare linguarum,
in eadem fide perseverare vos faciat,
et per illam a spe ad speciem pervenire concedat.
R. Amen.

Et benedictio Dei omnipotentis,
Patris, et Filii, ✠ et Spiritus Sancti,
descendat super vos et maneat semper.
R. Amen.

9. Per annum, I

Benedicat vobis Dominus, et custodiat vos.
R. Amen.

Illuminet faciem suam super vos, et misereatur vestri.
R. Amen.

Convertat vultum suum ad vos, et donet vobis suam pacem.
R. Amen.

Et benedictio Dei omnipotentis,
Patris, et Filii, ✠ et Spiritus Sancti,
descendat super vos et maneat semper.
R. Amen.

10. Per annum, II

Pax Dei, quæ exsuperat omnem sensum,
custodiat corda vestra et intellegentias vestras
in scientia et caritate Dei,
et Filii sui, Domini nostri Iesu Christi.
R. Amen.

Et benedictio Dei omnipotentis,
Patris, et Filii, ✠ et Spiritus Sancti,
descendat super vos et maneat semper.
R. Amen.

11. Per annum, III

Omnipotens Deus sua vos clementia benedicat,
et sensum in vobis sapientiæ salutaris infundat.
R. Amen.

May the wondrous flame that appeared above the disciples,
powerfully cleanse your hearts from every evil
and pervade them with its purifying light.
R. Amen.

And may God, who has been pleased to unite many tongues
in the profession of one faith,
give you perseverance in that same faith
and, by believing, may you journey from hope to clear vision.
R. Amen.

And may the blessing of almighty God,
the Father, and the Son, ✠ and the Holy Spirit,
come down on you and remain with you for ever.
R. Amen.

9. Ordinary Time I
May the Lord bless you and keep you.
R. Amen.

May he let his face shine upon you
and show you his mercy.
R. Amen.

May he turn his countenance towards you
and give you his peace.
R. Amen.

And may the blessing of almighty God,
the Father, and the Son, ✠ and the Holy Spirit,
come down on you and remain with you for ever.
R. Amen.

10. Ordinary Time II
May the peace of God,
which surpasses all understanding,
keep your hearts and minds
in the knowledge and love of God,
and of his Son, our Lord Jesus Christ.
R. Amen.

And may the blessing of almighty God,
the Father, and the Son, ✠ and the Holy Spirit,
come down on you and remain with you for ever.
R. Amen.

11. Ordinary Time III
May almighty God bless you in his kindness
and pour out saving wisdom upon you.
R. Amen.

Fidei documentis vos semper enutriat,
et in sanctis operibus, ut perseveretis, efficiat.
R. Amen.

Gressus vestros ad se convertat,
et viam vobis pacis et caritatis ostendat.
R. Amen.

Et benedictio Dei omnipotentis,
Patris, et Filii, ✠ et Spiritus Sancti,
descendat super vos et maneat semper.
R. Amen.

12. Per annum, IV

Deus totius consolationis dies vestros in sua pace disponat,
et suæ vobis benedictionis dona concedat.
R. Amen.

Ab omni semper perturbatione vos liberet,
et corda vestra in suo amore confirmet.
R. Amen.

Quatenus donis spei, fidei et caritatis divites,
et præsentem vitam transigatis in opere efficaces,
et possitis ad æternam pervenire felices.
R. Amen.

Et benedictio Dei omnipotentis,
Patris, et Filii, ✠ et Spiritus Sancti,
descendat super vos et maneat semper.
R. Amen.

13. Per annum, V

Omnipotens Deus universa a vobis adversa semper excludat,
et suæ super vos benedictionis dona propitiatus infundat.
R. Amen.

Corda vestra efficiat divinis intenta eloquiis,
ut repleri possint gaudiis sempiternis.
R. Amen.

Quatenus, quæ bona et recta intellegentes,
viam mandatorum Dei inveniamini semper currentes,
et civium supernorum efficiamini coheredes.
R. Amen.

Et benedictio Dei omnipotentis,
Patris, et Filii, ✠ et Spiritus Sancti,
descendat super vos et maneat semper.
R. Amen.

May he nourish you always with the teachings of the faith
and make you persevere in holy deeds.
R. Amen.

May he turn your steps towards himself
and show you the path of charity and peace.
R. Amen.

And may the blessing of almighty God,
the Father, and the Son, ✠ and the Holy Spirit,
come down on you and remain with you for ever.
R. Amen.

12. Ordinary Time IV

May the God of all consolation order your days in his peace
and grant you the gifts of his blessing.
R. Amen.

May he free you always from every distress
and confirm your hearts in his love.
R. Amen.

So that on this life's journey
you may be effective in good works,
rich in the gifts of hope, faith and charity,
and may come happily to eternal life.
R. Amen.

And may the blessing of almighty God,
the Father, and the Son, ✠ and the Holy Spirit,
come down on you and remain with you for ever.
R. Amen.

13. Ordinary Time V

May almighty God always keep every adversity far from you
and in his kindness pour out upon you the gifts of his blessing.
R. Amen.

May God keep your hearts attentive to his words,
that they may be filled with everlasting gladness.
R. Amen.

And so, may you always understand what is good and right,
and be found ever hastening along
in the path of God's commands,
made coheirs with the citizens of heaven.
R. Amen.

And may the blessing of almighty God,
the Father, and the Son, ✠ and the Holy Spirit,
come down on you and remain with you for ever.
R. Amen.

14. Per annum, VI

Benedicat vos Deus omni benedictione cælesti,
sanctosque vos et puros
in conspectu suo semper efficiat;
divitias gloriæ suæ in vos abundanter effundat,
verbis veritatis instruat, Evangelio salutis erudiat,
et caritate fraterna semper locupletet.
Per Christum Dominum nostrum.
R. Amen.

Et benedictio Dei omnipotentis,
Patris, et Filii, ✠ et Spiritus Sancti,
descendat super vos et maneat semper.
R. Amen.

II. For Celebrations of the Saints

15. De beata Maria Virgine

Deus, qui per beatæ Mariæ Virginis partum
genus humanum sua voluit benignitate redimere,
sua vos dignetur benedictione ditare.
R. Amen.

Eiusque semper et ubique patrocinia sentiatis,
per quam auctorem vitæ suscipere meruistis.
R. Amen.

Et qui hodierna die devotis mentibus convenistis,
spiritalium gaudiorum cælestiumque præmiorum
vobiscum munera reportetis.
R. Amen.

Et benedictio Dei omnipotentis,
Patris, et Filii, ✠ et Spiritus Sancti,
descendat super vos et maneat semper.
R. Amen.

16. De sanctis Petro et Paulo

Benedicat vos omnipotens Deus,
qui in beati Petri confessione vos saluberrima stabilivit,
et per eam in Ecclesiæ soliditate fidei fundavit.
R. Amen.

Et quos beati Pauli instruxit indefessa prædicatione,
suo semper exemplo doceat Christo fratres lucrifacere.
R. Amen.

14. Ordinary Time VI
May God bless you with every heavenly blessing,
make you always holy and pure in his sight,
pour out in abundance upon you the riches of his glory,
and teach you with the words of truth;
may he instruct you in the Gospel of salvation,
and ever endow you with fraternal charity.
Through Christ our Lord.
R. Amen.

And may the blessing of almighty God,
the Father, and the Son, ✠ and the Holy Spirit,
come down on you and remain with you for ever.
R. Amen.

II. For Celebrations of the Saints

15. The Blessed Virgin Mary

May God, who through the childbearing of the Blessed Virgin Mary
willed in his great kindness to redeem the human race,
be pleased to enrich you with his blessing.
R. Amen.

May you know always and everywhere
the protection of her,
through whom you have been found worthy to receive
the author of life.
R. Amen.

May you, who have devoutly gathered on this day,
carry away with you the gifts of spiritual joys and heavenly rewards.
R. Amen.

And may the blessing of almighty God,
the Father, and the Son, ✠ and the Holy Spirit,
come down on you and remain with you for ever.
R. Amen.

16. Saints Peter and Paul, Apostles

May almighty God bless you,
for he has made you steadfast in Saint Peter's saving confession
and through it has set you on the solid rock of the Church's faith.
R. Amen.

And having instructed you
by the tireless preaching of Saint Paul,
may God teach you constantly by his example
to win brothers and sisters for Christ.
R. Amen.

Ut Petrus clave, Paulus verbo,
ope intercessionis uterque
in illam patriam nos certent inducere,
ad quam meruerunt illi, alter cruce, alter gladio,
feliciter pervenire.
R. Amen.

Et benedictio Dei omnipotentis,
Patris, et Filii, ✠ et Spiritus Sancti,
descendat super vos et maneat semper.
R. Amen.

17. De Apostolis

Deus, qui vos in apostolicis tribuit consistere fundamentis,
benedicere vobis dignetur
beatorum Apostolorum N. et N. (beati Apostoli N.)
meritis intercedentibus gloriosis.
R. Amen.

Et apostolicis præsidiis vos pro cunctis faciat testes veritatis,
qui vos eorum munerari documentis voluit et exemplis.
R. Amen.

Ut eorum intercessione
ad æternæ patriæ hereditatem pervenire possitis,
per quorum doctrinam fidei firmitatem possidetis.
R. Amen.

Et benedictio Dei omnipotentis,
Patris, et Filii, ✠ et Spiritus Sancti,
descendat super vos et maneat semper.
R. Amen.

18. De omnibus Sanctis

Deus, gloria et exsultatio Sanctorum,
benedicat vos benedictione perpetua,
qui vobis tribuit eximiis suffragiis roborari.
R. Amen.

Eorum intercessione a præsentibus malis liberati,
et exemplis sanctæ conversationis instructi,
in servitio Dei fratrumque inveniamini semper intenti.
R. Amen.

So that by the keys of St Peter and the words of St Paul,
and by the support of their intercession,
God may bring us happily to that homeland
that Peter attained on a cross
and Paul by the blade of a sword.
R. Amen.

And may the blessing of almighty God,
the Father, and the Son, ✠ and the Holy Spirit,
come down on you and remain with you for ever.
R. Amen.

17. The Apostles

May God, who has granted you
to stand firm on apostolic foundations,
graciously bless you through the glorious merits
of the holy Apostles N. and N. (the holy Apostle N.).
R. Amen.

And may he, who endowed you
with the teaching and example of the Apostles,
make you, under their protection,
witnesses to the truth before all.
R. Amen.

So that through the intercession of the Apostles,
you may inherit the eternal homeland,
for by their teaching you possess firmness of faith.
R. Amen.

And may the blessing of almighty God,
the Father, and the Son, ✠ and the Holy Spirit,
come down on you and remain with you for ever.
R. Amen.

18. All Saints

May God, the glory and joy of the Saints,
who has caused you to be strengthened
by means of their outstanding prayers,
bless you with unending blessings.
R. Amen.

Freed through their intercession from present ills
and formed by the example of their holy way of life,
may you be ever devoted
to serving God and your neighbour.
R. Amen.

Quatenus cum iis omnibus
valeatis illius patriæ vos gaudia possidere,
in qua filios suos supernis coniungi civibus
in pace perpetua sancta lætatur Ecclesia.
R. Amen.

Et benedictio Dei omnipotentis,
Patris, et Filii, ✠ et Spiritus Sancti,
descendat super vos et maneat semper.
R. Amen.

III. Other Blessings

19. In dedicatione ecclesiæ

Deus, Dominus cæli et terræ,
qui vos hodie ad huius domus dedicationem adunavit,
ipse vos cælesti benedictione faciat abundare.
R. Amen.

Concedatque vobis fieri templum suum
et habitaculum Spiritus Sancti,
qui omnes filios dispersos voluit in Filio suo congregari.
R. Amen.

Quatenus feliciter emundati,
habitatorem Deum in vobismetipsis possitis habere,
et æternæ beatitudinis hereditatem
cum omnibus Sanctis possidere.
R. Amen.

Et benedictio Dei omnipotentis,
Patris, et Filii, ✠ et Spiritus Sancti,
descendat super vos et maneat semper.
R. Amen.

20. In celebrationibus pro defunctis

Benedicat vos Deus totius consolationis,
qui hominem ineffabili bonitate creavit,
et in resurrectione Unigeniti sui
spem credentibus resurgendi concessit.
R. Amen.

Nobis, qui vivimus, veniam tribuat pro peccatis,
et omnibus defunctis locum concedat lucis et pacis.
R. Amen.

So that, together with all,
you may possess the joys of the homeland,
where Holy Church rejoices
that her children are admitted in perpetual peace
to the company of the citizens of heaven.
R. Amen.

And may the blessing of almighty God,
the Father, and the Son, ✠ and the Holy Spirit,
come down on you and remain with you for ever.
R. Amen.

III. Other Blessings

19. For the Dedication of a Church

May God, the Lord of heaven and earth,
who has gathered you today for the dedication of this church,
make you abound in heavenly blessings.
R. Amen.

And may he, who has willed that all his scattered children
should be gathered together in his Son,
grant that you may become his temple
and the dwelling place of the Holy Spirit.
R. Amen.

And so, when you are thoroughly cleansed,
may God dwell within you
and grant you to possess with all the Saints
the inheritance of eternal happiness.
R. Amen.

And may the blessing of almighty God,
the Father, and the Son, ✠ and the Holy Spirit,
come down on you and remain with you for ever.
R. Amen.

20. In Celebrations for the Dead

May the God of all consolation bless you,
for in his unfathomable goodness he created the human race,
and in the Resurrection of his Only Begotten Son
he has given believers the hope of rising again.
R. Amen.

To us who are alive, may God grant pardon for our sins,
and to all the dead, a place of light and peace.
R. Amen.

Ut omnes cum Christo sine fine feliciter vivamus,
quem resurrexisse a mortuis veraciter credimus.
R. Amen.

Et benedictio Dei omnipotentis,
Patris, et Filii, ✠ et Spiritus Sancti,
descendat super vos et maneat semper.
R. Amen.

So may we all live happily for ever with Christ,
whom we believe truly rose from the dead.

R. Amen.

And may the blessing of almighty God,
the Father, and the Son, ✠ and the Holy Spirit,
come down on you and remain with you for ever.

R. Amen.

THANKSGIVING AFTER MASS

Prayer of Saint Thomas Aquinas

I give you thanks,
Lord, holy Father,
　　almighty and eternal God,
who have been pleased
　　to nourish me,
a sinner and your
　　unworthy servant,
with the precious Body and Blood
of your Son, our Lord Jesus Christ:
this through no merits of mine,
but due solely to
　　the graciousness of your mercy.

And I pray that this
　　Holy Communion
may not be for me an offence
　　to be punished,
but a saving plea for forgiveness.
May it be for me the armour of faith,
and the shield of good will.
May it cancel my faults,
destroy concupiscence
　　and carnal passion,
increase charity and patience,
　　humility and obedience
and all the virtues,
may it be a firm defence against
　　the snares of all my enemies,
both visible and invisible,
the complete calming of
　　my impulses,
both of the flesh and of the spirit,
a firm adherence to you,
　　the one true God,
and the joyful completion of my
　　life's course.

Oratio S. Thomas Aquinatis

Gratias tibi ago, Domine,
sancte Pater,
　　omnipotens æterne Deus,
qui me peccatorem,
　　indignum famulum tuum,
nullis meis meritis, sed sola
　　dignatione misericordiæ tuæ
satiare dignatus es pretioso Corpore
　　et Sanguine Filii tui,
Domini nostri Iesu Christi.

Et precor,
　　ut hæc sancta communio
non sit mihi reatus ad pœnam,
sed intercessio salutaris ad veniam.
Sit mihi armatura fidei,
　　et scutum bonæ voluntatis.
Sit vitiorum meorum evacuatio,
concupiscentiæ
　　et libidinis exterminatio,
caritatis et patientiæ,
　　humilitatis et obœdientiæ,
omniumque virtutum
　　augmentatio:
contra insidias
　　inimicorum omnium
tam visibilium quam invisibilium,
　　firma defensio:
motuum meorum, tam carnalium
　　quam spiritalium,
perfecta quietatio:
in te uno ac vero Deo
　　firma adhæsio,
atque finis mei felix consummatio.

And I beseech you to lead me,
a sinner,
to that banquet beyond all telling,
where with your Son and the
Holy Spirit
you are the true light of
your Saints,
fullness of satisfied desire,
eternal gladness,
consummate delight and
perfect happiness.
Through Christ our Lord.
Amen.

Et precor te,
ut ad illud ineffabile convivium
me peccatorem perducere digneris,
ubi tu, cum Filio tuo et
Spiritu Sancto,
Sanctis tuis es lux vera,
satietas plena,
gaudium sempiternum,
iucunditas consummata et
felicitas perfecta.
Per Christum Dominum nostrum.
Amen.

Prayer to the Most Holy Redeemer

Soul of Christ, sanctify me.
Body of Christ, save me.
Blood of Christ, embolden me.
Water from the side of Christ,
wash me.

Passion of Christ, strengthen me.
O good Jesus, hear me.
Within your wounds hide me.
Never permit me to be parted
from you.

From the evil Enemy defend me.
At the hour of my death call me
and bid me come to you,
that with your Saints
I may praise you
for age upon age.
Amen.

Aspirationes ad Ss.mum Redemptorem

Anima Christi, sanctifica me.
Corpus Christi, salva me.
Sanguis Christi, inebria me.
Aqua lateris Christi, lava me.

Passio Christi, conforta me.
O bone Iesu, exaudi me.
Intra tua vulnera absconde me.
Ne permittas me separari a te.

Ab hoste maligno defende me.
In hora mortis meæ voca me.
Et iube me venire ad te,
ut cum Sanctis tuis laudem te
in sæcula sæculorum.

Amen.

Prayer of Self-Offering

Receive, Lord, my entire freedom.
Accept the whole of my memory,
my intellect and my will.

Oblatio sui

Suscipe, Domine,
universam meam libertatem.
Accipe memoriam, intellectum
atque voluntatem omnem.

Whatever I have or possess,
it was you who gave it to me;
I restore it to you in full,
and I surrender it completely
to the guidance of your will.
Give me only love of you
together with your grace,
and I am rich enough
and ask for nothing more.
Amen.

Quidquid habeo vel possideo,
    mihi largitus es:
id tibi totum restituo,
ac tuæ prorsus voluntati
    trado gubernandum.
Amorem tui solum cum gratia tua
    mihi dones,
et dives sum satis, nec aliud
    quidquam ultra posco.
Amen.

Prayer to Our Lord Jesus Christ Crucified

Oratio ad Dominum nostrum Iesum Christum Crucifixum

Behold, O good and loving Jesus,
that I cast myself on my knees
    before you
and, with the greatest fervour
    of spirit,
I pray and beseech you to instill
    into my heart
ardent sentiments of faith,
    hope and charity,
with true repentance for my sins
and a most firm purpose
    of amendment.

En ego, o bone et dulcissime Iesu,
ante conspectum tuum genibus
    me provolvo,
ac maximo animi ardore te oro
    atque obtestor,
ut meum in cor vividos fidei,
    spei et caritatis sensus,
atque veram peccatorum
    meorum pœnitentiam,
eaque emendandi firmissimam
    voluntatem velis imprimere;

With deep affection and sorrow
I ponder intimately
and contemplate in my mind
    your five wounds,
having before my eyes what
    the prophet David
had already put in your mouth
    about yourself, O good Jesus:
They have pierced my hands and
    my feet;
they have numbered all my bones
    (Ps 21:17-18).

dum magno animi affectu et dolore
tua quinque vulnera mecum
    ipse considero
ac mente contemplor,
illud præ oculis habens,
quod iam in ore ponebat tuo David
    propheta de te, o bone Iesu:

Foderunt manus meas
    et pedes meos:
dinumeraverunt omnia ossa mea
    (Ps 21:17-18).

The Universal Prayer Attributed to Pope Clement XI

I believe, O Lord,
but may I believe more firmly;
I hope,
but may I hope more securely;
I love,
but may I love more ardently;
I sorrow,
but may I sorrow more deeply.

I adore you as my first beginning;
I long for you as my last end;
I praise you as my
constant benefactor;
I invoke you as my
gracious protector.

By your wisdom direct me,
by your righteousness restrain me,
by your indulgence console me,
by your power protect me.

I offer you, Lord, my thoughts to
be directed to you,
my words, to be about you,
my deeds, to respect your will,
my trials, to be endured for you.

I will whatever you will,
I will it because you will it,
I will it in the way you will it,
I will it for as long as you will it.

Lord, enlighten my understanding,
I pray:
arouse my will,
cleanse my heart,
sanctify my soul.

Oratio universalis sub nomine Clementis Pp. XI vulgata

Credo, Domine,
sed credam firmius;
spero, sed sperem securius;
amo, sed amem ardentius;
doleo, sed doleam vehementius.

Adoro te ut primum principium;
desidero ut finem ultimum;
laudo ut benefactorem perpetuum;
invoco ut defensorem propitium.

Tua me sapientia dirige,
iustitia contine,
clementia solare,
potentia protege.

Offero tibi, Domine, cogitanda,
ut sint ad te;
dicenda, ut sint de te;
facienda, ut sint secundum te;
ferenda, ut sint propter te.

Volo quidquid vis,
volo quia vis,
volo quomodo vis,
volo quamdiu vis.

Oro, Domine:
intellectum illumines,
voluntatem inflammes,
cor emundes,
animam sanctifices.

May I weep for past sins,
repel future temptations,
correct evil inclinations,
nurture appropriate virtues.

Give me, good God,
love for you, hatred for myself,
zeal for my neighbour,
contempt for the world.

May I strive to obey superiors,
to help those dependent on me,
to have care for my friends,
forgiveness for my enemies.

May I conquer sensuality
     by austerity,
avarice by generosity,
anger by gentleness,
lukewarmness by fervour.

Render me prudent in planning,
steadfast in dangers,
patient in adversity,
humble in prosperity.

Make me, O Lord, attentive at prayer,
moderate at meals,
diligent in work,
steadfast in intent.

May I be careful to maintain
     interior innocence,
outward modesty,
exemplary behaviour,
a regular life.

May I be always watchful in
     subduing nature,
in nourishing grace,
in observing your law,
in winning salvation.

Defleam præteritas iniquitates,
repellam futuras tentationes,
corrigam vitiosas propensiones,
excolam idoneas virtutes.

Tribue mihi, bone Deus,
amorem tui, odium mei,
zelum proximi,
contemptum mundi.

Studeam superioribus obœdire,
inferioribus subvenire,
amicis consulere,
inimicis parcere.

Vincam voluptatem austeritate,
avaritiam largitate,
iracundiam lenitate,
tepiditatem fervore.

Redde me prudentem in consiliis,
constantem in periculis,
patientem in adversis,
humilem in prosperis.

Fac, Domine,
     ut sim in oratione attentus,
in epulis sobrius,
in munere sedulus,
in proposito firmus.

Curem habere innocentiam
     interiorem,
modestiam exteriorem,
conversationem exemplarem,
vitam regularem.

Assidue invigilem naturæ
     domandæ,
gratiæ fovendæ,
legi servandæ,
saluti promerendæ.

May I learn from you
how precarious are earthly things,
how great divine things,
how fleeting is time,
how lasting things eternal.

Grant that I may prepare for death,
fear judgement,
flee hell,
gain paradise.
Through Christ our Lord.
Amen.

Prayers to the Blessed Virgin Mary

O Mary, Virgin and
    Mother most holy,
behold, I have received your
    most dear Son,
whom you conceived in
    your immaculate womb,
brought forth, nursed and
    embraced most tenderly.
Behold him at whose sight
you used to rejoice and be filled
    with all delight;
him whom, humbly and lovingly,
once again I present
and offer him to you
to be clasped in your arms,
to be loved by your heart,
and to be offered up to
    the Most Holy Trinity
as the supreme worship of adoration,
for your own honour and glory
and for my needs and for those of
    the whole world.
I ask you therefore,
    most loving Mother:

Discam a te quam tenue quod
    terrenum,
quam grande quod divinum,
quam breve quod temporaneum,
quam durabile quod æternum.

Da, ut mortem præveniam,
iudicium pertimeam,
infernum effugiam,
paradisum obtineam.
Per Christum Dominum nostrum.
Amen.

Orationes ad B. Mariam Virginem

O Maria, Virgo
    et Mater sanctissima,
ecce suscepi dilectissimum
    Filium tuum,
quem immaculato utero
    tuo concepisti,
genuisti, lactasti atque suavissimis
    amplexibus strinxisti.
Ecce, cuius aspectu lætabaris
    et omnibus deliciis replebaris,
illum ipsum tibi humiliter
    et amanter repræsento et offero,

tuis bracchiis constringendum,
    tuo corde amandum,

sanctissimæque Trinitati in
    supremum latriæ cultum,
pro tui ipsius honore et gloria
et pro meis totiusque mundi
    necessitatibus, offerendum.
Rogo ergo te, piissima Mater,

entreat for me the forgiveness
   of all my sins
and, in abundant measure,
   the grace
of serving him in the future
   more faithfully,
and at the last, final grace,
so that with you I may praise him
for all the ages of ages.
Amen.

Hail, Mary, full of grace, the Lord is
   with thee;
blessed art thou amongst women,
and blessed is the fruit of thy
   womb, Jesus.
Holy Mary, Mother of God,
pray for us sinners
now and at the hour of our death.
Amen.

impetra mihi veniam omnium
   peccatorum meorum,
uberemque gratiam ipsi deinceps
   fidelius serviendi,
ac denique gratiam finalem,
ut eum tecum laudare possim
per omnia sæcula sæculorum.

Amen.

Ave Maria, gratia plena, Dominus
   tecum;
benedicta tu in mulieribus,
et benedictus fructus ventris tui,
   Iesus.
Sancta Maria, Mater Dei,
ora pro nobis peccatoribus
nunc et in hora mortis nostræ.
Amen.

AFTER HOLY COMMUNION

Act of Faith

O Jesus, I believe that I have received your Flesh to eat and your Blood to drink, because you have said it, and your word is true. All that I have and all that I am are your gift and now you have given me yourself.

Act of Adoration

O Jesus, my God, my Creator, I adore you, because from your hands I came and with you I am to be happy for ever.

Act of Humility

O Jesus, I am not worthy to receive you, and yet you have come to me that my poor heart may learn of you to be meek and humble.

Act of Love

Jesus, I love you; I love you with all my heart. You know that I love you, and wish to love you daily more and more.

Act of Thanksgiving

My good Jesus, I thank you with all my heart. How good, how kind you are to me. Blessed be Jesus in the most holy Sacrament of the Altar.

Act of Offering

O Jesus, receive my poor offering.
Jesus, you have given yourself to me,
and now let me give myself to you:
I give you my body, that I may be chaste and pure.
I give you my soul, that I may be free from sin.
I give you my heart, that I may always love you.
I give you my every breath that I shall breathe,
and especially my last.
I give you myself in life and in death,
that I may be yours for ever and ever.

For Yourself

O Jesus, wash away my sins with your Precious Blood.

O Jesus, the struggle against temptation is not yet finished. My Jesus, when temptation comes near me, make me strong against it. In the moment of temptation may I always say: "My Jesus, mercy! Mary, help!"

O Jesus, may I lead a good life; may I die a happy death. May I receive you before I die. May I say when I am dying: "Jesus, Mary and Joseph, I give you my heart and my soul".

Listen now for a moment to Jesus Christ; perhaps he has something to say to you. Answer Jesus in your heart, and tell him all your troubles. Then say:

For Perseverance

Jesus, I am going away for a time, but, I trust, not without you. You are with me by your grace. I resolve never to leave you by mortal sin. Although I am so weak I have such hope in you. Give me grace to persevere. Amen.

IF I CAN'T GET TO MASS

Spiritual Communion

Spiritual Communion is the heartfelt desire to receive Our Lord, even when we are unable because of the distance or for some other reason. This desire to receive him through spiritual Communion is an act of love which prolongs our thanksgiving even when we are not in the Eucharistic presence of Our Lord. The wish to live constantly in his presence can be fuelled by acts of love and desire to be united with him and is a means of drawing more deeply from the life of the Holy Spirit dwelling within our souls in the state of grace. 'The effects of a sacrament can be received by desire. Although in such a case the sacrament is not received physically . . . nevertheless the actual reception of the sacrament itself brings with it fuller effect than receiving it through desire alone' (St Thomas Aquinas). The writings of the saints reveal many formulae for making a spiritual Communion:

Acts of Spiritual Communion

My Jesus, I believe that You are truly present in the Most Holy Sacrament. I love You above all things, and I desire to receive You into my soul. Since I cannot at this moment receive You sacramentally, come at least spiritually into my heart. I embrace You as being already there and unite myself wholly to You. Never permit me to be separated from You. Amen.

(St Alphonsus Liguori)

I wish, my Lord, to receive You with the purity, humility and devotion with which your Most Holy Mother received You, with the spirit and fervour of the saints. Come, Lord Jesus.

Give me, good Lord, a longing to be with You ... give me warmth, delight and quickness in thinking upon You. And give me Your grace to long for Your holy sacraments, and specially to rejoice in the presence of Your very blessed Body, Sweet Saviour Christ, in the Holy Sacrament of the altar.

(St Thomas More)

27 November

FIRST SUNDAY OF ADVENT

The Lord comes; today, the first day of the Liturgical Year, this proclamation marks our starting point: we know that over and above every favourable or adverse event, the Lord does not leave us on our own. He came two thousand years ago and he will come again at the end of time, but he also comes today into my life and into yours. Yes, this life of ours, with all its problems, anxiety and uncertainty, is visited by the Lord. This is the source of our joy: the Lord has never tired and will never tire of us, he wants to come, he wants to visit us.

(Pope Francis)

Entrance Antiphon   Cf. Ps 24:1-3

TO you, I lift up my soul,
O my God.
In you, I have trusted;
  let me not be put to shame.
Nor let my enemies exult over me;
and let none who hope in you
  be put to shame.

Ant. ad introitum

AD te levavi animam meam,
Deus meus, in te confido,
  non erubescam.
Neque irrideant me inimici mei,
etenim universi qui te exspectant
  non confundentur.

The Gloria in excelsis (Glory to God in the highest) is not said.

Collect

Grant your faithful, we pray,
  almighty God,
the resolve to run forth
  to meet your Christ
with righteous deeds at his coming,
so that, gathered at his right hand,
they may be worthy to possess
  the heavenly Kingdom.
Through our Lord Jesus Christ,
  your Son,
who lives and reigns with you
  in the unity of the Holy Spirit,
God, for ever and ever.

Collecta

Da, quæsumus, omnipotens Deus,
hanc tuis fidelibus voluntatem,
ut, Christo tuo venienti iustis
  operibus occurrentes,
eius dexteræ sociati, regnum
  mereantur possidere cæleste.
Per Dominum nostrum Iesum
  Christum Filium tuum,
qui tecum vivit et regnat in unitate
  Spiritus Sancti, Deus,
per omnia sæcula sæculorum.

FIRST READING

A reading from the prophet Isaiah   2:1-5

The Lord gathers all nations together into the eternal peace of God's kingdom.

The vision of Isaiah son of Amoz, concerning Judah and Jerusalem.

In the days to come
the mountain of the Temple of the Lord
shall tower above the mountains
and be lifted higher than the hills.
All the nations will stream to it,
peoples without number will come to it, and they will say:

> 'Come, let us go up to the mountain of the Lord,
> to the Temple of the God of Jacob
> that he may teach us his ways
> so that we may walk in his paths;
> since the Law will go out from Sion,
> and the oracle of the Lord from Jerusalem.'

He will wield authority over the nations
and adjudicate between many peoples;
these will hammer their swords into ploughshares,
their spears into sickles.
Nation will not lift sword against nation,
there will be no more training for war.
O House of Jacob, come,
let us walk in the light of the Lord.

> The word of the Lord.

Responsorial Psalm   Ps 121:1-2,4-5,6-9. R. Cf. v.1

R. **I rejoiced when I heard them say:
   'Let us go to God's house.'**

I rejoiced when I heard them say:
'Let us go to God's house.'
And now our feet are standing
within your gates, O Jerusalem. R.

It is there that the tribes go up,
the tribes of the Lord.
For Israel's law it is
there to praise the Lord's name.

There were set the thrones of judgement
of the house of David. R.

For the peace of Jerusalem pray:
'Peace be to your homes!'
May peace reign in your walls,
in your palaces, peace!' R.

For love of my brethren and friends
I say: 'Peace upon you!'
For love of the house of the Lord
I will ask for your good. R.

SECOND READING

A reading from the letter of St Paul to the Romans   13:11-14

Our salvation is near.

You know 'the time' has come: you must wake up now: our salvation is
even nearer than it was when we were converted. The night is almost over,
it will be daylight soon – let us give up all the things we prefer to do under
cover of the dark; let us arm ourselves and appear in the light. Let us live
decently as people do in the daytime: no drunken orgies, no promiscuity
or licentiousness, and no wrangling or jealousy. Let your armour be the
Lord Jesus Christ.

The word of the Lord.

Gospel Acclamation   Ps 84:8

R. **Alleluia, alleluia!**
Let us see, O Lord, your mercy
and give us your saving help.
R. **Alleluia!**

GOSPEL

A reading from the holy Gospel according to Matthew   24:37-44

Stay awake so that you may be ready.

Jesus said to his disciples: 'As it was in Noah's day, so will it be when the
Son of Man comes. For in those days before the Flood people were eating,
drinking, taking wives, taking husbands, right up to the day Noah went
into the ark, and they suspected nothing till the Flood came and swept all
away. It will be like this when the Son of Man comes. Then of two men in
the fields one is taken, one left; of two women at the millstone grinding,
one is taken, one left.

'So stay awake, because you do not know the day when your master is coming. You may be quite sure of this that if the householder had known at what time of the night the burglar would come, he would have stayed awake and would not have allowed anyone to break through the wall of his house. Therefore, you too must stand ready because the Son of Man is coming at an hour you do not expect.'

The Gospel of the Lord.

The Creed is said.

Prayer over the Offerings

Accept, we pray, O Lord,
  these offerings we make,
gathered from among
  your gifts to us,
and may what you grant us
  to celebrate devoutly here below,
gain for us the prize
  of eternal redemption.
Through Christ our Lord.

Preface I of Advent, pp.42-43.

Super oblata

Suscipe, quæsumus,
  Domine, munera
quæ de tuis offerimus
  collata beneficiis,
et, quod nostræ devotioni concedis
  effici temporali,
tuæ nobis fiat præmium
  redemptionis æternæ.
Per Christum Dominum nostrum.

Communion Antiphon   Ps 84:13

The Lord will bestow his bounty,
and our earth shall yield its increase.

Ant. ad communionem

Dominus dabit benignitatem,
et terra nostra dabit fructum suum

Prayer after Communion

May these mysteries, O Lord,
in which we have participated,
profit us, we pray,
for even now, as we walk amid
  passing things,
you teach us by them to love
  the things of heaven
and hold fast to what endures.
Through Christ our Lord.

Post communionem

Prosint nobis, quæsumus, Domine,
  frequentata mysteria,
quibus nos,
  inter prætereuntia ambulantes,
iam nunc instituis amare cælestia
  et inhærere mansuris.
Per Christum Dominum nostrum.

A formula of Solemn Blessing, pp.132-133, may be used.

30 November

In Scotland

SAINT ANDREW, APOSTLE AND MARTYR, PATRON OF SCOTLAND

The lesson of the grain of wheat that dies in order to bear fruit also has a parallel in the life of Saint Andrew. Tradition tells us that he followed the fate of his Lord and Master, ending his days in Patras, Greece. Like Peter, he endured martyrdom on a cross, the diagonal cross that we venerate today as the cross of Saint Andrew. From his example we learn that the path of each single Christian, like that of the Church as a whole, leads to new life, to eternal life, through the imitation of Christ and the experience of his cross. *(Pope Benedict XVI)*

Solemnity

Entrance Antiphon Cf. Mt 4:18-19

BESIDE the Sea of Galilee,
the Lord saw two brothers,
Peter and Andrew,
and he said to them:
Come after me and I will make you
    fishers of men.

Ant. ad introitum

DOMINUS secus mare Galilææ
vidit duos fratres,
Petrum et Andream,
et vocavit eos:
Venite post me, faciam vos fieri
    piscatores hominum.

The Gloria in excelsis (Glory to God in the highest) is said.

Collect

We humbly implore your majesty,
    O Lord,
that, just as the blessed
    Apostle Andrew
was for your Church a preacher
    and pastor,
so he may be for us a constant
    intercessor before you.
Through our Lord Jesus Christ,
    your Son,
who lives and reigns with you
    in the unity of the Holy Spirit,
God, for ever and ever.

Collecta

Maiestatem tuam, Domine,
    suppliciter exoramus,
ut, sicut Ecclesiæ tuæ beatus
    Andreas apostolus
exstitit prædicator et rector,
ita apud te sit pro nobis
    perpetuus intercessor.
Per Dominum nostrum Iesum
    Christum Filium tuum,
qui tecum vivit et regnat
    in unitate Spiritus Sancti,
Deus, per omnia sæcula sæculorum.

FIRST READING

A reading from the book of Wisdom   3:1-9

He accepted them as a holocaust.

The souls of the virtuous are in the hands of God,
no torment shall ever touch them.
In the eyes of the unwise, they did appear to die,
their going looked like a disaster,
their leaving us, like annihilation;
but they are in peace.
If they experienced punishment as men see it,
their hope was rich with immortality;
slight was their affliction, great will their blessings be.
God has put them to the test
and proved them worthy to be with him;
he has tested them like gold in a furnace,
and accepted them as a holocaust.
When the time comes for his visitation they will shine out;
as sparks run through the stubble, so will they.
They shall judge nations, rule over peoples,
and the Lord will be their king for ever.
They who trust in him will understand the truth,
those who are faithful will live with him in love;
for grace and mercy await those he has chosen.

The word of the Lord.

Responsorial Psalm   Ps 30:3-4,6,8,17,21. R. v.6

R. **Into your hands, O Lord,
    I commend my spirit.**

Be a rock of refuge for me,
a mighty stronghold to save me,
for you are my rock, my stronghold.
For your name's sake, lead me and guide me. R.

Into your hands I commend my spirit.
It is you who will redeem me, Lord.
As for me, I trust in the Lord:
let me be glad and rejoice in your love. R.

Let your face shine on your servant.
Save me in your love.

You hide them in the shelter of your presence
from the plotting of men. R.

SECOND READING

A reading from the letter of St Paul to the Romans   10:9-18

Faith comes from what is preached, and what is preached comes from the word of Christ.

If your lips confess that Jesus is Lord and if you believe in your heart that God raised him from the dead, then you will be saved. By believing from the heart you are made righteous; by confessing with your lips you are saved. When scripture says: those who believe in him will have no cause for shame, it makes no distinction between Jew and Greek: all belong to the same Lord who is rich enough, however many ask his help, for everyone who calls on the name of the Lord will be saved.

But they will not ask his help unless they believe in him, and they will not believe in him unless they have heard him, and they will not hear him unless they get a preacher, and they will never have a preacher unless one is sent, but as scripture says: The footsteps of those who bring good news are a welcome sound. Not everyone, of course, listens to the Good News. As Isaiah says: Lord, how many believe what we proclaimed? So faith comes from what is preached, and what is preached comes from the word of Christ.

Let me put the question: is it possible that they did not hear? Indeed they did; in the words of the psalm, their voice has gone out through all the earth, and their message to the ends of the world.

The word of the Lord.

Gospel Acclamation   Mt 4:19
R. **Alleluia, alleluia!**
Follow me, says the Lord,
and I will make you fishers of men.
R. **Alleluia!**

GOSPEL

A reading from the holy Gospel according to Matthew   4:18-22

And they left their nets at once and followed him.

As Jesus was walking by the Sea of Galilee he saw two brothers, Simon, who was called Peter, and his brother Andrew; they were making a cast in the lake with their net, for they were fishermen. And he said to them, 'Follow me and I will make you fishers of men.' And they left their nets at once and followed him.

Going on from there he saw another pair of brothers, James son of Zebedee and his brother John; they were in their boat with their father Zebedee, mending their nets, and he called them. At once, leaving the boat and their father, they followed him.

The Gospel of the Lord.

The Creed is said.

Prayer over the Offerings

Grant us, almighty God,
　　that through these offerings,
which we bring on the feast day
　　of Saint Andrew,
we may please you by what
　　we have brought
and be given life by what
　　you have accepted.
Through Christ our Lord.

Preface of the Apostles, pp.70-71.

Super oblata

Concede nobis, omnipotens Deus,
ut his muneribus,
quæ in beati Andreæ festivitate
　　deferimus,
et tibi placeamus exhibitis,
　　et vivificemur acceptis.
Per Christum Dominum nostrum.

Communion Antiphon Cf. Jn 1:41-42

Andrew told his brother Simon:
We have found the Messiah,
　　the Christ,
and he brought him to Jesus.

Ant. ad communionem

Dixit Andreas Simoni fratri suo:
Invenimus Messiam,
　　qui dicitur Christus.
Et adduxit eum ad Iesum.

Prayer after Communion

May communion in your Sacrament
　　strengthen us, O Lord,
so that by the example of the
　　blessed Apostle Andrew
we, who carry in our body
　　the Death of Christ,
may merit to live with him in glory.
Who lives and reigns
　　for ever and ever.

Post communionem

Roboret nos, Domine,
　　sacramenti tui communio,
ut, exemplo beati Andreæ apostoli,
Christi mortificationem ferentes,
cum ipso vivere mereamur
　　in gloria.
Qui vivit et regnat
　　in sæcula sæculorum.

A formula of Solemn Blessing, pp.146-147, may be used.

4 December

SECOND SUNDAY OF ADVENT

In the Gospel this Sunday, John the Baptist's invitation resounds: "Repent, for the kingdom of heaven is at hand!". The condition for entering and being a part of this kingdom is to implement a change in our life, which is to convert, to convert every day, to take a step forward each day. It is a question of leaving behind the comfortable but misleading ways of the idols of this world: success at all costs; power to the detriment of the weak; the desire for wealth; pleasure at any price. And instead, preparing the way of the Lord: this does not take away our freedom, but gives us true happiness. With the birth of Jesus in Bethlehem, it is God himself who abides among us to free us from self interest, sin and corruption, from these manners of the devil.

(Pope Francis)

Entrance Antiphon   Cf. Is 30:19,30

O PEOPLE of Sion, behold,
   the Lord will come to save
the nations,
and the Lord will make the glory
   of his voice heard
in the joy of your heart.

Ant. ad introitum

P OPULUS Sion, ecce Dominus
   veniet ad salvandas gentes;
et auditam faciet Dominus gloriam
   vocis suæ
in lætitia cordis vestri.

The Gloria in excelsis (Glory to God in the highest) is not said.

Collect

Almighty and merciful God,
may no earthly undertaking
   hinder those
who set out in haste
   to meet your Son,
but may our learning
   of heavenly wisdom
gain us admittance to his company.
Who lives and reigns with you
   in the unity of the Holy Spirit,
God, for ever and ever.

Collecta

Omnipotens et misericors Deus,
in tui occursum Filii festinantes
nulla opera terreni actus impediant,
sed sapientiæ cælestis eruditio nos
   faciat eius esse consortes.
Qui tecum vivit et regnat
   in unitate Spiritus Sancti,
Deus, per omnia sæcula sæculorum.

FIRST READING

A reading from the prophet Isaiah   11:1-10

He judges the wretched with integrity.

A shoot springs from the stock of Jesse,
a scion thrusts from his roots:
on him the spirit of the Lord rests,
a spirit of wisdom and insight,
a spirit of counsel and power,
a spirit of knowledge and of the fear of the Lord.
(The fear of the Lord is his breath.)
He does not judge by appearances,
he gives no verdict on hearsay,
but judges the wretched with integrity,
and with equity gives a verdict for the poor of the land.
His word is a rod that strikes the ruthless,
his sentences bring death to the wicked.

Integrity is the loincloth round his waist,
faithfulness the belt about his hips.

The wolf lives with the lamb,
the panther lies down with the kid,
calf and lion cub feed together
with a little boy to lead them.
The cow and the bear make friends,
their young lie down together.
The lion eats straw like the ox.
The infant plays over the cobra's hole;
into the viper's lair
the young child puts his hand.
They do not hurt, no harm,
on all my holy mountain,
for the country is filled with the knowledge of the Lord
as the waters swell the sea.

That day, the root of Jesse
shall stand as a signal to the peoples.
It will be sought out by the nations
and its home will be glorious.

The word of the Lord.

Responsorial Psalm   Ps 71:1-2,7-8,12-13,17. R. Cf. v.7

R. **In his days justice shall flourish
and peace till the moon fails.**

O God, give your judgement to the king,
to a king's son your justice,
that he may judge your people in justice
and your poor in right judgement. R.

In his days justice shall flourish
and peace till the moon fails.
He shall rule from sea to sea,
from the Great River to earth's bounds. R.

For he shall save the poor when they cry
and the needy who are helpless.
He will have pity on the weak
and save the lives of the poor. R.

May his name be blessed for ever
and endure like the sun.
Every tribe shall be blessed in him,
all nations bless his name. R.

SECOND READING

A reading from the letter of St Paul to the Romans   15:4-9

Christ is the saviour of all men.

Everything that was written long ago in the scriptures was meant to teach
us something about hope from the examples scripture gives of how people
who did not give up were helped by God. And may he who helps us when
we refuse to give up, help you all to be tolerant with each other, following
the example of Christ Jesus, so that united in mind and voice you may give
glory to the God and Father of our Lord Jesus Christ.

It can only be to God's glory, then, for you to treat each other in the
same friendly way as Christ treated you. The reason Christ became the
servant of circumcised Jews was not only so that God could faithfully carry
out the promises made to the patriarchs, it was also to get the pagans to
give glory to God for his mercy, as scripture says in one place: For this I
shall praise you among the pagans and sing to your name.

The word of the Lord.

Gospel Acclamation   Lk 3:4,6

R. **Alleluia, alleluia!**
Prepare a way for the Lord, make his paths straight,
and all mankind shall see the salvation of God.
R. **Alleluia!**

GOSPEL

A reading from the holy Gospel according to Matthew   3:1-12
Repent, for the kingdom of heaven is close at hand.

In due course John the Baptist appeared; he preached in the wilderness
of Judaea and this was his message: 'Repent, for the kingdom of heaven is
close at hand.' This was the man the prophet Isaiah spoke of when he said:

A voice cries in the wilderness:
Prepare a way for the Lord,
make his paths straight.

This man John wore a garment made of camel-hair with a leather belt
round his waist, and his food was locusts and wild honey. Then Jerusalem
and all Judaea and the whole Jordan district made their way to him, and as
they were baptised by him in the river Jordan they confessed their sins. But
when he saw a number of Pharisees and Sadducees coming for baptism he
said to them, 'Brood of vipers, who warned you to fly from the retribution
that is coming? But if you are repentant, produce the appropriate fruit,
and do not presume to tell yourselves, "We have Abraham for our father,"
because, I tell you, God can raise children for Abraham from these stones.
Even now the axe is laid to the roots of the trees, so that any tree which fails
to produce good fruit will be cut down and thrown on the fire. I baptise
you in water for repentance, but the one who follows me is more powerful
than I am, and I am not fit to carry his sandals; he will baptise you with
the Holy Spirit and fire. His winnowing-fan is in his hand; he will clear his
threshing-floor and gather his wheat into the barn; but the chaff he will
burn in a fire that will never go out.'

The Gospel of the Lord.

The Creed is said.

Prayer over the Offerings

Be pleased, O Lord, with our
    humble prayers and offerings,
and, since we have no merits
    to plead our cause,
come, we pray, to our rescue
with the protection of your mercy.
Through Christ our Lord.

Preface I of Advent, pp.42-43.

Communion Antiphon Ba 5:5;4:36

Jerusalem, arise and stand upon
    the heights,
and behold the joy which comes
    to you from God.

Prayer after Communion

Replenished by the food
    of spiritual nourishment,
we humbly beseech you, O Lord,
that, through our partaking
    in this mystery,
you may teach us to judge wisely
    the things of earth
and hold firm to the things
    of heaven.
Through Christ our Lord.

A formula of Solemn Blessing, pp.132-133, may be used.

Super oblata

Placare, Domine, quæsumus,
nostræ precis humilitatis
    et hostiis,
et, ubi nulla suppetunt
    suffragia meritorum,
tuæ nobis indulgentiæ
    succurre præsidiis.
Per Christum Dominum nostrum.

Ant. ad communionem

Ierusalem, surge et sta in excelso,
et vide iucunditatem,
    quæ veniet tibi a Deo tuo.

Post communionem

Repleti cibo spiritalis alimoniæ,
supplices te, Domine, deprecamur,
ut, huius participatione mysterii,
doceas nos terrena
    sapienter perpendere,
et cælestibus inhærere.
Per Christum Dominum nostrum.

8 December

THE IMMACULATE CONCEPTION OF THE BLESSED VIRGIN MARY

In order to work marvellous deeds, the Lord has no need of grand means and our lofty abilities, but rather of our humility, of our eyes open to him, and also open to others. With the annunciation, within the poor walls of a small house, God changed history. Today too, he wants to do great things with us in our daily lives: that is, in our families, at work, in everyday environments. God's grace loves to operate there more than in great historical events. But do we believe this? Or do we think that holiness is a utopia, something for insiders, a pious illusion incompatible with ordinary life? Let us ask Our Lady for a grace: that she may free us from the misleading idea that the Gospel is one thing and life is another; that she kindle our enthusiasm for the ideal of holiness which is about living what happens each day, humbly and joyfully, *like Our Lady, free from ourselves, with our eyes fixed on God and the neighbour we meet.*

(Pope Francis)

Solemnity

Entrance Antiphon   Is 61:10

I REJOICE heartily in the Lord,
  in my God is the joy of my soul;
for he has clothed me with a robe
    of salvation,
and wrapped me in a mantle
    of justice,
like a bride adorned with her jewels.

Ant. ad introitum

G AUDENS gaudebo in Domino,
  et exsultabit anima mea
  in Deo meo;
quia induit me vestimentis salutis,
et indumento iustitiæ
    circumdedit me,
quasi sponsam ornatam
    monilibus suis.

The **Gloria in excelsis** (Glory to God in the highest) is said.

Collect

O God, who by the Immaculate
  Conception of the Blessed Virgin
prepared a worthy dwelling
    for your Son,
grant, we pray,

Collecta

Deus, qui per immaculatam
  Virginis Conceptionem
dignum Filio tuo
    habitaculum præparasti,
quæsumus, ut, qui ex morte

that, as you preserved her
    from every stain
by virtue of the Death of your Son,
    which you foresaw,
so, through her intercession,
we, too, may be cleansed
    and admitted to your presence.
Through our Lord Jesus Christ,
    your Son,
who lives and reigns with you
    in the unity of the Holy Spirit,
God, for ever and ever.

eiusdem Filii tui prævisa,
eam ab omni labe præservasti,
nos quoque mundos,
    eius intercessione,
ad te pervenire concedas.
Per Dominum nostrum Iesum
    Christum Filium tuum,
qui tecum vivit et regnat
    in unitate Spiritus Sancti,
Deus, per omnia sæcula sæculorum.

FIRST READING

A reading from the book of Genesis   3:9-15,20

I will make you enemies of each other; your offspring and her offspring.

After Adam had eaten of the tree, the Lord God called to him, 'Where are you?' he asked. 'I heard the sound of you in the garden,' he replied. 'I was afraid because I was naked, so I hid.' 'Who told you that you were naked?' he asked. 'Have you been eating of the tree I forbade you to eat?' The man replied, 'It was the woman you put with me; she gave me the fruit, and I ate it.' Then the Lord God asked the woman, 'What is this you have done?' The woman replied, 'The serpent tempted me and I ate.'

> Then the Lord God said to the serpent, 'Because you have done this,
> 'Be accursed beyond all cattle,
> all wild beasts.
> You shall crawl on your belly and eat dust
> every day of your life.
> I will make you enemies of each other:
> you and the woman,
> your offspring and her offspring.
> It will crush your head
> and you will strike its heel.'

The man named his wife 'Eve' because she was the mother of all those who live.

> The word of the Lord.

Responsorial Psalm   Ps 97:1-4. R. v.1

R. **Sing a new song to the Lord**
   for he has worked wonders.

Sing a new song to the Lord
for he has worked wonders.
His right hand and his holy arm
have brought salvation. R.

The Lord has made known his salvation;
has shown his justice to the nations.
He has remembered his truth and love
for the house of Israel. R.

All the ends of the earth have seen
the salvation of our God.
Shout to the Lord all the earth,
ring out your joy. R.

SECOND READING

A reading from the letter of St Paul to the Ephesians   1:3-6,11-12

Before the world was made, God chose us in Christ.

Blessed be God the Father of our Lord Jesus Christ,
who has blessed us with all the spiritual blessings of heaven in Christ.
Before the world was made, he chose us, chose us in Christ,
to be holy and spotless, and to live through love in his presence,
determining that we should become his adopted sons,
    through Jesus Christ
for his own kind purposes,
to make us praise the glory of his grace,
his free gift to us in the Beloved.
And it is in him that we were claimed as God's own,
chosen from the beginning,
under the predetermined plan of the one who guides all things
as he decides by his own will;
chosen to be,
for his greater glory,
the people who would put their hopes in Christ before he came.

The word of the Lord.

Gospel Acclamation   Cf. Lk 1:28

R. **Alleluia, alleluia!**
Hail, Mary, full of grace; the Lord is with thee!
Blessed art thou among women.
R. **Alleluia!**

GOSPEL

A reading from the holy Gospel according to Luke   1:26-38

Rejoice, so highly favoured! The Lord is with you.

The angel Gabriel was sent by God to a town in Galilee called Nazareth, to a virgin betrothed to a man named Joseph, of the house of David; and the virgin's name was Mary. He went in and said to her, 'Rejoice, so highly favoured! The Lord is with you.' She was deeply disturbed by these words and asked herself what this greeting could mean, but the angel said to her, 'Mary, do not be afraid; you have won God's favour. Listen! You are to conceive and bear a son, and you must name him Jesus. He will be great and will be called Son of the Most High. The Lord God will give him the throne of his ancestor David; he will rule over the House of Jacob for ever and his reign will have no end.' Mary said to the angel, 'But how can this come about, since I am a virgin?' 'The Holy Spirit will come upon you' the angel answered, 'and the power of the Most High will cover you with its shadow. And so the child will be holy and will be called Son of God. Know this too: your kinswoman Elizabeth has, in her old age, herself conceived a son, and she whom people called barren is now in her sixth month, for nothing is impossible to God.' 'I am the handmaid of the Lord,' said Mary, 'let what you have said be done to me.' And the angel left her.

The Gospel of the Lord.

The Creed is said.

Prayer over the Offerings	Super oblata
Graciously accept the saving sacrifice which we offer you, O Lord, on the Solemnity of the Immaculate Conception of the Blessed Virgin Mary, and grant that, as we profess her,	Salutarem hostiam, quam in sollemnitate immaculatæ Conceptionis beatæ Virginis Mariæ tibi, Domine, offerimus, suscipe dignanter, et præsta,

on account of your prevenient grace,
to be untouched by any stain of sin,
so, through her intercession,
we may be delivered from all
    our faults.
Through Christ our Lord.

ut, sicut illam tua gratia præveniente
ab omni labe
profitemur immunem,
ita, eius intercessione, a culpis
    omnibus liberemur.
Per Christum Dominum nostrum.

Preface: The Mystery of Mary
and the Church.

Præfatio: De mysterio Mariæ
et Ecclesiæ.

It is truly right and just,
    our duty and our salvation,
always and everywhere
    to give you thanks,
Lord, holy Father,
    almighty and eternal God.

Vere dignum et iustum est,
    æquum et salutare,
nos tibi semper et ubique
    gratias agere:
Domine, sancte Pater,
    omnipotens æterne Deus:

For you preserved the most Blessed
    Virgin Mary
from all stain of original sin,
so that in her, endowed with
    the rich fullness of your grace,
you might prepare a worthy
    Mother for your Son
and signify the beginning
    of the Church,
his beautiful Bride without spot
    or wrinkle.

Qui beatissimam Virginem Mariam
ab omni originalis culpæ
    labe præservasti,
ut in ea,
    gratiæ tuæ plenitudine ditata,
dignam Filio tuo
    Genetricem præparares
et Sponsæ eius Ecclesiæ,
sine ruga vel macula formosæ,
    signares exordium.

She, the most pure Virgin,
    was to bring forth a Son,
the innocent Lamb who would
    wipe away our offences;
you placed her above all others
to be for your people an advocate
    of grace
and a model of holiness.

Filium enim erat purissima
    Virgo datura,
qui crimina nostra Agnus
    innocens aboleret;
et ipsam præ omnibus tuo
    populo disponebas
advocatam gratiæ
    et sanctitatis exemplar.

And so, in company with the choirs
of Angels,
we praise you, and with joy
we proclaim:

Holy, Holy, Holy Lord God of hosts...

Et ideo, choris angelicis sociati,
te laudamus in gaudio confitentes:

Sanctus, Sanctus, Sanctus. . .

Communion Antiphon

Glorious things are spoken of you,
O Mary,
for from you arose the sun of justice,
Christ our God.

Ant. ad communionem

Gloriosa dicta sunt de te, Maria,
quia ex te ortus est sol iustitiæ,
Christus Deus noster.

Prayer after Communion

May the Sacrament we have received,
O Lord our God,
heal in us the wounds of that fault
from which in a singular way
you preserved Blessed Mary in her
Immaculate Conception.
Through Christ our Lord.

Post communionem

Sacramenta quæ sumpsimus,
Domine Deus noster,
illius in nobis culpæ
vulnera reparent,
a qua immaculatam beatæ
Mariæ Conceptionem
singulariter præservasti.
Per Christum Dominum nostrum.

A formula of Solemn Blessing, pp.144-145, may be used.

11 December

THIRD SUNDAY OF ADVENT

Salvation envelops the whole person and regenerates him. But this new birth, with the joy that accompanies it, always presupposes a death to ourselves and to the sin within us. Hence the call to conversion, which is the basis of the preaching of both the Baptist and Jesus; in particular, it is a question of converting our idea of God. Advent is a time of grace. It tells us that it is not enough to believe in God: it is necessary to purify our faith every day. It is a matter of preparing ourselves to welcome not a fairy-tale character, but the God who challenges us, involves us and before whom a choice is imposed.

(Pope Francis)

Entrance Antiphon Ph 4:4-5	Ant. ad introitum

REJOICE in the Lord always; again I say, rejoice. Indeed, the Lord is near.

GAUDETE in Domino semper: iterum dico, gaudete. Dominus enim prope est.

The Gloria in excelsis (Glory to God in the highest) is not said.

Collect	Collecta

O God, who see how your people
faithfully await the feast
    of the Lord's Nativity,
enable us, we pray,
to attain the joys of so great
    a salvation
and to celebrate them always
with solemn worship
    and glad rejoicing.
Through our Lord Jesus Christ,
    your Son,
who lives and reigns with you
    in the unity of the Holy Spirit,
God, for ever and ever.

Deus, qui conspicis populum tuum
nativitatis dominicæ festivitatem
    fideliter exspectare,
præsta, quæsumus,
ut valeamus ad tantæ salutis
    gaudia pervenire,
et ea votis sollemnibus alacri
    semper lætitia celebrare.

Per Dominum nostrum
    Iesum Christum Filium tuum,
qui tecum vivit et regnat
    in unitate Spiritus Sancti,
Deus, per omnia sæcula sæculorum.

FIRST READING

A reading from the prophet Isaiah   35:1-6,10

God himself is coming to save you.

Let the wilderness and the dry-lands exult,
let the wasteland rejoice and bloom,
let it bring forth flowers like the jonquil,
let it rejoice and sing for joy.

The glory of Lebanon is bestowed on it,
the splendour of Carmel and Sharon;
they shall see the glory of the Lord,
the splendour of our God.

Strengthen all weary hands,
steady all trembling knees
and say to all faint hearts,
'Courage! Do not be afraid.

'Look, your God is coming,
vengeance is coming,
the retribution of God;
he is coming to save you.'

Then the eyes of the blind shall be opened,
the ears of the deaf unsealed,
then the lame shall leap like a deer
and the tongues of the dumb sing for joy,
for those the Lord has ransomed shall return.

They will come to Sion shouting for joy,
everlasting joy on their faces;
joy and gladness will go with them
and sorrow and lament be ended.

The word of the Lord.

Responsial Psalm   Ps 145:6-10. R. Cf. Is 35:4

R. **Come, Lord, and save us.**
   or **Alleluia!**

   It is the Lord who keeps faith for ever,
   who is just to those who are oppressed.
   It is he who gives bread to the hungry,
   the Lord, who sets prisoners free. R.

It is the Lord who gives sight to the blind,
who raises up those who are bowed down,
the Lord, who protects the stranger
and upholds the widow and orphan. R.

It is the Lord who loves the just
but thwarts the path of the wicked.
The Lord will reign for ever,
Sion's God, from age to age. R.

R. **Come, Lord, and save us.**
   or **Alleluia!**

SECOND READING

A reading from the letter of St James   5:7-10
Do not lose heart, because the Lord's coming will be soon

Be patient, brothers, until the Lord's coming. Think of a farmer: how
patiently he waits for the precious fruit of the ground until it has had the
autumn rains and the spring rains! You too have to be patient; do not lose
heart, because the Lord's coming will be soon. Do not make complaints
against one another, brothers, so as not to be brought to judgement
yourselves; the Judge is already to be seen waiting at the gates. For your
example, brothers, in submitting with patience, take the prophets who
spoke in the name of the Lord.

   The word of the Lord.

Gospel Acclamation   Is 61:1 (Lk 4:18)

R. **Alleluia, alleluia!**
The Spirit of the Lord has been given to me.
He has sent me to bring good news to the poor.
R. **Alleluia!**

GOSPEL

A reading from the holy Gospel according to Matthew   11:2-11
Are you the one who is to come, or have we got to wait for someone else?

John in his prison had heard what Christ was doing and he sent his disciples
to ask him, 'Are you the one who is to come, or have we got to wait for
someone else?' Jesus answered, 'Go back and tell John what you hear and
see; the blind see again, and the lame walk, lepers are cleansed, and the
deaf hear, and the dead are raised to life and the Good News is proclaimed
to the poor; and happy is the man who does not lose faith in me.'

As the messengers were leaving, Jesus began to talk to the people about John: 'What did you go out into the wilderness to see? A reed swaying in the breeze? No? Then what did you go out to see? A man wearing fine clothes? Oh no, those who wear fine clothes are to be found in palaces. Then what did you go out for? To see a prophet? Yes, I tell you, and much more than a prophet: he is the one of whom scripture says: Look, I am going to send my messenger before you; he will prepare your way before you. I tell you solemnly, of all the children born of women, a greater than John the Baptist has never been seen; yet the least in the kingdom of heaven is greater than he is.'

The Gospel of the Lord.

The Creed is said.

Prayer over the Offerings

May the sacrifice of our worship,
    Lord, we pray,
be offered to you unceasingly,
to complete what was begun
    in sacred mystery
and powerfully accomplish for us
    your saving work.
Through Christ our Lord.

Preface I of Advent, pp.42-43.

Super oblata

Devotionis nostræ tibi,
    Domine, quæsumus,
hostia iugiter immoletur,
quæ et sacri peragat
    instituta mysterii
et salutare tuum nobis
    potenter operetur.
Per Christum Dominum nostrum.

Communion Antiphon   Cf. Is 35:4

Say to the faint of heart:
    Be strong and do not fear.
Behold, our God will come,
    and he will save us.

Ant. ad communionem

Dicite: Pusillanimes,
    confortamini et nolite timere:
ecce Deus noster veniet
et salvabit nos.

Prayer after Communion

We implore your mercy, Lord,
that this divine sustenance may
    cleanse us of our faults
and prepare us for
    the coming feasts.
Through Christ our Lord.

Post communionem

Tuam, Domine,
    clementiam imploramus,
ut hæc divina subsidia,
    a vitiis expiatos,
ad festa ventura nos præparent.
Per Christum Dominum nostrum.

A formula of Solemn Blessing, pp.132-133, may be used.

18 December

FOURTH SUNDAY OF ADVENT

Joseph trusts God totally, obeys the Angel's words and takes Mary with him. It was precisely this unshakable trust in God that enabled him to accept a humanly difficult and incomprehensible situation. Joseph understands, in faith, that the child born in Mary's womb is not his child, but the Son of God, and he, Joseph, will be its guardian, fully assuming its earthly paternity. The example of this gentle and wise man exhorts us to lift up our gaze and push it further. It is a question of recovering the surprising logic of God which, far from small or great calculations, is made up of openness towards new horizons, towards Christ and his Word.

(Pope Francis)

Entrance Antiphon   Cf. Is 45:8

DROP down dew from above,
you heavens,
and let the clouds rain down
the Just One;
let the earth be opened
and bring forth a Saviour.

Ant. ad introitum

RORATE, cæli, desuper,
et nubes pluant iustum;
aperiatur terra
et germinet Salvatorem.

The Gloria in excelsis (Glory to God in the highest) is not said.

Collect

Pour forth, we beseech you, O Lord,
your grace into our hearts,
that we, to whom the Incarnation
of Christ your Son
was made known by the message
of an Angel,
may by his Passion and Cross
be brought to the glory
of his Resurrection.

Collecta

Gratiam tuam,
quæsumus, Domine,
mentibus nostris infunde, ut qui,
Angelo nuntiante,
Christi Filii tui
incarnationem cognovimus,
per passionem eius et crucem
ad resurrectionis
gloriam perducamur.

| Who lives and reigns with you
   in the unity of the Holy Spirit,
God, for ever and ever. | Per Dominum nostrum Iesum
   Christum Filium tuum,
qui tecum vivit et regnat
   in unitate Spiritus Sancti,
Deus, per omnia sæcula sæculorum. |

FIRST READING

A reading from the prophet Isaiah   7:10-14

The maiden is with child.

The Lord spoke to Ahaz and said, 'Ask the Lord your God for a sign for
yourself coming either from the depths of Sheol or from the heights
above.' 'No,' Ahaz answered 'I will not put the Lord to the test.'

   Then Isaiah said:

'Listen now, House of David:
are you not satisfied with trying the patience of men
without trying the patience of my God, too?
The Lord himself, therefore,
will give you a sign.
It is this: the maiden is with child
and will soon give birth to a son
whom she will call Emmanuel,
a name which means "God-is-with-us".'

   The word of the Lord.

Responsorial Psalm   Ps 23:1-6. R. Cf. vv.7,10

R. **Let the Lord enter!**
  He is the king of glory.

The Lord's is the earth and its fullness,
the world and all its peoples.
It is he who set it on the seas;
on the waters he made it firm. R.

Who shall climb the mountain of the Lord?
Who shall stand in his holy place?
The man with clean hands and pure heart,
who desires not worthless things. R.

He shall receive blessings from the Lord
and reward from the God who saves him.
Such are the men who seek him,
seek the face of the God of Jacob. R.

SECOND READING

A reading from the letter of St Paul to the Romans   1:1-7

Jesus Christ, descendant of David, Son of God.

From Paul, a servant of Christ Jesus who has been called to be an apostle,
and specially chosen to preach the Good News that God promised long ago
through his prophets in the scriptures.

This news is about the Son of God who, according to the human
nature he took, was a descendant of David: it is about Jesus Christ our Lord
who, in the order of the spirit, the spirit of holiness that was in him, was
proclaimed Son of God in all his power through his resurrection from the
dead. Through him we received grace and our apostolic mission to preach
the obedience of faith to all pagan nations in honour of his name. You
are one of these nations, and by his call belong to Jesus Christ. To you all,
then, who are God's beloved in Rome, called to be saints, may God our
Father and the Lord Jesus Christ send grace and peace.

The word of the Lord.

Gospel Acclamation   Mt 1:23

R. **Alleluia, alleluia!**
The virgin will conceive and give birth to a son
and they will call him Emmanuel,
a name which means 'God-is-with-us'.
R. **Alleluia!**

GOSPEL

A reading from the holy Gospel according to Matthew   1:18-24

Jesus is born of Mary who was betrothed to Joseph, son of David.

This is how Jesus Christ came to be born. His mother Mary was betrothed
to Joseph; but before they came to live together she was found to be with
child through the Holy Spirit. Her husband Joseph, being a man of honour
and wanting to spare her publicity, decided to divorce her informally. He
had made up his mind to do this when the angel of the Lord appeared
to him in a dream and said, 'Joseph son of David, do not be afraid to
take Mary home as your wife, because she has conceived what is in her
by the Holy Spirit. She will give birth to a son and you must name him
Jesus, because he is the one who is to save his people from their sins.'
Now all this took place to fulfil the words spoken by the Lord through
the prophet:

The virgin will conceive and give birth to a son
and they will call him Emmanuel,

a name which means 'God-is-with-us'. When Joseph woke up he did what
the angel of the Lord had told him to do: he took his wife to his home.

The Gospel of the Lord.

The Creed is said.

Prayer over the Offerings

May the Holy Spirit, O Lord,
sanctify these gifts laid upon
    your altar,
just as he filled with his power the
    womb of the Blessed Virgin Mary.
Through Christ our Lord.

Preface II of Advent, pp.44-45.

Super oblata

Altari tuo, Domine,
    superposita munera
Spiritus ille sanctificet,
qui beatæ Mariæ viscera
    sua virtute replevit.
Per Christum Dominum nostrum.

Communion Antiphon   Is 7:14

Behold, a Virgin shall conceive
    and bear a son;
and his name will be
    called Emmanuel.

Ant. ad communionem

Ecce Virgo concipiet,
    et pariet filium;
et vocabitur nomen
    eius Emmanuel.

Prayer after Communion

Having received this pledge
    of eternal redemption,
we pray, almighty God,
that, as the feast day of our
    salvation draws ever nearer,
so we may press forward
    all the more eagerly
to the worthy celebration of the
    mystery of your Son's Nativity.
Who lives and reigns
    for ever and ever.

Post communionem

Sumpto pignore
    redemptionis æternæ,
quæsumus, omnipotens Deus,
ut quanto magis dies salutiferæ
    festivitatis accedit,
tanto devotius proficiamus
ad Filii tui digne nativitatis
    mysterium celebrandum.
Qui vivit et regnat
    in sæcula sæculorum.

A formula of Solemn Blessing, pp.132-133, may be used.

25 December

THE NATIVITY OF THE LORD

Solemnity

At the Vigil Mass

24 December

Today, anyone wishing to enter the Church of Jesus's Nativity in Bethlehem will find that the doorway five and a half metres high, through which emperors and caliphs used to enter the building, is now largely walled up. Only a low opening of one and a half metres has remained. The intention was probably to provide the church with better protection from attack, but above all to prevent people from entering God's house on horseback. Anyone wishing to enter the place of Jesus's birth has to bend down. It seems to me that a deeper truth is revealed here, which should touch our hearts on this holy night: if we want to find the God who appeared as a child, then we must dismount from the high horse of our "enlightened" reason. We must set aside our false certainties, our intellectual pride, which prevents us from recognising God's closeness. We must follow the interior path of Saint Francis - the path leading to that ultimate outward and inward simplicity which enables the heart to see. We must bend down, spiritually we must as it were go on foot, in order to pass through the portal of faith and encounter the God who is so different from our prejudices and opinions - the God who conceals himself in the humility of a newborn baby. In this spirit let us celebrate the liturgy of the holy night, let us strip away our fixation on what is material, on what can be measured and grasped. Let us allow ourselves to be made simple by the God who reveals himself to the simple of heart.

(Pope Benedict XVI)

This Mass is used on the evening of 24 December, either before or after First Vespers (Evening Prayer I) of the Nativity.

Entrance Antiphon Cf. Ex 16:6-7	Ant. ad introitum
TODAY you will know that the Lord will come, and he will save us, and in the morning you will see his glory.	HODIE scietis, quia veniet Dominus, et salvabit nos, et mane videbitis gloriam eius.

The **Gloria in excelsis** (Glory to God in the highest) is said.

Collect	Collecta
O God, who gladden us year by year as we wait in hope for our redemption, grant that, just as we joyfully welcome your Only Begotten Son as our Redeemer, we may also merit to face him confidently when he comes again as our Judge. Who lives and reigns with you in the unity of the Holy Spirit, God, for ever and ever.	Deus, qui nos redemptionis nostræ annua exspectatione lætificas, præsta, ut Unigenitum tuum, quem læti suscipimus Redemptorem, venientem quoque Iudicem securi videre mereamur, Dominum nostrum, Iesum Christum. Qui tecum vivit et regnat in unitate Spiritus Sancti, Deus, per omnia sæcula sæculorum.

FIRST READING

A reading from the prophet Isaiah   62:1-5

The Lord takes delight in you.

About Sion I will not be silent,
about Jerusalem I will not grow weary,
until her integrity shines out like the dawn
and her salvation flames like a torch.
The nations then will see your integrity,
all the kings your glory,
and you will be called by a new name,
one which the mouth of the Lord will confer.
You are to be a crown of splendour in the hand of the Lord,
a princely diadem in the hand of your God;
no longer are you to be named 'Forsaken'
nor your land 'Abandoned',
but you shall be called 'My Delight'
and your land 'The Wedded';
for the Lord takes delight in you
and your land will have its wedding.
Like a young man marrying a virgin,
so will the one who built you wed you,
and as the bridegroom rejoices in his bride,
so will your God rejoice in you.

    The word of the Lord.

Responsional Psalm   Ps 88:4-5,16-17,27,29. R. Cf. v.2

R. **I will sing for ever of your love, O Lord.**

'I have made a covenant with my chosen one;
I have sworn to David my servant:
I will establish your dynasty for ever
and set up your throne through all ages.' R.

Happy the people who acclaim such a king,
who walk, O Lord, in the light of your face,
who find their joy every day in your name,
who make your justice the source of their bliss. R.

'He will say to me: "You are my father,
my God, the rock who saves me."
I will keep my love for him always;
for him my covenant shall endure.' R.

SECOND READING

A reading from the Acts of the Apostles   13:16-17,22-25

Paul's witness to Christ, the son of David.

When Paul reached Antioch in Pisidia, he stood up in the synagogue, held
up a hand for silence and began to speak:

'Men of Israel, and fearers of God, listen! The God of our nation Israel
chose our ancestors, and made our people great when they were living as
foreigners in Egypt; then by divine power he led them out.

'Then he made David their king, of whom he approved in these words,
"I have selected David son of Jesse, a man after my own heart, who will
carry out my whole purpose." To keep his promise, God has raised up for
Israel one of David's descendants, Jesus, as Saviour, whose coming was
heralded by John when he proclaimed a baptism of repentance for the
whole people of Israel. Before John ended his career he said, "I am not the
one you imagine me to be; that one is coming after me and I am not fit to
undo his sandal."'

The word of the Lord.

Gospel Acclamation

R. **Alleluia, alleluia!**
Tomorrow there will be an end to the sin of the world
and the saviour of the world will be our king.
R. **Alleluia!**

GOSPEL

A reading from the holy Gospel according to Matthew   1:1-25

The ancestry of Jesus Christ, the son of David.

A genealogy of Jesus Christ, the son of David, son of Abraham:

Abraham was the father of Isaac,
Isaac the father of Jacob,
Jacob the father of Judah and his brothers,
Judah the father of Perez and Zerah, Tamar being their mother,
Perez the father of Hezron,
Hezron the father of Ram,
Ram the father of Amminadab,
Amminadab the father of Nahshon,
Nahshon the father of Salmon,
Salmon was the father of Boaz, Rahab being his mother,
Boaz the father of Obed, Ruth being his mother,
Obed was the father of Jesse;
and Jesse was the father of King David.

David was the father of Solomon, whose mother had been Uriah's wife,
Solomon was the father of Rehoboam,
Rehoboam the father of Abijah,
Abijah the father of Asa,
Asa was the father of Jehoshaphat,
Jehoshaphat the father of Joram,
Joram the father of Azariah,
Azariah was the father of Jotham,
Jotham the father of Ahaz,
Ahaz the father of Hezekiah,
Hezekiah was the father of Manasseh,
Manasseh the father of Amon,
Amon the father of Josiah;
and Josiah was the father of Jechoniah and his brothers.
Then the deportation to Babylon took place.

After the deportation to Babylon:
Jechoniah was the father of Shealtiel,
Shealtiel the father of Zerubbabel,
Zerubbabel was the father of Abiud,
Abiud the father of Eliakim,
Eliakim the father of Azor,
Azor was the father of Zadok,
Zadok the father of Achim,

Achim the father of Eliud,
Eliud was the father of Eleazar,
Eleazar the father of Matthan,
Matthan the father of Jacob,
and Jacob was the father of Joseph the husband of Mary; of her was born
Jesus who is called Christ.

The sum of generations is therefore: fourteen from Abraham to David;
fourteen from David to the Babylonian deportation; and fourteen from
the Babylonian deportation to Christ.

[This is how Jesus Christ came to be born. His mother Mary was
betrothed to Joseph; but before they came to live together she was found
to be with child through the Holy Spirit. Her husband Joseph, being a
man of honour and wanting to spare her publicity, decided to divorce her
informally. He had made up his mind to do this when the angel of the Lord
appeared to him in a dream and said, 'Joseph son of David, do not be afraid
to take Mary home as your wife, because she has conceived what is in her by
the Holy Spirit. She will give birth to a son and you must name him Jesus,
because he is the one who is to save his people from their sins.' Now all this
took place to fulfil the words spoken by the Lord through the prophet:

The Virgin will conceive and give birth to a son
and they will call him Emmanuel,

a name which means 'God-is-with-us'. When Joseph woke up he did what
the angel of the Lord had told him to do: he took his wife to his home and,
though he had not had intercourse with her, she gave birth to a son; and
he named him Jesus.

The Gospel of the Lord.]

Shorter Form, verses 18-25. Read between [ ]

The Creed is said.

All kneel at the words **and by the Holy Spirit was incarnate**.

Prayer over the Offerings	Super oblata
As we look forward, O Lord, to the coming festivities, may we serve you all the more eagerly for knowing that in them you make manifest the beginnings of our redemption. Through Christ our Lord.	Tanto nos, Domine, quæsumus, promptiore servitio hæc præcurrere concede sollemnia, quanto in his constare principium nostræ redemptionis ostendis. Per Christum Dominum nostrum.

Preface I, II or III of the Nativity of the Lord, pp.44-47

Communion Antiphon Cf. Is 40:5	Ant. ad communionem

The glory of the Lord
   will be revealed,
and all flesh will see the salvation
   of our God.
	Revelabitur gloria Domini,
	et videbit omnis caro salutare
	   Dei nostri.

Prayer after Communion	Post communionem

Grant, O Lord, we pray,
that we may draw new vigour
from celebrating the Nativity
   of your Only Begotten Son,
by whose heavenly mystery
   we receive both food and drink.
Who lives and reigns
   for ever and ever.
	Da nobis, quæsumus, Domine,
	Unigeniti Filii tui recensita
	   nativitate vegetari,
	cuius cælesti mysterio pascimur
	   et potamur.
	Qui vivit et regnat
	   in sæcula sæculorum.

A formula of Solemn Blessing, pp.132-135, may be used.

At the Mass during the Night

25 December

If, as in Bethlehem, the darkness of night overwhelms you, if you feel surrounded by cold indifference, if the hurt you carry inside cries out, "You are of little account; you are worthless; you will never be loved the way you want", tonight, if this is what you are feeling, God answers back. He tells you: "I love you just as you are. Your littleness does not frighten me, your failings do not trouble me. I became little for your sake. To be your God, I became your brother. Don't be afraid of me. Find in me your measure of greatness. I am close to you, and one thing only do I ask: trust me and open your heart to me".

(Pope Francis)

On the Nativity of the Lord all Priests may celebrate or concelebrate three Masses, provided the Masses are celebrated at their proper times.

Entrance Antiphon Ps 2:7	Ant. ad introitum

THE Lord said to me:
   You are my Son.
It is I who have begotten you this day.
	DOMINUS dixit ad me:
	   Filius meus es tu,
	ego hodie genui te.

Or:

Let us all rejoice in the Lord,
   for our Saviour has been born
   in the world.
Today true peace has come down
   to us from heaven.

The Gloria in excelsis (Glory to God in the highest) is said.

Collect

O God, who have made
   this most sacred night
radiant with the splendour
   of the true light,
grant, we pray, that we,
   who have known the mysteries
   of his light on earth,
may also delight in his gladness
   in heaven.
Who lives and reigns with you
   in the unity of the Holy Spirit,
God, for ever and ever.

Vel:

Gaudeamus omnes in Domino,
quia Salvator noster natus
   est in mundo.
Hodie nobis de cælo pax
   vera descendit.

Collecta

Deus, qui hanc sacratissimam
   noctem
veri luminis fecisti
   illustratione clarescere,
da, quæsumus, ut, cuius in terra
   mysteria lucis agnovimus,
eius quoque gaudiis perfruamur
   in cælo.
Qui tecum vivit et regnat
   in unitate Spiritus Sancti,
Deus, per omnia sæcula sæculorum.

FIRST READING

A reading from the prophet Isaiah   9:1-7

A Son is given to us.

The people that walked in darkness
has seen a great light;
on those who live in a land of deep shadow
a light has shone.
You have made their gladness greater,
you have made their joy increase;
they rejoice in your presence
as men rejoice at harvest time,
as men are happy when they are dividing the spoils.
For the yoke that was weighing on him,
the bar across his shoulders,
the rod of his oppressor,
these you break as on the day of Midian.

For all the footgear of battle,
every cloak rolled in blood,
is burnt,
and consumed by fire.
For there is a child born for us,
a son given to us
and dominion is laid on his shoulders;
and this is the name they give him:
Wonder-Counsellor, Mighty-God,
Eternal-Father, Prince-of-Peace.
Wide is his dominion
in a peace that has no end,
for the throne of David
and for his royal power,
which he establishes and makes secure
in justice and integrity.
From this time onwards and for ever,
the jealous love of the Lord of hosts will do this.

    The word of the Lord.

Responsorial Psalm   Ps 95:1-3,11-13. R. Lk 2:11

R. **Today a saviour has been born to us;**
   he is Christ the Lord.

    O sing a new song to the Lord,
    sing to the Lord all the earth.
    O sing to the Lord, bless his name. R.

    Proclaim his help day by day,
    tell among the nations his glory
    and his wonders among all the peoples. R.

    Let the heavens rejoice and earth be glad,
    let the sea and all within it thunder praise,
    let the land and all it bears rejoice,
    all the trees of the wood shout for joy
    at the presence of the Lord for he comes,
    he comes to rule the earth. R.

    With justice he will rule the world,
    he will judge the peoples with his truth. R.

SECOND READING

A reading from the letter of St Paul to Titus   2:11-14

God's grace has been revealed to the whole human race.

God's grace has been revealed, and it has made salvation possible for the whole human race and taught us that what we have to do is to give up everything that does not lead to God, and all our worldly ambitions; we must be self-restrained and live good and religious lives here in this present world, while we are waiting in hope for the blessing which will come with the Appearing of the glory of our great God and saviour Christ Jesus. He sacrificed himself for us in order to set us free from all wickedness and to purify a people so that it could be his very own and would have no ambition except to do good.

The word of the Lord.

Gospel Acclamation   Lk 2:10-11

R. **Alleluia, alleluia!**
I bring you news of great joy:
today a saviour has been born to us, Christ the Lord.
R. **Alleluia!**

GOSPEL

A reading from the holy Gospel according to Luke   2:1-14

Today a saviour has been born to you.

Caesar Augustus issued a decree for a census of the whole world to be taken. This census – the first – took place while Quirinius was governor of Syria, and everyone went to his own town to be registered. So Joseph set out from the town of Nazareth in Galilee and travelled up to Judaea, to the town of David called Bethlehem, since he was of David's House and line, in order to be registered together with Mary, his betrothed, who was with child. While they were there the time came for her to have her child, and she gave birth to a son, her first-born. She wrapped him in swaddling clothes, and laid him in a manger because there was no room for them at the inn. In the countryside close by there were shepherds who lived in the fields and took it in turns to watch their flocks during the night. The angel of the Lord appeared to them and the glory of the Lord shone round them. They were terrified, but the angel said, 'Do not be afraid. Listen, I bring you news of great joy, a joy to be shared by the whole people. Today in the town of David a saviour has been born to you; he is Christ the Lord. And here is a sign for you: you will find a baby wrapped in swaddling clothes and lying in a manger.' And suddenly with the angel there was a great throng of the heavenly host, praising God and singing:

'Glory to God in the highest heaven,
and peace to men who enjoy his favour'.

The Gospel of the Lord.

The Creed is said. All kneel at the words **and by the Holy Spirit was incarnate**.

Prayer over the Offerings

May the oblation of this day's feast
be pleasing to you, O Lord, we pray,
that through this most holy exchange
we may be found in the likeness
     of Christ,
in whom our nature is united to you.
Who lives and reigns
     for ever and ever.

Super oblata

Grata tibi sit, Domine, quæsumus,
hodiernæ festivitatis oblatio,
ut, per hæc sacrosancta commercia,
in illius inveniamur forma,
in quo tecum est nostra substantia.
Qui vivit et regnat
     in sæcula sæculorum.

Preface I, II or III of the Nativity of the Lord, pp.44-47.

Communion Antiphon   Jn 1:14

The Word became flesh,
     and we have seen his glory.

Ant. ad communionem

Verbum caro factum est,
     et vidimus gloriam eius.

Prayer after Communion

Grant us, we pray, O Lord our God,
that we, who are gladdened
     by participation
in the feast of
     our Redeemer's Nativity,
may through an honourable way
     of life become worthy of union
     with him.
Who lives and reigns
     for ever and ever.

Post communionem

Da nobis, quæsumus,
     Domine Deus noster,
ut, qui nativitatem
     Redemptoris nostri
frequentare gaudemus,
dignis conversationibus
ad eius mereamur
     pervenire consortium.
Per Christum Dominum nostrum.

A formula of Solemn Blessing, pp.132-135, may be used.

At the Mass at Dawn

Let us ask ourselves: can we accept God's way of doing things? This is the challenge of Christmas: God reveals himself, but men and women fail to understand. He makes himself little in the eyes of the world, while we continue to seek grandeur in the eyes of the world, perhaps even in his name. God lowers himself and we try to become great. The Most High goes in search of shepherds, the unseen in our midst, and we look for visibility; we want to be seen. Jesus is born in order to serve, and we spend a lifetime pursuing success. God does not seek power and might; he asks for tender love and interior littleness.

(Pope Francis)

Entrance Antiphon Cf. Is 9:1,5; Lk 1:33

TODAY a light will shine upon us,
   for the Lord is born for us;
and he will be called Wondrous God,
Prince of peace, Father of future ages:
and his reign will be without end.

Ant. ad introitum

LUX fulgebit hodie super nos,
   quia natus est nobis Dominus;
et vocabitur admirabilis, Deus,
   Princeps pacis,
Pater futuri sæculi:
   cuius regni non erit finis.

The Gloria in excelsis (Glory to God in the highest) is said.

Collect

Grant, we pray, almighty God,
that, as we are bathed in the new
   radiance of your incarnate Word,
the light of faith, which illumines
   our minds,
may also shine through in our deeds.
Through our Lord Jesus Christ,
   your Son,
who lives and reigns with you
   in the unity of the Holy Spirit,
God, for ever and ever.

Collecta

Da, quæsumus, omnipotens Deus,
ut dum nova incarnati Verbi
   tui luce perfundimur,
hoc in nostro resplendeat opere,
quod per fidem fulget in mente.
Per Dominum nostrum Iesum
   Christum Filium tuum,
qui tecum vivit et regnat
   in unitate Spiritus Sancti,
Deus, per omnia sæcula sæculorum.

FIRST READING

A reading from the prophet Isaiah   62:11-12

Look, your saviour comes.

This the Lord proclaims
to the ends of the earth:

> Say to the daughter of Sion, 'Look,
> your saviour comes,
> the prize of his victory with him,
> his trophies before him.'
> They shall be called 'The Holy People',
> 'The Lord's Redeemed'.
> And you shall be called 'The-sought-after',
> 'City-not-forsaken'.

The word of the Lord.

Responsional Psalm   Ps 96:1,6,11-12

R. **This day new light will shine upon the earth:
the Lord is born for us.**

> The Lord is king, let earth rejoice,
> the many coastlands be glad.
> The skies proclaim his justice;
> all peoples see his glory. R.

> Light shines forth for the just
> and joy for the upright of heart.
> Rejoice, you just, in the Lord;
> give glory to his holy name. R.

SECOND READING

A reading from the letter of St Paul to Titus   3:4-7

It was for no reason except his own compassion that he saved us.

When the kindness and love of God our saviour for mankind were revealed,
it was not because he was concerned with any righteous actions we might
have done ourselves; it was for no reason except his own compassion that
he saved us, by means of the cleansing water of rebirth and by renewing
us with the Holy Spirit which he has so generously poured over us through
Jesus Christ our saviour. He did this so that we should be justified by his
grace, to become heirs looking forward to inheriting eternal life.

The word of the Lord.

Gospel Acclamation   Lk 2:14

R. **Alleluia, alleluia!**
Glory to God in the highest heaven,
and peace to men who enjoy his favour.

R. **Alleluia!**

GOSPEL

A reading from the holy Gospel according to Luke   2:15-20
The shepherds found Mary and Joseph and the baby.

Now when the angels had gone from them into heaven, the shepherds
said to one another, 'Let us go to Bethlehem and see this thing that has
happened which the Lord has made known to us.' So they hurried away
and found Mary and Joseph, and the baby lying in the manger. When
they saw the child they repeated what they had been told about him, and
everyone who heard it was astonished at what the shepherds had to say. As
for Mary, she treasured all these things and pondered them in her heart.
And the shepherds went back glorifying and praising God for all they had
heard and seen; it was exactly as they had been told.

The Gospel of the Lord.

The Creed is said. All kneel at the words **and by the Holy Spirit was incarnate**.

Prayer over the Offerings

May our offerings be worthy,
    we pray, O Lord,
of the mysteries of the Nativity
    this day,
that, just as Christ was born a man
    and also shone forth as God,
so these earthly gifts may confer
    on us what is divine.
Through Christ our Lord.

Super oblata

Munera nostra, quæsumus, Domine,
nativitatis hodiernæ mysteriis
    apta proveniant,
ut sicut homo genitus idem
    præfulsit et Deus,
sic nobis hæc terrena substantia
conferat quod divinum est.
Per Christum Dominum nostrum.

Preface I, II or III of the Nativity of the Lord, pp.44-47.

Communion Antiphon Cf. Zc 9:9

Rejoice, O Daughter Sion; lift up
    praise, Daughter Jerusalem:
Behold, your King will come,
    the Holy One and Saviour
    of the world.

Ant. ad communionem

Exsulta, filia Sion, lauda,
    filia Ierusalem:
ecce Rex tuus veniet sanctus
    et salvator mundi.

Prayer after Communion	Post communionem

Grant us, Lord, as we honour
with joyful devotion
the Nativity of your Son,
that we may come to know
with fullness of faith
the hidden depths of this mystery
and to love them
ever more and more.
Through Christ our Lord.

Da nobis, Domine,
Filii tui nativitatem
læta devotione colentibus,
huius arcana mysterii
et plena fide cognoscere,
et pleniore caritatis ardore diligere.
Per Christum Dominum nostrum.

A formula of Solemn Blessing, pp.132-135 may be used.

At the Mass during the Day

*The Word of God, who created the world and who gives meaning to history
and to humanity's journey, became flesh and came to dwell among us. He
came like a whisper, like the murmur of a gentle breeze, to fill with wonder the
heart of every man and woman who is open to this mystery. The Word became
flesh in order to dialogue with us. God does not desire to carry on a monologue,
but a dialogue. For God himself, Father, Son and Holy Spirit, is dialogue, an
eternal and infinite communion of love and life. By the coming of Jesus, the
Person of the Word made flesh, into our world, God showed us the way of
encounter and dialogue. Indeed, he made that way incarnate in himself, so
that we might know it and follow it, in trust and hope.*

(Pope Francis)

Entrance Antiphon Cf. Is 9:5	Ant. ad introitum

A CHILD is born for us,
and a son is given to us;
his sceptre of power rests
upon his shoulder,
and his name will be called
Messenger of great counsel.

P UER natus est nobis,
et filius datus est nobis,
cuius imperium super
humerum eius,
et vocabitur nomen eius magni
consilii Angelus.

The Gloria in excelsis (Glory to God in the highest) is said.

Collect

O God, who wonderfully created
    the dignity of human nature
and still more wonderfully
    restored it,
grant, we pray,
that we may share in the divinity
    of Christ,
who humbled himself to share
    in our humanity.
Who lives and reigns with you
    in the unity of the Holy Spirit,
God, for ever and ever.

Collecta

Deus, qui humanæ
    substantiæ dignitatem
et mirabiliter condidisti,
    et mirabilius reformasti,
da, quæsumus, nobis eius
    divinitatis esse consortes,
qui humanitatis nostræ fieri
    dignatus est particeps.
Qui tecum vivit et regnat
    in unitate Spiritus Sancti,
Deus, per omnia sæcula sæculorum.

FIRST READING

A reading from the prophet Isaiah   52:7-10
All the ends of the earth shall see the salvation of our God.

How beautiful on the mountains,
are the feet of one who brings good news,
who heralds peace, brings happiness,
proclaims salvation,
and tells Sion,
'Your God is king!'
Listen! Your watchmen raise their voices,
they shout for joy together,
for they see the Lord face to face,
as he returns to Sion.
Break into shouts of joy together,
you ruins of Jerusalem;
for the Lord is consoling his people,
redeeming Jerusalem.
The Lord bares his holy arm
in the sight of all the nations,
and all the ends of the earth shall see
the salvation of our God.

    The word of the Lord.

Responsorial Psalm

Ps 97:1-6. R. v.3

R. **All the ends of the earth have seen
the salvation of our God.**

Sing a new song to the Lord
for he has worked wonders.
His right hand and his holy arm
have brought salvation. R.

The Lord has made known his salvation;
has shown his justice to the nations.
He has remembered his truth and love
for the house of Israel. R.

All the ends of the earth have seen
the salvation of our God.
Shout to the Lord all the earth,
ring out your joy. R.

Sing psalms to the Lord with the harp,
with the sound of music.
With trumpets and the sound of the horn
acclaim the King, the Lord. R.

SECOND READING

A reading from the letter to the Hebrews

1:1-6

God has spoken to us through his Son.

At various times in the past and in various different ways, God spoke to
our ancestors through the prophets; but in our own time, the last days, he
has spoken to us through his Son, the Son that he has appointed to inherit
everything and through whom he made everything there is. He is the
radiant light of God's glory and the perfect copy of his nature, sustaining
the universe by his powerful command; and now that he has destroyed the
defilement of sin, he has gone to take his place in heaven at the right hand
of divine Majesty. So he is now as far above the angels as the title which he
has inherited is higher than their own name.

God has never said to any angel: You are my Son, today I have become your father; or: I will be a father to him and he a son to me. Again, when he brings the First-born into the world, he says: Let all the angels of God worship him.

The word of the Lord.

Gospel Acclamation.

R. **Alleluia, alleluia!**
A hallowed day has dawned upon us.
Come, you nations, worship the Lord,
for today a great light has shone down upon the earth.

R. **Alleluia!**

GOSPEL

A reading from the holy Gospel according to John   1:1-18

The Word was made flesh, and lived among us.

[In the beginning was the Word:
the Word was with God
and the Word was God.
He was with God in the beginning.
Through him all things came to be,
not one thing had its being but through him.
All that came to be had life in him
and that life was the light of men,
a light that shines in the dark,
a light that darkness could not overpower.]

A man came, sent by God.
His name was John.
He came as a witness,
as a witness to speak for the light,
so that everyone might believe through him.
He was not the light,
only a witness to speak for the light.

[The Word was the true light
that enlightens all men;
and he was coming into the world.

He was in the world
that had its being through him,
and the world did not know him.
He came to his own domain
and his own people did not accept him.
But to all who did accept him
he gave power to become children of God,
to all who believe in the name of him
who was born not out of human stock
or urge of the flesh
or will of man
but of God himself.
The Word was made flesh,
he lived among us,
and we saw his glory,
the glory that is his as the only Son of the Father,
full of grace and truth.]

John appears as his witness. He proclaims:
'This is the one of whom I said:
He who comes after me
ranks before me
because he existed before me.'
Indeed, from his fullness we have, all of us, received –
yes, grace in return for grace,
since, though the Law was given through Moses,
grace and truth have come through Jesus Christ.
No one has ever seen God,
it is the only Son, who is nearest to the Father's heart,
who has made him known.

   [The Gospel of the Lord.]

Shorter Form, verses 1-5,9-14. Read between [ ]

The Creed is said. All kneel at the words **and by the Holy Spirit was incarnate**.

Prayer over the Offerings

Make acceptable, O Lord,
  our oblation on this solemn day,
when you manifested
  the reconciliation
that makes us wholly pleasing
  in your sight
and inaugurated for us the fullness
  of divine worship.
Through Christ our Lord.

Super oblata

Oblatio tibi sit, Domine,
  hodiernæ sollemnitatis accepta,
qua et nostræ reconciliationis
  processit perfecta placatio,
et divini cultus nobis
  est indita plenitudo.
Per Christum Dominum nostrum.

Preface I, II or III of the Nativity of the Lord, pp.44-47.

Communion Antiphon Cf. Ps 97:3

All the ends of the earth have seen
  the salvation of our God.

Ant. ad communionem

Viderunt omnes fines terræ
  salutare Dei nostri.

Prayer after Communion

Grant, O merciful God,
that, just as the Saviour of the
  world, born this day,
is the author of divine generation
  for us,
so he may be the giver even
  of immortality.
Who lives and reigns
  for ever and ever.

Post communionem

Præsta, misericors Deus,
  ut natus hodie Salvator mundi,
sicut divinæ nobis generationis
  est auctor,
ita et immortalitatis sit ipse largitor.
Qui vivit et regnat
  in sæcula sæculorum.

A formula of Solemn Blessing, pp.132-135, may be used.

30 December

THE HOLY FAMILY OF JESUS, MARY AND JOSEPH

We learn how to be a family, each day. In the Gospel, we see that even in the Holy Family things did not all go well: there were unexpected problems, anxiety, suffering. The Holy Family of holy cards does not exist. Mary and Joseph lose Jesus and search for him anxiously, only to find him three days later. And when, seated among the teachers in the Temple, he responds that he had to be about his Father's business, they do not understand. They need time to learn to know their son. So it is with us too: every day, families have to learn to listen and understand one another, to walk together, to face conflicts and difficulties. It is a daily challenge and it is overcome with the right attitude, through simple actions, simple gestures, caring for the details of our relationships.

(Pope Francis)

Feast

Entrance Antiphon Lk 2:16	Ant. ad introitum
THE shepherds went in haste, and found Mary and Joseph and the Infant lying in a manger.	VENERUNT pastores festinantes, et invenerunt Mariam et Ioseph et Infantem positum in præsepio.

The Gloria in excelsis (Glory to God in the highest) is said.

Collect	Collecta
O God, who were pleased to give us the shining example of the Holy Family, graciously grant that we may imitate them in practising the virtues of family life and in the bonds of charity, and so, in the joy of your house, delight one day in eternal rewards.	Deus, qui præclara nobis sanctæ Familiæ dignatus es exempla præbere, concede propitius, ut, domesticis virtutibus caritatisque vinculis illam sectantes, in lætitia domus tuæ præmiis fruamur æternis.

Through our Lord Jesus Christ, your Son, who lives and reigns with you in the unity of the Holy Spirit, God, for ever and ever.	Per Dominum nostrum Iesum Christum Filium tuum, qui tecum vivit et regnat in unitate Spiritus Sancti, Deus, per omnia sæcula sæculorum.

FIRST READING

Either:

A reading from the book of Ecclesiasticus   3:3-7,14-17

He who fears the Lord respects his parents.

The Lord honours the father in his children,
and upholds the rights of a mother over her sons.
Whoever respects his father is atoning for his sins,
he who honours his mother is like someone amassing a fortune.
Whoever respects his father will be happy with children of his own,
he shall be heard on the day when he prays.
Long life comes to him who honours his father,
he who sets his mother at ease is showing obedience to the Lord.
My son, support your father in his old age,
do not grieve him during his life.
Even if his mind should fail, show him sympathy,
do not despise him in your health and strength;
for kindness to a father shall not be forgotten
but will serve as reparation for your sins.

The word of the Lord.

Or:

A reading from the letter of St Paul to the Colossians   3:12-21

Family life in the Lord.

You are God's chosen race, his saints; he loves you, and you should be clothed in sincere compassion, in kindness and humility, gentleness and patience. Bear with one another; forgive each other as soon as a quarrel begins. The Lord has forgiven you; now you must do the same. Over all these clothes, to keep them together and complete them, put on love. And may the peace of Christ reign in your hearts, because it is for this that you were called together as parts of one body. Always be thankful.

Let the message of Christ, in all its richness, find a home with you. Teach each other, and advise each other, in all wisdom. With gratitude in your hearts sing psalms and hymns and inspired songs to God; and never say or do anything except in the name of the Lord Jesus, giving thanks to God the Father through him.

Wives, give way to your husbands, as you should in the Lord. Husbands, love your wives and treat them with gentleness. Children, be obedient to your parents always, because that is what will please the Lord. Parents, never drive your children to resentment or you will make them feel frustrated.

The word of the Lord.

Responsorial Psalm   Ps 127:1-5. R. Cf. v.1

R. **O blessed are those who fear the Lord
and walk in his ways!**

O blessed are those who fear the Lord
and walk in his ways!
By the labour of your hands you shall eat.
You will be happy and prosper. R.

Your wife like a fruitful vine
in the heart of your house;
your children like shoots of the olive,
around your table. R.

Indeed thus shall be blessed
the man who fears the Lord.
May the Lord bless you from Sion
all the days of your life. R.

Gospel Acclamation   Col 3:15,16

R. **Alleluia, alleluia!**
May the peace of Christ reign in your hearts;
let the message of Christ find a home with you.
R. **Alleluia!**

GOSPEL

A reading from the holy Gospel according to Matthew   2:13-15,19-23

Take the child and his mother and escape into Egypt.

After the wise men had left, the angel of the Lord appeared to Joseph in a dream and said, 'Get up, take the child and his mother with you, and escape into Egypt, and stay there until I tell you, because Herod intends to search for the child and do away with him.' So Joseph got up and, taking the child and his mother with him, left that night for Egypt, where he stayed until Herod was dead. This was to fulfil what the Lord had spoken through the prophet:

I called my son out of Egypt.

After Herod's death, the angel of the Lord appeared in a dream to Joseph in Egypt and said, 'Get up, take the child and his mother with you and go back to the land of Israel, for those who wanted to kill the child are dead.' So Joseph got up and, taking the child and his mother with him, went back to the land of Israel. But when he learnt that Archelaus had succeeded his father Herod as ruler of Judaea he was afraid to go there, and being warned in a dream he left for the region of Galilee. There he settled in a town called Nazareth. In this way the words spoken through the prophets were to be fulfilled:

He will be called a Nazarene.

The Gospel of the Lord.

The Creed is not said.

Prayer over the Offerings

We offer you, Lord,
   the sacrifice of conciliation,
humbly asking that,
through the intercession
   of the Virgin Mother of God
   and Saint Joseph,
you may establish our families firmly
   in your grace and your peace.
Through Christ our Lord.

Super oblata

Hostiam tibi placationis offerimus,
   Domine,
suppliciter deprecantes,
ut, Deiparæ Virginis beatique
   Ioseph interveniente suffragio,
familias nostras in tua gratia
   firmiter et pace constituas.
Per Christum Dominum nostrum.

Preface I, II or III of the Nativity of the Lord, pp.44-47.

Communion Antiphon   Ba 3:38

Our God has appeared on the earth,
   and lived among us.

Ant. ad communionem

Deus noster in terris visus est,
et cum hominibus conversatus est.

Prayer after Communion

Bring those you refresh
   with this heavenly Sacrament,
most merciful Father,
to imitate constantly the example
   of the Holy Family,
so that, after the trials of this world,
we may share their company for ever.
Through Christ our Lord.

Post communionem

Quos cælestibus reficis sacramentis,
fac, clementissime Pater,
sanctæ Familiæ exempla
   iugiter imitari,
ut, post ærumnas sæculi,
eius consortium
   consequamur æternum.
Per Christum Dominum nostrum.

1 January

SOLEMNITY OF MARY, THE HOLY MOTHER OF GOD

The New Year begins under the sign of the Holy Mother of God, under the sign of the Mother. A mother's gaze is the path to rebirth and growth. We need mothers, women who look at the world not to exploit it, but so that it can have life. Women who, seeing with the heart, can combine dreams and aspirations with concrete reality, without drifting into abstraction and sterile pragmatism. And the Church is a Mother, this is what makes the Church feminine. For this reason, we cannot find a place for women in the Church without allowing the heart of the Woman and Mother to shine. This is the place of women in the Church, the great place, from which other places, more concrete and less important, are derived.

(Pope Francis)

Solemnity

Entrance Antiphon

HAIL, Holy Mother,
who gave birth to the King
who rules heaven and earth for ever.

Or: Cf. Is 9:1,5; Lk 1:33

Today a light will shine upon us,
    for the Lord is born for us;
and he will be called Wondrous God,
Prince of peace, Father of future ages:
and his reign will be without end.

Ant. ad introitum

SALVE, sancta Parens,
enixa puerpera Regem,
qui cælum terramque regit
    in sæcula sæculorum.

Vel:

Lux fulgebit hodie super nos,
quia natus est nobis Dominus;
et vocabitur admirabilis, Deus,
    Princeps pacis,
Pater futuri sæculi:
    cuius regni non erit finis.

The **Gloria in excelsis** (**Glory to God in the highest**) is said.

Collect

O God, who through the fruitful
    virginity of Blessed Mary
bestowed on the human race
the grace of eternal salvation,
grant, we pray,
that we may experience
    the intercession of her,
through whom we were
    found worthy
to receive the author of life,
our Lord Jesus Christ, your Son.
Who lives and reigns with you
    in the unity of the Holy Spirit,
God, for ever and ever.

Collecta

Deus, qui salutis æternæ,
beatæ Mariæ virginitate fecunda,
humano generi præmia præstitisti,
    tribue, quæsumus,
ut ipsam pro nobis
    intercedere sentiamus,
per quam meruimus
    auctorem vitæ suscipere,
Dominum nostrum Iesum
    Christum, Filium tuum.
Qui tecum vivit et regnat
    in unitate Spiritus Sancti,
Deus, per omnia sæcula sæculorum.

FIRST READING

A reading from the book of Numbers   6:22-27

They are to call down my name on the sons of Israel, and I will bless them.

The Lord spoke to Moses and said, 'Say this to Aaron and his sons: "This is
how you are to bless the sons of Israel. You shall say to them:

    May the Lord bless you and keep you.
    May the Lord let his face shine on you and be gracious to you.
    May the Lord uncover his face to you and bring you peace."

This is how they are to call down my name on the sons of Israel, and I will
bless them.'

    The word of the Lord.

Responsorial Psalm   Ps 66:2-3,5,6,8. R. v.2

R. **O God, be gracious and bless us.**

    God, be gracious and bless us
    and let your face shed its light upon us.
    So will your ways be known upon earth
    and all nations learn your saving help. R.

    Let the nations be glad and exult
    for you rule the world with justice.
    With fairness you rule the peoples,
    you guide the nations on earth. R.

Let the peoples praise you, O God;
let all the peoples praise you.
May God still give us his blessing
till the ends of the earth revere him. R.

SECOND READING

A reading from the letter of St Paul to the Galatians   4:4-7

God sent his Son, born of a woman.

When the appointed time came, God sent his Son, born of a woman, born
a subject of the Law, to redeem the subjects of the Law and to enable us to
be adopted as sons. The proof that you are sons is that God has sent the
Spirit of his Son into our hearts: the Spirit that cries, 'Abba, Father', and it
is this that makes you a son, you are not a slave any more; and if God has
made you son, then he has made you heir.

The word of the Lord.

Gospel Acclamation   Heb 1:1-2

R. **Alleluia, alleluia!**

At various times in the past
and in various different ways,
God spoke to our ancestors through the prophets;
but in our own time, the last days,
he has spoken to us through his Son.

R. **Alleluia!**

GOSPEL

A reading from the holy Gospel according to Luke   2:16-21

*They found Mary and Joseph and the baby ... When the eighth day came, they gave
him the name Jesus.*

The shepherds hurried away to Bethlehem and found Mary and Joseph,
and the baby lying in the manger. When they saw the child they repeated
what they had been told about him, and everyone who heard it was
astonished at what the shepherds had to say. As for Mary, she treasured
all these things and pondered them in her heart. And the shepherds went
back glorifying and praising God for all they had heard and seen; it was
exactly as they had been told.

When the eighth day came and the child was to be circumcised, they gave him the name Jesus, the name the angel had given him before his conception.

The Gospel of the Lord.

The Creed is said.

Prayer over the Offerings

O God, who in your kindness begin
   all good things
and bring them to fulfilment,
grant to us, who find joy
   in the Solemnity of the holy
   Mother of God,
that, just as we glory in the
   beginnings of your grace,
so one day we may rejoice
   in its completion.
Through Christ our Lord.

Super oblata

Deus, qui bona cuncta inchoas
   benignus et perficis,
da nobis, de sollemnitate sanctæ
   Dei Genetricis lætantibus,
sicut de initiis tuæ gratiæ gloriamur,
ita de perfectione gaudere.
Per Christum Dominum nostrum.

Preface: The Motherhood of the Blessed Virgin Mary.

It is truly right and just,
   our duty and our salvation,
always and everywhere to give
   you thanks,
Lord, holy Father,
   almighty and eternal God,
and to praise, bless,
   and glorify your name
on the Solemnity of the Motherhood
of the Blessed ever-Virgin Mary.

For by the overshadowing
   of the Holy Spirit
she conceived your
   Only Begotten Son,
and without losing the glory
   of virginity,
brought forth into the world
   the eternal Light,
Jesus Christ our Lord.

Præfatio: De Maternitate beatæ Mariæ Virginis.

Vere dignum et iustum est,
   æquum et salutare,
nos tibi semper
   et ubique gratias agere:
Domine, sancte Pater,
   omnipotens æterne Deus:

Et te in Maternitate
beatæ Mariæ semper Virginis
   collaudare,
benedicere et prædicare.

Quæ et Unigenitum tuum Sancti
   Spiritus obumbratione concepit,
et, virginitatis gloria permanente,
lumen æternum mundo effudit,
Iesum Christum Dominum nostrum.

Through him the Angels praise
  your majesty,
Dominions adore and Powers
  tremble before you.
Heaven and the Virtues of heaven
  and the blessed Seraphim
worship together with exultation.
May our voices, we pray,
  join with theirs
in humble praise, as we acclaim:

Holy, Holy, Holy Lord God of hosts...

Per quem maiestatem
  laudant Angeli,
adorant Dominationes,
  tremunt Potestates.
Cæli cælorumque Virtutes,
  ac beata Seraphim,
socia exsultatione concelebrant.
Cum quibis et nostras voces ut
  admitti iubeas, deprecamur,
supplici confessione dicentes:

Sanctus, Sanctus, Sanctus. . .

Communion Antiphon   Heb 13:8

Jesus Christ is the same yesterday,
  today, and for ever.

Ant. ad communionem

Iesus Christus heri et hodie,
  ipse et in sæcula.

Prayer after Communion

We have received this heavenly
  Sacrament with joy, O Lord:
grant, we pray,
that it may lead us to eternal life,
for we rejoice to proclaim
  the blessed ever-Virgin Mary
Mother of your Son
  and Mother of the Church.
Through Christ our Lord.

Post communionem

Sumpsimus, Domine,
  læti sacramenta cælestia:
præsta, quæsumus,
ut ad vitam nobis
  proficiant sempiternam,
qui beatam semper Virginem Mariam
Filii tui Genetricem
  et Ecclesiæ Matrem
profiteri gloriamur.
Per Christum Dominum nostrum.

A formula of Solemn Blessing, pp.134-135, may be used.

In England, Wales & Ireland
6 January

In Scotland
8 January

THE EPIPHANY OF THE LORD

Worship is an act of love that changes our lives. It is to do what the Magi did. To bring gold to the Lord and to tell him that nothing is more precious than he is. To offer him incense and to tell him that only in union with him can our lives rise up to heaven. To present him with myrrh, balm for the bruised and wounded, and to promise him that we will aid our marginalised and suffering neighbours, in whom he himself is present. We usually know how to pray – we ask the Lord, we thank him – but the Church must move forward in her prayer of worship; we must grow in worshipping. This is wisdom that we must learn each day. Praying by worshipping: the prayer of worship.

(Pope Francis)

Solemnity

At the Vigil Mass

This Mass is used on the evening of the day before the Solemnity, either before or after First Vespers (Evening Prayer I) of the Epiphany.

Entrance Antiphon Cf. Ba 5:5	Ant. ad introitum
ARISE, Jerusalem, and look to the East and see your children gathered from the rising to the setting of the sun.	SURGE, Ierusalem, et circumspice ad orientem et vide congregatos filios tuos a solis ortu usque ad occasum.

The **Gloria in excelsis** (**Glory to God in the highest**) is said.

Collect	Collecta
May the splendour of your majesty, O Lord, we pray, shed its light upon our hearts, that we may pass through the shadows of this world and reach the brightness of our eternal home.	Corda nostra, quæsumus, Domine, tuæ maiestatis splendor illustret, quo per mundi huius tenebras transire valeamus, et perveniamus ad patriam claritatis æternæ.

Through our Lord Jesus Christ,
  your Son,
who lives and reigns with you
  in the unity of the Holy Spirit,
God, for ever and ever.
	Per Dominum nostrum Iesum
	  Christum Filium tuum,
	qui tecum vivit et regnat
	  in unitate Spiritus Sancti,
	Deus, per omnia sæcula sæculorum.

FIRST READING

A reading from the prophet Isaiah   60:1-6

Above you the glory of the Lord appears.

Arise, shine out Jerusalem, for your light has come,
the glory of the Lord is rising on you,
though night still covers the earth
and darkness the peoples.

Above you the Lord now rises
and above you his glory appears.
The nations come to your light
and kings to your dawning brightness.

Lift up your eyes and look around:
all are assembling and coming towards you,
your sons from far away
and daughters being tenderly carried.

At this sight you will glow radiant,
your heart throbbing and full;
since the riches of the sea will flow to you;
the wealth of the nations come to you;

camels in throngs will cover you,
and dromedaries of Midian and Ephah;
everyone in Sheba will come,
bringing gold and incense
and singing the praise of the Lord.

  The word of the Lord.

Responsorial Psalm   Ps 71:1-2,7-8,10-13. R. Cf. v.11

R. **All nations shall fall prostrate before you, O Lord.**

O God, give your judgement to the king,
to a king's son your justice,
that he may judge your people in justice
and your poor in right judgement. R.

In his days justice shall flourish
and peace till the moon fails.
He shall rule from sea to sea,
from the Great River to earth's bounds. R.

The Kings of Tarshish and the sea coasts
shall pay him tribute.
The kings of Sheba and Seba
shall bring him gifts.
Before him all kings shall fall prostrate,
all nations shall serve him. R.

For he shall save the poor when they cry
and the needy who are helpless.
He will have pity on the weak
and save the lives of the poor. R.

SECOND READING

A reading from the letter of St Paul to the Ephesians   3:2-3,5-6

It has now been revealed that pagans share the same inheritance.

You have probably heard how I have been entrusted by God with the
grace he meant for you, and that it was by a revelation that I was given
the knowledge of the mystery. This mystery that has now been revealed
through the Spirit to his holy apostles and prophets was unknown to
any men in past generations; it means that pagans now share the same
inheritance, that they are parts of the same body, and that the same
promise has been made to them, in Christ Jesus, through the gospel.

The word of the Lord.

Gospel Acclamation   Mt 2:2

R. **Alleluia, alleluia!**
We saw his star as it rose
and have come to do the Lord homage.
R. **Alleluia!**

GOSPEL

A reading from the holy Gospel according to Matthew   2:1-12

We saw his star and have come to do the king homage.

After Jesus had been born at Bethlehem in Judaea during the reign of King
Herod, some wise men came to Jerusalem from the east. 'Where is the infant
king of the Jews?' they asked. 'We saw his star as it rose and have come to
do him homage.' When King Herod heard this he was perturbed, and so
was the whole of Jerusalem. He called together all the chief priests and the
scribes of the people, and enquired of them where the Christ was to be born.
'At Bethlehem in Judaea,' they told him 'for this is what the prophet wrote:

And you, Bethlehem, in the land of Judah
you are by no means least among the leaders of Judah,
for out of you will come a leader
who will shepherd my people Israel.'

Then Herod summoned the wise men to see him privately. He asked
them the exact date on which the star had appeared, and sent them on to
Bethlehem. 'Go and find out all about the child,' he said 'and when you
have found him, let me know, so that I too may go and do him homage.'
Having listened to what the king had to say, they set out. And there in
front of them was the star they had seen rising; it went forward and halted
over the place where the child was. The sight of the star filled them with
delight, and going into the house they saw the child with his mother
Mary, and falling to their knees they did him homage. Then, opening their
treasures, they offered him gifts of gold and frankincense and myrrh. But
they were warned in a dream not to go back to Herod, and returned to their
own country by a different way.

The Gospel of the Lord.

The Creed is said.

Prayer over the Offerings	Super oblata
Accept we pray, O Lord, our offerings, in honour of the appearing of your Only Begotten Son and the first fruits of the nations, that to you praise may be rendered and eternal salvation be ours. Through Christ our Lord.	Suscipe, quæsumus, Domine, munera nostra pro apparitione Unigeniti Filii tui et primitiis gentium dicata, ut et tibi celebretur laudatio et nobis fiat æterna salvatio. Per Christum Dominum nostrum.

Preface of the Epiphany of the Lord, pp.48-49.

Communion Antiphon Cf. Rv 21:23

The brightness of God illumined
    the holy city Jerusalem,
and the nations will walk by its light.

Ant. ad communionem

Claritas Dei illuminavit civitatem
    sanctam Ierusalem
et ambulabant gentes in lumine eius.

Prayer after Communion

Renewed by sacred nourishment,
we implore your mercy, O Lord,
that the star of your justice
may shine always bright in our minds
and that our true treasure may ever
    consist in our confession of you.
Through Christ our Lord.

Post communionem

Sacra alimonia renovati,
tuam, Domine,
    misericordiam deprecamur,
ut semper in mentibus nostris
    tuæ appareat stella iustitiæ
et noster in tua sit
    confessione thesaurus.
Per Christum Dominum nostrum.

A formula of Solemn Blessing, pp.134-137, may be used.

At the Mass during the Day

Entrance Antiphon Cf.Ml 3:1;1Ch 29:12

BEHOLD, the Lord,
  the Mighty One, has come;
and kingship is in his grasp,
    and power and dominion.

Ant. ad introitum

ECCE advenit
  Dominator Dominus;
et regnum in manu eius
    et potestas et imperium.

The Gloria in excelsis (Glory to God in the highest) is said.

Collect

O God, who on this day
revealed your Only Begotten Son
    to the nations
by the guidance of a star,
grant in your mercy
that we, who know you already
    by faith,
may be brought to behold
    the beauty of your sublime glory.
Through our Lord Jesus Christ,
    your Son,
who lives and reigns with you
    in the unity of the Holy Spirit,
God, for ever and ever.

Collecta

Deus, qui hodierna die
    Unigenitum tuum
gentibus stella duce revelasti,
concede propitius, ut qui iam
    te ex fide cognovimus,
usque ad contemplandam speciem
    tuæ celsitudinis perducamur.
Per Dominum nostrum Iesum
    Christum Filium tuum,
qui tecum vivit et regnat
    in unitate Spiritus Sancti,
Deus, per omnia sæcula sæculorum.

FIRST READING

A reading from the prophet Isaiah   60:1-6

Above you the glory of the Lord appears.

Arise, shine out Jerusalem, for your light has come,
the glory of the Lord is rising on you,
though night still covers the earth
and darkness the peoples.
Above you the Lord now rises
and above you his glory appears.
The nations come to your light
and kings to your dawning brightness.

Lift up your eyes and look around:
all are assembling and coming towards you,
your sons from far away
and daughters being tenderly carried.

At this sight you will glow radiant,
your heart throbbing and full;
since the riches of the sea will flow to you;
the wealth of the nations come to you;

camels in throngs will cover you,
and dromedaries of Midian and Ephah;
everyone in Sheba will come,
bringing gold and incense
and singing the praise of the Lord.

   The word of the Lord.

Responsorial Psalm   Ps 71:1-2,7-8,10-13. R. Cf. v.11

R. **All nations shall fall prostrate before you, O Lord.**

   O God, give your judgement to the king,
   to a king's son your justice,
   that he may judge your people in justice
   and your poor in right judgement. R.

   In his days justice shall flourish
   and peace till the moon fails.
   He shall rule from sea to sea,
   from the Great River to earth's bounds. R.

The Kings of Tarshish and the sea coasts
shall pay him tribute.
The kings of Sheba and Seba
shall bring him gifts.
Before him all kings shall fall prostrate,
all nations shall serve him. R.

For he shall save the poor when they cry
and the needy who are helpless.
He will have pity on the weak
and save the lives of the poor. R.

R. **All nations shall fall prostrate before you, O Lord.**

SECOND READING

A reading from the letter of St Paul to the Ephesians   3:2-3,5-6
It has now been revealed that pagans share the same inheritance.

You have probably heard how I have been entrusted by God with the
grace he meant for you, and that it was by a revelation that I was given
the knowledge of the mystery. This mystery that has now been revealed
through the Spirit to his holy apostles and prophets was unknown to
any men in past generations; it means that pagans now share the same
inheritance, that they are parts of the same body, and that the same
promise has been made to them, in Christ Jesus, through the gospel.

The word of the Lord.

Gospel Acclamation   Mt 2:2

R. **Alleluia, alleluia!**
We saw his star as it rose
and have come to do the Lord homage.
R. **Alleluia!**

GOSPEL

A reading from the holy Gospel according to Matthew   2:1-12
We saw his star and have come to do the king homage.

After Jesus had been born at Bethlehem in Judaea during the reign of King
Herod, some wise men came to Jerusalem from the east. 'Where is the
infant king of the Jews?' they asked. 'We saw his star as it rose and have
come to do him homage.' When King Herod heard this he was perturbed,

and so was the whole of Jerusalem. He called together all the chief priests and the scribes of the people, and enquired of them where the Christ was to be born. 'At Bethlehem in Judaea,' they told him 'for this is what the prophet wrote:

> And you, Bethlehem, in the land of Judah
> you are by no means least among the leaders of Judah,
> for out of you will come a leader
> who will shepherd my people Israel.'

Then Herod summoned the wise men to see him privately. He asked them the exact date on which the star had appeared, and sent them on to Bethlehem. 'Go and find out all about the child,' he said 'and when you have found him, let me know, so that I too may go and do him homage.' Having listened to what the king had to say, they set out. And there in front of them was the star they had seen rising; it went forward and halted over the place where the child was. The sight of the star filled them with delight, and going into the house they saw the child with his mother Mary, and falling to their knees they did him homage. Then, opening their treasures, they offered him gifts of gold and frankincense and myrrh. But they were warned in a dream not to go back to Herod, and returned to their own country by a different way.

The Gospel of the Lord.

The Creed is said.

Prayer over the Offerings

Look with favour, Lord, we pray,
on these gifts of your Church,
in which are offered now not gold
or frankincense or myrrh,
but he who by them is proclaimed,
sacrificed and received, Jesus Christ.
Who lives and reigns
for ever and ever.

Super oblata

Ecclesiæ tuæ, quæsumus, Domine,
dona propitius intuere,
quibus non iam aurum,
thus et myrrha profertur,
sed quod eisdem muneribus
declaratur, immolatur et sumitur,
Iesus Christus.
Qui vivit et regnat
in sæcula sæculorum.

Preface of the Epiphany of the Lord, pp.48-49.

Communion Antiphon Cf. Mt 2:2	Ant. ad communionem
We have seen his star in the East, and have come with gifts to adore the Lord.	Vidimus stellam eius in Oriente, et venimus cum muneribus adorare Dominum.

Prayer after Communion	Post communionem
Go before us with heavenly light, O Lord, always and everywhere, that we may perceive with clear sight and revere with true affection the mystery in which you have willed us to participate. Through Christ our Lord.	Cælesti lumine, quæsumus, Domine, semper et ubique nos præveni, ut mysterium, cuius nos participes esse voluisti, et puro cernamus intuitu, et digno percipiamus affectu. Per Christum Dominum nostrum.

A formula of Solemn Blessing, pp.134-137, may be used.

In England, Wales & Ireland
8 January

In Scotland
9 January

THE BAPTISM OF THE LORD

Let us remember that God is the God of surprises. John had stated that there was an abyssal, unbridgeable difference between him and Jesus. But the Son of God came precisely to fill this gap between man and God. If Jesus is completely on God's side, he is also completely on the side of mankind and he reunites what was divided. The Messiah asks to be baptised so that all righteousness be fulfilled, that God's design which passes through filial obedience and solidarity with fragile and sinful mankind, be fulfilled. It is the path of humility and of God's complete closeness to his children.

(Pope Francis)

Feast

Entrance Antiphon Cf. Mt 3:16-17

AFTER the Lord was baptised,
the heavens were opened,
and the Spirit descended upon him
   like a dove,
and the voice of the Father thundered:
This is my beloved Son,
   with whom I am well pleased.

Ant. ad introitum

BAPTIZATO Domino,
aperti sunt cæli,
et sicut columba super eum
   Spiritus mansit,
et vox Patris intonuit:
Hic est Filius meus dilectus,
in quo mihi bene complacui.

The **Gloria in excelsis** (Glory to God in the highest) is said.

Collect

Almighty ever-living God,
who, when Christ had been
   baptised in the River Jordan
and as the Holy Spirit descended
   upon him,
solemnly declared him your
   beloved Son,
grant that your children
   by adoption,
reborn of water and the Holy Spirit,
may always be well pleasing to you.
Through our Lord Jesus Christ,
   your Son,
who lives and reigns with you in
   the unity of the Holy Spirit,
God, for ever and ever.

Or:

O God, whose Only Begotten Son
has appeared in our very flesh,
grant, we pray, that we may be
   inwardly transformed
through him whom we recognise
   as outwardly like ourselves.
Who lives and reigns with you in
   the unity of the Holy Spirit,
God, for ever and ever.

Collecta

Omnipotens sempiterne Deus,
qui Christum, in Iordane
   flumine baptizatum,
Spiritu Sancto super
   eum descendente,
dilectum Filium tuum
   sollemniter declarasti,
concede filiis adoptionis tuæ,
ex aqua et Spiritu Sancto renatis,
ut in beneplacito tuo
   iugiter perseverent.
Per Dominum nostrum
   Iesum Christum Filium tuum,
qui tecum vivit et regnat
   in unitate Spiritus Sancti,
Deus, per omnia sæcula sæculorum.

Vel:

Deus, cuius Unigenitus in
   substantia nostræ carnis apparuit,
præsta, quæsumus,
ut per eum, quem similem nobis
   foris agnovimus,
intus reformari mereamur.
Qui tecum vivit et regnat
   in unitate Spiritus Sancti,
Deus, per omnia sæcula sæculorum.

In Scotland only one reading is read before the Gospel. Either Isaiah 42:1-4,6-7 or Acts 10:34-38.

FIRST READING

A reading from the prophet Isaiah   42:1-4,6-7

Here is my servant in whom my soul delights.

Thus says the Lord:

> Here is my servant whom I uphold,
> my chosen one in whom my soul delights.
> I have endowed him with my spirit
> that he may bring true justice to the nations.
>
> He does not cry out or shout aloud,
> or make his voice heard in the streets.
> He does not break the crushed reed,
> nor quench the wavering flame.
>
> Faithfully he brings true justice;
> he will neither waver, nor be crushed
> until true justice is established on earth,
> for the islands are awaiting his law.
>
> I, the Lord, have called you to serve the cause of right;
> I have taken you by the hand and formed you;
> I have appointed you as covenant of the people and light of the nations,
> to open the eyes of the blind
> to free captives from prison,
> and those who live in darkness from the dungeon.

The word of the Lord.

Responsorial Psalm   Ps 28:1-4,9-10. R. v.11

R. **The Lord will bless his people with peace.**

> O give the Lord you sons of God,
> give the Lord glory and power;
> give the Lord the glory of his name.
> Adore the Lord in his holy court. R.

> The Lord's voice resounding on the waters,
> the Lord on the immensity of waters;
> the voice of the Lord, full of power,
> the voice of the Lord, full of splendour. R.

> The God of glory thunders.
> In his temple they all cry: 'Glory!'
> The Lord sat enthroned over the flood;
> the Lord sits as king for ever. R.

SECOND READING

A reading from Acts of the Apostles   10:34-38

God had anointed him with the Holy Spirit.

Peter addressed Cornelius and his household: 'The truth I have now come
to realise' he said 'is that God does not have favourites, but that anybody of
any nationality who fears God and does what is right is acceptable to him.

'It is true, God sent his word to the people of Israel, and it was to them
that the good news of peace was brought by Jesus Christ – but Jesus Christ
is Lord of all men. You must have heard about the recent happenings in
Judaea; about Jesus of Nazareth and how he began in Galilee, after John
had been preaching baptism. God had anointed him with the Holy Spirit
and with power, and because God was with him, Jesus went about doing
good and curing all who had fallen into the power of the devil.'

The word of the Lord.

Gospel Acclamation   Cf. Mk 9:7

R. **Alleluia, alleluia!**
The heavens opened and the Father's voice resounded:
'This is my Son, the Beloved. Listen to him.'
R. **Alleluia!**

GOSPEL

A reading from the holy Gospel according to Matthew   3:13-17

As soon as Jesus was baptised he saw the Spirit of God coming down on him.

Jesus came from Galilee to the Jordan to be baptised by John. John tried to dissuade him. 'It is I who need baptism from you' he said 'and yet you come to me!' But Jesus replied, 'Leave it like this for the time being; it is fitting that we should, in this way, do all that righteousness demands.' At this, John gave in to him.

As soon as Jesus was baptised he came up from the water, and suddenly the heavens opened and he saw the Spirit of God descending like a dove and coming down on him. And a voice spoke from heaven, 'This is my Son, the Beloved; my favour rests on him.'

The Gospel of the Lord.

The Creed is said in England, Wales and Ireland.

Prayer over the Offerings

Accept, O Lord, the offerings
we have brought to honour the
    revealing of your beloved Son,
so that the oblation of your faithful
may be transformed into the
    sacrifice of him
who willed in his compassion
to wash away the sins of the world.
Who lives and reigns
    for ever and ever.

Super oblata

Suscipe munera, Domine,
in dilecti Filii tui revelatione delata,
ut fidelium tuorum oblatio
    in eius sacrificium transeat,
qui mundi voluit peccata
    miseratus abluere.
Qui vivit et regnat
    in sæcula sæculorum.

Preface: The Baptism of the Lord. | Præfatio: de Baptismate Domini.

It is truly right and just,
　　our duty and our salvation,
always and everywhere
　　to give you thanks,
Lord, holy Father,
　　almighty and eternal God.

For in the waters of the Jordan
　　you revealed with signs
　　and wonders a new Baptism,
so that through the voice
　　that came down from heaven
we might come to believe in your
　　Word dwelling among us,
and by the Spirit's descending
　　in the likeness of a dove
we might know that Christ
　　your Servant
has been anointed with the oil
　　of gladness
and sent to bring the good news
　　to the poor.

And so, with the Powers of heaven,
we worship you constantly on earth,
and before your majesty
without end we acclaim:

Holy, Holy, Holy Lord God of hosts...

Vere dignum et iustum est,
æquum et salutare,
nos tibi semper et ubique
　　gratias agere:
Domine, sancte Pater,
　　omnipotens æterne deus:

Qui miris signasti mysteriis novum
　　in Iordane lavacrum,
ut, per vocem de cælo delapsam,
habitare Verbum tuum inter
　　homines crederetur;

et, per Spiritum in columbæ
specie descendentem,
Christus Servus tuus oleo
　　perungi lætitiæ
ac mitti ad evangelizandum
　　pauperibus nosceretur.

Et ideo cum cælorum virtutibus
in terris te iugiter celebramus,
maiestati tuæ sine fine clamantes:

Sanctus, Sanctus, Sanctus. . .

Communion Antiphon Jn 1:32,34

Behold the One of whom
   John said:
I have seen and testified that this is
   the Son of God.

Prayer after Communion

Nourished with these sacred gifts,
we humbly entreat your mercy,
   O Lord,
that, faithfully listening to your
   Only Begotten Son,
we may be your children
   in name and in truth.
Through Christ our Lord.

Ant. ad communionem

Ecce de quo dicebat Ioannes:
Ego vidi et testimonium perhibui,
   quia hic est Filius Dei.

Post communionem

Sacro munere satiati,
clementiam tuam, Domine,
   suppliciter exoramus,
ut, Unigenitum tuum
   fideliter audientes,
filii tui vere nominemur et simus.
Per Christum Dominum nostrum.

---

15 January

SECOND SUNDAY IN ORDINARY TIME

Entrance Antiphon   Ps 65:4

ALL the earth shall bow down
  before you, O God,
and shall sing to you,
shall sing to your name,
   O Most High!

Collect

Almighty ever-living God,
who govern all things,
both in heaven and on earth,
mercifully hear the pleading
   of your people
and bestow your peace on our times.
Through our Lord Jesus Christ,
   your Son,
who lives and reigns with you
   in the unity of the Holy Spirit,
God, for ever and ever.

Ant. ad introitum

OMNIS terra adoret te, Deus,
  et psallat tibi;
psalmum dicat nomini tuo,
   Altissime.

Collecta

Omnipotens sempiterne Deus,
qui cælestia simul
   et terrena moderaris,
supplicationes populi tui
   clementer exaudi,
et pacem tuam nostris
   concede temporibus.
Per Dominum nostrum Iesum
   Christum Filium tuum,
qui tecum vivit et regnat
   in unitate Spiritus Sancti,
Deus, per omnia sæcula sæculorum.

FIRST READING

A reading from the prophet Isaiah   49:3,5-6

I will make you the light of the nations so that my salvation may reach to the ends of the earth.

The Lord said to me, 'You are my servant, Israel,
in whom I shall be glorified';
I was honoured in the eyes of the Lord,
my God was my strength.
And now the Lord has spoken,
he who formed me in the womb to be his servant,
to bring Jacob back to him,
to gather Israel to him:

> 'It is not enough for you to be my servant,
> to restore the tribes of Jacob and bring back the survivors of Israel;
> I will make you the light of the nations
> so that my salvation may reach to the ends of the earth.'

The word of the Lord.

Responsorial Psalm   Ps 39:2,4,7-10. R. vv.8,9

R. **Here I am, Lord!**
I come to do your will.

I waited, I waited for the Lord
and he stooped down to me;
he heard my cry.
He put a new song into my mouth,
praise of our God. R.

You do not ask for sacrifice and offerings,
but an open ear.
You do not ask for holocaust and victim.
Instead, here am I. R.

In the scroll of the book it stands written
that I should do your will.
My God, I delight in your law
in the depth of my heart. R.

Your justice I have proclaimed
in the great assembly.
My lips I have not sealed;
you know it, O Lord. R.

SECOND READING

A reading from the first letter of St Paul to the Corinthians   1:1-3

May God our Father and the Lord Jesus Christ send you grace and peace.

I, Paul, appointed by God to be an apostle, together with brother Sosthenes, send greetings to the church of God in Corinth, to the holy people of Jesus Christ, who are called to take their place among all the saints everywhere who pray to our Lord Jesus Christ; for he is their Lord no less than ours. May God our Father and the Lord Jesus Christ send you grace and peace.

The word of the Lord.

Gospel Acclamation

R. **Alleluia, alleluia!**
Blessings on the King who comes,
in the name of the Lord!
Peace in heaven
and glory in the highest heavens!
R. **Alleluia!**

Or: Jn 1:14,12

R. **Alleluia, alleluia!**
The Word was made flesh and lived among us;
to all who did accept him
he gave power to become children of God.
R. **Alleluia!**

GOSPEL

A reading from the holy Gospel according to John   1:29-34

Look, there is the lamb of God that takes away the sin of the world.

Seeing Jesus coming towards him, John said, 'Look, there is the lamb of God that takes away the sin of the world. This is the one I spoke of when I said: A man is coming after me who ranks before me because he existed before me. I did not know him myself, and yet it was to reveal him to Israel that I came baptising with water.' John also declared, 'I saw the Spirit coming down on him from heaven like a dove and resting on him. I did not know him myself, but he who sent me to baptise with water had said to me, "The man on whom you see the Spirit come down and rest is the one who is going to baptise with the Holy Spirit." Yes, I have seen and I am the witness that he is the Chosen One of God.'

The Gospel of the Lord.

Prayer over the Offerings

Grant us, O Lord, we pray,
that we may participate worthily
in these mysteries,
for whenever the memorial
of this sacrifice is celebrated
the work of our redemption
is accomplished.
Through Christ our Lord.

Super oblata

Concede nobis,
quæsumus, Domine,
hæc digne frequentare mysteria,
quia, quoties huius hostiæ
commemoratio celebratur,
opus nostræ
redemptionis exercetur.
Per Christum Dominum nostrum.

Preface of Sundays in Ordinary Time I-VIII, pp.60-67.

Communion Antiphon Cf. Ps 22:5

You have prepared a table before me,
and how precious is the chalice
that quenches my thirst.

Or: 1 Jn 4:16

We have come to know
and to believe
in the love that God has for us.

Ant. ad communionem

Parasti in conspectu meo mensam,
et calix meus inebrians quam
præclarus est!

Vel:

Nos cognovimus
et credidimus caritati,
quam Deus habet in nobis.

Prayer after Communion

Pour on us, O Lord,
the Spirit of your love,
and in your kindness
make those you have nourished
by this one heavenly Bread
one in mind and heart.
Through Christ our Lord.

Post communionem

Spiritum nobis, Domine,
tuæ caritatis infunde,
ut, quos uno cælesti pane satiasti,
una facias pietate concordes.
Per Christum Dominum nostrum.

22 January

THIRD SUNDAY IN ORDINARY TIME

Entrance Antiphon   Cf. Ps 95:1,6

O SING a new song to the Lord;
sing to the Lord, all the earth.
In his presence are majesty
    and splendour,
strength and honour
    in his holy place.

Ant. ad introitum

CANTATE Domino
    canticum novum,
cantate Domino, omnis terra.
Confessio et pulchritudo
    in conspectu eius,
sanctitas et magnificentia
    in sanctificatione eius.

Collect

Almighty ever-living God,
direct our actions according
    to your good pleasure,
that in the name of your beloved Son
we may abound in good works.
Through our Lord Jesus Christ,
    your Son,
who lives and reigns with you
    in the unity of the Holy Spirit,
God, for ever and ever.

Collecta

Omnipotens sempiterne Deus,
dirige actus nostros
    in beneplacito tuo,
ut in nomine dilecti Filii tui
mereamur bonis operibus abundare.
Per Dominum nostrum Iesum
    Christum Filium tuum,
qui tecum vivit et regnat
    in unitate Spiritus Sancti,
Deus, per omnia sæcula sæculorum.

FIRST READING

A reading from the prophet Isaiah   8:23-9:3

In Galilee of the nations the people has seen a great light.

In days past the Lord humbled the land of Zebulun and the land of
Naphtali, but in days to come he will confer glory on the Way of the Sea
on the far side of Jordan, province of the nations.

The people that walked in darkness
has seen a great light;
on those who live in a land of deep shadow
a light has shone.
You have made their gladness greater,
you have made their joy increase;
they rejoice in your presence
as men rejoice at harvest time,
as men are happy when they are dividing the spoils.

For the yoke that was weighing on him,
the bar across his shoulders,
the rod of his oppressor,
these you break as on the day of Midian.

   The word of the Lord.

Responsorial Psalm   Ps 26:1,4,13-14. R. v.1

R. **The Lord is my light and my help.**

   The Lord is my light and my help;
   whom shall I fear?
   The Lord is the stronghold of my life;
   before whom shall I shrink? R.

   There is one thing I ask of the Lord,
   for this I long,
   to live in the house of the Lord,
   all the days of my life,
   to savour the sweetness of the Lord,
   to behold his temple. R.

   I am sure I shall see the Lord's goodness
   in the land of the living.
   Hope in him, hold firm and take heart.
   Hope in the Lord! R.

SECOND READING

A reading from the first letter of St Paul to the Corinthians   1:10-13,17
Make up the differences between you instead of disagreeing among yourselves.

I appeal to you, brothers, for the sake of our Lord Jesus Christ, to make up
the differences between you, and instead of disagreeing among yourselves,
to be united again in your belief and practice. From what Chloe's people
have been telling me, my dear brothers, it is clear that there are serious
differences among you. What I mean are all these slogans that you have,
like: 'I am for Paul,' 'I am for Apollos,' 'I am for Cephas,' 'I am for Christ.'
Has Christ been parcelled out? Was it Paul that was crucified for you? Were
you baptised in the name of Paul?

   For Christ did not send me to baptise, but to preach the Good News,
and not to preach that in the terms of philosophy in which the crucifixion
of Christ cannot be expressed.

   The word of the Lord.

Gospel Acclamation   Cf. Mt 4:23

R. **Alleluia, alleluia!**
Jesus proclaimed the Good News of the kingdom,
and cured all kinds of sickness among the people.
R. **Alleluia!**

GOSPEL

A reading from the holy Gospel according to Matthew   4:12-23

He went and settled in Capernaum: in this way the prophecy of Isaiah was to be fulfilled.

[Hearing that John had been arrested Jesus went back to Galilee, and leaving Nazareth he went and settled in Capernaum, a lakeside town on the borders of Zebulun and Naphtali. In this way the prophecy of Isaiah was to be fulfilled:

> Land of Zebulun! Land of Naphtali!
> Way of the sea on the far side of Jordan,
> Galilee of the nations!
> The people that lived in darkness
> has seen a great light;
> on those who dwell in the land and shadow of death
> a light has dawned.

From that moment Jesus began his preaching with the message, 'Repent, for the kingdom of heaven is close at hand.]

As he was walking by the Sea of Galilee he saw two brothers, Simon, who was called Peter, and his brother Andrew; they were making a cast in the lake with their net, for they were fishermen. And he said to them, 'Follow me and I will make you fishers of men.' And they left their nets at once and followed him.

Going on from there he saw another pair of brothers, James son of Zebedee and his brother John; they were in their boat with their father Zebedee, mending their nets, and he called them. At once, leaving the boat and their father, they followed him.

He went round the whole of Galilee teaching in their synagogues, proclaiming the Good News of the kingdom and curing all kinds of diseases and sickness among the people.

[The Gospel of the Lord.]

Shorter Form, verses 12-17. Read between [ ]

Prayer over the Offerings

Accept our offerings, O Lord,
we pray,
and in sanctifying them
grant that they may profit us
for salvation.
Through Christ our Lord.

Super oblata

Munera nostra, Domine,
suscipe placatus,
quæ sanctificando
nobis, quæsumus,
salutaria fore concede.
Per Christum Dominum nostrum.

Preface of Sundays in Ordinary Time I-VIII, pp.60-67.

Communion Antiphon Cf. Ps 33:6

Look toward the Lord
and be radiant;
let your faces not be abashed.

Ant. ad communionem

Accedite ad Dominum
et illuminamini,
et facies vestræ non confundentur.

Or: Jn 8:12

I am the light of the world,
says the Lord;
whoever follows me will not walk
in darkness,
but will have the light of life.

Vel:

Ego sum lux mundi, dicit Dominus:
qui sequitur me non ambulat
in tenebris,
sed habebit lumen vitæ.

Prayer after Communion

Grant, we pray, almighty God,
that, receiving the grace
by which you bring us to new life,
we may always glory in your gift.
Through Christ our Lord.

Post communionem

Præsta nobis, quæsumus,
omnipotens Deus,
ut, vivificationis tuæ
gratiam consequentes,
in tuo semper munere gloriemur.
Per Christum Dominum nostrum.

29 January

FOURTH SUNDAY IN ORDINARY TIME

Entrance Antiphon   Ps 105:47

S AVE us, O Lord our God!
   And gather us from the nations,
to give thanks to your holy name,
and make it our glory to praise you.

Ant. ad introitum

S ALVOS nos fac,
   Domine Deus noster,
et congrega nos de nationibus,
ut confiteamur nomini sancto tuo,
et gloriemur in laude tua.

Collect

Grant us, Lord our God,
that we may honour you
     with all our mind,
and love everyone in truth of heart.
Through our Lord Jesus Christ,
     your Son,
who lives and reigns with you
     in the unity of the Holy Spirit,
God, for ever and ever.

Collecta

Concede nobis,
     Domine Deus noster,
ut te tota mente veneremur,
et omnes homines rationabili
     diligamus affectu.
Per Dominum nostrum Iesum
     Christum Filium tuum,
qui tecum vivit et regnat
     in unitate Spiritus Sancti,
Deus, per omnia sæcula sæculorum.

FIRST READING

A reading from the prophet Zephaniah   2:3; 3:12-13

In your midst I will leave a humble and lowly people.

Seek the Lord
all you, the humble of the earth,
who obey his commands.
Seek integrity,
seek humility:
you may perhaps find shelter
on the day of the anger of the Lord.
In your midst I will leave
a humble and lowly people,
and those who are left in Israel will seek refuge in the name of the Lord.
They will do no wrong,
will tell no lies;
and the perjured tongue will no longer

be found in their mouths.
But they will be able to graze and rest
with no one to disturb them.

The word of the Lord.

Responsorial Psalm   Ps 145:7-10. R. Mt 5:3

R. **How happy are the poor in spirit;**
   theirs is the kingdom of heaven.
   Or: **Alleluia!**

It is the Lord who keeps faith for ever,
who is just to those who are oppressed.
It is he who gives bread to the hungry,
the Lord, who sets prisoners free. R.

It is the Lord who gives sight to the blind,
who raises up those who are bowed down,
the Lord, who protects the stranger
and upholds the widow and orphan. R.

It is the Lord who loves the just
but thwarts the path of the wicked.
The Lord will reign for ever,
Sion's God, from age to age. R.

SECOND READING

A reading from the first letter of St Paul to the Corinthians   1:26-31

God chose what is foolish by human reckoning.

Take yourselves, brothers, at the time when you were called: how many of
you were wise in the ordinary sense of the word, how many were influential
people, or came from noble families? No, it was to shame the wise that
God chose what is foolish by human reckoning, and to shame what is
strong that he chose what is weak by human reckoning; those whom the
world thinks common and contemptible are the ones that God has chosen
– those who are nothing at all to show up those who are everything. The
human race has nothing to boast about to God. but you, God has made
members of Christ Jesus and by God's doing he has become our wisdom,
and our virtue, and our holiness, and our freedom. As scripture says: if
anyone wants to boast, let him boast about the Lord.

The word of the Lord.

Gospel Acclamation   Mt 11:25

R. **Alleluia, alleluia!**
Blessed are you, Father,
Lord of heaven and earth,
for revealing the mysteries of the kingdom
to mere children.
R. **Alleluia!**

Or: Mt 5:12

R. **Alleluia, alleluia!**
Rejoice and be glad:
your reward will be great in heaven.
R. **Alleluia!**

GOSPEL

A reading from the holy Gospel according to Matthew   5:1-12

How happy are the poor in spirit.

Seeing the crowds, Jesus went up the hill. There he sat down and was joined
by his disciples. Then he began to speak. This is what he taught them:

'How happy are the poor in spirit:
theirs is the kingdom of heaven.
Happy the gentle:
they shall have the earth for their heritage.
Happy those who mourn:
they shall be comforted.
Happy those who hunger and thirst for what is right:
they shall be satisfied.
Happy the merciful:
they shall have mercy shown them.
Happy the pure in heart:
they shall see God.
Happy the peacemakers:
they shall be called sons of God.
Happy those who are persecuted in the cause of right:
theirs is the kingdom of heaven.

'Happy are you when people abuse you and persecute you and speak all
kinds of calumny against you on my account. Rejoice and be glad, for your
reward will be great in heaven.'

The Gospel of the Lord.

Prayer over the Offerings

O Lord, we bring to your altar
these offerings of our service:
be pleased to receive them, we pray,
and transform them
into the Sacrament
    of our redemption.
Through Christ our Lord.

Super oblata

Altaribus tuis, Domine,
munera nostræ
    servitutis inferimus,
quæ, placatus assumens,
sacramentum nostræ
    redemptionis efficias.
Per Christum Dominum nostrum.

Preface of Sundays in Ordinary Time I-VIII, pp.60-67.

Communion Antiphon Cf. Ps 30:17-18

Let your face shine on your servant.
Save me in your merciful love.
O Lord, let me never be put to shame,
    for I call on you.

Ant. ad communionem

Illumina faciem tuam super
    servum tuum,
et salvum me fac in tua misericordia.
Domine, non confundar,
    quoniam invocavi te.

Or: Mt 5:3-4

Blessed are the poor in spirit,
for theirs is the Kingdom
    of Heaven.
Blessed are the meek,
    for they shall possess the land.

Vel:

Beati pauperes spiritu,
quoniam ipsorum
    est regnum cælorum.
Beati mites,
    quoniam ipsi possidebunt terram.

Prayer after Communion

Nourished by these redeeming gifts,
we pray, O Lord,
that through this help
    to eternal salvation
true faith may ever increase.
Through Christ our Lord.

Post communionem

Redemptionis nostræ munere
    vegetati, quæsumus, Domine,
ut hoc perpetuæ salutis auxilio
fides semper vera proficiat.
Per Christum Dominum nostrum.

2 February

THE PRESENTATION OF THE LORD

Simeon goes to the Temple, "moved by the spirit". The Holy Spirit is the protagonist in this scene. He makes Simeon's heart burn with desire for God. He keeps expectation alive in his heart: he impels him to go to the Temple and he enables his eyes to recognise the Messiah, even in the guise of a poor little baby. That is what the Holy Spirit does: he enables us to discern God's presence and activity not in great things, in outward appearances or shows of force, but in littleness and vulnerability. Think of the cross. There too we find littleness and vulnerability, but also something dramatic: the power of God.

(Pope Francis)

Feast

THE BLESSING OF CANDLES AND THE PROCESSION

First Form: The Procession

1. At an appropriate hour, a gathering takes place at a smaller church or other suitable place other than inside the church to which the procession will go. The faithful hold in their hands unlighted candles.

2. The Priest, wearing white vestments as for Mass, approaches with the ministers. Instead of the chasuble, the Priest may wear a cope, which he leaves aside after the procession is over.

3. While the candles are being lit, the following antiphon or another appropriate chant is sung.

Behold, our Lord will come with power, to enlighten the eyes of his servants, alleluia.	Ecce Dominus noster cum virtute veniet, ut illuminet oculos servorum suorum, alleluia.

4. When the chant is concluded, the Priest, facing the people, says: **In the name of the Father, and of the Son, and of the Holy Spirit**. Then the Priest greets the people in the usual way, and next he gives an introductory address, encouraging the faithful to celebrate the rite of this feast day actively and consciously. He may use these or similar words:

Dear brethren (brothers and sisters),
forty days have passed since
   we celebrated the joyful feast
of the Nativity of the Lord.
Today is the blessed day
when Jesus was presented in
   the Temple by Mary and Joseph.
Outwardly he was fulfilling the Law,
but in reality he was coming
   to meet his believing people.
Prompted by the Holy Spirit,
Simeon and Anna came
   to the Temple.
Enlightened by the same Spirit,
they recognised the Lord
and confessed him with exultation
So let us also, gathered together
   by the Holy Spirit,
proceed to the house of God
   to encounter Christ.
There we shall find him
and recognise him in the breaking
   of the bread,
until he comes again, revealed in glory.

Fratres carissimi:
Ante dies quadraginta celebravimus
cum gaudio festum
   Nativitatis Domini.
Hodie vero occurrit dies ille beatus,
quo Iesus a Maria et Ioseph
   præsentatus est in templo,
exterius quidem legem implens,
rerum veritate autem occurrens
   populo suo credenti.
Spiritu Sancto impulsi, in templum
   venerunt beati illi senes
et cognoverunt Dominum eodem
   Spiritu illuminati,
et confessi sunt eum
   in exsultatione.
Ita et nos, congregati in unum
   per Spiritum Sanctum,
procedamus ad domum
   Dei obviam Christo.
Inveniemus eum et cognoscemus
   in fractione panis,
donec veniat manifestus in gloria.

5. After the address the Priest blesses the candles, saying, with hands extended:

Let us pray.

O God, source and origin of all light,
who on this day showed
   to the just man Simeon
the Light for revelation to the Gentiles,
we humbly ask that,
in answer to your people's prayers,
you may be pleased to sanctify
   with your blessing ✠ these candles,
which we are eager to carry
   in praise of your name,
so that, treading the path of virtue,
we may reach that light
   which never fails.
Through Christ our Lord.
R. Amen.

Oremus

Deus, omnis luminis fons et origo,
qui iusto Simeoni Lumen
   ad revelationem gentium
hodie demonstrasti,
te supplices deprecamur,
ut hos cereos sanctificare tua ✠
   benedictione digneris,
tuæ plebis vota suscipiens,
quæ ad tui nominis laudem eos
   gestatura concurrit,
quatenus per virtutum semitam
ad lucem indeficientem
   pervenire mereatur.
Per Christum Dominum nostrum.
R. Amen.

Or:

O God, true light,
    who create light eternal,
spreading it far and wide,
pour, we pray, into the hearts
    of the faithful
the brilliance of perpetual light,
so that all who are brightened
    in your holy temple
by the splendour of these candles
may happily reach the light
    of your glory.
Through Christ our Lord.
R. Amen.

Vel:

Deus, lumen verum, æternæ lucis
    propagator et auctor,
cordibus infunde fidelium perpetui
    luminis claritatem,
ut, quicumque in templo
    sancto tuo
splendore præsentium
    luminum adornantur,
ad lumen gloriæ tuæ feliciter
    valeant pervenire.
Per Christum Dominum nostrum.
R. Amen.

He sprinkles the candles with holy water without saying anything, and puts incense into the thurible for the procession.

6. Then the Priest receives from the Deacon or a minister the lighted candle prepared for him and the procession begins, with the Deacon announcing (or, if there is no Deacon, the Priest himself):

Let us go in peace to meet the Lord.

Procedamus in pace
    ad occurrendum Domino.

Or:

Let us go in peace.

Vel:

Procedamus in pace.

In this case, all respond:

In the name of Christ. Amen.

In nomine Christi. Amen.

7. All carry lighted candles. As the procession moves forward, one or other of the antiphons that follow is sung, namely the antiphon **A light for revelation** with the canticle (Lk 2:29-32), or the antiphon **Sion, adorn your bridal chamber** or another appropriate chant.

I

Antiphon   Lk 2:29-32

Ant. A light for revelation
    to the Gentiles
and the glory of your people Israel.
Lord, now you let your servant
    go in peace,
in accordance with your word. Ant.
For my eyes have seen
    your salvation. Ant.

Antiphona

Ant. Lumen ad
    revelationem gentium,
et gloriam plebis tuæ Israël.
Nunc dimittis servum tuum, Domine,
secundum verbum tuum
    in pace. Ant.
Quia viderunt oculi mei
    salutare tuum. Ant.

Which you have prepared
    in the sight of all peoples. Ant.
	Quod parasti ante faciem
	    omnium populorum. Ant.

II

Ant. Sion, adorn your bridal chamber
    and welcome Christ the King;
take Mary in your arms,
    who is the gate of heaven,
for she herself is carrying
    the King of glory and new light.
A Virgin she remains, though
    bringing in her hands the Son
    before the morning star begotten,
whom Simeon, taking in his arms
announced to the peoples as Lord
    of life and death and Saviour
    of the world.
	Ant. Adorna thalamum tuum, Sion,
	    et suscipe Regem Christum:
	amplectere Mariam,
	    quæ est cælestis porta:
	ipsa enim portat Regem gloriæ
	    novi luminis:
	subsistit Virgo, adducens manibus
	    Filium ante luciferum genitum:
	quem accipiens Simeon in ulnas
	    suas, prædicavit populis,
	Dominum eum esse vitæ et mortis,
	et Salvatorem mundi.

8. As the procession enters the church, the Entrance Antiphon of the Mass is sung. When the Priest has arrived at the altar, he venerates it and, if appropriate, incenses it. Then he goes to the chair, where he takes off the cope, if he used it in the procession, and puts on a chasuble. After the singing of the hymn **Gloria in excelsis** (**Glory to God in the highest**), he says the Collect as usual. The Mass continues in the usual manner.

Second Form: The Solemn Entrance

9. Whenever a procession cannot take place, the faithful gather in church, holding candles in their hands. The Priest, wearing white sacred vestments as for Mass, together with the ministers and a representative group of the faithful, goes to a suitable place, either in front of the church door or inside the church itself, where at least a large part of the faithful can conveniently participate in the rite.

10. When the Priest reaches the place appointed for the blessing of the candles, candles are lit while the antiphon **Behold, our Lord** (no. 3) or another appropriate chant is sung.

11. Then, after the greeting and address, the Priest blesses the candles, as above nos. 4-5; and then the procession to the altar takes place, with singing (nos. 6-7). For Mass, what is indicated in no. 8 above is observed.

At the Mass

Entrance Antiphon Cf. Ps 47:10-11

Your merciful love, O God,
we have received in the midst of
    your temple.
Your praise, O God, like your name,
reaches the ends of the earth;
your right hand is filled
    with saving justice.

Ant. ad introitum

Suscepimus, Deus,
    misericordiam tuam
in medio templi tui.
Secundum nomen tuum, Deus,
ita et laus tua in fines terræ;
iustitia plena est dextera tua.

The **Gloria in excelsis** (Glory to God in the highest) is said.

Collect

Almighty ever-living God,
we humbly implore your majesty
that, just as your Only Begotten Son
was presented on this day
    in the Temple
in the substance of our flesh,
so, by your grace,
we may be presented to you
    with minds made pure.
Through our Lord Jesus Christ,
    your Son,
who lives and reigns with you
    in the unity of the Holy Spirit,
God, for ever and ever.

Collecta

Omnipotens sempiterne Deus,
maiestatem tuam
    supplices exoramus,
ut, sicut Unigenitus Filius tuus
hodierna die cum nostræ
    carnis substantia
in templo est præsentatus,
ita nos facias purificatis tibi
    mentibus præsentari.
Per Dominum nostrum Iesum
    Christum Filium tuum,
qui tecum vivit et regnat
    in unitate Spiritus Sancti,
Deus, per omnia sæcula sæculorum.

FIRST READING

Either:

A reading from the prophet Malachi   3:1-4

The Lord you are seeking will suddenly enter his Temple.

The Lord God says this: Look, I am going to send my messenger to prepare a way before me. And the Lord you are seeking will suddenly enter his Temple; and the angel of the covenant whom you are longing for, yes, he is coming, says the Lord of hosts. Who will be able to resist the day of his coming? Who will remain standing when he appears? For he is like the refiner's fire and the fuller's alkali. He will take his seat as refiner and purifier; he will purify the sons of Levi and refine them like gold and silver, and then they will make the offering to the Lord as it should be made. The offering of Judah and Jerusalem will then be welcomed by the Lord as in former days, as in the years of old.

The word of the Lord.

Or:

A reading from the letter to the Hebrews 2:14-18

It was essential that he should in this way become completely like his brothers.

Since all the children share the same blood and flesh, Jesus too shared equally in it, so that by his death he could take away all the power of the devil, who had power over death, and set free all those who had been held in slavery all their lives by the fear of death. For it was not the angels that he took to himself; he took to himself descent from Abraham. It was essential that he should in this way become completely like his brothers so that he could be a compassionate and trustworthy high priest of God's religion, able to atone for human sins. That is, because he has himself been through temptation he is able to help others who are tempted.

The word of the Lord.

Responsorial Psalm Ps 23:7-10. R. v.10

R. **Who is the king of glory?**
It is the Lord.

O gates, lift up your heads;
grow higher, ancient doors.
Let him enter, the king of glory! R.

Who is the king of glory?
The Lord, the mighty, the valiant,
the Lord, the valiant in war. R.

O gates, lift high your heads;
grow higher, ancient doors.
Let him enter, the king of glory! R.

Who is he, the king of glory?
He, the Lord of armies,
he is the king of glory. R.

Gospel Acclamation Lk 2:32

R. **Alleluia, alleluia!**
The light to enlighten the Gentiles
and give glory to Israel, your people.
R. **Alleluia!**

GOSPEL

A reading from the holy Gospel according to Luke   2:22-40

My eyes have seen your salvation.

[When the day came for them to be purified as laid down by the Law of Moses, the parents of Jesus took him up to Jerusalem to present him to the Lord – observing what stands written in the Law of the Lord: Every first-born male must be consecrated to the Lord – and also to offer in sacrifice, in accordance with what is said in the Law of the Lord, a pair of turtle-doves or two young pigeons. Now in Jerusalem there was a man named Simeon. He was an upright and devout man; he looked forward to Israel's comforting and the Holy Spirit rested on him. It had been revealed to him by the Holy Spirit that he would not see death until he had set eyes on the Christ of the Lord. Prompted by the Spirit he came to the Temple; and when the parents brought in the child Jesus to do for him what the Law required, he took him into his arms and blessed God; and he said:

'Now, Master, you can let your servant go in peace,
just as you promised;
because my eyes have seen the salvation
which you have prepared for all the nations to see,
a light to enlighten the pagans
and the glory of your people Israel.']

As the child's father and mother stood there wondering at the things that were being said about him, Simeon blessed them and said to Mary his mother, 'You see this child: he is destined for the fall and for the rising of many in Israel, destined to be a sign that is rejected – and a sword will pierce your own soul too so that the secret thoughts of many may be laid bare.'

There was a prophetess also, Anna the daughter of Phanuel, of the tribe of Asher. She was well on in years. Her days of girlhood over, she had been married for seven years before becoming a widow. She was now eighty-four years old and never left the Temple, serving God night and day with fasting and prayer. She came by just at that moment and began to praise God; and she spoke of the child to all who looked forward to the deliverance of Jerusalem.

When they had done everything the Law of the Lord required, they went back to Galilee, to their own town of Nazareth. Meanwhile the child grew to maturity, and he was filled with wisdom; and God's favour was with him.

[The Gospel of the Lord.]

Shorter Form, verses 2:22-32. Read between [ ]

The Creed is not said.

Prayer over the Offerings

May the offering made
   with exultation by your Church
be pleasing to you, O Lord, we pray,
for you willed that your
   Only Begotten Son
be offered to you for the life
   of the world
as the Lamb without blemish.
Who lives and reigns
   for ever and ever.

Super oblata

Gratum tibi sit,
   Domine, quæsumus,
exsultantis Ecclesiæ
   munus oblatum,
qui Unigenitum Filium
   tuum voluisti
Agnum immaculatum tibi
   offerri pro sæculi vita.
Qui vivit et regnat
   in sæcula sæculorum.

Preface: The Mystery of the Presentation of the Lord.

It is truly right and just,
   our duty and our salvation,
always and everywhere
   to give you thanks,
Lord, holy Father,
   almighty and eternal God.

For your co-eternal Son was presented
   on this day in the Temple
and revealed by the Spirit
as the glory of Israel
   and Light of the nations.

And so, we, too, go forth, rejoicing
   to encounter your Salvation,
and with the Angels and Saints
praise you, as without end
   we acclaim:

Holy, Holy, Holy Lord God of hosts...

Præfatio: De mysterio Præsentationis Domini.

Vere dignum et iustum est,
   æquum et salutare,
nos tibi semper et ubique
   gratias agere:
Domine, sancte Pater,
   omnipotens æterne Deus:

Quia coæternus hodie in templo
   tuus Filius præsentatus
gloria Israel et lumen gentium
   a Spiritu declaratur.

Unde et nos, Salutari tuo
   in gaudiis occurrentes,
cum Angelis et Sanctis te laudamus,
   sine fine dicentes:

Sanctus, Sanctus, Sanctus. . .

Communion Antiphon Lk 2:30-31

My eyes have seen your salvation,
which you prepared in the sight
    of all the peoples.

Prayer after Communion

By these holy gifts which
    we have received, O Lord,
bring your grace to perfection
    within us,
and, as you fulfilled
    Simeon's expectation
that he would not see death
until he had been privileged
    to welcome the Christ,
so may we,
    going forth to meet the Lord,
obtain the gift of eternal life.
Through Christ our Lord.

Ant. ad communionem

Viderunt oculi mei salutare tuum,
quod parasti ante faciem
    omnium populorum.

Post communionem

Per hæc sancta quæ sumpsimus,
    Domine,
perfice in nobis gratiam tuam,
qui exspectationem
    Simeonis implesti,
ut, sicut ille mortem non vidit
nisi prius Christum
    suscipere mereretur,
ita et nos, in occursum
    Domini procedentes,
vitam obtineamus æternam.
Per Christum Dominum nostrum.

5 February

FIFTH SUNDAY IN ORDINARY TIME

Entrance Antiphon   Ps 94:6-7

O COME, let us worship God
  and bow low before the God
  who made us,
for he is the Lord our God.

Ant. ad introitum

V ENITE, adoremus Deum,
  et procidamus ante Dominum,
  qui fecit nos;
quia ipse est Dominus Deus noster.

Collect

Keep your family safe, O Lord,
  with unfailing care,
that, relying solely on the hope
  of heavenly grace,
they may be defended always
  by your protection.
Through our Lord Jesus Christ,
  your Son,
who lives and reigns with you
  in the unity of the Holy Spirit,
God, for ever and ever.

Collecta

Familiam tuam,
  quæsumus, Domine,
continua pietate custodi,
ut, quæ in sola spe gratiæ
  cælestis innititur,
tua semper protectione muniatur.
Per Dominum nostrum Iesum
  Christum Filium tuum,
qui tecum vivit et regnat
  in unitate Spiritus Sancti,
Deus, per omnia sæcula sæculorum.

FIRST READING

A reading from the prophet Isaiah   58:7-10

Then will your light shine like the dawn.

Thus says the Lord:

Share your bread with the hungry,
and shelter the homeless poor,

clothe the man you see to be naked
and turn not from your own kin.
Then will your light shine like the dawn
and your wound be quickly healed over.

Your integrity will go before you
and the glory of the Lord behind you.
Cry, and the Lord will answer;
call, and he will say, 'I am here.'

If you do away with the yoke,
the clenched fist, the wicked word,
if you give your bread to the hungry,
and relief to the oppressed,
your light will rise in the darkness,
and your shadows become like noon.

The word of the Lord.

Responsorial Psalm   Ps 111:4-9. R. v.4

R. **The good man is a light in the darkness for the upright.**
   Or: **Alleluia!**

He is a light in the darkness for the upright:
he is generous, merciful and just.
The good man takes pity and lends,
he conducts his affairs with honour. R.

The just man will never waver:
he will be remembered for ever.
He has no fear of evil news;
with a firm heart he trusts in the Lord. R.

With a steadfast heart he will not fear;
open-handed, he gives to the poor;
his justice stands firm for ever.
His head will be raised in glory. R.

SECOND READING

A reading from the first letter of St Paul to the Corinthians   2:1-5
During my stay with you, the only knowledge I claimed to have was about Jesus as the crucified Christ.

When I came to you, brothers, it was not with any show of oratory or
philosophy, but simply to tell you what God had guaranteed. During my
stay with you, the only knowledge I claimed to have was about Jesus, and
only about him as the crucified Christ. Far from relying on any power of my
own, I came among you in great 'fear and trembling' and in my speeches
and the sermons that I gave, there were none of the arguments that belong
to philosophy; only a demonstration of the power of the Spirit. And I did
this so that your faith should not depend on human philosophy but on
the power of God.

The word of the Lord.

Gospel Acclamation   Jn 8:12

R. **Alleluia, alleluia!**
I am the light of the world, says the Lord,
anyone who follows me
will have the light of life.
R. **Alleluia!**

GOSPEL

A reading from the holy Gospel according to Matthew   5:13-16
You are the light of the world.

Jesus said to his disciples: 'You are the salt of the earth. But if salt becomes
tasteless, what can make it salty again? It is good for nothing, and can only
be thrown out to be trampled underfoot by men.

'You are the light of the world. A city built on a hill-top cannot be
hidden. No one lights a lamp to put it under a tub; they put it on the lamp-
stand where it shines for everyone in the house. In the same way your light
must shine in the sight of men, so that, seeing your good works, they may
give the praise to your Father in heaven.'

The Gospel of the Lord.

Prayer over the Offerings	Super oblata

O Lord our God,
who once established these
   created things
to sustain us in our frailty,
grant, we pray,
that they may become for us now
the Sacrament of eternal life.
Through Christ our Lord.
	Domine Deus noster,
	   qui has potius creaturas
	ad fragilitatis nostræ
	   subsidium condidisti,
	tribue, quæsumus,
	ut etiam æternitatis nobis
	   fiant sacramentum.
	Per Christum Dominum nostrum.

Preface of Sundays in Ordinary Time I-VIII, pp.60-67.

Communion Antiphon Cf. Ps 106:8-9	Ant. ad communionem

Let them thank the Lord
   for his mercy,
his wonders for the children of men
   for he satisfies the thirsty soul,
and the hungry he fills
   with good things.
	Confiteantur Domino
	   misericordiæ eius,
	et mirabilia eius filiis hominum,
	quia satiavit animam inanem,
	et animam esurientem
	   satiavit bonis.

Or: Mt 5:5-6

Blessed are those who mourn,
    for they shall be consoled.
Blessed are those who hunger
    and thirst for righteousness,
for they shall have their fill.

Vel:

Beati qui lugent,
    quoniam ipsi consolabuntur.
Beati qui esuriunt
    et sitiunt iustitiam,
quoniam ipsi saturabuntur.

Prayer after Communion

O God, who have willed
    that we be partakers
in the one Bread and the one Chalice,
grant us, we pray, so to live that,
    made one in Christ,
we may joyfully bear fruit
for the salvation of the world.
Through Christ our Lord.

Post communionem

Deus, qui nos de uno pane
    et de uno calice
participes esse voluisti,
da nobis, quæsumus, ita vivere, ut,
    unum in Christo effecti,
fructum afferamus pro mundi
    salute gaudentes.
Per Christum Dominum nostrum.

12 February

SIXTH SUNDAY IN ORDINARY TIME

Entrance Antiphon   Cf. Ps 30:3-4

BE my protector, O God,
a mighty stronghold to save me.
For you are my rock, my stronghold!
Lead me, guide me,
    for the sake of your name.

Ant. ad introitum

ESTO mihi
in Deum protectorem,
et in locum refugii,
    ut salvum me facias.
Quoniam firmamentum meum
    et refugium meum es tu,
et propter nomen tuum dux
    mihi eris, et enutries me.

Collect

O God, who teach us that you abide
in hearts that are just and true,
grant that we may be so fashioned
    by your grace
as to become a dwelling pleasing
    to you.
Through our Lord Jesus Christ,
    your Son,
who lives and reigns with you
    in the unity of the Holy Spirit,
God, for ever and ever.

Collecta

Deus, qui te in rectis et sinceris
    manere pectoribus asseris,
da nobis tua gratia tales exsistere,
in quibus habitare digneris.
Per Dominum nostrum Iesum
    Christum Filium tuum,
qui tecum vivit et regnat
    in unitate Spiritus Sancti,
Deus, per omnia sæcula sæculorum.

FIRST READING

A reading from the book of Ecclesiasticus   15:15-20
He never commanded anyone to be godless.

If you wish, you can keep the commandments,
to behave faithfully is within your power.
He has set fire and water before you;
put out your hand to whichever you prefer.
Man has life and death before him;
whichever a man likes better will be given him.
For vast is the wisdom of the Lord;
he is almighty and all-seeing.
His eyes are on those who fear him,
he notes every action of man.
He never commanded anyone to be godless,
he has given no one permission to sin.

    The word of the Lord.

Responsorial Psalm   Ps 118:1-2,4-5,17-18,33-34. R. v.1

R. **They are happy who follow God's law!**

    They are happy whose life is blameless,
    who follow God's law!
    They are happy those who do his will,
    seeking him with all their hearts. R.

    You have laid down your precepts
    to be obeyed with care.
    May my footsteps be firm
    to obey your statutes. R.

Bless your servant and I shall live
and obey your word.
Open my eyes that I may consider
the wonders of your law. R.

Teach me the demands of your statutes
and I will keep them to the end.
Train me to observe your law,
to keep it with my heart. R.

R. **They are happy who follow God's law!**

SECOND READING

A reading from the first letter of St Paul to the Corinthians   2:6-10
God predestined wisdom to be for our glory before the ages began.

We have a wisdom to offer those who have reached maturity: not a
philosophy of our age, it is true, still less of the masters of our age, which
are coming to their end. The hidden wisdom of God which we teach in our
mysteries is the wisdom that God predestined to be for our glory before
the ages began. It is a wisdom that none of the masters of this age have
ever known, or they would not have crucified the Lord of Glory; we teach
what scripture calls: the things that no eye has seen and no ear has heard,
things beyond the mind of man, all that God has prepared for those who
love him.

These are the very things that God has revealed to us through the Spirit,
for the Spirit reaches the depths of everything, even the depths of God.

The word of the Lord.

Gospel Acclamation   1 S 3:9; Jn 6:68

R. **Alleluia, alleluia!**
Speak, Lord, your servant is listening:
you have the message of eternal life.
R. **Alleluia!**

Or: Cf. Mt 11:25

R. **Alleluia, alleluia!**
Blessed are you, Father,
Lord of heaven and earth,
for revealing the mysteries of the kingdom.
to mere children.
R. **Alleluia!**

GOSPEL

A reading from the holy Gospel according to Matthew   5:17-37

You have learnt how it was said to our ancestors; but I say this to you.

[Jesus said to his disciples:] 'Do not imagine that I have come to abolish the Law or the Prophets. I have come not to abolish them but to complete them. I tell you solemnly, till heaven and earth disappear, not one dot, one little stroke, shall disappear from the Law until its purpose is achieved. Therefore, the man who infringes even one of the least of these commandments and teaches others to do the same will be considered the least in the kingdom of heaven; but the man who keeps them and teaches them will be considered great in the kingdom of heaven.

['For I tell you, if your virtue goes no deeper than that of the scribes and Pharisees, you will never get into the kingdom of heaven.

'You have learnt how it was said to our ancestors: You must not kill; and if anyone does kill he must answer for it before the court. But I say this to you: anyone who is angry with his brother will answer for it before the court;] if a man calls his brother "Fool" he will answer for it before the Sanhedrin; and if a man calls him "Renegade" he will answer for it in hell fire. So then, if you are bringing your offering to the altar and there remember that your brother has something against you, leave your offering there before the altar, go and be reconciled with your brother first, and then come back and present your offering. Come to terms with your opponent in good time while you are still on the way to the court with him, or he may hand you over to the judge and the judge to the officer, and you will be thrown into prison. I tell you solemnly, you will not get out till you have paid the last penny.

[You have learnt how it was said: You must not commit adultery. But I say this to you: if a man looks at a woman lustfully, he has already committed adultery with her in his heart.] If your right eye should cause you to sin, tear it out and throw it away; for it will do you less harm to lose one part of you than to have your whole body thrown into hell. And if your right hand should cause you to sin, cut it off and throw it away; for it will do you less harm to lose one part of you than to have your whole body go to hell.

'It has also been said: Anyone who divorces his wife must give her a writ of dismissal. But I say this to you: everyone who divorces his wife, except for the case of fornication, makes her an adulteress; and anyone who marries a divorced woman commits adultery.

['Again, you have learnt how it was said to our ancestors: You must not break your oath, but must fulfil your oaths to the Lord. But I say this to you: do not swear at all,] either by heaven, since that is God's throne; or by the earth, since that is his footstool; or by Jerusalem, since that is the city of the great king. Do not swear by your own head either, since you cannot turn a single hair white or black. [All you need say is "Yes" if you mean yes, "No" if you mean no; anything more than this comes from the evil one.'

The Gospel of the Lord.]

Shorter Form, verses 20-22,27-28,33-34,37. Read between [ ]

Prayer over the Offerings	Super oblata
May this oblation, O Lord, we pray, cleanse and renew us and may it become for those who do your will the source of eternal reward. Through Christ our Lord.	Hæc nos oblatio, quæsumus, Domine, mundet et renovet, atque tuam exsequentibus voluntatem fiat causa remunerationis æternæ. Per Christum Dominum nostrum.

Preface of Sundays in Ordinary Time I-VIII, pp.60-67.

Communion Antiphon Cf. Ps 77:29-30	Ant. ad communionem
They ate and had their fill, and what they craved the Lord gave them; they were not disappointed in what they craved.	Manducaverunt, et saturati sunt nimis, et desiderium eorum attulit eis Dominus; non sunt fraudati a desiderio suo.

Or: Jn 3:16	Vel:
God so loved the world that he gave his Only Begotten Son, so that all who believe in him may not perish, but may have eternal life.	Sic Deus dilexit mundum, ut Filium suum Unigenitum daret, ut omnis qui credit in eum non pereat, sed habeat vitam æternam.

Prayer after Communion	Post communionem
Having fed upon these heavenly delights, we pray, O Lord, that we may always long for that food by which we truly live. Through Christ our Lord.	Cælestibus, Domine, pasti deliciis, quæsumus, ut semper eadem, per quæ veraciter vivimus, appetamus. Per Christum Dominum nostrum.

19 February

SEVENTH SUNDAY IN ORDINARY TIME

Entrance Antiphon   Ps 12:6

O LORD, I trust in your
   merciful love.
My heart will rejoice
   in your salvation.
I will sing to the Lord
   who has been bountiful with me.

Ant. ad introitum

D OMINE, in tua
   misericordia speravi.
Exsultavit cor meum in salutari tuo,
cantabo Domino,
   qui bona tribuit mihi.

Collect

Grant, we pray, almighty God,
that, always pondering
   spiritual things,
we may carry out in both
   word and deed
that which is pleasing to you.
Through our Lord Jesus Christ,
   your Son,
who lives and reigns with you
   in the unity of the Holy Spirit,
God, for ever and ever.

Collecta

Præsta, quæsumus,
   omnipotens Deus,
ut, semper rationabilia meditantes,
quæ tibi sunt placita,
   et dictis exsequamur et factis.
Per Dominum nostrum Iesum
   Christum Filium tuum,
qui tecum vivit et regnat
   in unitate Spiritus Sancti,
Deus, per omnia sæcula sæculorum.

FIRST READING

A reading from the book of Leviticus   19:1-2,17-18

You must love your neighbour as yourself.

The Lord spoke to Moses; he said: 'Speak to the whole community of the
sons of Israel and say to them: "Be holy, for I, the Lord your God, am holy.

   "You must not bear hatred for your brother in your heart. You must
openly tell him, your neighbour, of his offence; this way you will not take
a sin upon yourself. You must not exact vengeance, nor must you bear a
grudge against the children of your people. You must love your neighbour
as yourself. I am the Lord."'

   The word of the Lord.

Responsorial Psalm   Ps 102:1-4,8,10,12-13. R. v.8

R. **The Lord is compassion and love.**

> My soul, give thanks to the Lord,
> all my being, bless his holy name.
> My soul, give thanks to the Lord
> and never forget all his blessings. R.

> It is he who forgives all your guilt,
> who heals every one of your ills,
> who redeems your life from the grave,
> who crowns you with love and compassion. R.

> The Lord is compassion and love,
> slow to anger and rich in mercy.
> He does not treat us according to our sins
> nor repay us according to our faults. R.

> As far as the east is from the west
> so far does he remove our sins.
> As a father has compassion on his sons,
> the Lord has pity on those who fear him. R.

SECOND READING

A reading from the first letter of St Paul to the Corinthians   3:16-23

All are your servants, but you belong to Christ and Christ belongs to God.

Didn't you realise that you were God's temple and that the Spirit of God was living among you? If anybody should destroy the temple of God, God will destroy him, because the temple of God is sacred; and you are that temple.

Make no mistake about it: if any one of you thinks of himself as wise, in the ordinary sense of the word, then he must learn to be a fool before he really can be wise. Why? Because the wisdom of this world is foolishness to God. As scripture says: The Lord knows wise men's thoughts: he knows how useless they are, or again: God is not convinced by the arguments of the wise. So there is nothing to boast about in anything human: Paul, Apollos, Cephas, the world, life and death, the present and the future, are all your servants; but you belong to Christ and Christ belongs to God.

The word of the Lord.

Gospel Acclamation   Jn 14:23

R. **Alleluia, alleluia!**
If anyone loves me he will keep my word,
and my Father will love him,
and we shall come to him.
R. **Alleluia!**

Or: 1 Jn 2:5

R. **Alleluia, alleluia!**
When anyone obeys what Christ has said,
God's love comes to perfection in him.
R. **Alleluia!**

GOSPEL

A reading from the holy Gospel according to Matthew   5:38-48

Love your enemies.

Jesus said to his disciples: 'You have learnt how it was said: Eye for eye and tooth for tooth. But I say this to you: offer the wicked man no resistance. On the contrary, if anyone hits you on the right cheek, offer him the other as well; if a man takes you to law and would have your tunic, let him have your cloak as well. And if anyone orders you to go one mile, go two miles with him. Give to anyone who asks, and if anyone wants to borrow, do not turn away.

'You have learnt how it was said: You must love your neighbour and hate your enemy. But I say this to you: love your enemies and pray for those who persecute you; in this way you will be sons of your Father in heaven, for he causes his sun to rise on bad men as well as good, and his rain to fall on honest and dishonest men alike. For if you love those who love you, what right have you to claim any credit? Even the tax collectors do as much, do they not? And if you save your greetings for your brothers, are you doing anything exceptional? Even the pagans do as much, do they not? You must therefore be perfect just as your heavenly Father is perfect.'

The Gospel of the Lord.

Prayer over the Offerings

As we celebrate your mysteries,
     O Lord,
with the observance that is your due,
we humbly ask you,
that what we offer to the honour
     of your majesty
may profit us for salvation.
Through Christ our Lord.

Preface of Sundays in Ordinary Time I-VIII, pp.60-67.

Super oblata

Mysteria tua, Domine,
     debitis servitiis exsequentes,
supplices te rogamus,
ut, quod ad honorem tuæ
     maiestatis offerimus,
nobis proficiat ad salutem.
Per Christum Dominum nostrum.

Communion Antiphon   Ps 9:2-3

I will recount all your wonders,
I will rejoice in you and be glad,
and sing psalms to your name,
     O Most High.

Or: Jn 11:27

Lord, I have come to believe
     that you are the Christ,
the Son of the living God,
     who is coming into this world.

Ant. ad communionem

Narrabo omnia mirabilia tua.
Lætabor et exsultabo in te,
psallam nomini tuo, Altissime.

Vel:

Domine, ego credidi quia
     tu es Christus Filius Dei vivi,
qui in hunc mundum venisti.

Prayer after Communion

Grant, we pray, almighty God,
that we may experience the effects
     of the salvation
which is pledged to us
     by these mysteries.
Through Christ our Lord.

Post communionem

Præsta, quæsumus,
     omnipotens Deus,
ut illius salutis capiamus effectum,
cuius per hæc mysteria
     pignus accepimus.
Per Christum Dominum nostrum.

22 February

ASH WEDNESDAY

The journey of Lent is an exodus, an exodus from slavery to freedom. These forty days correspond to the forty years that God's people trekked through the desert to return to their homeland. How difficult it was to leave Egypt! It was more difficult for God's people to leave the Egypt of the heart, that Egypt they carried within them, than to leave the land of Egypt. It is hard to leave Egypt behind. During their journey, there was an ever-present temptation to yearn for leeks, to turn back, to cling to memories of the past or to this or that idol. So it is with us: our journey back to God is blocked by our unhealthy attachments, held back by the seductive snares of our sins, by the false security of money and appearances, by the paralysis of our discontents. To embark on this journey, we have to unmask these illusions.

(Pope Francis)

In the course of today's Mass, ashes are blessed and distributed. These are made from the olive branches or branches of other trees that were blessed the previous year.

Entrance Antiphon Ws 11:24,25,27

YOU are merciful to all, O Lord,
and despise nothing that you
   have made.
You overlook people's sins,
   to bring them to repentance,
and you spare them,
   for you are the Lord our God.

Ant. ad introitum

MISERERIS omnium, Domine,
et nihil odisti eorum
   quæ fecisti,
dissimulans peccata hominum
   propter pænitentiam
et parcens illis,
   quia tu es Dominus Deus noster.

The Penitential Act is omitted, and the Distribution of Ashes takes its place.

Collect

Grant, O Lord, that we may begin
   with holy fasting
this campaign of Christian service,
so that, as we take up battle
   against spiritual evils,
we may be armed with weapons
   of self-restraint.

Collecta

Concede nobis, Domine,
præsidia militiæ christianæ sanctis
   inchoare ieiuniis,
ut, contra spiritales
   nequitias pugnaturi,
continentiæ muniamur auxiliis.

Through our Lord Jesus Christ,
   your Son,
who lives and reigns with you
   in the unity of the Holy Spirit,
God, for ever and ever.

Per Dominum nostrum
   Iesum Christum Filium tuum,
qui tecum vivit et regnat
   in unitate Spiritus Sancti,
Deus, per omnia sæcula sæculorum.

FIRST READING

A reading from the prophet Joel   2:12-18

Let your hearts be broken, not your garments torn.

'Now, now – it is the Lord who speaks –
come back to me with all your heart,
fasting, weeping, mourning.'
Let your hearts be broken not your garments torn,
turn to the Lord your God again,
for he is all tenderness and compassion,
slow to anger, rich in graciousness,
and ready to relent.
Who knows if he will not turn again, will not relent,
will not leave a blessing as he passes,
oblation and libation
for the Lord your God?
Sound the trumpet in Sion!
Order a fast,
proclaim a solemn assembly,
call the people together,
summon the community,
assemble the elders,
gather the children,
even the infants at the breast.
Let the bridegroom leave his bedroom
and the bride her alcove.
Between vestibule and altar let the priests,
the ministers of the Lord, lament.
Let them say,
'Spare your people, Lord!
Do not make your heritage a thing of shame,
a byword for the nations.
Why should it be said among the nations,

"Where is their God?"'
Then the Lord, jealous on behalf of his land,
took pity on his people.

   The word of the Lord.

Responsorial Psalm   Ps 50:3-6,12-14,17. R. v.3

R. **Have mercy on us, O Lord, for we have sinned.**

   Have mercy on me, God, in your kindness.
   In your compassion blot out my offence.
   O wash me more and more from my guilt
   and cleanse me from my sin. R.

   My offences truly I know them;
   my sin is always before me.
   Against you, you alone, have I sinned:
   what is evil in your sight I have done. R.

   A pure heart create for me, O God,
   put a steadfast spirit within me.
   Do not cast me away from your presence,
   nor deprive me of your holy spirit. R.

   Give me again the joy of your help;
   with a spirit of fervour sustain me.
   O Lord, open my lips
   and my mouth shall declare your praise. R.

SECOND READING

A reading from the second letter of St Paul to the Corinthians   5:20-6:2
Be reconciled to God ... now is the favourable time.

We are ambassadors for Christ; it is as though God were appealing through
us, and the appeal that we make in Christ's name is: be reconciled to God.
For our sake God made the sinless one into sin, so that in him we might
become the goodness of God. As his fellow workers, we beg you once again
not to neglect the grace of God that you have received. For he says: At the
favourable time, I have listened to you, on the day of salvation I came to
your help. Well, now is the favourable time; this is the day of salvation.

   The word of the Lord.

Gospel Acclamation   Ps 50:12,14

R. **Praise to you, O Christ, king of eternal glory!**
A pure heart create for me, O God,
and give me again the joy of your help.
R. **Praise to you, O Christ, king of eternal glory!**

Or: Cf. Ps 94:8

R. **Praise to you, O Christ, king of eternal glory!**
Harden not your hearts today,
but listen to the voice of the Lord.
R. **Praise to you, O Christ, king of eternal glory!**

GOSPEL

A reading from holy Gospel according to Matthew   6:1-6,16-18

Your Father, who sees all that is done in secret, will reward you.

Jesus said to his disciples:

'Be careful not to parade your good deeds before men to attract their notice; by doing this you will lose all reward from your Father in heaven. So when you give alms, do not have it trumpeted before you; this is what the hypocrites do in the synagogues and in the streets to win men's admiration. I tell you solemnly, they have had their reward. But when you give alms, your left hand must not know what your right is doing; your almsgiving must be secret, and your Father who sees all that is done in secret will reward you.

'And when you pray, do not imitate the hypocrites: they love to say their prayers standing up in the synagogues and at the street corners for people to see them. I tell you solemnly, they have had their reward. But when you pray go to your private room and, when you have shut your door, pray to your Father who is in that secret place, and your Father who sees all that is done in secret will reward you.

'When you fast do not put on a gloomy look as the hypocrites do: they pull long faces to let men know they are fasting. I tell you solemnly, they have had their reward. But when you fast, put oil on your head and wash your face, so that no one will know you are fasting except your Father who sees all that is done in secret; and your Father who sees all that is done in secret will reward you.'

The Gospel of the Lord.

Blessing and Distribution of Ashes

After the Homily, the Priest, standing with hands joined, says:

Dear brethren (brothers and sisters),
    let us humbly ask God our Father
that he be pleased to bless
    with the abundance of his grace
these ashes, which we will put
    on our heads in penitence.

Deum Patrem, fratres carissimi,
    suppliciter deprecemur,
ut hos cineres, quos pænitentiæ causa
capitibus nostris imponimus,
ubertate gratiæ suæ
    benedicere dignetur.

After a brief prayer in silence, and, with hands extended, he continues:

O God, who are moved
    by acts of humility
and respond with forgiveness
    to works of penance,
lend your merciful ear to our prayers
and in your kindness pour out
    the grace of your ✠ blessing
on your servants who are marked
    with these ashes,
that, as they follow
    the Lenten observances,
they may be worthy to come
    with minds made pure
to celebrate the Paschal Mystery
    of your Son.
Who lives and reigns
    for ever and ever.

R. Amen.

Or:

O God, who desire not
    the death of sinners,
but their conversion,
mercifully hear our prayers
and in your kindness be pleased
    to bless ✠ these ashes,
which we intend to receive
    upon our heads,
that we, who acknowledge
    we are but ashes
and shall return to dust,

Deus, qui humiliatione flecteris
    et satisfactione placaris,
aurem tuæ pietatis precibus
    nostris inclina,
et super famulos tuos,
horum cinerum aspersione contactos,
gratiam tuæ benedictionis ✠
    effunde propitius,
ut, quadragesimalem
    observantiam prosequentes,
ad Filii tui paschale
    mysterium celebrandum
purificatis mentibus
    pervenire mereantur.
Per Christum Dominum nostrum.

R. Amen.

Vel:

Deus, qui non mortem
    sed conversionem
desideras peccatorum,
preces nostras clementer exaudi,
et hos cineres,
quos capitibus nostris
    imponi decernimus,
benedicere ✠ pro tua pietate dignare,
ut qui nos cinerem esse
et in pulverem
    reversuros cognoscimus,

may, through a steadfast
    observance of Lent,
gain pardon for sins
    and newness of life
after the likeness of your Risen Son.
Who lives and reigns
    for ever and ever.

R. Amen.

quadragesimalis exercitationis studio,
peccatorum veniam
et novitatem vitæ,
ad imaginem Filii tui resurgentis,
    consequi valeamus.
Qui vivit et regnat
    in sæcula sæculorum.

R. Amen.

He sprinkles the ashes with holy water, without saying anything.

Then the Priest places ashes on the head of all those present who come to him, and says to each one:

Repent, and believe in the Gospel.

Or:

Remember that you are dust,
    and to dust you shall return.

Pænitemini, et credite Evangelio.

Vel:

Memento, homo, quia pulvis es,
    et in pulverem reverteris.

Meanwhile, the following are sung:

Antiphon 1

Let us change our garments
    to sackcloth and ashes,
let us fast and weep before the Lord,
that our God, rich in mercy,
    might forgive us our sins.

Antiphona 1

Immutemur habitu,
    in cinere et cilicio,
ieiunemus,
    et ploremus ante Dominum,
quia multum misericors est
dimittere peccata nostra
    Deus noster.

Antiphon 2   Cf. Jl 2:17; Est 4:17

Let the priests,
    the ministers of the Lord,
stand between the porch and
    the altar and weep and cry out:
Spare, O Lord, spare your people;
do not close the mouths of those
    who sing your praise, O Lord

Antiphona 2

Inter vestibulum et altare
plorabunt sacerdotes
    ministri Domini,
et dicent: Parce, Domine,
    parce populo tuo,
et ne claudas ora canentium te,
    Domine.

Antiphon 3   Ps 50:3

Blot out my transgressions, O Lord.

Antiphona 3

Dele, Domine, iniquitatem meam.

This may be repeated after each verse of Psalm 50

(Have mercy on me, O God) . | Miserere mei, Deus.

Responsory Cf. Ba 3:2; Ps 78:9	Responsorium
R. Let us correct our faults which we have committed in ignorance, let us not be taken unawares by the day of our death, looking in vain for leisure to repent. * Hear us, O Lord, and show us your mercy, for we have sinned against you.	R. Emendemus in melius, quæ ignoranter peccavimus, ne subito præoccupati die mortis quæramus spatium pænitentiæ, et invenire non possimus. * Attende, Domine, et miserere, quia peccavimus tibi.
V. Help us, O God our Saviour; for the sake of your name, O Lord, set us free. * Hear us, O Lord. . .	V. Adiuva nos, Deus salutaris noster, et propter honorem nominis tui, Domine, libera nos. * Attende, Domine. . .

Another appropriate chant may also be sung.

After the distribution of ashes, the Priest washes his hands and proceeds to the Universal Prayer, and continues the Mass in the usual way.

The Creed is not said.

The Liturgy of the Eucharist

Prayer over the Offerings	Super oblata
As we solemnly offer the annual sacrifice for the beginning of Lent, we entreat you, O Lord, that, through works of penance and charity, we may turn away from harmful pleasures and, cleansed from our sins, may become worthy to celebrate devoutly the Passion of your Son. Who lives and reigns for ever and ever.	Sacrificium quadragesimalis initii sollemniter immolamus, te, Domine, deprecantes, ut per pænitentiæ caritatisque labores a noxiis voluptatibus temperemus, et, a peccatis mundati, ad celebrandam Filii tui passionem mereamur esse devoti. Qui vivit et regnet in sæcula sæculorum.

Preface III or IV of Lent, pp.50-52.

Communion Antiphon Cf. Ps 1:2-3 | Ant. ad communionem

He who ponders the law
of the Lord day and night
will yield fruit in due season.

Qui meditabitur in lege
Domini die ac nocte,
dabit fructum suum in tempore suo.

Prayer after Communion | Post communionem

May the Sacrament we have
received sustain us, O Lord,
that our Lenten fast may
be pleasing to you
and be for us a healing remedy.
Through Christ our Lord.

Percepta nobis, Domine,
præbeant sacramenta subsidium,
ut tibi grata sint nostra ieiunia,
et nobis proficiant ad medelam.
Per Christum Dominum nostrum.

For the dismissal, the Priest stands facing the people and, extending his hands over them, says this prayer:

Prayer over the People | Oratio super populum

Pour out a spirit of compunction,
O God,
on those who bow before
your majesty,
and by your mercy may they
merit the rewards you promise
to those who do penance.
Through Christ our Lord.

Super inclinantes se tuæ maiestati,
Deus,
spiritum compunctionis
propitius effunde,
et præmia pænitentibus repromissa
misericorditer consequi mereantur.
Per Christum Dominum nostrum.

The blessing and distribution of ashes may also take place outside Mass. In this case, the rite is preceded by a Liturgy of the Word, with the Entrance Antiphon, the Collect, and the readings with their chants as at Mass. Then there follow the Homily and the blessing and distribution of ashes. The rite is concluded with the Universal Prayer, the Blessing, and the Dismissal of the Faithful.

26 February

FIRST SUNDAY OF LENT

Jesus does not dialogue with the devil. Jesus responds to the devil with the Word of God, not with his own words. In temptation, we often begin to dialogue with temptation, to dialogue with the devil: "yes, I may do this..., then I will go to confession, then this, then that...". We must never dialogue with the devil. Jesus does two things with the devil: he either sends him away or, like in this case, he responds with the Word of God. Be attentive to this: never dialogue with temptation, never dialogue with the devil.

(Pope Francis)

Entrance Antiphon Cf. Ps 90:15-16

WHEN he calls on me,
    I will answer him;
I will deliver him
    and give him glory,
I will grant him length of days.

The Gloria in excelsis (Glory to God in the highest) is not said.

Collect

Grant, almighty God,
through the yearly observances
    of holy Lent,
that we may grow in understanding
of the riches hidden in Christ
and by worthy conduct pursue
    their effects.
Through our Lord Jesus Christ,
    your Son,
who lives and reigns with you
    in the unity of the Holy Spirit,
God, for ever and ever.

Ant. ad introitum

INVOCABIT me,
    et ego exaudiam eum;
eripiam eum, et glorificabo eum,
longitudine dierum
    adimplebo eum.

Collecta

Concede nobis, omnipotens Deus,
ut, per annua quadragesimalis
    exercitia sacramenti,
et ad intellegendum Christi
    proficiamus arcanum,
et effectus eius digna
    conversatione sectemur.
Per Dominum nostrum Iesum
    Christum Filium tuum,
qui tecum vivit et regnat
    in unitate Spiritus Sancti,
Deus, per omnia sæcula sæculorum.

FIRST READING

A reading from the book of Genesis   2:7-9; 3:1-7

The creation and sin of our first parents.

The Lord God fashioned man of dust from the soil. Then he breathed into his nostrils a breath of life, and thus man became a living being.

The Lord God planted a garden in Eden which is in the east, and there he put the man he had fashioned. The Lord God caused to spring up from the soil every kind of tree, enticing to look at and good to eat, with the tree of life and the tree of the knowledge of good and evil in the middle of the garden.

The serpent was the most subtle of all the wild beasts that the Lord God had made. It asked the woman, 'Did God really say you were not to eat from any of the trees in the garden?' The woman answered the serpent, 'We may eat the fruit of the trees in the garden. But of the fruit of the tree in the middle of the garden God said, "You must not eat it, nor touch it, under pain of death."' Then the serpent said to the woman, 'No! You will not die! God knows in fact that on the day you eat it your eyes will be opened and you will be like gods, knowing good and evil.' The woman saw that the tree was good to eat and pleasing to the eye, and that it was desirable for the knowledge that it could give. So she took some of its fruit and ate it. She gave some also to her husband who was with her, and he ate it. Then the eyes of both of them were opened and they realised that they were naked. So they sewed fig-leaves together to make themselves loin-cloths.

The word of the Lord.

Responsorial Psalm   Ps 50:3-6,12-14,17. R. Cf. v.3

R. **Have mercy on us, O Lord, for we have sinned.**

Have mercy on me, God, in your kindness.
In your compassion blot out my offence.
O wash me more and more from my guilt
and cleanse me from my sin. R.

My offences truly I know them;
my sin is always before me.
Against you, you alone, have I sinned;
what is evil in your sight I have done. R.

A pure heart create for me, O God,
put a steadfast spirit within me.
Do not cast me away from your presence,
nor deprive me of your holy spirit. R.

Give me again the joy of your help;
with a spirit of fervour sustain me.
O Lord, open my lips
and my mouth shall declare your praise. R.

SECOND READING

A reading from the letter of St Paul to the Romans   5:12-19

However great the number of sins committed, grace was even greater.

[Sin entered the world through one man, and through sin death, and thus death has spread through the whole human race because everyone has sinned.] Sin existed in the world long before the Law was given. There was no law and so no one could be accused of the sin of 'law-breaking', yet death reigned over all from Adam to Moses, even though their sin, unlike that of Adam, was not a matter of breaking a law.

Adam prefigured the One to come, but the gift itself considerably outweighed the fall. If it is certain that through one man's fall so many died, it is even more certain that divine grace, coming through the one man, Jesus Christ, came to so many as an abundant free gift. The results of the gift also outweigh the results of one man's sin: for after one single fall came judgement with a verdict of condemnation, now after many falls comes grace with its verdict of acquittal. [If it is certain that death reigned over everyone as the consequence of one man's fall, it is even more certain that one man, Jesus Christ, will cause everyone to reign in life who receives the free gift that he does not deserve, of being made righteous. Again, as one man's fall brought condemnation on everyone, so the good act of one man brings everyone life and makes them justified. As by one man's disobedience many were made sinners, so by one man's obedience many will be made righteous.

The word of the Lord.]

Shorter Form, verses 12,17-19. Read between [ ]

Gospel Acclamation   Mt 4:4

R. **Praise to you, O Christ, king of eternal glory!**
Man does not live on bread alone
but on every word that comes from the mouth of God.
R. **Praise to you, O Christ, king of eternal glory!**

GOSPEL

A reading from the holy Gospel according to Matthew   4:1-11

Jesus fasts for forty days and is tempted.

Jesus was led by the Spirit out into the wilderness to be tempted by the devil. He fasted for forty days and forty nights, after which he was very hungry, and the tempter came and said to him, 'If you are the Son of God, tell these stones to turn into loaves.' But he replied, 'Scripture says:

Man does not live on bread alone
but on every word that comes from the mouth of God.'

The devil then took him to the holy city and made him stand on the parapet of the Temple. 'If you are the Son of God' he said 'throw yourself down; for scripture says:

He will put you in his angels' charge,
and they will support you on their hands
in case you hurt your foot against a stone.'

Jesus said to him, 'Scripture also says:

You must not put the Lord your God to the test.'

Next, taking him to a very high mountain, the devil showed him all the kingdoms of the world and their splendour. 'I will give you all these' he said, 'if you fall at my feet and worship me.' Then Jesus replied, 'Be off, Satan! For scripture says:

You must worship the Lord your God,
and serve him alone.'

Then the devil left him, and angels appeared and looked after him.

The Gospel of the Lord.

The Creed is said.

Prayer over the Offerings	Super oblata
Give us the right dispositions, O Lord, we pray, to make these offerings, for with them we celebrate the beginning of this venerable and sacred time. Through Christ our Lord.	Fac nos, quæsumus, Domine, his muneribus offerendis convenienter aptari, quibus ipsius venerabilis sacramenti celebramus exordium. Per Christum Dominum nostrum.

Preface: The Temptation of the Lord.

It is truly right and just,
  our duty and our salvation,
always and everywhere
  to give you thanks,
Lord, holy Father,
  almighty and eternal God,
through Christ our Lord.

By abstaining forty long days
  from earthly food,
he consecrated through his fast
the pattern of our Lenten observance
and, by overturning all the snares
  of the ancient serpent,
taught us to cast out the leaven
  of malice,
so that, celebrating worthily
  the Paschal Mystery,
we might pass over at last
  to the eternal paschal feast.

And so, with the company
  of Angels and Saints,
we sing the hymn of your praise,
as without end we acclaim:

Holy, Holy, Holy Lord God of hosts...

Communion Antiphon   Mt 4:4

One does not live by bread alone,
but by every word that comes forth
  from the mouth of God.

Or: Cf. Ps 90:4

The Lord will conceal you
  with his pinions,
and under his wings you will trust.

Praefatio: De tentatione Domini.

Vere dignum et iustum est,
  aequum et salutare,
nos tibi semper et ubique
  gratias agere:
Domine, sancte Pater, omnipotens
  aeterne Deus:
per Christum Dominum nostrum:

Qui quadraginta diebus,
terrenis abstinens alimentis,
formam huius observantiae
  ieiunio dedicavit,
et, omnes evertens antiqui
  serpentis insidias,
fermentum malitiae nos
  docuit superare,
ut, paschale mysterium dignis
  mentibus celebrantes,
ad pascha demum
  perpetuum transeamus.

Et ideo, cum Angelorum
  atque Sanctorum turba,
hymnum laudis tibi canimus,
  sine fine dicentes:

Sanctus, Sanctus, Sanctus. . .

Ant. ad communionem

Non in solo pane vivit homo,
sed in omni verbo quod procedit
  de ore Dei.

Vel:

Scapulis suis obumbrabit
  tibi Dominus,
et sub pennis eius sperabis.

Prayer after Communion

Renewed now with heavenly bread,
by which faith is nourished,
    hope increased,
and charity strengthened,
we pray, O Lord,
that we may learn to hunger
    for Christ,
the true and living Bread,
and strive to live by every word
which proceeds from your mouth.
Through Christ our Lord.

Post communionem

Cælesti pane refecti,
quo fides alitur, spes provehitur
    et caritas roboratur,
quæsumus, Domine,
ut ipsum, qui est panis vivus
    et verus, esurire discamus,
et in omni verbo,
    quod procedit de ore tuo,
vivere valeamus.
Per Christum Dominum nostrum.

Prayer over the People

May bountiful blessing, O Lord,
    we pray,
come down upon your people,
that hope may grow in tribulation,
virtue be strengthened in temptation,
and eternal redemption be assured.
Through Christ our Lord.

Oratio super populum

Super populum tuum,
    Domine, quæsumus,
benedictio copiosa descendat,
ut spes in tribulatione succrescat,
virtus in tentatione firmetur,
æterna redemptio tribuatur.
Per Christum Dominum nostrum.

In Wales

1 March

SAINT DAVID, BISHOP, PATRON OF WALES

Saint David was one of the great saints of the sixth century, that golden age of saints and missionaries in these isles, and he was thus a founder of the Christian culture which lies at the root of modern Europe. David's preaching was simple yet profound: his dying words to his monks were, "Be joyful, keep the faith, and do the little things". It is the little things that reveal our love for the one who loved us first (Cf. 1 Jn 4:19) and that bind people into a community of faith, love and service. May Saint David's message, in all its simplicity and richness, continue to resound today, drawing the hearts of people to renewed love for Christ and his Church.

(Pope Benedict XVI)

Solemnity

Entrance Antiphon   Is 52:7

How beautiful upon the mountains are the feet of him
who brings glad tidings of peace,
bearing good news, announcing salvation!

The Gloria in excelsis (Glory to God in the highest) is said.

Collect

O God, who graciously bestowed on your Bishop Saint David of Wales
the virtue of wisdom and the gift of eloquence
and made him an example of prayer and pastoral zeal,
grant that, through his intercession
your Church may ever prosper and render you joyful praise.
Through our Lord Jesus Christ, your Son,
who lives and reigns with you in the unity of the Holy Spirit,
God, for ever and ever.

Readings such as the following may be chosen from the Common of Pastors, or from the Common of Holy Men and Women. First readings outside Easter are always from the Old Testament.

FIRST READING

A reading from the book of Genesis   12:1-4

The call of Abraham, the father the People of God.

The Lord said to Abram, 'Leave your country, your family and your father's house, for the land I will show you. I will make you a great nation; I will bless you and make your name so famous that it will be used as a blessing.

'I will bless those who bless you:
I will curse those who slight you.
All the tribes of the earth
shall bless themselves by you.'

So Abram went as the Lord told him.

The word of the Lord.

Responsorial Psalm   Ps 1. R. Ps 39:5

R. **Happy the man who has placed
his trust in the Lord.**

Happy indeed is the man
who follows not the counsel of the wicked;
nor lingers in the way of sinners
nor sits in the company of scorners,
but whose delight is the law of the Lord
and who ponders his law day and night. R.

He is like a tree that is planted
beside the flowing waters,
that yields its fruit in due season
and whose leaves shall never fade;
and all that he does shall prosper. R.

Not so are the wicked, not so!
For they like winnowed chaff
shall be driven away by the wind;
for the Lord guards the way of the just
but the way of the wicked leads to doom. R.

SECOND READING

A reading from the letter of St Paul to the Philippians 3:8-14

I am racing for the finish, for the prize to which God calls us upwards to receive in Christ Jesus.

I believe nothing can happen that will outweigh the supreme advantage of knowing Christ Jesus my Lord. For him I have accepted the loss of everything, and I look on everything as so much rubbish if only I can have Christ and be given a place in him. I am no longer trying for perfection by my own efforts, the perfection that comes from the Law, but I want only the perfection that comes through faith in Christ, and is from God and based on faith. All I want is to know Christ and the power of his resurrection and to share his sufferings by reproducing the pattern of his death. That is the way I can hope to take my place in the resurrection of the dead. Not that I have become perfect yet: I have not yet won, but I am still running, trying to capture the prize for which Christ Jesus captured me. I can assure you my brothers, I am far from thinking that I have already won. All I can say is that I forget the past and I strain ahead for what is still to come; I am racing for the finish, for the prize to which God calls us upwards to receive in Christ Jesus.

The word of the Lord.

Gospel Acclamation Jn 8:31-32

R. **Glory and praise to you, O Christ!**
If you make my word your home
you will indeed be my disciples,
and you will learn the truth, says the Lord.
R. **Glory and praise to you, O Christ!**

GOSPEL

A reading from the holy Gospel according to Matthew 5:13-16

You are the light of the world.

Jesus said to his disciples: 'You are the salt of the earth. But if salt becomes tasteless, what can make it salty again? It is good for nothing, and can only be thrown out to be trampled underfoot by men.

'You are the light of the world. A city built on a hill-top cannot be hidden. No one lights a lamp to put it under a tub; they put it on the lamp-stand where it shines for everyone in the house. In the same way your light must shine in the sight of men, so that, seeing your good works, they may give the praise to your Father in heaven.'

The Gospel of the Lord.

The Creed is said.

Prayer over the Offerings

Look with favour, O Lord, we pray,
on the offerings we set upon this sacred altar
on the feast day of the Bishop Saint David,
that, bestowing on us your pardon,
our oblations may give honour to your name.
Through Christ our Lord.

Communion Antiphon   Cf. 1 Co 1:23-24

We proclaim Christ crucified,
Christ, the power of God, and the wisdom of God.

Prayer after Communion

We pray, almighty God,
that we, who are fortified by the power of this Sacrament,
may learn through the example of your Bishop Saint David
to seek you always above all things
and to bear in this world the likeness of the New Man.
Who lives and reigns for ever and ever.

5 March

SECOND SUNDAY OF LENT

To be witnesses to Jesus is a gift we have not deserved; we may feel inadequate but we cannot back out with the excuse of our incapacity. We have not been on Mount Tabor, we have not seen with our own eyes the face of Jesus shining like the sun. However, we too were given the Word of Salvation, faith was given to us, and we have experienced the joy of meeting Jesus in different ways. Jesus also says to us: "Rise, and have no fear". In this world, marked by selfishness and greed, the light of God is obscured by the worries of everyday life. We often say: I do not have time to pray, I am unable to carry out a service in the parish, to respond to the requests of others...But we must not forget that the Baptism and Confirmation we have received has made us witnesses, not because of our ability, but as a result of the gift of the Spirit.

(Pope Francis)

Entrance Antiphon   Cf. Ps 26:8-9

OF you my heart has spoken:
Seek his face.
It is your face, O Lord, that I seek;
   hide not your face from me.

Or: Cf. Ps 24:6,2,22

Remember your compassion,
   O Lord,
and your merciful love,
   for they are from of old.
Let not our enemies exult over us.
Redeem us, O God of Israel,
   from all our distress.

Ant. ad introitum

TIBI dixit cor meum quæsivi
  vultum tuum,
vultum tuum, Domine, requiram.
Ne avertas faciem tuam a me.

Vel:

Reminiscere miserationum tuarum,
   Domine,
et misericordiæ tuæ,
   quæ a sæculo sunt.
Ne umquam dominentur nobis
   inimici nostri;
libera nos, Deus Israel,
   ex omnibus angustiis nostris.

The Gloria in excelsis (Glory to God in the highest) is not said.

Collect

O God, who have commanded us
to listen to your beloved Son,
be pleased, we pray,
to nourish us inwardly by your word,
that, with spiritual sight made pure,
we may rejoice to behold your glory.

Collecta

Deus, qui nobis dilectum Filium
   tuum audire præcepisti,
verbo tuo interius nos
   pascere digneris,
ut, spiritali purificato intuitu,
gloriæ tuæ lætemur aspectu.

Through our Lord Jesus Christ, your Son, who lives and reigns with you in the unity of the Holy Spirit, God, for ever and ever.	Per Dominum nostrum Iesum Christum Filium tuum, qui tecum vivit et regnat in unitate Spiritus Sancti, Deus, per omnia sæcula sæculorum.

FIRST READING

A reading from the book of Genesis   12:1-4

The call of Abraham, the father the People of God.

The Lord said to Abram, 'Leave your country, your family and your father's house, for the land I will show you. I will make you a great nation; I will bless you and make your name so famous that it will be used as a blessing.

'I will bless those who bless you:
I will curse those who slight you.
All the tribes of the earth
shall bless themselves by you.'

So Abram went as the Lord told him.

The word of the Lord.

Responsorial Psalm   Ps 32:4-5,18-20,22. R. v.22

R. **May your love be upon us, O Lord,
as we place all our hope in you.**

The word of the Lord is faithful
and all his works to be trusted.
The Lord loves justice and right
and fills the earth with his love. R.

The Lord looks on those who revere him,
on those who hope in his love,
to rescue their souls from death,
to keep them alive in famine. R.

Our soul is waiting for the Lord.
The Lord is our help and our shield.
May your love be upon us, O Lord,
as we place all our hope in you. R.

SECOND READING

A reading from the second letter of St Paul to Timothy   1:8-10

God calls and enlightens us.

With me, bear the hardships for the sake of the Good News, relying on the power of God who has saved us and called us to be holy - not because of anything we ourselves have done but for his own purpose and by his own grace. This grace had already been granted to us, in Christ Jesus, before the beginning of time, but it has only been revealed by the Appearing of our saviour Christ Jesus. He abolished death, and he has proclaimed life and immortality through the Good News.

The word of the Lord.

Gospel Acclamation   Mt 17:5

R. **Glory and praise to you, O Christ!**
From the bright cloud the Father's voice was heard:
'This is my Son, the Beloved. Listen to him.'
R. **Glory and praise to you, O Christ!**

GOSPEL

A reading from the holy Gospel according to Matthew   17:1-9

His face shone like the sun.

Jesus took with him Peter and James and his brother John and led them up a high mountain where they could be alone. There in their presence he was transfigured; his face shone like the sun and his clothes became as white as the light. Suddenly Moses and Elijah appeared to them; they were talking with him. Then Peter spoke to Jesus. 'Lord,' he said 'it is wonderful for us to be here; if you wish, I will make three tents here, one for you, one for Moses and one for Elijah.' He was still speaking when suddenly a bright cloud covered them with shadow, and from the cloud there came a voice which said, 'This is my Son, the Beloved; he enjoys my favour. Listen to him.' When they heard this, the disciples fell on their faces, overcome with fear. But Jesus came up and touched them. 'Stand up,' he said 'do not be afraid.' And when they raised their eyes they saw no one but only Jesus.

As they came down from the mountain Jesus gave them this order. 'Tell no one about the vision until the Son of Man has risen from the dead.'

The Gospel of the Lord.

The Creed is said.

Prayer over the Offerings

May this sacrifice, O Lord, we pray,
cleanse us of our faults
and sanctify your faithful
    in body and mind
for the celebration
    of the paschal festivities.
Through Christ our Lord.

Preface: The Transfiguration
of the Lord.

It is truly right and just,
    our duty and our salvation,
always and everywhere
    to give you thanks,
Lord, holy Father,
    almighty and eternal God,
through Christ our Lord.

For after he had told the disciples
    of his coming Death,
on the holy mountain
    he manifested to them his glory,
to show, even by the testimony
    of the law and the prophets,
that the Passion leads to the glory
    of the Resurrection.

And so, with the Powers of heaven,
we worship you constantly on earth,
and before your majesty
without end we acclaim:

Holy, Holy, Holy Lord God of hosts...

Super oblata

Hæc hostia, Domine, quæsumus,
    emundet nostra delicta,
et ad celebranda festa paschalia
fidelium tuorum corpora
    mentesque sanctificet.
Per Christum Dominum nostrum.

Praefatio: De transfiguratione Domini.

Vere dignum et iustum est,
    aequum et salutare,
nos tibi semper et ubique
    gratias agere:
Domine, sancte Pater,
    omnipotens aeterne Deus:
per Christum Dominum nostrum:

Qui, propria morte
    praenuntiata discipulis,
in monte sancto suam eis
    aperuit claritatem,
ut per passionem, etiam lege
    prophetisque testantibus,
ad gloriam resurrectionis
    perveniri constaret.

Et ideo, cum caelorum Virtutibus,
in terris te iugiter celebramus,
maiestati tuae sine fine clamantes:

Sanctus, Sanctus, Sanctus. . .

Communion Antiphon   Mt 17:5

This is my beloved Son,
  with whom I am well pleased;
listen to him.

Prayer after Communion

As we receive these
  glorious mysteries,
we make thanksgiving to you,
  O Lord,
for allowing us while still on earth
to be partakers even now
  of the things of heaven.
Through Christ our Lord.

Prayer over the People

Bless your faithful, we pray, O Lord,
with a blessing that endures for ever,
and keep them faithful
to the Gospel of your
  Only Begotten Son,
so that they may always desire
  and at last attain
that glory whose beauty he showed
  in his own Body,
to the amazement of his Apostles.
Through Christ our Lord.

Ant. ad communionem

Hic est Filius meus dilectus,
in quo mihi bene complacui;
ipsum audite.

Post communionem

Percipientes, Domine,
  gloriosa mysteria,
gratias tibi referre satagimus,
quod, in terra positos,
iam cælestium præstas
  esse participes.
Per Christum Dominum nostrum.

Oratio super populum

Benedic, Domine, fideles tuos
  benedictione perpetua,
et fac eos Unigeniti tui Evangelio
  sic adhærere,
ut ad illam gloriam, cuius in se
  speciem Apostolis ostendit,
et suspirare iugiter et feliciter
  valeant pervenire.
Per Christum Dominum nostrum.

12 March

THIRD SUNDAY OF LENT

The Gospel passage from today tells us of Jesus's meeting with a Samaritan woman. Like the Samaritan woman, whoever personally encounters the living Jesus feels the need to talk about him to others, so that everyone might reach the point of proclaiming that Jesus "is truly the saviour of the world". Generated to new life through Baptism, we too are called to witness the life and hope that are within us. If our quest and our thirst are thoroughly quenched in Christ, we will manifest that salvation is not found in the "things" of this world, which ultimately produce drought, but in he who has loved us and will always love us: Jesus, our Saviour, in the living water, that he offers us.

(Pope Francis)

Entrance Antiphon Cf. Ps 24:15-16

MY eyes are always on the Lord,
for he rescues my feet
from the snare.
Turn to me and have mercy on me,
for I am alone and poor.

Or: Cf. Ezk 36:23-26

When I prove my holiness
    among you,
I will gather you from all
    the foreign lands;
and I will pour clean water upon you
and cleanse you from all
    your impurities,
and I will give you a new spirit,
    says the Lord.

Ant. ad introitum

OCULI mei semper
ad Dominum,
quia ipse evellet de laqueo
    pedes meos.
Respice in me et miserere mei,
quoniam unicus et pauper sum ego.

Vel:

Cum sanctificatus fuero in vobis,
congregabo vos de universis terris;
et effundam super vos
    aquam mundam,
et mundabimini ab omnibus
    inquinamentis vestris,
et dabo vobis spiritum novum,
    dicit Dominus.

The Gloria in excelsis (Glory to God in the highest) is not said.

Collect

O God, author of every mercy
and of all goodness,
who in fasting, prayer and almsgiving
have shown us a remedy for sin,
look graciously on this confession
of our lowliness,
that we, who are bowed down
by our conscience,
may always be lifted up
by your mercy.
Through our Lord Jesus Christ,
your Son,
who lives and reigns with you
in the unity of the Holy Spirit,
God, for ever and ever.

Collecta

Deus, omnium misericordiarum
et totius bonitatis auctor,
qui peccatorum remedia in ieiuniis,
orationibus et eleemosynis
demonstrasti,
hanc humilitatis nostræ
confessionem propitius intuere,
ut, qui inclinamur conscientia nostra,
tua semper misericordia sublevemur.
Per Dominum nostrum Iesum
Christum Filium tuum,
qui tecum vivit et regnat
in unitate Spiritus Sancti,
Deus, per omnia sæcula sæculorum.

FIRST READING

A reading from the book of Exodus   17:3-7

Give us water to drink.

Tormented by thirst, the people complained against Moses. 'Why did you bring us out of Egypt?' they said. 'Was it so that I should die of thirst, my children too, and my cattle?' Moses appealed to the Lord. 'How am I to deal with this people?' he said. 'A little more and they will stone me!' The Lord said to Moses, 'Take with you some of the elders of Israel and move on to the forefront of the people; take in your hand the staff with which you struck the river, and go. I shall be standing before you there on the rock, at Horeb. You must strike the rock, and water will flow from it for the people to drink.' This is what Moses did, in the sight of the elders of Israel. The place was named Massah and Meribah because of the grumbling of the sons of Israel and because they put the Lord to the test by saying, 'Is the Lord with us, or not?'

The word of the Lord.

Responsorial Psalm   Ps 94:1-2,6-9. R. v.8

R. O that today you would listen to his voice:
   'Harden not your hearts.'

   Come, ring out our joy to the Lord;
   hail the rock who saves us.
   Let us come before him, giving thanks,
   with songs let us hail the Lord. R.

Come in; let us bow and bend low;
let us kneel before the God who made us
for he is our God and we
the people who belong to his pasture,
the flock that is led by his hand. R.

O that today you would listen to his voice!
'Harden not your hearts as at Meribah,
as on that day at Massah in the desert
when your fathers put me to the test;
when they tried me, though they saw my work.' R.

R. **O that today you would listen to his voice:**
  'Harden not your hearts.'

SECOND READING

A reading from the letter of St Paul to the Romans   5:1-2,5-8

The love of God has been poured into our hearts by the Holy Spirit which has been given us.

Through our Lord Jesus Christ by faith we are judged righteous and at peace with God, since it is by faith and through Jesus that we have entered this state of grace in which we can boast about looking forward to God's glory. This hope is not deceptive, because the love of God has been poured into our hearts by the Holy Spirit which has been given us. We were still helpless when at his appointed moment Christ died for sinful men. It is not easy to die even for a good man – though of course for someone really worthy, a man might be prepared to die – but what proves that God loves us is that Christ died for us while we were still sinners.

The word of the Lord.

Gospel Acclamation   Cf. Jn 4:42,15

R. **Glory to you, O Christ, you are the Word of God!**
Lord, you are really the saviour of the world;
give me the living water, so that I may never get thirsty.
R. **Glory to you, O Christ, you are the Word of God!**

GOSPEL

A reading from the holy Gospel according to John   4:5-42

A spring of water welling up to eternal life.

[Jesus came to the Samaritan town called Sychar, near the land that Jacob gave to his son Joseph. Jacob's well is there and Jesus, tired by the journey, sat straight down by the well. It was about the sixth hour. When a Samaritan woman came to draw water, Jesus said to her, 'Give me a drink.'

His disciples had gone into the town to buy food. The Samaritan woman said to him, 'What? You are a Jew and you ask me, a Samaritan for a drink?' – Jews in fact, do not associate with Samaritans. Jesus replied:

> 'If you only knew what God is offering
> and who it is that is saying to you:
> Give me a drink,
> you would have been the one to ask,
> and he would have given you living water.'

'You have no bucket, sir,' she answered, 'and the well is deep: how could you get this living water? Are you a greater man than our father Jacob who gave us this well and drank from it himself with his sons and his cattle?' Jesus replied:

> 'Whoever drinks this water
> will get thirsty again;
> but anyone who drinks the water that I shall give
> will never be thirsty again:
> the water that I shall give
> will turn into a spring inside him, welling up to eternal life.'

'Sir,' said the woman, 'give me some of that water, so that I may never get thirsty and never have to come here again to draw water.'] 'Go and call your husband' said Jesus to her 'and come back here.' The woman answered, 'I have no husband.' He said to her, 'You are right to say, "I have no husband"; for although you have had five, the one you have now is not your husband. You spoke the truth there.' ['I see you are a prophet, sir' said the woman. 'Our fathers worshipped on this mountain, while you say that Jerusalem is the place where one ought to worship.' Jesus said:

> 'Believe me, woman, the hour is coming
> when you will worship the Father
> neither on this mountain nor in Jerusalem.
> You worship what you do not know;
> we worship what we do know;
> for salvation comes from the Jews.
> But the hour will come – in fact it is here already –
> when true worshippers will worship the Father in spirit and truth:
> that is the kind of worshipper
> the Father wants.
> God is spirit,
> and those who worship
> must worship in spirit and truth.'

The woman said to him, 'I know that Messiah – that is, Christ – is coming; and when he comes he will tell us everything.' 'I who am speaking to you,' said Jesus 'I am he.']

At this point his disciples returned, and were surprised to find him speaking to a woman, though none of them asked, 'What do you want from her?' or, 'Why are you talking to her?' The woman put down her water jar and hurried back to the town to tell the people, 'Come and see a man who has told me everything I ever did; I wonder if he is the Christ?' This brought people out of the town and they started walking towards him.

Meanwhile, the disciples were urging him, 'Rabbi, do have something to eat'; but he said, 'I have food to eat that you do not know about.' So the disciples asked one another, 'Has someone been bringing him food?' But Jesus said:

'My food
is to do the will of the one who sent me,
and to complete his work.
Have you not got a saying:
Four months and then the harvest?
Well, I tell you:
Look around you, look at the fields;
already they are white, ready for harvest!
Already the reaper is being paid his wages,
already he is bringing in the grain for eternal life,
and thus sower and reaper rejoice together.
For here the proverb holds good:
one sows, another reaps;
I sent you to reap
a harvest you had not worked for.
Others worked for it;
and you have come into the rewards of their trouble.'

[Many Samaritans of that town had believed in him on the strength of the woman's testimony when she said, 'He told me all I have ever done,' so, when the Samaritans came up to him, they begged him to stay with them. He stayed for two days, and when he spoke to them many more came to believe; and they said to the woman, 'Now we no longer believe because of what you told us; we have heard him ourselves and we know that he really is the saviour of the world.'

The Gospel of the Lord.]

Shorter Form, verses 5-15,19-26,39-42. Read between [ ]

The Creed is said.

Prayer over the Offerings

Be pleased, O Lord,
    with these sacrificial offerings,
and grant that we who beseech
    pardon for our own sins,
may take care to forgive
    our neighbour.
Through Christ our Lord.

Super oblata

His sacrificiis, Domine,
    concede placatus,
ut, qui propriis oramus
    absolvi delictis,
fraterna dimittere studeamus.
Per Christum Dominum nostrum.

Preface: The Samaritan Woman.

It is truly right and just,
    our duty and our salvation,
always and everywhere
    to give you thanks,
Lord, holy Father,
    almighty and eternal God,
through Christ our Lord.

For when he asked the Samaritan
    woman for water to drink,
he had already created
    the gift of faith within her
and so ardently did he thirst
    for her faith,
that he kindled in her the fire
    of divine love.

And so we, too, give you thanks
and with the Angels
praise your mighty deeds,
    as we acclaim:

Holy, Holy, Holy Lord God of hosts...

Praefatio: De Samaritana.

Vere dignum et iustum est,
    aequum et salutare,
nos tibi semper et ubique
    gratias agere:
Domine, sancte Pater,
    omnipotens aeterne Deus:
per Christum Dominum nostrum:

Qui, dum aquae sibi petiit potum
    a Samaritana praeberi,
iam in ea fidei donum ipse creaverat,
et ita eius fidem sitire dignatus est,
ut ignem in illa divini
    amoris accenderet.

Unde et nos tibi gratias agimus,
et tuas virtutes cum Angelis
    praedicamus, dicentes:

Sanctus, Sanctus, Sanctus. . .

Communion Antiphon Jn 4:13-14

For anyone who drinks it,
    says the Lord,
the water I shall give will become
    in him
a spring welling up to eternal life.

Ant. ad communionem

Qui biberit aquam, quam ego dabo
    ei, dicit Dominus,
fiet in eo fons aquæ salientis
    in vitam æternam.

Prayer after Communion

As we receive the pledge
of things yet hidden in heaven
and are nourished while still
   on earth
with the Bread that comes
   from on high,
we humbly entreat you, O Lord,
that what is being brought about
   in us in mystery
may come to true completion.
Through Christ our Lord.

Post communionem

Sumentes pignus cælestis arcani,
et in terra positi iam superno
   pane satiati,
te, Domine, supplices deprecamur,
ut, quod in nobis mysterio geritur,
   opere impleatur.
Per Christum Dominum nostrum.

Prayer over the People

Direct, O Lord, we pray,
   the hearts of your faithful,
and in your kindness grant
   your servants this grace:
that, abiding in the love of you
   and their neighbour,
they may fulfil the whole
   of your commands.
Through Christ our Lord.

Oratio super populum

Rege, Domine, quæsumus,
   tuorum corda fidelium,
et servis tuis hanc gratiam
   largire propitius,
ut in tui et proximi
   dilectione manentes
plenitudinem mandatorum
   tuorum adimpleant.
Per Christum Dominum nostrum.

In Ireland

17 March

SAINT PATRICK, BISHOP, PATRON OF IRELAND

From his days as a shepherd boy at Slemish right up to his death at Saul, Patrick was a witness to Jesus Christ. Not far from this spot, on the Hill of Slane, it is said that he lit, for the first time in Ireland, the Paschal Fire, so that the light of Christ might shine forth on all of Ireland and unite all of its people in the love of the one Jesus Christ. He is the Lord of history, the Light of the world, the Hope of the future of all humanity. In the words of the Easter Liturgy, celebrated for the first time in Ireland by Saint Patrick on the Hill of Slane, we greet Christ today: he is the Alpha and the Omega, the beginning of all things and their end. All time is his and all the ages. To him be glory for ever and ever. Lumen Christi: Deo gratias. That he might be faithful to the

end of his life to the light of Christ was Saint Patrick's prayer for himself. That
the people of Ireland might remain faithful always to the light of Christ was
his constant prayer for the Irish.

(Pope St John Paul II)

Solemnity

Entrance Antiphon   Gn 12:1-2

GO from your country and your kindred and your father's house to
the land that I will show you.
I will make of you a great nation, and I will bless you,
and make your name great, so that you will be a blessing.

The Gloria in excelsis (Glory to God in the highest) is said.

Collect

Lord, through the work of Saint Patrick in Ireland
we have come to acknowledge the mystery of the one true God
and give thanks for our salvation in Christ;
grant by his prayers
that we who celebrate this festival
may keep alive the fire of faith he kindled.
Through our Lord Jesus Christ, your Son,
who lives and reigns with you in the unity of the Holy Spirit,
God, for ever and ever.

FIRST READING

A reading from the book of Ecclesiasticus   39:6-10

His memory will not disappear, generation after generation his name will live.

If it is the will of the great Lord,
the scholar will be filled with the spirit of understanding,
he will shower forth words of wisdom,
and in prayer give thanks to the Lord.
He will grow upright in purpose and learning,
he will ponder the Lord's hidden mysteries.
He will display the instruction he has received,
taking his pride in the Law of the Lord's covenant.
Many will praise his understanding,
and it will never be forgotten.
His memory will not disappear,
generation after generation his name will live.
Nations will proclaim his wisdom,
the assembly will celebrate his praises.

The word of the Lord.

Responsorial Psalm   Ps 115:12-19. R. 12

R. **How can I repay the Lord for his goodness to me?**

How can I repay the Lord
for his goodness to me?
The cup of salvation I will raise;
I will call on the Lord's name. R.

My vows to the Lord I will fulfil
before all his people.
O precious in the eyes of the Lord
is the death of his faithful. R.

Your servant, O Lord, your servant am I;
you have loosened my bonds.
A thanksgiving sacrifice I make;
I will call on the Lord's name. R.

My vows to the Lord I will fulfil
before all his people,
in the courts of the house of the Lord,
in your midst, O Jerusalem. R.

SECOND READING

A reading from the second letter of St Paul to Timothy   4:1-8

Refute falsehood, correct error, call to obedience - but do all with patience and with the intention of teaching.

Before God and before Christ Jesus who is to be judge of the living and the dead, I put this duty to you, in the name of his Appearing and of his kingdom: proclaim the message and, welcome or unwelcome, insist on it. Refute falsehood, correct error, call to obedience – but do all with patience and with the intention of teaching. The time is sure to come when, far from being content with sound teaching, people will be avid for the latest novelty and collect themselves a whole series of teachers according to their own tastes; and then, instead of listening to the truth, they will turn to myths. Be careful always to choose the right course; be brave under trials; make the preaching of the Good News your life's work, in thoroughgoing service.

As for me, my life is already being poured away as a libation, and the time has come for me to be gone. I have fought the good fight to the end; I have run the race to the finish; I have kept the faith; all there is to come now is the crown of righteousness reserved for me, which the Lord, the righteous judge, will give me on that Day; and not only to me but to all those who have longed for his Appearing.

The word of the Lord.

Gospel Acclamation   Jm 1:21

R. **Glory to you, O Christ, you are the Word of God!**
Accept and submit to the word which has been planted in you
and can save your souls.
R. **Glory to you, O Christ, you are the Word of God!**

GOSPEL

A reading from the holy Gospel according to Matthew   13:24-32
It is the smallest of all seeds, but when it has grown it is the greatest of shrubs.

Jesus put a parable before the crowds, 'The kingdom of heaven may be
compared to a man who sowed good seed in his field. While everybody was
asleep his enemy came, sowed darnel all among the wheat, and made off.
When the new wheat sprouted and ripened, the darnel appeared as well.
The owner's servants went to him and said, "Sir, was it not good seed that
you sowed in your field? If so, where does the darnel come from?" "Some
enemy has done this" he answered. And the servants said, "Do you want
us to go and weed it out?" But he said, "No, because when you weed out
the darnel you might pull up the wheat with it. Let them both grow till the
harvest; and at harvest time I shall say to the reapers: First collect the darnel
and tie it in bundles to be burnt, then gather the wheat into my barn."'

He put another parable before them, 'The kingdom of heaven is like a
mustard seed which a man took and sowed in his field. It is the smallest
of all the seeds, but when it has grown it is the biggest shrub of all and
becomes a tree so that the birds of the air come and shelter in its branches.'

The Gospel of the Lord.

The Creed is said.

Prayer over the Offerings

Lord, accept this pure sacrifice
which, through the labours of Saint Patrick,
your grateful people make
to the glory of your name.
Through Christ our Lord.

Preface

It is truly right and just, our duty and our salvation,
always and everywhere to give you thanks,
Lord, holy Father, almighty and eternal God,
and proclaim your greatness with due praise
as we honour Saint Patrick.

For you drew him through daily prayer
in captivity and hardship
to know you as a loving Father.

You chose him out of all the world
to return to the land of his captors,
that they might acknowledge Jesus Christ, their Redeemer.

In the power of your Spirit you directed his paths
to win the sons and daughters of the Irish
to the service of the Triune God.

And so, with the Angels and Archangels,
and with the great multitude of the Saints,
we sing the hymn of your praise, as without end we acclaim:

Holy, Holy, Holy Lord God of hosts ...

Communion Antiphon   Cf. Mt 8:11

Many will come from east and west
and sit down with Abraham, Isaac and Jacob
at the feast in the Kingdom of Heaven, says the Lord.

Prayer after Communion

Strengthen us, O Lord, by this sacrament
so that we may profess the faith taught by Saint Patrick
and to proclaim it in our way of living.
Through Christ our Lord.

Solemn Blessing

May God the Father, who called us together
to celebrate this feast of Saint Patrick,
bless you, protect you and keep you faithful.

R. **Amen.**

May Christ the Lord, the High King of Heaven,
be near you at all times and shield you from evil.

R. **Amen.**

May the Holy Spirit, who is the source of all holiness,
make you rich in the love of God's people.

R. **Amen.**

And may the blessing of almighty God,
the Father, and the Son, ✠ and the Holy Spirit,
come down on you and remain with you for ever.

R. **Amen.**

19 March

FOURTH SUNDAY OF LENT

With the light of faith he who was blind discovers his new identity. He is no longer a beggar marginalised by the community; he is no longer a slave to blindness and prejudice. His path of enlightenment is a metaphor for the path of liberation from sin to which we are called. Sin is like a dark veil that covers our face and prevents us from clearly seeing ourselves and the world; the Lord's forgiveness takes away this blanket of shadow and darkness and gives us new light. The healed blind man, who now sees both with the eyes of the body and with those of the soul, is the image of every baptised person, who immersed in grace has been pulled out of the darkness and placed in the light of faith. But it is not enough to receive the light, one must become light. Each one of us is called to receive the divine light in order to manifest it with our whole life.

(Pope Francis)

Entrance Antiphon Cf. Is 66:10-11	Ant. ad introitum

REJOICE, Jerusalem,
and all who love her.
Be joyful, all who were
    in mourning;
exult and be satisfied at her
    consoling breast.
	LÆTARE, Ierusalem,
	et conventum facite,
	    omnes qui diligitis eam;
	gaudete cum lætitia,
	    qui in tristitia fuistis,
	ut exsultetis, et satiemini ab
	    uberibus consolationis vestræ.

The Gloria in excelsis (Glory to God in the highest) is not said.

Collect	Collecta

O God, who through your Word
reconcile the human race
    to yourself in a wonderful way,
grant, we pray,
that with prompt devotion
    and eager faith
the Christian people may hasten
toward the solemn celebrations
    to come.
Through our Lord Jesus Christ,
    your Son,
who lives and reigns with you
    in the unity of the Holy Spirit,
God, for ever and ever.
	Deus, qui per Verbum tuum
	humani generis reconciliationem
	    mirabiliter operaris,
	præsta, quæsumus,
	    ut populus christianus
	prompta devotione et alacri fide
	ad ventura sollemnia valeat festinare.
	Per Dominum nostrum Iesum
	    Christum Filium tuum,
	qui tecum vivit et regnat
	    in unitate Spiritus Sancti,
	Deus, per omnia sæcula sæculorum.

FIRST READING

A reading from the first book of Samuel   16:1,6-7,10-13

David is anointed king of Israel.

The Lord said to Samuel, 'Fill your horn with oil and go. I am sending you to Jesse of Bethlehem, for I have chosen myself a king among his sons.' When Samuel arrived, he caught sight of Eliab and thought, 'Surely the Lord's anointed one stands there before him,' but the Lord said to Samuel, 'Take no notice of his appearance or his height for I have rejected him; God does not see as man sees; man looks at appearances but the Lord looks at the heart.' Jesse presented his seven sons to Samuel, but Samuel said to Jesse, 'The Lord has not chosen these.' He then asked Jesse, 'Are these all the sons you have?' He answered, 'There is still one left, the youngest; he is out looking after the sheep.' Then Samuel said to Jesse, 'Send for him; we will not sit down to eat until he comes.' Jesse had him sent for, a boy of fresh complexion, with fine eyes and pleasant bearing. The Lord said, 'Come, anoint him, for this is the one.' At this, Samuel took the horn of oil and anointed him where he stood with his brothers; and the spirit of the Lord seized on David and stayed with him from that day on.

The word of the Lord.

Responsorial Psalm   Ps 22. R. v.1

R. **The Lord is my shepherd;**
   there is nothing I shall want.

   The Lord is my shepherd;
   there is nothing I shall want.
   Fresh and green are the pastures
   where he gives me repose.
   Near restful waters he leads me,
   to revive my drooping spirit. R.

   He guides me along the right path;
   he is true to his name.
   If I should walk in the valley of darkness
   no evil would I fear.
   You are there with your crook and your staff;
   with these you give me comfort. R.

   You have prepared a banquet for me
   in the sight of my foes.

My head you have anointed with oil;
my cup is overflowing. R.

Surely goodness and kindness shall follow me
all the days of my life.
In the Lord's own house shall I dwell
for ever and ever. R.

SECOND READING

A reading from the letter of St Paul to the Ephesians   5:8-14

Rise from the dead and Christ will shine on you.

You were darkness once, but now you are light in the Lord; be like children
of light, for the effects of the light are seen in complete goodness and right
living and truth. Try to discover what the Lord wants of you, having nothing
to do with the futile works of darkness but exposing them by contrast.
The things which are done in secret are things that people are ashamed
even to speak of; but anything exposed by the light will be illuminated and
anything illuminated turns into light. That is why it is said:

Wake up from your sleep,
rise from the dead,
and Christ will shine on you.

The word of the Lord.

Gospel Acclamation   Jn 8:12

R. **Glory to you, O Christ, you are the Word of God!**
I am the light of the world, says the Lord;
anyone who follows me will have the light of life.
R. **Glory to you, O Christ, you are the Word of God!**

GOSPEL

A reading from the holy Gospel according to John   9:1-41

The blind man went off and washed himself, and came away with his sight restored.

| [As Jesus went along, he saw a man who had been blind from birth.] His
disciples asked him, 'Rabbi, who sinned, this man or his parents, for him to
have been born blind?' 'Neither he nor his parents sinned,' Jesus answered
'he was born blind so that the works of God might be displayed in him.

'As long as the day lasts
I must carry out the work of the one who sent me;

the night will soon be here when no one can work.
As long as I am in the world
I am the light of the world.'

Having said this, [he spat on the ground, made a paste with the spittle, put this over the eyes of the blind man and said to him, 'Go and wash in the Pool of Siloam' (a name that means 'sent'). So the blind man went off and washed himself, and came away with his sight restored.

His neighbours and people who earlier had seen him begging said, 'Isn't this the man who used to sit and beg?' Some said, 'Yes, it is the same one.' Others said, 'No, he only looks like him.' The man himself said, 'I am the man.'] So they said to him, 'Then how do your eyes come to be open?' 'The man called Jesus' he answered 'made a paste, daubed my eyes with it and said to me, "Go and wash at Siloam"; so I went, and when I washed I could see.' They asked, 'Where is he?' 'I don't know' he answered.

[They brought the man who had been blind to the Pharisees. It had been a sabbath day when Jesus made the paste and opened the man's eyes, so when the Pharisees asked him how he had come to see, he said, 'He put a paste on my eyes, and I washed, and I can see.' Then some of the Pharisees said, 'This man cannot be from God: he does not keep the sabbath.' Others said, 'How could a sinner produce signs like this?' And there was disagreement among them. So they spoke to the blind man again, 'What have you to say about him yourself, now that he has opened your eyes?' 'He is a prophet' replied the man.]

However, the Jews would not believe that the man had been blind and had gained his sight, without first sending for his parents and asking them, 'Is this man really your son who you say was born blind? If so, how is it that he is now able to see?' His parents answered, 'We know he is our son and we know he was born blind, but we don't know how it is that he can see now, or who opened his eyes. He is old enough: let him speak for himself.' His parents spoke like this out of fear of the Jews, who had already agreed to expel from the synagogue anyone who should acknowledge Jesus as the Christ. This was why his parents said, 'He is old enough; ask him.'

So the Jews again sent for the man and said to him, 'Give glory to God! For our part, we know that this man is a sinner.' The man answered, 'I don't know if he is a sinner; I only know that I was blind and now I can see.' They said to him, 'What did he do to you? How did he open your eyes?' He replied, 'I have told you once and you wouldn't listen. Why do you want to hear it all again? Do you want to become his disciples too?' At this they hurled abuse at him: 'You can be his disciple,' they said 'we are disciples of Moses: we know that God spoke to Moses, but as for this man, we don't know where he comes from.' The man replied, 'Now here is an astonishing thing! He has opened my eyes and you don't know where he comes from! We know that God doesn't listen to sinners, but God does listen to men who are devout and do his will. Ever since the world began it is unheard of for anyone to open the eyes of a man who was born blind; if this man were not from God, he couldn't do a thing.' ['Are you trying to teach us,' they replied 'and you a sinner through and through, since you were born!' And they drove him away.

Jesus heard they had driven him away, and when he found him he said to him, 'Do you believe in the Son of Man?' 'Sir,' the man replied 'tell me who he is so that I may believe in him.' Jesus said, 'You are looking at him; he is speaking to you.' The man said, 'Lord, I believe', and worshipped him.]

> Jesus said:
>
> 'It is for judgement
> that I have come into this world,
> so that those without sight may see
> and those with sight turn blind.'

Hearing this, some Pharisees who were present said to him, 'We are not blind, surely?' Jesus replied:

> 'Blind? If you were,
> you would not be guilty,
> but since you say, "We see",
> your guilt remains.'

| [The Gospel of the Lord.]

Shorter Form, verses 1,6-9,13-17,34-38. Read between [ ]

The Creed is said.

Prayer over the Offerings

We place before you with joy
   these offerings,
which bring eternal remedy, O Lord,
praying that we may both faithfully
   revere them
and present them to you, as is fitting,
for the salvation of all the world.
Through Christ our Lord.

Preface: The Man Born Blind.

It is truly right and just,
   our duty and our salvation,
always and everywhere
   to give you thanks,
Lord, holy Father,
   almighty and eternal God,
through Christ our Lord.

By the mystery of the Incarnation,
he has led the human race
   that walked in darkness
into the radiance of the faith
and has brought those born
   in slavery to ancient sin
through the waters of regeneration
to make them your adopted children.

Therefore, all creatures
   of heaven and earth
sing a new song in adoration,
and we, with all the host of Angels,
cry out, and without end acclaim:

Holy, Holy, Holy Lord God of hosts...

Super oblata

Remedii sempiterni munera,
   Domine,
lætantes offerimus,
   suppliciter exorantes,
ut eadem nos et fideliter venerari,
et pro salute mundi congruenter
   exhibere perficias.
Per Christum Dominum nostrum.

Praefatio: De caeco nato.

Vere dignum et iustum est,
   aequum et salutare,
nos tibi semper et ubique
   gratias agere:
Domine, sancte Pater,
   omnipotens aeterne Deus:
per Christum Dominum nostrum:

Qui genus humanum,
   in tenebris ambulans,
ad fidei claritatem
per mysterium incarnationis adduxit,
et, qui servi peccati
   veteris nascebantur,
per lavacrum regenerationis
in filios adoptionis assumpsit.

Propter quod caelestia tibi
   atque terrestria
canticum novum
   concinunt adorando,
et nos cum omni exercitu Angelorum
proclamamus, sine fine dicentes:

Sanctus, Sanctus, Sanctus. . .

Communion Antiphon Cf. Jn 9:11,38 | Ant. ad communionem

The Lord anointed my eyes:
    I went, I washed,
I saw and I believed in God.

Dominus linivit oculos meos:
et abii, et lavi, et vidi, et credidi Deo.

Prayer after Communion | Post communionem

O God, who enlighten everyone
    who comes into this world,
illuminate our hearts, we pray,
with the splendour of your grace,
that we may always ponder
what is worthy and pleasing
    to your majesty
and love you in all sincerity.
Through Christ our Lord.

Deus, qui illuminas
    omnem hominem
venientem in hunc mundum,
illumina, quæsumus, corda nostra
    gratiæ tuæ splendore,
ut digna ac placita maiestati tuæ
    cogitare semper,
et te sincere diligere valeamus.
Per Christum Dominum nostrum.

Prayer over the People | Oratio super populum

Look upon those who call to you,
    O Lord,
and sustain the weak;
give life by your unfailing light
to those who walk in the shadow
    of death,
and bring those rescued by your
    mercy from every evil
to reach the highest good.
Through Christ our Lord.

Tuere, Domine, supplices tuos,
    sustena fragiles,
et inter tenebras mortalium
    ambulantes
tua semper luce vivifica,
atque a malis omnibus
    clementer ereptos,
ad summa bona pervenire concede.
Per Christum Dominum nostrum.

20 March

SAINT JOSEPH,
SPOUSE OF THE BLESSED VIRGIN MARY

The Lord chose a just man, a man of faith, a man who was capable of being a man, and also capable of speaking with God, of entering into God's mystery. This was Joseph's life: living his profession, his life as a man and entering into the mystery. A man capable of dialoguing with mystery, of interacting with the mystery of God. He was not a dreamer. He entered into the mystery with the same naturalness with which he pursued his craft, with the precision of his craft. He was able to adjust a wooden angle within a millimetre, he knew how to do it. He was able to sand down, to reduce a wooden surface by a millimetre. He was precise, but also able to enter into the mystery that he could not control. This was Joseph's holiness: going through life, being just and professional at his job, and at the right moment, entering into the mystery. When the Gospel talks about Joseph's dreams, it enables us to understand this: he enters into the mystery.

(Pope Francis)

Solemnity

Entrance Antiphon Cf. Lk 12:42	Ant. ad introitum
BEHOLD, a faithful and prudent steward, whom the Lord set over his household.	ECCE fidelis servus et prudens, quem constituit Dominus super familiam suam.

The Gloria in excelsis (Glory to God in the highest) is said.

Collect	Collecta
Grant, we pray, almighty God, that by Saint Joseph's intercession your Church may constantly watch over the unfolding of the mysteries of human salvation, whose beginnings you entrusted to his faithful care.	Præsta, quæsumus, omnipotens Deus, ut humanæ salutis mysteria, cuius primordia beati Ioseph fideli custodiæ commisisti, Ecclesia tua, ipso intercedente, iugiter servet implenda.

Through our Lord Jesus Christ,
    your Son,
who lives and reigns with you
    in the unity of the Holy Spirit,
God, for ever and ever.
	Per Dominum nostrum Iesum
	    Christum Filium tuum,
	qui tecum vivit et regnat
	    in unitate Spiritus Sancti,
	Deus, per omnia sæcula sæculorum.

FIRST READING

A reading from the second book of Samuel   7:4-5,12-14,16
The Lord will give him the throne of his ancestor David.

The word of the Lord came to Nathan:

'Go and tell my servant David, "Thus the Lord speaks: When your days are ended and you are laid to rest with your ancestors, I will preserve the offspring of your body after you and make his sovereignty secure. (It is he who shall build a house for my name and I will make his royal throne secure for ever.) I will be a father to him and he a son to me. Your House and your sovereignty will always stand secure before me and your throne be established for ever."'

The word of the Lord.

Responsorial Psalm   Ps 88:2-5,27,29. R. v.37

R. **His dynasty shall last for ever.**

I will sing for ever of your love, O Lord;
    through all ages my mouth will proclaim your truth.
Of this I am sure, that your love lasts for ever,
    that your truth is firmly established as the heavens. R.

'I have made a covenant with my chosen one;
I have sworn to David my servant:
I will establish your dynasty for ever
    and set up your throne through all ages.' R.

He will say to me: 'You are my father,
    my God, the rock who saves me.'
I will keep my love for him always;
    for him my covenant shall endure. R.

SECOND READING

A reading from the letter of St Paul to the Romans   4:13,16-18,22
Though it seemed Abraham's hope could not be fulfilled, he hoped and he believed.

The promise of inheriting the world was not made to Abraham and his descendants on account of any law but on account of the righteousness which consists in faith. That is why what fulfils the promise depends on faith, so that it may be a free gift and be available to all of Abraham's descendants, not only those who belong to the Law but also to those who belong to the faith of Abraham who is the father of all of us. As scripture says: I have made you the ancestor of many nations – Abraham is our father in the eyes of God, in whom he put his faith, and who brings the dead to life and calls into being what does not exist.

Though it seemed Abraham's hope could not be fulfilled, he hoped and he believed, and through doing so he did become the father of many nations exactly as he had been promised: Your descendants will be as many as the stars. This is the faith that was 'considered as justifying him'.

The word of the Lord.

Gospel Acclamation   Ps 83:5

R. **Glory and praise to you, O Christ.**
They are happy who dwell in your house, O Lord,
for ever singing your praise.
R. **Glory and praise to you, O Christ.**

GOSPEL

A reading from the holy Gospel according to Matthew   1:16,18-21,24
Joseph did what the angel of the Lord had told him to do.

Jacob was the father of Joseph the husband of Mary; of her was born Jesus who is called Christ.

This is how Jesus Christ came to be born. His mother Mary was betrothed to Joseph; but before they came to live together she was found to be with child through the Holy Spirit. Her husband Joseph, being a man of honour and wanting to spare her publicity, decided to divorce her informally. He had made up his mind to do this when the angel of the Lord appeared to him in a dream and said, 'Joseph son of David, do not be afraid to take Mary home as your wife, because she has conceived what is in her by the Holy Spirit. She will give birth to a son and you must name him Jesus, because he is the one who is to save his people from their sins.' When Joseph woke up he did what the angel of the Lord had told him to do.

The Gospel of the Lord

ALTERNATIVE GOSPEL

A reading from the holy Gospel according to Luke   2:41-51
See how worried your father and I have been, looking for you.

Every year the parents of Jesus used to go to Jerusalem for the feast of the Passover. When he was twelve years old, they went up for the feast as usual.

When they were on their way home after the feast, the boy Jesus stayed behind in Jerusalem without his parents knowing it. They assumed he was with the caravan, and it was only after a day's journey that they went to look for him among their relations and acquaintances. When they failed to find him they went back to Jerusalem looking for him everywhere.

Three days later, they found him in the Temple, sitting among the doctors, listening to them, and asking them questions; and all those who heard him were astounded at his intelligence and his replies. They were overcome when they saw him and his mother said to him, 'My child, why have you done this to us? See how worried your father and I have been, looking for you.' 'Why were you looking for me?' he replied. 'Did you not know that I must be busy with my Father's affairs?' But they did not understand what he meant.

He then went down with them and came to Nazareth and lived under their authority.

The Gospel of the Lord.

The Creed is said.

Prayer over the Offerings	Super oblata
We pray, O Lord, that, just as Saint Joseph served with loving care your Only Begotten Son, born of the Virgin Mary, so we may be worthy to minister with a pure heart at your altar. Through Christ our Lord.	Quæsumus, Domine, ut, sicut beatus Ioseph Unigenito tuo, nato de Maria Virgine, pia devotione deserviit, ita et nos mundo corde tuis altaribus mereamur ministrare. Per Christum Dominum nostrum.
Preface: The mission of Saint Joseph.	**Præfatio:** De missione sancti Ioseph.
It is truly right and just, our duty and our salvation, always and everywhere to give you thanks, Lord, holy Father, almighty and eternal God, and on the Solemnity of Saint Joseph to give you fitting praise, to glorify you and bless you.	Vere dignum et iustum est, æquum et salutare, nos tibi semper et ubique gratias agere: Domine, sancte Pater, omnipotens æterne Deus: Et te in sollemnitate beati Ioseph debitis magnificare præconiis, benedicere et prædicare.

For this just man was given by you
as spouse to the Virgin Mother of God
and set as a wise and faithful servant
in charge of your household
to watch like a father over your
    Only Begotten Son,
who was conceived by the
    overshadowing of the Holy Spirit,
our Lord Jesus Christ.

Through him the Angels praise
    your majesty,
Dominions adore and Powers
    tremble before you.
Heaven and the Virtues of heaven
    and the blessed Seraphim
worship together with exultation.

May our voices, we pray,
    join with theirs
in humble praise, as we acclaim:

Holy, Holy, Holy Lord God of hosts...

Qui et vir iustus, a te Deiparæ
    Virgini Sponsus est datus,
et fidelis servus ac prudens,
super Familiam tuam est constitutus,
ut Unigenitum tuum,
Sancti Spiritus obumbratione
    conceptum,
paterna vice custodiret,
Iesum Christum Dominum nostrum.

Per quem maiestatem tuam
    laudant Angeli,
adorant Dominationes,
    tremunt Potestates.
Cæli cælorumque Virtutes,
    ac beata Seraphim,
socia exsultatione concelebrant.

Cum quibus et nostras voces ut
    admitti iubeas, deprecamur,
supplici confessione dicentes:

Sanctus, Sanctus, Sanctus. . .

Communion Antiphon   Mt 25:21

Well done, good and faithful servant.
    Come, share your master's joy.

Ant. ad communionem

Euge, serve bone et fidelis:
    intra in gaudium Domini tui.

Prayer after Communion

Defend with unfailing protection,
O Lord, we pray,
the family you have nourished
with food from this altar,
as they rejoice at the Solemnity
    of Saint Joseph,
and graciously keep safe your gifts
    among them.
Through Christ our Lord.

Post communionem

Familiam tuam, quæsumus,
    Domine,
quam de beati Ioseph
    sollemnitate lætantem
ex huius altaris alimonia satiasti,
perpetua protectione defende,
et tua in ea propitiatus
    dona custodi.
Per Christum Dominum nostrum.

25 March

THE ANNUNCIATION OF THE LORD

On 25 March in the Church we solemnly celebrate the Annunciation, the mystery of the Incarnation begins. The Archangel Gabriel visits a humble girl in Nazareth and proclaims to her that she will conceive and bear the Son of God. With this Annunciation the Lord illuminates and strengthens Mary's faith, as he will also do for her spouse Joseph, so that Jesus could be born into a human family. This is very beautiful: it shows us how deeply the mystery of the Incarnation, as God desired, encompasses not only conception in the mother's womb, but also acceptance in a real family. Today I would like to contemplate with you the beauty of this bond, the beauty of God's condescension.

(Pope Francis)

Solemnity

Entrance Antiphon Heb 10:5,7	Ant. ad introitum

THE Lord said,
   as he entered the world:
Behold, I come to do your will,
   O God.
	DOMINUS ingrediens
	   mundum dixit:
	Ecce venio ut faciam, Deus,
	   voluntatem tuam.

The **Gloria in excelsis** (Glory to God in the highest) is said.

Collect	Collecta

O God, who willed that your Word
should take on the reality
   of human flesh
in the womb of the Virgin Mary,
grant, we pray,
that we, who confess our Redeemer
to be God and man,
may merit to become partakers
   even in his divine nature.
Who lives and reigns with you
   in the unity of the Holy Spirit,
God, for ever and ever.
	Deus, qui Verbum tuum in utero
	   Virginis Mariæ
	veritatem carnis humanæ
	   suscipere voluisti,
	concede, quæsumus,
	ut, qui Redemptorem nostrum
	Deum et hominem confitemur,
	ipsius etiam divinæ naturæ
	   mereamur esse consortes.
	Per Dominum nostrum Iesum
	   Christum Filium tuum,
	qui tecum vivit et regnat
	   in unitate Spiritus Sancti,
	Deus, per omnia sæcula sæculorum.

FIRST READING

A reading from the prophet Isaiah   7:10-14,8:10

The maiden is with child.

The Lord spoke to Ahaz and said, 'Ask the Lord your God for a sign for yourself coming either from the depths of Sheol or from the heights above.' 'No,' Ahaz answered, 'I will not put the Lord to the test.'

> Then Isaiah said:
>
> Listen now, House of David:
> are you not satisfied with trying the patience of men
> without trying the patience of my God, too?
> The Lord himself, therefore,
> will give you a sign.
> It is this: the maiden is with child
> and will soon give birth to a son
> whom she will call Emmanuel,
> a name which means 'God-is-with-us'.

The word of the Lord.

Responsorial Psalm   Ps 39:7-11. R. vv.8,9

R. **Here I am, Lord!**
   I come to do your will.

You do not ask for sacrifice and offerings,
but an open ear.
You do not ask for holocaust and victim.
Instead, here am I. R.

In the scroll of the book it stands written
that I should do your will.
My God, I delight in your law
in the depth of my heart. R.

Your justice I have proclaimed
in the great assembly.
My lips I have not sealed;
you know it, O Lord. R.

I have not hidden your justice in my heart
but declared your faithful help.
I have not hidden your love and your truth
from the great assembly. R.

SECOND READING

A reading from the letter to the Hebrews   10:4-10

I was commanded in the scroll of the book, 'God, here I am! I am coming to obey your will.'

Bulls' blood and goats' blood are useless for taking away sins, and this is what Christ said, on coming into the world:

> You who wanted no sacrifice or oblation,
> prepared a body for me.
> you took no pleasure in holocausts or sacrifices for sin;
> then I said,
> just as I was commanded in the scroll of the book,
>   'God, here I am! I am coming to obey your will.'

Notice that he says first: You did not want what the Law lays down as the things to be offered, that is: the sacrifices, the oblations, the holocausts and the sacrifices for sin, and you took no pleasure in them; and then he says: Here I am! I am coming to obey your will. He is abolishing the first sort to replace it with the second. And this will was for us to be made holy by the offering of his body made once and for all by Jesus Christ.

The word of the Lord.

Gospel Acclamation   Jn 1:14

R. **Praise to you, O Christ, king of eternal glory!**
The Word was made flesh,
he lived among us,
and we saw his glory.
R. **Praise to you, O Christ, king of eternal glory!**

GOSPEL

A reading from the Gospel according to Luke   1:26-38

Listen! You are to conceive and bear a son.

The angel Gabriel was sent by God to a town in Galilee called Nazareth, to a virgin betrothed to a man named Joseph, of the house of David; and the virgin's name was Mary. He went in and said to her, "Rejoice, so highly favoured! The Lord is with you.' She was deeply disturbed by these words and asked herself what this greeting could mean, but the angel said to her, 'Mary, do not be afraid; you have won God's favour. Listen! You are to conceive and bear a son, and you must name him Jesus. He will be great and will be called Son of the Most High. The Lord God will give him the throne of his ancestor David; he will rule over the House of Jacob for ever and his reign will have no end.' Mary said to the angel, 'But how can this come about, since I am a virgin?' 'The Holy Spirit will come upon you, the angel answered, 'and the power of the Most High will cover you with its shadow. And so the child will be holy and will be called Son of God. Know this too: your kinswoman Elizabeth also, in her old age, herself conceived a son, and she whom people called barren is now in her sixth month, for nothing is impossible to God.' 'I am the handmaid of the Lord,' said Mary, 'let what you have said be done to me.' And the angel left her.

The Gospel of the Lord.

The Creed is said. At the words **and was incarnate** all genuflect.

Prayer over the Offerings

Be pleased, almighty God,
to accept your Church's offering,
so that she,
  who is aware that her beginnings
lie in the Incarnation of your Only
  Begotten Son,
may rejoice to celebrate his mysteries
  on this Solemnity.
Who lives and reigns
  for ever and ever.

Super oblata

Ecclesiæ tuæ munus, omnipotens
  Deus, dignare suscipere,
ut, quæ in Unigeniti
  tui incarnatione
primordia sua constare cognoscit,
ipsius gaudeat hac sollemnitate
  celebrare mysteria.
Per Christum Dominum nostrum.

Preface: The Mystery of the Incarnation.

It is truly right and just,
  our duty and our salvation,
always and everywhere
  to give you thanks,
Lord, holy Father,
  almighty and eternal God,
through Christ our Lord.

For the Virgin Mary heard with faith
that the Christ was to be born
  among men and for men's sake
by the overshadowing power
  of the Holy Spirit.

Præfatio: De mysterio Incarnationis.

Vere dignum et iustum est,
  æquum et salutare,
nos tibi semper et ubique
  gratias agere:
Domine, sancte Pater,
  omnipotens æterne Deus:
per Christum Dominum nostrum.

Quem inter homines et propter
  homines nasciturum,
Spiritus Sancti obumbrante virtute,
a cælesti nuntio Virgo
  fidenter audivit

Lovingly she bore him in her
    immaculate womb,
that the promises to the children
    of Israel might come about
and the hope of nations be
    accomplished beyond all telling.
Through him the host of Angels
    adores your majesty
and rejoices in your presence for ever.

May our voices, we pray,
    join with theirs
in one chorus of exultant praise,
    as we acclaim:

Holy, Holy, Holy Lord God of hosts...

et immaculatis visceribus
    amanter portavit,
ut et promissiones filiis Israel
    perficeret veritas,
et gentium exspectatio pateret
    ineffabiliter adimplenda.
Per quem maiestatem tuam adorat
    exercitus Angelorum,
ante conspectum tuum
    in æternitate lætantium.

Cum quibus et nostras voces
    ut admitti iubeas, deprecamur,
socia exsultatione dicentes:

Sanctus, Sanctus, Sanctus. . .

Communion Antiphon   Is 7:14

Behold, a Virgin shall conceive
    and bear a son;
and his name will be
    called Emmanuel.

Ant. ad communionem

Ecce Virgo concipiet,
    et pariet Filium;
et vocabitur nomen
    eius Emmanuel.

Prayer after Communion

Confirm in our minds
    the mysteries of the true faith,
we pray, O Lord,
so that, confessing that he who was
    conceived of the Virgin Mary
is true God and true man,
we may, through the saving power
    of his Resurrection,
merit to attain eternal joy.
Through Christ our Lord.

Post communionem

In mentibus nostris, quæsumus,
    Domine,
veræ fidei sacramenta confirma,
ut, qui conceptum de Virgine
Deum verum
    et hominem confitemur,
per eius salutiferæ
    resurrectionis potentiam,
ad æternam mereamur
    pervenire lætitiam.
Per Christum Dominum nostrum.

26 March

FIFTH SUNDAY OF LENT

Today, Jesus repeats to us: "Take away the stone". God did not create us for the tomb, but rather he created us for life, which is beautiful, good, joyful. But "through the devil's envy death entered the world" says the Book of Wisdom, and Jesus Christ came to free us from its bonds. We are thus called to take away the stones of all that suggests death: for example, the hypocrisy with which faith is lived, is death; the destructive criticism of others, is death; insults, slander, are death; the marginalisation of the poor, is death. The Lord asks us to remove these stones from our hearts, and life will then flourish again around us. Christ lives, and those who welcome him and follow him come into contact with life. Without Christ, or outside of Christ, not only is life not present, but one falls back into death.

(Pope Francis)

Entrance Antiphon   Cf. Ps 42:1-2

GIVE me justice, O God,
and plead my cause against
a nation that is faithless.
From the deceitful and cunning
rescue me,
for you, O God, are my strength.

Ant. ad introitum

IUDICA me, Deus,
et discerne causam meam
de gente non sancta;
ab homine iniquo et doloso eripe me,
quia tu es Deus meus
et fortitudo mea.

The Gloria in excelsis (Glory to God in the highest) is not said.

Collect

By your help, we beseech you,
Lord our God,
may we walk eagerly
in that same charity
with which, out of love for the world,
your Son handed himself
over to death.
Through our Lord Jesus Christ,
your Son,
who lives and reigns with you
in the unity of the Holy Spirit,
God, for ever and ever.

Collecta

Quæsumus, Domine Deus noster,
ut in illa caritate
qua Filius tuus diligens mundum
morti se tradidit,
inveniamur ipsi, te opitulante,
alacriter ambulantes.
Per Dominum nostrum Iesum
Christum Filium tuum,
qui tecum vivit et regnat
in unitate Spiritus Sancti,
Deus, per omnia sæcula sæculorum.

FIRST READING

A reading from the prophet Ezekiel   37:12-14

I shall put my spirit in you, and you will live.

The Lord says this: I am now going to open your graves; I mean to raise you
from your graves, my people, and lead you back to the soil of Israel. And
you will know that I am the Lord, when I open your graves and raise you
from your graves, my people. And I shall put my spirit in you, and you will
live, and I shall resettle you on your own soil; and you will know that I, the
Lord, have said and done this – it is the Lord who speaks.

The word of the Lord.

Responsorial Psalm   Ps 129. R. v.7

R. **With the Lord there is mercy**
   and fullness of redemption.

   Out of the depths I cry to you, O Lord,
   Lord, hear my voice!
   O let your ears be attentive
   to the voice of my pleading. R.

   If you, O Lord, should mark our guilt,
   Lord, who would survive?
   But with you is found forgiveness:
   for this we revere you. R.

   My soul is waiting for the Lord,
   I count on his word.
   My soul is longing for the Lord
   more than watchman for daybreak.
   (Let the watchman count on daybreak
   and Israel on the Lord.) R.

   Because with the Lord there is mercy
   and fullness of redemption,
   Israel indeed he will redeem
   from all its iniquity. R.

SECOND READING

A reading from the letter of St Paul to the Romans   8:8-11

The Spirit of him who raised Jesus from the dead is living in you.

People who are interested only in unspiritual things can never be pleasing to
God. Your interests, however, are not in the unspiritual, but in the spiritual,

since the Spirit of God has made his home in you. In fact, unless you possessed the Spirit of Christ you would not belong to him. Though your body may be dead it is because of sin, but if Christ is in you then your spirit is life itself because you have been justified; and if the Spirit of him who raised Jesus from the dead is living in you, then he who raised Jesus from the dead will give life to your own mortal bodies through his Spirit living in you.

The word of the Lord.

Gospel Acclamation   Jn 11:25-26

R. **Glory and praise to you, O Christ!**
I am the resurrection and the life, says the Lord:
whoever believes in me will never die.
R. **Glory and praise to you, O Christ!**

GOSPEL

A reading from the holy Gospel according to John   11:1-45

I am the resurrection and the life.

There was a man named Lazarus who lived in the village of Bethany with the two sisters, Mary and Martha, and he was ill. It was the same Mary, the sister of the sick man Lazarus, who anointed the Lord with ointment and wiped his feet with her hair. [The sisters sent this message to Jesus, 'Lord, the man you love is ill.' On receiving the message, Jesus said, 'This sickness will end not in death but in God's glory, and through it the Son of God will be glorified.'

Jesus loved Martha and her sister and Lazarus, yet when he heard that Lazarus was ill he stayed where he was for two more days before saying to the disciples, 'Let us go to Judaea.'] The disciples said, 'Rabbi, it is not long since the Jews wanted to stone you; are you going back again?' Jesus replied:

'Are there not twelve hours in the day?
A man can walk in the daytime without stumbling
because he has the light of this world to see by;
but if he walks at night he stumbles,
because there is no light to guide him.'

He said that and then added, 'Our friend Lazarus is resting, I am going to wake him.' The disciples said to him, 'Lord, if he is able to rest he is sure to get better.' The phrase Jesus used referred to the death of Lazarus, but they thought that by 'rest' he meant 'sleep', so Jesus put it plainly, 'Lazarus is dead; and for your sake I am glad I was not there because now you will believe. But let us go to him.' Then Thomas – known as the Twin – said to the other disciples, 'Let us go too, and die with him.'

[On arriving, Jesus found that Lazarus had been in the tomb for four days already.] Bethany is only about two miles from Jerusalem, and many Jews had come to Martha and Mary to sympathise with them over their brother. [When Martha heard that Jesus had come she went to meet him. Mary remained sitting in the house. Martha said to Jesus, 'If you had been here, my brother would not have died, but I know that, even now, whatever you ask of God, he will grant you.' 'Your brother' said Jesus to her 'will rise again.' Martha said, 'I know he will rise again at the resurrection on the last day.' Jesus said:

'I am the resurrection and the life.
If anyone believes in me, even though he dies he will live,
and whoever lives and believes in me
will never die.
Do you believe this?'

'Yes Lord,' she said 'I believe that you are the Christ, the Son of God, the one who was to come into this world.]

When she had said this, she went and called her sister Mary, saying in a low voice, 'The Master is here and wants to see you.' Hearing this, Mary got up quickly and went to him. Jesus had not yet come into the village; he was still at the place where Martha had met him. When the Jews who were in the house sympathising with Mary saw her get up so quickly and go out, they followed her, thinking that she was going to the tomb to weep there.

Mary went to Jesus, and as soon as she saw him she threw herself at his feet, saying, 'Lord, if you had been here, my brother would not have died.' At the sight of her tears, and those of the Jews who followed her, [Jesus said in great distress, with a sigh that came straight from the heart, 'Where have you put him?' They said, 'Lord, come and see.' Jesus wept; and the Jews said, 'See how much he loved him!' But there were some who remarked, 'He opened the eyes of the blind man, could he not have prevented this man's death?' Still sighing, Jesus reached the tomb: it was a cave with a stone to close the opening. Jesus said, 'Take the stone away.' Martha said to him, 'Lord, by now he will smell; this is the fourth day.' Jesus replied, 'Have I not told you that if you believe you will see the glory of God?' So they took away the stone. Then Jesus lifted up his eyes and said:

'Father, I thank you for hearing my prayer.
I knew indeed that you always hear me,
but I speak
for the sake of all these who stand round me,
so that they may believe it was you who sent me.'

When he had said this, he cried in a loud voice, 'Lazarus, here! Come out!' The dead man came out, his feet and hands bound with bands of stuff and a cloth round his face. Jesus said to them, 'Unbind him, let him go free.'

Many of the Jews who had come to visit Mary and had seen what he did believed in him.

The Gospel of the Lord.]

Shorter Form, verses 3-7,17,20-27,33-45. Read between [ ]
The Creed is said.

Prayer over the Offerings	Super oblata
Hear us, almighty God, and, having instilled in your servants the teachings of the Christian faith, graciously purify them by the working of this sacrifice. Through Christ our Lord.	Exaudi nos, omnipotens Deus, et famulos tuos, quos fidei christianæ eruditionibus imbuisti, huius sacrificii tribuas operatione mundari. Per Christum Dominum nostrum.
Preface: Lazarus.	Praefatio: De Lazaro.
It is truly right and just, our duty and our salvation, always and everywhere to give you thanks, Lord, holy Father, almighty and eternal God, through Christ our Lord.	Vere dignum et iustum est, aequum et salutare, nos tibi semper et ubique gratias agere: Domine, sancte Pater, omnipotens aeterne Deus: per Christum Dominum nostrum:
For as true man he wept for Lazarus his friend and as eternal God raised him from the tomb, just as, taking pity on the human race, he leads us by sacred mysteries to new life.	Ipse enim verus homo Lazarum flevit amicum, et Deus aeternus e tumulo suscitavit, qui, humani generis miseratus, ad novam vitam sacris mysteriis nos adducit.

Through him the host
   of Angels adores your majesty
and rejoices in your presence
   for ever.
May our voices, we pray,
   join with theirs
in one chorus of exultant praise,
   as we acclaim:

Holy, Holy, Holy Lord God of hosts...

Per quem maiestatem tuam adorat
   exercitus Angelorum,
ante conspectum tuum
   in aeternitate laetantium.
Cum quibus et nostras voces
   ut admitti iubeas, deprecamur,
socia exsultatione dicentes:

Sanctus, Sanctus, Sanctus. . .

Communion Antiphon Cf. Jn 11:26

Everyone who lives and believes
   in me
will not die for ever, says the Lord.

Ant. ad communionem

Omnis qui vivit et credit in me,
non morietur in æternum,
   dicit Dominus.

Prayer after Communion

We pray, almighty God,
that we may always be counted
   among the members of Christ,
in whose Body and Blood
   we have communion.
Who lives and reigns
   for ever and ever.

Post communionem

Quæsumus, omnipotens Deus,
ut inter eius membra
   semper numeremur,
cuius Corpori communicamus
   et Sanguini.
Qui vivit et regnat
   in sæcula sæculorum.

Prayer over the People

Bless, O Lord, your people,
who long for the gift of your mercy,
and grant that what,
   at your prompting, they desire
they may receive
   by your generous gift.
Through Christ our Lord.

Oratio super populum

Benedic, Domine, plebem tuam,
quæ munus tuæ
   miserationis exspectat,
et concede, ut, quod,
   te inspirante, desiderat,
te largiente percipiat.
Per Christum Dominum nostrum.

2 April

PALM SUNDAY OF THE PASSION OF THE LORD

Jesus says one thing from the Cross, one thing alone: "My God, my God, why have you forsaken me?" Why did all this take place? It was done for our sake, to serve us. So that when we have our back to the wall, when we find ourselves at a dead end, with no light and no way of escape, when it seems that God himself is not responding, we should remember that we are not alone. Jesus experienced total abandonment in a situation he had never before experienced in order to be one with us in everything. He did it for me, for you, for all of us; he did it to say to us: "Do not be afraid, you are not alone. I experienced all your desolation in order to be ever close to you". That is the extent to which Jesus served us: he descended into the abyss of our most bitter sufferings, culminating in betrayal and abandonment. Today, in the face of the many false securities that have crumbled, in the face of so many hopes betrayed, in the sense of abandonment that weighs upon our hearts, Jesus says to each one of us: "Courage, open your heart to my love. You will feel the consolation of God who sustains you".

(Pope Francis)

On this day the Church recalls the entrance of Christ the Lord into Jerusalem to accomplish his Paschal Mystery. Accordingly, the memorial of this entrance of the Lord takes place at all Masses, by means of the Procession or the Solemn Entrance before the principal Mass or the Simple Entrance before other Masses. The Solemn Entrance, but not the Procession, may be repeated before other Masses that are usually celebrated with a large gathering of people.

It is desirable that, where neither the Procession nor the Solemn Entrance can take place, there be a sacred celebration of the Word of God on the messianic entrance and on the Passion of the Lord, either on Saturday evening or on Sunday at a convenient time.

The Commemoration of the Lord's Entrance into Jerusalem

First Form: The Procession

At an appropriate hour, a gathering takes place at a smaller church or other suitable place other than inside the church to which the procession will go. The faithful hold branches in their hands.

Wearing the red sacred vestments as for Mass, the Priest and the Deacon, accompanied by other ministers, approach the place where the people are gathered.

Instead of the chasuble, the Priest may wear a cope, which he leaves aside when the procession is over, and puts on a chasuble.

Meanwhile, the following antiphon or another appropriate chant is sung.

Ant.   Mt 21:9 | Ant.

Hosanna to the Son of David; | Hosanna filio David:
blessed is he who comes | benedictus qui venit
in the name of the Lord, | in nomine Domini.
the King of Israel. | Rex Israel:
Hosanna in the highest. | Hosanna in excelsis.

After this, the Priest and people sign themselves, while the Priest says: **In the name of the Father, and of the Son, and of the Holy Spirit**. Then he greets the people in the usual way. A brief address is given, in which the faithful are invited to participate actively and consciously in the celebration of this day, in these or similar words:

Dear brethren (brothers and sisters), | Fratres carissimi,
since the beginning of Lent until now | postquam iam ab initio
we have prepared our hearts | Quadragesimæ corda nostra
   by penance and charitable works. | pænitentia et operibus
Today we gather together to herald | caritatis præparavimus,
   with the whole Church | hodierna die congregamur,
the beginning of the celebration | ut cum tota Ecclesia præludamus
of our Lord's Paschal Mystery, | paschale Domini nostri mysterium,
that is to say, of his Passion | eius nempe passionem
   and Resurrection. | atque resurrectionem,
For it was to accomplish this mystery | ad quod implendum
that he entered his own city | ipse ingressus est civitatem
   of Jerusalem. | suam Ierusalem.
Therefore, with all faith | Quare cum omni fide et devotione
   and devotion, | memoriam agentes
let us commemorate | huius salutiferi ingressus,
the Lord's entry into the city | sequamur Dominum,
   for our salvation, | ut, per gratiam consortes
following in his footsteps, | effecti crucis,
so that, being made by his grace | partem habeamus resurrectionis
   partakers of the Cross, | et vitæ.
we may have a share also in his |
   Resurrection and in his life. |

After the address, the Priest says one of the following prayers with hands extended.

Let us pray.

Almighty ever-living God,
sanctify ✠ these branches
    with your blessing,
that we, who follow Christ the King
    in exultation,
may reach the eternal Jerusalem
    through him.
Who lives and reigns
    for ever and ever.
R. Amen.

Or:

Increase the faith of those who
    place their hope in you, O God,
and graciously hear the prayers
    of those who call on you,
that we, who today hold high
    these branches
to hail Christ in his triumph,
may bear fruit for you by good
    works accomplished in him.
Who lives and reigns
for ever and ever.
R. Amen.

Oremus.

Omnipotens sempiterne Deus,
hos palmites tua
    benedictione ✠ sanctifica,
ut nos, qui Christum Regem
    exsultando prosequimur,
per ipsum valeamus ad æternam
    Ierusalem pervenire.
Qui vivit et regnat
    in sæcula sæculorum.
R. Amen.

Vel:

Auge fidem in te sperantium, Deus,
et supplicum preces
    clementer exaudi,
ut, qui hodie Christo triumphanti
    palmites exhibemus,
in ipso fructus tibi bonorum
    operum afferamus.
Qui vivit et regnat
    in sæcula sæculorum.
R. Amen.

He sprinkles the branches with holy water without saying anything.

Then a Deacon or, if there is no Deacon, a Priest, proclaims in the usual way the Gospel concerning the Lord's entrance according to one of the four Gospels. If appropriate, incense may be used.

GOSPEL

A reading from the holy Gospel according to Matthew

21:1-11

'Blessed is he who comes in the name of the Lord.'

When they drew near to Jerusalem
and came to Bethphage, to the Mount of Olives,
Jesus sent two disciples, saying to them,
'Go into the village opposite you,
and immediately you will find an ass tied,
and a colt with her; untie them and bring them to me.
If any one says anything to you, you shall say,
"The Lord has need of them,"
and he will send them immediately.'
This took place to fulfil
what was spoken by the prophet, saying,

'Tell the daughter of Sion,
Behold, your king is coming to you,
humble, and mounted on an ass,
and on a colt, the foal of an ass.'

The disciples went and did as Jesus had directed them;
they brought the ass and the colt,
and put their garments on them, and he sat thereon.
Most of the crowd spread their garments on the road,
and others cut branches from the trees
and spread them on the road.
And the crowds that went before him
and that followed him shouted,
'Hosanna to the Son of David!
Blessed is he who comes in the name of the Lord!
Hosanna in the highest!'
And when he entered Jerusalem,
all the city was stirred, saying, 'Who is this?'
And the crowds said,
'This is the prophet Jesus from Nazareth of Galilee.'

The Gospel of the Lord.

After the Gospel, a brief homily may be given. Then, to begin the Procession, an invitation may be given by a Priest or a Deacon or a lay minister, in these or similar words:

Dear brethren (brothers and sisters), like the crowds who acclaimed Jesus in Jerusalem, let us go forth in peace.	Imitemur, fratres carissimi, turbas acclamantes Iesum, et procedamus in pace.
Or:	Vel:
Let us go forth in peace.	Procedamus in pace.
In this latter case, all respond:	
In the name of Christ. Amen.	In nomine Christi. Amen.

The Procession to the church where Mass will be celebrated then sets off in the usual way. If incense is used, the thurifer goes first, carrying a thurible with burning incense, then an acolyte or another minister, carrying a cross decorated with palm branches according to local custom, between two ministers with lighted candles. Then follow the Deacon carrying the Book of the Gospels, the Priest with the ministers, and, after them, all the faithful carrying branches.

As the Procession moves forward, the following or other suitable chants in honour of Christ the King are sung by the choir and people.

Antiphon 1

Antiphona 1

The children of the Hebrews, carrying olive branches, went to meet the Lord, crying out and saying: Hosanna in the highest.	Pueri Hebræorum, portantes ramos olivarum, obviaverunt Domino, clamantes et dicentes: Hosanna in excelsis.

If appropriate, this antiphon is repeated between the strophes of the following Psalm.

PSALM 23

The Lord's is the earth and its fullness,* the world, and those who dwell in it. It is he who set it on the seas;* on the rivers he made it firm. Ant.	Domini est terra et plenitudo eius,* orbis terrarum et qui habitant in eo. Quia ipse super maria fundavit eum* et super flumina firmavit eum. Ant.

Who shall climb the mountain
of the Lord?*
The clean of hands and pure of heart,
whose soul is not set on vain things,†
who has not sworn
deceitful words.* Ant.

Blessings from the Lord
shall he receive,*
and right reward from the God
who saves him.
Such are the people who seek him,*
who seek the face of the God
of Jacob. Ant.

O gates, lift high your heads,†
grow higher, ancient doors.*
Let him enter, the king of glory!
Who is this king of glory?*
The Lord, the mighty, the valiant;
the Lord, the valiant in war. Ant.

O gates, lift high your heads;†
grow higher, ancient doors.*
Let him enter, the king of glory!
Who is this king of glory?*
He, the Lord of hosts,
he is the king of glory. Ant.

Antiphon 2

The children of the Hebrews spread
their garments on the road,
crying out and saying:
Hosanna to the Son of David;
blessed is he who comes
in the name of the Lord.

Quis ascendet in montem Domini,*
aut quis stabit in loco sancto eius?
Innocens manibus et mundo corde,†
qui non levavit ad vana
animam suam,*
nec iuravit in dolum. Ant.

Hic accipiet benedictionem
a Domino*
et iustificationem a Deo salutari suo.
Hæc est generatio
quærentium eum,*
quærentium faciem Dei Iacob. Ant.

Attollite, portæ, capita vestra,†
et elevamini, portæ æternales,*
et introibit rex gloriæ.
Quis est iste rex gloriæ?*
Dominus fortis et potens,
Dominus potens in prœlio. Ant.

Attollite, portæ, capita vestra, †
et elevamini, portæ æternales,*
et introibit rex gloriæ.
Quis est iste rex gloriæ?*
Dominus virtutum ipse est
rex gloriæ. Ant.

Antiphona 2

Pueri Hebræorum vestimenta
prosternebant in via,
et clamabant dicentes:
Hosanna filio David;
benedictus, qui venit
in nomine Domini.

If appropriate, this antiphon is repeated between the strophes of the following Psalm.

PSALM 46

All peoples, clap your hands.*
Cry to God with shouts of joy!
For the Lord, the Most High,
   is awesome,*
the great king over all the earth. Ant.

He humbles peoples under us*
and nations under our feet.
Our heritage he chose for us,*
the pride of Jacob whom he loves.
God goes up with shouts of joy.*
The Lord goes up
   with trumpet blast. Ant.

Sing praise for God; sing praise!*
Sing praise to our king; sing praise!
God is king of all earth.*
Sing praise with all your skill. Ant.

God reigns over the nations.*
God sits upon his holy throne.
The princes of the peoples
   are assembled
with the people of the God
   of Abraham. †
The rulers of the earth belong
   to God,*
who is greatly exalted. Ant.

Omnes gentes, plaudite manibus,*
iubilate Deo in voce exsultationis,
quoniam Dominus Altissimus,
   terribilis,*
rex magnus super omnem terram. Ant.

Subiecit populos nobis,*
et gentes sub pedibus nostris.
Elegit nobis hereditatem nostram,*
gloriam Iacob, quem dilexit.
Ascendit Deus in iubilo,*
et Dominus in voce tubæ. Ant.

Psallite Deo, psallite;*
psallite regi nostro, psallite.
Quoniam rex omnis terræ Deus,*
psallite sapienter. Ant.

Regnavit Deus super gentes,*
Deus sedet super sedem
   sanctam suam.
Principes populorum congregati sunt
cum populo Dei Abraham,†
quoniam Dei sunt scuta terræ:*
vehementer elevatus est. Ant.

Hymn to Christ the King

Chorus:

Glory and honour and praise be to
   you, Christ, King and Redeemer,
to whom young children cried out
   loving Hosannas with joy.
All repeat: Glory and honour. . .
Chorus:

Israel's King are you, King David's
   magnificent offspring;
you are the ruler who come blest
   in the name of the Lord. . .
All repeat: Glory and honour. . .

Hymnus ad Christum Regem

Gloria, laus et honor tibi sit,
   rex Christe redemptor,
cui puerile decus prompsit
   Hosanna pium.
Omnes repetunt: Gloria, laus. . .

Israel es tu rex, Davidis
   et inclita proles,
nomine qui in Domini,
   rex benedicte, venis.
Omnes repetunt: Gloria, laus. . .

Chorus:

Heavenly hosts on high unite
in singing your praises;
men and women on earth
and all creation join in.

All repeat: Glory and honour. . .

Chorus:

Bearing branches of palm, Hebrews
came crowding to greet you;
see how with prayers and hymns
we come to pay you our vows.

All repeat: Glory and honour. . .

Chorus:

They offered gifts of praise to you,
so near to your Passion;
see how we sing this song now
to you reigning on high.

All repeat: Glory and honour. . .

Chorus:

Those you were pleased to accept;
now accept our gifts of devotion,
good and merciful King,
lover of all that is good.

All repeat: Glory and honour. . .

Cœtus in excelsis te laudat
cælicus omnis,
et mortalis homo,
et cuncta creata simul.

Omnes repetunt: Gloria, laus. . .

Plebs Hebræa tibi cum palmis
obvia venit;
cum prece, voto,
hymnis adsumus ecce tibi.

Omnes repetunt: Gloria, laus. . .

Hi tibi passuro solvebant
munia laudis;
nos tibi regnanti
pangimus ecce melos.

Omnes repetunt: Gloria, laus. . .

Hi placuere tibi,
placeat devotio nostra:
rex bone, rex clemens,
cui bona cuncta placent.

Omnes repetunt: Gloria, laus. . .

As the procession enters the church, there is sung the following responsory or
another chant, which should speak of the Lord's entrance.

R. As the Lord entered the holy city,
the children of the Hebrews
proclaimed the resurrection of life.
*Waving their branches of palm,
they cried:
Hosanna in the Highest.

V. When the people heard that
Jesus was coming to Jerusalem,
they went out to meet him.

*Waving their branches. . .

R. Ingrediente Domino
in sanctam civitatem,
Hebræorum pueri, resurrectionem
vitæ pronuntiantes,
*Cum ramis palmarum:
Hosanna, clamabant, in excelsis.

V. Cum audisset populus, quod
Iesus veniret Hierosolymam,
exierunt obviam ei.

*Cum ramis. . .

When the Priest arrives at the altar, he venerates it and, if appropriate, incenses it. Then he goes to the chair, where he puts aside the cope, if he has worn one, and puts on the chasuble. Omitting the other Introductory Rites of the Mass and, if appropriate, the **Kyrie (Lord, have mercy)**, he says the Collect of the Mass, and then continues the Mass in the usual way.

Second Form: The Solemn Entrance

When a procession outside the church cannot take place, the entrance of the Lord is celebrated inside the church by means of a Solemn Entrance before the principal Mass.

Holding branches in their hands, the faithful gather either outside, in front of the church door, or inside the church itself. The Priest and ministers and a representative group of the faithful go to a suitable place in the church outside the sanctuary, where at least the greater part of the faithful can see the rite.

While the Priest approaches the appointed place, the antiphon **Hosanna** or another appropriate chant is sung. Then the blessing of branches and the proclamation of the Gospel of the Lord's entrance into Jerusalem take place. After the Gospel, the Priest processes solemnly with the ministers and the representative group of the faithful through the church to the sanctuary, while the responsory **As the Lord entered** or another appropriate chant is sung.

Arriving at the altar, the Priest venerates it. He then goes to the chair and, omitting the Introductory Rites of the Mass and, if appropriate, the **Kyrie (Lord, have mercy)**, he says the Collect of the Mass, and then continues the Mass in the usual way.

Third Form: The Simple Entrance

At all other Masses of this Sunday at which the Solemn Entrance is not held, the memorial of the Lord's entrance into Jerusalem takes place by means of a Simple Entrance.

While the Priest proceeds to the altar, the Entrance Antiphon with its Psalm or another chant on the same theme is sung. Arriving at the altar, the Priest venerates it and goes to the chair. After the Sign of the Cross, he greets the people and continues the Mass in the usual way.

At other Masses, in which singing at the entrance cannot take place, the Priest, as soon as he has arrived at the altar and venerated it, greets the people, reads the Entrance Antiphon, and continues the Mass in the usual way.

Entrance Antiphon Cf. Jn 12:1,12-13; Ps 23:9-10

Six days before the Passover,
when the Lord came into
the city of Jerusalem,
the children ran to meet him;
in their hands they carried
palm branches
and with a loud voice cried out:

*Hosanna in the highest!
Blessed are you, who have come
in your abundant mercy!

O gates, lift high your heads;
grow higher, ancient doors.
Let him enter, the king of glory!
Who is this king of glory?
He, the Lord of hosts,
he is the king of glory.

*Hosanna in the highest!
Blessed are you, who have come
in your abundant mercy!

Ant. ad introitum

Ante sex dies sollemnis Paschæ,
quando venit Dominus
in civitatem Ierusalem,
occurrerunt ei pueri:
et in manibus portabant
ramos palmarum
et clamabant voce magna, dicentes:

*Hosanna in excelsis:
Benedictus, qui venisti
in multitudine misericordiæ tuæ.

Attollite, portæ, capita vestra,
et elevamini, portæ æternales,
et introibit rex gloriæ.
Quis est iste rex gloriæ?
Dominus virtutum ipse est
rex gloriæ.

*Hosanna in excelsis:
Benedictus, qui venisti
in multitudine misericordiæ tuæ.

At the Mass

After the Procession or Solemn Entrance the Priest begins the Mass with the Collect.

Collect

Almighty ever-living God,
who as an example of humility
for the human race to follow
caused our Saviour to take flesh
and submit to the Cross,
graciously grant that we may heed
his lesson of patient suffering
and so merit a share
in his Resurrection.
Who lives and reigns with you
in the unity of the Holy Spirit,
God, for ever and ever.

Collecta

Omnipotens sempiterne Deus,
qui humano generi, ad imitandum
humilitatis exemplum,
Salvatorem nostrum carnem sumere,
et crucem subire fecisti,
concede propitius,
ut et patientiæ ipsius
habere documenta
et resurrectionis consortia mereamur.
Qui tecum vivit et regnat
in unitate Spiritus Sancti,
Deus, per omnia sæcula sæculorum.

FIRST READING

A reading from the prophet Isaiah   50:4-7

I did not cover my face against insult - I know I shall not be shamed.

The Lord has given me
a disciple's tongue.
So that I may know how to reply to the wearied
he provides me with speech.
Each morning he wakes me to hear,
to listen like a disciple.
The Lord has opened my ear.
For my part, I made no resistance,
neither did I turn away.
I offered my back to those who struck me,
my cheeks to those who tore at my beard;
I did not cover my face
against insult and spittle.
The Lord comes to my help,
so that I am untouched by the insults.
So, too, I set my face like flint,
I know I shall not be shamed.

     The word of the Lord.

Responsorial Psalm   Ps 21:8-9,17-20,23-24. R. v.2

R. **My God, my God, why have you forsaken me?**

All who see me deride me.
They curl their lips, they toss their heads.
'He trusted in the Lord, let him save him;
let him release him if this is his friend.' R.

Many dogs have surrounded me,
a band of the wicked beset me.
They tear holes in my hands and my feet.
I can count every one of my bones. R.

They divide my clothing among them.
They cast lots for my robe.
O Lord, do not leave me alone,
my strength, make haste to help me! R.

I will tell of your name to my brethren
and praise you where they are assembled.
'You who fear the Lord give him praise;
all sons of Jacob, give him glory.
Revere him, Israel's sons.' R.

SECOND READING

A reading from the letter of St Paul to the Philippians   2:6-11

He humbled himself, but God raised him high.

His state was divine,
yet Christ Jesus did not cling
to his equality with God
but emptied himself
to assume the condition of a slave,
and became as men are;
and being as all men are,
he was humbler yet,
even to accepting death,
death on a cross.
But God raised him high
and gave him the name
which is above all other names
so that all beings
in the heavens, on earth and in the underworld,
should bend the knee at the name of Jesus
and that every tongue should acclaim
Jesus Christ as Lord,
to the glory of God the Father.

The word of the Lord.

Gospel Acclamation   Ph 2:8-9

R. **Praise to you, O Christ, king of eternal glory.**
Christ was humbler yet,
even to accepting death, death on a cross.
But God raised him high
and gave him the name which is above all names.
R. **Praise to you, O Christ, king of eternal glory.**

The narrative of the Lord's Passion is read without candles and without incense,
with no greeting or signing of the book. It is read by a Deacon or, if there is no
Deacon, by a Priest. It may also be read by readers, with the part of Christ, if possible,
reserved to a Priest.

Deacons, but not others, ask for the blessing of the Priest before singing the Passion,
as at other times before the Gospel.

GOSPEL

The passion of our Lord Jesus Christ according to Matthew　　26:14-27:66

The symbols in the following passion narrative represent:

N Narrator　　J Jesus　　O Other single speaker

C Crowd, or more than one speaker

N One of the Twelve, the man called Judas Iscariot, went to the chief priests and said:

O What are you prepared to give me if I hand him over to you?

N They paid him thirty silver pieces, and from that moment he looked for an opportunity to betray him.

　　Now on the first day of Unleavened Bread the disciples came to Jesus to say,

C Where do you want us to make the preparations for you to eat the Passover?

N He replied:

J Go to so-and-so in the city and say to him, 'The Master says: My time is near. It is at your house that I am keeping Passover with my disciples.'

N The disciples did what Jesus told them and prepared the Passover. When the evening came he was at table with the twelve disciples. And while they were eating he said:

J I tell you solemnly, one of you is about to betray me.

N They were greatly distressed and started asking him in turn,

C Not I, Lord, surely?

N He answered:

J Someone who has dipped his hand into the dish with me, will betray me. The Son of Man is going to his fate, as the scriptures say he will, but alas for that man by whom the Son of Man is betrayed! Better for that man if he had never been born!

N Judas, who was to betray him, asked in his turn,

O Not I, Rabbi, surely?

N Jesus answered:

J They are your own words.

N Now as they were eating, Jesus took some bread, and when he had said the blessing he broke it and gave it to the disciples and said:

J Take it and eat; this is my body.

N Then he took a cup, and when he had returned thanks he gave it to them saying:

J Drink all of you from this, for this is my blood, the blood of the covenant, which is to be poured out for many for the forgiveness of sins. From now on, I tell you, I shall not drink wine until the day I drink the new wine with you in the kingdom of my Father.

N   After psalms had been sung they left for the Mount of Olives. Then Jesus said to them,

J   You will all lose faith in me this night, for the scripture says: I shall strike the shepherd and the sheep of the flock will be scattered. But after my resurrection I shall go before you to Galilee.

N   At this, Peter said:

O   Though all lose faith in you, I will never lose faith.

N   Jesus answered him,

J   I tell you solemnly, this very night, before the cock crows, you will have disowned me three times.

N   Peter said to him,

O   Even if I have to die with you, I will never disown you.

N   And all the disciples said the same.
        Then Jesus came with them to a small estate called Gethsemane; and he said to his disciples,

J   Stay here while I go over there to pray.

N   He took Peter and the two sons of Zebedee with him. And sadness came over him, and great distress. Then he said to them:

J   My soul is sorrowful to the point of death. Wait here and keep awake with me.

N   And going on a little further he fell on his face and prayed:

J   My Father, if it is possible let this cup pass me by. Nevertheless, let it be as you, not I, would have it.

N   He came back to the disciples and found them sleeping, and he said to Peter:

J   So you had not the strength to keep awake with me one hour? You should be awake, and praying not to be put to the test. The spirit is willing, but the flesh is weak.

N   Again, a second time, he went away and prayed:

J   My Father, if this cup cannot pass by without my drinking it, your will be done!

N   And he came again back and found them sleeping, their eyes were so heavy. Leaving them there, he went away again and prayed for the third time, repeating the same words. Then he came back to the disciples and said to them,

J   You can sleep on now and take your rest. Now the hour has come when the Son of Man is to be betrayed into the hands of sinners. Get up! Let us go! My betrayer is already close at hand.

N   He was still speaking when Judas, one of the Twelve, appeared, and with him a large number of men armed with swords and clubs, sent by the chief priests and elders of the people Now the traitor had arranged a sign with them. He had said:

O   'The one I kiss, he is the man. Take him in charge.'

N   So he went straight up to Jesus and said:

O   Greetings, Rabbi,

N   and kissed him. Jesus said to him,

J   My friend, do what you are here for.

N   Then they came forward, seized Jesus and took him in charge. At that, one of the followers of Jesus grasped his sword and drew it; he struck out at the high priest's servant and cut off his ear. Jesus then said:

J   Put your sword back, for all who draw the sword will die by the sword. Or do you think that I cannot appeal to my Father who would promptly send more than twelve legions of angels to my defence? But then, how would the scriptures be fulfilled that say this is the way it must be?

N   It was at this time that Jesus said to the crowds:

J   Am I a brigand, that you had to set out to capture me with swords and clubs? I sat teaching in the Temple day after day and you never laid hands on me.

N   Now all this happened to fulfil the prophecies in scripture. Then all the disciples deserted him and ran away.

       The men who had arrested Jesus led him off to Caiaphas the high priest, where the scribes and the elders were assembled. Peter followed him at a distance, and when he reached the high priest's palace, he went in and sat down with the attendants to see what the end would be.

       The chief priests and the whole Sanhedrin were looking for evidence against Jesus, however false, on which they might pass the death-sentence. But they could not find any, though several lying witnesses came forward. Eventually two stepped forward and made a statement,

O   This man said: 'I have power to destroy the Temple of God and in three days build it up.'

N   The high priest then stood up and said to him:

O   Have you no answer to that? What is this evidence these men are bringing against you?

N   But Jesus was silent. And the high priest said to him:

O   I put you on oath by the living God to tell us if you are the Christ, the Son of God.

N   Jesus answered:

J   The words are your own. Moreover, I tell you that from this time onward you will see the Son of Man seated at the right hand of the Power and coming on the clouds of heaven.

N   At this, the high priest tore his clothes and said:

O   He has blasphemed. What need of witnesses have we now? There! You have just heard the blasphemy. What is your opinion?

N   They answered:

C   He deserves to die

N   Then they spat in his face and hit him with their fists; others said as they struck him:

C   Play the prophet, Christ! Who hit you then?

N   Meanwhile Peter was sitting outside in the courtyard, and a servant-girl came up to him and said:

O   You too were with Jesus the Galilean.

N   But he denied it in front of them all, saying:

O   I do not know what you are talking about.

N   When he went out to the gateway another servant-girl saw him and said to the people there:

O   This man was with Jesus the Nazarene.

N   And again, with an oath, he denied it,

O   I do not know the man.

N   A little later the bystanders came up and said to Peter:

C   You are one of them for sure! Why, your accent gives you away.

N   Then he started calling down curses on himself and swearing:

O   I do not know the man.

N   At that moment the cock crew, and Peter remembered what Jesus had said, 'Before the cock crows you will have disowned me three times.' And he went outside and wept bitterly.

    When morning came, all the chief priests and the elders of the people met in council to bring about the death of Jesus. They had him bound, and led him away to hand him over to Pilate, the governor. When he found that Jesus had been condemned, Judas his betrayer was filled with remorse and took the thirty pieces of silver back to the chief priests and elders, saying:

O   I have sinned. I have betrayed innocent blood.

N   They replied:

C   What is that to us? That is your concern.

N   And flinging down the silver pieces in the sanctuary he made off, and went and hanged himself. The chief priests picked up the silver pieces and said:

C   It is against the Law to put this into the treasury; it is blood money.

N   So they discussed the matter and bought the potter's field with it as a graveyard for foreigners, and this is why the field is called the Field of Blood today. The words of the prophet Jeremiah were then fulfilled: And they took the thirty silver pieces, the sum at which the precious One was priced by children of Israel, and they gave them for the potter's field, just as the Lord directed me.

[Jesus, then, was brought before the governor, and the governor put to him this question:

O   Are you the king of the Jews?

N   Jesus replied:

J   It is you who say it.

N   But when he was accused by the chief priests and the elders he refused to answer at all. Pilate then said to him:

O   Do you not hear how many charges they have brought against you?

N   But to the governor's complete amazement, he offered no reply to any of the charges.

     At festival time it was the governor's practice to release a prisoner for the people, anyone they chose. Now there was at that time a notorious prisoner whose name was Barabbas. So when the crowd gathered, Pilate said to them,

O   Which do you want me to release for you: Barabbas or Jesus who is called Christ?

N   For Pilate knew it was out of jealousy that they had handed him over. Now as he was seated in the chair of judgement, his wife sent him a message,

O   Have nothing to do with that man; I have been upset all day by a dream I had about him.

N   The chief priests and the elders, however, had persuaded the crowd to demand the release of Barabbas and the execution of Jesus. So when the governor spoke and asked them:

O   Which of the two do you want me to release for you?

N   They said:

C Barabbas.
N Pilate said to them:
O What am I to do with Jesus who is called Christ?
N They all said:
C Let him be crucified!
N Pilate asked:
O Why? What harm has he done?
N But they shouted all the louder,
C Let him be crucified!
N Then Pilate saw that he was making no impression, that in fact a riot was imminent. So he took some water, washed his hands in front of the crowd and said:
O I am innocent of this man's blood. It is your concern.
N And the people, to a man, shouted back:
C His blood be on us and on our children!
N Then he released Barabbas for them. He ordered Jesus to be first scourged and then handed over to be crucified.

The governor's soldiers took Jesus with them into the Praetorium and collected the whole cohort round him. Then they stripped him and made him wear a scarlet cloak, and having twisted some thorns into a crown they put this on his head and placed a reed in his right hand. To make fun of him they knelt to him saying:

C Hail, king of the Jews!
N And they spat on him and took the reed and struck him on the head with it. And when they had finished making fun of him, they took off the cloak and dressed him in his own clothes and led him away to crucify him.

On their way out, they came across a man from Cyrene, Simon by name, and enlisted him to carry his cross. When they had reach a place called Golgotha, that is, the place of the skull, they gave him wine to drink. When they had finished crucifying him they shared out his clothing by casting lots, and then sat down and stayed there keeping guard over him. Above his head was placed the charge against him; it read: 'This is Jesus, the King of the Jews.' At the same time two robbers were crucified with him, one on the right and one on the left.

The passers-by jeered at him; they shook their heads and said:

C So you would destroy the Temple and rebuild it in three days! Then save yourself! If you are God's son, come down from the cross!

N   The chief priests with the scribes and elders mocked him in the same way, saying:

C   He saved others; he cannot save himself. He is the King of Israel; let him come down from the cross now, and we will believe in him. He put his trust in God; now let God rescue him if he wants him. For he did say, 'I am the son of God.'

N   Even the robbers who were crucified with him taunted him in the same way.

      From the sixth hour there was darkness over all the land until the ninth hour. And about the ninth hour, Jesus cried out in a loud voice:

J   Eli, Eli, lama sabachthani?

N   That is: 'My God, my God, why have you deserted me?' When some of those who stood there heard this, they said:

C   The man is calling on Elijah,

N   and one of them quickly ran to get a sponge which he dipped in vinegar and, putting it on a reed, gave it him to drink. The rest of them said:

C   Wait! See if Elijah will come to save him.

N   But Jesus, again crying out in a loud voice, yielded up his spirit.

All kneel and pause a moment.

N   At that, the veil of the Temple was torn in two from top to bottom; the earth quaked; the rocks were split; the tombs opened and the bodies of many holy men rose from the dead, and these, after his resurrection, came out of the tombs, entered the Holy City and appeared to a number of people.

      Meanwhile the centurion, together with the others guarding Jesus, had seen the earthquake and all that was taking place, and they were terrified and said:

C   In truth this was a son of God.]

N   And many women were there, watching from a distance, the same women who had followed Jesus from Galilee and looked after him. Among them were Mary of Magdala, Mary the mother of James and Joseph, and the mother of Zebedee's sons.

      When it was evening, there came a rich man of Arimathaea called Joseph, who had himself become a disciple of Jesus. This man went to Pilate and asked for the body of Jesus. Pilate thereupon ordered it to be handed over. So Joseph took the body, wrapped it in a clean shroud and put it in his own new tomb which he had hewn out of the rock. He then rolled a large stone across the entrance of the tomb and went away. Now Mary of Magdala and the other Mary were there, sitting opposite the sepulchre.

Next day, that is, when Preparation Day was over, the chief priests and the Pharisees went in a body to Pilate and said to him,

C   Your Excellency, we recall that this impostor said, while he was still alive, 'After three days I shall rise again.' Therefore give the order to have the sepulchre kept secure until the third day, for fear his disciples come and steal him away and tell the people, 'He has risen from the dead.' This last piece of fraud would be worse than what went before.

N   Pilate said to them:

O   You may have your guards. Go and make it all as secure as you know how.

N   So they went and made the sepulchre secure, putting seals on the stone and mounting a guard.

| [The Gospel of the Lord.]

Shorter Form, verses 27:11-54. Read between [ ]

After the narrative of the Passion, a brief homily should take place, if appropriate. A period of silence may also be observed.

The Creed is said, and the Universal Prayer takes place.

Prayer over the Offerings

Through the Passion of your Only
      Begotten Son, O Lord,
may our reconciliation with you
      be near at hand,
so that, though we do not merit it
      by our own deeds,
yet by this sacrifice made once
      for all,
we may feel already the effects
      of your mercy.
Through Christ our Lord.

Super oblata

Per Unigeniti tui passionem
placatio tua nobis, Domine,
      sit propinqua,
quam, etsi nostris operibus
      non meremur,
interveniente sacrificio singulari,
tua percipiamus
      miseratione præventi.
Per Christum Dominum nostrum.

Preface: The Passion of the Lord.

It is truly right and just,
      our duty and our salvation,
always and everywhere to give
      you thanks,
Lord, holy Father, almighty
      and eternal God,
through Christ our Lord.

Præfatio: De dominica Passione.

Vere dignum et iustum est,
      æquum et salutare,
nos tibi semper et ubique
      gratias agere:
Domine, sancte Pater, omnipotens
      æterne Deus:
per Christum Dominum nostrum.

For, though innocent, he suffered
willingly for sinners
and accepted unjust condemnation
to save the guilty.
His Death has washed away our sins,
and his Resurrection has purchased
our justification.

And so, with all the Angels,
we praise you, as in joyful
celebration we acclaim:

Holy, Holy, Holy Lord God of hosts...

Qui pati pro impiis dignatus
est innocens,
et pro sceleratis
indebite condemnari.
Cuius mors delicta nostra detersit,
et iustificationem nobis
resurrectio comparavit.

Unde et nos cum omnibus Angelis
te laudamus,
iucunda celebratione clamantes:

Sanctus, Sanctus, Sanctus. . .

Communion Antiphon   Mt 26:42

Father, if this chalice cannot pass
without my drinking it,
your will be done.

Ant. ad communionem

Pater, si non potest
hic calix transire,
nisi bibam illum, fiat voluntas tua.

Prayer after Communion

Nourished with these sacred gifts,
we humbly beseech you, O Lord,
that, just as through the death
of your Son
you have brought us to hope
for what we believe,
so by his Resurrection
you may lead us to where you call.
Through Christ our Lord.

Post communionem

Sacro munere satiati,
supplices te, Domine, deprecamur,
ut, qui fecisti nos
morte Filii tui sperare
quod credimus,
facias nos, eodem resurgente,
pervenire quo tendimus.
Per Christum Dominum nostrum.

Prayer over the People

Look, we pray, O Lord,
on this your family,
for whom our Lord Jesus Christ
did not hesitate to be delivered
into the hands of the wicked
and submit to the agony
of the Cross.
Who lives and reigns
for ever and ever.

Oratio super populum

Respice, quæsumus, Domine,
super hanc familiam tuam,
pro qua Dominus noster
Iesus Christus
non dubitavit manibus
tradi nocentium,
et crucis subire tormentum.
Qui vivit et regnat
in sæcula sæculorum.

THE SACRED PASCHAL TRIDUUM

In the Sacred Triduum, the Church solemnly celebrates the greatest mysteries of our redemption, keeping by means of special celebrations the memorial of her Lord, crucified, buried, and risen.

The Paschal Fast should also be kept sacred. It is to be celebrated everywhere on the Friday of the Lord's Passion and, where appropriate, prolonged also through Holy Saturday as a way of coming, with spirit uplifted, to the joys of the Lord's Resurrection.

For a fitting celebration of the Sacred Triduum, a sufficient number of lay ministers is required, who must be carefully instructed as to what they are to do.

The singing of the people, the ministers, and the Priest Celebrant has a special importance in the celebrations of these days, for when texts are sung, they have their proper impact.

Pastors should, therefore, not fail to explain to the Christian faithful, as best they can, the meaning and order of the celebrations and to prepare them for active and fruitful participation.

The celebrations of the Sacred Triduum are to be carried out in cathedral and parochial churches and only in those churches in which they can be performed with dignity, that is, with a good attendance of the faithful, an appropriate number of ministers, and the means to sing at least some of the parts.

Consequently, it is desirable that small communities, associations, and special groups of various kinds join together in these churches to carry out the sacred celebrations in a more noble manner.

6 April

THURSDAY OF THE LORD'S SUPPER
(MAUNDY THURSDAY)

*We are not scandalised, because Jesus himself was not scandalised by
seeing that his joyful preaching of salvation to the poor was not received
wholeheartedly, but amid the shouts and threats of those who refused to hear
his word or wanted to reduce it to legalisms such as moralism or clericalism.
We are not scandalised because Jesus was not scandalised by having to heal
the sick and to set prisoners free amid the moralistic, legalistic and clerical
squabbles that arose every time he did some good. We are not scandalised
because Jesus was not scandalised by having to give sight to the blind amid
people who closed their eyes in order not to see, or looked the other way. We are
not scandalised because the preaching of the Gospel is effective not because of
our eloquent words but because of the power of the cross.*

(Pope Francis)

In accordance with a most ancient tradition of the Church, on this day all Masses
without the people are forbidden.

At the Evening Mass

The Mass of the Lord's Supper is celebrated in the evening, at a convenient time,
with the full participation of the whole local community and with all the Priests
and ministers exercising their office.

All Priests may concelebrate even if they have already concelebrated the Chrism Mass on
this day, or if they have to celebrate another Mass for the good of the Christian faithful.

Where a pastoral reason requires it, the local Ordinary may permit another Mass
to be celebrated in churches and oratories in the evening and, in case of genuine
necessity, even in the morning, but only for the faithful who are in no way able
to participate in the evening Mass. Care should, nevertheless, be taken that
celebrations of this sort do not take place for the advantage of private persons or
special small groups, and do not prejudice the evening Mass.

Holy Communion may only be distributed to the faithful during Mass; but it may
be brought to the sick at any hour of the day.

The altar may be decorated with flowers with a moderation that accords with the
character of this day. The tabernacle should be entirely empty; but a sufficient
amount of bread should be consecrated in this Mass for the Communion of the
clergy and the people on this and the following day.

<table>
<tr><td>

Entrance Antiphon   Cf. Ga 6:14

WE should glory in the Cross
of our Lord Jesus Christ,
in whom is our salvation,
   life and resurrection,
through whom we are saved
   and delivered.

</td><td>

Ant. ad introitum

NOS autem gloriari oportet
in cruce Domini nostri
   Iesu Christi,
in quo est salus,
   vita et resurrectio nostra,
per quem salvati et liberati sumus.

</td></tr>
</table>

The **Gloria in excelsis** (**Glory to God in the highest**) is said. While the hymn is being sung, bells are rung, and when it is finished, they remain silent until the **Gloria in excelsis** of the Easter Vigil, unless, if appropriate, the Diocesan Bishop has decided otherwise. Likewise, during this same period, the organ and other musical instruments may be used only so as to support the singing.

<table>
<tr><td>

Collect

O God, who have called us
   to participate
in this most sacred Supper,
in which your Only Begotten Son,
when about to hand himself over
   to death,
entrusted to the Church a sacrifice
   new for all eternity,
the banquet of his love,
grant, we pray,
that we may draw from so great
   a mystery,
the fullness of charity and of life.
Through our Lord Jesus Christ,
   your Son,
who lives and reigns with you
   in the unity of the Holy Spirit,
God, for ever and ever.

</td><td>

Collecta

Sacratissimam, Deus,
   frequentantibus Cenam,
in qua Unigenitus tuus,
   morti se traditurus,
novum in sæcula sacrificium
dilectionisque suæ convivium
   Ecclesiæ commendavit,
da nobis, quæsumus,
   ut ex tanto mysterio
plenitudinem caritatis hauriamus
   et vitæ.
Per Dominum nostrum Iesum
   Christum Filium tuum,
qui tecum vivit et regnat
   in unitate Spiritus Sancti,
Deus, per omnia sæcula sæculorum.

</td></tr>
</table>

FIRST READING

A reading from the book of Exodus   12:1-8,11-14

Instructions concerning the Passover meal.

The Lord said to Moses and Aaron in the land of Egypt, 'This month is to be the first of all the others for you, the first month of your year. Speak to the whole community of Israel and say, "On the tenth day of this month each man must take an animal from the flock, one for each family: one animal for each household. If the household is too small to eat the animal, a man must join with his neighbour, the nearest to his house, as the number of persons requires. You must take into account what each can eat in deciding the number for the animal. It must be an animal without blemish, a male one year old; you may take it from either sheep or goats. You must keep it till the fourteenth day of the month when the whole assembly of the community of Israel shall slaughter it between the two evenings. Some of the blood must then be taken and put on the two doorposts and the lintel of the houses where it is eaten. That night, the flesh is to be eaten, roasted over the fire; it must be eaten with unleavened bread and bitter herbs. You shall eat it like this: with a girdle round your waist, sandals on your feet, a staff in your hand. You shall eat it hastily; it is a passover in honour of the Lord. That night, I will go through the land of Egypt and strike down all the first-born in the land of Egypt, man and beast alike, and I shall deal out punishment to all the gods of Egypt, I am the Lord. The blood shall serve to mark the houses that you live in. When I see the blood I will pass over you and you shall escape the destroying plague when I strike the land of Egypt. This day is to be a day of remembrance for you, and you must celebrate it as a feast in the Lord's honour. For all generations you are to declare it a day of festival, for ever.'"

The word of the Lord.

Responsional Psalm   Ps 115:12-13,15-18. R. Cf. 1 Co 10:16

R. **The blessing-cup that we bless**
   is a communion with the blood of Christ.

How can I repay the Lord
for his goodness to me?
The cup of salvation I will raise;
I will call on the Lord's name. R.

O precious in the eyes of the Lord
is the death of his faithful.
Your servant, Lord, your servant am I;
you have loosened my bonds. R.

A thanksgiving sacrifice I make:
I will call on the Lord's name.
My vows to the Lord I will fulfil
before all his people. R.

SECOND READING

A reading from the first letter of St Paul to the Corinthians   11:23-26

Every time you eat this bread and drink this cup, you are proclaiming the death of the Lord.

This is what I received from the Lord, and in turn passed on to you: that on the same night that he was betrayed, the Lord Jesus took some bread, and thanked God for it and broke it, and he said, 'This is my body, which is for you; do this as a memorial of me.' In the same way he took the cup after supper, and said,'This cup is the new covenant in my blood. Whenever you drink it, do this as a memorial of me.' Until the Lord comes, therefore, every time you eat this bread and drink this cup, you are proclaiming his death.

The word of the Lord.

Gospel Acclamation   Jn 13:34

R. **Praise and honour to you, Lord Jesus!**
I give you a new commandment:
love one another just as I have loved you, says the Lord.
R. **Praise and honour to you, Lord Jesus!**

GOSPEL

A reading from the holy Gospel according to John   13:1-15

Now he showed how perfect his love was.

It was before the festival of the Passover, and Jesus knew that the hour had come for him to pass from this world to the Father. He had always loved those who were his in the world, but now he showed how perfect his love was.

They were at supper, and the devil had already put it into the mind of Judas Iscariot son of Simon, to betray him. Jesus knew that the Father had put everything into his hands, and that he had come from God and was returning to God, and he got up from table, removed his outer garment and, taking a towel, wrapped it round his waist; he then poured water into a basin and began to wash the disciples' feet and to wipe them with the towel he was wearing.

He came to Simon Peter, who said to him, 'Lord, are you going to wash my feet?' Jesus answered, 'At the moment you do not know what I am doing, but later you will understand.' 'Never!' said Peter 'You shall never wash my feet.' Jesus replied, 'If I do not wash you, you can have nothing in common with me.' 'Then, Lord,' said Simon Peter 'not only my feet, but my hands and my head as well!' Jesus said, 'No one who has taken a bath needs washing, he is clean all over. You too are clean, though not all of you are.' He knew who was going to betray him, that was why he said, 'though not all of you are.'

When he had washed their feet and put on his clothes again he went back to the table. 'Do you understand' he said 'what I have done to you? You call me Master and Lord, and rightly; so I am. If I, then, the Lord and Master, have washed your feet, you should wash each other's feet. I have given you an example so that you may copy what I have done to you.'

The Gospel of the Lord.

After the proclamation of the Gospel, the Priest gives a homily in which light is shed on the principal mysteries that are commemorated in this Mass, namely, the institution of the Holy Eucharist and of the priestly Order, and the commandment of the Lord concerning fraternal charity.

The Washing of Feet

After the Homily, where a pastoral reason suggests it, the Washing of Feet follows.

Those who have been chosen are led by the ministers to seats prepared in a suitable place. Then the Priest (removing his chasuble if necessary) goes to each one, and, with the help of the ministers, pours water over each one's feet and then dries them. Meanwhile some of the following antiphons or other appropriate chants are sung.

Antiphon 1 Cf. Jn 13:4,5,15	Antiphona 1
After the Lord had risen from supper, he poured water into a basin and began to wash the feet of his disciples: he left them this example.	Postquam surrexit Dominus a cena, misit aquam in pelvim, et cœpit lavare pedes discipulorum: hoc exemplum reliquit eis.
Antiphon 2 Cf. Jn 13:12,13,15	Antiphona 2
The Lord Jesus, after eating supper with his disciples, washed their feet and said to them: Do you know what I, your Lord and Master, have done for you? I have given you an example, that you should do likewise.	Dominus Iesus, postquam cenavit cum discipulis suis, lavit pedes eorum, et ait illis: 'Scitis quid fecerim vobis ego, Dominus et Magister? Exemplum dedi vobis, ut et vos ita faciatis.'

Antiphon 3   Jn 13:6,7,8

Lord, are you to wash my feet?
    Jesus said to him in answer:
If I do not wash your feet,
    you will have no share with me.

V. So he came to Simon Peter
    and Peter said to him:
– Lord, are you to wash my feet?. . .

V. What I am doing,
    you do not know for now,
    but later you will come to know.
– Lord, are you to wash my feet?. . .

Antiphon 4   Cf. Jn 13:14

If I, your Lord and Master,
    have washed your feet,
how much more should you wash
    each other's feet?

Antiphon 5   Jn 13:35

This is how all will know that you
    are my disciples:
if you have love for one another.

V. Jesus said to his disciples:
– This is how all will know. . .

Antiphon 6   Jn 13:34

I give you a new commandment,
that you love one another
as I have loved you, says the Lord.

Antiphon 7   1 Co 13:13

Let faith, hope and charity,
    these three, remain among you,
but the greatest of these is charity.

V. Now faith, hope and charity,
    these three, remain;
but the greatest of these is charity.
– Let faith, hope and charity. . .

Antiphona 3

Domine, tu mihi lavas pedes?
    Respondit Iesus et dixit ei:
Se non lavero tibi pedes,
    non habebis partem mecum.

V. Venit ergo ad Simonem Petrum,
    et dixit ei Petrus:
– Domine, tu mihi lavas pedes?. . .

V. Quod ego facio,
    tu nescis modo:
    scies autem postea.
– Domine, tu mihi lavas pedes?. . .

Antiphona 4

Si ego, Dominus et Magister vester,
    lavi vobis pedes:
quanto magis debetis alter alterius
    lavare pedes?

Antiphona 5

In hoc cognoscent omnes,
    quia discipuli mei estis,
si dilectionem habueritis
    ad invicem.

V. Dixit Iesus discipulis suis.
– In hoc cognoscent omnes. . .

Antiphona 6

Mandatum novum do vobis,
    ut diligatis invicem,
sicut dilexi vos, dicit Dominus.

Antiphona 7

Maneant in vobis fides, spes,
    caritas, tria hæc:
maior autem horum est caritas.

V. Nunc autem manent fides, spes,
    caritas, tria hæc:
maior horum est caritas.
– Maneant in vobis fides. . .

After the Washing of Feet, the Priest washes and dries his hands, puts the chasuble back on, and returns to the chair, and from there he directs the Universal Prayer.

The Creed is not said.

The Liturgy of the Eucharist

At the beginning of the Liturgy of the Eucharist, there may be a procession of the faithful in which gifts for the poor may be presented with the bread and wine.

Meanwhile the following, or another appropriate chant, is sung.

Ant. Where true charity is dwelling,
      God is present there.

V. By the love of Christ we have
   been brought together:

V. let us find in him our gladness
   and our pleasure;

V. may we love him and revere him,
   God the living,

V. and in love respect each other
   with sincere hearts.

Ant. Where true charity is dwelling,
      God is present there.

V. So when we as one are gathered
   all together,

V. let us strive to keep our minds
   free of division;

V. may there be an end to malice,
   strife and quarrels,

V. and let Christ our God
   be dwelling here among us.

Ant. Where true charity is dwelling,
      God is present there.

V. May your face thus be our vision,
   bright in glory,

V. Christ our God, with all
   the blessed Saints in heaven:

V. such delight is pure and faultless,
   joy unbounded,

V. which endures through
   countless ages
   world without end. Amen.

Ant. Ubi caritas est vera,
      Deus ibi est.

V. Exsultemus et in
   ipso iucundemur.

V. Congregavit nos in unum
   Christi amor.

V. Timeamus et amemus
   Deum vivum.

V. Et ex corde diligamus nos sincero.

Ant. Ubi caritas est vera,
      Deus ibi est.

V. Simul ergo cum in
   unum congregamur:

V. Ne nos mente dividamur,
   caveamus.

V. Cessent iurgia maligna,
   cessent lites.

V. Et in medio nostri sit
   Christus Deus.

Ant. Ubi caritas est vera,
      Deus ibi est.

V. Simul quoque cum beatis
   videamus

V. Glorianter vultum tuum,
   Christe Deus:

V. Gaudium, quod est immensum
   atque probum,

V. Sæcula per infinita sæculorum.
   Amen.

Prayer over the Offerings

Grant us, O Lord, we pray,
that we may participate worthily
    in these mysteries,
for whenever the memorial
    of this sacrifice is celebrated
the work of our redemption
    is accomplished.
Through Christ our Lord.

Super oblata

Concede nobis,
    quæsumus, Domine,
hæc digne frequentare mysteria,
quia, quoties huius hostiæ
    commemoratio celebratur,
opus nostræ redemptionis exercetur.
Per Christum Dominum nostrum.

Preface I of the Most Holy Eucharist, pp.68-69.
If the Roman Canon is said, the following special forms are used.

Celebrating the most sacred day
on which our Lord Jesus Christ
was handed over for our sake,
and in communion with those
    whose memory we venerate,
especially the glorious
    ever-Virgin Mary,
Mother of our God and Lord,
    Jesus Christ,
and blessed Joseph, her Spouse,
your blessed Apostles and Martyrs,
Peter and Paul, Andrew,
(James, John,
Thomas, James, Philip,
Bartholomew, Matthew,
Simon and Jude;
Linus, Cletus, Clement, Sixtus,
Cornelius, Cyprian,
Lawrence, Chrysogonus,
John and Paul,
Cosmas and Damian)
and all your Saints;
we ask that through their merits
    and prayers,
in all things we may be defended
by your protecting help.
(Through Christ our Lord. Amen.)

Communicantes, et diem
    sacratissimum celebrantes,
quo Dominus noster Iesus Christus
pro nobis est traditus,
sed et memoriam venerantes,
in primis gloriosæ semper
    Virginis Mariæ,
Genetricis eiusdem Dei et Domini
    nostri Iesu Christi:
sed et beati Ioseph,
    eiusdem Virginis Sponsi,
et beatorum Apostolorum ac
    Martyrum tuorum,
Petri et Pauli, Andreæ,
(Iacobi, Ioannis,
Thomæ, Iacobi, Philippi,
Bartholomæi, Matthæi,
Simonis et Thaddæi:
Lini, Cleti, Clementis, Xysti,
Cornelii, Cypriani,
Laurentii, Chrysogoni,
Ioannis et Pauli,
Cosmæ et Damiani)
et omnium Sanctorum tuorum;
quorum meritis precibusque concedas,
ut in omnibus protectionis tuæ
    muniamur auxilio.
(Per Christum Dominum nostrum.
    Amen.)

Therefore, Lord, we pray:
graciously accept this oblation of
    our service,
that of your whole family,
which we make to you
as we observe the day
on which our Lord Jesus Christ
handed on the mysteries
    of his Body and Blood
for his disciples to celebrate;
order our days in your peace,
and command that we be delivered
    from eternal damnation
and counted among the flock of
    those you have chosen.
(Through Christ our Lord. Amen.)

Be pleased, O God, we pray,
to bless, acknowledge,
and approve this offering
    in every respect;
make it spiritual and acceptable,
so that it may become for us
the Body and Blood of your most
    beloved Son,
our Lord Jesus Christ.

On the day before he was to suffer
for our salvation and the salvation
    of all,
that is today,
he took bread in his holy
    and venerable hands,
and with eyes raised to heaven
to you, O God, his almighty Father,
giving you thanks,
    he said the blessing,
broke the bread
and gave it to his disciples, saying:

TAKE THIS, ALL OF YOU,
    AND EAT OF IT,
FOR THIS IS MY BODY,
WHICH WILL BE GIVEN UP FOR YOU.

Hanc igitur oblationem
    servitutis nostræ,
sed et cunctæ familiæ tuæ,
quam tibi offerimus ob diem,
in qua Dominus noster Iesus Christus
tradidit discipulis suis
Corporis et Sanguinis
    sui mysteria celebranda,
quæsumus, Domine,
    ut placatus accipias:
diesque nostros in tua pace
    disponas,
atque ab æterna damnatione
    nos eripi
et in electorum tuorum iubeas
    grege numerari.
(Per Christum Dominum nostrum.
    Amen.)

Quam oblationem tu, Deus,
    in omnibus, quæsumus,
benedictam, adscriptam, ratam,
rationabilem, acceptabilemque
    facere digneris:
ut nobis Corpus et Sanguis fiat
    dilectissimi Filii tui,
Domini nostri Iesu Christi.

Qui, pridie quam pro nostra
omniumque salute pateretur,
hoc est hodie,
accepit panem in sanctus ac
    venerabiles manus suas,
et elevatis oculis in cælum
ad te Deum Patrem
    suum omnipotentem,
tibi gratias agens benedixit,
fregit, deditque discipulis suis, dicens:

ACCIPITE ET MANDUCATE
    EX HOC OMNES:
HOC EST ENIM CORPUS MEUM,
QUOD PRO VOBIS TRADETUR.

Then follows the remainder of the Roman Canon as usual (see pp.86-93) and the Communion Rite, pp.120-121.

At an appropriate moment during Communion, the Priest entrusts the Eucharist from the table of the altar to Deacons or acolytes or other extraordinary ministers, so that afterwards it may be brought to the sick who are to receive Holy Communion at home.

Communion Antiphon 1 Co 11:24-25	Ant. ad communionem
This is the Body that will be given up for you;	Hoc Corpus, quod pro vobis tradetur:
this is the Chalice of the new covenant in my Blood, says the Lord;	hic calix novi testamenti est in meo Sanguine, dicit Dominus;
do this, whenever you receive it, in memory of me.	hoc facite, quotiescumque sumitis, in meam commemorationem.

After the distribution of Communion, the ciborium with hosts for Communion on the following day is left on the altar. The Priest, standing at the chair, says the Prayer after Communion.

Prayer after Communion	Post communionem
Grant, almighty God, that, just as we are renewed by the Supper of your Son in this present age, so we may enjoy his banquet for all eternity. Who lives and reigns for ever and ever.	Concede nobis, omnipotens Deus, ut, sicut Cena Filii tui reficimur temporali, ita satiari mereamur æterna. Per Christum Dominum nostrum.

The Transfer of the Most Blessed Sacrament

After the Prayer after Communion, the Priest puts incense in the thurible while standing, blesses it and then, kneeling, incenses the Blessed Sacrament three times. Then, having put on a white humeral veil, he rises, takes the ciborium, and covers it with the ends of the veil.

A procession is formed in which the Blessed Sacrament, accompanied by torches and incense, is carried through the church to a place of repose prepared in a part of the church or in a chapel suitably decorated. A lay minister with a cross, standing between two other ministers with lighted candles leads off. Others carrying lighted candles follow. Before the Priest carrying the Blessed Sacrament comes the thurifer with a smoking thurible. Meanwhile, the hymn Pange, lingua (exclusive of the last two stanzas) or another eucharistic chant is sung.

When the procession reaches the place of repose, the Priest, with the help of the Deacon if necessary, places the ciborium in the tabernacle, the door of which remains open. Then he puts incense in the thurible and, kneeling, incenses the

Blessed Sacrament, while **Tantum ergo Sacramentum** or another eucharistic chant is sung. Then the Deacon or the Priest himself places the Sacrament in the tabernacle and closes the door.

After a period of adoration in silence, the Priest and ministers genuflect and return to the sacristy.

At an appropriate time, the altar is stripped and, if possible, the crosses are removed from the church. It is expedient that any crosses which remain in the church be veiled.

Vespers (Evening Prayer) is not celebrated by those who have attended the Mass of the Lord's Supper.

The faithful are invited to continue adoration before the Blessed Sacrament for a suitable length of time during the night, according to local circumstances, but after midnight the adoration should take place without solemnity.

If the celebration of the Passion of the Lord on the following Friday does not take place in the same church, the Mass is concluded in the usual way and the Blessed Sacrament is placed in the tabernacle.

7 April

FRIDAY OF THE PASSION OF THE LORD
(GOOD FRIDAY)

What is most amazing about the Lord and his Passover? It is the fact that he achieves glory through humiliation. He triumphs by accepting suffering and death, things that we, in our quest for admiration and success, would rather avoid. Jesus did it for us, to plumb the depths of our human experience, our entire existence, all our evil. To draw near to us and not abandon us in our suffering and our death. Jesus was lifted high on the cross in order to descend to the abyss of our suffering. He experienced our deepest sorrows: failure, loss of everything, betrayal by a friend, even abandonment by God. By experiencing in the flesh our deepest struggles and conflicts, he redeemed and transformed them. His love draws close to our frailty; it touches the very things of which we are most ashamed. Yet now we know that we are not alone: God is at our side in every affliction, in every fear; no evil, no sin will ever have the final word. God triumphs, but the palm of victory passes through the wood of the cross. For the palm and the cross are inseparable.

(Pope Francis)

On this and the following day, by a most ancient tradition, the Church does not celebrate the Sacraments at all, except for Penance and the Anointing of the Sick.

On this day, Holy Communion is distributed to the faithful only within the celebration of the Lord's Passion; but it may be brought at any hour of the day to the sick who cannot participate in this celebration.

The altar should be completely bare: without a cross, without candles and without cloths.

The Celebration of the Passion of the Lord

On the afternoon of this day, about three o'clock (unless a later hour is chosen for a pastoral reason), there takes place the celebration of the Lord's Passion consisting of three parts, namely, the Liturgy of the Word, the Adoration of the Cross, and Holy Communion.

The Priest and the Deacon, if a Deacon is present, wearing red vestments as for Mass, go to the altar in silence and, after making a reverence to the altar, prostrate themselves or, if appropriate, kneel and pray in silence for a while. All others kneel.

Then the Priest, with the ministers, goes to the chair where, facing the people, who are standing, he says, with hands extended, one of the following prayers, omitting the invitation **Let us pray**.

Prayer

Remember your mercies, O Lord,
and with your eternal protection
    sanctify your servants,
for whom Christ your Son,
by the shedding of his Blood,
established the Paschal Mystery.
Who lives and reigns
    for ever and ever.
R. Amen.

Or:

O God, who by the Passion
    of Christ your Son, our Lord,
abolished the death inherited
    from ancient sin
by every succeeding generation,
grant that just as,
    being conformed to him,
we have borne by the law of nature
the image of the man of earth,
so by the sanctification of grace
we may bear the image of the Man
    of heaven.
Through Christ our Lord.
R. Amen.

Oratio

Reminiscere miserationum
    tuarum, Domine,
et famulos tuos æterna
    protectione sanctifica,
pro quibus Christus, Filius tuus,
per suum cruorem instituit
    paschale mysterium.
Qui vivit et regnat
    in sæcula sæculorum.
R. Amen.

Vel:

Deus, qui peccati veteris
    hereditariam mortem,
in qua posteritatis genus
    omne successerat,
Christi Filii tui, Domini nostri,
    passione solvisti,
da, ut conformes eidem facti,
sicut imaginem terreni hominis
naturæ necessitate portavimus,
ita imaginem cælestis
gratiæ sanctificatione portemus.
Per Christum Dominum nostrum.
R. Amen.

FIRST PART:

The Liturgy of the Word

FIRST READING

A reading from the prophet Isaiah   52:13-53:12
He was pierced through our faults.

See, my servant will prosper,
he shall be lifted up, exalted, rise to great heights.
As the crowds were appalled on seeing him
 – so disfigured did he look
that he seemed no longer human –
so will the crowds be astonished at him,
and kings stand speechless before him;
for they shall see something never told
and witness something never heard before:
'Who could believe what we have heard,
and to whom has the power of the Lord been revealed?'

Like a sapling he grew up in front of us,
like a root in arid ground.
Without beauty, without majesty (we saw him),
no looks to attract our eyes;
a thing despised and rejected by men,
a man of sorrows and familiar with suffering,
a man to make people screen their faces;
he was despised and we took no account of him.

And yet ours were the sufferings he bore,
ours the sorrows he carried.
But we, we thought of him as someone punished,
struck by God, and brought low.
Yet he was pierced through for our faults,
crushed for our sins.
On him lies a punishment that brings us peace,
and through his wounds we are healed.

We had all gone astray like sheep,
each taking his own way,
and the Lord burdened him
with the sins of all of us.

Harshly dealt with, he bore it humbly,
he never opened his mouth,
like a lamb that is led to the slaughter-house,
like a sheep that is dumb before its shearers
never opening its mouth.

By force and by law he was taken;
would anyone plead his cause?
Yes, he was torn away from the land of the living;
for our faults struck down in death.
They gave him a grave with the wicked,
a tomb with the rich,
though he had done no wrong
and there had been no perjury in his mouth.
The Lord has been pleased to crush him with suffering.
If he offers his life in atonement,
he shall see his heirs, he shall have a long life
and through him what the Lord wishes will be done.
His soul's anguish over
he shall see the light and be content.
By his sufferings shall my servant justify many,
taking their faults on himself.

Hence I will grant whole hordes for his tribute,
he shall divide the spoil with the mighty,
for surrendering himself to death
and letting himself be taken for a sinner,
while he was bearing the faults of many
and praying all the time for sinners.

    The word of the Lord.

Responsorial Psalm   Ps 30:2,6,12-13,15-17,25. R. Lk 23:46

R. **Father, into your hands I commend my spirit.**

    In you, O Lord, I take refuge.
    Let me never be put to shame.
    In your justice, set me free.
    Into your hands I commend my spirit.
    It is you who will redeem me, Lord. R.

In the face of all my foes
I am a reproach,
an object of scorn to my neighbours
and of fear to my friends. R.

Those who see me in the street
run far away from me.
I am like a dead man, forgotten in men's hearts,
like a thing thrown away. R.

But as for me, I trust in you, Lord,
I say: 'You are my God.'
My life is in your hands, deliver me
from the hands of those who hate me. R.

Let your face shine on your servant.
Save me in your love.
Be strong, let your heart take courage,
all who hope in the Lord. R.

R. **Father, into your hands I commend my spirit.**

SECOND READING

A reading from the letter to the Hebrews   4:14-16; 5:7-9

He learnt to obey through suffering and became for all who obey him the source of eternal salvation.

Since in Jesus, the Son of God, we have the supreme high priest who has gone through to the highest heaven, we must never let go of the faith that we have professed. For it is not as if we had a high priest who was incapable of feeling our weaknesses with us; but we have one who has been tempted in every way that we are, though he is without sin. Let us be confident, then, in approaching the throne of grace, that we shall have mercy from him and find grace when we are in need of help.

During his life on earth, he offered up prayer and entreaty, aloud and in silent tears, to the one who had the power to save him out of death, and he submitted so humbly that his prayer was heard. Although he was Son, he learnt to obey through suffering; but having been made perfect, he became for all who obey him the source of eternal salvation.

The word of the Lord.

Gospel Acclamation   Ph 2:8-9

R. **Glory and praise to you, O Christ!**
Christ was humbler yet,
even accepting death, death on a cross.
But God raised him high
and gave him the name which is above all names.
R. **Glory and praise to you, O Christ!**

GOSPEL

The symbols in the following passion narrative represent:

N Narrator   J Jesus   O Other single speaker
C Crowd, or more than one speaker

The passion of our Lord Jesus Christ according to John   18:1-19:42

N Jesus left with his disciples and crossed the Kedron valley. There was a
   garden there, and he went into it with his disciples. Judas the traitor
   knew the place well, since Jesus had often met his disciples there, and
   he brought the cohort to this place together with a detachment of
   guards sent by the chief priests and the Pharisees, all with lanterns and
   torches and weapons. Knowing everything that was going to happen to
   him, Jesus then came forward and said,
J Who are you looking for?
N They answered,
C Jesus the Nazarene.
N He said,
J I am he.
N Now Judas the traitor was standing among them. When Jesus said,
   'I am he', they moved back and fell to the ground. He asked them a
   second time,
J Who are you looking for?
N They said,
C Jesus the Nazarene.
N Jesus replied,
J I have told you that I am he. If I am the one you are looking for, let
   these others go.
N This was to fulfil the words he has spoken: 'Not one of those you gave
   me have I lost.'
       Simon Peter, who carried a sword, drew it and wounded the high
   priest's servant, cutting off his right ear. The servant's name was
   Malchus. Jesus said to Peter,

J   Put your sword back in its scabbard; am I not to drink the cup that the Father has given me?

N   The cohort and its captain and the Jewish guards seized Jesus and bound him. They took him first to Annas, because Annas was the father-in-law of Caiaphas, who was high priest that year. It was Caiaphas who had suggested to the Jews, 'It is better for one man to die for the people.'

       Simon Peter, with another disciple, followed Jesus. This disciple, who was known to the high priest, went with Jesus into the high priest's palace, but Peter stayed outside the door. So the other disciple, the one known to the high priest, went out, spoke to the woman who was keeping the door and brought Peter in. The maid on duty at the door said to Peter,

O   Aren't you another of that man's disciples?

N   He answered,

O   I am not.

N   Now it was cold, and the servants and guards had lit a charcoal fire and were standing there warming themselves; so Peter stood there too, warming himself with the others.

       The high priest questioned Jesus about his disciples and his teaching. Jesus answered,

J   I have spoken openly for all the world to hear; I have always taught in the synagogue and in the Temple where all the Jews meet together: I have said nothing in secret. But why ask me? Ask my hearers what I taught: they know what I said.

N   At these words, one of the guards standing by gave Jesus a slap in the face, saying,

O   Is that the way to answer the high priest?

N   Jesus replied,

J   If there is something wrong in what I said, point it out; but if there is no offence in it, why do you strike me?

N   Then Annas sent him, still bound, to Caiaphas, the high priest. As Simon Peter stood there warming himself, someone said to him,

O   Aren't you another of his disciples?

N   He denied it saying,

O   I am not.

N   One of the high priest's servants, a relation of the man whose ear Peter had cut off, said,

O   Didn't I see you in the garden with him?

N   Again Peter denied it, and at once a cock crew.

They then led Jesus from the house of Caiaphas to the Praetorium.
It was now morning. They did not go into the Praetorium themselves
or they would be defiled and unable to eat the passover. So Pilate came
outside to them and said,

O What charge do you bring against this man?

N They replied,

C If he were not a criminal, we should not be handing him over to you.

N Pilate said,

O Take him yourselves, and try him by your own Law.

N The Jews answered,

C We are not allowed to put a man to death.

N This was to fulfil the words Jesus had spoken indicating the way he was
going to die.

So Pilate went back into the Praetorium and called Jesus to him,
and asked,

O Are you the king of Jews?

N Jesus replied,

J Do you ask this of your own accord, or have others spoken to you
about me?

N Pilate answered,

O Am I a Jew? It is your own people and the chief priests who have handed
you over to me: what have you done?

N Jesus replied,

J Mine is not a kingdom of this world; if my kingdom were of this world,
my men would have fought to prevent me being surrendered to the
Jews. But my kingdom is not of this kind.

N Pilate said,

O So you are the king then?

N Jesus answered,

J It is you who say it. Yes, I am a king. I was born for this; I came into the
world for this; to bear witness to the truth, and all who are on the side
of truth listen to my voice.

N Pilate said,

O Truth? What is that?

N And with that he went out again to the Jews and said,

O I find no case against him. But according to a custom of yours I should
release one prisoner at the Passover; would you like me, then, to release
the king of Jews?

N At this they shouted:

C   Not this man, but Barabbas.

N   Barabbas was a brigand.

     Pilate then had Jesus taken away and scourged; and after this, the soldiers twisted some thorns into a crown and put it on his head, and dressed him in a purple robe. They kept coming up to him and saying,

C   Hail, king of the Jews!

N   and they slapped him in the face.

     Pilate came outside again and said to them,

O   Look, I am going to bring him out to you to let you see that I find no case.

N   Jesus then came out wearing the crown of thorns and the purple robe. Pilate said,

O   Here is the man.

N   When they saw him the chief priests and the guards shouted,

C   Crucify him! Crucify him!

N   Pilate said,

O   Take him yourselves and crucify him: I can find no case against him

N   The Jews replied,

C   We have a Law, and according to the Law he ought to die, because he has claimed to be the son of God.

N   When Pilate heard them say this his fears increased. Re-entering the Praetorium, he said to Jesus,

O   Where do you come from?

N   But Jesus made no answer. Pilate then said to him,

O   Are you refusing to speak to me? Surely you know I have power to release you and I have power to crucify you?

N   Jesus replied,

J   You would have no power over me if it had not been given you from above; that is why the one who handed me over to you has the greater guilt.

N   From that moment Pilate was anxious to set him free, but the Jews shouted,

C   If you set him free you are no friend of Caesar's; anyone who makes himself king is defying Caesar.

N   Hearing these words, Pilate had Jesus brought out, and seated himself on the chair of judgement at a place called the Pavement, in Hebrew Gabbatha. It was Passover Preparation Day, about the sixth hour. Pilate said to the Jews,

O   Here is your king.

N   They said,

C   Take him away, take him away. Crucify him!

N   Pilate said,

O   Do you want me to crucify your king?

N   The chief priests answered,

C   We have no king except Caesar.

N   So in the end Pilate handed him over to them to be crucified.

They then took charge of Jesus, and carrying his own cross he went out of the city to the place of the skull, or, as it was called in Hebrew, Golgotha, where they crucified him with two others, one on either side with Jesus in the middle. Pilate wrote out a notice and had it fixed to the cross; it ran: 'Jesus the Nazarene, King of the Jews.' This notice was read by many of the Jews, because the place where Jesus was crucified was not far from the city, and the writing was in Hebrew, Latin and Greek. So the Jewish chief priests said to Pilate,

C   You should not write 'King of the Jews', but 'This man said: I am King of the Jews'.

N   Pilate answered,

O   What I have written, I have written.

N   When the soldiers had finished crucifying Jesus they took his clothing and divided it into four shares, one for each soldier. His undergarment was seamless, woven in one piece from neck to hem; so they said to one another,

C   Instead of tearing it, let's throw dice to decide who is to have it.

N   In this way the words of scripture were fulfilled:

They shared out my clothing among them.

They cast lots for my clothes.

This is exactly what the soldiers did.

Near the cross of Jesus stood his mother and his mother's sister, Mary the wife of Clopas, and Mary of Magdala. Seeing his mother and the disciple he loved standing near her, Jesus said to his mother,

J   Woman, this is your son.

N   Then to the disciple he said,

J   This is your mother.

N   And from that moment the disciple made a place for her in his home.

After this, Jesus knew that everything had now been completed, and to fulfil the scripture perfectly he said:

J   I am thirsty.

N   A jar full of vinegar stood there, so putting a sponge soaked in vinegar on a hyssop stick they held it up to his mouth. After Jesus had taken the vinegar he said,

J   It is accomplished;

N   and bowing his head he gave up the spirit.

All kneel and pause a moment.

N   It was Preparation Day, and to prevent the bodies remaining on the cross during the sabbath – since that sabbath was a day of special solemnity – the Jews asked Pilate to have the legs broken and the bodies taken away. Consequently the soldiers came and broke the legs of the first man who had been crucified with him and then of the other. When they came to Jesus, they found that he was already dead, and so instead of breaking his legs one of the soldiers pierced his side with a lance; and immediately there came out blood and water. This is the evidence of one who saw it – trustworthy evidence, and he knows he speaks the truth – and he gives it so that you may believe as well. Because all this happened to fulfil the words of scripture:

Not one bone of his will be broken,

and again, in another place scripture says:

They will look on the one whom they have pierced.

After this, Joseph of Arimathaea, who was a disciple of Jesus – though a secret one because he was afraid of the Jews – asked Pilate to let him remove the body of Jesus. Pilate gave permission, so they came and took it away. Nicodemus came as well – the same one who had first come to Jesus at night – time – and he brought a mixture of myrrh and aloes, weighing about a hundred pounds. They took the body of Jesus and wrapped it with the spices in linen cloths, following the Jewish burial custom. At the place where he had been crucified there was a garden, and in the garden a new tomb in which no one had yet been buried. Since it was the Jewish Day of Preparation and the tomb was near at hand, they laid Jesus there.

The Gospel of the Lord.

After the reading of the Lord's Passion, the Priest gives a brief homily and, at its end, the faithful may be invited to spend a short time in prayer.

The Solemn Intercessions

The Liturgy of the Word concludes with the Solemn Intercessions, which take place in this way: the Deacon, if a Deacon is present, or if he is not, a lay minister, stands at the ambo, and sings or says the invitation in which the intention is expressed. Then all pray in silence for a while, and afterwards the Priest, standing at the chair or, if appropriate, at the altar, with hands extended, sings or says the prayer.

The faithful may remain either kneeling or standing throughout the entire period of the prayers.

Before the Priest's prayer, in accord with tradition, it is permissible to use the Deacon's invitations **Let us kneel – Let us stand**, (**Flectamus genua – Levate**), with all kneeling for silent prayer.

The Conferences of Bishops may provide other invitations to introduce the prayer of the Priest.

In a situation of grave public need, the Diocesan Bishop may permit or order the addition of a special intention.

The prayer is sung in the simple tone or, if the invitations **Let us kneel – Let us stand**, (**Flectamus genua – Levate**), are used, in the solemn tone.

I. For Holy Church

Let us pray, dearly beloved,
   for the holy Church of God,
that our God and Lord be pleased
   to give her peace,
to guard her and to unite her
   throughout the whole world
and grant that, leading our life
   in tranquillity and quiet,
we may glorify God
   the Father almighty.

Prayer in silence. Then the Priest says:

Almighty ever-living God,
who in Christ revealed your glory
   to all the nations,
watch over the works of your mercy,
that your Church, spread
   throughout all the world,
may persevere with steadfast faith
   in confessing your name.
Through Christ our Lord.
R. Amen.

II. For the Pope

Let us pray also for our most
   Holy Father Pope N.,
that our God and Lord,
who chose him for the
   Order of Bishops,

I. Pro sancta Ecclesia

Oremus, dilectissimi nobis,
   pro Ecclesia sancta Dei,
ut eam Deus et Dominus noster
pacificare, adunare
   et custodire dignetur
toto orbe terrarum,
detque nobis, quietam et tranquillam
   vitam degentibus,
glorificare Deum
   Patrem omnipotentem.

Omnipotens sempiterne Deus,
qui gloriam tuam omnibus
   in Christo gentibus revelasti:
custodi opera misericordiæ tuæ,
ut Ecclesia tua, toto orbe diffusa,
stabili fide in confessione
   tui nominis perseveret.
Per Christum Dominum nostrum.
R. Amen.

II. Pro Papa

Oremus et pro beatissimo
   Papa nostro N.,
ut Deus et Dominus noster,
qui elegit eum
   in ordine episcopatus,

may keep him safe and unharmed
    for the Lord's holy Church,
to govern the holy People of God.

salvum atque incolumem custodiat
    Ecclesiæ suæ sanctæ,
ad regendum populum
    sanctum Dei.

Prayer in silence. Then the Priest says:

Almighty ever-living God,
by whose decree all things
    are founded,
look with favour on our prayers
and in your kindness protect
    the Pope chosen for us,
that, under him,
    the Christian people,
governed by you their maker,
may grow in merit by reason
    of their faith.
Through Christ our Lord.
R. Amen.

Omnipotens sempiterne Deus,
cuius iudicio universa fundantur,
respice propitius ad preces nostras,
et electum nobis Antistitem
    tua pietate conserva,
ut christiana plebs,
    quæ te gubernatur auctore,
sub ipso Pontifice,
    fidei suæ meritis augeatur.
Per Christum Dominum nostrum.
R. Amen.

III. For all orders and degrees of the faithful

III. Pro omnibus ordinibus gradibusque fidelium

Let us pray also for our Bishop N.,
for all Bishops, Priests,
    and Deacons of the Church
and for the whole
    of the faithful people.

Oremus et pro Episcopo nostro N.,
pro omnibus Episcopis, presbyteris,
    diaconis Ecclesiæ,
et universa plebe fidelium.

Prayer in silence. Then the Priest says:

Almighty ever-living God,
by whose Spirit the whole body
    of the Church
is sanctified and governed,
hear our humble prayer
    for your ministers,
that, by the gift of your grace,
all may serve you faithfully.
Through Christ our Lord.
R. Amen.

Omnipotens sempiterne Deus,
cuius Spiritu totum corpus Ecclesiæ
sanctificatur et regitur,
exaudi nos pro ministris
    tuis supplicantes,
ut, gratiæ tuæ munere, ab omnibus
    tibi fideliter serviatur.
Per Christum Dominum nostrum.
R. Amen.

IV. For catechumens

Let us pray also
for (our) catechumens,
that our God and Lord
may open wide the ears
of their inmost hearts
and unlock the gates of his mercy,
that, having received forgiveness
of all their sins
through the waters of rebirth,
they, too, may be one with Christ
Jesus our Lord.

Prayer in silence. Then the Priest says:

Almighty ever-living God,
who make your Church ever
fruitful with new offspring,
increase the faith and understanding
of (our) catechumens,
that, reborn in the font of Baptism,
they may be added to the number
of your adopted children.
Through Christ our Lord.
R. Amen.

V. For the unity of Christians

Let us pray also for all our brothers
and sisters who believe in Christ,
that our God and Lord may
be pleased,
as they live the truth,
to gather them together and keep
them in his one Church.

Prayer in silence. Then the Priest says:

Almighty ever-living God,
who gather what is scattered
and keep together what you
have gathered,
look kindly on the flock of your Son,

IV. Pro catechumenis

Oremus et pro
catechumenis (nostris),
ut Deus et Dominus noster
adaperiat aures
præcordiorum ipsorum
ianuamque misericordiæ,
ut, per lavacrum regenerationis
accepta remissione
omnium peccatorum,
et ipsi inveniantur in Christo Iesu
Domino nostro.

Omnipotens sempiterne Deus,
qui Ecclesiam tuam nova semper
prole fecundas,
auge fidem et intellectum
catechumenis (nostris),
ut, renati fonte baptismatis,
adoptionis tuæ filiis aggregentur.
Per Christum Dominum nostrum.
R. Amen.

V. Pro unitate Christianorum

Oremus et pro universis fratribus
in Christum credentibus,
ut Deus et Dominus noster eos,
veritatem facientes,
in una Ecclesia sua congregare
et custodire dignetur.

Omnipotens sempiterne Deus,
qui dispersa congregas
et congregata conservas,
ad gregem Filii tui placatus intende,
ut, quos unum baptisma sacravit,

that those whom one Baptism
  has consecrated
may be joined together by integrity
  of faith
and united in the bond of charity.
Through Christ our Lord.
R. Amen.

| eos et fidei iungat integritas
| et vinculum societ caritatis.
| Per Christum Dominum nostrum.
| R. Amen.

VI. For the Jewish people

Let us pray also for the Jewish people,
to whom the Lord our God
  spoke first,
that he may grant them to advance
  in love of his name
and in faithfulness to his covenant.

Prayer in silence. Then the Priest says:

Almighty ever-living God,
who bestowed your promises on
  Abraham and his descendants,
graciously hear the prayers
  of your Church,
that the people you first made
  your own
may attain the fullness
  of redemption.
Through Christ our Lord.
R. Amen.

| ## VI. Pro Iudæis
|
| Oremus et pro Iudæis,
| ut, ad quos prius locutus est
| Dominus Deus noster,
| eis tribuat in sui nominis amore
| et in sui fœderis fidelitate proficere.
|
|
| Omnipotens sempiterne Deus,
| qui promissiones tuas Abrahæ
| eiusque semini contulisti,
| Ecclesiæ tuæ preces
| clementer exaudi,
| ut populus acquisitionis prioris
| ad redemptionis mereatur
| plenitudinem pervenire.
| Per Christum Dominum nostrum.
| R. Amen.

VII. For those who do not believe in Christ

Let us pray also for those who
  do not believe in Christ,
that, enlightened by the Holy Spirit,
they, too, may enter on the way
  of salvation.

Prayer in silence. Then the Priest says:

Almighty ever-living God,
grant to those who do not
  confess Christ
that, by walking before you
  with a sincere heart,

| ## VII. Pro iis qui Christum non credunt
|
| Oremus et pro iis qui in Christum
| non credunt,
| ut, luce Sancti Spiritus illustrati,
| viam salutis et ipsi valeant introire.
|
|
| Omnipotens sempiterne Deus,
| fac ut qui Christum
| non confitentur,
| coram te sincero corde ambulantes,
| inveniant veritatem,

they may find the truth,
and that we ourselves, being
    constant in mutual love
and striving to understand more
    fully the mystery of your life,
may be made more perfect witnesses
    to your love in the world.
Through Christ our Lord. R. Amen.

nosque, mutuo proficientes
    semper amore
et ad tuæ vitæ mysterium plenius
    percipiendum sollicitos,
perfectiores effice tuæ testes
    caritatis in mundo.
Per Christum Dominum nostrum.
R. Amen.

VIII. For those who do not believe in God

Let us pray also for those who
    do not acknowledge God,
that, following what is right
    in sincerity of heart,
they may find the way
    to God himself.

VIII. Pro iis qui in Deum non credunt

Oremus et pro iis qui Deum
    non agnoscunt,
ut, quæ recta sunt sincero
    corde sectantes,
ad ipsum Deum
    pervenire mereantur.

Prayer in silence. Then the Priest says:

Almighty ever-living God,
who created all people
to seek you always by desiring you
and, by finding you, come to rest,
grant, we pray,
that, despite every harmful obstacle,
all may recognise the signs
    of your fatherly love
and the witness of the good works
done by those who believe in you,
and so in gladness confess you,
the one true God and Father
    of our human race.
Through Christ our Lord. R. Amen.

Omnipotens sempiterne Deus,
qui cunctos homines condidisti,
ut te semper desiderando quærerent
et inveniendo quiescerent,
præsta, quæsumus,
ut inter noxia quæque obstacula
omnes, tuæ signa pietatis
et in te credentium testimonium
bonorum operum percipientes,
te solum verum Deum nostrique
    generis Patrem
gaudeant confiteri.
Per Christum Dominum nostrum.
R. Amen.

IX. For those in public office

Let us pray also for those
    in public office,
that our God and Lord
may direct their minds and hearts
    according to his will
for the true peace and freedom of all.

IX. Pro rempublicam moderantibus

Oremus et pro omnibus
    rempublicam moderantibus,
ut Deus et Dominus noster
mentes et corda eorum secundum
    voluntatem suam dirigat
ad veram omnium pacem
    et libertatem.

Prayer in silence. Then the Priest says:

Almighty ever-living God,
in whose hand lies every
    human heart
and the rights of peoples,
look with favour, we pray,
on those who govern
    with authority over us,
that throughout the whole world,
the prosperity of peoples,
the assurance of peace,
and freedom of religion
may through your gift
    be made secure.
Through Christ our Lord. R. Amen.

Omnipotens sempiterne Deus,
in cuius manu sunt hominum
    corda et iura populorum,
respice benignus ad eos,
    qui nos in potestate moderantur,
ut ubique terrarum populorum
    prosperitas,
pacis securitas et religionis libertas,
te largiente, consistant.
Per Christum Dominum nostrum.
R. Amen.

X. For those in tribulation

X. Pro tribulatis

Let us pray, dearly beloved,
to God the Father almighty,
that he may cleanse the world
    of all errors,
banish disease, drive out hunger,
unlock prisons, loosen fetters,
granting to travellers safety,
    to pilgrims return,
health to the sick,
    and salvation to the dying.

Oremus, dilectissimi nobis,
    Deum Patrem omnipotentem,
ut cunctis mundum
    purget erroribus,
morbos auferat, famem depellat,
aperiat carceres, vincula solvat,
viatoribus securitatem,
    peregrinantibus reditum,
infirmantibus sanitatem
atque morientibus
    salutem indulgeat.

Prayer in silence. Then the Priest says:

Almighty ever-living God,
comfort of mourners,
    strength of all who toil,
may the prayers of those who cry out
    in any tribulation
come before you,
that all may rejoice,
because in their hour of need
your mercy was at hand.
Through Christ our Lord.
R. Amen.

Omnipotens sempiterne Deus,
mæstorum consolatio,
    laborantium fortitudo,
perveniant ad te preces
de quacumque
    tribulatione clamantium,
ut omnes sibi in necessitatibus suis
misericordiam tuam
    gaudeant affuisse.
Per Christum Dominum nostrum.
R. Amen.

SECOND PART:

THE ADORATION OF THE HOLY CROSS

After the Solemn Intercessions, the solemn Adoration of the Holy Cross takes place. Of the two forms of the showing of the Cross presented here, the more appropriate one, according to pastoral needs, should be chosen.

The Showing of the Holy Cross

First Form

The Deacon accompanied by ministers, or another suitable minister, goes to the sacristy, from which, in procession, accompanied by two ministers with lighted candles, he carries the Cross, covered with a violet veil, through the church to the middle of the sanctuary.

The Priest, standing before the altar and facing the people, receives the Cross, uncovers a little of its upper part and elevates it while beginning the **Ecce lignum Crucis** (Behold the wood of the Cross). He is assisted in singing by the Deacon or, if need be, by the choir. All respond, **Come, let us adore**. At the end of the singing, all kneel and for a brief moment adore in silence, while the Priest stands and holds the Cross raised.

Behold the wood of the Cross, on which hung the salvation of the world.	Ecce lignum Crucis, in quo salus mundi pependit.
R. Come, let us adore.	R. Venite, adoremus.

Then the Priest uncovers the right arm of the Cross and again, raising up the Cross, begins, **Behold the wood of the Cross** and everything takes place as above.

Finally, he uncovers the Cross entirely and, raising it up, he begins the invitation **Behold the wood of the Cross** a third time and everything takes place like the first time.

Second Form

The Priest or the Deacon accompanied by ministers, or another suitable minister, goes to the door of the church, where he receives the unveiled Cross, and the ministers take lighted candles; then the procession sets off through the church to the sanctuary. Near the door, in the middle of the church, and before the entrance of the sanctuary, the one who carries the Cross elevates it, singing, **Behold the wood of the Cross**, to which all respond, **Come, let us adore**. After each response all kneel and for a brief moment adore in silence, as above.

The Adoration of the Holy Cross

Then, accompanied by two ministers with lighted candles, the Priest or the Deacon carries the Cross to the entrance of the sanctuary or to another suitable place and there puts it down or hands it over to the ministers to hold. Candles are placed on the right and left sides of the Cross.

For the Adoration of the Cross, first the Priest Celebrant alone approaches, with the chasuble and his shoes removed, if appropriate. Then the clergy, the lay ministers, and the faithful approach, moving as if in procession, and showing reverence to the Cross by a simple genuflection or by some other sign appropriate to the usage of the region, for example, by kissing the Cross.

Only one Cross should be offered for adoration. If, because of the large number of people, it is not possible for all to approach individually, the Priest, after some of the clergy and faithful have adored, takes the Cross and, standing in the middle before the altar, invites the people in a few words to adore the Holy Cross and afterwards holds the Cross elevated higher for a brief time, for the faithful to adore it in silence.

While the adoration of the Holy Cross is taking place, the antiphon **Crucem tuam adoramus** (We adore your Cross, O Lord), the Reproaches, the hymn **Crux fidelis** (**Faithful Cross**) or other suitable chants are sung, during which all who have already adored the Cross remain seated.

Chants to be Sung during the Adoration of the Holy Cross

Ant. We adore your Cross, O Lord,
we praise and glorify your
   holy Resurrection,
for behold, because of the wood
   of a tree
joy has come to the whole world.

Ant. Crucem tuam
   adoramus, Domine,
et sanctam resurrectionem tuam
   laudamus et glorificamus:
ecce enim propter lignum
venit gaudium in universo mundo.

Cf. Ps 66:2

May God have mercy on us
   and bless us;
may he let his face shed its light
   upon us
and have mercy on us.
And the antiphon is repeated:
We adore. . .

Deus misereatur nostri,
   et benedicat nobis:
illuminet vultum suum super nos,
et misereatur nostri.

Crucem tuam. . .

THE REPROACHES

Parts assigned to one of the two choirs separately are indicated by the numbers 1 (first choir) and 2 (second choir); parts sung by both choirs together are marked: 1 and 2. Some of the verses may also be sung by two cantors.

1 and 2 My people,
   what have I done to you?
Or how have I grieved you?
   Answer me!

1 et 2 Popule meus,
   quid feci tibi?
Aut in quo contristavi te?
   Responde mihi!

1 Because I led you out of the land
of Egypt,
you have prepared a Cross
for your Saviour.

1 Quia eduxi te de terra Ægypti:
parasti Crucem Salvatori tuo.

1 Hagios o Theos,
2 Holy is God,
1 Hagios Ischyros,
2 Holy and Mighty,
1 Hagios Athanatos,
eleison himas.
2 Holy and Immortal One,
have mercy on us.

1 Hagios o Theos.
2 Sanctus Deus.
1 Hagios Ischyros.
2 Sanctus Fortis.
1 Hagios Athanatos,
eleison himas.
2 Sanctus Immortalis,
miserere nobis.

1 and 2 Because I led you out
through the desert forty years
and fed you with manna and
brought you into a land of plenty,
you have prepared a Cross
for your Saviour.

1 et 2 Quia eduxi te per desertum
quadraginta annis,
et manna cibavi te,
et introduxi te in terram
satis bonam:
parasti Crucem Salvatori tuo.

1 Hagios o Theos,
2 Holy is God,
1 Hagios Ischyros,
2 Holy and Mighty,
1 Hagios Athanatos, eleison himas.
2 Holy and Immortal One,
have mercy on us.

1 Hagios o Theos.
2 Sanctus Deus.
1 Hagios Ischyros.
2 Sanctus Fortis.
1 Hagios Athanatos, eleison himas.
2 Sanctus Immortalis,
miserere nobis.

1 and 2 What more should I have
done for you and have not done?
Indeed, I planted you as my most
beautiful chosen vine
and you have turned very bitter
for me,
for in my thirst you gave me
vinegar to drink
and with a lance you pierced your
Saviour's side.

1 et 2 Quid ultra debui facere tibi,
et non feci?
Ego quidem plantavi te
vineam electam
meam speciosissimam:
et tu facta es mihi nimis amara:
aceto namque sitim meam potasti,
et lancea perforasti latus
Salvatori tuo.

1 Hagios o Theos,
2 Holy is God,

1 Hagios o Theos.
2 Sanctus Deus.

1 Hagios Ischyros,	1 Hagios Ischyros.
2 Holy and Mighty,	2 Sanctus Fortis.
1 Hagios Athanatos,	1 Hagios Athanatos,
eleison himas.	eleison himas.
2 Holy and Immortal One, have	2 Sanctus Immortalis,
mercy on us.	miserere nobis.

II

Cantors:	Cantores:
I scourged Egypt for your sake with its firstborn sons,	Ego propter te flagellavi Ægyptum cum primogenitis suis:
and you scourged me and handed me over.	et tu me flagellatum tradidisti.
1 and 2 repeat:	1 et 2 repetunt:
My people, what have I done to you?	Popule meus, quid feci tibi?
Or how have I grieved you?	Aut in quo contristavi te?
Answer me!	Responde mihi!
Cantors:	Cantores:
I led you out from Egypt as Pharaoh lay sunk in the Red Sea,	Ego eduxi te de Ægypto, demerso Pharaone in Mare Rubrum:
and you handed me over to the chief priests.	et tu me tradidisti principibus sacerdotum.
1 and 2 repeat:	1 et 2 repetunt:
My people. . .	Popule meus. . .
Cantors:	Cantores:
I opened up the sea before you,	Ego ante te aperui mare:
and you opened my side with a lance.	et tu aperuisti lancea latus meum.
1 and 2 repeat:	1 et 2 repetunt:
My people. . .	Popule meus. . .
Cantors:	Cantores:
I went before you in a pillar of cloud,	Ego ante te præivi in columna nubis:
and you led me into Pilate's palace.	et tu me duxisti ad prætorium Pilati.
1 and 2 repeat:	1 et 2 repetunt:
My people. . .	Popule meus. . .

Cantors:

I fed you with manna in the desert,
and on me you rained blows
    and lashes.

1 and 2 repeat:

My people. . .

Cantors:

I gave you saving water
    from the rock to drink,
and for drink you gave me gall
    and vinegar.

1 and 2 repeat:

My people. . .

Cantors:

I struck down for you the kings
    of the Canaanites,
and you struck my head with a reed.

1 and 2 repeat:

My people. . .

Cantors:

I put in your hand a royal sceptre,
and you put on my head
    a crown of thorns.

1 and 2 repeat:

My people. . .

Cantors:

I exalted you with great power,
and you hung me on the scaffold
    of the Cross.

1 and 2 repeat:

My people. . .

Cantores:

Ego te pavi manna per desertum:
et tu me cecidisti alapis et flagellis.

1 et 2 repetunt:

Popule meus. . .

Cantores:

Ego te potavi aqua salutis de petra:
et tu me potasti felle et aceto.

1 et 2 repetunt:

Popule meus. . .

Cantores:

Ego propter te Chananæorum
    reges percussi:
et tu percussisti arundine
    caput meum.

1 et 2 repetunt:

Popule meus. . .

Cantores:

Ego dedi tibi sceptrum regale:
et tu dedisti capiti meo spineam
    coronam.

1 et 2 repetunt:

Popule meus. . .

Cantores:

Ego te exaltavi magna virtute:
et tu me suspendisti
    in patibulo Crucis.

1 et 2 repetunt:

Popule meus. . .

HYMN

All:

Faithful Cross the Saints rely on,
Noble tree beyond compare!
Never was there such a scion,
Never leaf or flower so rare.
Sweet the timber, sweet the iron,
Sweet the burden that they bear!

Cantors:

Sing, my tongue, in exultation
Of our banner and device!
Make a solemn proclamation
Of a triumph and its price:
How the Saviour of creation
Conquered by his sacrifice!

All:

Faithful Cross the Saints rely on,
Noble tree beyond compare!
Never was there such a scion,
Never leaf or flower so rare.

Cantors:

For, when Adam first offended,
Eating that forbidden fruit,
Not all hopes of glory ended
With the serpent at the root:
Broken nature would be mended
By a second tree and shoot.

All:

Sweet the timber, sweet the iron,
Sweet the burden that they bear!

Cantors:

Thus the tempter was outwitted
By a wisdom deeper still:
Remedy and ailment fitted,
Means to cure and means to kill;
That the world might be acquitted,
Christ would do his Father's will.

Omnes:

Crux fidelis, inter omnes
    arbor una nobilis,
Nulla talem silva profert,
    flore, fronde, germine!
Dulce lignum dulci clavo
    dulce pondus sustinens!

Cantores:

Pange, lingua, gloriosi
    prœlium certaminis,
Et super crucis tropæo
    dic triumphum nobilem,
Qualiter Redemptor orbis
    immolatus vicerit.

Omnes:

Crux fidelis, inter omnes
    arbor una nobilis,
Nulla talem silva profert,
    flore, fronde, germine!

Cantores:

De parentis protoplasti
    fraude factor condolens,
Quando pomi noxialis
    morte morsu corruit,
Ipse lignum tunc notavit,
    damna ligni ut solveret.

Omnes:

Dulce lignum dulci clavo
    dulce pondus sustinens!

Cantores:

Hoc opus nostræ salutis
    ordo depoposcerat,
Multiformis perditoris
    arte ut artem falleret,
Et medelam ferret inde,
    hostis unde læserat.

All:
Faithful Cross the Saints rely on,
Noble tree beyond compare!
Never was there such a scion,
Never leaf or flower so rare.

Cantors:
So the Father, out of pity
For our self-inflicted doom,
Sent him from the heavenly city
When the holy time had come:
He, the Son and the Almighty,
Took our flesh in Mary's womb.

All:
Sweet the timber, sweet the iron,
Sweet the burden that they bear!

Cantors:
Hear a tiny baby crying,
Founder of the seas and strands;
See his virgin Mother tying
Cloth around his feet and hands;
Find him in a manger lying
Tightly wrapped in swaddling-bands!

All:
Faithful Cross the Saints rely on,
Noble tree beyond compare!
Never was there such a scion,
Never leaf or flower so rare.

Cantors:
So he came, the long-expected,
Not in glory, not to reign;
Only born to be rejected,
Choosing hunger, toil and pain,
Till the scaffold was erected
And the Paschal Lamb was slain.

All:
Sweet the timber, sweet the iron,
Sweet the burden that they bear!

Cantors:
No disgrace was too abhorrent:
Nailed and mocked and

Omnes:
Crux fidelis, inter omnes
    arbor una nobilis,
Nulla talem silva profert,
    flore, fronde, germine!

Cantores:
Quando venit ergo sacri
    plenitudo temporis,
Missus est ab arce Patris
Natus, orbis conditor,
Atque ventre virginali
    carne factus prodiit.

Omnes:
Dulce lignum dulci clavo
    dulce pondus sustinens!

Cantores:
Vagit infans inter arta
    conditus præsepia,
Membra pannis involuta
    Virgo Mater alligat,
Et manus pedesque et crura
    stricta cingit fascia.

Omnes:
Crux fidelis, inter omnes
    arbor una nobilis,
Nulla talem silva profert,
    flore, fronde, germine!

Cantores:
Lustra sex qui iam peracta,
    tempus implens corporis,
se volente, natus ad hoc,
    passioni deditus,
agnus in crucis levatur
    immolandus stipite.

Omnes:
Dulce lignum dulci clavo
    dulce pondus sustinens!

Cantores:
En acetum, fel, arundo,
Mite corpus perforatur,

parched he died;
Blood and water, double warrant,
Issue from his wounded side,
Washing in a mighty torrent
Earth and stars and oceantide.

sputa, clavi, lancea;
sanguis unde profluit;
Terra, pontus, astra, mundus
    quo lavantur flumine!

All:

Faithful Cross the Saints rely on,
Noble tree beyond compare!
Never was there such a scion,
Never leaf or flower so rare.

Omnes:

Crux fidelis, inter omnes
    arbor una nobilis,
Nulla talem silva profert,
    flore, fronde, germine!

Cantors:

Lofty timber,
    smooth your roughness,
Flex your boughs for blossoming;
Let your fibres lose their toughness,
Gently let your tendrils cling;
Lay aside your native gruffness,
Clasp the body of your King!

Cantores:

Flecte ramos, arbor alta,
    tensa laxa viscera,
Et rigor lentescat ille,
    quem dedit nativitas,
Ut superni membra Regis
    miti tendas stipite.

All:

Sweet the timber, sweet the iron,
Sweet the burden that they bear!

Omnes:

Dulce lignum dulci clavo
    dulce pondus sustinens!

Cantors:

Noblest tree of all created,
Richly jewelled and embossed:
Post by Lamb's blood consecrated;
Spar that saves the tempest-tossed;
Scaffold-beam which, elevated,
Carries what the world has cost!

Cantores:

Sola digna tu fuisti
    ferre sæcli pretium
Atque portum præparare
    nauta mundo naufrago,
Quem sacer cruor perunxit
    fusus Agni corpore.

All:

Faithful Cross the Saints rely on,
Noble tree beyond compare!
Never was there such a scion,
Never leaf or flower so rare.

Omnes:

Crux fidelis, inter omnes
    arbor una nobilis,
Nulla talem silva profert,
    flore, fronde, germine!

The following conclusion is never to be omitted:

All:

Wisdom, power, and adoration
To the blessed Trinity

Omnes:

Æqua Patri Filioque,
    inclito Paraclito,

For redemption and salvation
Through the Paschal Mystery,
Now, in every generation,
And for all eternity. Amen.

Sempiterna sit beatæ
   Trinitati gloria;
cuius alma nos redemit
   atque servat gratia. Amen.

In accordance with local circumstances or popular traditions and if it is pastorally appropriate, the **Stabat Mater** may be sung, as found in the Graduale Romanum, or another suitable chant in memory of the compassion of the Blessed Virgin Mary.

When the adoration has been concluded, the Cross is carried by the Deacon or a minister to its place at the altar. Lighted candles are placed around or on the altar or near the Cross.

THIRD PART:

Holy Communion

A cloth is spread on the altar, and a corporal and the Missal put in place. Meanwhile the Deacon or, if there is no Deacon, the Priest himself, putting on a humeral veil, brings the Blessed Sacrament back from the place of repose to the altar by a shorter route, while all stand in silence. Two ministers with lighted candles accompany the Blessed Sacrament and place their candlesticks around or upon the altar.

When the Deacon, if a Deacon is present, has placed the Blessed Sacrament upon the altar and uncovered the ciborium, the Priest goes to the altar and genuflects.

Then the Priest, with hands joined, says aloud:

At the Saviour's command
and formed by divine teaching,
we dare to say:

Præceptis salutaribus moniti,
et divina institutione formati,
audemus dicere:

The Priest, with hands extended says, and all present continue:

Our Father, who art in heaven,
hallowed be thy name;
thy kingdom come,
thy will be done
on earth as it is in heaven.
Give us this day our daily bread,
and forgive us our trespasses,
as we forgive those who trespass
   against us;
and lead us not into temptation,
but deliver us from evil.

Pater noster, qui es in cælis:
sanctificetur nomen tuum;
adveniat regnum tuum;
fiat voluntas tua, sicut in cælo,
   et in terra.
Panem nostrum cotidianum
   da nobis hodie;
et dimitte nobis debita nostra,
sicut et nos dimittimus
   debitoribus nostris;
et ne nos inducas in tentationem;
sed libera nos a malo.

With hands extended, the Priest continues alone:

Deliver us, Lord, we pray,
   from every evil,

Libera nos, quæsumus, Domine,
   ab omnibus malis,

graciously grant peace in our days,	da propitius pacem in diebus nostris,
that, by the help of your mercy,	ut, ope misericordiæ tuæ adiuti,
we may be always free from sin	et a peccato simus semper liberi
and safe from all distress,	et ab omni perturbatione securi:
as we await the blessed hope	exspectantes beatam spem
and the coming of our Saviour,	et adventum Salvatoris nostri
Jesus Christ.	Iesu Christi.

He joins his hands.

The people conclude the prayer, acclaiming:

For the kingdom,	Quia tuum est regnum,
the power and the glory are yours	et potestas,
now and for ever.	et gloria in sæcula.

Then the Priest, with hands joined, says quietly:

May the receiving of your Body	Perceptio Corporis tui,
and Blood,	Domine Iesu Christe,
Lord Jesus Christ,	non mihi proveniat in iudicium
not bring me to judgement	et condemnationem:
and condemnation,	sed pro tua pietate prosit mihi
but through your loving mercy	ad tutamentum mentis et corporis,
be for me protection in mind	et ad medelam percipiendam.
and body	
and a healing remedy.	

The Priest then genuflects, takes a particle, and, holding it slightly raised over the ciborium, while facing the people, says aloud:

Behold the Lamb of God,	Ecce Agnus Dei, ecce qui tollit
behold him who takes away	peccata mundi.
the sins of the world.	Beati qui ad cenam
Blessed are those called	Agni vocati sunt.
to the supper of the Lamb.	

And together with the people he adds once:

Lord, I am not worthy	Domine, non sum dignus,
that you should enter under my roof,	ut intres sub tectum meum,
but only say the word	sed tantum dic verbo,
and my soul shall be healed.	et sanabitur anima mea.

And facing the altar, he reverently consumes the Body of Christ, saying quietly:

May the Body of Christ keep me	Corpus Christi custodiat me
safe for eternal life.	in vitam æternam.

He then proceeds to distribute Communion to the faithful. During Communion, Psalm 21 or another appropriate chant may be sung.

When the distribution of Communion has been completed, the ciborium is taken by the Deacon or another suitable minister to a place prepared outside the church or, if circumstances so require, it is placed in the tabernacle.

Then the Priest says: **Let us pray**, and, after a period of sacred silence, if circumstances so suggest, has been observed, he says the Prayer after Communion.

Almighty ever-living God, who have restored us to life by the blessed Death and Resurrection of your Christ, preserve in us the work of your mercy, that, by partaking of this mystery, we may have a life unceasingly devoted to you. Through Christ our Lord. R. **Amen.**	Omnipotens sempiterne Deus, qui nos Christi tui beata morte et resurrectione reparasti, conserva in nobis opus misericordiæ tuæ, ut huius mysterii participatione perpetua devotione vivamus. Per Christum Dominum nostrum. R. Amen.

For the Dismissal the Deacon or, if there is no Deacon, the Priest himself, may say the invitation **Bow down for the blessing**.

Then the Priest, standing facing the people and extending his hands over them, says this Prayer over the People:

May abundant blessing, O Lord, we pray, descend upon your people, who have honoured the Death of your Son in the hope of their resurrection: may pardon come, comfort be given, holy faith increase, and everlasting redemption be made secure. Through Christ our Lord. R. **Amen.**	Super populum tuum, quæsumus, Domine, qui mortem Filii tui in spe suæ resurrectionis recoluit, benedictio copiosa descendat, indulgentia veniat, consolatio tribuatur, fides sancta succrescat, redemptio sempiterna firmetur. Per Christum Dominum nostrum. R. Amen.

And all, after genuflecting to the Cross, depart in silence.

After the celebration, the altar is stripped, but the Cross remains on the altar with two or four candlesticks.

Vespers (Evening Prayer) is not celebrated by those who have been present at the solemn afternoon liturgical celebration.

EASTER SUNDAY OF THE RESURRECTION OF THE LORD

8 April

THE EASTER VIGIL IN THE HOLY NIGHT

This is the first Easter message that I would offer you: it is always possible to begin anew, because there is always a new life that God can awaken in us in spite of all our failures. From the rubble of our hearts – and each one of us knows the rubble of our hearts – God can create a work of art; from the ruined remnants of our humanity, God can prepare a new history. He never ceases to go ahead of us: in the cross of suffering, desolation and death, and in the glory of a life that rises again, a history that changes, a hope that is reborn. Going to Galilee also means setting out on new paths. It means walking away from the tomb. There is a kind of faith that can become the memory of something once beautiful, now simply to be recalled. Many people – including us – experience such a "faith of memories", as if Jesus were someone from the past, an old friend from their youth who is now far distant, an event that took place long ago, when they attended catechism as a child. Going to Galilee, on the other hand, means realising that faith, if it is to be alive, must get back on the road. It must daily renew the first steps of the journey, the amazement of the first encounter.

(Pope Francis)

By most ancient tradition, this is the night of keeping vigil for the Lord (Ex 12:42), in which, following the Gospel admonition (Lk 12:35-37), the faithful, carrying lighted lamps in their hands, should be like those looking for the Lord when he returns, so that at his coming he may find them awake and have them sit at his table.

Of this night's Vigil, which is the greatest and most noble of all solemnities, there is to be only one celebration in each church. It is arranged, moreover, in such a way that after the Lucernarium and Easter Proclamation (which constitutes the first part of this Vigil), Holy Church meditates on the wonders the Lord God has done for his people from the beginning, trusting in his word and promise (the second part, that is, the Liturgy of the Word) until, as day approaches, with new members reborn in Baptism (the third part), the Church is called to the table the Lord has prepared for his people, the memorial of his Death and Resurrection until he comes again (the fourth part).

The entire celebration of the Easter Vigil must take place during the night, so that it begins after nightfall and ends before daybreak on the Sunday.

The Mass of the Vigil, even if it is celebrated before midnight, is a paschal Mass of the Sunday of the Resurrection.

Anyone who participates in the Mass of the night may receive Communion again at Mass during the day. A Priest who celebrates or concelebrates the Mass of the night may again celebrate or concelebrate Mass during the day.

The Easter Vigil takes the place of the Office of Readings.

The Priest is usually assisted by a Deacon. If, however, there is no Deacon, the duties of his Order, except those indicated below, are assumed by the Priest Celebrant or by a concelebrant.

The Priest and Deacon vest as at Mass, in white vestments.

Candles should be prepared for all who participate in the Vigil. The lights of the church are extinguished.

FIRST PART:

THE SOLEMN BEGINNING OF THE VIGIL OR LUCERNARIUM

The Blessing of the Fire and Preparation of the Candle

A blazing fire is prepared in a suitable place outside the church. When the people are gathered there, the Priest approaches with the ministers, one of whom carries the paschal candle. The processional cross and candles are not carried.

Where, however, a fire cannot be lit outside the church, the rite is carried out as below.

The Priest and faithful sign themselves while the Priest says: **In the name of the Father, and of the Son, and of the Holy Spirit,** and then he greets the assembled people in the usual way and briefly instructs them about the night vigil in these or similar words:

Dear brethren (brothers and sisters), on this most sacred night, in which our Lord Jesus Christ passed over from death to life, the Church calls upon her sons and daughters, scattered throughout the world, to come together to watch and pray. If we keep the memorial of the Lord's paschal solemnity in this way, listening to his word and celebrating his mysteries, then we shall have the sure hope of sharing his triumph over death and living with him in God.	Fratres carissimi, hac sacratissima nocte, in qua Dominus noster Iesus Christus de morte transivit ad vitam, Ecclesia invitat filios dispersos per orbem terrarum, ut ad vigilandum et orandum conveniant. Si ita memoriam egerimus Paschatis Domini, audientes verbum et celebrantes mysteria eius, spem habebimus participandi triumphum eius de morte et vivendi cum ipso in Deo.

Then the Priest blesses the fire, saying with hands extended:

Let us pray.	Oremus.
O God, who through your Son bestowed upon the faithful the fire of your glory, sanctify ✠ this new fire, we pray, and grant that, by these paschal celebrations, we may be so inflamed with heavenly desires, that with minds made pure we may attain festivities of unending splendour. Through Christ our Lord.	Deus, qui per Filium tuum claritatis tuæ ignem fidelibus contulisti, novum hunc ignem ✠ sanctifica, et concede nobis, ita per hæc festa paschalia cælestibus desideriis inflammari, ut ad perpetuæ claritatis puris mentibus valeamus festa pertingere. Per Christum Dominum nostrum.
R. Amen.	R. Amen.

After the blessing of the new fire, one of the ministers brings the paschal candle to the Priest, who cuts a cross into the candle with a stylus. Then he makes the Greek letter Alpha above the cross, the letter Omega below, and the four numerals of the current year between the arms of the cross, saying meanwhile:

1. Christ yesterday and today	1. Christus heri et hodie
2. the Beginning and the End	2. Principium et Finis
3. the Alpha	3. Alpha
4. and the Omega	4. et Omega
5. All time belongs to him	5. Ipsius sunt tempora
6. and all the ages	6. et sæcula
7. To him be glory and power	7. Ipsi gloria et imperium
8. through every age and for ever. Amen	8. per universa æternitatis sæcula. Amen

When the cutting of the cross and of the other signs has been completed, the Priest may insert five grains of incense into the candle in the form of a cross, meanwhile saying:

1. By his holy	1. Per sua sancta vulnera
2. and glorious wounds,	2. gloriosa
3. may Christ the Lord	3. custodiat
4. guard us	4. et conservet nos
5. and protect us. Amen.	5. Christus Dominus. Amen.

Where, because of difficulties that may occur, a fire is not lit, the blessing of fire is adapted to the circumstances. When the people are gathered in the church as on other occasions, the Priest comes to the door of the church, along with the ministers carrying the paschal candle. The people, insofar as is possible, turn to face the Priest.

The greeting and address take place as above; then the fire is blessed and the candle is prepared, as above.

The Priest lights the paschal candle from the new fire, saying:

May the light of Christ rising in glory dispel the darkness of our hearts and minds.	**Lumen Christi gloriose resurgentis dissipet tenebras cordis et mentis.**

As regards the preceding elements, Conferences of Bishops may also establish other forms more adapted to the culture of the different peoples.

Procession

When the candle has been lit, one of the ministers takes burning coals from the fire and places them in the thurible, and the Priest puts incense into it in the usual way. The Deacon or, if there is no Deacon, another suitable minister, takes the paschal candle and a procession forms. The thurifer with the smoking thurible precedes the Deacon or other minister who carries the paschal candle. After them follows the Priest with the ministers and the people, all holding in their hands unlit candles.

At the door of the church the Deacon, standing and raising up the candle, sings:

The Light of Christ.	**Lumen Christi.**

And all reply:

Thanks be to God.	**Deo gratias.**

The Priest lights his candle from the flame of the paschal candle.

Then the Deacon moves forward to the middle of the church and, standing and raising up the candle, sings a second time:

The Light of Christ.	**Lumen Christi.**

And all reply:

Thanks be to God.	**Deo gratias.**

All light their candles from the flame of the paschal candle and continue in procession.

When the Deacon arrives before the altar, he stands facing the people, raises up the candle and sings a third time:

The Light of Christ.	**Lumen Christi.**

And all reply:

Thanks be to God.	**Deo gratias.**

Then the Deacon places the paschal candle on a large candlestand prepared next to the ambo or in the middle of the sanctuary.

And lights are lit throughout the church, except for the altar candles.

The Easter Proclamation (Exsultet)

Arriving at the altar, the Priest goes to his chair, gives his candle to a minister, puts incense into the thurible and blesses the incense as at the Gospel at Mass. The Deacon goes to the Priest and saying, **Your blessing, Father,** asks for and receives a blessing from the Priest, who says in a low voice:

May the Lord be in your heart and on your lips,	Dominus sit in corde tuo et in labiis tuis,
that you may proclaim his paschal praise worthily and well,	ut digne et competenter annunties suum paschale præconium:
in the name of the Father and of the Son, ✠ and of the Holy Spirit.	in nomine Patris, et Filii, ✠ et Spiritus Sancti.
The Deacon replies: **Amen.**	Amen.

This blessing is omitted if the Proclamation is made by someone who is not a Deacon.

The Deacon, after incensing the book and the candle, proclaims the Easter Proclamation (Exsultet) at the ambo or at a lectern, with all standing and holding lighted candles in their hands.

The Easter Proclamation may be made, in the absence of a Deacon, by the Priest himself or by another concelebrating Priest. If, however, because of necessity, a lay cantor sings the Proclamation, the words **Therefore, dearest friends** up to the end of the invitation are omitted, along with the greeting **The Lord be with you**.

The Proclamation may also be sung in the shorter form p.388.

Longer Form of the Easter Proclamation

Exult, let them exult, the hosts of heaven, exult, let Angel ministers of God exult, let the trumpet of salvation sound aloud our mighty King's triumph! Be glad, let earth be glad, as glory floods her, ablaze with light from her eternal King, let all corners of the earth be glad, knowing an end to gloom and darkness.	Exsultet iam angelica turba cælorum: exsultent divina mysteria: et pro tanti Regis victoria tuba insonet salutaris. Gaudeat et tellus tantis irradiata fulgoribus: et, æterni Regis splendore illustrata, totius orbis se sentiat amisisse caliginem.

Rejoice, let Mother Church
    also rejoice,
arrayed with the lightning
    of his glory,
let this holy building shake with joy,
filled with the mighty voices
    of the peoples.

(Therefore, dearest friends,
standing in the awesome glory
    of this holy light,
invoke with me, I ask you,
the mercy of God almighty,
that he, who has been pleased
    to number me,
though unworthy, among the Levites,
may pour into me his light
    unshadowed,
that I may sing this candle's
    perfect praises.)

(V. The Lord be with you.
R. And with your spirit.)
V. Lift up your hearts.
R. We lift them up to the Lord.
V. Let us give thanks to the Lord
    our God.
R. It is right and just.

It is truly right and just,
with ardent love of mind and heart
and with devoted service of our voice,
to acclaim our God invisible,
    the almighty Father,
and Jesus Christ, our Lord, his Son,
    his Only Begotten.

Who for our sake paid Adam's debt
    to the eternal Father,
and, pouring out his own dear Blood,
wiped clean the record of our
    ancient sinfulness.

Lætetur et mater Ecclesia,
tanti luminis adornata fulgoribus:
et magnis populorum vocibus hæc
    aula resultet.

(Quapropter astantes vos,
    fratres carissimi,
ad tam miram huius sancti
    luminis claritatem,
una mecum, quæso,
Dei omnipotentis
    misericordiam invocate.
Ut, qui me non meis meritis
intra Levitarum numerum dignatus
    est aggregare,
luminis sui claritatem infundens,
cerei huius laudem
    implere perficiat.)

(V. Dominus vobiscum.
R. Et cum spiritu tuo.)
V. Sursum corda.
R. Habemus ad Dominum.
V. Gratias agamus Domino
    Deo nostro.
R. Dignum et iustum est.

Vere dignum et iustum est,
invisibilem Deum
    Patrem omnipotentem
Filiumque eius Unigenitum,
Dominum nostrum
    Iesum Christum,
toto cordis ac mentis affectu
    et vocis ministerio personare.

Qui pro nobis æterno Patri Adæ
    debitum solvit,
et veteris piaculi cautionem
    pio cruore detersit.

These then are the feasts of Passover,
in which is slain the Lamb,
    the one true Lamb,
whose Blood anoints the doorposts
    of believers.

This is the night,
when once you led our forebears,
    Israel's children,
from slavery in Egypt
and made them pass dry-shod
    through the Red Sea.

This is the night
that with a pillar of fire
banished the darkness of sin.

This is the night
that even now, throughout the world,
sets Christian believers apart
    from worldly vices
and from the gloom of sin,
leading them to grace
and joining them to his holy ones.

This is the night,
when Christ broke the prison-bars
    of death
and rose victorious
    from the underworld.

Our birth would have been no gain,
had we not been redeemed.
O wonder of your humble care for us!
O love, O charity beyond all telling,
to ransom a slave you gave away
    your Son!

O truly necessary sin of Adam,
destroyed completely by the Death
    of Christ!

Hæc sunt enim festa paschalia,
in quibus verus ille Agnus occiditur,
cuius sanguine postes
    fidelium consecrantur.

Hæc nox est,
in qua primum patres nostros,
filios Israel eductos de Ægypto,
Mare Rubrum sicco vestigio
    transire fecisti.

Hæc igitur nox est,
quæ peccatorum tenebras columnæ
    illuminatione purgavit.

Hæc nox est,
quæ hodie per universum mundum
    in Christo credentes,
a vitiis sæculi et caligine
    peccatorum segregatos,
reddit gratiæ, sociat sanctitati.

Hæc nox est,
in qua, destructis vinculis mortis,
Christus ab inferis victor ascendit.

Nihil enim nobis nasci profuit,
    nisi redimi profuisset.
O mira circa nos tuæ pietatis
    dignatio!
O inæstimablilis dilectio caritatis:
ut servum redimeres,
    Filium tradidisti!

O certe necessarium
    Adæ peccatum,
quod Christi morte deletum est!

O happy fault
that earned so great,
    so glorious a Redeemer!

O truly blessed night,
worthy alone to know the time
    and hour
when Christ rose
    from the underworld!

This is the night
of which it is written:
The night shall be as bright as day,
dazzling is the night for me,
and full of gladness.

The sanctifying power of this night
dispels wickedness,
    washes faults away,
restores innocence to the fallen,
    and joy to mourners,
drives out hatred, fosters concord,
    and brings down the mighty.

On this, your night of grace,
    O holy Father,
accept this candle, a solemn offering,
the work of bees and of your
    servants' hands,
an evening sacrifice of praise,
this gift from your most holy Church.

But now we know the praises
    of this pillar,
which glowing fire ignites
    for God's honour,
a fire into many flames divided,
yet never dimmed by sharing
    of its light,
for it is fed by melting wax,
drawn out by mother bees
to build a torch so precious.

O felix culpa,
quæ talem ac tantum meruit
    habere Redemptorem!

O vere beata nox,
quæ sola meruit scire tempus
    et horam,
in qua Christus ab inferis resurrexit!

Hæc nox est, de qua scriptum est:
Et nox sicut dies illuminabitur:
et nox illuminatio mea
    in deliciis meis.

Huius igitur sanctificatio noctis
    fugat scelera, culpas lavat:
et reddit innocentiam lapsis
    et mæstis lætitiam.
Fugat odia, concordiam parat
    et curvat imperia.

In huius igitur noctis gratia,
suscipe, sancte Pater, laudis huius
    sacrificium vespertinum,
quod tibi in hac cerei
    oblatione sollemni,
per ministrorum manus
de operibus apum,
    sacrosancta reddit Ecclesia.

Sed iam columnæ huius
    præconia novimus,
quam in honorem Dei rutilans
    ignis accendit.
Qui, licet sit divisus in partes,
mutuati tamen luminis detrimenta
    non novit.
Alitur enim liquantibus ceris,
quas in substantiam pretiosæ
    huius lampadis
apis mater eduxit.

O truly blessed night,
when things of heaven are wed
    to those of earth,
and divine to the human.

Therefore, O Lord,
we pray you that this candle,
hallowed to the honour of
    your name,
may persevere undimmed,
to overcome the darkness
    of this night.
Receive it as a pleasing fragrance,
and let it mingle with
    the lights of heaven.
May this flame be found still burning
by the Morning Star:
the one Morning Star who never sets,
Christ your Son,
who, coming back
    from death's domain,
has shed his peaceful light
    on humanity,
and lives and reigns
    for ever and ever.
R. Amen.

O vere beata nox,
in qua terrenis cælestia,
    humanis divina iunguntur!

Oramus ergo te, Domine,
ut cereus iste in honorem tui
    nominis consecratus,
ad noctis huius
    caliginem destruendam,
indeficiens perseveret.

Et in odorem suavitatis acceptus,
supernis luminaribus misceatur.
Flammas eius lucifer
    matutinus inveniat:

Ille, inquam, lucifer,
    qui nescit occasum:
Christus Filius tuus,
qui, regressus ab inferis, humano
    generi serenus illuxit,
et vivit et regnat
    in sæcula sæculorum.

R. Amen.

Shorter Form of the Easter Proclamation

Exult, let them exult,
    the hosts of heaven,
exult, let Angel ministers
    of God exult,
let the trumpet of salvation
sound aloud our mighty
    King's triumph!

Be glad, let earth be glad, as glory
    floods her,
ablaze with light from her
    eternal King,
let all corners of the earth be glad,
knowing an end to gloom
    and darkness.

Exsultet iam angelica
    turba cælorum:
exsultent divina mysteria:
et pro tanti Regis victoria tuba
    insonet salutaris.

Gaudeat et tellus tantis
    irradiata fulgoribus:
et, æterni Regis splendore illustrata,
totius orbis se sentiat
    amisisse caliginem.

Rejoice, let Mother Church
     also rejoice,
arrayed with the lightning
     of his glory,
let this holy building shake with joy,
filled with the mighty voices
     of the peoples.

(V. The Lord be with you.
R. And with your spirit.)

V. Lift up your hearts.
R. We lift them up to the Lord.
V. Let us give thanks to the Lord
     our God.
R. It is right and just.

It is truly right and just,
with ardent love of mind and heart
and with devoted service of our voice,
to acclaim our God invisible,
     the almighty Father,
and Jesus Christ, our Lord, his Son,
     his Only Begotten.

Who for our sake paid Adam's debt
     to the eternal Father,
and, pouring out his own dear Blood,
wiped clean the record
     of our ancient sinfulness.

These then are the feasts of Passover,
in which is slain the Lamb,
     the one true Lamb,
whose Blood anoints the doorposts
     of believers.

This is the night,
when once you led our forebears,
     Israel's children,
from slavery in Egypt
and made them pass dry-shod
     through the Red Sea.

Lætetur et mater Ecclesia,
tanti luminis adornata fulgoribus:
et magnis populorum vocibus hæc
     aula resultet.

(V. Dominus vobiscum.
R. Et cum spiritu tuo.)

V. Sursum corda.
R. Habemus ad Dominum.
V. Gratias agamus Domino
     Deo nostro.
R. Dignum et iustum est.

Vere dignum et iustum est,
invisibilem Deum
     Patrem omnipotentem
Filiumque eius Unigenitum,
Dominum nostrum
     Iesum Christum,
toto cordis ac mentis affectu
     et vocis ministerio personare.

Qui pro nobis æterno Patri Adæ
     debitum solvit,
et veteris piaculi cautionem pio
     cruore detersit.

Hæc sunt enim festa paschalia,
in quibus verus ille
     Agnus occiditur,
cuius sanguine postes
     fidelium consecrantur.

Hæc nox est,
in qua primum patres nostros,
     filios Israel
eductos de Ægypto,
Mare Rubrum sicco vestigio
     transire fecisti.

This is the night that with a pillar of fire banished the darkness of sin.	Hæc igitur nox est, quæ peccatorum tenebras columnæ illuminatione purgavit.
This is the night that even now, throughout the world, sets Christian believers apart from worldly vices and from the gloom of sin, leading them to grace and joining them to his holy ones.	Hæc nox est, quæ hodie per universum mundum in Christo credentes, a vitiis sæculi et caligine peccatorum segregatos, reddit gratiæ, sociat sanctitati.
This is the night, when Christ broke the prison-bars of death and rose victorious from the underworld.	Hæc nox est, in qua, destructis vinculis mortis, Christus ab inferis victor ascendit.
O wonder of your humble care for us! O love, O charity beyond all telling, to ransom a slave you gave away your Son!	O mira circa nos tuæ pietatis dignatio! O inæstimablilis dilectio caritatis: ut servum redimeres, Filium tradidisti!
O truly necessary sin of Adam, destroyed completely by the Death of Christ!	O certe necessarium Adæ peccatum, quod Christi morte deletum est!
O happy fault that earned so great, so glorious a Redeemer!	O felix culpa, quæ talem ac tantum meruit habere Redemptorem!
The sanctifying power of this night dispels wickedness, washes faults away, restores innocence to the fallen, and joy to mourners.	Huius igitur sanctificatio noctis fugat scelera, culpas lavat: et reddit innocentiam lapsis et mæstis lætitiam.
O truly blessed night, when things of heaven are wed to those of earth, and divine to the human.	O vere beata nox, in qua terrenis cælestia, humanis divina iunguntur!
On this, your night of grace, O holy Father, accept this candle, a solemn offering, the work of bees and of your	In huius igitur noctis gratia, suscipe, sancte Pater, laudis huius sacrificium vespertinum, quod tibi in hac cerei

servants' hands,
an evening sacrifice of praise,
this gift from your most
    holy Church.

Therefore, O Lord,
we pray you that this candle,
hallowed to the honour
    of your name,
may persevere undimmed,
to overcome the darkness
    of this night.
Receive it as a pleasing fragrance,
and let it mingle with the lights
    of heaven.
May this flame be found
    still burning
by the Morning Star:
the one Morning Star who never sets,
Christ your Son,
who, coming back from
    death's domain,
has shed his peaceful light
    on humanity,
and lives and reigns
    for ever and ever.
R. Amen.

oblatione sollemni,
per ministrorum manus
de operibus apum,
    sacrosancta reddit Ecclesia.

Oramus ergo te, Domine,
ut cereus iste in honorem tui
    nominis consecratus,
ad noctis huius
    caliginem destruendam,
indeficiens perseveret.
Et in odorem suavitatis acceptus,
supernis luminaribus misceatur.
Flammas eius lucifer
    matutinus inveniat:
Ille, inquam, lucifer,
    qui nescit occasum:
Christus Filius tuus,
qui, regressus ab inferis,
    humano generi serenus illuxit,
et vivit et regnat
    in sæcula sæculorum.
R. Amen.

SECOND PART:
The Liturgy of the Word

In this Vigil, the mother of all Vigils, nine readings are provided, namely seven from the Old Testament and two from the New (the Epistle and Gospel), all of which should be read whenever this can be done, so that the character of the Vigil, which demands an extended period of time, may be preserved.

Nevertheless, where more serious pastoral circumstances demand it, the number of readings from the Old Testament may be reduced, always bearing in mind that the reading of the Word of God is a fundamental part of this Easter Vigil. At least three readings should be read from the Old Testament, both from the Law and from the Prophets, and their respective Responsorial Psalms should be sung. Never, moreover, should the reading of chapter 14 of Exodus with its canticle be omitted.

After setting aside their candles, all sit. Before the readings begin, the Priest instructs the people in these or similar words:

Dear brethren (brothers and sisters),
now that we have begun
    our solemn Vigil,
let us listen with quiet hearts
    to the Word of God.
Let us meditate on how God in
    times past saved his people
and in these, the last days, has sent
    us his Son as our Redeemer.
Let us pray that our God may
    complete this paschal work
    of salvation
by the fullness of redemption.

Vigiliam sollemniter ingressi,
    fratres carissimi,
quieto corde nunc verbum
    Dei audiamus.
Meditemur, quomodo Deus
    populum suum
elapsis temporibus salvum fecerit,
et novissime nobis Filium suum
    miserit Redemptorem.
Oremus, ut Deus noster hoc
    paschale salvationis opus
ad plenam redemptionem perficiat.

Then the readings follow. A reader goes to the ambo and proclaims the reading. Afterwards a psalmist or a cantor sings or says the Psalm with the people making the response. Then all rise, the Priest says, Let us pray and, after all have prayed for a while in silence, he says the prayer corresponding to the reading. In place of the Responsorial Psalm a period of sacred silence may be observed, in which case the pause after Let us pray is omitted.

FIRST READING

A reading from the book of Genesis   1:1-2:2
God saw all he made, and indeed it was very good.

[In the beginning God created the heavens and the earth.] Now the earth was a formless void, there was darkness over the deep, and God's spirit hovered over the water.

God said, 'Let there be light,' and there was light. God saw that light was good, and God divided light from darkness. God called light 'day', and darkness he called 'night'. Evening came and morning came: the first day. God said, 'Let there be a vault in the waters to divide the waters in two.' And so it was. God made the vault, and it divided the waters above the vault from the waters under the vault. God called the vault 'heaven'. Evening came and morning came: the second day.

God said, 'Let the waters under heaven come together into a single mass, and let dry land appear.' And so it was. God called the dry land 'earth' and the mass of waters 'seas', and God saw that it was good.

God said, 'Let the earth produce vegetation: seed-bearing plants, and fruit trees bearing fruit with their seed inside, on the earth.' And so it was.

The earth produced vegetation: plants bearing seed in their several kinds, and trees bearing fruit with their seed inside in their several kinds. God saw that it was good. Evening came and morning came: the third day.

God said, 'Let there be lights in the vault of heaven to divide day from night, and let them indicate festivals, days and years. Let them be lights in the vault of heaven to shine on the earth.' And so it was. God made the two great lights: the greater light to govern the day, the smaller light to govern the night, and the stars. God set them in the vault of heaven to shine on the earth, to govern the day and the night and to divide light from darkness. God saw that it was good. Evening came and morning came: the fourth day.

God said, 'Let the waters teem with living creatures, and let birds fly above the earth within the vault of heaven.' And so it was. God created great sea-serpents and every kind of living creature with which the waters teem, and every kind of winged creature. God saw that it was good. God blessed them, saying, 'Be fruitful, multiply, and fill the waters of the seas, and let the birds multiply upon the earth.' Evening came and morning came: the fifth day.

God said, 'Let the earth produce every kind of living creature: cattle, reptiles, and every kind of wild beast.' And so it was. God made every kind of wild beast, every kind of cattle, and every kind of land reptile. God saw that it was good.

[God said, 'Let us make man in our own image, in the likeness of ourselves, and let them be masters of the fish of the sea, the birds of heaven, the cattle, all the wild beasts and all the reptiles that crawl upon the earth.'

God created man in the image of himself,
in the image of God he created him,
male and female he created them.

God blessed them, saying to them, 'Be fruitful, multiply, fill the earth and conquer it. Be masters of the fish of the sea, the birds of heaven and all living animals on the earth.' God said, 'See, I give you all the seed-bearing plants that are upon the whole earth, and all the trees with seed-bearing fruit; this shall be your food. To all wild beasts, all birds of heaven and all living reptiles on the earth I give all the foliage of plants for food.' And so it was. God saw all he had made, and indeed it was very good. Evening came and morning came: the sixth day.

Thus heaven and earth were completed with all their array. On the seventh day God completed the work he had been doing. He rested on the seventh day after all the work he had been doing.

The word of the Lord.]

Shorter Form, verses 1, 26-31. Read between [ ]

Responsorial Psalm   Ps 103:1-2,5-6,10,12-14,24,35. R. Cf. v.30

R. **Send forth your spirit, O Lord,**
   and renew the face of the earth.

   Bless the Lord, my soul!
   Lord God, how great you are,
   clothed in majesty and glory,
   wrapped in light as in a robe! R.

   You founded the earth on its base,
   to stand firm from age to age.
   You wrapped it with the ocean like a cloak:
   the waters stood higher than the mountains. R.

   You make springs gush forth in the valleys:
   they flow in between the hills.
   On their banks dwell the birds of heaven;
   from the branches they sing their song. R.

   From your dwelling you water the hills;
   earth drinks its fill of your gift.
   You make the grass grow for the cattle
   and the plants to serve man's needs. R.

   How many are your works, O Lord!
   In wisdom you have made them all.
   The earth is full of your riches.
   Bless the Lord, my soul! R.

Alternative Psalm   Ps 32:4-7,12-13,20,22. R. v.5

R. **The Lord fills the earth with his love.**

   The word of the Lord is faithful
   and all his works to be trusted.
   The Lord loves justice and right
   and fills the earth with his love. R.

   By his word the heavens were made,
   by the breath of his mouth all the stars.
   He collects the waves of the ocean;
   he stores up the depths of the sea. R.

   They are happy, whose God is the Lord,
   the people he has chosen as his own.
   From the heavens the Lord looks forth,
   he sees all the children of men. R.

Our soul is waiting for the Lord.
The Lord is our help and our shield.
May your love be upon us, O Lord,
as we place all our hope in you. R.

Prayer

Let us pray.

Almighty ever-living God,
who are wonderful in the ordering
    of all your works,
may those you have
    redeemed understand
that there exists nothing
    more marvellous
than the world's creation
    in the beginning
except that, at the end of the ages,
Christ our Passover
    has been sacrificed.
Who lives and reigns
    for ever and ever.
R. Amen.

Or, On the creation of man:

O God, who wonderfully created
    human nature
and still more wonderfully
    redeemed it,
grant us, we pray,
to set our minds against
    the enticements of sin,
that we may merit to attain
    eternal joys.
Through Christ our Lord.
R. Amen.

Oremus.

Omnipotens sempiterne Deus,
qui es in omnium operum tuorum
    dispensatione mirabilis,
intellegant redempti tui,
    non fuisse excellentius,
quod initio factus est mundus,
quam quod in fine sæculorum
Pascha nostrum immolatus
    est Christus.
Qui vivit et regnat
    in sæcula sæculorum.
R. Amen.

Deus, qui mirabiliter creasti hominem
et mirabilius redemisti,
da nobis, quæsumus,
contra oblectamenta peccati mentis
    ratione persistere,
ut mereamur ad æterna
    gaudia pervenire.
Per Christum Dominum nostrum.
R. Amen.

SECOND READING

A reading from the book of Genesis   22:1-18

The sacrifice of Abraham, our father in faith.

[God put Abraham to the test. 'Abraham, Abraham,' he called. 'Here I am'
he replied. 'Take your son,' God said 'your only child Isaac, whom you

love, and go to the land of Moriah. There you shall offer him as a burnt offering, on a mountain I will point out to you.']

Rising early next morning Abraham saddled his ass and took with him two of his servants and his son Isaac. He chopped wood for the burnt offering and started on his journey to the place God had pointed out to him. On the third day Abraham looked up and saw the place in the distance. Then Abraham said to his servants, 'Stay here with the donkey. The boy and I will go over there; we will worship and come back to you.'

Abraham took the wood for the burnt offering, loaded it on Isaac, and carried in his own hands the fire and the knife. Then the two of them set out together. Isaac spoke to his father Abraham, 'Father' he said. 'Yes, my son' he replied. 'Look,' he said 'here are the fire and the wood, but where is the lamb for the burnt offering?' Abraham answered, 'My son, God himself will provide the lamb for the burnt offering.' Then the two of them went on together.

[When they arrived at the place God had pointed out to him, Abraham built an altar there, and arranged the wood. Then he bound his son Isaac and put him on the altar on top of the wood. Abraham stretched out his hand and seized the knife to kill his son.

But the angel of the Lord called to him from heaven. 'Abraham, Abraham' he said. 'I am here' he replied. 'Do not raise your hand against the boy' the angel said. 'Do not harm him, for now I know you fear God. You have not refused me your son, your only son.' Then looking up, Abraham saw a ram caught by its horns in a bush. Abraham took the ram and offered it as a burnt-offering in place of his son.] Abraham called this place 'The Lord provides', and hence the saying today: On the mountain the Lord provides.

[The angel of the Lord called Abraham a second time from heaven. 'I swear by my own self – it is the Lord who speaks – because you have done this, because you have not refused me your son, your only son, I will shower blessings on you, I will make your descendants as many as the stars of heaven and the grains of sand on the seashore. Your descendants shall gain possession of the gates of their enemies. All the nations of the earth shall bless themselves by your descendants, as a reward for your obedience.

The word of the Lord.]

Shorter Form, verses 1-2,9-13,15-18. Read between [ ]

Responsorial Psalm   Ps 15:5,8-11, R. v.1

R. **Preserve me, God, I take refuge in you.**

O Lord, it is you who are my portion and cup;
it is you yourself who are my prize.
I keep the Lord ever in my sight:
since he is at my right hand, I shall stand firm. R.

And so my heart rejoices, my soul is glad;
even my body shall rest in safety.
For you will not leave my soul among the dead,
nor let your beloved know decay. R.

You will show me the path of life,
the fullness of joy in your presence,
at your right hand happiness for ever. R.

Prayer

Let us pray.

O God, supreme Father
    of the faithful,
who increase the children
    of your promise
by pouring out the grace
    of adoption
throughout the whole world
and who through the Paschal Mystery
make your servant Abraham father
    of nations,
as once you swore,
grant, we pray,
that your peoples may enter worthily
into the grace to which you call them.
Through Christ our Lord.
R. Amen.

Oremus.

Deus, Pater summe fidelium,
qui promissionis tuæ filios diffusa
    adoptionis gratia
in toto terrarum orbe multiplicas,
et per paschale sacramentum
Abraham puerum tuum
universarum, sicut iurasti,
    gentium efficis patrem,
da populis tuis digne ad gratiam
    tuæ vocationis intrare.
Per Christum Dominum nostrum.
R. Amen.

The following reading must always be read.

THIRD READING

A reading from book of Exodus   14:15-15:1

The sons of Israel went on dry ground right into the sea.

The Lord said to Moses, 'Why do you cry to me so? Tell the sons of Israel to
march on. For yourself, raise your staff and stretch out your hand over the

sea and part it for the sons of Israel to walk through the sea on dry ground. I for my part will make the heart of the Egyptians so stubborn that they will follow them. So shall I win myself glory at the expense of Pharaoh, of all his army, his chariots, his horsemen. And when I have won glory for myself, at the expense of Pharaoh and his chariots and his army, the Egyptians will learn that I am the Lord.'

Then the angel of the Lord, who marched at the front of the army of Israel, changed station and moved to their rear. The pillar of cloud changed station from the front to the rear of them, and remained there. It came between the camp of the Egyptians and the camp of Israel. The cloud was dark, and the night passed without the armies drawing any closer the whole night long. Moses stretched out his hand over the sea. The Lord drove back the sea with a strong easterly wind all night, and he made dry land of the sea. The waters parted and the sons of Israel went on dry ground right into the sea, walls of water to right and to left of them. The Egyptians gave chase: after them they went, right into the sea, all Pharaoh's horses, his chariots, and his horsemen. In the morning watch, the Lord looked down on the army of the Egyptians from the pillar of fire and of cloud, and threw the army into confusion. He so clogged their chariot wheels that they could scarcely make headway. 'Let us flee from the Israelites,' the Egyptians cried 'the Lord is fighting for them against the Egyptians!' 'Stretch out your hand over the sea,' the Lord said to Moses 'that the waters may flow back on the Egyptians and their chariots and their horsemen.' Moses stretched out his hand over the sea and, as day broke, the sea returned to its bed. The fleeing Egyptians marched right into it, and the Lord overthrew the Egyptians in the very middle of the sea. The returning waters overwhelmed the chariots and the horsemen of Pharaoh's whole army, which had followed the Israelites into the sea; not a single one of them was left. But the sons of Israel had marched through the sea on dry ground, walls of water to right and to left of them. That day, the Lord rescued Israel from the Egyptians, and Israel saw the Egyptians lying dead on the shore. Israel witnessed the great act that the Lord had performed against the Egyptians, and the people venerated the Lord; they put their faith in the Lord and in Moses, his servant.

It was then that Moses and the sons of Israel sang this song in honour of the Lord:

The choir takes up the Responsorial Psalm immediately.

Responsorial Psalm   Ex 15:1-6,17-18. R. v.1

R. **I will sing to the Lord, glorious his triumph!**

I will sing to the Lord, glorious his triumph!
Horse and rider he has thrown into the sea!
The Lord is my strength, my song, my salvation.
This is my God and I extol him,
my father's God and I give him praise. R.

The Lord is a warrior! The Lord is his name.
The chariots of Pharaoh he hurled into the sea,
the flower of his army is drowned in the sea.
The deeps hide them; they sank like a stone. R.

Your right hand, Lord, glorious in its power,
your right hand, Lord, has shattered the enemy.
In the greatness of your glory you crushed the foe. R.

You will lead your people and plant them on your mountain,
the place, O Lord, where you have made your home,
the sanctuary, Lord, which your hands have made.
The Lord will reign for ever and ever. R.

Prayer

Let us pray.

O God, whose ancient wonders
remain undimmed in splendour
   even in our day,
for what you once bestowed
   on a single people,
freeing them from
   Pharaoh's persecution
by the power of your right hand,
now you bring about as the salvation
   of the nations
through the waters of rebirth,
grant, we pray,
   that the whole world
may become children of Abraham
and inherit the dignity
   of Israel's birthright.
Through Christ our Lord.
R. Amen.

Oremus.

Deus, cuius antiqua miracula
etiam nostris temporibus
   coruscare sentimus,
dum, quod uni populo
a persecutione Pharaonis liberando
dexteræ tuæ potentia contulisti,
id in salutem gentium
per aquam regenerationis operaris,
præsta, ut in Abrahæ filios
et in Israeliticam dignitatem
totius mundi transeat plenitudo.
Per Christum Dominum nostrum.
R. Amen.

Or:

O God, who by the light
of the New Testament
have unlocked the meaning
of wonders worked in former times,
so that the Red Sea prefigures
the sacred font
and the nation delivered from slavery
foreshadows the Christian people,
grant, we pray, that all nations,
obtaining the privilege of Israel
by merit of faith,
may be reborn by partaking
of your Spirit.
Through Christ our Lord.
R. Amen.

Vel:

Deus, qui primis temporibus
impleta miracula novi testamenti
luce reserasti,
ut et Mare Rubrum forma sacri
fontis exsisteret,
et plebs a servitute liberata
christiani populi
sacramenta præferret,
da, ut omnes gentes,
Israelis privilegium merito
fidei consecutæ,
Spiritus tui participatione
regenerentur.
Per Christum Dominum nostrum.
R. Amen.

FOURTH READING

A reading from the prophet Isaiah   54:5-14

With everlasting love the Lord your redeemer has taken pity on you.

Now your creator will be your husband,
his name, the Lord of hosts;
your redeemer will be the Holy One of Israel,
he is called the God of the whole earth.
Yes, like a forsaken wife, distressed in spirit,
the Lord calls you back.
Does a man cast off the wife of his youth?
says your God.

I did forsake you for a brief moment,
but with great love will I take you back.
In excess of anger, for a moment
I hid my face from you.
But with everlasting love I have taken pity on you,
says the Lord, your redeemer.

I am now as I was in the days of Noah
when I swore that Noah's waters
should never flood the world again.
So now I swear concerning my anger with you
and the threats I made against you;

for the mountains may depart,
the hills be shaken,

but my love for you will never leave you;
and my covenant of peace with you will never be shaken,
says the Lord who takes pity on you.
Unhappy creature, storm-tossed, disconsolate,
see, I will set your stones on carbuncles
and your foundations on sapphires.
I will make rubies your battlements,
your gates crystal,
and your entire wall precious stones.
Your sons will all be taught by the Lord.
The prosperity of your sons will be great.
You will be founded on integrity;
remote from oppression, you will have nothing to fear;
remote from terror, it will not approach you.

   The word of the Lord.

Responsional Psalm   Ps 29:2,4-6,11-13. R. v.2

R. **I will praise you, Lord, you have rescued me.**

   I will praise you, Lord, you have rescued me
   and have not let my enemies rejoice over me.
   O Lord, you have raised my soul from the dead,
   restored me to life from those who sink into the grave. R.

   Sing psalms to the Lord, you who love him,
   give thanks to his holy name.
   His anger lasts but a moment; his favour through life.
   At night there are tears, but joy comes with dawn. R.

   The Lord listened and had pity.
   The Lord came to my help.
   For me you have changed my mourning into dancing,
   O Lord my God, I will thank you for ever. R.

Prayer

Let us pray.	Oremus.
Almighty ever-living God,	Omnipotens sempiterne Deus,
surpass, for the honour of your name,	multiplica in honorem nominis tui
what you pledged to the Patriarchs	quod patrum fidei spopondisti,
by reason of their faith,	et promissionis filios sacra
and through sacred adoption increase	adoptione dilata,
the children of your promise,	ut, quod priores sancti non

so that what the Saints of old never
  doubted would come to pass
your Church may now see in great
  part fulfilled.
Through Christ our Lord. R. **Amen.**

dubitaverunt futurum,
Ecclesia tua magna ex parte iam
  cognoscat impletum.
Per Christum Dominum nostrum.
R. **Amen.**

Alternatively, other prayers may be used from among those which follow the readings that have been omitted.

FIFTH READING

A reading from the prophet Isaiah   55:1-11

Come to me and your soul will live, and I will make an everlasting covenant with you.

Thus says the Lord:
  Oh, come to the water all you who are thirsty;
    though you have no money, come!
  Buy corn without money, and eat,
  and, at no cost, wine and milk.
  Why spend money on what is not bread,
    your wages on what fails to satisfy?
  Listen, listen to me, and you will have good things to eat
  and rich food to enjoy.
  Pay attention, come to me;
  and your soul will live.

  With you I will make an everlasting covenant
  out of the favours promised to David.
  See, I have made of you a witness to the peoples,
  a leader and a master of the nations.
  See, you will summon a nation you never knew,
  those unknown will come hurrying to you,
  for the sake of the Lord your God,
  of the Holy One of Israel who will glorify you.

  Seek the Lord while he is still to be found,
  call to him while he is still near.
  Let the wicked man abandon his way,
  the evil man his thoughts.
  Let him turn back to the Lord who will take pity on him,
  to our God who is rich in forgiving;
  for my thoughts are not your thoughts,
  my ways not your ways – it is the Lord who speaks.
  Yes, the heavens are as high above earth
  as my ways are above your ways,
  my thoughts above your thoughts.

Yes, as the rain and the snow come down from the heavens and do not return without watering the earth, making it yield and giving growth to provide seed for the sower and bread for the eating, so the word that goes from my mouth does not return to me empty, without carrying out my will and succeeding in what it was sent to do.

The word of the Lord.

Responsorial Psalm

Is 12:2-6. R. v.3

R. **With joy you will draw water from the wells of salvation.**

Truly God is my salvation,
I trust, I shall not fear.
For the Lord is my strength, my song,
he became my saviour.
With joy you will draw water
from the wells of salvation. R.

Give thanks to the Lord, give praise to his name!
Make his mighty deeds known to the peoples,
declare the greatness of his name. R.

Sing a psalm to the Lord
for he has done glorious deeds,
make them known to all the earth!
People of Sion, sing and shout for joy
for great in your midst is the Holy One of Israel. R.

Prayer

Let us pray.

Almighty ever-living God,
sole hope of the world,
who by the preaching
     of your Prophets
unveiled the mysteries
     of this present age,
graciously increase the longing
     of your people,
for only at the prompting
     of your grace
do the faithful progress in any
     kind of virtue.
Through Christ our Lord.
R. Amen.

Oremus.

Omnipotens sempiterne Deus,
spes unica mundi,
qui prophetarum tuorum præconio
præsentium temporum
     declarasti mysteria,
auge populi tui vota placatus,
quia in nullo fidelium nisi ex tua
     inspiratione proveniunt
quarumlibet incrementa virtutum.
Per Christum Dominum nostrum.
R. Amen.

SIXTH READING

A reading from the prophet Baruch   3:9-15,32-4:4

In the radiance of the Lord make your way to light.

Listen, Israel, to commands that bring life;
hear, and learn what knowledge means.
Why, Israel, why are you in the country of your enemies,
growing older and older in an alien land,
sharing defilement with the dead,
reckoned with those who go to Sheol?
Because you have forsaken the fountain of wisdom.
Had you walked in the way of God,
you would have lived in peace for ever.
Learn where knowledge is, where strength,
where understanding, and so learn
where length of days is, where life,
where the light of the eyes and where peace.
But who has found out where she lives,
who has entered her treasure house?

But the One who knows all knows her,
he has grasped her with his own intellect,
he has set the earth firm for ever
and filled it with four-footed beasts,
he sends the light – and it goes,
he recalls it – and trembling it obeys;
the stars shine joyfully at their set times:
when he calls them, they answer, 'Here we are';
they gladly shine for their creator.
It is he who is our God,
no other can compare with him.
He has grasped the whole way of knowledge,
and confided it to his servant Jacob,
to Israel his well-beloved;
so causing her to appear on earth
and move among men.

This is the book of the commandments of God,
the Law that stands for ever;
those who keep her live,
those who desert her die.
Turn back, Jacob, seize her,
in her radiance make your way to light:

do not yield your glory to another,
your privilege to a people not your own.
Israel, blessed are we:
what pleases God has been revealed to us.

The word of the Lord.

Responsional Psalm   Ps 18:8-11. R. Jn 6:69

R. **You have the message of eternal life, O Lord.**

The law of the Lord is perfect,
it revives the soul.
The rule of the Lord is to be trusted,
it gives wisdom to the simple. R.

The precepts of the Lord are right,
they gladden the heart.
The command of the Lord is clear,
it gives light to the eyes. R.

The fear of the Lord is holy,
abiding for ever.
The decrees of the Lord are truth
and all of them just. R.

They are more to be desired than gold,
than the purest of gold
and sweeter are they than honey,
than honey from the comb. R.

Prayer

Let us pray.

O God, who constantly increase
    your Church
by your call to the nations,
graciously grant
to those you wash clean
    in the waters of Baptism
the assurance of your
    unfailing protection.
Through Christ our Lord.
R. Amen.

Oremus.

Deus, qui Ecclesiam tuam
semper gentium
    vocatione multiplicas,
concede propitius,
ut, quos aqua baptismatis abluis,
continua protectione tuearis.
Per Christum Dominum nostrum.
R. Amen.

SEVENTH READING

A reading from the prophet Ezekiel
36:16-28

I shall pour clean water over you, and I shall give you a new heart.

The word of the Lord was addressed to me as follows: 'Son of man, the members of the House of Israel used to live in their own land, but they defiled it by their conduct and actions. I then discharged my fury at them because of the blood they shed in their land and the idols with which they defiled it. I scattered them among the nations and dispersed them in foreign countries. I sentenced them as their conduct and actions deserved. And now they have profaned my holy name among the nations where they have gone, so that people say of them, "These are the people of the Lord; they have been exiled from his land." But I have been concerned about my holy name, which the House of Israel has profaned among the nations where they have gone. And so, say to the House of Israel, "The Lord says this: I am not doing this for my sake, House of Israel, but for the sake of my holy name, which you have profaned among the nations where you have gone. I mean to display the holiness of my great name, which has been profaned among the nations, which you have profaned among them. And the nations will learn that I am the Lord – it is the Lord who speaks – when I display my holiness for your sake before their eyes. Then I am going to take you from among the nations and gather you together from all the foreign countries, and bring you home to your own land. I shall pour clean water over you and you will be cleansed; I shall cleanse you of all your defilement and all your idols. I shall give you a new heart, and put a new spirit in you; I shall remove the heart of stone from your bodies and give you a heart of flesh instead. I shall put my spirit in you, and make you keep my laws and sincerely respect my observances. You will live in the land which I gave your ancestors. You shall be my people and I will be your God."'

The word of the Lord.

Responsorial Psalm   Pss 41:3,5; 42:3,4. R. Ps 41:1

R. **Like the deer that yearns for running streams,**
   so my soul is yearning for you, my God.

   My soul is thirsting for God.
   the God of my life;
   when can I enter and see
   the face of God? R.

These things I will remember
as I pour out my soul:
how I would lead the rejoicing crowd
into the house of God,
amid cries of gladness and thanksgiving,
the throng wild with joy. R.

O send forth your light and your truth;
let these be my guide.
Let them bring me to your holy mountain
to the place where you dwell. R.

And I will come to the altar of God,
the God of my joy.
My redeemer, I will thank you on the harp,
O God, my God. R.

If a Baptism takes place the Responsorial Psalm which follows the Fifth Reading (see p.403), is used, or Psalm 50 as follows.

Responsorial Psalm
Ps 50:12-15,18,19. R. v.12

R. **A pure heart create for me, O God.**

A pure heart create for me, O God,
put a steadfast spirit within me.
Do not cast me away from your presence,
nor deprive me of your holy spirit. R.

Give me again the joy of your help;
with a spirit of fervour sustain me,
that I may teach transgressors your ways
and sinners may return to you. R.

For in sacrifice you take no delight,
burnt offering from me you would refuse,
my sacrifice, a contrite spirit.
A humbled, contrite heart you will not spurn. R.

Prayer

Let us pray.

O God of unchanging power
   and eternal light,
look with favour on the wondrous
   mystery of the whole Church

Oremus.

Deus, incommutabilis virtus
   et lumen æternum,
respice propitius ad totius
   Ecclesiæ mirabile sacramentum,

and serenely accomplish the work
of human salvation,
which you planned from all eternity;
may the whole world know and see
that what was cast down is raised up,
what had become old is made new,
and all things are restored
    to integrity through Christ,
just as by him they came into being.
Who lives and reigns
    for ever and ever.
R. Amen.

Or:

O God, who by the pages
    of both Testaments
instruct and prepare us to celebrate
    the Paschal Mystery,
grant that we may comprehend
    your mercy,
so that the gifts we receive
    from you this night
may confirm our hope of the gifts
    to come.
Through Christ our Lord.
R. Amen.

et opus salutis humanæ
perpetuæ dispositionis effectu
tranquillius operare;
totusque mundus experiatur
    et videat
deiecta erigi, inveterata renovari
et per ipsum Christum redire
    omnia in integrum,
a quo sumpsere principium.
Qui vivit et regnat
    in sæcula sæculorum.
R. Amen.

Vel:

Deus, qui nos ad celebrandum
    paschale sacramentum
utriusque Testamenti
    paginis instruis,
da nobis intellegere
    misericordiam tuam,
ut ex perceptione
    præsentium munerum
firma sit exspectatio futurorum.
Per Christum Dominum nostrum.
R. Amen.

After the last reading from the Old Testament with its Responsorial Psalm and its prayer, the altar candles are lit, and the Priest intones the hymn **Gloria in excelsis Deo** (Glory to God in the highest), which is taken up by all, while bells are rung, according to local custom.

The complete musical setting of the Latin text is found in the Graduale Romanum.

When the hymn is concluded, the Priest says the Collect in the usual way.

Collect

Let us pray.

O God, who make this most sacred
    night radiant
with the glory
    of the Lord's Resurrection,
stir up in your Church a spirit
    of adoption,

Collecta

Oremus.

Deus, qui hanc
    sacratissimam noctem
gloria dominicæ
    resurrectionis illustras,
excita in Ecclesia tua
    adoptionis spiritum,

so that, renewed in body and mind,	ut, corpore et mente renovati,
we may render you undivided service.	puram tibi exhibeamus servitutem.
Through our Lord Jesus Christ,	Per Dominum nostrum Iesum
your Son,	Christum Filium tuum,
who lives and reigns with you	qui tecum vivit et regnat
in the unity of the Holy Spirit,	in unitate Spiritus Sancti,
God, for ever and ever.	Deus, per omnia sæcula sæculorum.

FIRST READING

A reading from the letter of St Paul to the Romans   6:3-11

Christ, having been raised from the dead, will never die again.

When we were baptised in Christ Jesus we were baptised in his death; in other words, when we were baptised we went into the tomb with him and joined him in death, so that as Christ was raised from the dead by the Father's glory, we too might live a new life.

If in union with Christ we have imitated his death, we shall also imitate him in his resurrection. We must realise that our former selves have been crucified with him to destroy this sinful body and to free us from the slavery of sin. When a man dies, of course, he has finished with sin.

But we believe that having died with Christ we shall return to life with him: Christ, as we know, having been raised from the dead will never die again. Death has no power over him any more. When he died, he died, once for all, to sin, so his life now is life with God; and in that way, you too must consider yourselves to be dead to sin but alive for God in Christ Jesus.

The word of the Lord.

After the Epistle has been read, all rise, then the Priest solemnly intones the **Alleluia** three times, raising his voice by a step each time, with all repeating it. If necessary, the psalmist intones the **Alleluia**.

Responsorial Psalm   Ps 117:1-2,16-17,22-23

R. **Alleluia, alleluia, alleluia!**

   Give thanks to the Lord for he is good,
   for his love has no end.
   Let the sons of Israel say:
   'His love has no end.'   R.

The Lord's right hand has triumphed;
his right hand raised me up.
I shall not die, I shall live
and recount his deeds. R.

The stone which the builders rejected
has become the corner stone.
This is the work of the Lord,
a marvel in our eyes. R.

R. **Alleluia, alleluia, alleluia!**

The Priest, in the usual way, puts incense in the thurible and blesses the Deacon. At
the Gospel lights are not carried, but only incense.

GOSPEL

A reading from the holy Gospel according to Matthew   28:1-10

He has risen from the dead and now he is going before you into Galilee.

After the sabbath, and towards dawn on the first day of the week, Mary of
Magdala and the other Mary went to visit the sepulchre. And all at once
there was a violent earthquake, for the angel of the Lord, descending from
heaven, came and rolled away the stone and sat on it. His face was like
lightning, his robe white as snow. The guards were so shaken, so frightened
of him, that they were like dead men. But the angel spoke; and he said to
the women, 'There is no need for you to be afraid. I know you are looking
for Jesus, who was crucified. He is not here, for he has risen, as he said he
would. Come and see the place where he lay, then go quickly and tell his
disciples, "He has risen from the dead and now he is going before you to
Galilee; it is there you will see him." Now I have told you.' Filled with awe
and great joy, the women came quickly away from the tomb and ran to tell
the disciples.

    And there, coming to meet them, was Jesus. 'Greetings' he said. And
the women came up to him and, falling down before him, clasped his feet.
Then Jesus said to them, 'Do not be afraid; go and tell my brothers that
they must leave for Galilee; they will see me there.'

    The Gospel of the Lord.

After the Gospel, the Homily, even if brief, is not to be omitted.

THIRD PART:

Baptismal Liturgy

After the Homily the Baptismal Liturgy begins. The Priest goes with the ministers to the baptismal font, if this can be seen by the faithful. Otherwise a vessel with water is placed in the sanctuary.

Catechumens, if there are any, are called forward and presented by their godparents in front of the assembled Church or, if they are small children, are carried by their parents and godparents.

Then, if there is to be a procession to the baptistery or to the font, it forms immediately. A minister with the paschal candle leads off, and those to be baptised follow him with their godparents, then the ministers, the Deacon, and the Priest. During the procession, the Litany is sung. When the Litany is completed, the Priest gives the address.

If, however, the Baptismal Liturgy takes place in the sanctuary, the Priest immediately makes an introductory statement in these or similar words.

If there are candidates to be baptised:

Dearly beloved,
with one heart and one soul,
   let us by our prayers
come to the aid of these our brothers
   and sisters in their blessed hope,
so that, as they approach the font
   of rebirth,
the almighty Father may bestow
   on them
all his merciful help.

Precibus nostris, carissimi,
fratrum nostrorum beatam spem
   unanimes adiuvemus,
ut Pater omnipotens ad fontem
   regenerationis euntes
omni misericordiæ suæ
   auxilio prosequatur.

If the font is to be blessed, but no one is to be baptised:

Dearly beloved,
let us humbly invoke upon
   this font
the grace of God the almighty Father,
that those who from it are born anew
may be numbered among the
   children of adoption in Christ.

Dei Patris omnipotentis gratiam,
   carissimi,
super hunc fontem
   supplices invocemus,
ut qui ex eo renascentur
adoptionis filiis in
   Christo aggregentur.

The Litany

The Litany is sung by two cantors, with all standing (because it is Easter Time) and responding.

If, however, there is to be a procession of some length to the baptistery, the Litany is sung during the procession; in this case, those to be baptised are called forward before the procession begins, and the procession takes place led by the paschal candle, followed by the catechumens with their godparents, then the ministers, the Deacon, and the Priest. The address should occur before the Blessing of Water.

If no one is to be baptised and the font is not to be blessed, the Litany is omitted, and the Blessing of Water takes place at once.

In the Litany the names of some Saints may be added, especially the Titular Saint of the church and the Patron Saints of the place and of those to be baptised.

Lord, have mercy.		Kyrie, eleison.	
	Lord, have mercy.		Kyrie, eleison.
Christ, have mercy.		Christe, eleison.	
	Christ, have mercy.		Christe, eleison.
Lord, have mercy.		Kyrie, eleison.	
	Lord have mercy.		Kyrie, eleison.
Holy Mary,		Sancta Maria,	
Mother of God,	pray for us.	Mater Dei,	ora pro nobis.
Saint Michael,	pray for us.	Sancte Michael,	ora pro nobis.
Holy Angels of God,	pray for us.	Sancti Angeli Dei,	orate pro nobis.
Saint John the Baptist,	pray for us.	Sancte Ioannes Baptista,	ora pro nobis.
Saint Joseph,	pray for us.	Sancte Ioseph,	ora pro nobis.
Saint Peter and		Sancti Petre et Paule,	orate pro nobis.
Saint Paul,	pray for us.		
Saint Andrew,	pray for us.	Sancte Andrea,	ora pro nobis.
Saint John,	pray for us.	Sancte Ioannes,	ora pro nobis.
Saint Mary Magdalene,	pray for us.	Sancta Maria Magdalena,	ora pro nobis.
Saint Stephen,	pray for us.	Sancte Stephane,	ora pro nobis.
Saint Ignatius of		Sancte Ignati	
Antioch,	pray for us.	Antiochene,	ora pro nobis.
Saint Lawrence,	pray for us.	Sancte Laurenti,	ora pro nobis.
Saint Perpetua and		Sanctæ Perpetua	
Saint Felicity,	pray for us.	et Felicitas,	orate pro nobis.
Saint Agnes,	pray for us.	Sancta Agnes,	ora pro nobis.
Saint Gregory,	pray for us.	Sancte Gregori,	ora pro nobis.
Saint Augustine,	pray for us.	Sancte Augustine,	ora pro nobis.

Saint Athanasius,	pray for us.	Sancte Athanasi,	ora pro nobis.
Saint Basil,	pray for us.	Sancte Basili,	ora pro nobis.
Saint Martin,	pray for us.	Sancte Martine,	ora pro nobis.
Saint Benedict,	pray for us.	Sancte Benedicte,	ora pro nobis.
Saint Francis and Saint Dominic,	pray for us.	Sancti Francisce et Dominice,	orate pro nobis.
Saint Francis Xavier,	pray for us.	Sancte Francisce (Xavier),	ora pro nobis.
Saint John Vianney,	pray for us.	Sancte Ioannes Maria (Vianney),	ora pro nobis.
Saint Catherine of Siena,	pray for us.	Sancta Catharina (Senensis),	ora pro nobis.
Saint Teresa of Jesus,	pray for us.	Sancta Teresia a Iesu,	ora pro nobis.
All holy men and women, Saints of God,	pray for us.	Omnes Sancti et Sanctæ Dei,	orate pro nobis.
Lord, be merciful Lord, deliver us, we pray.		Propitius esto,	libera nos, Domine.
From all evil, Lord, deliver us, we pray.		Ab omni malo,	libera nos, Domine.
From every sin, Lord, deliver us, we pray.		Ab omni peccato,	libera nos, Domine.
From everlasting death, Lord, deliver us, we pray.		A morte perpetua,	libera nos, Domine.
By your Incarnation, Lord, deliver us, we pray.		Per incarnationem tuam,	libera nos, Domine.
By your Death and Resurrection, Lord, deliver us, we pray.		Per mortem et resurrectionem tuam,	libera nos, Domine.
By the out-pouring of the Holy Spirit, Lord, deliver us, we pray.		Per effusionem Spiritus Sancti,	libera nos, Domine.
Be merciful to us sinners, Lord we ask you to hear our prayer.		Peccatores,	te rogamus, audi nos.

If there are candidates to be baptised

Bring these chosen ones to new birth through the grace of Baptism, Lord, we ask you, hear our prayer.	Ut hos electos per gratiam Baptismi regenerare digneris te rogamus, audi nos.

If there is no one to be baptised:

Make this font holy by your grace
    for the new birth of your children,
    Lord, we ask you, hear our prayer.
	Ut hunc fontem,
	    regenerandis tibi filiis,
	    gratia tua sanctificare digneris
	              te rogamus, audi nos.

Jesus, Son of the Living God,
    Lord, we ask you, hear our prayer.
	Iesu, Fili Dei vivi,
	              te rogamus, audi nos.

Christ, hear us.   Christ, hear us.
Christ, graciously hear us.
       Christ graciously hear us.
	Christe, audi nos. Christe, audi nos.
	Christe, exaudi nos.
	            Christe, exaudi nos.

If there are candidates to be baptised, the Priest, with hands extended, says the following prayer:

Almighty ever-living God,
be present by the mysteries of your
    great love
and send forth the spirit of adoption
to create the new peoples
brought to birth for you in the font
    of Baptism,
so that what is to be carried out
    by our humble service
may be brought to fulfilment
    by your mighty power.
Through Christ our Lord.
R. Amen.
	Omnipotens sempiterne Deus,
	adesto magnæ pietatis
	    tuæ sacramentis,
	et ad recreandos novos populos,
	quos tibi fons baptismatis parturit,
	spiritum adoptionis emitte,
	ut, quod nostræ humilitatis
	    gerendum est ministerio,
	virtutis tuæ impleatur effectu.
	Per Christum Dominum nostrum.
	R. Amen.

Blessing of Baptismal Water

The Priest then blesses the baptismal water, saying the following prayer with hands extended:

O God, who by invisible power
accomplish a wondrous effect
through sacramental signs
and who in many ways have
    prepared water, your creation,
to show forth the grace of Baptism;
	Deus, qui invisibili potentia
	per sacramentorum signa
	    mirabilem operaris effectum,
	et creaturam aquæ multis
	    modis præparasti,
	ut baptismi gratiam demonstraret;

O God, whose Spirit
in the first moments
    of the world's creation
hovered over the waters,
	Deus, cuius Spiritus
	super aquas inter ipsa mundi
	    primordia ferebatur,
	ut iam tunc virtutem sanctificandi

so that the very substance of water
would even then take to itself
     the power to sanctify;

O God, who by the outpouring
     of the flood
foreshadowed regeneration,
so that from the mystery of one
     and the same element of water
would come an end to vice
     and a beginning of virtue;

O God, who caused the children
     of Abraham
to pass dry-shod through the Red Sea,
so that the chosen people,
set free from slavery to Pharaoh,
would prefigure the people
     of the baptised;

O God, whose Son,
baptised by John in the waters
     of the Jordan,
was anointed with the Holy Spirit,
and, as he hung upon the Cross,
gave forth water from his side
     along with blood,
and after his Resurrection,
     commanded his disciples:
'Go forth, teach all nations,
     baptising them
in the name of the Father and of the
     Son and of the Holy Spirit',
look now, we pray, upon the face
     of your Church
and graciously unseal for her
     the fountain of Baptism.

May this water receive
     by the Holy Spirit
the grace of your Only Begotten Son,

aquarum natura conciperet;

Deus, qui regenerationis speciem
in ipsa diluvii effusione signasti,
ut unius eiusdemque
     elementi mysterio
et finis esset vitiis et origo virtutum;

Deus, qui Abrahæ filios
per Mare Rubrum sicco vestigio
     transire fecisti,
ut plebs, a Pharaonis
     servitute liberata,
populum baptizatorum
     præfiguraret;

Deus, cuius Filius, in aqua Iordanis
     a Ioanne baptizatus,
Sancto Spiritu est inunctus,
et, in cruce pendens,
una cum sanguine aquam de latere
     suo produxit,
ac, post resurrectionem suam,
     discipulis iussit:

'Ite, docete omnes gentes,
     baptizantes eos
in nomine Patris et Filii
     et Spiritus Sancti':
respice in faciem Ecclesiæ tuæ,
eique dignare fontem
     baptismatis aperire.

Sumat hæc aqua Unigeniti tui
     gratiam de Spiritu Sancto,
ut homo, ad imaginem

so that human nature,
   created in your image,
and washed clean through
   the Sacrament of Baptism
from all the squalor of the life of old,
may be found worthy to rise
   to the life of newborn children
through water and the Holy Spirit.

tuam conditus,
sacramento baptismatis
a cunctis squaloribus
   vetustatis ablutus,
in novam infantiam
ex aqua et Spiritu Sancto
   resurgere mereatur.

And, if appropriate, lowering the paschal candle into the water either once or three times, he continues:

May the power of the Holy Spirit,
O Lord, we pray,
come down through your Son
into the fullness of this font,

Descendat, quæsumus, Domine,
in hanc plenitudinem fontis
per Filium tuum virtus
   Spiritus Sancti,

and, holding the candle in the water, he continues:

so that all who have been buried
   with Christ
by Baptism into death
may rise again to life with him.
Who lives and reigns with you
   in the unity of the Holy Spirit,
God, for ever and ever.
R. **Amen.**

ut omnes, cum Christo consepulti
per baptismum in mortem,
ad vitam cum ipso resurgant.
Qui tecum vivit et regnat
   in unitate Spiritus Sancti,
Deus, per omnia sæcula sæculorum.
R. **Amen.**

Then the candle is lifted out of the water, as the people acclaim:

Springs of water, bless the Lord;
praise and exalt him above all
   for ever.

Benedicite, fontes, Domino,
laudate et superexaltate eum
   in sæcula.

After the blessing of baptismal water and the acclamation of the people, the Priest, standing, puts the prescribed questions to the adults and the parents or godparents of the children, as is set out in the respective Rites of the Roman Ritual, in order for them to make the required renunciation.

If the anointing of the adults with the Oil of Catechumens has not taken place beforehand, as part of the immediately preparatory rites, it occurs at this moment.

Then the Priest questions the adults individually about the faith and, if there are children to be baptised, he requests the triple profession of faith from all the parents and godparents together, as is indicated in the respective Rites.

Where many are to be baptised on this night, it is possible to arrange the rite so that, immediately after the response of those to be baptised and of the godparents and the parents, the Celebrant asks for and receives the renewal of baptismal promises of all present.

When the interrogation is concluded, the Priest baptises the adult elect and the children.

After the Baptism, the Priest anoints the infants with chrism. A white garment is given to each, whether adults or children. Then the Priest or Deacon receives the paschal candle from the hand of the minister, and the candles of the newly baptised are lighted. For infants the rite of Ephphetha is omitted.

Afterwards, unless the baptismal washing and the other explanatory rites have occurred in the sanctuary, a procession returns to the sanctuary, formed as before, with the newly baptised or the godparents or parents carrying lighted candles. During this procession, the baptismal canticle **Vidi aquam (I saw water)** or another appropriate chant is sung.

If adults have been baptised, the Bishop or, in his absence, the Priest who has conferred Baptism, should at once administer the Sacrament of Confirmation to them in the sanctuary, as is indicated in the Roman Pontifical or Roman Ritual.

The Blessing of Water

If no one present is to be baptised and the font is not to be blessed, the Priest introduces the faithful to the blessing of water, saying:

Dear brothers and sisters, let us humbly beseech the Lord our God to bless this water he has created, which will be sprinkled upon us as a memorial of our Baptism. May he graciously renew us, that we may remain faithful to the Spirit whom we have received.	Dominum Deum nostrum, fratres carissimi, suppliciter exoremus, ut hanc creaturam aquæ benedicere dignetur, super nos aspergendam in nostri memoriam baptismi. Ipse autem nos adiuvare dignetur, ut Spiritui, quem accepimus, fideles maneamus.

And after a brief pause in silence, he proclaims the following prayer, with hands extended:

Lord our God, in your mercy be present to your people who keep vigil on this most sacred night, and, for us who recall the wondrous work of our creation	Domine Deus noster, populo tuo hac nocte sacratissima vigilanti adesto propitius; et nobis, mirabile nostræ creationis opus, sed et redemptionis nostræ

and the still greater work
   of our redemption,
graciously bless this water.
For you created water to make
   the fields fruitful
and to refresh and cleanse our bodies.
You also made water the instrument
   of your mercy:
for through water you freed
   your people from slavery
and quenched their thirst
   in the desert;
through water the Prophets
   proclaimed the new covenant
you were to enter upon
   with the human race;
and last of all,
through water, which Christ made
   holy in the Jordan,
you have renewed our
   corrupted nature
in the bath of regeneration.
Therefore, may this water be for us
a memorial of the Baptism
   we have received,
and grant that we may share
in the gladness of our brothers
   and sisters,
who at Easter have received
   their Baptism.
Through Christ our Lord.
R. Amen.

mirabilius, memorantibus,
hanc aquam benedicere tu dignare.

Ipsam enim tu fecisti,
ut et arva fecunditate donaret,
et levamen corporibus nostris
   munditiamque præberet.

Aquam etiam tuæ ministram
   misericordiæ condidisti;
nam per ipsam solvisti tui
   populi servitutem
illiusque sitim in deserto sedasti;
per ipsam novum fœdus
   nuntiaverunt prophetæ,
quod eras cum hominibus initurus;
per ipsam denique, quam Christus
   in Iordane sacravit,
corruptam naturæ
   nostræ substantiam
in regenerationis lavacro renovasti.

Sit igitur hæc aqua nobis suscepti
   baptismatis memoria,
et cum fratribus nostris,
   qui sunt in Paschate baptizati,
gaudia nos tribuas sociare.
Per Christum Dominum nostrum.
R. Amen.

The Renewal of Baptismal Promises

When the Rite of Baptism (and Confirmation) has been completed or, if this has not taken place, after the blessing of water, all stand, holding lighted candles in their hands, and renew the promise of baptismal faith, unless this has already been done together with those to be baptised.

The Priest addresses the faithful in these or similar words:

Dear brethren (brothers and sisters),
through the Paschal Mystery
we have been buried with Christ
in Baptism,
so that we may walk with him
in newness of life.
And so, now that our Lenten
observance is concluded,
let us renew the promises
of Holy Baptism,
by which we once renounced Satan
and his works
and promised to serve God
in the holy Catholic Church.
And so I ask you:

Priest: Do you renounce Satan?
All: **I do.**

Priest: And all his works?
All: **I do.**

Priest: And all his empty show?
All: **I do.**

Or:

Priest: Do you renounce sin,
so as to live in the freedom
of the children of God?
All: **I do.**

Priest: Do you renounce the lure
of evil,
so that sin may have no mastery
over you?
All: **I do.**

Priest: Do you renounce Satan,
the author and prince of sin?
All: **I do.**

Per paschale mysterium,
fratres carissimi,
in baptismo consepulti sumus
cum Christo,
ut cum eo in novitate
vitæ ambulemus.
Quapropter, quadragesimali
observatione absoluta,
sancti baptismatis
promissiones renovemus,
quibus olim Satanæ et operibus
eius abrenuntiavimus,
et Deo in sancta Ecclesia catholica
servire promisimus.
Quapropter:

Sacerdos: Abrenutiatis Satanæ?
Omnes: **Abrenuntio.**

Sacerdos: Et omnibus operibus eius?
Omnes: **Abrenuntio.**

Sacerdos: Et omnibus pompis eius?
Omnes: **Abrenuntio.**

Vel:

Sacerdos: Abrenuntiatis peccato,
ut in libertate filiorum Dei vivatis?
Omnes: **Abrenuntio.**

Sacerdos: Abrenuntiatis
seductionibus iniquitatis,
ne pecccatum vobis dominetur?
Omnes: **Abrenuntio.**

Sacerdos: Abrenuntiatis Satanæ,
qui est auctor et princeps peccati?
Omnes: **Abrenuntio.**

If the situation warrants, this second formula may be adapted by Conferences of Bishops according to local needs.

Then the Priest continues:

Priest: Do you believe in God, the Father almighty,
Creator of heaven and earth?
All: **I do.**

Priest: Do you believe in Jesus Christ, his only Son, our Lord,
who was born of the Virgin Mary,
suffered death and was buried,
rose again from the dead
and is seated at the right hand of the Father?
All: **I do.**

Priest: Do you believe in the Holy Spirit,
the holy Catholic Church,
the communion of saints,
the forgiveness of sins,
the resurrection of the body,
and life everlasting?
All: **I do.**

And the Priest concludes:

And may almighty God, the Father of our Lord Jesus Christ,
who has given us new birth by water and the Holy Spirit
and bestowed on us forgiveness of our sins,
keep us by his grace,
in Christ Jesus our Lord,
for eternal life.
All: **Amen.**

Sacerdos: Creditis in Deum Patrem omnipotentem,
creatorem cæli et terræ?
Omnes: **Credo.**

Sacerdos: Creditis in Iesum Christum, Filium eius unicum,
Dominum nostrum,
natum ex Maria Virgine,
passum et sepultum,
qui a mortuis resurrexit
et sedet ad dexteram Patris?
Omnes: **Credo.**

Sacerdos: Creditis in Spiritum Sanctum,
sanctam Ecclesiam catholicam,
sanctorum communionem,
remissionem peccatorum,
carnis resurrectionem et
vitam æternam?
Omnes: **Credo.**

Et Deus omnipotens, Pater Domini nostri Iesu Christi,
qui nos regeneravit ex aqua et Spiritu Sancto,
quique nobis dedit remissionem peccatorum,
ipse nos custodiat gratia sua,
in Christo Iesu Domino nostro,
in vitam æternam.
Omnes: **Amen.**

The Priest sprinkles the people with the blessed water, while all sing:

Antiphon

I saw water flowing from the Temple,
from its right-hand side, alleluia;
and all to whom this water came were saved
and shall say: Alleluia, alleluia.

Vidi aquam egredientem de templo,
a latere dextro, alleluia;
et omnes, ad quos pervenit aqua ista, salvi facti sunt
et dicent: Alleluia, alleluia.

Another chant that is baptismal in character may also be sung.

Meanwhile the newly baptised are led to their place among the faithful.

If the blessing of baptismal water has not taken place in the baptistery, the Deacon and the ministers reverently carry the vessel of water to the font.

If the blessing of the font has not occurred, the blessed water is put aside in an appropriate place.

After the sprinkling, the Priest returns to the chair where, omitting the Creed, he directs the Universal Prayer, in which the newly baptised participate for the first time.

FOURTH PART:
The Liturgy of the Eucharist

The Priest goes to the altar and begins the Liturgy of the Eucharist in the usual way.

It is desirable that the bread and wine be brought forward by the newly baptised or, if they are children, by their parents or godparents.

Prayer over the Offerings	Super oblata
Accept, we ask, O Lord, the prayers of your people with the sacrificial offerings, that what has begun in the paschal mysteries may, by the working of your power, bring us to the healing of eternity. Through Christ our Lord.	Suscipe, quæsumus, Domine, preces populi tui cum oblationibus hostiarum, ut, paschalibus initiata mysteriis, ad æternitatis nobis medelam, te operante, proficiant. Per Christum Dominum nostrum.

Preface I of Easter: The Paschal Mystery (. . .on this night above all. . .), pp.52-55.

In the Eucharistic Prayer, a commemoration is made of the baptised and their godparents in accord with the formulas which are found in the Roman Missal and Roman Ritual for each of the Eucharistic Prayers.

Before the **Ecce Agnus Dei** (**Behold the Lamb of God**), the Priest may briefly address the newly baptised about receiving their first Communion and about the excellence of this great mystery, which is the climax of Initiation and the centre of the whole of Christian life.

It is desirable that the newly baptised receive Holy Communion under both kinds, together with their godfathers, godmothers, and Catholic parents and spouses, as well as their lay catechists. It is even appropriate that, with the consent of the Diocesan Bishop, where the occasion suggests this, all the faithful be admitted to Holy Communion under both kinds.

Communion Antiphon 1 Co 5:7-8	Ant. ad communionem
Christ our Passover has been sacrificed; therefore let us keep the feast with the unleavened bread of purity and truth, alleluia.	Pascha nostrum immolatus est Christus; itaque epulemur in azymis sinceritatis et veritatis, alleluia.

Psalm 117 may appropriately be sung.

Prayer after Communion

Pour out on us, O Lord,
   the Spirit of your love,
and in your kindness make those
   you have nourished
by this paschal Sacrament
one in mind and heart.
Through Christ our Lord.

Post communionem

Spiritum nobis, Domine,
   tuæ caritatis infunde,
ut, quos sacramentis
   paschalibus satiasti,
tua facias pietate concordes.
Per Christum Dominum nostrum.

Solemn Blessing

May almighty God bless you
through today's Easter Solemnity
and, in his compassion,
defend you from every assault of sin.
R. Amen.

And may he, who restores you
   to eternal life
in the Resurrection
   of his Only Begotten,
endow you with the prize
   of immortality.
R. Amen.

Now that the days of the Lord's
   Passion have drawn to a close,
may you who celebrate
   the gladness of the Paschal Feast
come with Christ's help,
   and exulting in spirit,
to those feasts that are celebrated
   in eternal joy.
R. Amen.

And may the blessing
   of almighty God,
the Father, and the Son,
   ✠ and the Holy Spirit,
come down on you and remain
   with you for ever.
R. Amen.

Benedictio sollemnis

Benedicat vos omnipotens Deus,
hodierna interveniente
   sollemnitate paschali,
et ab omni miseratus defendat
   incursione peccati.
R. Amen.

Et qui ad æternam vitam
in Unigeniti sui resurrectione
   vos reparat,
vos præmiis
   immortalitatis adimpleat.
R. Amen.

Et qui, expletis passionis
   dominicæ diebus,
paschalis festi gaudia celebratis,
ad ea festa, quæ lætitiis
   peraguntur æternis,
ipso opitulante, exsultantibus
animis veniatis.
R. Amen.

Et benedictio Dei omnipotentis,
Patris, et Filii, ✠ et Spiritus Sancti,
descendat super vos
   et maneat semper.
R. Amen.

The final blessing formula from the Rite of Baptism of Adults or of Children may also be used, according to circumstances.

To dismiss the people the Deacon or, if there is no Deacon, the Priest himself sings or says:

Go forth, the Mass is ended, alleluia, alleluia.	Ite, missa est, alleluia, alleluia.
Or:	Vel:
Go in peace, alleluia, alleluia.	Ite in pace, alleluia, alleluia
All reply:	Omnes respondent:
Thanks be to God, alleluia, alleluia.	Deo gratias, alleluia, alleluia.

This practice is observed throughout the Octave of Easter.
The paschal candle is lit in all the more solemn liturgical celebrations of this period.

9 April

At the Mass during the Day

Today, throughout the world, the Church's proclamation resounds: "Jesus, who was crucified, has risen as he said. Alleluia!" The crucified Jesus, none other, has risen from the dead. God the Father raised Jesus, his Son, because he fully accomplished his saving will. Jesus took upon himself our weakness, our infirmities, even our death. He endured our sufferings and bore the weight of our sins. Because of this, God the Father exalted him and now Jesus Christ lives forever; he is the Lord. The witnesses report an important detail: the risen Jesus bears the marks of the wounds in his hands, feet and side. These wounds are the everlasting seal of his love for us. All those who experience a painful trial in body or spirit can find refuge in these wounds and, through them, receive the grace of the hope that does not disappoint.

(Pope Francis)

Entrance Antiphon Cf. Ps 138:18,5-6	Ant. ad introitum
I HAVE risen, and I am with you still, alleluia.	RESURREXI, et adhuc tecum sum, alleluia:
You have laid your hand upon me, alleluia.	posuisti super me manum tuam, alleluia:
Too wonderful for me, this knowledge, alleluia, alleluia.	mirabilis facta est scientia tua, alleluia, alleluia.

Or: Lk 24:34; Cf. Rv 1:6	Vel:
The Lord is truly risen, alleluia.	Surrexit Dominus vere, alleluia.
To him be glory and power	Ipsi gloria et imperium
for all the ages of eternity, alleluia, alleluia.	per universa æternitatis sæcula, alleluia, alleluia.

The Gloria in excelsis (Glory to God in the highest) is said.

Collect	Collecta
O God, who on this day, through your Only Begotten Son, have conquered death and unlocked for us the path to eternity, grant, we pray, that we who keep the solemnity of the Lord's Resurrection may, through the renewal brought by your Spirit, rise up in the light of life. Through our Lord Jesus Christ, your Son, who lives and reigns with you in the unity of the Holy Spirit, God, for ever and ever.	Deus, qui hodierna die, per Unigenitum tuum, æternitatis nobis aditum, devicta morte, reserasti, da nobis, quæsumus, ut, qui resurrectionis dominicæ sollemnia colimus, per innovationem tui Spiritus in lumine vitæ resurgamus. Per Dominum nostrum Iesum Christum Filium tuum, qui tecum vivit et regnat in unitate Spiritus Sancti, Deus, per omnia sæcula sæculorum.

FIRST READING

A reading from the Acts of the Apostles   10:34,37-43

We have eaten and drunk with him after his resurrection.

Peter addressed Cornelius and his household: 'You must have heard about the recent happenings in Judaea; about Jesus of Nazareth and how he began in Galilee, after John had been preaching baptism. God had anointed him with the Holy Spirit and with power, and because God was with him, Jesus went about doing good and curing all who had fallen into the power of the devil. Now I, and those with me, can witness to everything he did throughout the countryside of Judaea and in Jerusalem itself: and also to the fact that they killed him by hanging him on a tree, yet three days afterwards God raised him to life and allowed him to be seen, not by the whole people but only by certain witnesses God had chosen beforehand. Now we are those witnesses – we have eaten and drunk with him after his resurrection from the dead – and he has ordered us to proclaim this to his people and to tell them that God has appointed him to judge everyone, alive or dead. It is to him that all the prophets bear this witness: that all who believe in Jesus will have their sins forgiven through his name.'

The word of the Lord.

Responsorial Psalm   Ps 117:1-2,16-17,22-23. R. v. 24

R. **This day was made by the Lord;**
   we rejoice and are glad.
   Or: **Alleluia, alleluia, alleluia!**

Give thanks to the Lord for he is good,
for his love has no end.
Let the sons of Israel say:
'His love has no end.' R.

The Lord's right hand has triumphed;
his right hand raised me up.
I shall not die, I shall live
and recount his deeds. R.

The stone which the builders rejected
has become the corner stone.
This is the work of the Lord,
a marvel in our eyes. R.

SECOND READING

A reading from the letter of St Paul to the Colossians   3:1-4
You must look for the things that are in heaven, where Christ is.

Since you have been brought back to true life with Christ, you must look for the things that are in heaven, where Christ is, sitting at God's right hand. Let your thoughts be on heavenly things, not on the things that are on the earth, because you have died, and now the life you have is hidden with Christ in God. But when Christ is revealed – and he is your life – you too will be revealed in all your glory with him.

The word of the Lord.

ALTERNATIVE SECOND READING

A reading from the first letter of St Paul to the Corinthians   5:6-8
Get rid of the old yeast, and make yourselves into a completely new batch of bread.

You must know how even a small amount of yeast is enough to leaven all the dough, so get rid of all the old yeast, and make yourselves into a completely new batch of bread, unleavened as you are meant to be. Christ, our Passover, has been sacrificed; let us celebrate the feast, by getting rid of all the old yeast of evil and wickedness, having only the unleavened bread of sincerity and truth.

The word of the Lord.

The sequence is said or sung on this day. On the weekdays of the Octave of Easter, its use is optional.

SEQUENCE

Christians, to the Paschal Victim
    offer sacrifice and praise.
The sheep are ransomed
    by the Lamb;
and Christ, the undefiled,
hath sinners to his Father reconciled.

Death with life contended:
    combat strangely ended!
Life's own Champion, slain,
    yet lives to reign.

Tell us, Mary:
    say what thou didst see
    upon the way.

The tomb the Living did enclose;
I saw Christ's glory as he rose!

The angels there attesting;
shroud with grave-clothes resting.
Christ, my hope, has risen:
he goes before you into Galilee.

That Christ is truly risen
    from the dead we know.
Victorious king, thy mercy show!

Victimæ paschali laudes
    immolent Christiani.
Agnus redemit oves:
    Christus innocens Patri
    reconciliavit peccatores.

Mors et vita duello
    conflixere mirando:
    dux vitæ mortuus regnat vivus.

Dic nobis, Maria,
    quid vidisti in via?

Sepulcrum Christi viventis,
    gloriam vidi resurgentis.

Angelicos testes,
    sudarium et vestes.
Surrexit Christus spes mea:
    præcedet vos in Galilæam.

Scimus Christum surrexisse
    a mortuis vere:
tu nobis, victor Rex, miserere.

Gospel Acclamation   1 Co 5:7-8

R. **Alleluia, alleluia!**
Christ, our passover, has been sacrificed;
let us celebrate the feast then, in the Lord.
R. **Alleluia!**

GOSPEL

A reading from the holy Gospel according to John   20:1-9
He must rise from the dead.

It was very early on the first day of the week and still dark, when Mary of Magdala came to the tomb. She saw that the stone had been moved away from the tomb and came running to Simon Peter and the other disciple, the one Jesus loved. 'They have taken the Lord out of the tomb' she said 'and we don't know where they have put him.'

So Peter set out with the other disciple to go to the tomb. They ran together, but the other disciple, running faster than Peter, reached the tomb first; he bent down and saw the linen cloths lying on the ground, but did not go in. Simon Peter who was following now came up, went right into the tomb, saw the linen cloths on the ground, and also the cloth that had been over his head; this was not with the linen cloths but rolled up in a place by itself. Then the other disciple who had reached the tomb first also went in; he saw and he believed. Till this moment they had failed to understand the teaching of scripture, that he must rise from the dead.

The Gospel of the Lord.

The Creed is said. However, in Easter Sunday Masses which are celebrated with a congregation, the rite of the renewal of baptismal promises may take place after the homily, according to the text used at the Easter Vigil (pp.418-421). In that case the Creed is omitted.

Prayer over the Offerings

Exultant with paschal gladness,
O Lord,
we offer the sacrifice
by which your Church
is wondrously reborn and nourished.
Through Christ our Lord.

Super oblata

Sacrificia, Domine,
paschalibus gaudiis
exsultantes offerimus,
quibus Ecclesia tua
mirabiliter renascitur et nutritur.
Per Christum Dominum nostrum.

Preface I of Easter, The Paschal Mystery, pp.52-55.

When the Roman Canon is used, the proper forms of the **Communicantes** (**In communion with those**) and **Hanc igitur** (**Therefore, Lord, we pray**) are said.

Communion Antiphon 1 Co 5:7-8

Christ our Passover has been
sacrificed, alleluia;
therefore let us keep the feast
with the unleavened bread
of purity and truth, alleluia, alleluia.

Ant. ad communionem

Pascha nostrum immolatus
est Christus, alleluia;
itaque epulemur
in azymis sinceritatis
et veritatis, alleluia, alleluia.

Prayer after Communion

Look upon your Church, O God,
with unfailing love and favour,
so that, renewed by the paschal
mysteries,
she may come to the glory
of the resurrection.
Through Christ our Lord.

Post communionem

Perpetuo, Deus, Ecclesiam tuam
pio favore tuere,
ut, paschalibus renovata mysteriis,
ad resurrectionis perveniat claritatem.
Per Christum Dominum nostrum.

To impart the blessing at the end of Mass, the Priest may appropriately use the formula of Solemn Blessing for the Mass of the Easter Vigil, p.422.

For the dismissal of the people, the following is sung or said:

Go forth, the Mass is ended, alleluia, alleluia.	Ite, missa est, alleluia, alleluia.
Or:	Vel:
Go in peace, alleluia, alleluia.	Ite in pace, alleluia, alleluia
R. Thanks be to God, alleluia, alleluia.	R. Deo gratias, alleluia, alleluia.

16 April

SECOND SUNDAY OF EASTER

(or of Divine Mercy)

Do you want proof that God has touched your life? See if you can stoop to bind the wounds of others. Today is the day to ask, "Am I, who so often have received God's peace, his mercy, merciful to others? Do I, who have so often been fed by the Body of Jesus, make any effort to relieve the hunger of the poor?" Let us not remain indifferent. Let us not live a one-way faith, a faith that receives but does not give, a faith that accepts the gift but does not give it in return. Having received mercy, let us now become merciful. For if love is only about us, faith becomes arid, barren and sentimental. Without others, faith becomes disembodied. Without works of mercy, it dies. Dear brothers and sisters, let us be renewed by the peace, forgiveness and wounds of the merciful Jesus.

(Pope Francis)

Entrance Antiphon 1 P 2:2	Ant. ad introitum
LIKE newborn infants, you must long for the pure, spiritual milk, that in him you may grow to salvation, alleluia.	QUASI modo geniti infantes, rationabile, sine dolo lac concupiscite, ut in eo crescatis in salutem, alleluia.
Or: 4 Esdr 2:36-37	Vel:
Receive the joy of your glory, giving thanks to God, who has called you into the heavenly kingdom, alleluia.	Accipite iucunditatem gloriæ vestræ, gratias agentes Deo, qui vos ad cælestia regna vocavit, alleluia.

The Gloria in excelsis (Glory to God in the highest) is said.

Collect	Collecta
God of everlasting mercy,	Deus misericordiæ sempiternæ,
who, in the very recurrence	qui in ipso paschalis festi recursu
of the paschal feast	fidem sacratæ tibi plebis accendis,
kindle the faith of the people you	auge gratiam quam dedisti,
have made your own,	ut digna omnes
increase, we pray, the grace you	intellegentia comprehendant,
have bestowed,	quo lavacro abluti,
that all may grasp	quo Spiritu regenerati,
and rightly understand	quo sanguine sunt redempti.
in what font they have been washed,	Per Dominum nostrum Iesum
by whose Spirit they have	Christum Filium tuum,
been reborn,	qui tecum vivit et regnat
by whose Blood they have	in unitate Spiritus Sancti,
been redeemed.	Deus, per omnia sæcula sæculorum.
Through our Lord Jesus Christ,	
your Son,	
who lives and reigns with you	
in the unity of the Holy Spirit,	
God, for ever and ever.	

FIRST READING

A reading from the Acts of the Apostles   2:42-47

The faithful all lived together and owned everything in common.

The whole community remained faithful to the teaching of the apostles, to the brotherhood, to the breaking of bread and to the prayers.

The many miracles and signs worked through the apostles made a deep impression on everyone.

The faithful all lived together and owned everything in common; they sold their goods and possessions and shared out the proceeds among themselves according to what each one needed.

They went as a body to the Temple every day but met in their houses for the breaking of bread; they shared their food gladly and generously; they praised God and were looked up to by everyone. Day by day the Lord added to their community those destined to be saved.

The word of the Lord.

Responsorial Psalm   Ps 117:2-4,13-15,22-24. R. v.1

R. **Give thanks to the Lord for he is good,**
   for his love has no end.
   Or: **Alleluia, alleluia, alleluia!**

Let the sons of Israel say:
'His love has no end.'
Let the sons of Aaron say:
'His love has no end.'
Let those who fear the Lord say:
'His love has no end.' R.

I was thrust, thrust down and falling
but the Lord was my helper.
The Lord is my strength and my song;
he was my saviour.
There are shouts of joy and victory
in the tents of the just. R.

The stone which the builders rejected
has become the corner stone.
This is the work of the Lord
a marvel in our eyes.
This day was made by the Lord;
we rejoice and are glad. R.

SECOND READING

A reading from the first letter of St Peter   1:3-9

In his great mercy he has given us a new birth as his sons by raising Jesus from the dead.

Blessed be God the Father of our Lord Jesus Christ, who in his great mercy
has given us a new birth as his sons, by raising Jesus Christ from the dead,
so that we have a sure hope and the promise of an inheritance that can
never be spoilt or soiled and never fade away, because it is being kept for
you in the heavens. Through your faith, God's power will guard you until
the salvation which had been prepared is revealed at the end of time. This
is a cause of great joy for you, even though you may for a short time have
to bear being plagued by all sorts of trials; so that, when Jesus Christ is
revealed, your faith will have been tested and proved like gold – only it
is more precious than gold, which is corruptible even though it bears
testing by fire – and then you will have praise and glory and honour. You
did not see him, yet you love him; and still without seeing him, you are

already filled with a joy so glorious that it cannot be described, because you believe; and you are sure of the end to which your faith looks forward, that is, the salvation of your souls.

The word of the Lord.

Easter Sequence can be sung here, see p.426.

Gospel Acclamation   Jn 20:29
R. **Alleluia, alleluia!**
Jesus said: 'You believe because you can see me.
Happy are those who have not seen and yet believe.'
R. **Alleluia!**

GOSPEL

A reading from the holy Gospel according to John   20:19-31
Eight days later, Jesus came.

In the evening of that same day, the first day of the week, the doors were closed in the room where the disciples were, for fear of the Jews. Jesus came and stood among them. He said to them, 'Peace be with you,' and showed them his hands and his side. The disciples were filled with joy when they saw the Lord, and he said to them again,

'Peace be with you.
As the Father sent me,
so am I sending you.'

After saying this he breathed on them and said:

'Receive the Holy Spirit.
For those whose sins you forgive,
they are forgiven;
for those whose sins you retain,
they are retained.'

Thomas, called the Twin, who was one of the Twelve, was not with them when Jesus came. When the disciples said, 'We have seen the Lord,' he answered, 'Unless I see the holes that the nails made in his hands and can put my finger into the holes they made, and unless I can put my hand into his side, I refuse to believe.' Eight days later the disciples were in the house again and Thomas was with them. The doors were closed, but Jesus came in and stood among them. 'Peace be with you,' he said. Then he spoke to Thomas, 'Put your finger here; look, here are my hands. Give me your hand; put it into my side. Doubt no longer but believe.' Thomas replied, 'My Lord and my God!'

Jesus said to him:

'You believe because you can see me.
Happy are those who have not seen and yet believe.'

There were many other signs that Jesus worked and the disciples saw, but they are not recorded in this book. These are recorded so that you may believe that Jesus is the Christ, the Son of God, and that believing this you may have life through his name.

The Gospel of the Lord.

The Creed is said.

Prayer over the Offerings

Accept, O Lord, we pray,
the oblations of your people
(and of those you have brought
   to new birth),
that, renewed by confession of your
   name and by Baptism,
they may attain unending happiness.
Through Christ our Lord.

Super oblata

Suscipe, quæsumus, Domine,
   plebis tuæ
(et tuorum renatorum) oblationes,
ut, confessione tui nominis
   et baptismate renovati,
sempiternam beatitudinem
   consequantur.
Per Christum Dominum nostrum.

Preface I of Easter: The Paschal Mystery (. . .on this day above all. . .), pp.52-55.
When the Roman Canon is used, the proper forms of the **Communicantes** (In communion with those) and **Hanc igitur** (Therefore, Lord, we pray) are said.

Communion Antiphon Cf. Jn 20:27

Bring your hand and feel the place
   of the nails,
and do not be unbelieving
   but believing, alleluia.

Ant. ad communionem

Mitte manum tuam, et cognosce
   loca clavorum,
et noli esse incredulus, sed fidelis,
   alleluia.

Prayer after Communion

Grant, we pray, almighty God,
that our reception of this paschal
   Sacrament
may have a continuing effect
in our minds and hearts.
Through Christ our Lord.

Post communionem

Concede, quæsumus,
   omnipotens Deus,
ut paschalis perceptio sacramenti
continua in nostris
   mentibus perseveret.
Per Christum Dominum nostrum.

A formula of Solemn Blessing, pp.136-139, may be used.
For the dismissal of the people, the following is sung or said: **Go forth, the Mass is ended, alleluia, alleluia**. Or: **Go in peace, alleluia, alleluia**. The people respond: **Thanks be to God, alleluia, alleluia**.

23 April

THIRD SUNDAY OF EASTER

In the first journey, there is the Lord walking beside them, but they do not recognise him; in the second one they do not see him anymore, but they feel him near them. The two different paths of those first disciples tell us, Jesus's disciples today, that in life we have two opposite directions before us: there is the path of those who, like those two on the outbound journey, allow themselves to be paralysed by life's disappointments and proceed sadly; and there is the path of those who do not put themselves and their problems first, but rather Jesus who visits us, and the brothers who await his visit, that is, our brothers who are waiting for us to take care of them. Here is the turning point: to stop orbiting around one's self; the disappointments of the past, the unrealised ideals, the many bad things that have happened in our life. Very often we tend to keep going around and around.... To leave that behind and to go forward looking at the greatest and truest reality of life: Jesus lives, Jesus loves me.

(Pope Francis)

Entrance Antiphon Cf. Ps 65:1-2

CRY out with joy to God,
   all the earth;
O sing to the glory of his name.
O render him glorious praise,
   alleluia.

Ant. ad introitum

IUBILATE Deo, omnis terra,
   psalmum dicite nomini eius,
date gloriam laudi eius, alleluia.

The Gloria in excelsis (Glory to God in the highest) is said.

Collect

May your people exult for ever,
   O God,
in renewed youthfulness of spirit,
so that, rejoicing now in the restored
   glory of our adoption,
we may look forward
   in confident hope
to the rejoicing of the day
   of resurrection.
Through our Lord Jesus Christ,
   your Son,
who lives and reigns with you
   in the unity of the Holy Spirit,
God, for ever and ever.

Collecta

Semper exsultet populus tuus, Deus,
   renovata animæ iuventute,
ut, qui nunc lætatur in adoptionis
   se gloriam restitutum,
resurrectionis diem spe certæ
   gratulationis exspectet.
Per Dominum nostrum Iesum
   Christum Filium tuum,
qui tecum vivit et regnat
   in unitate Spiritus Sancti,
Deus, per omnia sæcula sæculorum.

FIRST READING

A reading from the Acts of the Apostles   2:14,22-33

It was impossible for him to be held in the power of Hades.

On the day of Pentecost Peter stood up with the Eleven and addressed the crowd in a loud voice: 'Men of Israel, listen to what I am going to say: Jesus the Nazarene was a man commended to you by God by the miracles and portents and signs that God worked through him when he was among you, as you all know. This man, who was put into your power by the deliberate intention and foreknowledge of God, you took and had crucified by men outside the Law. You killed him, but God raised him to life, freeing him from the pangs of Hades; for it was impossible for him to be held in its power since, as David says of him:

> I saw the Lord before me always,
> for with him at my right hand nothing can shake me.
> So my heart was glad
> and my tongue cried out with joy;
> my body, too, will rest in the hope
> that you will not abandon my soul to Hades
> nor allow your holy one to experience corruption.
> You have made known the way of life to me,
> you will fill me with gladness through your presence.

'Brothers, no one can deny that the patriarch David himself is dead and buried: his tomb is still with us. But since he was a prophet, and knew that God had sworn him an oath to make one of his descendants succeed him on the throne, what he foresaw and spoke about was the resurrection of the Christ: he is the one who was not abandoned to Hades, and whose body did not experience corruption. God raised this man Jesus to life, and all of us are witnesses to that. Now raised to the heights by God's right hand, he has received from the Father the Holy Spirit, who was promised, and what you see and hear is the outpouring of that Spirit.'

The word of the Lord.

Responsorial Psalm   Ps 15:1-2,5,7-11. R. v.11

R. **Show us, Lord, the path of life.**
   Or: **Alleluia!**

> Preserve me, God, I take refuge in you.
> I say to the Lord: 'You are my God.

O Lord, it is you who are my portion and cup;
it is you yourself who are my prize.' R.

I will bless the Lord who gives me counsel,
who even at night directs my heart.
I keep the Lord ever in my sight:
since he is at my right hand, I shall stand firm. R.

And so my heart rejoices, my soul is glad;
even my body shall rest in safety.
For you will not leave my soul among the dead,
nor let your beloved know decay. R.

You will show me the path of life,
the fullness of joy in your presence,
at your right hand happiness for ever. R.

SECOND READING

A reading from the first letter of St Peter   1:17-21

Your ransom was paid in the precious blood of a lamb without spot or stain,
namely, Christ.

If you are acknowledging as your Father one who has no favourites and
judges everyone according to what he has done, you must be scrupulously
careful as long as you are living away from your home. Remember, the
ransom that was paid to free you from the useless way of life your ancestors
handed down was not paid in anything corruptible, neither in silver nor
gold, but in the precious blood of a lamb without spot or stain, namely
Christ; who though known since before the world was made, has been
revealed only in our time, the end of the ages, for your sake. Through him
you now have faith in God, who raised him from the dead and gave him
glory for that very reason – so that you would have faith and hope in God.

The word of the Lord.

Gospel Acclamation   Cf. Lk 24:32

R. **Alleluia, alleluia!**
Lord Jesus, explain the scriptures to us.
Make our hearts burn within us as you talk to us.
R. **Alleluia!**

GOSPEL

A reading from the holy Gospel according to Luke   24:13-35

They recognised him at the breaking of bread.

Two of the disciples of Jesus were on their way to a village called Emmaus, seven miles from Jerusalem, and they were talking together about all that had happened. Now as they talked this over, Jesus himself came up and walked by their side; but something prevented them from recognising him. He said to them, 'What matters are you discussing as you walk along?' They stopped short, their faces downcast.

Then one of them, called Cleopas, answered him, 'You must be the only person staying in Jerusalem who does not know the things that have been happening there these last few days.' 'What things?' he asked. 'All about Jesus of Nazareth' they answered 'who proved he was a great prophet by the things he said and did in the sight of God and of the whole people; and how our chief priests and our leaders handed him over to be sentenced to death, and had him crucified. Our own hope had been that he would be the one to set Israel free. And this is not all: two whole days have gone by since it all happened; and some women from our group have astounded us: they went to the tomb in the early morning, and when they did not find the body, they came back to tell us they had seen a vision of angels who declared he was alive. Some of our friends went to the tomb and found everything exactly as the women had reported, but of him they saw nothing.'

Then he said to them, 'You foolish men! So slow to believe the full message of the prophets! Was it not ordained that the Christ should suffer and so enter into his glory?' Then, starting with Moses and going through all the prophets, he explained to them the passages throughout the scriptures that were about himself.

When they drew near to the village to which they were going, he made as if to go on; but they pressed him to stay with them. 'It is nearly evening' they said 'and the day is almost over.' So he went in to stay with them. Now while he was with them at table, he took the bread and said the blessing; then he broke it and handed it to them. And their eyes were opened and they recognised him; but he had vanished from their sight. Then they said to each other, 'Did not our hearts burn within us as he talked to us on the road and explained the scriptures to us?'

They set out that instant and returned to Jerusalem. There they found the Eleven assembled together with their companions, who said to them, 'Yes, it is true. The Lord has risen and has appeared to Simon.' Then they told their story of what had happened on the road and how they had recognised him at the breaking of bread.

The Gospel of the Lord.

The Creed is said.

Prayer over the Offerings	Super oblata

Receive, O Lord, we pray,
   these offerings of your
      exultant Church,
and, as you have given her cause
   for such great gladness,
grant also that the gifts we bring
may bear fruit in perpetual happiness.
Through Christ our Lord.
	Suscipe munera, Domine,
	   quæsumus, exsultantis Ecclesiæ,
	et cui causam tanti gaudii præstitisti,
	perpetuæ fructum concede lætitiæ.
	Per Christum Dominum nostrum.

Preface of Easter, pp.52-57.

Communion Antiphon Lk 24:35	Ant. ad communionem

The disciples recognised
   the Lord Jesus
in the breaking of the bread, alleluia.
	Cognoverunt discipuli
	   Dominum Iesum
	in fractione panis, alleluia.

Prayer after Communion	Post communionem

Look with kindness upon
   your people, O Lord,
and grant, we pray,
that those you were pleased
   to renew by eternal mysteries
may attain in their flesh
the incorruptible glory
   of the resurrection.
Through Christ our Lord.
	Populum tuum, quæsumus,
	   Domine, intuere benignus,
	et, quem æternis dignatus
	   es renovare mysteriis,
	ad incorruptibilem glorificandæ
	   carnis resurrectionem
	pervenire concede.
	Per Christum Dominum nostrum.

A formula of Solemn Blessing, pp.136-139, may be used.

In England

24 April

SAINT GEORGE, MARTYR, PATRON OF ENGLAND

The Church's action is credible and effective only to the extent to which those who belong to her are prepared to pay in person for their fidelity to Christ in every circumstance. When this readiness is lacking, the crucial argument of truth on which the Church herself depends is also absent. Dear brothers and sisters, as in early times, today too Christ needs apostles ready to sacrifice themselves. He needs witnesses and martyrs.

(Pope Benedict XVI)

Solemnity

Entrance Antiphon   Cf. Mt 25:34

REJOICE, you Saints, in the presence of the Lamb;
a kingdom has been prepared for you
from the foundation of the world, alleluia.

Or: Ps 90:13

On the asp and the viper you will tread,
and trample the young lion and the dragon, alleluia.

The Gloria in excelsis (Glory to God in the highest) is said.

Collect

God of hosts,
who so kindled the fire of charity
in the heart of Saint George your martyr
that he bore witness to the risen Lord
both by his life and by his death,
grant us through his intercession, we pray,
the same faith and power of love,
that we who rejoice in his triumph

may be led to share with him
in the fullness of the resurrection.
Through our Lord Jesus Christ, your Son,
who lives and reigns with you in the unity of the Holy Spirit,
God, for ever and ever.

FIRST READING

A reading from the book of the Apocalypse 12:10-12

In the face of death they would not cling to life.

I, John, heard a voice shout from heaven, 'Victory and power and empire for ever have been won by our God, and all authority for his Christ, now that the persecutor, who accused our brothers day and night before our God, has been brought down. They have triumphed over him by the blood of the Lamb and by the witness of their martyrdom, because even in the face of death they would not cling to life. Let the heavens rejoice and all who live there.'

The word of the Lord.

Responsial Psalm Ps 125. R. v. 5

R. **Those who are sowing in tears
will sing when they reap.**

When the Lord delivered Sion from bondage,
it seemed like a dream.
Then was our mouth filled with laughter,
on our lips there were songs. R.

The heathens themselves said: 'What marvels
the Lord worked for them!'
What marvels the Lord worked for us!
Indeed we were glad. R.

Deliver us, O Lord, from our bondage
as streams in dry land.
Those who are sowing in tears
will sing when they reap. R.

They go out, they go out, full of tears,
carrying seed for the sowing;
they come back, they come back, full of song,
carrying their sheaves. R.

A second reading is chosen from the Common of Martyrs.

Gospel Acclamation   Mt 23:9-10

R. **Alleluia, alleluia!**
Happy the man who stands firm,
for he has proved himself,
and will win the crown of life.
R. **Alleluia!**

GOSPEL

A reading from the holy Gospel according to John   15:18-21
If they persecuted me, they will persecute you.

Jesus said to his disciples:
'If the world hates you,
  remember that it hated me before you.
If you belonged to the world,
  the world would love you as its own;
but because you do not belong to the world,
because my choice withdrew you from the world,
  therefore the world hates you.
Remember the words I said to you:
A servant is not greater than his master.
If they persecuted me,
  they will persecute you too;
if they kept my word,
  they will keep yours as well.
But it will be on my account that they will do all this,
  because they do not know the one who sent me.'

The Gospel of the Lord.

ALTERNATIVE GOSPEL

A reading from the holy Gospel according to John   15:1-8

Whoever remains in me, with me in him, bears fruit in plenty.

Jesus said to his disciples:
  'I am the true vine,
  and my Father is the vinedresser.
  Every branch in me that bears no fruit
  he cuts away,
  and every branch that does bear fruit he prunes
  to make it bear even more.
  You are pruned already,
  by means of the word that I have spoken to you.
  Make your home in me, as I make mine in you.
  As a branch cannot bear fruit all by itself,
  but must remain part of the vine,
  neither can you unless you remain in me.
  I am the vine,
  you are the branches.
  Whoever remains in me, with me in him,
  bears fruit in plenty;
  for cut off from me you can do nothing.
  Anyone who does not remain in me
  is like a branch that has been thrown away
  – he withers;
  these branches are collected and thrown on the fire,
  and they are burnt.
  If you remain in me
  and my words remain in you,
  you may ask what you will
  and you shall get it.
  It is to the glory of my Father that you should bear much fruit,
  and then you will be my disciples.'

  The Gospel of the Lord.

The Creed is said.

Prayer over the Offerings

Receive, we pray, O Lord,
the sacrifice of conciliation and praise,
which we offer to your majesty
in commemoration of the blessed Martyr Saint George,
that it may lead us to forgiveness
and confirm us in constant thanksgiving.
Through Christ our Lord.

Preface I or II of Holy Martyrs, pp.72-73.

Communion Antiphon   Cf. 2 Tm 2:11-12

If we have died with Christ, we shall also live with him;
if we persevere, we shall also reign with him, alleluia.

Prayer after Communion

Rejoicing on this festival day, O Lord,
we have received your heavenly gifts;
grant, we pray,
that we who in this divine banquet
proclaim the death of your Son
may merit with Saint George to be partakers
in his resurrection and glory.
Through Christ our Lord.

30 April

FOURTH SUNDAY OF EASTER

Different voices resonate within us. There is the voice of God, who speaks kindly to the conscience, and there is the tempting voice that leads to evil. How can we recognise the voice of the Good Shepherd from that of the thief, how can we distinguish the inspiration of God from the suggestion of the evil one? The voice of God never forces us: God proposes himself, he does not impose himself. Instead, the evil voice seduces, assails, forces: it arouses dazzling illusions, emotions that are tempting but transient. At first it flatters, it makes us believe that we are all-powerful, but then it leaves us empty inside and accuses us: "You are worth nothing". The voice of God, instead, corrects us, with great patience, but always encourages us, consoles us: it always nourishes hope. Another difference: the voice of the enemy distracts us from the present and wants us to focus on fears of the future or sadness about the past — the enemy does not want the present — it brings to surface the bitterness, the memories of the wrongs suffered, of those who have hurt us...many bad memories. On the other hand, the voice of God speaks in the present: "Now you can do good, now you can exercise the creativity of love, now you can forego the regrets and remorse that hold your heart captive". It inspires us, it leads us ahead, but it speaks in the present: now.

(Pope Francis)

Entrance Antiphon   Cf. Ps 32:5-6

THE merciful love of the Lord
fills the earth;
by the word of the Lord
   the heavens were made, alleluia.

The Gloria in excelsis (Glory to God in the highest) is said.

Collect

Almighty ever-living God,
lead us to a share in the joys
   of heaven,
so that the humble flock may reach
where the brave Shepherd
   has gone before.
Who lives and reigns with you
   in the unity of the Holy Spirit,
God, for ever and ever.

Ant. ad introitum

MISERICORDIA Domini plena
  est terra;
verbo Domini cæli firmati sunt,
  alleluia.

Collecta

Omnipotens sempiterne Deus,
deduc nos ad societatem
   cælestium gaudiorum,
ut eo perveniat humilitas gregis,
quo processit fortitudo pastoris.
Per Dominum nostrum Iesum
   Christum Filium tuum,
qui tecum vivit et regnat
   in unitate Spiritus Sancti,
Deus, per omnia sæcula sæculorum.

FIRST READING

A reading from the Acts of the Apostles   2:14,36-41
God has made him both Lord and Christ.

On the day of Pentecost Peter stood up with the Eleven and addressed the crowd with a loud voice: 'The whole House of Israel can be certain that God has made this Jesus whom you crucified both Lord and Christ.'

Hearing this, they were cut to the heart and said to Peter and the apostles, 'What must we do, brothers?' 'You must repent,' Peter answered 'and every one of you must be baptised in the name of Jesus Christ for the forgiveness of your sins, and you will receive the gift of the Holy Spirit. The promise that was made is for you and your children, and for all those who are far away, for all those whom the Lord our God will call to himself.' He spoke to them for a long time using many arguments, and he urged them, 'Save yourselves from this perverse generation.' They were convinced by his arguments, and they accepted what he said and were baptised. That very day about three thousand were added to their number.

The word of the Lord.

Responsorial Psalm   Ps 22:1-6. R. v.1

R. **The Lord is my shepherd;**
   there is nothing I shall want.
   Or: **Alleluia!**

   The Lord is my shepherd;
   there is nothing I shall want.
   Fresh and green are the pastures
   where he gives me repose.
   Near restful waters he leads me,
   to revive my drooping spirit. R.

   He guides me along the right path;
   he is true to his name.
   If I should walk in the valley of darkness
   no evil would I fear.
   You are there with your crook and your staff;
   with these you give me comfort. R.

   You have prepared a banquet for me
   in the sight of my foes.
   My head you have anointed with oil;
   my cup is overflowing. R.

   Surely goodness and kindness shall follow me
   all the days of my life.

In the Lord's own house shall I dwell
for ever and ever. R.

SECOND READING

A reading from the first letter of St Peter   2:20-25

You have come back to the shepherd of your souls.

The merit, in the sight of God, is in bearing punishment patiently when
you are punished after doing your duty.

This, in fact, is what you were called to do, because Christ suffered for
you and left an example for you to follow the way he took. He had not
done anything wrong, and there had been no perjury in his mouth. He
was insulted and did not retaliate with insults; when he was tortured he
made no threats but he put his trust in the righteous judge. He was bearing
our faults in his own body on the cross, so that we might die to our faults
and live for holiness; through his wounds you have been healed. You had
gone astray like sheep but now you have come back to the shepherd and
guardian of your souls.

The word of the Lord.

Gospel Acclamation   Jn 10:14

R. **Alleluia, alleluia!**
I am the good shepherd, says the Lord;
I know my own sheep and my own know me.
R. **Alleluia!**

GOSPEL

A reading from the holy Gospel according to John   10:1-10

I am the gate of the sheepfold.

Jesus said: 'I tell you most solemnly, anyone who does not enter the
sheepfold through the gate, but gets in some other way is a thief and a
brigand. The one who enters through the gate is the shepherd of the flock;
the gatekeeper lets him in, the sheep hear his voice, one by one he calls
his own sheep and leads them out. When he has brought out his flock, he
goes ahead of them, and the sheep follow because they know his voice.
They never follow a stranger but run away from him: they do not recognise
the voice of strangers.'

Jesus told them this parable but they failed to understand what he
meant by telling it to them.

So Jesus spoke to them again:

'I tell you most solemnly,
I am the gate of the sheepfold.

All others who have come
are thieves and brigands;
but the sheep took no notice of them.
I am the gate.
Anyone who enters through me will be safe:
he will go freely in and out
and be sure of finding pasture.
The thief comes
only to steal and kill and destroy.
I have come so that they may have life
and have it to the full.'

The Gospel of the Lord.

The Creed is said.

Prayer over the Offerings

Grant, we pray, O Lord,
that we may always find delight
    in these paschal mysteries,
so that the renewal constantly
    at work within us
may be the cause of our unending joy.
Through Christ our Lord.

Preface of Easter, pp.52-57.

Super oblata

Concede, quæsumus, Domine,
semper nos per hæc mysteria
        paschalia gratulari,
ut continua nostræ
        reparationis operatio
perpetuæ nobis fiat causa lætitiæ.
Per Christum Dominum nostrum.

Communion Antiphon

The Good Shepherd has risen,
who laid down his life for his sheep
and willingly died for his flock,
        alleluia.

Ant. ad communionem

Surrexit Pastor bonus, qui animam
    suam posuit pro ovibus suis,
et pro grege suo mori dignatus est,
    alleluia.

Prayer after Communion

Look upon your flock,
    kind Shepherd,
and be pleased to settle
    in eternal pastures
the sheep you have redeemed
by the Precious Blood of your Son.
Who lives and reigns
    for ever and ever.

Post communionem

Gregem tuum, Pastor bone,
        placatus intende,
et oves, quas pretioso Filii
        tui sanguine redemisti,
in æternis pascuis collocare digneris.
Per Christum Dominum nostrum.

A formula of Solemn Blessing, pp.136-139, may be used.

7 May

FIFTH SUNDAY OF EASTER

In today's Gospel Jesus says, "Do not let your hearts be troubled". He says it to us too. But how can we ensure that our hearts are not troubled? Because the heart does become troubled. The Lord indicates two remedies. The first is: "Believe in me". He knows that, in life, the worst anxiety, anguish, arises from the sensation of not being able to cope, of feeling alone and without points of reference when faced with events. We cannot overcome this anguish alone, when one difficulty is added to another. We need Jesus's help, and this is why Jesus asks us to have faith in him, that is, to lean not on ourselves but on him. Jesus is risen and lives precisely to be always by our side. There is then a second remedy for being troubled: "My Father's house has many rooms... I am going there to prepare a place for you". This is what Jesus did for us: he reserved a place in heaven for us. He took our humanity upon himself to carry it beyond death. It is the certainty that comforts us: there is a place reserved for each of us.

(Pope Francis)

Entrance Antiphon Cf. Ps 97:1-2	Ant. ad introitum
O SING a new song to the Lord, for he has worked wonders; in the sight of the nations he has shown his deliverance, alleluia.	C ANTATE Domino canticum novum, quia mirabilia fecit Dominus; ante conspectum gentium revelavit iustitiam suam, alleluia.

The Gloria in excelsis (Glory to God in the highest) is said.

Collect	Collecta
Almighty ever-living God, constantly accomplish the Paschal Mystery within us, that those you were pleased to make new in Holy Baptism may, under your protective care, bear much fruit and come to the joys of life eternal. Through our Lord Jesus Christ, your Son, who lives and reigns with you in the unity of the Holy Spirit, God, for ever and ever.	Omnipotens sempiterne Deus, semper in nobis paschale perfice sacramentum, ut, quos sacro baptismate dignatus es renovare, sub tuæ protectionis auxilio multos fructus afferant, et ad æternæ vitæ gaudia pervenire concedas. Per Dominum nostrum Iesum Christum Filium tuum, qui tecum vivit et regnat in unitate Spiritus Sancti, Deus, per omnia sæcula sæculorum.

FIRST READING

A reading from the Acts of the Apostles   6:1-7

They elected seven men full of the Holy Spirit.

About this time, when the number of disciples was increasing, the Hellenists made a complaint against the Hebrews: in the daily distribution their own widows were being overlooked. So the Twelve called a full meeting of the disciples and addressed them, 'It would not be right for us to neglect the word of God so as to give out food; you, brothers, must select from among yourselves seven men of good reputation, filled with the Spirit and with wisdom; we will hand over this duty to them, and continue to devote ourselves to prayer and to the service of the word.' The whole assembly approved of this proposal and elected Stephen, a man full of faith and of the Holy Spirit, together with Philip, Prochorus, Nicanor, Timon, Parmenas, and Nicolaus of Antioch, a convert to Judaism. They presented these to the apostles, who prayed and laid their hands on them.

The word of the Lord continued to spread: the number of disciples in Jerusalem was greatly increased, and a large group of priests made their submission to the faith.

The word of the Lord.

Responsorial Psalm   Ps 32:1-2,4-5,18-19. R. v.22

R. **May your love be upon us, O Lord,**
   as we place all our hope in you.
   Or: **Alleluia!**

Ring out your joy to the Lord, O you just;
for praise is fitting for loyal hearts.
Give thanks to the Lord upon the harp,
with a ten-stringed lute sing him songs. R.

For the word of the Lord is faithful
and all his works to be trusted.
The Lord loves justice and right
and fills the earth with his love. R.

The Lord looks on those who revere him,
on those who hope in his love,
to rescue their souls from death,
to keep them alive in famine. R.

SECOND READING

A reading from the first letter of St Peter 2:4-9

But you are a chosen race, a royal priesthood.

The Lord is the living stone, rejected by men but chosen by God and precious to him; set yourselves close to him so that you too, the holy priesthood that offers the spiritual sacrifices which Jesus Christ has made acceptable to God, may be living stones making a spiritual house. As scripture says: See how I lay in Sion a precious cornerstone that I have chosen and the man who rests his trust on it will not be disappointed. That means that for you who are believers, it is precious; but for unbelievers, the stone rejected by the builders has proved to be the keystone, a stone to stumble over, a rock to bring men down. They stumble over it because they do not believe in the word; it was the fate in store for them.

But you are a chosen race, a royal priesthood, a consecrated nation, a people set apart to sing the praises of God who called you out of the darkness into his wonderful light.

The word of the Lord.

Gospel Acclamation Jn 14:6

R. **Alleluia, alleluia!**
Jesus said: 'I am the Way, the Truth, and the Life.
No one can come to the Father except through me.'
R. **Alleluia!**

GOSPEL

A reading from the holy Gospel according to John 14:1-12

I am the Way, the Truth and the Life.

Jesus said to his disciples:

'Do not let your hearts be troubled.
Trust in God still, and trust in me.
There are many rooms in my Father's house;
if there were not, I should have told you.
I am going now to prepare a place for you,
and after I have gone and prepared you a place,
I shall return to take you with me;
so that where I am
you may be too.
You know the way to the place where I am going.'

Thomas said, 'Lord, we do not know where you are going, so how can we know the way?' Jesus said:

'I am the Way, the Truth and the Life.
No one can come to the Father except through me.
If you know me, you know my Father too.
From this moment you know him and have seen him.'

Philip said, 'Lord, let us see the Father and then we shall be satisfied.'
'Have I been with you all this time, Philip,' said Jesus to him 'and you still
do not know me?

'To have seen me is to have seen the Father,
so how can you say, "Let us see the Father"?
Do you not believe
that I am in the Father and the Father is in me?
The words I say to you I do not speak as from myself:
it is the Father, living in me, who is doing this work.
You must believe me when I say
that I am in the Father and the Father is in me;
believe it on the evidence of this work, if for no other reason.

'I tell you most solemnly,
whoever believes in me
will perform the same works as I do myself,
he will perform even greater works,
because I am going to the Father.'

The Gospel of the Lord.

The Creed is said.

Prayer over the Offerings

O God, who by the wonderful
    exchange effected in this sacrifice
have made us partakers of the one
    supreme Godhead,
grant, we pray,
that, as we have come to know
    your truth,
we may make it ours by a worthy
    way of life.
Through Christ our Lord.

Preface of Easter, pp.52-57.

Super oblata

Deus, qui nos, per huius sacrificii
    veneranda commercia,
unius summæque divinitatis
    participes effecisti,
præsta, quæsumus,
ut, sicut tuam cognovimus veritatem,
sic eam dignis moribus assequamur.
Per Christum Dominum nostrum.

Communion Antiphon Cf. Jn 15:1,5

I am the true vine and you
    are the branches, says the Lord.
Whoever remains in me, and I in
    him, bears fruit in plenty, alleluia.

Prayer after Communion

Graciously be present to your
    people, we pray, O Lord,
and lead those you have imbued
    with heavenly mysteries
to pass from former ways
    to newness of life.
Through Christ our Lord.

Ant. ad communionem.

Ego sum vitis vera et vos palmites,
    dicit Dominus;
qui manet in me et ego in eo,
hic fert fructum multum, alleluia.

Post communionem

Populo tuo, quæsumus, Domine,
    adesto propitius,
et, quem mysteriis
    cælestibus imbuisti,
fac ad novitatem vitæ
    de vetustate transire.
Per Christum Dominum nostrum.

A formula of Solemn Blessing, pp.136-139, may be used.

14 May

SIXTH SUNDAY OF EASTER

*Faced with the experience of error and sin — which we all do — the Holy Spirit
helps us not to succumb and enables us to grasp and fully live the meaning
of Jesus's words: "If you love me, you will keep my commandments". The
commandments are not given to us as a kind of mirror in which to see the
reflection of our miseries, our inconsistencies. No, they are not like that. The
Word of God is given to us as the Word of life, which transforms the heart, life;
which renews, which does not judge in order to condemn, but heals and has
forgiveness as its aim. God's mercy is thus. A Word that is light for our steps.
All this is the work of the Holy Spirit! He is the Gift of God; he is God himself,
who helps us to be free people, people who want and know how to love, people
who understand that life is a mission to proclaim the wonders that the Lord
accomplishes in those who trust in him.*

(Pope Francis)

Entrance Antiphon   Cf. Is 48:20

PROCLAIM a joyful sound
    and let it be heard;
proclaim to the ends of the earth:
The Lord has freed his people,
    alleluia.

Ant. ad introitum

VOCEM iucunditatis annuntiate,
    et audiatur,
annuntiate usque ad extremum terræ:
liberavit Dominus populum suum,
    alleluia.

The **Gloria in excelsis** (Glory to God in the highest) is said.

Collect

Grant, almighty God,
that we may celebrate with heartfelt
    devotion these days of joy,
which we keep in honour
    of the risen Lord,
and that what we relive
    in remembrance
we may always hold to in what we do.
Through our Lord Jesus Christ,
    your Son,
who lives and reigns with you
    in the unity of the Holy Spirit,
God, for ever and ever.

Collecta

Fac nos, omnipotens Deus,
    hos lætitiæ dies,
quos in honorem Domini
    resurgentis exsequimur,
affectu sedulo celebrare,
ut quod recordatione percurrimus
semper in opere teneamus.
Per Dominum nostrum Iesum
    Christum Filium tuum,
qui tecum vivit et regnat
    in unitate Spiritus Sancti,
Deus, per omnia sæcula sæculorum.

FIRST READING

A reading from the Acts of the Apostles   8:5-8,14-17

They laid hands on them, and they received the Holy Spirit.

Philip went to a Samaritan town and proclaimed the Christ to them. The
people united in welcoming the message Philip preached, either because
they had heard of the miracles he worked or because they saw them for
themselves. There were, for example, unclean spirits that came shrieking
out of many who were possessed, and several paralytics and cripples were
cured. As a result there was great rejoicing in that town.

When the apostles in Jerusalem heard that Samaria had accepted the
word of God, they sent Peter and John to them, and they went down there,
and prayed for the Samaritans to receive the Holy Spirit, for as yet he had
not come down on any of them: they had only been baptised in the name
of the Lord Jesus. Then they laid hands on them, and they received the
Holy Spirit.

The word of the Lord.

Responsorial Psalm   Ps 65:1-7,16,20. R. v.1

R. **Cry out with joy to God all the earth.**
    Or: **Alleluia!**

Cry out with joy to God all the earth,
O sing to the glory of his name.
O render him glorious praise.
Say to God: 'How tremendous your deeds! R.

'Before you all the earth shall bow;
shall sing to you, sing to your name!'
Come and see the works of God,
tremendous his deeds among men. R.

He turned the sea into dry land,
they passed through the river dry-shod.
Let our joy then be in him;
he rules for ever by his might. R.

Come and hear, all who fear God.
I will tell what he did for my soul:
Blessed be God who did not reject my prayer
nor withhold his love from me. R.

SECOND READING

A reading from the first letter of St Peter   3:15-18

In the body he was put to death, in the spirit he was raised to life.

Reverence the Lord Christ in your hearts, and always have your answer ready
for people who ask you the reason for the hope that you all have. But give
it with courtesy and respect and with a clear conscience, so that those who
slander you when you are living a good life in Christ may be proved wrong
in the accusations that they bring. And if it is the will of God that you should
suffer, it is better to suffer for doing right than for doing wrong.

Why, Christ himself, innocent though he was, had died once for sins,
died for the guilty, to lead us to God. In the body he was put to death, in
the spirit he was raised to life.

The word of the Lord.

Gospel Acclamation   Jn 14:23

R. **Alleluia, alleluia!**
Jesus said: 'If anyone loves me he will keep my word,
and my Father will love him, and we shall come to him.'
R. **Alleluia.**

GOSPEL

A reading from the holy Gospel according to John   14:15-21

I shall ask the Father, and he will give you another Advocate.

Jesus said to his disciples:

'If you love me you will keep my commandments.
I shall ask the Father,
and he will give you another Advocate

to be with you for ever,
that Spirit of truth
whom the world can never receive
since it neither sees nor knows him,
but you know him,
because he is with you, he is in you.
I will not leave you orphans;
I will come back to you.
In a short time the world will no longer see me;
but you will see me,
because I live and you will live.
On that day
you will understand that I am in my Father
and you in me and I in you.
Anybody who receives my commandments and keeps them
will be one who loves me;
and anybody who loves me will be loved by my Father,
and I shall love him and show myself to him.'

The Gospel of the Lord.

When the Ascension is celebrated on the Seventh Sunday of Easter, the Second
Reading and Gospel assigned to the Seventh Sunday may be read on the Sixth Sunday.

The Creed is said.

Prayer over the Offerings

May our prayers rise up to you,
    O Lord,
together with the sacrificial offerings,
so that, purified by
    your graciousness,
we may be conformed to the
    mysteries of your mighty love.
Through Christ our Lord.

Preface of Easter, pp.52-57.

Super oblata

Ascendant ad te, Domine,
    preces nostræ
cum oblationibus hostiarum,
ut, tua dignatione mundati,
sacramentis magnæ
    pietatis aptemur.
Per Christum Dominum nostrum.

Communion Antiphon Jn 14:15-16

If you love me, keep my
    commandments, says the Lord,
and I will ask the Father and he will
    send you another Paraclete,
to abide with you for ever, alleluia.

Ant. ad communionem

Si diligitis me, mandata mea
    servate, dicit Dominus.
Et ego rogabo Patrem,
    et alium Paraclitum dabit vobis,
ut maneat vobiscum in æternum,
    alleluia.

Prayer after Communion	Post communionem
Almighty ever-living God, who restore us to eternal life in the Resurrection of Christ, increase in us, we pray, the fruits of this paschal Sacrament and pour into our hearts the strength of this saving food. Through Christ our Lord.	Omnipotens sempiterne Deus, qui ad æternam vitam in Christi resurrectione nos reparas, fructus in nobis paschalis multiplica sacramenti, et fortitudinem cibi salutaris nostris infunde pectoribus. Per Christum Dominum nostrum.

A formula of Solemn Blessing, pp.136-139, may be used.

In England, Wales & Scotland

18 May

In Ireland

21 May

THE ASCENSION OF THE LORD

The Ascension completes Jesus's mission among us. Indeed, if it is for us that Jesus descended from heaven, it is also for us that he ascends there. After having descended into our humanity and redeemed it, he now ascends into heaven, taking our flesh with him. He is the first man who enters heaven, because Jesus is man, true man; he is God, true God; our flesh is in heaven and this gives us joy. Now a human body sits at the right hand of the Father for the first time, the body of Jesus, and in this mystery we each contemplate our own future destination. This is not at all an abandonment; Jesus remains forever with the disciples – with us. He remains in prayer, because as man, he prays to the Father, and as God, man and God, he shows him his wounds, the wounds by which he has redeemed us. Jesus's prayer is there, with our flesh: he is one of us, God-man, and he prays for us.

(Pope Francis)

Solemnity

Where the Solemnity of the Ascension is not to be observed as a Holyday of Obligation, it is assigned to the Seventh Sunday of Easter as its proper day.

At the Vigil Mass

This Mass is used on the evening of the day before the Solemnity, either before or after First Vespers (Evening Prayer I) of the Ascension.

Entrance Antiphon Ps 67:33,35	Ant. ad introitum
YOU kingdoms of the earth, sing to God; praise the Lord, who ascends above the highest heavens; his majesty and might are in the skies, alleluia.	REGNA terræ cantate Deo, psallite Domino, qui ascendit super cælum cæli; magnificentia et virtus eius in nubibus, alleluia.

The **Gloria in excelsis** (Glory to God in the highest) is said.

Collect	Collecta
O God, whose Son today ascended to the heavens as the Apostles looked on, grant, we pray, that, in accordance with his promise, we may be worthy for him to live with us always on earth, and we with him in heaven. Who lives and reigns with you in the unity of the Holy Spirit, God, for ever and ever.	Deus, cuius Filius hodie in cælos, Apostolis astantibus, ascendit, concede nobis, quæsumus, ut secundum eius promissionem et ille nobiscum semper in terris et nos cum eo in cælo vivere mereamur. Qui tecum vivit et regnat in unitate Spiritus Sancti, Deus, per omnia sæcula sæculorum.

FIRST READING

A reading from the Acts of the Apostles   1:1-11

He was lifted up while they looked on.

In my earlier work, Theophilus, I dealt with everything Jesus had done and taught from the beginning until the day he gave his instructions to the apostles he had chosen through the Holy Spirit, and was taken up to heaven. He had shown himself alive to them after his Passion by many demonstrations: for forty days he had continued to appear to them and tell them about the kingdom of God. When he had been at table with them, he had told them not to leave Jerusalem, but to wait there for what the Father had promised. 'It is' he had said 'what you have heard me speak about: John baptised with water but you, not many days from now, will be baptised with the Holy Spirit.'

Now having met together, they asked him, 'Lord, has the time come? Are you going to restore the kingdom to Israel?' He replied, 'It is not for you to know times or dates that the Father has decided by his own authority, but you will receive power when the Holy Spirit comes on you, and then you will be my witnesses not only in Jerusalem but throughout Judaea and Samaria, and indeed to the ends of the earth.'

As he said this he was lifted up while they looked on, and a cloud took him from their sight. They were still staring into the sky when suddenly two men in white were standing near them and they said, 'Why are you men from Galilee standing here looking into the sky? Jesus who has been taken up from you into heaven, this same Jesus will come back in the same way as you have seen him go there.'

The word of the Lord.

Responsial Psalm   Ps 46:2-3,6-9. R. v.6

R. **God goes up with shouts of joy;**
  the Lord goes up with trumpet blast.
   Or: **Alleluia!**

All peoples, clap your hands,
cry to God with shouts of joy!
For the Lord, the Most High, we must fear,
great king over all the earth. R.

God goes up with shouts of joy;
the Lord goes up with trumpet blast.
Sing praise for God, sing praise,
sing praise to our king, sing praise. R.

God is king of all the earth.
Sing praise with all your skill.
God is king over the nations;
God reigns on his holy throne. R.

SECOND READING

A reading from the letter of St Paul to the Ephesians   1:17-23

He made him sit at his right hand in heaven.

May the God of our Lord Jesus Christ, the Father of glory, give you a spirit of wisdom and perception of what is revealed, to bring you to full knowledge of him. May he enlighten the eyes of your mind so that you can see what hope his call holds for you, what rich glories he has promised the saints will inherit and how infinitely great is the power that he has exercised for us believers. This you can tell from the strength of his power at work in Christ, when he used it to raise him from the dead and to make him sit at his right hand, in heaven, far above every Sovereignty, Authority, Power, or Domination, or any other name that can be named, not only in this age, but also in the age to come. He has put all things under his feet, and made him as the ruler of everything, the head of the Church; which is his body, the fullness of him who fills the whole creation.

    The word of the Lord.

Gospel Acclamation   Mt 28:19,20

R. **Alleluia, alleluia!**
Go, make disciples of all the nations;
I am with you always; yes, to the end of time.
R. **Alleluia!**

GOSPEL

A reading from the holy Gospel according to Matthew   28:16-20

All authority in heaven and earth has been given to me.

The eleven disciples set out for Galilee, to the mountain where Jesus had arranged to meet them. When they saw him they fell down before him, though some hesitated. Jesus came up and spoke to them. He said, 'All authority in heaven and on earth has been given to me. Go, therefore, make disciples of all the nations; baptise them in the name of the Father and of the Son and of the Holy Spirit, and teach them to observe all the commands I gave you. And know that I am with you always; yes, to the end of time.'

    The Gospel of the Lord.

The Creed is said.

Prayer over the Offerings

O God, whose Only Begotten Son,
  our High Priest,
is seated ever-living at your right
  hand to intercede for us,
grant that we may approach with
  confidence the throne of grace
and there obtain your mercy.
Through Christ our Lord.

Super oblata

Deus, cuius Unigenitus,
  Pontifex noster,
semper vivens sedet
  ad dexteram tuam
ad interpellandum pro nobis,
concede nos adire cum fiducia ad
  thronum gratiæ,
ut misericordiam tuam consequamur.
Per Christum Dominum nostrum.

Preface I or II of the Ascension of the Lord, pp.58-59.

When the Roman Canon is used, the proper form of the **Communicantes** (**In communion with those**) is said.

Communion Antiphon Cf. Heb 10:12

Christ, offering a single sacrifice
  for sins,
is seated for ever at God's right hand,
  alleluia.

Ant. ad communionem

Christus, unam pro peccatis
  offerens hostiam,
in sempiternum sedet in dextera Dei,
  alleluia.

Prayer after Communion

May the gifts we have received
  from your altar, Lord,
kindle in our hearts a longing
  for the heavenly homeland
and cause us to press forward,
  following in the
  Saviour's footsteps,
to the place where for our sake he
  entered before us.
Who lives and reigns
  for ever and ever.

Post communionem

Quæ ex altari tuo, Domine,
  dona percepimus,
accendant in cordibus nostris
  cælestis patriæ desiderium,
et quo præcursor pro nobis
  introivit Salvator,
faciant nos, eius vestigia
  sectantes, contendere.
Qui vivit et regnat
  in sæcula sæculorum.

A formula of Solemn Blessing, pp.138-139, may be used.

At the Mass during the Day

Entrance Antiphon   Ac 1:11

MEN of Galilee, why gaze
in wonder at the heavens?
This Jesus whom you saw ascending
into heaven
will return as you saw him go,
alleluia.

Ant. ad introitum

VIRI Galilæi, quid admiramini
aspicientes in cælum?
Quemadmodum vidistis eum
ascendentem in cælum,
ita veniet, alleluia.

The Gloria in excelsis (Glory to God in the highest) is said.

Collect

Gladden us with holy joys,
almighty God,
and make us rejoice with
devout thanksgiving,
for the Ascension of Christ your Son
is our exaltation,
and, where the Head has gone
before in glory,
the Body is called to follow in hope.
Through our Lord Jesus Christ,
your Son,
who lives and reigns with you
in the unity of the Holy Spirit,
God, for ever and ever.

Or:

Grant, we pray, almighty God,
that we, who believe that your Only
Begotten Son, our Redeemer,
ascended this day to the heavens,
may in spirit dwell already
in heavenly realms.
Who lives and reigns with you
in the unity of the Holy Spirit,
God, for ever and ever.

Collecta

Fac nos, omnipotens Deus,
sanctis exsultare gaudiis,
et pia gratiarum actione lætari,
quia Christi Filii tui ascensio
est nostra provectio,
et quo processit gloria capitis,
eo spes vocatur et corporis.
Per Dominum nostrum Iesum
Christum Filium tuum,
qui tecum vivit et regnat
in unitate Spiritus Sancti,
Deus, per omnia sæcula sæculorum.

Vel:

Concede, quæsumus,
omnipotens Deus,
ut, qui hodierna die
Unigenitum tuum
Redemptorem nostrum
ad cælos ascendisse credimus,
ipsi quoque mente in
cælestibus habitemus.
Qui tecum vivit et regnat
in unitate Spiritus Sancti,
Deus, per omnia sæcula sæculorum.

FIRST READING

A reading from the Acts of the Apostles   1:1-11

He was lifted up while they looked on.

In my earlier work, Theophilus, I dealt with everything Jesus had done and taught from the beginning until the day he gave his instructions to the apostles he had chosen through the Holy Spirit, and was taken up to heaven. He had shown himself alive to them after his Passion by many demonstrations: for forty days he had continued to appear to them and tell them about the kingdom of God. When he had been at table with them, he had told them not to leave Jerusalem, but to wait there for what the Father had promised. 'It is' he had said 'what you have heard me speak about: John baptised with water but you, not many days from now, will be baptised with the Holy Spirit.'

Now having met together, they asked him, 'Lord, has the time come? Are you going to restore the kingdom to Israel?' He replied, 'It is not for you to know times or dates that the Father has decided by his own authority, but you will receive power when the Holy Spirit comes on you, and then you will be my witnesses not only in Jerusalem but throughout Judaea and Samaria, and indeed to the ends of the earth.'

As he said this he was lifted up while they looked on, and a cloud took him from their sight. They were still staring into the sky when suddenly two men in white were standing near them and they said, 'Why are you men from Galilee standing here looking into the sky? Jesus who has been taken up from you into heaven, this same Jesus will come back in the same way as you have seen him go there.'

The word of the Lord.

Responsorial Psalm   Ps 46:2-3,6-9. R. v.6

R. **God goes up with shouts of joy;**
   the Lord goes up with trumpet blast.
   Or: **Alleluia!**

All peoples, clap your hands,
cry to God with shouts of joy!
For the Lord, the Most High, we must fear,
great king over all the earth. R.

God goes up with shouts of joy;
the Lord goes up with trumpet blast.
Sing praise for God, sing praise,
sing praise to our king, sing praise. R.

God is king of all the earth.
Sing praise with all your skill.
God is king over the nations;
God reigns on his holy throne. R.

R. **God goes up with shouts of joy;**
   the Lord goes up with trumpet blast.
   Or: **Alleluia!**

SECOND READING

A reading from the letter of St Paul to the Ephesians   1:17-23
He made him sit at his right hand in heaven.

May the God of our Lord Jesus Christ, the Father of glory, give you a spirit of
wisdom and perception of what is revealed, to bring you to full knowledge
of him. May he enlighten the eyes of your mind so that you can see what
hope his call holds for you, what rich glories he has promised the saints
will inherit and how infinitely great is the power that he has exercised for
us believers. This you can tell from the strength of his power at work in
Christ, when he used it to raise him from the dead and to make him sit at
his right hand, in heaven, far above every Sovereignty, Authority, Power, or
Domination, or any other name that can be named, not only in this age,
but also in the age to come. He has put all things under his feet, and made
him as the ruler of everything, the head of the Church; which is his body,
the fullness of him who fills the whole creation.

The word of the Lord.

Gospel Acclamation   Mt 28:19.20

R. **Alleluia, alleluia!**
Go, make disciples of all the nations;
I am with you always; yes, to the end of time.
R. **Alleluia!**

GOSPEL

A reading from the holy Gospel according to Matthew   28:16-20
All authority in heaven and earth has been given to me.

The eleven disciples set out for Galilee, to the mountain where Jesus had
arranged to meet them. When they saw him they fell down before him,
though some hesitated. Jesus came up and spoke to them. He said, 'All
authority in heaven and on earth has been given to me. Go, therefore,
make disciples of all the nations; baptise them in the name of the Father

and of the Son and of the Holy Spirit, and teach them to observe all the commands I gave you. And know that I am with you always; yes, to the end of time.'

The Gospel of the Lord.

The Creed is said.

Prayer over the Offerings

We offer sacrifice now
in supplication, O Lord,
to honour the wondrous Ascension
of your Son:
grant, we pray,
that through this most holy exchange
we, too, may rise up
to the heavenly realms.
Through Christ our Lord.

Super oblata

Sacrificium, Domine,
pro Filii tui supplices
venerabili nunc
ascensione deferimus:
præsta, quæsumus,
ut his commerciis sacrosanctis
ad cælestia consurgamus.
Per Christum Dominum nostrum.

Preface I or II of the Ascension of the Lord, pp.58-59.

When the Roman Canon is used, the proper form of the **Communicantes** (**In communion with those**) is said.

Communion Antiphon   Mt 28:20

Behold, I am with you always,
even to the end of the age, alleluia.

Ant. ad communionem

Ecce ego vobiscum sum
omnibus diebus,
usque ad consummationem sæculi,
alleluia.

Prayer after Communion

Almighty ever-living God,
who allow those on earth
to celebrate divine mysteries,
grant, we pray,
that Christian hope may draw
us onward
to where our nature is united
with you.
Through Christ our Lord.

Post communionem

Omnipotens sempiterne Deus,
qui in terra constitutos divina
tractare concedis,
præsta, quæsumus,
ut illuc tendat christianæ
devotionis affectus,
quo tecum est nostra substantia.
Per Christum Dominum nostrum.

A formula of Solemn Blessing, pp.138-139, may be used.

In England, Wales & Scotland

21 May

SEVENTH SUNDAY OF EASTER

In his farewell discourses to the disciples, Jesus stressed the importance of his "return to the Father", the culmination of his whole mission: indeed, he came into the world to bring man back to God, not on the ideal level – like a philosopher or a master of wisdom – but really, like a shepherd who wants to lead his sheep back to the fold. It was for our sake that he came down from Heaven and for our sake that he ascended to it, after making himself in all things like men, humbling himself even to death on a cross and after having touched the abyss of the greatest distance from God. For this very reason the Father was pleased with him and "highly exalted" him (Ph 2:9), restoring to him the fullness of his glory, but now with our humanity. God in man – man in God: this is even now a reality, not a theoretical truth.

(Pope Benedict XVI)

Entrance Antiphon Cf. Ps 26:7-9	Ant. ad introitum

O LORD, hear my voice,
    for I have called to you;
of you my heart has spoken:
    Seek his face;
hide not your face from me, alleluia.
	E XAUDI, Domine, vocem meam,
	    qua clamavi ad te.
	Tibi dixit cor meum,
	    quæsivi vultum tuum,
	vultum tuum requiram;
	ne avertas faciem tuam a me, alleluia.

The Gloria in excelsis (Glory to God in the highest) is said.

Collect	Collecta

Graciously hear our supplications,
    O Lord,
so that we, who believe that
    the Saviour of the human race
is with you in your glory,
may experience, as he promised,
until the end of the world,
his abiding presence among us.
Who lives and reigns with you
    in the unity of the Holy Spirit,
God, for ever and ever.
	Supplicationibus nostris, Domine,
	    adesto propitius,
	ut, sicut humani generis Salvatorem
	tecum in tua credimus maiestate,
	ita eum usque ad
	    consummationem sæculi
	manere nobiscum,
	sicut ipse promisit, sentiamus.
	Qui tecum vivit et regnat
	    in unitate Spiritus Sancti,
	Deus, per omnia sæcula sæculorum.

FIRST READING

A reading from the Acts of the Apostles   1:12-14

All joined in continuous prayer.

After Jesus was taken up into heaven, the apostles went back from the Mount of Olives, as it is called, to Jerusalem, a short distance away, no more than a sabbath walk; and when they reached the city they went to the upper room where they were staying; there were Peter and John, James and Andrew, Philip and Thomas, Bartholomew and Matthew, James son of Alphaeus and Simon the Zealot, and Jude son of James. All these joined in continuous prayer, together with several women, including Mary the mother of Jesus, and with his brothers.

The word of the Lord.

Responsional Psalm   Ps 26:1,4,7-8. R. v.13

R. **I am sure I shall see the Lord's goodness
   in the land of the living.**
   Or: **Alleluia!**

The Lord is my light and my help;
whom shall I fear?
The Lord is the stronghold of my life;
before whom shall I shrink? R.

There is one thing I ask of the Lord,
for this I long,
to live in the house of the Lord,
all the days of my life,
to savour the sweetness of the Lord,
to behold his temple. R.

O Lord, hear my voice when I call;
have mercy and answer.
Of you my heart has spoken;
'Seek his face.' R.

SECOND READING

A reading from the first letter of St Peter   4:13-16

It is a blessing for you when they insult you for bearing the name of Christ.

If you can have some share in the sufferings of Christ, be glad, because you will enjoy a much greater gladness when his glory is revealed. It is a blessing for you when they insult you for bearing the name of Christ, because it means that you have the Spirit of glory, the Spirit of God resting on you. None of you should ever deserve to suffer for being a murderer, a thief, a criminal or an informer; but if anyone of you should suffer for being a Christian, then he is not to be ashamed of it; he should thank God that he has been called one.

The word of the Lord.

Gospel Acclamation   Cf. Jn 14:18

R. **Alleluia, alleluia!**
I will not leave you orphans, says the Lord;
I will come back to you, and your hearts will be full of joy.
R. **Alleluia!**

GOSPEL

A reading from the holy Gospel according to John   17:1-11
Father, glorify your Son.

Jesus raised his eyes to heaven and said:
  'Father, the hour has come:
  glorify your Son
  so that your Son may glorify you;
  and, through the power over all mankind that you have given him,
  let him give eternal life to all those you have entrusted to him.
  And eternal life is this:
  to know you,
  the only true God,
  and Jesus Christ whom you have sent.
  I have glorified you on earth
  and finished the work
  that you gave me to do.
  Now, Father, it is time for you to glorify me
  with that glory I had with you
  before ever the world was.
  I have made your name known
  to the men you took from the world to give me.
  They were yours and you gave them to me,
  and they have kept your word.
  Now at last they know
  that all you have given me comes indeed from you;
  for I have given them
  the teaching you gave to me,
  and they have truly accepted this, that I came from you,
  and have believed that it was you who sent me.

I pray for them;
I am not praying for the world
but for those you have given me,
because they belong to you:
all I have is yours
and all you have is mine,
and in them I am glorified.
I am not in the world any longer,
but they are in the world,
and I am coming to you.'

The Gospel of the Lord.

The Creed is said.

Prayer over the Offerings

Accept, O Lord, the prayers
of your faithful
with the sacrificial offerings,
that through these acts
of devotedness
we may pass over to the glory
of heaven.
Through Christ our Lord.

Super oblata

Suscipe, Domine, fidelium preces
cum oblationibus hostiarum,
ut, per hæc piæ devotionis officia,
ad cælestem gloriam transeamus.
Per Christum Dominum nostrum.

Preface of Easter, or of the Ascension, pp.52-59.

Communion Antiphon   Jn 17:22

Father, I pray that they may be one
as we also are one, alleluia.

Ant. ad communionem

Rogo, Pater, ut sint unum,
sicut et nos unum sumus, alleluia.

Prayer after Communion

Hear us, O God our Saviour,
and grant us confidence,
that through these sacred mysteries
there will be accomplished
in the body of the whole Church
what has already come to pass
in Christ her Head.
Who lives and reigns
for ever and ever.

Post communionem

Exaudi nos, Deus, salutaris noster,
ut per hæc sacrosancta mysteria
in totius Ecclesiæ confidamus
corpore faciendum,
quod eius præcessit in capite.
Per Christum Dominum nostrum.

A formula of Solemn Blessing, pp.136-139, may be used.

28 May

PENTECOST SUNDAY

Look at the apostles: they were alone that morning, alone and bewildered, cowering behind closed doors, living in fear and overwhelmed by their weaknesses, failings and their sins, for they had denied Christ. The years they had spent with Jesus had not changed them: they were no different from what they had been. Then they received the Spirit and everything changed: the problems and failings remained, yet they were no longer afraid of them, nor of any who would be hostile to them. They sensed comfort within and they wanted to overflow with the comfort of God. Before, they were fearful; now their only fear was that of not testifying to the love they had received.

(Pope Francis)

Solemnity

At the Vigil Mass

EXTENDED FORM

This Vigil Mass may be celebrated on the Saturday evening, either before or after First Vespers (Evening Prayer I) of Pentecost Sunday.

In churches where the Vigil Mass is celebrated in an extended form, this may be done as follows.

a) If First Vespers (Evening Prayer I) celebrated in choir or in common immediately precede Mass, the celebration may begin either from the introductory verse and the hymn (**Veni, creator Spiritus**) or else from the singing of the Entrance Antiphon with the procession and greeting of the Priest; in either case the Penitential Act is omitted (Cf. General Instruction of the Liturgy of the Hours, nos. 94 and 96).

Then the Psalmody prescribed for Vespers follows, up to but not including the Short Reading.

After the Psalmody, omitting the Penitential Act, and if appropriate, the **Kyrie** (**Lord, have mercy**), the Priest says the prayer **Grant, we pray, almighty God, that the splendour**, as at the Vigil Mass.

b) If Mass is begun in the usual way, after the **Kyrie** (**Lord, have mercy**), the Priest says the prayer **Grant, we pray, almighty God, that the splendour**, as at the Vigil Mass.

Then the Priest may address the people in these or similar words:

Dear brethren (brothers and sisters),
we have now begun our
  Pentecost Vigil,
after the example of the Apostles
  and disciples
who with Mary, the Mother
  of Jesus, persevered in prayer,
awaiting the Spirit promised
  by the Lord;
like them, let us, too, listen with quiet
  hearts to the Word of God.
Let us meditate on how many
  great deeds
God in times past did for his people
and let us pray that the Holy Spirit,
whom the Father sent as the first
  fruits for those who believe,
may bring to perfection his work
  in the world.

Vigiliam Pentecostes ingressi,
  fratres carissimi, ad exemplum
Apostolorum et discipulorum qui,
  cum Maria, Matre Iesu,
instabant in oratione,
exspectantes Spiritum a Domino
  promissum, quieto corde nunc
  verbum Dei audiamus.
Meditemur quanta fecit
  Deus populo suo et oremus,
ut Spiritus Sanctus
quem Pater misit
  primitias credentibus,
opus suum
in mundo perficiat.

Then follow the readings proposed as options in the Lectionary. A reader goes to the ambo and proclaims the reading. Afterwards a psalmist or a cantor sings or says the Psalm with the people making the response. Then all rise, the Priest says, Let us pray and, after all have prayed for a while in silence, he says the prayer corresponding to the reading. In place of the Responsorial Psalm a period of sacred silence may be observed, in which case the pause after Let us pray is omitted.

FIRST READING

A reading from the book of Genesis   11:1-9

It was named Babel because there the language of the whole earth was confused.

Throughout the earth men spoke the same language, with the same vocabulary. Now as they moved eastwards they found a plain in the land of Shinar where they settled. They said to one another, 'Come, let us make bricks and bake them in the fire.' – For stone they used bricks, and for mortar they used bitumen. – 'Come,' they said 'let us build ourselves a town and a tower with its top reaching heaven. Let us make a name for ourselves, so that we may not be scattered about the whole earth.'

Now the Lord came down to see the town and the tower that the sons of man had built. 'So they are all a single people with a single language!' said the Lord. 'This is but the start of their undertakings! There will be nothing too hard for them to do. Come, let us go down and confuse their language on the spot so that they can no longer understand one another.'

The Lord scattered them thence over the whole face of the earth, and they stopped building the town. It was named Babel therefore, because there the Lord confused the language of the whole earth. It was from there that the Lord scattered them over the whole face of the earth.

The word of the Lord.

Responsorial Psalm   Ps 32:10-11,12-13,14-15 R. v.12b

R. **Happy the people the Lord has chosen as his own.**

He frustrates the designs of the nations,
he defeats the plans of the peoples.
His own designs shall stand for ever,
the plans of his heart from age to age. R.

They are happy, whose God is the Lord,
the people he has chosen as his own.
From the heavens the Lord looks forth,
he sees all the children of men. R.

From the place where he dwells he gazes
on all the dwellers on the earth,
he who shapes the hearts of them all
and considers all their deeds. R.

Prayer

Let us pray.
Grant, we pray, almighty God,
that your Church may always
    remain that holy people,
formed as one by the unity
    of Father, Son and Holy Spirit,
which manifests to the world
the Sacrament of your holiness
    and unity
and leads it to the perfection
    of your charity.
Through Christ our Lord.
R. Amen.

Oremus.
Concede, quæsumus,
    omnipotens Deus,
ut Ecclesia tua semper ea plebs
    sancta permaneat
de unitate Patris et Filii
    et Spiritus Sancti adunata,
quæ tuæ sanctitatis
    et unitatis sacramentum
mundo manifestet
et ipsum ad perfectionem
    tuæ conducat caritatis.
Per Christum Dominum nostrum.
R. Amen.

SECOND READING

A reading from the book of Exodus   19:3-8,16-20

The Lord came down on the mountain of Sinai before all the people.

Moses went up to God, and the Lord called to him from the mountain, saying, 'Say this to the House of Jacob, declare this to the sons of Israel,

"You yourselves have seen what I did with the Egyptians, how I carried you on eagle's wings and brought you to myself. From this you know that now, if you obey my voice and hold fast to my covenant, you of all the nations shall be my very own, for all the earth is mine. I will count you a kingdom of priests, a consecrated nation." Those are the words you are to speak to the sons of Israel.' So Moses went and summoned the elders of the people, putting before them all that the Lord had bidden him. Then all the people answered as one, 'All that the Lord has said, we will do.'

Now at daybreak on the third day there were peals of thunder on the mountain and lightning flashes, a dense cloud, and a loud trumpet blast, and inside the camp all the people trembled. Then Moses led the people out of the camp to meet God; and they stood at the bottom of the mountain. The mountain of Sinai was entirely wrapped in smoke, because the Lord had descended on it in the form of fire. Like smoke from a furnace the smoke went up, and the whole mountain shook violently. Louder and louder grew the sound of the trumpet. Moses spoke, and God answered him with peals of thunder. The Lord came down on the mountain of Sinai, on the mountain top, and the Lord called Moses to the top of the mountain.

The word of the Lord.

Responsorial Psalm   Dn 3:52,53,54,55,56. R. v.52b

R. **To you glory and praise for evermore.**

You are blest, Lord God of our fathers. R.
Blest your glorious holy name. R.
You are blest in the temple of your glory. R.
You are blest on the throne of your kingdom. R.
You are blest who gaze into the depths. R.
You are blest in the firmament of heaven. R.

Or   Ps 18:8,9,10,11. R. Jn v.6:68c

R. **You have the message of eternal life, O Lord.**

The law of the Lord is perfect,
it revives the soul.
The rule of the Lord is to be trusted,
it gives wisdom to the simple. R.

The precepts of the Lord are right,
they gladden the heart.
The command of the Lord is clear,
it gives light to the eyes. R.

The fear of the Lord is holy,
abiding for ever.

The decrees of the Lord are truth
and all of them just. R.

They are more to be desired than gold,
than the purest of gold
and sweeter are they than honey,
than honey from the comb. R.

R. **You have the message of eternal life, O Lord.**

Prayer

Let us pray.

O God, who in fire and lightning
gave the ancient Law to Moses
     on Mount Sinai
and on this day manifested
     the new covenant
in the fire of the Spirit,
grant, we pray,
that we may always be aflame
     with that same Spirit
whom you wondrously poured out
     on your Apostles,
and that the new Israel,
gathered from every people,
may receive with rejoicing
the eternal commandment
     of your love.
Through Christ our Lord.
R. Amen.

Oremus.

Deus, qui in fulgure ignis
     in monte Sinai
legem antiquam Moysi dedisti
et fœdus novum in igne Spiritus
hoc die manifestasti,
presta, quæsumus,
ut illo iugiter Spiritu ferveamus,
quem Apostolis tuis
     ineffabiliter infudisti,
et novus Israel,
ex omni populo congregatus,
mandatum æternum tui amoris
     lætanter accipiat.
Per Christum Dominum nostrum.
R. Amen.

THIRD READING

A reading from the prophet Ezekiel   37:1-14

Dry bones, I am going to make the breath enter you, and you will live.

The hand of the Lord was laid on me, and he carried me away by the
spirit of the Lord and set me down in the middle of a valley, a valley full
of bones. He made me walk up and down among them. There were vast
quantities of these bones on the ground the whole length of the valley;
and they were quite dried up. He said to me, 'Son of man, can these bones
live?' I said, 'You know, Lord.' He said, 'Prophesy over these bones. Say,
"Dry bones, hear the word of the Lord. The Lord says this to these bones:
I am now going to make the breath enter you, and you will live. I shall put

sinews on you, I shall make flesh grow on you, I shall cover you with skin and give you breath, and you will live, and you will learn that I am the Lord."' I prophesied as I had been ordered. While I was prophesying, there was a noise, a sound of clattering; and the bones joined together. I looked, and saw that they were covered with sinews; flesh was growing on them and skin was covering them, but there was no breath in them. He said to me, 'Prophesy to the breath; prophesy, son of man. Say to the breath, "The Lord says this: Come from the four winds, breath; breathe on these dead; let them live!"' I prophesied as he had ordered me, and the breath entered them; they came to life again and stood up on their feet, a great, an immense army.

Then he said, 'Son of man, these bones are the whole House of Israel. They keep saying, "Our bones are dried up, our hope has gone; we are as good as dead." So prophesy. Say to them, "The Lord says this: I am now going to open your graves; I mean to raise you from your graves, my people, and lead you back to the soil of Israel. And you will know that I am the Lord, when I open your graves and raise you from your graves, my people. And I shall put my spirit in you, and you will live, and I shall resettle you on your own soil; and you will know that I, the Lord have said and done this – it is the Lord who speaks."'

The word of the Lord.

Responsional Psalm   Ps 106:2-3,4-5,6–7,8–9. R. v.1

R. **O give thanks to the Lord, for he is good;**
    for his love has no end.
    Or: **Alleluia!**

Let them say this, the Lord's redeemed,
whom he redeemed from the hand of the foe
and gathered from far-off lands,
from east and west, north and south. R.

Some wandered in the desert, in the wilderness,
finding no way to a city they could dwell in.
Hungry they were and thirsty;
their soul was fainting within them. R.

Then they cried to the Lord in their need
and he rescued them from their distress
and he led them along the right way,
to reach a city they could dwell in. R.

Let them thank the Lord for his love,
for the wonders he does for men.

For he satisfies the thirsty soul;
he fills the hungry with good things. R.

R. **O give thanks to the Lord, for he is good;**
   for his love has no end.
   Or: **Alleluia!**

Prayer

Let us pray.
Lord, God of power,
who restore what has fallen
and preserve what you have restored,
increase, we pray, the peoples
to be renewed by the sanctification
    of your name,
that all who are washed clean
    by holy Baptism
may always be directed
    by your prompting.
Through Christ our Lord.
R. Amen.

Or:

O God, who have brought us
    to rebirth by the word of life,
pour out upon us your Holy Spirit,
that, walking in oneness of faith,
we may attain in our flesh
the incorruptible glory
    of the resurrection.
Through Christ our Lord.
R. Amen.

Or:

May your people exult for ever,
    O God,
in renewed youthfulness of spirit,
so that, rejoicing now in the restored
    glory of our adoption,
we may look forward
in confident hope

Oremus.
Domine, Deus virtutum,
qui collapsa reparas
    et reparata conservas,
auge populos in tui nominis
    sanctificatione renovandos,
ut omnes, qui sacro
    Baptismate diluuntur,
tua semper inspiratione dirigantur.
Per Christum Dominum nostrum.
R. Amen.

Vel:

Deus, qui nos verbo vitæ regenerasti,
effunde super nos
    Spiritum Sanctum tuum,
ut, in unitate fidei ambulantes,
ad incorruptibilem glorificandæ
    carnis resurrectionem
pervenire mereamur.
Per Christum Dominum nostrum.
R. Amen.

Vel:

Semper exsultet populus
    tuus, Deus,
Spiritu Sancto tuo renovata
    animæ iuventute,
ut, qui nunc lætatur in adoptionis
    se gloriam restitutum,
resurrectionis diem spe certæ

to the rejoicing of the day
   of resurrection.
Through Christ our Lord.
R. Amen.

gratulationis exspectet.
Per Christum Dominum nostrum.
R. Amen.

FOURTH READING

A reading from the prophet Joel   3:1-5

I will pour out my spirit on all people.

Thus says the Lord:

   'I will pour out my spirit on all mankind.
   Your sons and daughters shall prophesy,
   your old men shall dream dreams,
   and your young men see visions.
   Even on the slaves, men and women,
   will I pour out my spirit in those days.
   I will display portents in heaven and on earth,
   blood and fire and columns of smoke.'

The sun will be turned into darkness,
and the moon into blood,
before the day of the Lord dawns,
that great and terrible day.
All who call on the name of the Lord will be saved,
for on Mount Sion there will be some who have escaped,
as the Lord has said,
and in Jerusalem some survivors whom the Lord will call.

   The word of the Lord.

Responsorial Psalm   Ps 103:1-2a,24,35c,27-28,29bc-30. R. v.30

R. **Send forth your Spirit, O Lord,**
   and renew the face of the earth.
   Or: **Alleluia!**

   Bless the Lord, my soul!
   Lord God, how great you are,
   clothed in majesty and glory,
   wrapped in light as in a robe! R.

   How many are your works, O Lord!
   In wisdom you have made them all.
   The earth is full of your riches.
   Bless the Lord, my soul. R.

All of these look to you
to give them their food in due season.
You give it, they gather it up:
you open your hand, they have their fill. R.

You take back your spirit, they die,
returning to the dust from which they came.
You send forth your spirit, they are created;
and you renew the face of the earth. R.

R. **Send forth your Spirit, O Lord,
and renew the face of the earth.**
Or: **Alleluia!**

Prayer

Let us pray.	Oremus.
Fulfil for us your gracious promise, O Lord, we pray,	Promissionem tuam, quǽsumus, Domine,
so that by his coming	super nos propitiatus adimple,
the Holy Spirit may make us witnesses before the world	ut Spiritus Sanctus adveniens nos coram mundo testes efficiat
to the Gospel of our Lord Jesus Christ.	Evangelii Domini nostri Iesu Christi.
Who lives and reigns for ever and ever.	Qui tecum vivit et regnat in sǽcula sæculorum.
R. Amen.	R. Amen.

Then the Priest intones the hymn **Gloria in excelsis Deo** (Glory to God in the highest).

When the hymn is concluded, the Priest says the Collect in the usual way: **Almighty ever-living God, who willed**, as here below (p.477).

Then the reader proclaims the reading from the Apostle (Rm 8:22-27) pp.478-479, and Mass continues in the usual way.

If Vespers (Evening Prayer) are joined to Mass, after Communion with the Communion Antiphon (**On the last day**), the Magnificat is sung, with its Vespers antiphon (**Veni, Sancte Spiritus**); then the Prayer after Communion is said and the rest follows as usual.

At the Vigil Mass

SIMPLE FORM

This Mass is used on the Saturday evening, either before or after First Vespers (Evening Prayer I) of Pentecost Sunday.

Entrance Antiphon Rm 5:5; Cf. 8:11 | Ant. ad introitum

THE love of God has been poured into our hearts through the Spirit of God dwelling within us, alleluia.

CARITAS Dei diffusa est in cordibus nostris per inhabitantem Spiritum eius in nobis, alleluia.

The Gloria in excelsis (Glory to God in the highest) is said.

Collect | Collecta

Almighty ever-living God,
who willed the Paschal Mystery
to be encompassed as a sign
    in fifty days,
grant that from out
    of the scattered nations
the confusion of many tongues
may be gathered by heavenly grace
into one great confession
    of your name.
Through our Lord Jesus Christ,
    your Son,
who lives and reigns with you
    in the unity of the Holy Spirit,
God, for ever and ever.

Omnipotens sempiterne Deus,
qui paschale sacramentum
quinquaginta dierum voluisti
    mysterio contineri,
præsta, ut, gentium
    facta dispersione,
divisiones linguarum ad unam
    confessionem tui nominis
cælesti munere congregentur.
Per Dominum nostrum Iesum
    Christum Filium tuum,
qui tecum vivit et regnat
    in unitate Spiritus Sancti,
Deus, per omnia sæcula sæculorum.

Or: | Vel:

Grant, we pray, almighty God,
that the splendour of your glory
may shine forth upon us
and that, by the bright rays
    of the Holy Spirit,
the light of your light may confirm
    the hearts
of those born again by your grace.

Præsta, quæsumus,
    omnipotens Deus,
ut claritatis tuæ super nos
    splendor effulgeat,
et lux tuæ lucis corda eorum,
qui per tuam gratiam sunt renati,
Sancti Spiritus
    illustratione confirmet.

| Through our Lord Jesus Christ, your Son, who lives and reigns with you in the unity of the Holy Spirit, God, for ever and ever. | Per Dominum nostrum Iesum Christum Filium tuum, qui tecum vivit et regnat in unitate Spiritus Sancti, Deus, per omnia sæcula sæculorum. |

FIRST READING

There is a choice of four texts for the First Reading: Either Genesis 11:1-9 (On Babel), p.469; or Exodus 19:3-8,16-20 (On God's descent on Mount Sinai), p.470; or Ezekiel 37:1-14 (On the dry bones and God's spirit), p.472; or Joel 3:1-5 (On the outpouring of the Spirit), p.475.

Responsorial Psalm   Ps 103:1-2,24,27-30,35. R. Cf. v.30

R. **Send forth your spirit, O Lord,
   and renew the face of the earth.**
   Or: **Alleluia!**

   Bless the Lord, my soul!
   Lord God, how great you are,
   clothed in majesty and glory,
   wrapped in light as in a robe! R.

   How many are your works, O Lord!
   In wisdom you have made them all.
   The earth is full of your riches.
   Bless the Lord, my soul. R.

   All of these look to you
   to give them their food in due season.
   You give it, they gather it up:
   you open your hand, they have their fill. R.

   You take back your spirit, they die,
   returning to the dust from which they came.
   You send forth your spirit, they are created;
   and you renew the face of the earth. R.

SECOND READING

A reading from the letter of St Paul to the Romans   8:22-27

The Spirit himself expresses our plea in a way that could never be put into words.

From the beginning till now the entire creation, as we know, has been groaning in one great act of giving birth; and not only creation, but all of us who possess the first-fruits of the Spirit, we too groan inwardly as we wait for our bodies to be set free. For we must be content to hope that we shall be saved – our salvation is not in sight, we should not have to be hoping for it if it were – but, as I say, we must hope to be saved since we are not saved yet – it is something we must wait for with patience.

The Spirit too comes to help us in our weakness. For when we cannot choose words in order to pray properly, the Spirit himself expresses our plea in a way that could never be put into words, and God who knows everything in our hearts knows perfectly well what he means, and that the pleas of the saints expressed by the Spirit are according to the mind of God.

The word of the Lord.

Gospel Acclamation

R. **Alleluia, alleluia!**
Come, Holy Spirit, fill the hearts of your faithful
and kindle in them the fire of your love.
R. **Alleluia!**

GOSPEL

A reading from the holy Gospel according to John   7:37-39
From his breast shall flow fountains of living water.

On the last day and greatest day of the festival, Jesus stood there and cried out:

'If any man is thirsty, let him come to me!
Let the man come and drink who believes in me!'

As scripture says: From his breast shall flow fountains of living water.

He was speaking of the Spirit which those who believed in him were to receive; for there was no Spirit as yet because Jesus had not yet been glorified.

The Gospel of the Lord.

The Creed is said.

Prayer over the Offerings	Super oblata
Pour out upon these gifts the blessing of your Spirit, we pray, O Lord, so that through them your Church may be imbued with such love that the truth of your saving mystery may shine forth for the whole world. Through Christ our Lord.	Præsentia munera, quæsumus, Domine, Spiritus tui benedictione perfunde, ut per ipsa Ecclesiæ tuæ ea dilectio tribuatur, per quam salutaris mysterii toto mundo veritas enitescat. Per Christum Dominum nostrum.

Preface: The Mystery of Pentecost.

It is truly right and just,
  our duty and our salvation,
always and everywhere
  to give you thanks,
Lord, holy Father,
  almighty and eternal God.
For, bringing your Paschal Mystery
  to completion,
you bestowed the Holy Spirit today
on those you made
  your adopted children
by uniting them to your Only
  Begotten Son.
This same Spirit,
  as the Church came to birth,
opened to all peoples
  the knowledge of God
and brought together the many
  languages of the earth
in profession of the one faith.

Therefore, overcome with paschal joy,
every land, every people exults
  in your praise
and even the heavenly Powers,
  with the angelic hosts,
sing together the unending hymn
  of your glory,
as they acclaim:

Holy, Holy, Holy Lord God of hosts...

Præfatio: De mysterio Pentecostes.

Vere dignum et iustum est,
  æquum et salutare,
nos tibi semper et ubique
  gratias agere:
Domine, sancte Pater,
  omnipotens æterne Deus.
Tu enim, sacramentum
  paschale consummans,
quibus, per Unigeniti tui consortium,
filios adoptionis esse tribuisti,
hodie Spiritum Sanctum es largitus;
qui, principio nascentis Ecclesiæ,
et cunctis gentibus scientiam
  indidit deitatis,
et linguarum diversitatem in unius
  fidei confessione sociavit.

Quapropter, profusis
  paschalibus gaudiis,
totus in orbe terrarum
  mundus exsultat.
Sed et supernæ virtutes atque
  angelicæ potestates
hymnum gloriæ tuæ concinunt,
  sine fine dicentes:

Sanctus, Sanctus, Sanctus. . .

When the Roman Canon is used, the proper form of the **Communicantes** (**In communion with those**) is said.

Communion Antiphon   Jn 7:37

On the last day of the festival,
  Jesus stood and cried out:
If anyone is thirsty, let him come
  to me and drink, alleluia.

Ant. ad communionem

Ultimo festivitatis die, stabat Iesus
  et clamabat dicens:
Si quis sitit, veniat ad me et bibat,
  alleluia.

Prayer after Communion

May these gifts we have consumed
benefit us, O Lord,
that we may always be aflame
    with the same Spirit,
whom you wondrously poured out
    on your Apostles.
Through Christ our Lord.

Post communionem

Hæc nobis, Domine,
    munera sumpta proficiant,
ut illo iugiter Spiritu ferveamus,
quem Apostolis tuis
    ineffabiliter infudisti.
Per Christum Dominum nostrum.

A formula of Solemn Blessing, pp.138-141, may be used.

To dismiss the people the Deacon or, if there is no Deacon, the Priest himself sings or says:

Go forth, the Mass is ended,
    alleluia, alleluia.

Ite, missa est, alleluia, alleluia.

Or:

Go in peace, alleluia, alleluia.

Vel:

Ite in pace, alleluia, alleluia.

And the people reply:

Thanks be to God, alleluia, alleluia.

Omnes respondent:

R. Deo gratias, alleluia, alleluia.

At the Mass during the Day

Entrance Antiphon   Ws 1:7

THE Spirit of the Lord has filled
    the whole world
and that which contains all things
understands what is said, alleluia.

Ant. ad introitum

SPIRITUS Domini replevit
    orbem terrarum,
et hoc quod continet omnia
scientiam habet vocis, alleluia.

Or: Rm 5:5; Cf. 8:11

The love of God has been poured
    into our hearts
through the Spirit of God dwelling
    within us, alleluia.

Vel:

Caritas Dei diffusa
    est in cordibus nostris
per inhabitantem Spiritum eius
    in nobis, alleluia.

The Gloria in excelsis (Glory to God in the highest) is said.

Collect

O God, who by the mystery
    of today's great feast
sanctify your whole Church
    in every people and nation,

Collecta

Deus, qui sacramento
    festivitatis hodiernæ
universam Ecclesiam tuam
in omni gente et natione sanctificas,

pour out, we pray, the gifts
    of the Holy Spirit
across the face of the earth
and, with the divine grace that
    was at work
when the Gospel
    was first proclaimed,
fill now once more the hearts
    of believers.
Through our Lord Jesus Christ,
    your Son,
who lives and reigns with you
    in the unity of the Holy Spirit,
God, for ever and ever.

in totam mundi latitudinem
    Spiritus Sancti dona defunde,
et, quod inter ipsa evangelicæ
    prædicationis exordia
operata est divina dignatio,
nunc quoque per credentium
    corda perfunde.
Per Dominum nostrum Iesum
    Christum Filium tuum,
qui tecum vivit et regnat
    in unitate Spiritus Sancti,
Deus, per omnia sæcula sæculorum.

FIRST READING

A reading from the Acts of the Apostles   2:1-11

They were all filled with the Holy Spirit and began to speak.

When Pentecost day came round, the apostles had all met in one room, when suddenly they heard what sounded like a powerful wind from heaven, the noise of which filled the entire house in which they were sitting; and something appeared to them that seemed like tongues of fire; these separated and came to rest on the head of each of them. They were all filled with the Holy Spirit, and began to speak foreign languages as the Spirit gave them the gift of speech.

Now there were devout men living in Jerusalem from every nation under heaven, and at this sound they all assembled, each one bewildered to hear these men speaking his own language. They were amazed and astonished. 'Surely' they said 'all these men speaking are Galileans? How does it happen that each of us hears them in his own native language? Parthians, Medes and Elamites; people from Mesopotamia, Judaea and Cappadocia, Pontus and Asia, Phrygia and Pamphylia, Egypt and the parts of Libya round Cyrene; as well as visitors from Rome – Jews and proselytes alike – Cretans and Arabs; we hear them preaching in our own language about the marvels of God.'

The word of the Lord.

Responsorial Psalm   Ps 103:1,24,29-31,34. R. Cf. v.30

R. **Send forth your Spirit, O Lord,
and renew the face of the earth.**
Or: **Alleluia!**

Bless the Lord, my soul!
Lord God, how great you are.
How many are your works, O Lord!
The earth is full of your riches. R.

You take back your spirit, they die,
returning to the dust from which they came.
You send forth your spirit, they are created;
and you renew the face of the earth. R.

May the glory of the Lord last for ever!
May the Lord rejoice in his works!
May my thoughts be pleasing to him.
I find my joy in the Lord. R.

SECOND READING

A reading from the first letter of St Paul to the Corinthians   12:3-7,12-13
In the one Spirit we were all baptised.

No one can say, 'Jesus is Lord' unless he is under the influence of the
Holy Spirit.

There is a variety of gifts but always the same Spirit; there are all sorts
of service to be done, but always to the same Lord; working in all sorts of
different ways in different people, it is the same God who is working in all
of them. The particular way in which the Spirit is given to each person is
for a good purpose.

Just as a human body, though it is made up of many parts, is a single
unit because all these parts, though many, make one body, so it is with
Christ. In the one Spirit we were all baptised, Jews as well as Greeks, slaves
as well as citizens, and one Spirit was given to us all to drink.

The word of the Lord.

SEQUENCE

The sequence may be said or sung.

Holy Spirit, Lord of light,
From the clear celestial height
Thy pure beaming radiance give.

Come, thou Father of the poor,
Come with treasures which endure;
Come, thou light of all that live!

Thou, of all consolers best,
Thou, the soul's delightful guest,
Dost refreshing peace bestow.

Thou in toil art comfort sweet;
Pleasant coolness in the heat;
Solace in the midst of woe.

Light immortal, light divine,
Visit thou these hearts of thine,
And our inmost being fill:

If thou take thy grace away,
Nothing pure in man will stay;
All his good is turned to ill.

Heal our wounds,
   our strength renew;
On our dryness pour thy dew;
Wash the stains of guilt away.

Bend the stubborn heart and will;
Melt the frozen, warm the chill;
Guide the steps that go astray.

Thou, on us who evermore
Thee confess and thee adore,
thy sevenfold gifts descend:

Give us comfort when we die,
Give us life with thee on high;
Give us joys that never end.

Veni, Sancte Spiritus,
   et emitte cælitus
lucis tuæ radium.

Veni, pater pauperum,
   veni, dator munerum,
veni, lumen cordium.

Consolator optime,
   dulcis hospes animæ,
dulce refrigerium.

In labore requies,
   in æstu temperies,
in fletu solacium.

O lux beatissima,
   reple cordis intima
tuorum fidelium.

Sine tuo numine,
nihil est in homine,
nihi est innoxium.

Lava quod est sordidum,
riga quod est aridum,
sana quod est saucium.

Flecte quod est rigidum,
fove quod est frigidum,
rege quod est devium.

Da tuis fidelibus,
   in te confidentibus,
sacrum septenarium.

Da virtutis meritum
   da salutis exitum,
da perenne gaudium.

Gospel Acclamation

R. **Alleluia, alleluia!**
Come, Holy Spirit, fill the hearts of your faithful
and kindle in them the fire of your love.
R. **Alleluia!**

GOSPEL

A reading from the holy Gospel according to John   20:19-23
As the Father sent me, so am I sending you: receive the Holy Spirit.

In the evening of the first day of the week, the doors were closed in the room where the disciples were, for fear of the Jews. Jesus came and stood among them. He said to them, 'Peace be with you,' and showed them his hands and his side. The disciples were filled with joy when they saw the Lord, and he said to them again, 'Peace be with you.

> 'As the Father sent me,
> so am I sending you.'

After saying this he breathed on them and said:

> 'Receive the Holy Spirit.
> For those whose sins you forgive,
> they are forgiven;
> for those whose sins you retain,
> they are retained.'

The Gospel of the Lord.

The Creed is said.

Prayer over the Offerings	Super oblata
Grant, we pray, O Lord, that, as promised by your Son, the Holy Spirit may reveal to us more abundantly the hidden mystery of this sacrifice and graciously lead us into all truth. Through Christ our Lord.	Præsta, quæsumus, Domine, ut, secundum promissionem Filii tui, Spiritus Sanctus huius nobis sacrificii copiosius revelet arcanum, et omnem propitius reseret veritatem. Per Christum Dominum nostrum.
Preface: The Mystery of Pentecost.	Præfatio: De mysterio Pentecostes.
It is truly right and just, our duty and our salvation, always and everywhere to give you thanks, Lord, holy Father, almighty and eternal God. For, bringing your Paschal Mystery to completion, you bestowed the Holy Spirit today	Vere dignum et iustum est, æquum et salutare, nos tibi semper et ubique gratias agere: Domine, sancte Pater, omnipotens æterne Deus. Tu enim, sacramentum paschale consummans, quibus, per Unigeniti tui consortium,

on those you made
  your adopted children
by uniting them to your Only
  Begotten Son.
This same Spirit,
  as the Church came to birth,
opened to all peoples
  the knowledge of God
and brought together the many
  languages of the earth
in profession of the one faith.

Therefore, overcome with paschal joy,
every land, every people exults
  in your praise
and even the heavenly Powers,
  with the angelic hosts,
sing together the unending hymn
  of your glory,
as they acclaim:

Holy, Holy, Holy Lord God of hosts...

filios adoptionis esse tribuisti,
hodie Spiritum Sanctum es largitus;
qui, principio nascentis Ecclesiæ,
et cunctis gentibus scientiam
  indidit deitatis,
et linguarum diversitatem in unius
  fidei confessione sociavit.

Quapropter, profusis
  paschalibus gaudiis,
totus in orbe terrarum
  mundus exsultat.
Sed et supernæ virtutes atque
  angelicæ potestates
hymnum gloriæ tuæ concinunt,
sine fine dicentes:

Sanctus, Sanctus, Sanctus. . .

When the Roman Canon is used, the proper form of the **Communicantes** (In communion with those) is said.

Communion Antiphon   Ac 2:4,11

They were all filled
  with the Holy Spirit
and spoke of the marvels of God,
alleluia.

Ant. ad communionem

Repleti sunt omnes Spiritu Sancto,
loquentes magnalia Dei, alleluia.

Prayer after Communion

O God, who bestow heavenly gifts
  upon your Church,
safeguard, we pray, the grace you
  have given,
that the gift of the Holy Spirit
  poured out upon her
may retain all its force
and that this spiritual food
may gain her abundance
  of eternal redemption.
Through Christ our Lord.

Post communionem

Deus, qui Ecclesiæ tuæ cælestia
  dona largiris,
custodi gratiam quam dedisti,
ut Spiritus Sancti vigeat semper
  munus infusum,
et ad æternæ
  redemptionis augmentum
spiritalis esca proficiat.
Per Christum Dominum nostrum.

A formula of Solemn Blessing, pp.138-141, may be used.

To dismiss the people the Deacon or, if there is no Deacon, the Priest himself sings or says:

Go forth, the Mass is ended, alleluia, alleluia.	Ite, missa est, alleluia, alleluia.
Or:	Vel:
Go in peace, alleluia, aleluia.	Ite in pace, alleluia, alleluia.
And the people reply:	Omnes respondent:
Thanks be to God, alleluia, alleluia.	Deo gratias, alleluia, alleluia.

With Easter Time now concluded, the paschal candle is extinguished. It is desirable to keep the paschal candle in the baptistery with due honour so that it is lit at the celebration of Baptism and the candles of those baptised are lit from it.

4 June

THE MOST HOLY TRINITY

The world God created was good, beautiful, but after sin, the world is marked by evil and corruption. We men and women are sinners, all of us; hence, God could intervene to judge the world, to destroy evil and castigate sinners. Instead, he loves the world, despite its sins; God loves each one of us even when we make mistakes and distance ourselves from him. God the Father loves the world so much that, in order to save it, He gives what is most precious to him: his only-begotten Son, who gives his life for humanity, rises again, returns to the Father and together with him sends the Holy Spirit. The Trinity is therefore Love, wholly at the service of the world, which he wishes to save and re-create.

(Pope Francis)

Solemnity

Entrance Antiphon	Ant. ad introitum
BLEST be God the Father, and the Only Begotten Son of God, and also the Holy Spirit, for he has shown us his merciful love.	BENEDICTUS sit Deus Pater, Unigenitusque Dei Filius, Sanctus quoque Spiritus, quia fecit nobiscum misericordiam suam.

The Gloria in excelsis (Glory to God in the highest) is said.

Collect

God our Father, who by sending
   into the world
the Word of truth and the Spirit
   of sanctification
made known to the human race
   your wondrous mystery,
grant us, we pray, that in professing
   the true faith,
we may acknowledge the Trinity
   of eternal glory
and adore your Unity,
   powerful in majesty.
Through our Lord Jesus Christ,
   your Son,
who lives and reigns with you
   in the unity of the Holy Spirit,
God, for ever and ever.

Collecta

Deus Pater, qui Verbum veritatis
et Spiritum sanctificationis mittens
   in mundum,
admirabile mysterium tuum
   hominibus declarasti,
da nobis, in confessione veræ fidei,
æternæ gloriam Trinitatis agnoscere,
et Unitatem adorare
   in potentia maiestatis.
Per Dominum nostrum Iesum
   Christum Filium tuum,
qui tecum vivit et regnat
   in unitate Spiritus Sancti,
Deus, per omnia sæcula sæculorum.

FIRST READING

A reading from the book of Exodus   34:4-6,8-9

Lord, Lord, a God of tenderness and compassion.

With the two tablets of stone in his hands, Moses went up the mountain of Sinai in the early morning as the Lord had commanded him. And the Lord descended in the form of a cloud, and Moses stood with him there.

He called on the name of the Lord. The Lord passed before him and proclaimed, 'Lord, Lord, a God of tenderness and compassion, slow to anger, rich in kindness and faithfulness.' And Moses bowed down to the ground at once and worshipped. 'If I have indeed won your favour, Lord,' he said 'let my Lord come with us, I beg. True, they are a headstrong people, but forgive us our faults and our sins, and adopt us as your heritage.'

The word of the Lord.

Responsional Psalm   Dn 3:52-56. R. v.52

> You are blest, Lord God of our fathers.

R. **To you glory and praise for evermore.**

> Blest your glorious holy name.

R. **To you glory and praise for evermore.**

> You are blest in the temple of your glory.

R. **To you glory and praise for evermore.**

> You are blest on the throne of your kingdom.

R. **To you glory and praise for evermore.**

> You are blest who gaze into the depths.

R. **To you glory and praise for evermore.**

> You are blest in the firmament of heaven.

R. **To you glory and praise for evermore.**

SECOND READING

A reading from the second letter of St Paul to the Corinthians   13:11-13
The grace of Jesus Christ, the love of God, and the fellowship of the Holy Spirit.

Brothers, we wish you happiness; try to grow perfect; help one another.
Be united; live in peace, and the God of love and peace will be with you.

Greet one another with the holy kiss. All the saints send you greetings.

The grace of the Lord Jesus Christ, the love of God and the fellowship
of the Holy Spirit be with you all.

The word of the Lord.

Gospel Acclamation   Cf. Rv 1:8

R. **Alleluia, alleluia!**
Glory be to the Father, and to the Son, and to the Holy Spirit,
the God who is, who was, and who is to come.
R. **Alleluia!**

GOSPEL

A reading from the holy Gospel according to John   3:16-18
God sent his Son so that through him the world might be saved.

Jesus said to Nicodemus:

> 'God loved the world so much
> that he gave his only Son,
> so that everyone who believes in him may not be lost

but may have eternal life.
For God sent his Son into the world
not to condemn the world,
but so that through him the world might be saved.
No one who believes in him will be condemned;
but whoever refuses to believe is condemned already,
because he has refused to believe
in the name of God's only Son.

The Gospel of the Lord.

The Creed is said.

Prayer over the Offerings	**Super oblata**
Sanctify by the invocation	Sanctifica, quæsumus,
of your name,	Domine Deus noster,
we pray, O Lord our God,	per tui nominis invocationem,
this oblation of our service,	hæc munera nostræ servitutis,
and by it make of us an eternal	et per ea nosmetipsos tibi perfice
offering to you.	munus æternum.
Through Christ our Lord.	Per Christum Dominum nostrum.
Preface: The Mystery of the Most Holy Trinity.	**Præfatio:** De mysterio Sanctissimæ Trinitatis.
It is truly right and just,	Vere dignum et iustum est,
our duty and our salvation,	æquum et salutare,
always and everywhere	nos tibi semper et ubique
to give you thanks,	gratias agere:
Lord, holy Father,	Domine, sancte Pater,
almighty and eternal God.	omnipotens æterne Deus:
For with your Only Begotten Son	Qui cum Unigenito Filio tuo
and the Holy Spirit	et Spiritu Sancto
you are one God, one Lord:	unus es Deus, unus es Dominus:
not in the unity of a single person,	non in unius singularitate personæ,
but in a Trinity of one substance.	sed in unius Trinitate substantiæ.
For what you have revealed to us	Quod enim de tua gloria,
of your glory	revelante te, credimus,
we believe equally of your Son	hoc de Filio tuo,
and of the Holy Spirit,	hoc de Spiritu Sancto,
so that, in the confessing of the true	sine discretione sentimus.
and eternal Godhead,	

you might be adored in what
   is proper to each Person,
their unity in substance,
and their equality in majesty.

For this is praised by Angels
   and Archangels,
Cherubim, too, and Seraphim,
who never cease to cry out each day,
as with one voice they acclaim:

Holy, Holy, Holy Lord God of hosts...

Ut in confessione veræ
   sempiternæque Deitatis,
et in personis proprietas,
et in essentia unitas,
et in maiestate adoretur æqualitas.

Quem laudant Angeli
   atque Archangeli,
Cherubim quoque ac Seraphim,
qui non cessant clamare cotidie,
   una voce dicentes:

Sanctus, Sanctus, Sanctus . . .

Communion Antiphon   Ga 4:6

Since you are children of God,
God has sent into your hearts
   the Spirit of his Son,
the Spirit who cries out:
   Abba, Father.

Ant. ad communionem

Quoniam autem estis filii,
misit Deus Spiritum Filii sui
   in corda vestra
clamantem: Abba, Pater.

Prayer after Communion

May receiving this Sacrament,
   O Lord our God,
bring us health of body and soul,
as we confess your eternal holy
   Trinity and undivided Unity.
Through Christ our Lord.

Post communionem

Proficiat nobis ad salutem
   corporis et animæ,
Domine Deus noster,
   huius sacramenti susceptio,
et sempiternæ sanctæ Trinitatis
eiusdemque individuæ
   Unitatis confessio.
Per Christum Dominum nostrum

11 June

THE MOST HOLY BODY AND BLOOD OF CHRIST (CORPUS CHRISTI)

The Lord, offering himself to us in the simplicity of bread, also invites us not to waste our lives in chasing the myriad illusions that we think we cannot do without, yet that leave us empty within. The Eucharist satisfies our hunger for material things and kindles our desire to serve. It raises us from our comfortable and lazy lifestyle and reminds us that we are not only mouths to be fed, but also his hands, to be used to help feed others. It is especially urgent now to take care of those who hunger for food and for dignity, of those without work and those who struggle to carry on. And this we must do in a real way, as real as the Bread that Jesus gives us. Genuine closeness is needed, as are true bonds of solidarity. In the Eucharist, Jesus draws close to us: let us not turn away from those around us!

(Pope Francis)

Solemnity

Entrance Antiphon   Cf. Ps 80:17

Here fed them with the finest wheat
and satisfied them with honey
  from the rock.

Ant. ad introitum

Cibavit eos ex adipe frumenti, et de petra melle saturavit eos.

The Gloria in excelsis (Glory to God in the highest) is said.

Collect

O God, who in this
  wonderful Sacrament
have left us a memorial
  of your Passion,
grant us, we pray,
so to revere the sacred mysteries
  of your Body and Blood
that we may always experience
  in ourselves
the fruits of your redemption.
Who live and reign
  with God the Father
in the unity of the Holy Spirit,
  God, for ever and ever.

Collecta

Deus, qui nobis sub
  sacramento mirabili
passionis tuæ memoriam reliquisti,
tribue, quæsumus,
ita nos Corporis et Sanguinis tui
  sacra mysteria venerari,
ut redemptionis tuæ fructum
  in nobis iugiter sentiamus.
Qui vivis et regnas cum Deo Patre
in unitate Spiritus Sancti,
Deus, per omnia sæcula sæculorum.

FIRST READING

A reading from the book of Deuteronomy 8:2-3,14-16

He fed you with manna which neither you nor your fathers had known.

Moses said to the people: 'Remember how the Lord your God led you for forty years in the wilderness, to humble you, to test you and know your inmost heart – whether you would keep his commandments or not. He humbled you, he made you feel hunger, he fed you with manna which neither you nor your fathers had known, to make you understand that man does not live on bread alone but that man lives on everything that comes from the mouth of the Lord.

'Do not then forget the Lord your God who brought you out of the land of Egypt, out of the house of slavery: who guided you through this vast and dreadful wilderness, a land of fiery serpents, scorpions, thirst; who in this waterless place brought you water from the hardest rock; who in this wilderness fed you with manna that your fathers had not known.'

The word of the Lord.

Responsorial Psalm   Ps 147:12-15,19-20. R. v.12

R. **O praise the Lord, Jerusalem!**
  Or: **Alleluia!**

O praise the Lord, Jerusalem!
Sion, praise your God!
He has strengthened the bars of your gates,
he has blessed the children within you. R.

He established peace on your borders,
he feeds you with finest wheat.
He sends out his word to the earth
and swiftly runs his command. R.

He makes his word known to Jacob,
to Israel his laws and decrees.
He has not dealt thus with other nations;
He has not taught them his decrees. R.

SECOND READING

A reading from the first letter of St Paul to the Corinthians   10:16-17

That there is only one loaf means that, though there are many of us, we form a single body.

The blessing-cup that we bless is a communion with the blood of Christ, and the bread that we break is a communion with the body of Christ. The fact that there is only one loaf means that, though there are many of us, we form a single body because we all have a share in this one loaf.

The word of the Lord.

SEQUENCE

The Sequence may be said or sung in full, or using the shorter form indicated by the asterisked verses.

Sing forth, O Sion, sweetly sing	Lauda Sion Salvatorem
The praises of thy Shepherd-King,	Lauda ducem et pastorem
In hymns and canticles divine;	In hymnis et canticis.
Dare all thou canst, thou hast no song	Quantum potes, tantum aude:
Worthy his praises to prolong,	Quia major omni laude,
So far surpassing powers like thine.	Nec laudare sufficis.
Today no theme of common praise	Laudis thema specialis,
Forms the sweet burden of thy lays –	Panis vivus et vitalis,
The living, life-dispensing food –	Hodie proponitur.
That food which at the sacred board	Quem in sacræ mensa cenæ,
Unto the brethren twelve our Lord	Turbæ fratrum duodenæ
His parting legacy bestowed.	Datum non ambigitur.
Then be the anthem clear and strong,	Sit laus plena, sit sonora,
Thy fullest note, thy sweetest song,	Sit iucunda, sit decora
The very music of thy breast:	Mentis iubilatio.
For now shines forth the day sublime	Dies enim solemnis agitur,
That brings remembrance of the time	In qua mensæ prima recolitur
When Jesus first his table blessed.	Huius institutio.
Within our new King's banquet-hall	In hac mensa novi Regis,
They meet to keep the festival	Novum Pascha novæ legis,
That closed the ancient paschal rite:	Phase vetus terminat.
The old is by the new replaced;	Vetustatem novitas,
The substance hath	Umbram fugat veritas,
the shadows chased;	Noctem lux eliminat.
And rising day dispels the night.	

Christ willed what He Himself
    had done
Should be renewed while time
    should run,
    in memory of His parting hour:
Thus, tutored in His school divine,
We consecrate the bread and wine;
    And lo – a Host of saving power.

This faith to Christian men is given –
Bread is made flesh by words
    from heaven:
    Into his Blood the wine is turned:
What though it baffles
    nature's powers
Of sense and sight? This faith of ours
    Proves more than nature
    e'er discerned.

Concealed beneath the two-fold sign,
Meet symbols of the gifts divine,
    There lie the mysteries adored:
The living body is our food;
Our drink the ever precious blood;
    In each, one undivided Lord.

Not he that eateth it divides
The sacred food, which whole abides
    Unbroken still, nor knows decay;
Be one, or be a thousand fed,
They eat alike the Living Bread
    Which, still received,
    ne'er wastes away.

The good, the guilty share therein,
With sure increase of grace or sin,
    The ghostly life, or ghostly death:
Death to the guilty; to the good
Immortal life. See how one food
    Man's joy or woe accomplisheth.

Quod in cœna Christus gessit,
Faciendum hoc expressit
    In sui memoriam.
Docti sacris institutis,
Panem, vinum, in salutis
    Consecramus hostiam.

Dogma datur Christianis,
Quod in carnem transit panis,
    Et vinum in sanguinem.
Quod non capis, quod non vides,
Animosa firmat fides,
    Præter rerum ordinem.

Sub diversis speciebus,
Signis tantum, et non rebus,
    Latent res eximiæ.
Caro cibus, sanguis potus:
Manet tamen Christus totus,
    Sub utraque specie.

A sumente non concisus,
Non confractus, non divisus:
    Integer accipitur.
Sumit unus, sumunt mille:
Quantum isti, tantum ille:
    Nec sumptus consumitur.

Sumunt boni, sumunt mali:
Sorte tamen inæquali,
    Vitæ vel interitus.
Mors est malis, vita bonis:
Vide paris sumptionis
    Quam sit dispar exitus.

We break the Sacrament; but bold
And firm thy faith shall keep its hold;
Deem not the whole doth
 more enfold
  Than in the fractured part resides:
Deem not that Christ doth broken lie;
'Tis but the sign that meets the eye;
The hidden deep reality
 In all its fulness still abides.

*Behold the bread of angels, sent
For pilgrims in their banishment,
The bread for God's true
 children meant,
  That may not unto dogs be given:
Oft in the olden types foreshadowed;
In Isaac on the altar bowed,
And in the ancient paschal food,
 And in the manna sent
 from heaven.

*Come then, good shepherd,
 bread divine,
Still show to us thy mercy sign;
Oh, feed us still, still keep us thine;
So may we see thy glories shine
 In fields of immortality;

*O thou, the wisest, mightiest, best,
Our present food, our future rest,
Come, make us each thy
 chosen guest,
Coheirs of thine, and comrades blest
 With saints whose dwelling
 is with thee.

Fracto demum Sacramento,
Ne vacilles, sed memento,
Tantum esse sub fragmento,
 Quantum toto tegitur.
Nulla rei fit scissura:
Signi tantum fit fractura:
Qua nec status nec statura
 Signati minuitur.

*Ecce panis Angelorum,
Factus cibus viatorum:
Vere panis filiorum,
 Non mittendus canibus.
In figuris præsignatur,
Cum Isaac immolatur:
Agnus paschæ deputatur
 Datur manna patribus.

*Bone pastor, panis vere,
Iesu, nostri miserere:
Tu nos pasce, nos tuere:
Tu nos bona fac videre
 In terra viventium.

*Tu, qui cuncta scis et vales:
Qui nos pascis hic mortales:
Tuos ibi commensales,
Cohæredes et sodales,
 Fac sanctorum civium.
Amen. Alleluia.

Gospel Acclamation   Jn 6:51

R. **Alleluia, alleluia!**
I am the living bread which has come down from heaven, says the Lord.
Anyone who eats this bread will live for ever.
R. **Alleluia**

GOSPEL

A reading from the holy Gospel according to John   6:51-58

My flesh is real food and my blood is real drink.

Jesus said to the Jews:

'I am the living bread which has come down from heaven.
Anyone who eats this bread will live for ever;
and the bread that I shall give
is my flesh, for the life of the world.'

Then the Jews started arguing with one another: 'How can this man give us his flesh to eat?' they said. Jesus replied:

'I tell you most solemnly,
if you do not eat the flesh of the Son of Man
and drink his blood,
you will not have life in you.
Anyone who does eat my flesh and drink my blood
has eternal life,
and I shall raise him up on the last day.
For my flesh is real food
and my blood is real drink.
He who eats my flesh and drinks my blood
lives in me
and I live in him.
As I, who am sent by the living Father,
myself draw life from the Father,
so whoever eats me will draw life from me.
This is the bread come down from heaven,
not like the bread our ancestors ate:
they are dead,
but anyone who eats this bread will live for ever.'

The Gospel of the Lord.

The Creed is said.

Prayer over the Offerings

Grant your Church, O Lord,
    we pray,
the gifts of unity and peace,
whose signs are to be seen in mystery
in the offerings we here present.
Through Christ our Lord.

Super oblata

Ecclesiæ tuæ, quæsumus, Domine,
unitatis et pacis propitius
    dona concede,
quæ sub oblatis muneribus
    mystice designantur.
Per Christum Dominum nostrum.

Preface of the Holy Eucharist I or II, pp.68-71.

Communion Antiphon   Jn 6:57

Whoever eats my flesh
    and drinks my blood
remains in me and I in him,
    says the Lord.

Ant. ad communionem

Qui manducat meam carnem
    et bibit meum sanguinem,
in me manet et ego in eo,
    dicit Dominus.

Prayer after Communion

Grant, O Lord, we pray,
that we may delight for all eternity
in that share in your divine life,
which is foreshadowed
    in the present age
by our reception of your precious
    Body and Blood.
Who live and reign for ever and ever.

Post communionem

Fac nos, quæsumus, Domine,
divinitatis tuæ sempiterna
    fruitione repleri,
quam pretiosi Corporis
    et Sanguinis tui
temporalis perceptio præfigurat.
Qui vivis et regnas
    in sæcula sæculorum.

It is desirable that a procession take place after the Mass in which the Host to be carried in the procession is consecrated. However, nothing prohibits a procession from taking place even after a public and lengthy period of adoration following the Mass. If a procession takes place after Mass, when the Communion of the faithful is over, the monstrance in which the consecrated host has been placed is set on the altar. When the Prayer after Communion has been said, the Concluding Rites are omitted and the procession forms.

16 June

THE MOST SACRED HEART OF JESUS

Jesus remains faithful, he never betrays us: even when we were wrong, he always waits for us to forgive us: he is the face of the merciful Father. This love, this steadfastness of the Lord manifests the humility of his heart: Jesus did not come to conquer men like the kings and the powerful of this world, but he came to offer love with gentleness and humility. This is how he defined himself: "learn from me; for I am gentle and lowly in heart". And the significance of the feast of the Sacred Heart of Jesus, which we are celebrating today, is to discover ever more and to let ourselves be enfolded by the humble faithfulness and the gentleness of Christ's love, revelation of the Father's mercy.

(Pope Francis)

Solemnity

Entrance Antiphon   Ps 32:11,19

THE designs of his Heart
are from age to age,
to rescue their souls from death,
and to keep them alive in famine.

Ant. ad introitum

COGITATIONES Cordis eius in
generatione et generationem,
ut eruat a morte animas eorum
    et alat eos in fame.

The **Gloria in excelsis** (Glory to God in the highest) is said.

Collect

Grant, we pray, almighty God,
that we, who glory in the Heart
    of your beloved Son
and recall the wonders of his
    love for us,
may be made worthy to receive
an overflowing measure of grace
from that fount of heavenly gifts.

Collecta

Concede, quæsumus,
    omnipotens Deus,
ut qui, dilecti Filii tui
    Corde gloriantes,
eius præcipua in nos beneficia
    recolimus caritatis,
de illo donorum fonte cælesti
supereffluentem gratiam
    mereamur accipere.

Through our Lord Jesus Christ,
your Son,
who lives and reigns with you in the
unity of the Holy Spirit,
God, for ever and ever.

Per Dominum nostrum Iesum
Christum Filium tuum,
qui tecum vivit et regnat in unitate
Spiritus Sancti, Deus,
per omnia sæcula sæculorum.

Or:

Vel:

O God, who in the Heart of your Son,
wounded by our sins,
bestow on us in mercy
the boundless treasures of your love,
grant, we pray,
that, in paying him the homage
of our devotion
we may also offer
worthy reparation.
Through our Lord Jesus Christ,
your Son,
who lives and reigns with you
in the unity of the Holy Spirit,
God, for ever and ever.

Deus, qui nobis in Corde Filii tui,
nostris vulnerato peccatis,
infinitos dilectionis thesauros
misericorditer largiri dignaris,
concede, quæsumus,
ut, illi devotum pietatis nostræ
præstantes obsequium,
dignæ quoque satisfactionis
exhibeamus officium.
Per Dominum nostrum Iesum
Christum Filium tuum,
qui tecum vivit et regnat
in unitate Spiritus Sancti,
Deus, per omnia sæcula sæculorum.

FIRST READING

A reading from the book of Deuteronomy   7:6-11

The Lord set his heart on you and chose you.

Moses said to the people: 'You are a people consecrated to the Lord your God; it is you that the Lord our God has chosen to be his very own people out of all the peoples on the earth.

'If the Lord set his heart on you and chose you, it was not because you outnumbered other peoples: you were the least of all peoples. It was for love of you and to keep the oath he swore to your fathers that the Lord brought you out with his mighty hand and redeemed you from the house of slavery, from the power of Pharaoh king of Egypt. Know then that the Lord your God is God indeed, the faithful God who is true to his covenant and his graciousness for a thousand generations towards those who love him and keep his commandments, but who punishes in their own persons those that hate him; he makes him work out his punishment in person.

You are therefore to keep and observe the commandments and statutes
and ordinances that I lay down for you today.'

The word of the Lord.

Responsorial Psalm

Ps 102:1-4,6-8,10. R. v.17

R. **The love of the Lord is everlasting**
   upon those who hold him in fear.

My soul, give thanks to the Lord,
all my being, bless his holy name.
My soul, give thanks to the Lord
and never forget all his blessings. R.

It is he who forgives all your guilt,
who heals every one of your ills,
who redeems your life from the grave,
who crowns you with love and compassion. R.

The Lord does deeds of justice,
gives judgment for all who are oppressed.
He made known his ways to Moses
and his deeds to Israel's sons. R.

The Lord is compassion and love,
slow to anger and rich in mercy.
He does not treat us according to our sins
nor repay us according to our faults. R.

SECOND READING

A reading from the first letter of St John

4:7-16

Love comes from God.

My dear people,
let us love one another
since love comes from God
and everyone who loves is begotten by God and knows God.
Anyone who fails to love can never have known God,
because God is love.
God's love for us was revealed
when God sent into the world his only Son
so that we could have life through him;
this is the love I mean:

not our love for God,
but God's love for us when he sent his Son
to be the sacrifice that takes our sins away.
My dear people,
since God has loved us so much,
we too should love one another.
No one has ever seen God;
but as long as we love one another
God will live in us
and his love will be complete in us.
We can know that we are living in him
and he is living in us
because he lets us share his Spirit.
We ourselves saw and we testify
that the Father sent his Son
as saviour of the world.
If anyone acknowledges that Jesus is the Son of God,
God lives in him, and he in God.
We ourselves have known and put our faith in
God's love towards ourselves.
God is love
and anyone who lives in love lives in God,
and God lives in him.

The word of the Lord.

Gospel Acclamation   Mt 11:29

R. **Alleluia, alleluia!**
Shoulder my yoke and learn from me,
for I am gentle and humble in heart.
R. **Alleluia!**

GOSPEL

A reading from the holy Gospel according to Matthew   11:25-30

I am gentle and humble in heart.

Jesus exclaimed, 'I bless you, Father, Lord of heaven and of earth, for
hiding these things from the learned and the clever and revealing them to
mere children. Yes, Father, for that is what it pleased you to do. Everything
has been entrusted to me by my Father; and no one knows the Son except

the Father, just as no one knows the Father except the Son and those to whom the Son chooses to reveal him.

'Come to me, all you who labour and are overburdened, and I will give you rest. Shoulder my yoke and learn from me, for I am gentle and humble in heart, and you will find rest for your souls. Yes, my yoke is easy and my burden light.'

The Gospel of the Lord.

The Creed is said.

Prayer over the Offerings

Look, O Lord, we pray,
    on the surpassing charity
in the Heart of your beloved Son,
that what we offer may be a gift
    acceptable to you
and an expiation of our offences.
Through Christ our Lord.

Super oblata

Respice, quæsumus, Domine,
ad ineffabilem Cordis dilecti Filii
    tui caritatem,
ut quod offerimus sit tibi
    munus acceptum
et nostrorum expiatio delictorum.
Per Christum Dominum nostrum.

Preface: The boundless charity of Christ.

Præfatio: De immense caritate Christi.

It is truly right and just,
    our duty and our salvation,
always and everywhere
    to give you thanks,
Lord, holy Father,
    almighty and eternal God,
through Christ our Lord.

For raised up high on the Cross,
he gave himself up for us
    with a wonderful love
and poured out blood and water
    from his pierced side,
the wellspring of the Church's
    Sacraments,
so that, won over to the open heart
    of the Saviour,
all might draw water joyfully
    from the springs of salvation.

Vere dignum et iustum est,
    æquum et salutare,
nos tibi semper et ubique
    gratias agere:
Domine, sancte Pater,
    omnipotens æterne Deus:
per Christum Dominum nostrum:

Qui, mira caritate, exaltatus in cruce,
pro nobis tradidit semetipsum,
atque de transfixo latere sanguinem
    fudit et aquam,
ex quo manarent Ecclesiæ
    sacramenta,
ut omnes, ad Cor apertum
    Salvatoris attracti,
iugiter haurirent e fontibus salutis
    in gaudio.

And so, with all the Angels
and Saints,
we praise you, as without end
we acclaim:

Holy, Holy, Holy Lord God of hosts...

Et ideo, cum Sanctis
et Angelis universis,
te collaudamus, sine fine dicentes:

Sanctus, Sanctus, Sanctus . . .

Communion Antiphon Cf. Jn 7:37-38

Ant. ad communionem

Thus says the Lord:
Let whoever is thirsty come to me
and drink.
Streams of living water will flow
from within the one who believes
in me.

Dicit Dominus:
Si quis sitit, veniat ad me et bibat.
Qui credit in me, flumina de ventre
eius fluent aquæ vivæ.

Or: Jn 19:34

Vel:

One of the soldiers opened his side
with a lance,
and at once there came forth blood
and water.

Unus militum lancea
latus eius aperuit,
et continuo exivit sanguis et aqua.

Prayer after Communion

Post communionem

May this sacrament of charity,
O Lord,
make us fervent with the fire
of holy love,
so that, drawn always to your Son,
we may learn to see him in
our neighbour.
Through Christ our Lord.

Sacramentum caritatis, Domine,
sancta nos faciat dilectione fervere,
qua, ad Filium tuum
semper attracti,
ipsum in fratribus
agnoscere discamus.
Qui vivit et regnat
in sæcula sæculorum.

18 June

ELEVENTH SUNDAY IN ORDINARY TIME

Entrance Antiphon   Cf. Ps 26:7,9 | Ant. ad introitum

O LORD, hear my voice,
for I have called to you;
be my help.
Do not abandon or forsake me,
O God, my Saviour!

E XAUDI, Domine, vocem meam,
qua clamavi ad te.
Adiutor meus esto,
ne derelinquas me,
neque despicias me,
Deus salutaris meus.

Collect | Collecta

O God, strength of those
who hope in you,
graciously hear our pleas,
and, since without you mortal
frailty can do nothing,
grant us always the help
of your grace,
that in following your commands
we may please you by our resolve
and our deeds.
Through our Lord Jesus Christ,
your Son,
who lives and reigns with you
in the unity of the Holy Spirit,
God, for ever and ever.

Deus, in te sperantium fortitudo,
invocationibus nostris
adesto propitius,
et, quia sine te nihil potest
mortalis infirmitas,
gratiæ tuæ præsta semper auxilium,
ut, in exsequendis mandatis tuis,
et voluntate tibi
et actione placeamus.
Per Dominum nostrum Iesum
Christum Filium tuum,
qui tecum vivit et regnat
in unitate Spiritus Sancti,
Deus, per omnia sæcula sæculorum.

FIRST READING

A reading from the book of Exodus   19:2-6
I will count you a kingdom of priests, a consecrated nation.

From Rephidim the Israelites set out again; and when they reached the wilderness of Sinai, there in the wilderness they pitched their camp; there facing the mountain Israel pitched camp.

Moses then went up to God, and the Lord called to him from the mountain, saying, 'Say this to the House of Jacob, declare this to the sons of Israel, "You yourselves have seen what I did with the Egyptians, how

I carried you on eagle's wings and brought you to myself. From this you know that now, if you obey my voice and hold fast to my covenant, you of all the nations shall be my very own, for all the earth is mine. I will count you a kingdom of priests, a consecrated nation.'"

The word of the Lord.

Responsial Psalm   Ps 99:1-3,5. R. v.3

R. **We are his people:**
   the sheep of his flock.

Cry out with joy to the Lord, all the earth.
Serve the Lord with gladness.
Come before him, singing for joy.   R.

Know that he, the Lord, is God.
He made us, we belong to him,
we are his people, the sheep of his flock.   R.

Indeed, how good is the Lord,
eternal his merciful love.
He is faithful from age to age.   R.

SECOND READING

A reading from the letter of St Paul to the Romans   5:6-11

Now that we have been reconciled by the death of his Son, surely we may count on being saved by the life of his Son.

We were still helpless when at his appointed moment Christ died for sinful men. It is not easy to die even for a good man – though of course for someone really worthy, a man mighty be prepared to die – but what proves that God loves us is that Christ died for us while we were still sinners. Having died to make us righteous, is it likely that he would now fail to save us from God's anger? When we were reconciled to God by the death of his Son, we were still enemies; now that we have been reconciled, surely we may count on being saved by the life of his Son? Not merely because we have been reconciled but because we are filled with joyful trust in God through our Lord Jesus Christ, through whom we have already gained our reconciliation.

The word of the Lord.

Gospel Acclamation   Jn 10:27

R. **Alleluia, alleluia!**
The sheep that belong to me listen to my voice,
says the Lord,
I know them and they follow me.
R. **Alleluia!**

Or: Mk 1:15

R. **Alleluia, alleluia!**
The kingdom of God is close at hand.
Repent, and believe the Good News.
R. **Alleluia!**

GOSPEL

A reading from the holy Gospel according to Matthew   9:36-10:8
He summoned his twelve disciples and sent them out.

When Jesus saw the crowds he felt sorry for them because they were
harassed and dejected, like sheep without a shepherd. Then he said to his
disciples, 'The harvest is rich but the labourers are few, so ask the Lord of
the harvest to send labourers to his harvest.'

He summoned his twelve disciples, and gave them authority over
unclean spirits with power to cast them out and to cure all kinds of diseases
and sickness.

These are the names of the twelve apostles: first, Simon who is called
Peter, and his brother Andrew; James the son of Zebedee, and his brother
John; Philip and Bartholomew; Thomas, and Matthew the tax collector;
James the son of Alphaeus, and Thaddaeus; Simon the Zealot and Judas
Iscariot, the one who was to betray him. These twelve Jesus sent out,
instructing them as follows:

'Do not turn your steps to pagan territory, and do not enter any
Samaritan town; go rather to the lost sheep of the House of Israel. And
as you go, proclaim that the kingdom of heaven is close at hand. Cure
the sick, raise the dead, cleanse the lepers, cast out devils. You received
without charge, give without charge.'

The Gospel of the Lord.

Prayer over the Offerings

O God, who in the offerings
    presented here
provide for the twofold needs
    of human nature,
nourishing us with food
and renewing us
    with your Sacrament,
grant, we pray,
that the sustenance they provide
may not fail us in body or in spirit.
Through Christ our Lord.

Super oblata

Deus, qui humani generis
    utramque substantiam
præsentium munerum
et alimento vegetas
    et renovas sacramento,
tribue, quæsumus, ut eorum
et corporibus nostris subsidium
    non desit et mentibus.
Per Christum Dominum nostrum.

Preface of Sundays in Ordinary Time I-VIII, pp.60-67.

Communion Antiphon   Ps 26:4

There is one thing I ask of the Lord,
    only this do I seek:
to live in the house of the Lord
    all the days of my life.

Or: Jn 17:11

Holy Father, keep in your name
    those you have given me,
that they may be one as we are one,
    says the Lord.

Ant. ad communionem

Unum petii a Domino,
    hoc requiram,
ut inhabitem in domo Domini
omnibus diebus vitæ meæ.

Vel:

Pater sancte,
    serva eos in nomine tuo,
quos dedisti mihi, ut sint unum
    sicut et nos, dicit Dominus.

Prayer after Communion

As this reception of your
    Holy Communion, O Lord,
foreshadows the union
    of the faithful in you,
so may it bring about unity
    in your Church.
Through Christ our Lord.

Post communionem

Hæc tua, Domine,
    sumpta sacra communio,
sicut fidelium in te
    unionem præsignat,
sic in Ecclesia tua unitatis
    operetur effectum.
Per Christum Dominum nostrum.

24 June

THE NATIVITY OF SAINT JOHN THE BAPTIST

Today, the liturgy invites us to celebrate the Solemnity of the Birth of St John the Baptist, whose life was totally directed to Christ, as was that of Mary, Christ's Mother. John the Baptist was the forerunner, the "voice" sent to proclaim the Incarnate Word. Thus, commemorating his birth actually means celebrating Christ, the fulfilment of the promises of all the prophets, among whom the greatest was the Baptist, called to "prepare the way" for the Messiah. All the Gospels introduce the narrative of Jesus's public life with the account of his baptism by John in the River Jordan. When Jesus, after receiving baptism, emerged from the water, John saw the Spirit descending upon him in the form of a dove. It was then that he "knew" the full reality of Jesus of Nazareth and began to make him "known to Israel", pointing him out as the Son of God and Redeemer of man: "Behold, the Lamb of God, who takes away the sin of the world!"

(Pope Benedict XVI)

Solemnity

At the Vigil Mass

This Mass is used on the evening of 23 June, either before or after First Vespers (Evening Prayer I) of the Solemnity.

Entrance Antiphon Lk 1:15-14	Ant. ad introitum
HE will be great in the sight of the Lord and will be filled with the Holy Spirit, even from his mother's womb; and many will rejoice at his birth.	HIC erit magnus coram Domino, et Spiritu Sancto replebitur adhuc ex utero matris suæ, et multi in nativitate eius gaudebunt.

The Gloria in excelsis (Glory to God in the highest) is said.

Collect	Collecta
Grant, we pray, almighty God, that your family may walk in the way of salvation and, attentive to what Saint John the Precursor urged, may come safely to the One he foretold, our Lord Jesus Christ.	Præsta, quæsumus, omnipotens Deus, ut familia tua per viam salutis incedat, et, beati Ioannis Præcursoris hortamenta sectando, ad eum quem prædixit, secura perveniat,

Who lives and reigns with you
　　in the unity of the Holy Spirit,
God, for ever and ever.

Dominum nostrum
　　Iesum Christum.
Qui tecum vivit et regnat
　　in unitate Spiritus Sancti,
Deus, per omnia sæcula sæculorum.

FIRST READING

A reading from the prophet Jeremiah 　　　　　1:4-10

Before I formed you in the womb, I knew you.

In the days of Josiah, the word of the Lord was addressed to me, saying,

'Before I formed you in the womb I knew you;
before you came to birth I consecrated you;
I have appointed you as prophet to the nations.'

I said, 'Ah, Lord, look, I do not know how to speak: I am a child!'

But the Lord replied,

'Do not say, "I am a child."
Go now to those to whom I send you
and say whatever I command you.
Do not be afraid of them,
for I am with you to protect you –
it is the Lord who speaks!'

Then the Lord put out his hand and touched my mouth and said to me:

'There! I am putting my words into your mouth.
Look, today I am setting you
over nations and over kingdoms,
to tear up and to knock down,
to destroy and to overthrow,
to build and to plant.'

The word of the Lord.

Responsorial Psalm 　　　　　　　　　　Ps 70:1-6,15,17. R. v.6

R. **From my mother's womb you have been my help.**

In you, O Lord, I take refuge;
let me never be put to shame.
In your justice rescue me, free me:
pay heed to me and save me. R.

Be a rock where I can take refuge,
a mighty stronghold to save me;
for you are my rock, my stronghold.
Free me from the hand of the wicked. R.

It is you, O Lord, who are my hope,
my trust, O Lord, since my youth.
On you I have leaned from my birth,
from my mother's womb you have been my help. R.

My lips will tell of your justice
and day by day of your help.
O God, you have taught me from my youth
and I proclaim your wonders still. R.

SECOND READING

A reading from the first letter of St Peter   1:8-12

It was this salvation that the prophets were looking and searching so hard for.

You did not see Jesus Christ, yet you love him; and still without seeing
him, you are already filled with joy so glorious that it cannot be described,
because you believe; and you are sure of the end to which your faith looks
forward, that is, the salvation of your souls.

It was this salvation that the prophets were looking and searching so
hard for; their prophecies were about the grace which was to come to you.
The Spirit of Christ which was in them foretold the sufferings of Christ and
the glories that would come after them, and they tried to find out at what
time and in what circumstances all this was to be expected. It was revealed
to them that the news they brought of all the things which have now been
announced to you, by those who preached to you the Good News through
the Holy Spirit sent from heaven, was for you and not for themselves. Even
the angels long to catch a glimpse of these things.

The word of the Lord.

Gospel Acclamation   Cf. Jn 1:7; Lk 1:17

R. **Alleluia, alleluia!**
He came as a witness,
as a witness to speak for the light,
preparing for the Lord a people fit for him.
R. **Alleluia!**

GOSPEL

A reading from the holy Gospel according to Luke   1:5-17

She is to bear you a son and you must name him John.

In the days of King Herod of Judaea there lived a priest called Zechariah
who belonged to the Abijah section of the priesthood, and he had a wife,
Elizabeth by name, who was a descendant of Aaron. Both were worthy in

the sight of God, and scrupulously observed all the commandments and observances of the Lord. But they were childless: Elizabeth was barren and they were both getting on in years.

Now it was the turn of Zechariah's section to serve, and he was exercising his priestly office before God when it fell to him by lot, as the ritual custom was, to enter the Lord's sanctuary and burn incense there. And at the hour of incense the whole congregation was outside, praying.

Then there appeared to him the angel of the Lord, standing on the right of the altar of incense. The sight disturbed Zechariah and he was overcome with fear. But the angel said to him, 'Zechariah, do not be afraid, your prayer has been heard. Your wife Elizabeth is to bear you a son and you must name him John. He will be your joy and delight and many will rejoice at his birth, for he will be great in the sight of the Lord; he must drink no wine, no strong drink. Even from his mother's womb he will be filled with the Holy Spirit, and he will bring back many of the sons of Israel to the Lord their God. With the spirit and power of Elijah, he will go before him to turn the hearts of fathers towards their children and the disobedient back to the wisdom that the virtuous have, preparing for the Lord a people fit for him.'

The Gospel of the Lord.

The Creed is said.

Prayer over the Offerings

Look with favour, O Lord,
upon the offerings made
    by your people
on the Solemnity of Saint John
    the Baptist,
and grant that what we celebrate
    in mystery
we may follow with deeds
    of devoted service.
Through Christ our Lord.

Super oblata

Munera populi tui, Domine,
    propitius intende,
in beati Ioannis Baptistæ
    sollemnitate delata,
et præsta, ut,
    quæ mysterio gerimus,
debitæ servitutis actione sectemur.
Per Christum Dominum nostrum.

Proper Preface, as in the following Mass, pp.516-517.

Communion Antiphon   Lk 1:68

Blessed be the Lord,
    the God of Israel!
He has visited his people
    and redeemed them.

Ant. ad communionem

Benedictus Dominus Deus Israel,
quia visitavit et fecit redemptionem
    plebi suæ.

Prayer after Communion

May the marvellous prayer of Saint
  John the Baptist
accompany us who have
  eaten our fill
at this sacrificial feast, O Lord,
and, since Saint John
  proclaimed your Son
to be the Lamb who would
  take away our sins,
may he implore now for us
  your favour.
Through Christ our Lord.

Post communionem

Sacris dapibus satiatos,
beati Ioannis Baptistæ nos,
  Domine,
præclara comitetur oratio,
et, quem Agnum nostra ablaturum
  crimina nuntiavit,
ipsum Filium tuum poscat nobis
  fore placatum.
Qui vivit et regnat
  in sæcula sæculorum.

At the Mass during the Day

Entrance Antiphon Jn 1:6-7; Lk 1:17

A MAN was sent from God,
whose name was John.
He came to testify to the light,
to prepare a people fit for the Lord.

Ant. ad introitum

FUIT homo missus a Deo,
cui nomen erat Ioannes.
Hic venit, ut testimonium
  perhiberet de lumine,
parare Domino plebem perfectam.

The Gloria in excelsis (Glory to God in the highest) is said.

Collect

O God, who raised up
  Saint John the Baptist
to make ready a nation fit for
  Christ the Lord,
give your people, we pray,
the grace of spiritual joys
and direct the hearts
  of all the faithful
into the way of salvation and peace.
Through our Lord Jesus Christ,
  your Son,
who lives and reigns with you
  in the unity of the Holy Spirit,
God, for ever and ever.

Collecta

Deus, qui beatum Ioannem
  Baptistam suscitasti,
ut perfectam plebem
  Christo Domino præpararet,
da populis tuis spiritalium
  gratiam gaudiorum,
et omnium fidelium mentes
  dirige in viam salutis et pacis.
Per Dominum nostrum
  Iesum Christum Filium tuum,
qui tecum vivit et regnat
  in unitate Spiritus Sancti,
Deus, per omnia sæcula sæculorum.

FIRST READING

A reading from the prophet Isaiah   49:1-6

I will make you the light of the nations.

Islands, listen to me,
pay attention, remotest peoples.
The Lord called me before I was born,
from my mother's womb he pronounced my name.

He made my mouth a sharp sword,
and hid me in the shadow of his hand.
He made me into a sharpened arrow,
and concealed me in his quiver.

He said to me, 'You are my servant (Israel)
in whom I shall be glorified';
while I was thinking, 'I have toiled in vain,
I have exhausted myself for nothing';

and all the while my cause was with the Lord,
my reward with my God.
I was honoured in the eyes of the Lord,
my God was my strength.

And now the Lord has spoken,
he who formed me in the womb to be his servant,
to bring Jacob back to him,
to gather Israel to him:

'It is not enough for you to be my servant,
to restore the tribes of Jacob and bring back the survivors of Israel;
I will make you the light of the nations
so that my salvation may reach to the ends of the earth.'

The word of the Lord.

Responsaorial Psalm   Ps 138:1-3,13-15. R. v.14

R. **I thank you for the wonder of my being.**

O Lord, you search me and you know me,
you know my resting and my rising,
you discern my purpose from afar.
You mark when I walk or lie down,
all my ways lie open to you. R.

For it was you who created my being,
knit me together in my mother's womb.

I thank you for the wonder of my being,
for the wonders of all your creation. R.

Already you knew my soul,
my body held no secret from you
when I was being fashioned in secret
and moulded in the depths of the earth. R.

SECOND READING

A reading from the Acts of the Apostles   13:22-26
Jesus, whose coming was heralded by John.

Paul said: 'God made David the king of our ancestors, of whom he
approved in these words, "I have elected David son of Jesse, a man after my
own heart, who will carry out my whole purpose." To keep his promise,
God has raised up for Israel one of David's descendants, Jesus, as Saviour,
whose coming was heralded by John when he proclaimed a baptism of
repentance for the whole people of Israel. Before John ended his career he
said, "I am not the one you imagine me to be; that one is coming after me
and I am not fit to undo his sandal."

'My brothers, sons of Abraham's race, and all you who fear God, this
message of salvation is meant for you.'

The word of the Lord.

Gospel Acclamation   Cf. Lk 1:76

R. **Alleluia, alleluia!**
As for you, little child, you shall be called
a prophet of God, the Most High.
You shall go ahead of the Lord
to prepare his ways before him.
R. **Alleluia!**

GOSPEL

A reading from the holy Gospel according to Luke   1:57-66,80
His name is John.

The time came for Elizabeth to have her child, and she gave birth to a son;
and when her neighbours and relations heard that the Lord had shown her
so great a kindness, they shared her joy.

Now on the eighth day they came to circumcise the child; they were
going to call him Zechariah after his father, but his mother spoke up. 'No,'
she said 'he is to be called John.' They said to her, 'But no one in your
family has that name', and made signs to his father to find out what he

wanted him called. The father asked for a writing-tablet and wrote, 'His name is John.' And they were all astonished. At that instant his power of speech returned and he spoke and praised God. All their neighbours were filled with awe and the whole affair was talked about throughout the hill country of Judaea. All those who heard of it treasured it in their hearts. 'What will this child turn out to be?' they wondered. And indeed the hand of the Lord was with him. Meanwhile, the child grew up and his spirit matured. And he lived out in the wilderness until the day he appeared openly to Israel.

The Gospel of the Lord.

The Creed is said.

Prayer over the Offerings

We place these offerings on
   your altar, O Lord,
to celebrate with fitting honour
   the nativity of him
who both foretold the coming
   of the world's Saviour
and pointed him out
   when he came.
Who lives and reigns
   for ever and ever.

Super oblata

Tua, Domine, muneribus
   altaria cumulamus,
illius nativitatem honore
   debito celebrantes,
qui Salvatorem mundi
   et cecinit affuturum,
et adesse monstravit.
Qui vivit et regnat
   in sæcula sæculorum.

Preface: The mission of the Precursor

It is truly right and just,
   our duty and our salvation,
always and everywhere
   to give you thanks,
Lord, holy Father,
   almighty and eternal God,
through Christ our Lord.

In his Precursor, Saint John
   the Baptist,
we praise your great glory,
for you consecrated him
   for a singular honour
among those born of women.

Præfatio: De missione Præcursoris

Vere dignum et iustum est,
   æquum et salutare,
nos tibi semper et ubique
   gratias agere:
Domine, sancte Pater,
   omnipotens æterne Deus:
per Christum Dominum nostrum.

In cuius Præcursore beato Ioanne
tuam magnificentiam collaudamus,
quem inter natos mulierum honore
   præcipuo consecrasti.

His birth brought great rejoicing;
even in the womb he leapt for joy
at the coming of human salvation.
He alone of all the prophets
pointed out the Lamb of redemption.

And to make holy the flowing waters,
he baptised the very author
of Baptism
and was privileged to bear him
supreme witness
by the shedding of his blood.

And so, with the Powers of heaven,
we worship you constantly on earth,
and before your majesty
without end we acclaim:

Holy, Holy, Holy Lord God of hosts...

Qui cum nascendo multa
gaudia præstitisset,
et nondum editus exsultasset
ad humanæ salutis adventum,
ipse solus omnium prophetarum
Agnum redemptionis ostendit.

Sed et sanctificandis etiam
aquæ fluentis
ipsum baptismatis lavit auctorem,
et meruit fuso sanguine supremum
illi testimonium exhibere.

Et ideo, cum cælorum virtutibus,
in terris te iugiter prædicamus,
maiestati tuæ sine fine clamantes:

Sanctus, Sanctus, Sanctus. . .

Communion Antiphon Cf. Lk 1:78

Ant. ad communionem

Through the tender mercy
of our God,
the Dawn from on high will visit us.

Per viscera misericordiæ Dei nostri,
visitavit nos Oriens ex alto.

Prayer after Communion

Post communionem

Having feasted at the banquet
of the heavenly Lamb,
we pray, O Lord,
that, finding joy in the nativity
of Saint John the Baptist,
your Church may know as
the author of her rebirth
the Christ whose coming
John foretold.
Who lives and reigns
for ever and ever.

Cælestis Agni convivio refecti,
quæsumus, Domine,
ut Ecclesia tua,
sumens de beati Ioannis Baptistæ
generatione lætitiam,
quem ille prænuntiavit venturum,
suæ regenerationis
cognoscat auctorem.
Qui vivit et regnat
in sæcula sæculorum.

25 June

TWELFTH SUNDAY IN ORDINARY TIME

Entrance Antiphon Cf. Ps 27:8-9	Ant. ad introitum

THE Lord is the strength
of his people,
a saving refuge for the one
he has anointed.
Save your people, Lord,
and bless your heritage,
and govern them for ever.

DOMINUS fortitudo plebis suæ,
et protector salutarium Christi
sui est.
Salvum fac populum
tuum, Domine,
et benedic hereditati tuæ,
et rege eos usque in sæculum.

Collect | Collecta

Grant, O Lord,
that we may always revere and love
your holy name,
for you never deprive
of your guidance
those you set firm
on the foundation of your love.
Through our Lord Jesus Christ,
your Son,
who lives and reigns with you
in the unity of the Holy Spirit,
God, for ever and ever.

Sancti nominis tui, Domine,
timorem pariter et amorem fac nos
habere perpetuum,
quia numquam tua
gubernatione destituis,
quos in soliditate tuæ
dilectionis instituis.
Per Dominum nostrum Iesum
Christum Filium tuum,
qui tecum vivit et regnat
in unitate Spiritus Sancti,
Deus, per omnia sæcula sæculorum.

FIRST READING

A reading from the prophet Jeremiah   20:10-13

He has delivered the soul of the needy from the hands of evil men.

Jeremiah said:
I hear so many disparaging me,
'"Terror from every side!"
Denounce him! Let us denounce him!'
All those who used to be my friends
watched for my downfall,
'Perhaps he will be seduced into error.
Then we will master him
and take our revenge!'

But the Lord is at my side, a mighty hero;
my opponents will stumble, mastered,
confounded by their failure;
everlasting, unforgettable disgrace will be theirs.
But you, Lord of Hosts, you who probe with justice,
who scrutinise the loins and heart,
let me see the vengeance you will take on them,
for I have committed my cause to you.
Sing to the Lord,
praise the Lord,
for he has delivered the soul of the needy
from the hands of evil men.

The word of the Lord.

Responsional Psalm   Ps 68:8-10,14,17,33-35. R. v.14

R. **In your great love, answer me, O God.**

It is for you that I suffer taunts,
that shame covers my face,
that I have become a stranger to my brothers,
an alien to my own mother's sons.
I burn with zeal for your house
and taunts against you fall on me. R.

This is my prayer to you,
my prayer for your favour.
In your great love, answer me, O God,
with your help that never fails:
Lord, answer, for your love is kind;
in your compassion, turn towards me. R.

The poor when they see it will be glad
and God-seeking hearts will revive;
for the Lord listens to the needy
and does not spurn his servants in their chains.
Let the heavens and the earth give him praise,
the sea and all its living creatures. R.

SECOND READING

A reading from the letter of St Paul to the Romans   5:12-15

The gift considerably outweighed the fall.

Sin entered the world through one man, and through sin death, and thus death has spread through the whole human race because everyone has sinned. Sin existed in the world long before the Law was given. There was no law and so no one could be accused of the sin of 'law-breaking', yet death reigned over all from Adam to Moses, even though their sin, unlike that of Adam, was not a matter of breaking a law.

Adam prefigured the One to come, but the gift itself considerably outweighed the fall. If it is certain that through one man's fall so many died, it is even more certain that divine grace, coming through the one man, Jesus Christ, came to so many as an abundant free gift.

The word of the Lord.

Gospel Acclamation   Jn 1:14,12

R. **Alleluia, alleluia!**
The Word was made flesh and lived among us;
to all who did accept him
he gave power to become children of God.
R. **Alleluia!**

Or: Jn 15:26,27

R. **Alleluia, alleluia!**
The Spirit of truth will be my witness;
and you too will be my witnesses.
R. **Alleluia!**

GOSPEL

A reading from the holy Gospel according to Matthew   10:26-33

Do not be afraid of those who kill the body.

Jesus instructed the Twelve as follows: 'Do not be afraid. For everything that is now covered will be uncovered, and everything now hidden will be made clear. What I say to you in the dark, tell in the daylight; what you hear in whispers, proclaim from the house-tops.

'Do not be afraid of those who kill the body but cannot kill the soul; fear him rather who can destroy both body and soul in hell. Can you not buy two sparrows for a penny? And yet not one falls to the ground without your Father knowing. Why, every hair on your head has been counted. So there is no need to be afraid; you are worth more than hundreds of sparrows.

'So if anyone declares himself for me in the presence of men, I will declare myself for him in the presence of my Father in heaven. But the one who disowns me in the presence of men, I will disown in the presence of my Father in heaven.'

The Gospel of the Lord.

Prayer over the Offerings	Super oblata
Receive, O Lord, the sacrifice of conciliation and praise and grant that, cleansed by its action, we may make offering of a heart pleasing to you.	Suscipe, Domine, sacrificium placationis et laudis, et præsta, ut, huius operatione mundati, beneplacitum tibi nostræ mentis offeramus affectum.
Through Christ our Lord.	Per Christum Dominum nostrum.

Preface of Sundays in Ordinary Time I-VIII, pp.60-67.

Communion Antiphon Ps 144:15	Ant. ad communionem
The eyes of all look to you, Lord, and you give them their food in due season.	Oculi omnium in te sperant, Domine, et tu das illis escam in tempore opportuno.

Or: Jn 10:11,15	Vel:
I am the Good Shepherd, and I lay down my life for my sheep, says the Lord.	Ego sum pastor bonus, et animam meam pono pro ovibus meis, dicit Dominus.

Prayer after Communion	Post communionem
Renewed and nourished by the Sacred Body and Precious Blood of your Son, we ask of your mercy, O Lord, that what we celebrate with constant devotion may be our sure pledge of redemption.	Sacri Corporis et Sanguinis pretiosi alimonia renovati, quæsumus, Domine, clementiam tuam, ut, quod gerimus devotione frequenti, certa redemptione capiamus.
Through Christ our Lord.	Per Christum Dominum nostrum.

29 June

SAINTS PETER AND PAUL, APOSTLES

Jesus asked the disciples: "Who do people say that I am?" There are those who stop at this question, opinions, and talk about Jesus; and there are those who, instead, talk to Jesus, bringing their life to him, entering into a relationship with him, making the decisive step. This is what interests the Lord: to be at the centre of our thoughts, to become the reference point of our affections; to be, in short, the love of our lives. Not the opinions we have of him; they do not interest him. He is interested in our love, whether he is in our heart. The Saints we celebrate today took that step and became witnesses. They were not admirers, but imitators of Jesus. And they provoke us, because we run the risk of stalling at the first question: of giving views and opinions, of having grand ideas and saying beautiful words, but never putting ourselves on the line. And Jesus wants us to put ourselves on the line.

(Pope Francis)

Solemnity

At the Vigil Mass

This Mass is used on the evening of 28 June, either before or after First Vespers (Evening Prayer I) of the Solemnity.

Entrance Antiphon	Ant. ad introitum
PETER the Apostle, and Paul the teacher of the Gentiles, these have taught us your law, O Lord.	PETRUS apostolus et Paulus doctor gentium, ipsi nos docuerunt legem tuam, Domine.

The **Gloria in excelsis** (Glory to God in the highest) is said.

Collect

Grant, we pray, O Lord our God,
that we may be sustained
by the intercession of the blessed
   Apostles Peter and Paul,
that, as through them you gave
   your Church
the foundations of her
   heavenly office,
so through them you may help
   her to eternal salvation.
Through our Lord Jesus Christ,
   your Son,
who lives and reigns with you
   in the unity of the Holy Spirit,
God, for ever and ever.

Collecta

Da nobis, quæsumus, Domine
   Deus noster,
beatorum apostolorum Petri
   et Pauli
intercessionibus sublevari,
ut, per quos Ecclesiæ tuæ
superni muneris
   rudimenta donasti,
per eos subsidia perpetuæ
   salutis impendas.
Per Dominum nostrum Iesum
   Christum Filium tuum,
qui tecum vivit et regnat
   in unitate Spiritus Sancti,
Deus, per omnia sæcula sæculorum.

FIRST READING

A reading from the Acts of the Apostles   3:1-10

I will give you what I have: in the name of Jesus, walk!

Once, when Peter and John were going up to the Temple for the prayers at
the ninth hour, it happened that there was a man being carried past. He
was a cripple from birth; and they used to put him down every day near
the Temple entrance called the Beautiful Gate so that he could beg from
the people going in. When this man saw Peter and John on their way into
the Temple he begged from them. Both Peter and John looked straight at
him and said, 'Look at us.' He turned to them expectantly, hoping to get
something from them, but Peter said, 'I have neither silver nor gold, but I
will give you what I have: in the name of Jesus Christ the Nazarene, walk!'
Peter then took him by the hand and helped him to stand up. Instantly
his feet and ankles became firm, he jumped up, stood, and began to
walk, and he went with them into the Temple, walking and jumping and
praising God. Everyone could see him walking and praising God, and they
recognised him as the man who used to sit begging at the Beautiful Gate
of the Temple. They were all astonished and unable to explain what had
happened to him.

   The word of the Lord.

Responsorial Psalm   Ps 18:2-5. R. v.5

R. **Their word goes forth through all the earth.**

The heavens proclaim the glory of God
and the firmament shows forth the work of his hands.
Day unto day takes up the story
and night unto night makes known the message. R.

No speech, no word, no voice is heard
yet their span extends through all the earth,
their words to the utmost bounds of the world. R.

SECOND READING

A reading from the letter of St Paul to the Galatians   1:11-20
God specially chose me while I was still in my mother's womb.

The Good News I preached is not a human message that I was given by
men, it is something I learnt only through a revelation of Jesus Christ. You
must have heard of my career as a practising Jew, how merciless I was in
persecuting the Church of God, how much damage I did to it, how I stood
out among other Jews of my generation, and how enthusiastic I was for the
traditions of my ancestors.

Then God, who had specially chosen me while I was still in my mother's
womb, called me through his grace and chose to reveal his Son in me, so
that I might preach the Good News about him to the pagans. I did not
stop to discuss this with any human being, nor did I go up to Jerusalem to
see those who were already apostles before me, but I went off to Arabia at
once and later went straight back from there to Damascus. Even when after
three years I went up to Jerusalem to visit Cephas and stayed with him for
fifteen days, I did not see any of the other apostles; I only saw James, the
brother of the Lord, and I swear before God that what I have just written is
the literal truth.

The word of the Lord.

Gospel Acclamation   Jn 21:17

R. **Alleluia, alleluia!**
Lord, you know everything;
you know I love you.
R. **Alleluia!**

GOSPEL

A reading from the holy Gospel according to John 21:15-19

Feed my lambs, feed my sheep.

After Jesus had shown himself to his disciples and eaten with them, he said to Simon Peter, 'Simon son of John, do you love me more than these others do?' He answered, 'Yes Lord, you know I love you.' Jesus said to him, 'Feed my lambs.' A second time he said to him, 'Simon son of John, do you love me?' He replied, 'Yes, Lord, you know I love you.' Jesus said to him, 'Look after my sheep.' Then he said to him a third time, 'Simon son of John, do you love me?' Peter was upset that he asked him the third time, 'Do you love me?' and said, 'Lord, you know everything; you know I love you.' Jesus said to him, 'Feed my sheep.

> 'I tell you most solemnly,
> when you were young
> you put on your own belt
> and walked where you liked;
> but when you grow old
> you will stretch out your hands,
> and somebody else will put a belt round you
> and take you where you would rather not go.'

In these words he indicated the kind of death by which Peter would give glory to God. After this he said, 'Follow me.'

The Gospel of the Lord.

The Creed is said.

Prayer over the Offerings	Super oblata
We bring offerings to your altar, O Lord, as we glory in the solemn feast of the blessed Apostles Peter and Paul, so that the more we doubt our own merits, the more we may rejoice that we are to be saved by your loving kindness. Through Christ our Lord.	Munera, Domine, tuis altaribus adhibemus, de beatorum apostolorum Petri et Pauli sollemnitatibus gloriantes, ut quantum sumus de nostro merito formidantes, tantum de tua benignitate gloriemur salvandi. Per Christum Dominum nostrum.

Proper Preface, as in the following Mass, p.530.

Communion Antiphon Cf. Jn 21:15,17

Simon, Son of John,
  do you love me more than these?
Lord, you know everything;
  you know that I love you.

Ant. ad communionem

Simon Ioannis, diligis me plus his?
Domine, tu omnia nosti;
tu scis, Domine, quia amo te.

Prayer after Communion

By this heavenly Sacrament,
  O Lord, we pray,
strengthen your faithful,
whom you have enlightened
  with the teaching of the Apostles.
Through Christ our Lord.

Post communionem

Cælestibus sacramentis,
  quæsumus, Domine,
fideles tuos corrobora,
quos Apostolorum
  doctrina illuminasti.
Per Christum Dominum nostrum.

A formula of Solemn Blessing, pp.144-147, may be used.

At the Mass during the Day

Entrance Antiphon

THESE are the ones who,
  living in the flesh,
planted the Church with their blood;
they drank the chalice of the Lord
and became the friends of God.

Ant. ad introitum

ISTI sunt qui, viventes in carne,
  plantaverunt Ecclesiam
  sanguine suo:
calicem Domini biberunt,
  et amici Dei facti sunt.

The **Gloria in excelsis** (Glory to God in the highest) is said.

Collect

O God, who on the Solemnity
  of the Apostles Peter and Paul
give us the noble and holy joy
  of this day,
grant, we pray, that your Church
may in all things follow the teaching
of those through whom she received
the beginnings of right religion.
Through our Lord Jesus Christ,
  your Son,
who lives and reigns with you
  in the unity of the Holy Spirit,
God, for ever and ever.

Collecta

Deus, qui huius diei venerandam
  sanctamque lætitiam
in apostolorum Petri et Pauli
  sollemnitate tribuisti,
da Ecclesiæ tuæ eorum in omnibus
  sequi præceptum,
per quos religionis sumpsit exordium.

Per Dominum nostrum Iesum
  Christum Filium tuum,
qui tecum vivit et regnat
  in unitate Spiritus Sancti,
Deus, per omnia sæcula sæculorum.

FIRST READING

A reading from the Acts of the Apostles

12:1-11

Now I know the Lord really did save me from Herod.

King Herod started persecuting certain members of the Church. He beheaded James the brother of John, and when he saw that this pleased the Jews he decided to arrest Peter as well. This was during the days of Unleavened Bread, and he put Peter in prison, assigning four squads of four soldiers each to guard him in turns. Herod meant to try Peter in public after the end of Passover week. All the time Peter was under guard the Church prayed to God for him unremittingly.

On the night before Herod was to try him, Peter was sleeping between two soldiers, fastened with double chains, while guards kept watch at the main entrance to the prison. Then suddenly the angel of the Lord stood there, and the cell was filled with light. He tapped Peter on the side and woke him. 'Get up!' he said 'Hurry!' – and the chains fell from his hands. The angel then said, 'Put on your belt and sandals.' After he had done this, the angel next said, 'Wrap your cloak round you and follow me.' Peter followed him, but had no idea that what the angel did was all happening in reality; he thought he was seeing a vision. They passed through two guard posts one after the other, and reached the iron gate leading to the city. This opened of its own accord; they went through it and had walked the whole length of one street when suddenly the angel left him. It was only then that Peter came to himself. 'Now I know it is all true,' he said. 'The Lord really did send his angel and has saved me from Herod and from all that the Jewish people were so certain would happen to me.'

The word of the Lord.

Responsional Psalm

Ps 33:2-9. R. v.5. Alt. R. v.8

R. **From all my terrors the Lord set me free.**
   Or: **The angel of the Lord rescues those who revere him.**

I will bless the Lord at all times
his praise always on my lips;
in the Lord my soul shall make its boast.
The humble shall hear and be glad. R.

Glorify the Lord with me.
Together let us praise his name.
I sought the Lord and he answered me;
from all my terrors he set me free. R.

Look towards him and be radiant;
let your faces not be abashed.
This poor man called; the Lord heard him
and rescued him from all his distress. R.

The angel of the Lord is encamped
around those who revere him, to rescue them.
Taste and see that the Lord is good.
He is happy who seeks refuge in him. R.

R. **From all my terrors the Lord set me free.**
  Or: **The angel of the Lord rescues those who revere him.**

SECOND READING

A reading from the second letter of St Paul to Timothy   4:6-8,17-18

All there is to come now is the crown of righteousness reserved for me.

My life is already being poured away as a libation, and the time has come
for me to be gone. I have fought the good fight to the end; I have run
the race to the finish; I have kept the faith; all there is to come now is
the crown of righteousness reserved for me, which the Lord, the righteous
judge, will give to me on that Day; and not only to me but to all those who
have longed for his Appearing.

The Lord stood by me and gave me power, so that through me the
whole message might be proclaimed for all the pagans to hear; and so I
was rescued from the lion's mouth. The Lord will rescue me from all evil
attempts on me, and bring me safely to his heavenly kingdom. To him be
glory for ever and ever. Amen.

The word of the Lord.

Gospel Acclamation   Mt 16:18

R. **Alleluia, alleluia!**
You are Peter and on this rock I will build my Church.
And the gates of the underworld can never hold out against it.
R. **Alleluia!**

GOSPEL

A reading from the holy Gospel according to Matthew   16:13-19

You are Peter, and I will give you the keys of the kingdom of heaven.

When Jesus came to the region of Caesarea Philippi he put this question to his disciples, 'Who do people say the Son of Man is?' And they said, 'Some say he is John the Baptist, some Elijah, and others Jeremiah or one of the prophets.' 'But you,' he said 'who do you say I am?' Then Simon Peter spoke up, 'You are the Christ,' he said 'the Son of the living God.' Jesus replied, 'Simon son of Jonah, you are a happy man! Because it was not flesh and blood that revealed this to you but my Father in heaven. So I now say to you: You are Peter and on this rock I will build my Church. And the gates of the underworld can never hold out against it. I will give you the keys of the kingdom of heaven: whatever you bind on earth shall be considered bound in heaven; whatever you loose on earth shall be considered loosed in heaven.'

The Gospel of the Lord.

The Creed is said.

Prayer over the Offerings

May the prayer of the Apostles,
   O Lord,
accompany the sacrificial gift
that we present to your name
   for consecration,
and may their intercession make
   us devoted to you
in celebration of the sacrifice.
Through Christ our Lord.

Super oblata

Hostiam, Domine, quam nomini
   tuo exhibemus sacrandam,
apostolica prosequatur oratio,
nosque tibi reddat in sacrificio
   celebrando devotos.
Per Christum Dominum nostrum.

Preface: The twofold mission of Peter and Paul in the Church.

Præfatio: De duplici missione Petri et Pauli in Ecclesia.

It is truly right and just,
    our duty and our salvation,
always and everywhere to give
    you thanks,
Lord, holy Father,
    almighty and eternal God.

Vere dignum et iustum est,
    æquum et salutare,
nos tibi semper et ubique
    gratias agere:
Domine, sancte Pater,
    omnipotens æterne Deus.

For by your providence
the blessed Apostles Peter and Paul
    bring us joy:
Peter, foremost in confessing
    the faith,
Paul, its outstanding preacher,
Peter, who established the early
    Church from the remnant
    of Israel,
Paul, master and teacher
    of the Gentiles that you call.

Quia nos beati apostoli
    Petrus et Paulus
tua dispositione lætificant:
hic princeps fidei confitendæ,
ille intellegendæ clarus assertor;
hic reliquiis Israel instituens
    Ecclesiam primitivam,
ille magister et doctor
    gentium vocandarum.

And so, each in a different way
gathered together the one family
    of Christ;
and revered together throughout
    the world,
they share one Martyr's crown.
And therefore, with all the Angels
    and Saints,
we praise you, as without end
    we acclaim:

Sic diverso consilio unam Christi
    familiam congregantes,
par mundo venerabile,
    una corona sociavit.
Et ideo, cum Sanctis
    et Angelis universis
te collaudamus, sine fine dicentes:

Holy, Holy, Holy Lord God of hosts...

Sanctus, Sanctus, Sanctus. . .

Communion Antiphon Cf. Mt 16:16,18

Peter said to Jesus:
  You are the Christ,
  the Son of the living God.
And Jesus replied: You are Peter,
and upon this rock I will build
  my Church.

Prayer after Communion

Grant us, O Lord,
who have been renewed
  by this Sacrament,
so to live in the Church,
that, persevering in the breaking
  of the Bread
and in the teaching of the Apostles,
we may be one heart and one soul,
made steadfast in your love.
Through Christ our Lord.

Ant. ad communionem

Dixit Petrus ad Iesum:
  Tu es Christus, Filius Dei vivi.
Respondit Iesus: Tu es Petrus,
et super hanc petram ædificabo
  Ecclesiam meam.

Post communionem

Da nobis, Domine,
  hoc sacramento refectis,
ita in Ecclesia conversari,
ut, perseverantes in fractione panis
Apostolorumque doctrina,
cor unum simus et anima una,
  tua caritate firmati.
Per Christum Dominum nostrum.

A formula of Solemn Blessing, pp.144-147, may be used.

2 July

THIRTEENTH SUNDAY IN ORDINARY TIME

Entrance Antiphon   Ps 46:2

ALL peoples, clap your hands.
Cry to God with shouts of joy!

Ant. ad introitum

OMNES gentes,
plaudite manibus,
iubilate Deo in voce exsultationis.

Collect

O God, who through the grace
    of adoption
chose us to be children of light,
grant, we pray,
that we may not be wrapped
    in the darkness of error
but always be seen to stand
    in the bright light of truth.
Through our Lord Jesus Christ,
    your Son,
who lives and reigns with you
    in the unity of the Holy Spirit,
God, for ever and ever.

Collecta

Deus, qui, per adoptionem gratiæ,
lucis nos esse filios voluisti,
præsta, quæsumus, ut errorum
    non involvamur tenebris,
sed in splendore veritatis semper
    maneamus conspicui.
Per Dominum nostrum Iesum
    Christum Filium tuum,
qui tecum vivit et regnat
    in unitate Spiritus Sancti,
Deus, per omnia sæcula sæculorum.

FIRST READING

A reading from the second book of the Kings   4:8-11,14-16

This is a holy man of God, let him rest there.

One day as Elisha was on his way to Shunem, a woman of rank who lived there pressed him to stay and eat there. After this he always broke his journey for a meal when he passed that way. She said to her husband, 'Look, I am sure the man who is constantly passing our way must be a holy man of God. Let us build him a small room on the roof, and put him a bed in it, and a table and chair and lamp; whenever he comes to us he can rest there.'

One day when he came, he retired to the upper room and lay down. 'What can be done for her?' he asked. Gehazi, his servant, answered, 'Well, she has no son and her husband is old.' Elisha said, 'Call her.' The servant called her and she stood at the door. 'This time next year,' Elisha said 'you will hold a son in your arms.'

The word of the Lord.

Responsorial Psalm   Ps 88:2-3,16-19. R. v.2

R. **I will sing for ever of your love, O Lord.**

I will sing for ever of your love, O Lord;
through all ages my mouth will proclaim your truth.
Of this I am sure, that your love lasts for ever,
that your truth is firmly established as the heavens. R.

Happy the people who acclaim such a king,
who walk, O Lord, in the light of your face,
who find their joy every day in your name,
who make your justice the source of their bliss. R.

For it is you, O Lord, who are the glory of their strength;
it is by your favour that our might is exalted:
for our ruler is in the keeping of the Lord;
our king in the keeping of the Holy One of Israel. R.

SECOND READING

A reading from the letter of St Paul to the Romans   6:3-4,8-11

When we were baptised we went into the tomb with Christ, so that we too might live a new life.

When we were baptised in Christ Jesus we were baptised in his death; in other words, when we were baptised we went into the tomb with him and joined him in death, so that as Christ was raised from the dead by the Father's glory, we too might live a new life.

But we believe that having died with Christ we shall return to life with him: Christ, as we know, having been raised from the dead will never die again. Death has no power over him any more. When he died, he died, once for all, to sin, so his life now is life with God; and in that way, you too must consider yourselves to be dead to sin but alive for God in Christ Jesus.

The word of the Lord.

Gospel Acclamation   Cf. Ac 16:14

R. **Alleluia, alleluia!**
Open our heart, O Lord,
to accept the words of your Son.
R. **Alleluia!**

Or: 1 P 2:9

R. **Alleluia, alleluia!**
You are a chosen race, a royal priesthood, a people set apart
to sing the praises of God
who called you out of darkness into his wonderful light.
R. **Alleluia!**

GOSPEL

A reading from the holy Gospel according to Matthew   10:37-42
*Anyone who does not take his cross is not worthy of me. Anyone who welcomes you
welcomes me.*

Jesus instructed the Twelve as follows: 'Anyone who prefers father or
mother to me is not worthy of me. Anyone who prefers son or daughter
to me is not worthy of me. Anyone who does not take his cross and follow
in my footsteps is not worthy of me. Anyone who finds his life will lose it;
anyone who loses his life for my sake will find it.

'Anyone who welcomes you welcomes me; and those who welcome me
welcome the one who sent me.

'Anyone who welcomes a prophet because he is a prophet will have a
prophet's reward; and anyone who welcomes a holy man because he is a
holy man will have a holy man's reward.

'If anyone gives so much as a cup of cold water to one of these little ones
because he is a disciple, then I tell you solemnly, he will most certainly not
lose his reward.'

The Gospel of the Lord.

Prayer over the Offerings	Super oblata
O God, who graciously accomplish	Deus, qui mysteriorum tuorum
the effects of your mysteries,	dignanter operaris effectus,
grant, we pray,	præsta, quæsumus,
that the deeds by which we serve you	ut sacris apta muneribus fiant
may be worthy of these sacred gifts.	nostra servitia.
Through Christ our Lord.	Per Christum Dominum nostrum.

Preface of Sundays in Ordinary Time I-VIII, pp.60-67.

Communion Antiphon Cf. Ps 102:1	Ant. ad communionem
Bless the Lord, O my soul,	Benedic, anima mea, Domino,
and all within me, his holy name.	et ea quæ intra me sunt nomini
	sancto eius.

Or: Jn 17:20-21	Vel:

O Father, I pray for them,
    that they may be one in us,
that the world may believe that you
    have sent me, says the Lord.
	Pater, pro eis rogo,
	    ut ipsi in nobis unum sint,
	ut credat mundus quia tu me
	    misisti, dicit Dominus.

Prayer after Communion	Post communionem

May this divine sacrifice
    we have offered and received
fill us with life, O Lord, we pray,
so that, bound to you
    in lasting charity,
we may bear fruit that lasts for ever.
Through Christ our Lord.
	Vivificet nos, quæsumus, Domine,
	divina quam obtulimus et
	    sumpsimus hostia,
	ut, perpetua tibi caritate coniuncti,
	fructum qui semper
	    maneat afferamus.
	Per Christum Dominum nostrum.

9 July

FOURTEENTH SUNDAY IN ORDINARY TIME

Entrance Antiphon Cf. Ps 47:10-11	Ant. ad introitum

YOUR merciful love, O God,
    we have received in the midst
    of your temple.
Your praise, O God, like your name,
reaches the ends of the earth;
your right hand is filled
    with saving justice.
	SUSCEPIMUS, Deus,
	    misericordiam tuam
	in medio templi tui.
	Secundum nomen tuum, Deus,
	ita et laus tua in fines terræ;
	iustitia plena est dextera tua.

Collect	Collecta

O God, who in the abasement
    of your Son
have raised up a fallen world,
fill your faithful with holy joy,
for on those you have rescued
    from slavery to sin
you bestow eternal gladness.
Through our Lord Jesus Christ,
    your Son,
who lives and reigns with you
	Deus, qui in Filii tui humilitate
	iacentem mundum erexisti,
	fidelibus tuis sanctam
	    concede lætitiam,
	ut, quos eripuisti
	    a servitute peccati,
	gaudiis facias perfrui sempiternis.
	Per Dominum nostrum Iesum
	    Christum Filium tuum,
	qui tecum vivit et regnat

in the unity of the Holy Spirit, God, for ever and ever.	in unitate Spiritus Sancti, Deus, per omnia sæcula sæculorum.

FIRST READING

A reading from the prophet Zechariah   9:9-10

See now, your king comes humbly to you.

The Lord says this:
> 'Rejoice heart and soul, daughter of Sion!
> Shout with gladness, daughter of Jerusalem!
> See now, your king comes to you;
> he is victorious, he is triumphant,
> humble and riding on a donkey,
> on a colt, the foal of a donkey.
> He will banish chariots from Ephraim
> and horses from Jerusalem;
> the bow of war will be banished.
> He will proclaim peace for the nations.
> His empire shall stretch from sea to sea,
> from the River to the ends of the earth.'

    The word of the Lord.

Responsorial Psalm   Ps 144:1-2,8-11,13-14. R. v.1

R. **I will bless your name for ever,**
   O God my King.
   Or: **Alleluia!**

I will give you glory, O God my King,
I will bless your name for ever.
I will bless you day after day
and praise your name for ever. R.

The Lord is kind and full of compassion,
slow to anger, abounding in love.
How good is the Lord to all,
compassionate to all his creatures. R.

All your creatures shall thank you, O Lord,
and your friends shall repeat their blessing.
They shall speak of the glory of your reign
and declare your might, O God. R.

The Lord is faithful in all his words
and loving in all his deeds.
The Lord supports all who fall
and raises all who are bowed down. R.

SECOND READING

A reading from the letter of St Paul to the Romans 8:9,11-13

If by the Spirit you put an end to the misdeeds of the body you will live.

Your interests are not in the unspiritual, but in the spiritual, since the Spirit of God has made his home in you. In fact, unless you possessed the Spirit of Christ you would not belong to him, and if the Spirit of him who raised Jesus from the dead is living in you, then he who raised Jesus from the dead will give life to your own mortal bodies through his Spirit living in you.

So then, my brothers, there is no necessity for us to obey our unspiritual selves or to live unspiritual lives. If you do live in that way, you are doomed to die, but if by the Spirit you put an end to the misdeeds of the body you will live.

The word of the Lord.

Gospel Acclamation   Cf. Mt 11:25

R. **Alleluia, alleluia!**
Blessed are you, Father,
Lord of heaven and earth;
for revealing the mysteries of the kingdom.
to mere children.
R. **Alleluia!**

GOSPEL

A reading from the holy Gospel according to Matthew 11:25-30

I am gentle and humble in heart.

Jesus exclaimed, 'I bless you, Father, Lord of heaven and of earth, for hiding these things from the learned and the clever and revealing them to mere children. Yes, Father, for that is what it pleased you to do. Everything has been entrusted to me by my Father; and no one knows the Son except the Father, just as no one knows the Father except the Son and those to whom the Son chooses to reveal him.

'Come to me, all you who labour and are overburdened, and I will give you rest. Shoulder my yoke and learn from me, for I am gentle and humble in heart, and you will find rest for your souls. Yes, my yoke is easy and my burden light.'

The Gospel of the Lord.

Prayer over the Offerings

May this oblation dedicated
to your name
purify us, O Lord,
and day by day bring our conduct
closer to the life of heaven.
Through Christ our Lord.

Super oblata

Oblatio nos, Domine,
tuo nomini dicata purificet,
et de die in diem ad cælestis vitæ
transferat actionem.
Per Christum Dominum nostrum.

Preface of Sundays in Ordinary Time I-VIII, pp.60-67.

Communion Antiphon   Ps 33:9

Taste and see that the Lord is good;
blessed the man who seeks refuge
in him.

Ant. ad communionem

Gustate et videte, quoniam suavis
est Dominus;
beatus vir, qui sperat in eo.

Or: Mt 11:28

Come to me, all who labour
and are burdened,
and I will refresh you,
says the Lord.

Vel:

Venite ad me, omnes qui laboratis
et onerati estis,
et ego reficiam vos, dicit Dominus.

Prayer after Communion

Grant, we pray, O Lord,
that, having been replenished
by such great gifts,
we may gain the prize of salvation
and never cease to praise you.
Through Christ our Lord.

Post communionem

Tantis, Domine, repleti muneribus,
præsta, quæsumus, ut et salutaria
dona capiamus,
et a tua numquam laude cessemus.
Per Christum Dominum nostrum.

16 July

FIFTEENTH SUNDAY IN ORDINARY TIME

Entrance Antiphon   Cf. Ps 16:15

AS for me, in justice I shall
behold your face;
I shall be filled with the vision
of your glory.

Ant. ad introitum

EGO autem cum iustitia
apparebo in conspectu tuo;
satiabor dum manifestabitur
gloria tua.

Collect

O God, who show the light
  of your truth
to those who go astray,
so that they may return
  to the right path,
give all who for the faith they profess
are accounted Christians
the grace to reject whatever
  is contrary to the name of Christ
and to strive after all that does
  it honour.
Through our Lord Jesus Christ,
  your Son,
who lives and reigns with you
  in the unity of the Holy Spirit,
God, for ever and ever.

Collecta

Deus, qui errantibus,
  ut in viam possint redire,
veritatis tuæ lumen ostendis,
da cunctis qui christiana
  professione censentur,
et illa respuere, quæ huic inimica
  sunt nomini,
et ea quæ sunt apta sectari.
Per Dominum nostrum Iesum
  Christum Filium tuum,
qui tecum vivit et regnat
  in unitate Spiritus Sancti,
Deus, per omnia sæcula sæculorum.

FIRST READING

A reading from the prophet Isaiah   55:10-11

The rain makes the earth give growth.

Thus says the Lord: 'As the rain and the snow come down from the heavens
and do not return without watering the earth, making it yield and giving
growth to provide seed for the sower and bread for the eating, so the word
that goes from my mouth does not return to me empty, without carrying
out my will and succeeding in what it was sent to do.'

The word of the Lord.

Responsorial Psalm   Ps 64:10-14. R. Lk 8:8

R. **Some seed fell into rich soil
   and produced its crop.**

You care for the earth, give it water,
you fill it with riches.
Your river in heaven brims over
to provide its grain. R.

And thus you provide for the earth;
you drench its furrows,
you level it, soften it with showers,
you bless its growth. R.

You crown the year with your goodness.
Abundance flows in your steps,
in the pastures of the wilderness it flows. R.

The hills are girded with joy,
the meadows covered with flocks,
the valleys are decked with wheat.
They shout for joy, yes, they sing. R.

R. **Some seed fell into rich soil**
and produced its crop.

SECOND READING

A reading from the letter of St Paul to the Romans   8:18-23
The whole creation is eagerly waiting for God to reveal his sons.

I think that what we suffer in this life can never be compared to the glory,
as yet unrevealed, which is waiting for us. The whole creation is eagerly
waiting for God to reveal his sons. It was not for any fault on the part of
creation that it was made unable to attain its purpose, it was made so by
God; but creation still retains the hope of being freed, like us, from its
slavery to decadence, to enjoy the same freedom and glory as the children
of God. From the beginning till now the entire creation, as we know, has
been groaning in one great act of giving birth; and not only creation, but
all of us who possess the first-fruits of the Spirit, we too groan inwardly as
we wait for our bodies to be set free.

The word of the Lord.

Gospel Acclamation   1 S 3:9; Jn 6:68

R. **Alleluia, alleluia!**
Speak, Lord, your servant is listening:
you have the message of eternal life.
R. **Alleluia!**

Or:

R. **Alleluia, alleluia!**
The seed is the word of God, Christ the sower;
whoever finds this seed will remain for ever.
R. **Alleluia!**

GOSPEL

A reading from the holy Gospel according to Matthew   13:1-23
A sower went out to sow.

[Jesus left the house and sat by the lakeside, but such crowds gathered
round him that he got into a boat and sat there. The people all stood on
the beach, and he told them many things in parables.

He said, 'Imagine a sower going out to sow. As he sowed, some seeds fell on the edge of the path, and the birds came and ate them up. Others fell on patches of rock where they found little soil and sprang up straight away, because there was no depth of earth; but as soon as the sun came up they were scorched and, not having any roots, they withered away. Others fell among thorns, and the thorns grew up and choked them. Others fell on rich soil and produced their crop, some a hundredfold, some sixty, some thirty. Listen, anyone who has ears!']

Then the disciples went up to him and asked, 'Why do you talk to them in parables?' 'Because' he replied 'the mysteries of the kingdom of heaven are revealed to you, but they are not revealed to them. For anyone who has will be given more, and he will have more than enough; but from anyone who has not, even what he has will be taken away. The reason I talk to them in parables is that they look without seeing and listen without hearing or understanding. So in their case this prophecy of Isaiah is being fulfilled:

You will listen and listen again, but not understand,
see and see again, but not perceive.
For the heart of this nation has grown coarse,
their ears are dull of hearing, and they have shut their eyes,
for fear they should see with their eyes,
hear with their ears,
understand with their heart,
and be converted
and be healed by me.

'But happy are your eyes because they see, your ears because they hear! I tell you solemnly, many prophets and holy men longed to see what you see, and never saw it; to hear what you hear, and never heard it.

'You, therefore, are to hear the parable of the sower. When anyone hears the word of the kingdom without understanding, the evil one comes and carries off what was sown in his heart: this is the man who received the seed on the edge of the path. The one who received it on patches of rock is the man who hears the word and welcomes it at once with joy. But he has no root in him, he does not last; let some trial come, or some persecution on account of the word, and he falls away at once. The one who received the seed in thorns is the man who hears the word but the worries of this world and the lure of riches choke the word and so he produces nothing. And the one who received the seed in rich soil is the man who hears the word and understands it; he is the one who yields a harvest and produces now a hundredfold, now sixty, now thirty.'

| [The Gospel of the Lord.]

Shorter Form, verses 1-9. Read between [ ]

Prayer over the Offerings

Look upon the offerings
　of the Church, O Lord,
as she makes her prayer to you,
and grant that, when consumed
　by those who believe,
they may bring ever
　greater holiness.
Through Christ our Lord.

Super oblata

Respice, Domine, munera
　supplicantis Ecclesiæ,
et pro credentium
　sanctificationis incremento
sumenda concede.
Per Christum Dominum nostrum.

Preface of Sundays in Ordinary Time I-VIII, pp.60-67.

Communion Antiphon Cf. Ps 83:4-5

The sparrow finds a home,
and the swallow a nest for her young:
by your altars, O Lord of hosts,
　my King and my God.
Blessed are they who dwell
　in your house,
for ever singing your praise.

Ant. ad communionem

Passer invenit sibi domum,
et turtur nidum,
　ubi reponat pullos suos.
Altaria tua, Domine virtutum,
　Rex meus, et Deus meus!
Beati qui habitant in domo tua,
in sæculum sæculi laudabunt te.

Or:　　　　　　　　　　　Jn 6:57

Whoever eats my flesh
　and drinks my blood
remains in me and I in him,
　says the Lord.

Vel:

Qui manducat meam carnem
　et bibit meum sanguinem,
in me manet et ego in eo,
　dicit Dominus.

Prayer after Communion

Having consumed these gifts,
　we pray, O Lord,
that, by our participation
　in this mystery,
its saving effects upon us may grow.
Through Christ our Lord.

Post communionem

Sumptis muneribus,
　quæsumus, Domine,
ut, cum frequentatione mysterii,
crescat nostræ salutis effectus.
Per Christum Dominum nostrum.

23 July

SIXTEENTH SUNDAY IN ORDINARY TIME

Entrance Antiphon   Ps 53:6,8

SEE, I have God for my help.
The Lord sustains my soul.
I will sacrifice to you
    with willing heart,
and praise your name, O Lord,
    for it is good.

Collect

Show favour, O Lord, to your servants
and mercifully increase the gifts
    of your grace,
that, made fervent in hope,
    faith and charity,
they may be ever watchful
    in keeping your commands.
Through our Lord Jesus Christ,
    your Son,
who lives and reigns with you
    in the unity of the Holy Spirit,
God, for ever and ever.

Ant. ad introitum

ECCE Deus adiuvat me,
et Dominus susceptor est
    animæ meæ.
Voluntarie sacrificabo tibi,
et confitebor nomini tuo, Domine,
    quoniam bonum est.

Collecta

Propitiare, Domine, famulis tuis,
et clementer gratiæ tuæ super eos
    dona multiplica,
ut, spe, fide et caritate ferventes,
semper in mandatis tuis vigili
    custodia perseverent.
Per Dominum nostrum Iesum
    Christum Filium tuum,
qui tecum vivit et regnat
    in unitate Spiritus Sancti,
Deus, per omnia sæcula sæculorum.

FIRST READING

A reading from the book of Wisdom   12:13,16-19

After sin you will grant repentance.

There is no god, other than you, who cares for everything,
to whom you might have to prove that you never judged unjustly.
Your justice has its source in strength,
your sovereignty over all makes you lenient to all.
You show your strength when your sovereign power is questioned
and you expose the insolence of those who know it;
but, disposing of such strength, you are mild in judgement,
you govern us with great lenience,
for you have only to will, and your power is there.
By acting thus you have taught a lesson to your people
how the virtuous man must be kindly to his fellow men,
and you have given your sons the good hope
that after sin you will grant repentance.

    The word of the Lord.

Responsorial Psalm   Ps 85:5-6,9-10,15-16. R. v.5

R. **O Lord, you are good and forgiving.**

O Lord, you are good and forgiving,
full of love to all who call.
Give heed, O Lord, to my prayer
and attend to the sound of my voice. R.

All the nations shall come to adore you
and glorify your name, O Lord:
for you are great and do marvellous deeds,
you who alone are God. R.

But you, God of mercy and compassion,
slow to anger, O Lord,
abounding in love and truth,
turn and take pity on me. R.

SECOND READING

A reading from the letter of St Paul to the Romans   8:26-27
The Spirit expresses our plea in a way that could never be put into words.

The Spirit comes to help us in our weakness. For when we cannot choose
words in order to pray properly, the Spirit himself expresses our plea in a
way that could never be put into words, and God who knows everything in
our hearts knows perfectly well what he means, and that the pleas of the
saints expressed by the Spirit are according to the mind of God.

The word of the Lord.

Gospel Acclamation   Cf. Ep 1:17,18

R. **Alleluia, alleluia!**
May the Father of our Lord Jesus Christ
enlighten the eyes of our mind,
so that we can see what hope his call holds for us.
R. **Alleluia!**

Or: Cf. Mt 11:25

R. **Alleluia, alleluia!**
Blessed are you, Father,
Lord of heaven and earth,
for revealing the mysteries of the kingdom
to mere children.
R. **Alleluia!**

GOSPEL

A reading from the holy Gospel according to Matthew   13:24-43

Let them both grow till the harvest.

[Jesus put another parable before the crowds: 'The kingdom of heaven may be compared to a man who sowed good seed in his field. While everybody was asleep his enemy came, sowed darnel all among the wheat, and made off. When the new wheat sprouted and ripened, the darnel appeared as well. The owner's servants went to him and said, "Sir, was it not good seed that you sowed in your field? If so, where does the darnel come from?" "Some enemy has done this" he answered. And the servants said, "Do you want us to go and weed it out?" But he said, "No, because when you weed out the darnel you might pull up the wheat with it. Let them both grow till the harvest; and at harvest time I shall say to the reapers: First collect the darnel and tie it in bundles to be burnt, then gather the wheat into my barn."']

He put another parable before them, 'The kingdom of heaven is like a mustard seed which a man took and sowed in his field. It is the smallest of all the seeds, but when it has grown it is the biggest shrub of all and becomes a tree so that the birds of the air come and shelter in its branches.'

He told them another parable, 'The kingdom of heaven is like the yeast a woman took and mixed in with three measures of flour till it was leavened all through.'

In all this Jesus spoke to the crowds in parables; indeed, he would never speak to them except in parables. This was to fulfill the prophecy:

I will speak to you in parables
and expound things hidden since the foundation of the world.

Then, leaving the crowds, he went to the house; and his disciples came to him and said, 'Explain the parable about the darnel in the field to us.' He said in reply, 'The sower of the good seed is the Son of Man. The field is the world; the good seed is the subjects of the kingdom; the darnel, the subjects of the evil one; the enemy who sowed them, the devil; the harvest is the end of the world, the reapers are the angels. Well then, just as the darnel is gathered up and burnt in the fire, so it will be at the end of time. The Son of Man will send his angels and they will gather out of his kingdom all things that provoke offences and all who do evil, and throw them into the blazing furnace, where there will be weeping and grinding of teeth. Then the virtuous will shine like the sun in the kingdom of their Father. Listen, anyone who has ears!'

[The Gospel of the Lord.]

Shorter Form, verses 24-30. Read between [ ]

Prayer over the Offerings

O God, who in the one
　　perfect sacrifice
brought to completion varied
　　offerings of the law,
accept, we pray, this sacrifice
　　from your faithful servants
and make it holy, as you blessed
　　the gifts of Abel,
so that what each has offered
　　to the honour of your majesty
may benefit the salvation of all.
Through Christ our Lord.

Super oblata

Deus, qui legalium
　　differentiam hostiarum
unius sacrificii perfectione sanxisti,
accipe sacrificium a devotis
　　tibi famulis,
et pari benedictione,
　　sicut munera Abel, sanctifica,
ut, quod singuli obtulerunt
　　ad maiestatis tuæ honorem,
cunctis proficiat ad salutem.
Per Christum Dominum nostrum.

Preface of Sundays in Ordinary Time I-VIII, pp.60-67.

Communion Antiphon　Ps 110:4-5

The Lord, the gracious, the merciful,
has made a memorial of his wonders;
he gives food to those who fear him.

Ant. ad communionem

Memoriam fecit mirabilium suorum
misericors et miserator Dominus;
escam dedit timentibus se.

Or:　　　　　　　　　　　Rv 3:20

Behold, I stand at the door
　　and knock, says the Lord.
If anyone hears my voice
　　and opens the door to me,
I will enter his house and dine
　　with him, and he with me.

Vel:

Ecce sto ad ostium et pulso,
　　dicit Dominus:
si quis audierit vocem meam,
　　et aperuerit mihi ianuam,
intrabo ad illum, et cenabo
　　cum illo, et ipse mecum.

Prayer after Communion

Graciously be present to your people,
　　we pray, O Lord,
and lead those you have imbued
　　with heavenly mysteries
to pass from former ways
　　to newness of life.
Through Christ our Lord.

Post communionem

Populo tuo, quæsumus, Domine,
　　adesto propitius,
et, quem mysteriis
　　cælestibus imbuisti,
fac ad novitatem vitæ
　　de vetustate transire.
Per Christum Dominum nostrum.

30 July

SEVENTEENTH SUNDAY IN ORDINARY TIME

Entrance Antiphon Cf. Ps 67:6-7,36 | Ant. ad introitum

GOD is in his holy place,
God who unites those
who dwell in his house;
he himself gives might and strength
to his people.

DEUS in loco sancto suo;
Deus qui inhabitare facit
unanimes in domo,
ipse dabit virtutem et fortitudinem
plebi suæ.

Collect | Collecta

O God, protector of those
who hope in you,
without whom nothing has firm
foundation, nothing is holy,
bestow in abundance your mercy
upon us
and grant that, with you as our ruler
and guide,
we may use the good things that pass
in such a way as to hold fast even now
to those that ever endure.
Through our Lord Jesus Christ,
your Son,
who lives and reigns with you
in the unity of the Holy Spirit,
God, for ever and ever.

Protector in te sperantium, Deus,
sine quo nihil est validum,
nihil sanctum,
multiplica super nos
misericordiam tuam
ut, te rectore, te duce, sic bonis
transeuntibus nunc utamur,
ut iam possimus
inhærere mansuris.
Per Dominum nostrum Iesum
Christum Filium tuum,
qui tecum vivit et regnat
in unitate Spiritus Sancti,
Deus, per omnia sæcula sæculorum.

FIRST READING

A reading from the first book of the Kings   3:5,7-12

You have asked for a discerning judgement for yourself.

The Lord appeared to Solomon in a dream and said, 'Ask what you would like me to give you.' Solomon replied, 'Lord, my God, you have made your servant king in succession to David my father. But I am a very young man, unskilled in leadership. Your servant finds himself in the midst of this people of yours that you have chosen, a people so many its numbers cannot be counted or reckoned. Give your servant a heart to understand how to discern between good and evil, for who could govern this people of yours that is so great?' It pleased the Lord that Solomon should have asked for this. 'Since you have asked for this' the Lord said 'and not asked for long life for yourself or riches or the lives of your enemies, but have asked for a discerning judgement for yourself, here and now I do what you ask. I give you a heart wise and shrewd as none before you has had and none will have after you.'

The word of the Lord.

Ps 118:57,72,76-77,127-130. R. v.97

R. **Lord how I love your law!**

My part, I have resolved, O Lord,
is to obey your word.
The law from your mouth means more to me
than silver and gold. R.

Let your love be ready to console me
by your promise to your servant.
Let your love come to me and I shall live
for your law is my delight. R.

That is why I love your commands
more than finest gold,
That is why I rule my life by your precepts:
I hate false ways. R.

Your will is wonderful indeed;
therefore I obey it.
The unfolding of your word gives light
and teaches the simple. R.

SECOND READING

A reading from the letter of St Paul to the Romans   8:28-30
God intended us to become true images of his Son.

We know that by turning everything to their good God co-operates with all those who love him, with all those that he has called according to his purpose. They are the ones he chose specially long ago and intended to become true images of his Son, so that his Son might be the eldest of many brothers. He called those he intended for this; those he called he justified, and with those he justified he shared his glory.

The word of the Lord.

Gospel Acclamation

Jn 15:15

R.**Alleluia, alleluia!**
I call you friends, says the Lord,
because I have made known to you
everything I have learnt from my Father.
R.**Alleluia!**

Or:

Cf. Mt 11:25

R.**Alleluia, alleluia!**
Blessed are you, Father,
Lord of heaven and earth,
for revealing the mysteries of the kingdom
to mere children.
R.**Alleluia!**

GOSPEL

A reading from the holy Gospel according to Matthew 13:44-52
He sells everything he owns and buys the field.

|Jesus said to the crowds: 'The kingdom of heaven is like treasure hidden in a field which someone has found; he hides it again, goes off happy, sells everything he owns and buys the field.

'Again, the kingdom of heaven is like a merchant looking for fine pearls; when he finds one of great value he goes and sells everything he owns and buys it.]

'Again, the kingdom of heaven is like a dragnet cast into the sea that brings in a haul of all kinds. When it is full, the fishermen haul it ashore; then, sitting down, they collect the good ones in a basket and throw away those that are no use. This is how it will be at the end of time: the angels will appear and separate the wicked from the just to throw them into the blazing furnace where there will be weeping and grinding of teeth.

'Have you understood all this?' They said, 'Yes.' And he said to them, 'Well then, every scribe who becomes a disciple of the kingdom of heaven is like a householder who brings out from his storeroom things both new and old.'

| [The Gospel of the Lord.]

Shorter Form, verses 44-46. Read between [ ]

Prayer over the Offerings

Accept, O Lord, we pray, the
  offerings
which we bring from the abundance
  of your gifts,
that through the powerful working
  of your grace
these most sacred mysteries may
  sanctify our present way of life
and lead us to eternal gladness.
Through Christ our Lord.

Preface of Sundays in Ordinary Time I-VIII, pp.60-67.

Super oblata

Suscipe, quæsumus,
  Domine, munera,
quæ tibi de tua largitate deferimus,
ut hæc sacrosancta mysteria,
  gratiæ tuæ operante virtute,
et præsentis vitæ nos
  conversatione sanctificent,
et ad gaudia sempiterna perducant.
Per Christum Dominum nostrum.

Communion Antiphon   Ps 102:2

Bless the Lord, O my soul,
and never forget all his benefits.

Ant. ad communionem

Benedic, anima mea, Domino,
et noli oblivisci omnes
  retributiones eius.

Or: Mt 5:7-8

Blessed are the merciful,
  for they shall receive mercy.
Blessed are the clean of heart,
  for they shall see God.

Vel:

Beati misericordes,
quoniam ipsi
  misericordiam consequentur.
Beati mundo corde,
quoniam ipsi Deum videbunt.

Prayer after Communion

We have consumed, O Lord,
  this divine Sacrament,
the perpetual memorial
  of the Passion of your Son;
grant, we pray, that this gift,
which he himself gave us with love
  beyond all telling,
may profit us for salvation.
Through Christ our Lord.

Post communionem

Sumpsimus, Domine,
  divinum sacramentum,
passionis Filii tui
  memoriale perpetuum;
tribue, quæsumus,
ut ad nostram salutem hoc
  munus proficiat,
quod ineffabili nobis caritate
  ipse donavit.
Qui vivit et regnat
  in sæcula sæculorum.

6 August

THE TRANSFIGURATION OF THE LORD

When the Lord is transfigured before Peter, James and John, they hear the voice of God the Father say: "This is my beloved Son! listen to him!". Listen to Jesus. Why? To nourish our faith with the Word of God. And this is the duty of the Christian. What are the duties of the Christian? Perhaps you will say to me: to go to Mass on Sundays; to fast and abstain during Holy Week; to do this.... Yet the first duty of the Christian is to listen to the Word of God, to listen to Jesus, because he speaks to us and he saves us by his word. And by this word he makes our faith even stronger and more robust.

(Pope Francis)

Feast

Entrance Antiphon   Cf. Mt 17:5

IN a resplendent cloud the Holy
  Spirit appeared.
The Father's voice was heard:
    This is my beloved Son,
with whom I am well pleased.
    Listen to him.

Ant. ad introitum

IN splendenti nube Spiritus
  Sanctus visus est,
paterna vox audita est:
    Hic est Filius meus dilectus,
in quo mihi bene complacui:
    ipsum audite.

The **Gloria in excelsis** (**Glory to God in the highest**) is said.

Collect

O God, who in the glorious
    Transfiguration
of your Only Begotten Son
confirmed the mysteries of faith
    by the witness of the Fathers
and wonderfully prefigured our full
    adoption to sonship,
grant, we pray, to your servants,
that, listening to the voice
    of your beloved Son,
we may merit to become coheirs
    with him.

Collecta

Deus, qui fidei sacramenta
in Unigeniti tui gloriosa
    Transfiguratione
patrum testimonio roborasti,
et adoptionem filiorum perfectam
    mirabiliter præsignasti,
concede nobis famulis tuis,
ut, ipsius dilecti Filii
    tui vocem audientes,
eiusdem coheredes effici mereamur.

| Who lives and reigns with you in the unity of the Holy Spirit, God, for ever and ever. | Qui tecum vivit et regnat in unitate Spiritus Sancti, Deus, per omnia sæcula sæculorum. |

FIRST READING

A reading from the prophet Daniel   7:9-10,13-14

His robe was white as snow.

As I watched:
Thrones were set in place
and one of great age took his seat.
His robe was white as snow,
the hair of his head as pure as wool.
His throne was a blaze of flames,
its wheels were a burning fire.
A stream of fire poured out,
issuing from his presence.
A thousand thousand waited on him,
ten thousand times ten thousand stood before him.
A court was held and the books were opened.
I gazed into the visions of the night.
And I saw, coming on the clouds of heaven,
one like a son of man.
He came to the one of great age
and was led into his presence.
On him was conferred sovereignty,
glory and kingship,
and men of all peoples, nations and languages became his servants.
His sovereignty is an eternal sovereignty
which shall never pass away,
nor will his empire ever be destroyed.

  The word of the Lord.

Responsorial Psalm   Ps 96:1-2,5-6,9. R. vv.1,9

R. **The Lord is king,**
   most high above all the earth.

The Lord is king, let earth rejoice,
let all the coastlands be glad.
Cloud and darkness are his raiment;
his throne, justice and right. R.

The mountains melt like wax
before the Lord of all the earth.
The skies proclaim his justice;
all peoples see his glory. R.

For you indeed are the Lord
most high above all the earth
exalted far above all spirits. R.

SECOND READING

A reading from the second letter of St Peter   1:16-19

We heard this ourselves, spoken from heaven.

It was not any cleverly invented myths that we were repeating when we
brought you the knowledge of the power and the coming of our Lord Jesus
Christ; we had seen his majesty for ourselves. He was honoured and glorified
by God the Father, when the Sublime Glory itself spoke to him and said,
'This is my Son, the Beloved; he enjoys my favour.' We heard this ourselves,
spoken from heaven, when we were with him on the holy mountain.

So we have confirmation of what was said in prophecies; and you will be
right to depend on prophecy and take it as a lamp for lighting a way through
the dark until the dawn comes and the morning star rises in your minds.

The word of the Lord.

Gospel Acclamation   Mt 17:5

R. **Alleluia, alleluia!**
This is my Son, the Beloved,
he enjoys my favour;
listen to him.
R. **Alleluia!**

GOSPEL

A reading from the holy Gospel according to Matthew   17:1-9

His face shone like the sun.

Jesus took with him Peter and James and his brother John and led them up a high mountain where they could be alone. There in their presence he was transfigured: his face shone like the sun and his clothes became as white as the light. Suddenly Moses and Elijah appeared to them; they were talking with him. Then Peter spoke to Jesus. 'Lord,' he said 'it is wonderful for us to be here; if you wish, I will make three tents here, one for you, one for Moses and one for Elijah.' He was still speaking when suddenly a bright cloud covered them with shadow, and from the cloud there came a voice which said, 'This is my Son, the Beloved; he enjoys my favour. Listen to him.' When they heard this, the disciples fell on their faces, overcome with fear. But Jesus came up and touched them. 'Stand up,' he said 'do not be afraid.' And when they raised their eyes they saw no one but only Jesus.

As they came down from the mountain Jesus gave them this order, 'Tell no one about the vision until the Son of Man has risen from the dead.'

The Gospel of the Lord.

The Creed is said.

Prayer over the Offerings	Super oblata
Sanctify, O Lord, we pray, these offerings here made to celebrate the glorious Transfiguration of your Only Begotten Son, and by his radiant splendour cleanse us from the stains of sin. Through Christ our Lord.	Oblata munera, quæsumus, Domine, gloriosa Unigeniti tui Transfiguratione sanctifica, nosque a peccatorum maculis, splendoribus ipsius illustrationis, emunda. Per Christum Dominum nostrum.

Preface: The Mystery of
the Transfiguration.

It is truly right and just, our duty
    and our salvation,
always and everywhere to give
    you thanks,
Lord, holy Father, almighty
    and eternal God,
through Christ our Lord.

For he revealed his glory in
    the presence of chosen witnesses
and filled with the greatest
    splendour that bodily form
which he shares with all humanity,
that the scandal of the Cross
might be removed from the hearts
    of his disciples
and that he might show
how in the Body of the whole
    Church is to be fulfilled
what so wonderfully shone forth
    first in its Head.

And so, with the Powers of heaven,
we worship you constantly
    on earth,
and before your majesty
without end we acclaim:

Holy, Holy, Holy Lord God of hosts...

Communion Antiphon Cf. 1 Jn 3:2

When Christ appears, we shall
    be like him,
for we shall see him as he is.

Præfatio: De mysterio
Transfigurationis.

Vere dignum et iustum est,
    æquum et salutare,
nos tibi semper et ubique
    gratias agere:
Domine, sancte Pater,
    omnipotens æterne Deus:
per Christum Dominum nostrum.

Qui coram electis testibus suam
    gloriam revelavit,
et communem illam cum ceteris
    corporis formam
maximo splendore perfudit,
ut de cordibus discipulorum crucis
    scandalum tolleretur,
et in totius Ecclesiæ corpore
    declararet implendum
quod eius mirabiliter præfulsit
    in capite.

Et ideo cum cælorum Virtutibus
in terris te iugiter celebramus,
maiestati tuæ sine fine clamantes:

Sanctus, Sanctus, Sanctus. . .

Ant. ad communionem

Cum Christus apparuerit,
similes ei erimus,
quoniam videbimus eum sicuti est.

Prayer after Communion

May the heavenly nourishment
    we have received,
O Lord, we pray,
transform us into the likeness
    of your Son,
whose radiant splendour you willed
    to make manifest
in his glorious Transfiguration.
Who lives and reigns for ever and ever.

Post communionem

Cælestia, quæsumus, Domine,
alimenta quæ sumpsimus
in eius nos
    transformet imaginem,
cuius claritatem gloriosa
    Transfiguratione
manifestare voluisti.
Qui vivit et regnat
    in sæcula sæculorum.

13 August

NINETEENTH SUNDAY IN ORDINARY TIME

Entrance Antiphon Cf. Ps 73:20,19,22,23

LOOK to your covenant, O Lord,
and forget not the life of your
    poor ones for ever.
Arise, O God, and defend your cause,
and forget not the cries of those
    who seek you.

Ant. ad introitum

RESPICE, Domine,
in testamentum tuum,
et animas pauperum tuorum
    ne derelinquas in finem.
Exsurge, Domine,
    et iudica causam tuam,
et ne obliviscaris voces
    quærentium te.

Collect

Almighty ever-living God,
whom, taught by the Holy Spirit,
we dare to call our Father,
bring, we pray, to perfection
    in our hearts
the spirit of adoption as your sons
    and daughters,
that we may merit
    to enter into the inheritance
which you have promised.
Through our Lord Jesus Christ,
    your Son,
who lives and reigns with you
    in the unity of the Holy Spirit,
God, for ever and ever.

Collecta

Omnipotens sempiterne Deus,
quem, docente Spiritu Sancto,
paterno nomine
    invocare præsumimus,
perfice in cordibus nostris spiritum
    adoptionis filiorum,
ut promissam hereditatem
    ingredi mereamur.
Per Dominum nostrum Iesum
    Christum Filium tuum,
qui tecum vivit et regnat
    in unitate Spiritus Sancti,
Deus, per omnia sæcula sæculorum.

FIRST READING

A reading from the first book of the Kings   19:9,11-13
Stand on the mountain before the Lord.

When Elijah reached Horeb, the mountain of God, he went into the cave
and spent the night in it. Then he was told, 'Go out and stand on the
mountain before the Lord.' Then the Lord himself went by. There came
a mighty wind, so strong it tore the mountains and shattered the rocks
before the Lord. But the Lord was not in the wind. After the wind came an
earthquake. But the Lord was not in the earthquake. After the earthquake
came a fire. But the Lord was not in the fire. And after the fire there came
the sound of a gentle breeze. And when Elijah heard this, he covered his
face with his cloak and went out and stood at the entrance of the cave.

The word of the Lord.

Responsorial Psalm   Ps 84:9-14. R. v.8

R. **Let us see, O Lord your mercy
and give us your saving help.**

I will hear what the Lord God has to say,
a voice that speaks of peace.
His help is near for those who fear him
and his glory will dwell in our land. R.

Mercy and faithfulness have met;
justice and peace have embraced.
Faithfulness shall spring from the earth
and justice look down from heaven. R.

The Lord will make us prosper
and our earth shall yield its fruit.
Justice shall march before him
and peace shall follow his steps. R.

SECOND READING

A reading from the letter of St Paul to the Romans   9:1-5
I would willingly be condemned if it could help my brothers.

What I want to say is no pretence; I say it in union with Christ – it is the
truth – my conscience in union with the Holy Spirit assures me of it too.
What I want to say is this: my sorrow is so great, my mental anguish so
endless, I would willingly be condemned and be cut off from Christ if
it could help my brothers of Israel, my own flesh and blood. They were

adopted as sons, they were given the glory and the covenants; the Law and the ritual were drawn up for them, and the promises were made to them. They are descended from the patriarchs and from their flesh and blood came Christ who is above all, God for ever blessed! Amen.

The word of the Lord.

Gospel Acclamation　　　　　　　　　　　　　　　　　Lk 19:38

R. **Alleluia, alleluia!**
Blessings on the King who comes, in the name of the Lord!
Peace in heaven and glory in the highest heavens!
R. **Alleluia!**

Or:　　　　　　　　　　　　　　　　　　　　　　　Ps 129:5

R. **Alleluia, alleluia!**
My soul is waiting for the Lord,
I count on his word.
R. **Alleluia!**

GOSPEL

A reading from the holy Gospel according to Matthew　　14:22-33

Tell me to come to you across the water.

Jesus made the disciples get into the boat and go on ahead to the other side while he would send the crowds away. After sending the crowds away he went up into the hills by himself to pray. When evening came, he was there alone, while the boat, by now far out on the lake, was battling with a heavy sea, for there was a headwind. In the fourth watch of the night he went towards them, walking on the lake, and when the disciples saw him walking on the lake they were terrified. 'It is a ghost' they said, and cried out in fear. But at once Jesus called out to them, saying, 'Courage! It is I! Do not be afraid.' It was Peter who answered. 'Lord,' he said 'if it is you, tell me to come to you across the water.' 'Come' said Jesus. Then Peter got out of the boat and started walking towards Jesus across the water, but as soon as he felt the force of the wind, he took fright and began to sink. 'Lord! Save me!' he cried. Jesus put out his hand at once and held him. 'Man of little faith,' he said 'why did you doubt?' And as they got into the boat the wind dropped. The men in the boat bowed down before him and said, 'Truly, you are the Son of God.'

The Gospel of the Lord.

Prayer over the Offerings

Be pleased, O Lord, to accept
　　the offerings of your Church,
for in your mercy you have given
　　them to be offered
and by your power
　　you transform them
into the mystery of our salvation.
Through Christ our Lord.

Super oblata

Ecclesiæ tuæ, Domine, munera
　　placatus assume,
quæ et misericors
　　offerenda tribuisti,
et in nostræ salutis potenter efficis
　　transire mysterium.
Per Christum Dominum nostrum.

Preface of Sundays in Ordinary Time I-VIII, pp.60-67.

Communion Antiphon Ps 147:12,14

O Jerusalem, glorify the Lord,
who gives you your fill
　　of finest wheat.

Or: Cf. Jn 6:51

The bread that I will give,
　　says the Lord,
is my flesh for the life of the world.

Ant. ad communionem

Lauda, Ierusalem, Dominum,
qui adipe frumenti satiat te.

Vel:

Panis, quem ego dedero,
caro mea est pro sæculi vita,
dicit Dominus.

Prayer after Communion

May the communion
　　in your Sacrament
that we have consumed, save us,
　　O Lord,
and confirm us in the light
　　of your truth.
Through Christ our Lord.

Post communionem

Sacramentorum tuorum, Domine,
communio sumpta nos salvet,
et in tuæ veritatis luce confirmet.
Per Christum Dominum nostrum.

15 August

THE ASSUMPTION
OF THE BLESSED VIRGIN MARY

Mary's secret is humility. It is her humility that attracted God's gaze to her. The human eye always looks for grandeur and allows itself to be dazzled by what is flashy. Instead, God does not look at the appearance. God looks at the heart and is enchanted by humility. Humility of heart enchants God. Today, looking at Mary assumed into heaven, we can say that humility is the way that leads to heaven. The word "humility" comes from the Latin word humus, which means "earth". It is paradoxical: to arrive on high, into heaven, what is needed is to stay low, like the earth! Jesus teaches this: "he who humbles himself will be exalted". God does not exalt us because of our gifts, because of our wealth or because of our skills, but because of humility. God loves humility. God lifts up those who humble themselves; he lifts up those who serve.

(Pope Francis)

Solemnity

At the Vigil Mass

This Mass is used on the evening of 14 August, either before or after First Vespers (Evening Prayer I) of the Solemnity.

Entrance Antiphon

GLORIOUS things are spoken
of you, O Mary,
who today were exalted above
  the choirs of Angels
into eternal triumph with Christ.

Ant. ad introitum

GLORIOSA dicta sunt de te,
Maria,
quæ hodie exaltata es super
  choros Angelorum,
et in æternum cum Christo triumphas.

The Gloria in excelsis (Glory to God in the highest) is said.

Collect

O God, who, looking on the lowliness
  of the Blessed Virgin Mary,
raised her to this grace,
that your Only Begotten Son was
  born of her according to the flesh
and that she was crowned this day

Collecta

Deus, qui beatam
  Virginem Mariam,
eius humilitatem respiciens,
  ad hanc gratiam evexisti,
ut Unigenitus tuus ex ipsa
  secundum carnem nasceretur,

with surpassing glory,
grant through her prayers,
that, saved by the mystery
  of your redemption,
we may merit to be exalted by you
  on high.
Through our Lord Jesus Christ,
  your Son,
who lives and reigns with you
  in the unity of the Holy Spirit,
God, for ever and ever.

et hodierna die superexcellenti
  gloria coronasti,
eius nobis precibus concede,
ut, redemptionis tuæ
  mysterio salvati,
a te exaltari mereamur.
Per Dominum nostrum Iesum
  Christum Filium tuum,
qui tecum vivit et regnat
  in unitate Spiritus Sancti,
Deus, per omnia sæcula sæculorum.

FIRST READING

A reading from the first book of Chronicles   15:3-4,15-16; 16:1-2

They brought in the ark of God and set it inside the tent which David had pitched for it.

David gathered all Israel together in Jerusalem to bring the ark of God up to the place he had prepared for it. David called together the sons of Aaron and the sons of Levi. And the Levites carried the ark of God with the shafts on their shoulders, as Moses had ordered in accordance with the word of the Lord.

David then told the heads of the Levites to assign duties for their kinsmen as cantors, with their various instruments of music, harps and lyres and cymbals, to play joyful tunes. They brought the ark of God in and put it inside the tent that David had pitched for it; and they offered holocausts before God, and communion sacrifices. And when David had finished offering holocausts and communion sacrifices, he blessed the people in the name of the Lord.

The word of the Lord.

Responsorial Psalm   Ps 131:6-7,9-10,13-14. R. v.8

R. **Go up, Lord, to the place of your rest,**
   you and the ark of your strength.

At Ephrata we heard of the ark;
we found it in the plains of Yearim.
'Let us go to the place of his dwelling;
let us go to kneel at his footstool.' R.

Your priests shall be clothed with holiness:
your faithful shall ring out their joy.

For the sake of David your servant
do not reject your anointed. R.

For the Lord has chosen Sion;
he has desired it for his dwelling:
'This is my resting-place for ever,
here have I chosen to live.' R.

R. **Go up, Lord, to the place of your rest,**
you and the ark of your strength.

SECOND READING

A reading from the first letter of St Paul to the Corinthians   15:54-57

He gave us victory through our Lord Jesus Christ.

When this perishable nature has put on imperishability, and when this mortal nature has put on immortality, then the words of scripture will come true: Death is swallowed up in victory. Death, where is your victory? Death, where is your sting? Now the sting of death is sin, and sin gets its power from the Law. So let us thank God for giving us the victory through our Lord Jesus Christ.

The word of the Lord.

Gospel Acclamation   Lk 11:28

R. **Alleluia, alleluia!**
Happy are those
who hear the word of God,
and keep it.
R. **Alleluia!**

GOSPEL

A reading from the holy Gospel according to Luke   11:27-28

Happy the womb that bore you!

As Jesus was speaking, a woman in the crowd raised her voice and said, 'Happy the womb that bore you and the breasts you sucked!' But he replied, 'Still happier those who hear the word of God and keep it!'

The Gospel of the Lord.

The Creed is said.

Prayer over the Offerings

Receive, we pray, O Lord,
the sacrifice of conciliation
    and praise,
which we celebrate on
    the Assumption of the holy
    Mother of God,
that it may lead us to your pardon
and confirm us in perpetual
    thanksgiving.
Through Christ our Lord.

Proper Preface, as in the following Mass, p.567.

Super oblata

Suscipe, quæsumus, Domine,
sacrificium placationis et laudis,
quod in sanctæ Dei Genetricis
    Assumptione celebramus,
ut ad veniam nos
    obtinendam perducat,
et in perpetua gratiarum
    constituat actione.
Per Christum Dominum nostrum.

Communion Antiphon Cf. Lk 11:27

Blessed is the womb
    of the Virgin Mary,
which bore the Son
    of the eternal Father.

Ant. ad communionem

Beata viscera Mariæ Virginis,
quæ portaverunt æterni
    Patris Filium.

Prayer after Communion

Having partaken of this
    heavenly table,
we beseech your mercy,
    Lord our God,
that we, who honour
    the Assumption of the Mother
    of God,
may be freed from every threat
    of harm.
Through Christ our Lord.

A formula of Solemn Blessing, pp.144-145, may be used.

Post communionem

Mensæ cælestis participes effecti,
imploramus clementiam tuam,
    Domine Deus noster,
ut, qui Assumptionem Dei
    Genetricis colimus,
a cunctis malis
    imminentibus liberemur.
Per Christum Dominum nostrum.

At the Mass during the Day

Entrance Antiphon Cf. Rv 12:1

A GREAT sign appeared
    in heaven:
a woman clothed with the sun,
    and the moon beneath her feet,
and on her head a crown
    of twelve stars.

Ant. ad introitum

S IGNUM magnum apparuit
    in cælo:
mulier amicta sole, et luna sub
    pedibus eius,
et in capite eius corona
    stellarum duodecim.

Or:

Let us all rejoice in the Lord,
as we celebrate the feast day
    in honour of the Virgin Mary,
at whose Assumption
    the Angels rejoice
and praise the Son of God.

Vel:

Gaudeamus omnes in Domino,
diem festum celebrantes sub
    honore Mariæ Virginis,
de cuius Assumptione
    gaudent Angeli,
et collaudant Filium Dei.

The **Gloria in excelsis** (**Glory to God in the highest**) is said.

Collect

Almighty ever-living God,
who assumed the Immaculate Virgin
    Mary, the Mother of your Son,
body and soul into heavenly glory,
grant, we pray,
that, always attentive to the things
    that are above,
we may merit to be sharers
    of her glory.
Through our Lord Jesus Christ,
    your Son,
who lives and reigns with you
    in the unity of the Holy Spirit,
God, for ever and ever.

Collecta

Omnipotens sempiterne Deus,
qui immaculatam Virginem
    Mariam, Filii tui Genetricem,
corpore et anima ad cælestem
    gloriam assumpsisti,
concede, quæsumus, ut,
    ad superna semper intenti,
ipsius gloriæ mereamur
    esse consortes.
Per Dominum nostrum Iesum
    Christum Filium tuum,
qui tecum vivit et regnat
in unitate Spiritus Sancti,
Deus, per omnia sæcula sæculorum.

FIRST READING

A reading from the book of the Apocalypse   11:19; 12:1-6,10

A woman adorned with the sun standing on the moon.

The sanctuary of God in heaven opened, and the ark of the covenant could be seen inside it.

Now a great sign appeared in heaven: a woman, adorned with the sun, standing on the moon, and with the twelve stars on her head for a crown. She was pregnant, and in labour, crying aloud in the pangs of childbirth. Then a second sign appeared in the sky, a huge red dragon which had seven heads and ten horns, and each of the seven heads crowned with a coronet. Its tail dragged a third of the stars from the sky and dropped them to the earth, and the dragon stopped in front of the woman as she was having the child, so that he could eat it as soon as it was born from its mother. The woman brought a male child into the world, the son who was to rule all nations with an iron sceptre, and the child was taken straight up to God and to his throne, while the woman escaped into the desert, where God had made a place of safety ready. Then I heard a voice shout from heaven, 'Victory and power and empire for ever have been won by our God, and all authority for his Christ.'

The word of the Lord.

Responsional Psalm   Ps 44:10-12,16. R. v.10

R. **On your right stands the queen,**
   in garments of gold.

The daughters of kings are among your loved ones.
On your right stands the queen in gold of Ophir.
Listen, O daughter, give ear to my words:
forget your own people and your father's house. R.

So will the king desire your beauty:
He is your lord, pay homage to him.
They are escorted amid gladness and joy;
they pass within the palace of the king. R.

SECOND READING

A reading from the first letter of St Paul to the Corinthians   15:20-26

Christ as the first-fruits and then, those who belong to him.

Christ has been raised from the dead, the first-fruits of all who have fallen asleep. Death came through one man and in the same way the resurrection of the dead has come through one man. Just as all men die in Adam, so all men will be brought to life in Christ; but all of them in their proper order: Christ as the first-fruits and then, after the coming of Christ, those who belong to him. After that will come the end, when he hands over the kingdom to God the Father, having done away with every sovereignty, authority and power. For he must be king until he has put all his enemies under his feet and the last of the enemies to be destroyed is death, for everything is to be put under his feet.

The word of the Lord.

Gospel Acclamation

R. **Alleluia, alleluia!**
Mary has been taken up into heaven;
all the choirs of angels are rejoicing.
R. **Alleluia!**

GOSPEL

A reading from the holy Gospel according to Luke   1:39-56
The Almighty has done great things for me, he has exalted up the lowly.

Mary set out and went as quickly as she could to a town in the hill country
of Judah. She went into Zechariah's house and greeted Elizabeth. Now as
soon as Elizabeth heard Mary's greeting, the child leapt in her womb and
Elizabeth was filled with the Holy Spirit. She gave a loud cry and said, 'Of
all women you are the most blessed, and blessed is the fruit of your womb.
Why should I be honoured with a visit from the mother of my Lord? For
the moment your greeting reached my ears, the child in my womb leapt
for joy. Yes, blessed is she who believed that the promise made her by the
Lord would be fulfilled.'

And Mary said:

> 'My soul proclaims the greatness of the Lord
> and my spirit exults in God my saviour;
> because he has looked upon his lowly handmaid.
> Yes, from this day forward all generations will call me blessed,
> for the Almighty has done great things for me.
> Holy is his name,
> and his mercy reaches from age to age for those who fear him.
> He has shown the power of his arm,
> he has routed the proud of heart.
> He has pulled down princes from their thrones and exalted the lowly.
> The hungry he has filled with good things, the rich sent empty away.
> He has come to the help of Israel his servant, mindful of his mercy
> – according to the promise he made to our ancestors –
> of his mercy to Abraham and to his descendants for ever.'

Mary stayed with Elizabeth about three months and then went back home.

   The Gospel of the Lord.

The Creed is said.

Prayer over the Offerings

May this oblation, our tribute
    of homage,
rise up to you, O Lord,
and, through the intercession
    of the most Blessed Virgin Mary,
whom you assumed into heaven,
may our hearts,
    aflame with the fire of love,
constantly long for you.
Through Christ our Lord.

Preface: The Glory of Mary
assumed into heaven.

It is truly right and just, our duty
    and our salvation,
always and everywhere to give
    you thanks,
Lord, holy Father, almighty
    and eternal God,
through Christ our Lord.

For today the Virgin Mother of God
was assumed into heaven
as the beginning and image
of your Church's coming
    to perfection
and a sign of sure hope and comfort
    to your pilgrim people;
rightly you would not allow her
to see the corruption of the tomb,
since from her own body she
    marvellously brought forth
your incarnate Son,
    the Author of all life.

And so, in company with the choirs
    of Angels,
we praise you, and with joy
    we proclaim:

Holy, Holy, Holy Lord God of hosts...

Super oblata

Ascendat ad te, Domine, nostræ
    devotionis oblatio,
et, beatissima Virgine Maria
in cælum assumpta intercedente,
corda nostra, caritatis igne succensa,
ad te iugiter aspirent.
Per Christum Dominum nostrum.

Præfatio: De Gloria
Mariæ Assumptæ.

Vere dignum et iustum est,
    æquum et salutare,
nos tibi semper et ubique
    gratias agere:
Domine, sancte Pater,
    omnipotens æterne Deus:
per Christum Dominum nostrum.

Quoniam hodie Virgo Deipara
    in cælos assumpta est,
Ecclesiæ tuæ consummandæ
    initium et imago,
ac populo peregrinanti certæ spei
    et solacii documentum;
corruptionem enim sepulcri
eam videre merito noluisti,
quæ Filium tuum,
    vitæ omnis auctorem,
ineffabiliter de se
    genuit incarnatum.

Et ideo, choris angelicis sociati,
te laudamus, in gaudio confitentes:

Sanctus, Sanctus, Sanctus. . .

Communion Antiphon Lk 1:48-49

All generations will call me blessed,
for he who is mighty has done
　　great things for me.

Ant. ad communionem

Beatam me dicent
　　omnes generationes,
quia fecit mihi magna
　　qui potens est.

Prayer after Communion

Having received the Sacrament
　　of salvation,
we ask you to grant, O Lord,
that, through the intercession
　　of the Blessed Virgin Mary,
whom you assumed into heaven,
we may be brought to the glory
　　of the resurrection.
Through Christ our Lord.

Post communionem

Sumptis, Domine,
　　salutaribus sacramentis,
da, quæsumus,
ut, intercessione beatæ Mariæ
　　Virginis in cælum assumptæ,
ad resurrectionis
　　gloriam perducamur.
Per Christum Dominum nostrum.

A formula of Solemn Blessing, p.144-145, may be used.

20 August

TWENTIETH SUNDAY IN ORDINARY TIME

Entrance Antiphon　　　Ps 83:10-11

TURN your eyes, O God,
　　our shield;
and look on the face
　　of your anointed one;
one day within your courts
is better than a thousand elsewhere.

Ant. ad introitum

PROTECTOR noster,
　　aspice, Deus,
et respice in faciem Christi tui,
quia melior est dies una in atriis
　　tuis super millia.

Collect

O God, who have prèpared
　　for those who love you
good things which no eye can see,
fill our hearts, we pray,
　　with the warmth of your love,

Collecta

Deus, qui diligentibus te bona
　　invisibilia præparasti,
infunde cordibus nostris
　　tui amoris affectum,
ut, te in omnibus et super
　　omnia diligentes,

so that, loving you in all things
   and above all things,
we may attain your promises,
which surpass every human desire.
Through our Lord Jesus Christ,
   your Son,
who lives and reigns with you
   in the unity of the Holy Spirit,
God, for ever and ever.

promissiones tuas, quæ omne
   desiderium superant,
consequamur.
Per Dominum nostrum Iesum
   Christum Filium tuum,
qui tecum vivit et regnat
   in unitate Spiritus Sancti,
Deus, per omnia sæcula sæculorum.

FIRST READING

A reading from the prophet Isaiah   56:1,6-7

I will bring foreigners to my holy mountain.

Thus says the Lord: Have a care for justice, act with integrity, for soon my salvation will come and my integrity be manifest.

Foreigners who have attached themselves to the Lord to serve him and to love his name and be his servants – all who observe the sabbath, not profaning it, and cling to my covenant – these I will bring to my holy mountain. I will make them joyful in my house of prayer. Their holocausts and their sacrifices will be accepted on my altar, for my house will be called a house of prayer for all the peoples.

The word of the Lord.

Responsorial Psalm   Ps 66:2-3,5-6,8. R. v.4

R. **Let the peoples praise you, O God;**
   let all the peoples praise you.

   O God, be gracious and bless us
   and let your face shed its light upon us.
   So will your ways be known upon earth
   and all nations learn your saving help. R.

   Let the nations be glad and exult
   for you rule the world with justice.
   With fairness you rule the peoples,
   you guide the nations on earth. R.

   Let the peoples praise you, O God;
   let all the peoples praise you.
   May God still give us his blessing
   till the ends of the earth revere him. R.

SECOND READING

A reading from the letter of St Paul to the Romans   11:13-15,29-32
With Israel, God never takes back his gifts or revokes his choice.

Let me tell you pagans this: I have been sent to the pagans as their apostle,
and I am proud of being sent, but the purpose of it is to make my own
people envious of you, and in this way save some of them. Since their
rejection meant the reconciliation of the world, do you know what their
admission will mean? Nothing less than a resurrection from the dead!
God never takes back his gifts or revokes his choice.

Just as you changed from being disobedient to God, and now enjoy
mercy because of their disobedience, so those who are disobedient now
– and only because of the mercy shown to you – will also enjoy mercy
eventually. God has imprisoned all men in their own disobedience only to
show mercy to all mankind.

The word of the Lord.

Gospel Acclamation   Cf. Jn 10:27

R. **Alleluia, alleluia!**
The sheep that belong to me listen to my voice,
says the Lord,
I know them and they follow me.
R. **Alleluia!**

Or: Cf. Mt 4:23

R. **Alleluia, alleluia!**
Jesus proclaimed the Good News of the kingdom,
and cured all kinds of sicknesses among the people.
R. **Alleluia!**

GOSPEL

A reading from the holy Gospel according to Matthew   15:21-28
Woman, you have great faith.

Jesus left Gennesaret and withdrew to the region of Tyre and Sidon. Then
out came a Canaanite woman from that district and started shouting, 'Sir,
Son of David, take pity on me. My daughter is tormented by a devil.' But
he answered her not a word. And his disciples went and pleaded with him.
'Give her what she wants,' they said 'because she is shouting after us.'
He said in reply, 'I was sent only to the lost sheep of the House of Israel.'
But the woman had come up and was kneeling at his feet. 'Lord,' she said

'help me.' He replied, 'It is not fair to take the children's food and throw it to the house-dogs.' She retorted, 'Ah yes, sir; but even house-dogs can eat the scraps that fall from their master's table.' Then Jesus answered her, 'Woman, you have great faith. Let your wish be granted.' And from that moment her daughter was well again.

The Gospel of the Lord.

Prayer over the Offerings

Receive our oblation, O Lord,
by which is brought about
  a glorious exchange,
that, by offering what you have given,
we may merit to receive
  your very self.
Through Christ our Lord.

Super oblata

Suscipe, Domine, munera nostra,
quibus exercentur
  commercia gloriosa,
ut, offerentes quæ dedisti,
teipsum mereamur accipere.
Per Christum Dominum nostrum.

Preface of Sundays in Ordinary Time I-VIII, pp.60-67.

Communion Antiphon   Ps 129:7

With the Lord there is mercy;
in him is plentiful redemption.

Ant. ad communionem

Apud Dominum misericordia,
et copiosa apud eum redemptio.

Or: Jn 6:51-52

I am the living bread that came
  down from heaven, says the Lord.
Whoever eats of this bread
  will live for ever.

Vel:

Ego sum panis vivus, qui de cælo
  descendi, dicit Dominus:
si quis manducaverit ex hoc pane,
  vivet in æternum.

Prayer after Communion

Made partakers of Christ through
  these Sacraments,
we humbly implore your mercy, Lord,
that, conformed to his image
  on earth,
we may merit also to be his coheirs
  in heaven.
Who lives and reigns
  for ever and ever.

Post communionem

Per hæc sacramenta, Domine,
  Christi participes effecti,
clementiam tuam
  humiliter imploramus,
ut, eius imaginis conformes in terris,
et eius consortes
  in cælis fieri mereamur.
Qui vivit et regnat
  in sæcula sæculorum.

27 August

TWENTY-FIRST SUNDAY IN ORDINARY TIME

Entrance Antiphon   Cf. Ps 85:1-3

TURN your ear, O Lord,
and answer me;
save the servant who trusts in you,
    my God.
Have mercy on me, O Lord,
    for I cry to you all the day long.

Ant. ad introitum

INCLINA, Domine, aurem tuam
ad me, et exaudi me.
Salvum fac servum tuum,
    Deus meus, sperantem in te.
Miserere mihi, Domine,
    quoniam ad te clamavi tota die.

Collect

O God, who cause the minds
    of the faithful
to unite in a single purpose,
grant your people to love
    what you command
and to desire what you promise,
that, amid the uncertainties
    of this world,
our hearts may be fixed on that place
where true gladness is found.
Through our Lord Jesus Christ,
    your Son,
who lives and reigns with you
    in the unity of the Holy Spirit,
God, for ever and ever.

Collecta

Deus, qui fidelium mentes unius
    efficis voluntatis,
da populis tuis id amare
    quod præcipis,
id desiderare quod promittis,
ut, inter mundanas varietates,
ibi nostra fixa sint corda,
    ubi vera sunt gaudia.
Per Dominum nostrum Iesum
    Christum Filium tuum,
qui tecum vivit et regnat
    in unitate Spiritus Sancti,
Deus, per omnia sæcula sæculorum.

FIRST READING

A reading from the prophet Isaiah   22:19-23

I place the key of the House of David upon his shoulder.

Thus says the Lord of hosts to Shebna, the master of the palace:
    I dismiss you from your office,
    I remove you from your post,
    and the same day I call on my servant
    Eliakim son of Hilkiah.
    I invest him with your robe,
    gird him with your sash,
    entrust him with your authority,
    and he shall be a father

to the inhabitants of Jerusalem
and to the House of Judah.
I place the key of the House of David
on his shoulder;
should he open, no one shall close,
should he close, no one shall open.
I drive him like a peg
into a firm place;
he will become a throne of glory
for his father's house.

The word of the Lord.

Responsorial Psalm   Ps 137:1-3,6,8. R. v.8

R. **Your love, O Lord, is eternal,
discard not the work of your hands.**

I thank you, Lord, with all my heart,
you have heard the words of my mouth.
Before the angels I will bless you.
I will adore before your holy temple. R.

I thank you for your faithfulness and love
which excel all we ever knew of you.
On the day I called, you answered;
you increased the strength of my soul. R.

The Lord is high yet he looks on the lowly
and the haughty he knows from afar.
Your love, O Lord, is eternal,
discard not the work of your hands. R.

SECOND READING

A reading from the letter of St Paul to the Romans   11:33-36
All that exists comes from him; all is by him and from him.

How rich are the depths of God – how deep his wisdom and knowledge –
and how impossible to penetrate his motives or understand his methods!
Who could ever know the mind of the Lord? Who could ever be his
counsellor? Who could ever give him anything or lend him anything? All
that exists comes from him; all is by him and for him. To him be glory for
ever! Amen.

The word of the Lord.

Gospel Acclamation   2 Co 5:19

R. **Alleluia, alleluia!**
God in Christ was reconciling the world to himself,
and he has entrusted to us the news that they are reconciled.
R. **Alleluia!**

Or: Mt 16:18

R. **Alleluia, alleluia!**
You are Peter,
and on this rock I will build my Church.
And the gates of the underworld can never hold out against it.
R. **Alleluia!**

GOSPEL

A reading from the holy Gospel according to Matthew   16:13-20

You are Peter, and I will give you the keys of the kingdom of heaven.

When Jesus came to the region of Caesarea Philippi he put this question to his disciples, 'Who do people say the Son of Man is?' And they said, 'Some say he is John the Baptist, some Elijah, and others Jeremiah or one of the prophets.' 'But you,' he said, 'who do you say I am?' Then Simon Peter spoke up, 'You are the Christ,' he said 'the Son of the living God.' Jesus replied, 'Simon son of Jonah, you are a happy man! Because it was not flesh and blood that revealed this to you but my Father in heaven. So I now say to you: You are Peter and on this rock I will build my Church. And the gates of the underworld can never hold out against it. I will give you the keys of the kingdom of heaven: whatever you bind on earth shall be considered bound in heaven; whatever you loose on earth shall be considered loosed in heaven.' Then he gave the disciples strict orders not to tell anyone that he was the Christ.

The Gospel of the Lord.

Prayer over the Offerings

O Lord, who gained for yourself
    a people by adoption
through the one sacrifice offered
    once for all,
bestow graciously on us, we pray,
the gifts of unity and peace
    in your Church.
Through Christ our Lord.

Super oblata

Qui una semel hostia, Domine,
adoptionis tibi populum acquisisti,
unitatis et pacis in Ecclesia tua
propitius nobis dona concedas.
Per Christum Dominum nostrum.

Preface of Sundays in Ordinary Time I-VIII, pp.60-67.

Communion Antiphon Cf. Ps 103:13-15	Ant. ad communionem

The earth is replete with the fruits
    of your work, O Lord;
you bring forth bread from the earth
and wine to cheer the heart.
	De fructu operum tuorum,
	    Domine, satiabitur terra,
	ut educas panem de terra,
	    et vinum lætificet cor hominis.

Or: Cf. Jn 6:54	Vel:

Whoever eats my flesh
    and drinks my blood
has eternal life, says the Lord,
and I will raise him up
    on the last day.
	Qui manducat meam carnem
	    et bibit meum sanguinem,
	habet vitam æternam,
	    dicit Dominus;
	et ego resuscitabo eum
	    in novissimo die.

Prayer after Communion	Post communionem

Complete within us, O Lord,
    we pray,
the healing work of your mercy
and graciously perfect
    and sustain us,
so that in all things we may
    please you.
Through Christ our Lord.
	Plenum, quæsumus, Domine,
	in nobis remedium tuæ
	    miserationis operare
	ac tales nos esse perfice propitius
	    et sic foveri,
	ut tibi in omnibus
	    placere valeamus.
	Per Christum Dominum nostrum.

3 September

TWENTY-SECOND SUNDAY IN ORDINARY TIME

Entrance Antiphon Cf. Ps 85:3,5	Ant. ad introitum

HAVE mercy on me, O Lord,
for I cry to you all the day long.
O Lord, you are good and forgiving,
full of mercy to all who call to you.
	MISERERE mihi, Domine,
	quoniam ad te clamavi
	    tota die:
	quia tu, Domine, suavis ac mitis es,
	et copiosus in misericordia
	    omnibus invocantibus te.

Collect

God of might, giver of every
   good gift,
put into our hearts the love
   of your name,
so that, by deepening our sense
   of reverence,
you may nurture in us what is good
and, by your watchful care,
keep safe what you have nurtured.
Through our Lord Jesus Christ,
   your Son,
who lives and reigns with you
   in the unity of the Holy Spirit,
God, for ever and ever.

Collecta

Deus virtutum, cuius est totum
   quod est optimum,
insere pectoribus nostris tui
   nominis amorem,
et præsta, ut in nobis,
religionis augmento,
   quæ sunt bona nutrias,
ac, vigilanti studio,
   quæ sunt nutrita custodias.
Per Dominum nostrum Iesum
   Christum Filium tuum,
qui tecum vivit et regnat
   in unitate Spiritus Sancti,
Deus, per omnia sæcula sæculorum.

FIRST READING

A reading from the prophet Jeremiah   20:7-9

The word of the Lord has meant insult for me.

You have seduced me, Lord, and I have let myself be seduced;
you have overpowered me: you were the stronger.
I am a daily laughing-stock,
everybody's butt.
Each time I speak the word, I have to howl
and proclaim: 'Violence and ruin!'
The word of the Lord has meant for me
insult, derision, all day long.
I used to say, 'I will not think about him,
I will not speak in his name anymore.'
Then there seemed to be a fire burning in my heart,
imprisoned in my bones.
The effort to restrain it wearied me,
I could not bear it.

   The word of the Lord.

Responsorial Psalm   Ps 62:2-6,8-9. R. v.2

R. **For you my soul is thirsting, O Lord my God.**

O God, you are my God, for you I long;
for you my soul is thirsting.
My body pines for you
like a dry, weary land without water. R.

So I gaze on you in the sanctuary
to see your strength and your glory.
For your love is better than life,
my lips will speak your praise. R.

So I will bless you all my life,
in your name I will lift up my hands.
My soul shall be filled as with a banquet,
my mouth shall praise you with joy. R.

For you have been my help;
in the shadow of your wings I rejoice.
My soul clings to you;
your right hand holds me fast. R.

SECOND READING

A reading from the letter of St Paul to the Romans   12:1-2

Offer your bodies as a living sacrifice.

Think of God's mercy, my brothers, and worship him, I beg you, in a way
that is worthy of thinking beings, by offering your living bodies as a holy
sacrifice, truly pleasing to God. Do not model yourselves on the behaviour
of the world around you, but let your behaviour change, modelled by your
new mind. This is the only way to discover the will of God and know what
is good, what it is that God wants, what is the perfect thing to do.

The word of the Lord.

Gospel Acclamation   Cf. Ep 1:17-18

R. **Alleluia, alleluia!**
May the Father of our Lord Jesus Christ
enlighten the eyes of our mind,
so that we can see
what hope his call holds for us.
R. **Alleluia!**

GOSPEL

A reading from the holy Gospel according Matthew   16:21-27

If anyone wants to be a follower of mine, let him renounce himself.

Jesus began to make it clear to his disciples that he was destined to go to Jerusalem and suffer grievously at the hands of the elders and chief priests and scribes, to be put to death and to be raised up on the third day. Then, taking him aside, Peter started to remonstrate with him. 'Heaven preserve you, Lord,' he said. 'This must not happen to you.' But he turned and said to Peter, 'Get behind me, Satan! You are an obstacle in my path, because the way you think is not God's way but man's.'

Then Jesus said to his disciples, 'If anyone wants to be a follower of mine, let him renounce himself and take up his cross and follow me. For anyone who wants to save his life will lose it; but anyone who loses his life for my sake will find it. What, then, will a man gain if he wins the whole world and ruins his life? Or what has a man to offer in exchange for his life?

'For the Son of Man is going to come in the glory of his Father with his angels, and, when he does, he will reward each one according to his behaviour.'

The Gospel of the Lord.

Prayer over the Offerings	Super oblata
May this sacred offering, O Lord, confer on us always the blessing of salvation, that what it celebrates in mystery it may accomplish in power. Through Christ our Lord.	Benedictionem nobis, Domine, conferat salutarem sacra semper oblatio, ut, quod agit mysterio, virtute perficiat. Per Christum Dominum nostrum.

Preface of Sundays in Ordinary Time I-VIII, pp.60-67.

Communion Antiphon Ps 30:20	Ant. ad communionem
How great is the goodness, Lord, that you keep for those who fear you.	Quam magna multitudo dulcedinis tuæ, Domine, quam abscondisti timentibus te.
Or: Mt 5:9-10	Vel:
Blessed are the peacemakers, for they shall be called children of God. Blessed are they who are persecuted for the sake of righteousness, for theirs is the Kingdom of Heaven.	Beati pacifici, quoniam filii Dei vocabuntur. Beati qui persecutionem patiuntur propter iustitiam, quoniam ipsorum est regnum cælorum.

Prayer after Communion

Renewed by this bread
 from the heavenly table,
we beseech you, Lord,
that, being the food of charity,
it may confirm our hearts
and stir us to serve you
 in our neighbour.
Through Christ our Lord.

Post communionem

Pane mensæ cælestis refecti, te,
 Domine, deprecamur,
ut hoc nutrimentum caritatis corda
 nostra confirmet,
quatenus ad tibi ministrandum
 in fratribus excitemur.
Per Christum Dominum nostrum.

10 September

TWENTY-THIRD SUNDAY IN ORDINARY TIME

Entrance Antiphon Ps 118:137,124

YOU are just, O Lord,
 and your judgement is right;
treat your servant in accord
 with your merciful love.

Ant. ad introitum

IUSTUS es, Domine,
 et rectum iudicium tuum;
fac cum servo tuo secundum
 misericordiam tuam.

Collect

O God, by whom we are redeemed
 and receive adoption,
look graciously upon your beloved
 sons and daughters,
that those who believe in Christ
may receive true freedom
and an everlasting inheritance.
Through our Lord Jesus Christ,
 your Son,
who lives and reigns with you
 in the unity of the Holy Spirit,
God, for ever and ever.

Collecta

Deus, per quem nobis
et redemptio venit
 et præstatur adoptio,
filios dilectionis tuæ
 benignus intende,
ut in Christo credentibus
et vera tribuatur libertas,
 et hereditas æterna.
Per Dominum nostrum Iesum
 Christum Filium tuum,
qui tecum vivit et regnat
 in unitate Spiritus Sancti,
Deus, per omnia sæcula sæculorum.

FIRST READING

A reading from the prophet Ezekiel

33:7-9

If you do not speak to the wicked man, I will hold you responsible for his death.

The word of the Lord was addressed to me as follows, 'Son of man, I have appointed you as sentry to the House of Israel. When you hear a word from my mouth, warn them in my name. If I say to a wicked man:

Wicked wretch, you are to die, and you do not speak to warn the wicked man to renounce his ways, then he shall die for his sin, but I will hold you responsible for his death. If, however, you do warn a wicked man to renounce his ways and repent, and he does not repent, then he shall die for his sin but you yourself will have saved your life.'

The word of the Lord.

Responsional Psalm   Ps 94:1-2,6-9. R. v.8

R. **O that today you would listen to his voice!
Harden not your hearts.**

Come, ring out our joy to the Lord;
hail the rock who saves us.
Let us come before him, giving thanks,
with songs let us hail the Lord. R.

Come in; let us bow and bend low;
let us kneel before the God who made us
for he is our God and we
the people who belong to his pasture,
the flock that is led by his hand. R.

O that today you would listen to his voice!
'Harden not your hearts as at Meribah,
as on that day at Massah in the desert
when your fathers put me to the test;
when they tried me, though they saw my work.' R.

SECOND READING

A reading from the letter of St Paul to the Romans   13:8-10
Love is the answer to every one of the commandments.

Avoid getting into debt, except the debt of mutual love. If you love your fellow men you have carried out your obligations. All the commandments: You shall not commit adultery, you shall not kill, you shall not steal, you shall not covet, and so on, are summed up in this single command: You must love your neighbour as yourself. Love is the one thing that cannot hurt your neighbour; that is why it is the answer to every one of the commandments.

The word of the Lord.

Gospel Acclamation   Jn 17:17

R. **Alleluia, alleluia!**
Your word is truth, O Lord,
consecrate us in the truth.
R. **Alleluia!**

Or: 2 Co 5:19

R. **Alleluia, alleluia!**
God in Christ was reconciling the world to himself,
and he has entrusted to us the news that they are reconciled.
R. **Alleluia!**

GOSPEL

A reading from the holy Gospel according to Matthew   18:15-20
If he listens to you, you have won back your brother.

Jesus said to his disciples: 'If your brother does something wrong, go and
have it out with him alone, between your two selves. If he listens to you,
you have won back your brother. If he does not listen, take one or two
others along with you: the evidence of two or three witnesses is required
to sustain any charge. But if he refuses to listen to these, report it to the
community; and if he refuses to listen to the community, treat him like a
pagan or a tax collector.

'I tell you solemnly, whatever you bind on earth shall be considered
bound in heaven; whatever you loose on earth shall be considered loosed
in heaven.

'I tell you solemnly once again, if two of you on earth agree to ask
anything at all, it will be granted to you by my Father in heaven. For where
two or three meet in my name, I shall be there with them.'

The Gospel of the Lord.

Prayer over the Offerings	Super oblata

O God, who give us the gift
    of true prayer and of peace,
graciously grant that,
    through this offering,
we may do fitting homage to your
    divine majesty
and, by partaking
    of the sacred mystery,
we may be faithfully united
    in mind and heart.
Through Christ our Lord.
	Deus, auctor sinceræ
	    devotionis et pacis,
	da, quæsumus,
	    ut et maiestatem tuam
	convenienter hoc
	    munere veneremur,
	et sacri participatione mysterii
	    fideliter sensibus uniamur.
	Per Christum Dominum nostrum.

Preface of Sundays in Ordinary Time I-VIII, pp.60-67.

Communion Antiphon Cf. Ps 41:2-3

Like the deer that yearns
for running streams,
so my soul is yearning for you,
my God;
my soul is thirsting for God,
the living God.

Or: Jn 8:12

I am the light of the world,
says the Lord;
whoever follows me will not walk
in darkness,
but will have the light of life.

Prayer after Communion

Grant that your faithful, O Lord,
whom you nourish and endow
with life
through the food of your Word
and heavenly Sacrament,
may so benefit from your beloved
Son's great gifts
that we may merit an eternal share
in his life.
Who lives and reigns
for ever and ever.

Ant. ad communionem

Quemadmodum desiderat cervus
ad fontes aquarum,
ita desiderat anima mea
ad te, Deus:
sitivit anima mea ad Deum
fortem vivum.

Vel:

Ego sum lux mundi,
dicit Dominus:
qui sequitur me non ambulat
in tenebris,
sed habebit lumen vitæ.

Post communionem

Da fidelibus tuis, Domine,
quos et verbi tui et cælestis
sacramenti pabulo
nutris et vivificas,
ita dilecti Filii tui tantis
muneribus proficere,
ut eius vitæ semper consortes
effici mereamur.
Qui vivit et regnat
in sæcula sæculorum.

17 September

TWENTY-FOURTH SUNDAY IN ORDINARY TIME

Entrance Antiphon   Cf. Sir 36:18

GIVE peace, O Lord,
   to those who wait for you,
that your prophets be found true.
Hear the prayers of your servant,
and of your people Israel.

Ant. ad introitum

DA pacem, Domine,
   sustinentibus te,
ut prophetæ tui fideles inveniantur;
exaudi preces servi tui,
   et plebis tuæ Israel.

Collect

Look upon us, O God,
Creator and ruler of all things,
and, that we may feel the working
   of your mercy,
grant that we may serve you
   with all our heart.
Through our Lord Jesus Christ,
   your Son,
who lives and reigns with you
   in the unity of the Holy Spirit,
God, for ever and ever.

Collecta

Respice nos, rerum omnium Deus
   creator et rector,
et, ut tuæ propitiationis
   sentiamus effectum,
toto nos tribue tibi corde servire.
Per Dominum nostrum Iesum
   Christum Filium tuum,
qui tecum vivit et regnat
   in unitate Spiritus Sancti,
Deus, per omnia sæcula sæculorum.

FIRST READING

A reading from the book of Ecclesiasticus   27:30-28:7

Forgive your neighbour the hurt he does you, and when you pray, your sins will be forgiven.

Resentment and anger, these are foul things,
and both are found with the sinner.
He who exacts vengeance will experience the vengeance of the Lord,
who keeps strict account of sin.
Forgive your neighbour the hurt he does you,
and when you pray, your sins will be forgiven.
If a man nurses anger against another,
can he then demand compassion from the Lord?
Showing no pity for a man like himself,
can he then plead for his own sins?
Mere creature of flesh, he cherishes resentment;
who will forgive him his sins?
Remember the last things, and stop hating,
remember dissolution and death, and live by the commandments.
Remember the commandments, and do not bear your neighbour ill-will;
remember the covenant of the Most High, and overlook the offence.
   The word of the Lord.

Responsorial Psalm   Ps 102:1-4,9-12. R. v.8

R. **The Lord is compassion and love,**
    slow to anger and rich in mercy.

My soul, give the thanks to the Lord,
all my being, bless his holy name.
My soul, give thanks to the Lord
and never forget all his blessings. R.

It is he who forgives all your guilt,
who heals every one of your ills,
who redeems your life from the grave,
who crowns you with love and compassion. R.

His wrath will come to an end;
he will not be angry for ever.
He does not treat us according to our sins
nor repay us according to our faults. R.

For as the heavens are high above the earth
so strong is his love for those who fear him.
As far as the east is from the west
so far does he remove our sins. R.

SECOND READING

A reading from the letter of St Paul to the Romans   14:7-9
Alive or dead we belong to the Lord.

The life and death of each of us has its influence on others; if we live, we
live for the Lord; and if we die, we die for the Lord, so that alive or dead we
belong to the Lord. This explains why Christ both died and came to life, it
was so that he might be Lord both of the dead and of the living.

    The word of the Lord.

Gospel Acclamation   1 S 3:9; Jn 6:68

R. **Alleluia, alleluia!**
Speak, Lord, your servant is listening:
you have the message of eternal life.
R. **Alleluia!**

Or: Jn 13:34

R. **Alleluia, alleluia!**
I give you a new commandment:
love one another, just as I have loved you,
says the Lord.
R. **Alleluia!**

GOSPEL

A reading from the holy Gospel according to Matthew 18:21-35

I do not tell you to forgive seven times, but seventy-seven times.

Peter went up to Jesus and said, 'Lord, how often must I forgive my brother if he wrongs me? As often as seven times?' Jesus answered, 'Not seven, I tell you, but seventy-seven times.

'And so the kingdom of heaven may be compared to a king who decided to settle his accounts with his servants. When the reckoning began, they brought him a man who owed ten thousand talents; but he had no means of paying, so his master gave orders that he should be sold, together with his wife and children and all his possessions, to meet the debt. At this, the servant threw himself down at his master's feet. "Give me time," he said "and I will pay the whole sum." And the servant's master felt so sorry for him that he let him go and cancelled the debt. Now as this servant went out, he happened to meet a fellow servant who owed him one hundred denarii; and he seized him by the throat and began to throttle him. "Pay what you owe me," he said. His fellow servant fell at his feet and implored him, saying, "Give me time and I will pay you." But the other would not agree; on the contrary, he had him thrown into prison till he should pay the debt. His fellow servants were deeply distressed when they saw what had happened, and they went to their master and reported the whole affair to him. Then the master sent for him. "You wicked servant," he said "I cancelled all that debt of yours when you appealed to me. Were you not bound, then, to have pity on your fellow servant just as I had pity on you?" And in his anger the master handed him over to the torturers till he should pay all his debt. And that is how my heavenly Father will deal with you unless you each forgive your brother from your heart.'

The Gospel of the Lord.

Prayer over the Offerings	Super oblata
Look with favour on our supplications, O Lord, and in your kindness accept these, your servants' offerings, that what each has offered to the honour of your name may serve the salvation of all. Through Christ our Lord.	Propitiare, Domine, supplicationibus nostris, et has oblationes famulorum tuorum benignus assume, ut, quod singuli ad honorem tui nominis obtulerunt, cunctis proficiat ad salutem. Per Christum Dominum nostrum.

Preface of Sundays in Ordinary Time I-VIII, pp.60-67.

Communion Antiphon Cf. Ps 35:8

How precious is your mercy, O God!
The children of men seek shelter
    in the shadow of your wings.

Or: Cf. 1 Co 10:16

The chalice of blessing that we bless
is a communion in the Blood
    of Christ;
and the bread that we break
is a sharing in the Body of the Lord.

Prayer after Communion

May the working of this heavenly
    gift, O Lord, we pray,
take possession of our minds
    and bodies,
so that its effects,
    and not our own desires,
may always prevail in us.
Through Christ our Lord.

Ant. ad communionem

Quam pretiosa
    est misericordia tua, Deus!
Filii hominum sub umbra alarum
    tuarum confugient.

Vel:

Calix benedictionis,
    cui benedicimus,
communicatio Sanguinis Christi est;
et panis, quem frangimus,
participatio Corporis Domini est.

Post communionem

Mentes nostras et corpora possideat,
quæsumus, Domine,
    doni cælestis operatio,
ut non noster sensus in nobis,
sed eius præveniat semper effectus.
Per Christum Dominum nostrum.

24 September

TWENTY-FIFTH SUNDAY IN ORDINARY TIME

Entrance Antiphon

I AM the salvation of the people,
    says the Lord.
Should they cry to me in any distress,
I will hear them, and I will be their
    Lord for ever.

Collect

O God, who founded all the
    commands of your sacred Law
upon love of you
    and of our neighbour,
grant that, by keeping your precepts,
we may merit to attain eternal life.

Ant. ad introitum

S ALUS populi ego sum,
    dicit Dominus.
De quacumque tribulatione
    clamaverint ad me,
exaudiam eos, et ero illorum
    Dominus in perpetuum.

Collecta

Deus, qui sacræ legis omnia constituta
in tua et proximi dilectione posuisti,
da nobis, ut,
    tua præcepta servantes,
ad vitam mereamur
    pervenire perpetuam.

Through our Lord Jesus Christ,
　　your Son,
who lives and reigns with you
　　in the unity of the Holy Spirit,
God, for ever and ever.

Per Dominum nostrum Iesum
　　Christum Filium tuum,
qui tecum vivit et regnat
　　in unitate Spiritus Sancti,
Deus, per omnia sæcula sæculorum.

FIRST READING

A reading from the prophet Isaiah
My thoughts are not your thoughts.

55:6-9

Seek the Lord while he is still to be found,
call to him while he is still near.
Let the wicked man abandon his way,
the evil man his thoughts.
Let him turn back to the Lord who will take pity on him,
to our God who is rich in forgiving;
for my thoughts are not your thoughts,
my ways not your ways – it is the Lord who speaks.
Yes, the heavens are as high above earth
as my ways are above your ways,
my thoughts above your thoughts.

　　The word of the Lord.

Responsorial Psalm

Ps 144:2-3,8-9,17-18. R. v.18

R. **The Lord is close to all who call him.**

　　I will bless you day after day
　　and praise your name for ever.
　　The Lord is great, highly to be praised,
　　his greatness cannot be measured. R.

　　The Lord is kind and full of compassion,
　　slow to anger, abounding in love.
　　How good is the Lord to all,
　　compassionate to all his creatures. R.

　　The Lord is just in all his ways
　　and loving in all his deeds.
　　He is close to all who call him,
　　who call on him from their hearts. R.

SECOND READING

A reading from the letter of St Paul to the Philippians
Life to me is Christ

1:20-24,27

Christ will be glorified in my body, whether by my life or by my death. Life to me, of course, is Christ, but then death would bring me something more;

but then again, if living in this body means doing work which is having good
results – I do not know what I should choose. I am caught in this dilemma:
I want to be gone and be with Christ, which would be very much the better,
but for me to stay alive in this body is a more urgent need for your sake.

Avoid anything in your everyday lives that would be unworthy of the
gospel of Christ.

The word of the Lord.

R. **Alleluia, alleluia!**
Blessings on the King who comes,
in the name of the Lord!
Peace in heaven
and glory in the highest heavens!
R. **Alleluia!**

Or: Cf. Ac 16:14

R. **Alleluia, alleluia!**
Open our hearts, O Lord,
to accept the words of your Son.
R. **Alleluia!**

GOSPEL

A reading from the holy Gospel according to Matthew   20:1-16

Why be envious because I am generous?

Jesus told this parable to his disciples: 'The kingdom of heaven is like a
landowner going out at daybreak to hire workers for his vineyard. He made
an agreement with the workers for one denarius a day, and sent them to
his vineyard. Going out at about the third hour he saw others standing idle
in the market place and said to them, "You go to my vineyard too and I
will give you a fair wage." So they went. At about the sixth hour and again
at about the ninth hour, he went out and did the same. Then at about the
eleventh hour he went out and found more men standing round, and he
said to them, "Why have you been standing here idle all day?" "Because
no one has hired us" they answered. He said to them, "You go into my
vineyard too." In the evening, the owner of the vineyard said to his bailiff,
"Call the workers and pay them their wages, starting with the last arrivals
and ending with the first." So those who were hired at about the eleventh
hour came forward and received one denarius each. When the first came,
they expected to get more, but they too received one denarius each. They
took it, but grumbled at the landowner. "The men who came last" they

said "have done only one hour, and you have treated them the same as us, though we have done a heavy day's work in all the heat." He answered one of them and said, "My friend, I am not being unjust to you; did we not agree on one denarius? Take your earnings and go. I choose to pay the last-comer as much as I pay you. Have I no right to do what I like with my own? Why be envious because I am generous?" Thus the last will be first, and the first, last.'

The Gospel of the Lord.

Prayer over the Offerings

Receive with favour, O Lord, we pray,
the offerings of your people,
that what they profess
    with devotion and faith
may be theirs through
    these heavenly mysteries.
Through Christ our Lord.

Super oblata

Munera, quæsumus, Domine,
    tuæ plebis propitiatus assume,
ut, quæ fidei pietate profitentur,
sacramentis cælestibus
    apprehendant.
Per Christum Dominum nostrum.

Preface of Sundays in Ordinary Time I-VIII, pp.60-67.

Communion Antiphon Ps 118:4-5

You have laid down your precepts
    to be carefully kept;
may my ways be firm in keeping
    your statutes.

Or: Jn 10:14

I am the Good Shepherd,
    says the Lord;
I know my sheep,
    and mine know me.

Ant. ad communionem

Tu mandasti mandata tua
    custodiri nimis;
utinam dirigantur viæ meæ
ad custodiendas iustificationes tuas.

Vel:

Ego sum pastor bonus,
    dicit Dominus;
et cognosco oves meas,
    et cognoscunt me meæ.

Prayer after Communion

Graciously raise up, O Lord,
those you renew
    with this Sacrament,
that we may come to possess
    your redemption
both in mystery and in the manner
    of our life.
Through Christ our Lord.

Post communionem

Quos tuis, Domine,
    reficis sacramentis,
continuis attolle benignus auxiliis,
ut redemptionis effectum
et mysteriis capiamus et moribus.
Per Christum Dominum nostrum.

1 October

TWENTY-SIXTH SUNDAY IN ORDINARY TIME

Entrance Antiphon Dn 3:31,29,30,43,42

ALL that you have done to us,
O Lord,
you have done with true judgement,
for we have sinned against you
and not obeyed
    your commandments.
But give glory to your name
and deal with us according
    to the bounty of your mercy.

Ant. ad introitum

OMNIA, quæ fecisti nobis,
Domine,
in vero iudicio fecisti, quia
    peccavimus tibi,
et mandatis tuis non obœdivimus;
sed da gloriam nomini tuo,
et fac nobiscum secundum
    multitudinem misericordiæ tuæ.

Collect

O God, who manifest
    your almighty power
above all by pardoning
    and showing mercy,
bestow, we pray, your grace
    abundantly upon us
and make those hastening to attain
    your promises
heirs to the treasures of heaven.
Through our Lord Jesus Christ,
    your Son,
who lives and reigns with you
    in the unity of the Holy Spirit,
God, for ever and ever.

Collecta

Deus, qui omnipotentiam tuam
parcendo maxime
    et miserando manifestas,
multiplica super nos gratiam tuam,
ut, ad tua promissa currentes,
cælestium bonorum facias
    esse consortes.
Per Dominum nostrum Iesum
    Christum Filium tuum,
qui tecum vivit et regnat
    in unitate Spiritus Sancti,
Deus, per omnia sæcula sæculorum.

FIRST READING

A reading from the prophet Ezekiel   18:25-28

When the sinner renounces sin, he shall certainly live.

The word of the Lord was addressed to me as follows: 'You object, "What the Lord does is unjust." Listen, you House of Israel: is what I do unjust? Is it not what you do that is unjust? When the upright man renounces his integrity to commit sin and dies because of this, he dies because of the evil that he himself has committed. When the sinner renounces sin to become law-abiding and honest, he deserves to live. He has chosen to renounce all his previous sins; he shall certainly live; he shall not die.'

The word of the Lord.

Responsional Psalm

Ps 24:4-9. R. v.6

R. **Remember your mercy, Lord.**

Lord, make me know your ways.
Lord, teach me your paths.
Make me walk in your truth, and teach me:
for you are God my saviour. R.

Remember your mercy, Lord,
and the love you have shown from of old.
Do not remember the sins of my youth.
In your love remember me,
because of your goodness, O Lord. R.

The Lord is good and upright.
He shows the path to those who stray,
he guides the humble in the right path;
he teaches his way to the poor. R.

SECOND READING

A reading from the letter of St Paul to the Philippians 2:1-11

In your minds you must be the same as Christ Jesus.

[If our life in Christ means anything to you, if love can persuade at all, or the Spirit that we have in common, or any tenderness and sympathy, then be united in your convictions and united in your love, with a common purpose and a common mind. That is the one thing which would make me completely happy. There must be no competition among you, no conceit; but everybody is to be self-effacing. Always consider the other person to be better than your self, so that nobody thinks of his own interests first but everybody thinks of other people's interests instead. In your minds you must be the same as Christ Jesus:]

His state was divine,
yet he did not cling
to his equality with God
but emptied himself
to assume the condition of a slave,
and became as men are;

and being as all men are,
he was humbler yet,
even to accepting death,
death on a cross.
But God raised him high
and gave him the name
which is above all other names
so that all beings
in the heavens, on earth and in the underworld,
should bend the knee at the name of Jesus
and that every tongue should acclaim
Jesus Christ as Lord,
to the glory of God the Father.

| [The word of the Lord.]

Shorter Form, verses 1-5. Read between [ ]

Gospel Acclamation   Jn 14:23

R. **Alleluia, alleluia!**
If anyone loves me he will keep my word.
and my Father will love him,
and we shall come to him.
R. **Alleluia!**

Or: Jn 10:27

R. **Alleluia, alleluia!**
The sheep that belong to me listen to my voice,
says the Lord,
I know them and they follow me.
R. **Alleluia!**

GOSPEL

A reading from the holy Gospel according to Matthew   21:28-32

*He thought better of it and went. Tax collectors and prostitutes are making their way
into the kingdom of God before you.*

Jesus said to the chief priests and the elders of the people, 'What is your
opinion? A man had two sons. He went and said to the first, "My boy, you
go and work in the vineyard today." He answered, "I will not go", but
afterwards thought better of it and went. The man then went and said
the same thing to the second who answered, "Certainly, sir", but did not
go. Which of the two did the father's will?' 'The first' they said. Jesus said

to them, 'I tell you solemnly, tax collectors and prostitutes are making their way into the kingdom of God before you. For John came to you, a pattern of true righteousness, but you did not believe him, and yet the tax collectors and prostitutes did. Even after seeing that, you refused to think better of it and believe in him.'

The Gospel of the Lord.

Prayer over the Offerings	Super oblata
Grant us, O merciful God, that this our offering may find acceptance with you and that through it the wellspring of all blessing may be laid open before us. Through Christ our Lord.	Concede nobis, misericors Deus, ut hæc nostra oblatio tibi sit accepta, et per eam nobis fons omnis benedictionis aperiatur. Per Christum Dominum nostrum.

Preface of Sundays in Ordinary Time I-VIII, pp.60-67.

Communion Antiphon Cf. Ps 118:49-50	Ant. ad communionem
Remember your word to your servant, O Lord, by which you have given me hope. This is my comfort when I am brought low.	Memento verbi tui servo tuo, Domine, in quo mihi spem dedisti; hæc me consolata est in humilitate mea.
Or: 1 Jn 3:16	Vel:
By this we came to know the love of God: that Christ laid down his life for us; so we ought to lay down our lives for one another.	In hoc cognovimus caritatem Dei: quoniam ille animam suam pro nobis posuit; et nos debemus pro fratribus animas ponere.

Prayer after Communion	Post communionem
May this heavenly mystery, O Lord, restore us in mind and body, that we may be coheirs in glory with Christ, to whose suffering we are united whenever we proclaim his Death. Who lives and reigns for ever and ever.	Sit nobis, Domine, reparatio mentis et corporis cæleste mysterium, ut simus eius in gloria coheredes, cui, mortem ipsius annuntiando, compatimur. Qui vivit et regnat in sæcula sæculorum.

8 October

TWENTY-SEVENTH SUNDAY IN ORDINARY TIME

Entrance Antiphon   Cf. Est 4:17

WITHIN your will, O Lord,
all things are established,
and there is none that can resist
    your will.
For you have made all things,
    the heaven and the earth,
and all that is held within the circle
    of heaven;
you are the Lord of all.

Collect

Almighty ever-living God,
who in the abundance
    of your kindness
surpass the merits and the desires
    of those who entreat you,
pour out your mercy upon us
to pardon what conscience dreads
and to give what prayer does
    not dare to ask.
Through our Lord Jesus Christ,
    your Son,
who lives and reigns with you
    in the unity of the Holy Spirit,
God, for ever and ever.

Ant. ad introitum

IN voluntate tua, Domine,
universa sunt posita,
et non est qui possit resistere
    voluntati tuæ.
Tu enim fecisti omnia,
    cælum et terram,
et universa quæ cæli
    ambitu continentur;
Dominus universorum tu es.

Collecta

Omnipotens sempiterne Deus,
    qui abundantia pietatis tuæ
et merita supplicum excedis et vota,
effunde super nos
    misericordiam tuam,
ut dimittas quæ conscientia metuit,
et adicias quod oratio non præsumit.
Per Dominum nostrum Iesum
    Christum Filium tuum,
qui tecum vivit et regnat
    in unitate Spiritus Sancti,
Deus, per omnia sæcula sæculorum.

FIRST READING

A reading from the prophet Isaiah   5:1-7
The vineyard of the Lord of hosts is the House of Israel.

Let me sing to my friend
the song of his love for his vineyard.
My friend had a vineyard
on a fertile hillside.
He dug the soil, cleared it of stones,
and planted choice vines in it.

In the middle he built a tower,
he dug a press there too.
He expected it to yield grapes,
but sour grapes were all that it gave.

And now, inhabitants of Jerusalem
and men of Judah,
I ask you to judge
between my vineyard and me.
What could I have done for my vineyard
that I have not done?
I expected it to yield grapes.
Why did it yield sour grapes instead?

Very well, I will tell you
what I am going to do to my vineyard:
I will take away its hedge for it to be grazed on,
and knock down its wall for it to be trampled on.
I will lay it waste, unpruned, undug;
overgrown by the briar and the thorn.
I will command the clouds
to rain no rain on it.
Yes, the vineyard of the Lord of hosts
is the House of Israel,
and the men of Judah
that chosen plant.
He expected justice, but found bloodshed,
integrity, but only a cry of distress.

The word of the Lord.

Responsional Psalm   Ps 79:9,12-16,19-20. R. Is 5:7

R. **The vineyard of the Lord is the House of Israel.**

You brought a vine out of Egypt;
to plant it you drove out the nations.
It stretched out its branches to the sea,
to the Great River it stretched out its shoots. R.

Then why have you broken down its walls?
It is plucked by all who pass by.
It is ravaged by the boar of the forest,
devoured by the beasts of the field. R.

God of hosts, turn again, we implore,
look down from heaven and see.
Visit this vine and protect it,
the vine your right hand has planted. R.

And we shall never forsake you again:
give us life that we may call upon your name.
God of hosts, bring us back;
let your face shine on us and we shall be saved. R.

R. **The vineyard of the Lord is the House of Israel.**

SECOND READING

A reading from the letter of St Paul to the Philippians   4:6-9
The God of peace will be with you.

There is no need to worry; but if there is anything you need, pray for it,
asking God for it with prayer and thanksgiving, and that peace of God,
which is so much greater than we can understand, will guard your hearts
and your thoughts, in Christ Jesus. Finally, brothers, fill your minds with
everything that is true, everything that is noble, everything that is good
and pure, everything that we love and honour, and everything that can be
thought virtuous or worthy of praise. Keep doing all the things that you
learnt from me and have been taught by me and have heard or seen that I
do. Then the God of peace will be with you.

The word of the Lord.

Gospel Acclamation   Jn 15:15

R. **Alleluia, alleluia!**
I call you friends, says the Lord,
because I have made known to you
everything I have learnt from my Father.
R. **Alleluia!**

Or: Cf. Jn 15:16

R. **Alleluia, alleluia!**
I chose you from the world
to go out and bear fruit,
fruit that will last,
says the Lord.
R. **Alleluia!**

GOSPEL

A reading from the holy Gospel according to Matthew   21:33-43

He will lease the vineyard to other tenants.

Jesus said to the chief priests and the elders of the people, 'Listen to another parable. There was a man, a landowner, who planted a vineyard; he fenced it round, dug a winepress in it and built a tower; then he leased it to tenants and went abroad. When vintage time drew near he sent his servants to the tenants to collect his produce. But the tenants seized his servants, thrashed one, killed another and stoned a third. Next he sent some more servants, this time a larger number, and they dealt with them in the same way. Finally he sent his son to them. "They will respect my son" he said. But when the tenants saw the son, they said to each other, "This is the heir. Come on, let us kill him and take over his inheritance." So they seized him and threw him out of the vineyard and killed him. Now when the owner of the vineyard comes, what will he do to those tenants?' They answered, 'He will bring those wretches to a wretched end and lease the vineyard to other tenants who will deliver the produce to him when the season arrives.' Jesus said to them, 'Have you never read in the scriptures:

It was the stone rejected by the builders
that became the keystone.
This was the Lord's doing
and it is wonderful to see?

'I tell you, then, that the kingdom of God will be taken from you and given to a people who will produce its fruit.'

The Gospel of the Lord.

Prayer over the Offerings	Super oblata
Accept, O Lord, we pray, the sacrifices instituted by your commands and, through the sacred mysteries, which we celebrate with dutiful service, graciously complete the sanctifying work by which you are pleased to redeem us. Through Christ our Lord.	Suscipe, quæsumus, Domine, sacrificia tuis instituta præceptis, et sacris mysteriis, quæ debitæ servitutis celebramus officio, sanctificationem tuæ nobis redemptionis dignanter adimple. Per Christum Dominum nostrum.

Preface of Sundays in Ordinary Time I-VIII, pp.60-67.

Communion Antiphon   Lm 3:25

The Lord is good to those
    who hope in him,
to the soul that seeks him.

Or: Cf. 1 Co 10:17

Though many, we are one bread,
    one body,
for we all partake of the one Bread
    and one Chalice.

Prayer after Communion

Grant us, almighty God,
that we may be refreshed
    and nourished
by the Sacrament which
    we have received,
so as to be transformed
    into what we consume.
Through Christ our Lord.

Ant. ad communionem

Bonus est Dominus
    sperantibus in eum,
animæ quærenti illum.

Vel:

Unus panis et unum corpus
    multi sumus,
omnes qui de uno pane et de uno
    calice participamus.

Post communionem

Concede nobis, omnipotens Deus,
ut de perceptis sacramentis
    inebriemur atque pascamur,
quatenus in id quod
    sumimus transeamus.
Per Christum Dominum nostrum.

---

15 October

TWENTY-EIGHTH SUNDAY IN ORDINARY TIME

Entrance Antiphon   Ps 129:3-4

IF you, O Lord,
   should mark iniquities,
Lord, who could stand?
But with you is found forgiveness,
O God of Israel.

Collect

May your grace, O Lord, we pray,
at all times go before us
    and follow after
and make us always determined
to carry out good works.
Through our Lord Jesus Christ,
    your Son,
who lives and reigns with you
    in the unity of the Holy Spirit,
God, for ever and ever.

Ant. ad introitum

SI iniquitates observaveris,
   Domine,
Domine, quis sustinebit?
Quia apud te propitiatio est,
    Deus Israel.

Collecta

Tua nos, quæsumus,
    Domine, gratia
semper et præveniat et sequatur,
ac bonis operibus iugiter præstet
    esse intentos.
Per Dominum nostrum Iesum
    Christum Filium tuum,
qui tecum vivit et regnat
    in unitate Spiritus Sancti,
Deus, per omnia sæcula sæculorum.

FIRST READING

A reading from the prophet Isaiah   25:6-10

The Lord will prepare a banquet, and will wipe away tears from every cheek.

On this mountain,
the Lord of hosts will prepare for all people
a banquet of rich food, a banquet of fine wines,
of food rich and juicy, of fine strained wines.
On this mountain he will remove
the mourning veil covering all peoples,
and the shroud enwrapping all nations,
he will destroy Death for ever.
The Lord will wipe away
the tears from every cheek;
he will take away his people's shame
everywhere on earth,
for the Lord has said so.
That day, it will be said: See, this is our God
in whom we hoped for salvation;
the Lord is the one in whom we hoped.
We exult and we rejoice
that he has saved us;
for the hand of the Lord
rests on this mountain.

   The word of the Lord.

Responsorial Psalm   Ps 22. R. v.6

R. **In the Lord's own house shall I dwell
    for ever and ever.**

   The Lord is my shepherd;
   there is nothing I shall want.
   Fresh and green are the pastures
   where he gives me repose.
   Near restful waters he leads me,
   to revive my drooping spirit. R.

   He guides me along the right path;
   he is true to his name.
   If I should walk in the valley of darkness
   no evil would I fear.
   You are there with your crook and your staff;
   with these you give me comfort. R.

You have prepared a banquet for me
in the sight of my foes.
My head you have anointed with oil;
my cup is overflowing. R.

Surely goodness and kindness shall follow me
all the days of my life.
In the Lord's own house shall I dwell
for ever and ever. R.

R. **In the Lord's own house shall I dwell
for ever and ever.**

SECOND READING

A reading from the letter of St Paul to the Philippians   4:12-14,19-20
There is nothing I cannot master with the help of the One who gives me strength.

I know how to be poor and I know how to be rich too. I have been through
my initiation and now I am ready for anything anywhere: full stomach
or empty stomach, poverty or plenty. There is nothing I cannot master
with the help of the One who gives me strength. All the same, it was good
of you to share with me in my hardships. In return my God will fulfil all
your needs, in Christ Jesus, as lavishly as only God can. Glory to God, our
Father, for ever and ever. Amen.

The word of the Lord.

Gospel Acclamation   Jn 1:12,14

R. **Alleluia, alleluia!**
The Word has made flesh and lived among us;
to all who did accept him
he gave power to become children of God.
R. **Alleluia!**
Or: Cf. Ep 1:17-18

R. **Alleluia, alleluia!**
May the Father of our Lord Jesus Christ
enlighten the eyes of our mind,
so that we can see what hope his call holds for us.
R. **Alleluia!**

GOSPEL

A reading from holy Gospel according to Matthew   22:1-14
Invite everyone you can find to the wedding.

[Jesus said to the chief priests and elders of the people: 'The kingdom of
heaven may be compared to a king who gave a feast for his son's wedding.

He sent his servants to call those who had been invited, but they would not come. Next he sent some more servants. "Tell those who have been invited" he said "that I have my banquet all prepared, my oxen and fattened cattle have been slaughtered, everything is ready. Come to the wedding." But they were not interested: one went off to his farm, another to his business, and the rest seized his servants, maltreated them and killed them. The king was furious. He despatched his troops, destroyed those murderers and burnt their town. Then he said to his servants, "The wedding is ready; but as those who were invited proved to be unworthy, go to the crossroads in the town and invite everyone you can find to the wedding." So these servants went out on to the roads and collected together everyone they could find, bad and good alike; and the wedding hall was filled with guests.]When the king came in to look at the guests he noticed one man who was not wearing a wedding garment, and said to him, "How did you get in here, my friend, without a wedding garment?" And the man was silent. Then the king said to the attendants, "Bind him hand and foot and throw him out into the dark, where there will be weeping and grinding of teeth." For many are called, but few are chosen.'

[The Gospel of the Lord.]

Shorter Form, verses 1-10. Read between [ ]

Prayer over the Offerings

Accept, O Lord,
   the prayers of your faithful
with the sacrificial offerings,
that, through these acts
   of devotedness,
we may pass over to the glory
   of heaven.
Through Christ our Lord.

Super oblata

Suscipe, Domine,
fidelium preces cum
   oblationibus hostiarum,
ut, per hæc piæ devotionis officia,
ad cælestem gloriam transeamus.
Per Christum Dominum nostrum.

Preface of Sundays in Ordinary Time I-VIII, pp.60-67.

Communion Antiphon Cf. Ps 33:11

The rich suffer want and go hungry,
but those who seek the Lord lack
   no blessing.

Or: 1 Jn 3:2

When the Lord appears,
   we shall be like him,
for we shall see him as he is.

Ant. ad communionem

Divites eguerunt et esurierunt;
quærentes autem Dominum non
   minuentur omni bono.

Vel:

Cum apparuerit Dominus,
   similes ei erimus,
quoniam videbimus eum sicuti est.

Prayer after Communion

We entreat your majesty most
    humbly, O Lord,
that, as you feed us
    with the nourishment
which comes from the most holy
    Body and Blood of your Son,
so you may make us sharers
    of his divine nature.
Who lives and reigns
    for ever and ever.

Post communionem

Maiestatem tuam, Domine,
    suppliciter deprecamur,
ut, sicut nos Corporis
    et Sanguinis sacrosancti
pascis alimento,
ita divinæ naturæ facias
    esse consortes.
Per Christum Dominum nostrum.

---

22 October

TWENTY-NINTH SUNDAY IN ORDINARY TIME

Entrance Antiphon Cf. Ps 16:6.8

To you I call; for you will surely
    heed me, O God;
turn your ear to me; hear my words.
Guard me as the apple of your eye;
in the shadow of your wings
    protect me.

Ant. ad introitum

Ego clamavi,
    quoniam exaudisti me, Deus;
inclina aurem tuam,
    et exaudi verba mea.
Custodi me, Domine,
    ut pupillam oculi;
sub umbra alarum tuarum
    protege me.

Collect

Almighty ever-living God,
grant that we may always conform
    our will to yours
and serve your majesty in sincerity
    of heart.
Through our Lord Jesus Christ,
    your Son,
who lives and reigns with you
    in the unity of the Holy Spirit,
God, for ever and ever.

Collecta

Omnipotens sempiterne Deus,
fac nos tibi semper et devotam
    gerere voluntatem,
et maiestati tuæ sincero
    corde servire.
Per Dominum nostrum Iesum
    Christum Filium tuum,
qui tecum vivit et regnat
    in unitate Spiritus Sancti,
Deus, per omnia sæcula sæculorum.

FIRST READING

A reading from the prophet Isaiah

45:1.4-6

I have taken Cyrus by his right hand to subdue nations before him.

Thus says the Lord to his anointed, to Cyrus,
whom he has taken by his right hand
to subdue nations before him
and strip the loins of kings,
to force gateways before him
that their gates be closed no more:

It is for the sake of my servant Jacob,
of Israel my chosen one,
that I have called you by your name,
conferring a title though you do not know me.
I am the Lord, unrivalled;
there is no other God besides me.
Though you do not know me, I arm you
that men may know from the rising to the setting of the sun
that, apart from me, all is nothing.

The word of the Lord.

Responsorial Psalm

Ps 95:1,3-5,7-10. R. v.7

R. **Give the Lord glory and power.**

O sing a new song to the Lord,
sing to the Lord all the earth.
Tell among the nations his glory
and his wonders among all the peoples. R.

The Lord is great and worthy of praise,
to be feared above all gods;
the gods of the heathens are naught.
It was the Lord who made the heavens. R.

Give the Lord, you families of peoples,
give the Lord glory and power,
give the Lord the glory of his name.
Bring an offering and enter his courts. R.

Worship the Lord in his temple.
O earth, tremble before him.
Proclaim to the nations: 'God is king.'
He will judge the peoples in fairness. R.

SECOND READING

A reading from the first letter of St Paul to the Thessalonians   1:1-5

We constantly remember your faith, your love and your hope.

From Paul, Silvanus and Timothy, to the Church in Thessalonika which is in God the Father and the Lord Jesus Christ; wishing you grace and peace from God the Father and the Lord Jesus Christ.

We always mention you in our prayers and thank God for you all, and constantly remember before God our Father how you have shown your faith in action, worked for love and persevered through hope, in our Lord Jesus Christ.

We know, brothers, that God loves you and that you have been chosen, because when we brought the Good News to you, it came to you not only as words, but as power and as the Holy Spirit and as utter conviction.

The word of the Lord.

Gospel Acclamation   Jn 17:17

R. **Alleluia, alleluia!**
Your word is truth, O Lord,
consecrate us in the truth.
R. **Alleluia!**

Or: Ph 2:15-16

R. **Alleluia, alleluia!**
You will shine on the world like bright stars
because you are offering it the word of life.
R. **Alleluia!**

GOSPEL

A reading from the holy Gospel according to Matthew   22:15-21

Give back to Caesar what belongs to Caesar – and to God what belongs to God.

The Pharisees went away to work out between them how to trap Jesus in what he said. And they sent their disciples to him, together with the Herodians, to say, 'Master, we know that you are an honest man and teach the way of God in an honest way, and that you are not afraid of anyone, because a man's rank means nothing to you. Tell us your opinion, then. Is it permissible to pay taxes to Caesar or not?' But Jesus was aware of their malice and replied, 'You hypocrites! Why do you set this trap for me? Let me see the money you pay the tax with.' They handed him a denarius, and he said, 'Whose head is this? Whose name?' 'Caesar's' they replied. He then said to them, 'Very well, give back to Caesar what belongs to Caesar – and to God what belongs to God.'

The Gospel of the Lord.

Prayer over the Offerings

Grant us, Lord, we pray,
a sincere respect for your gifts,
that, through the purifying action
   of your grace,
we may be cleansed by the very
   mysteries we serve.
Through Christ our Lord.

Super oblata

Tribue nos, Domine, quæsumus,
donis tuis libera mente servire,
ut, tua purificante nos gratia,
iisdem quibus famulamur
   mysteriis emundemur.
Per Christum Dominum nostrum.

Preface of Sundays in Ordinary Time I-VIII, pp.60-67.

Communion Antiphon Cf. Ps 32:18-19

Behold, the eyes of the Lord
are on those who fear him,
who hope in his merciful love,
to rescue their souls from death,
to keep them alive in famine.

Ant. ad communionem

Ecce oculi Domini super
   timentes eum,
et in eis qui sperant super
   misericordia eius;
ut eruat a morte animas eorum,
   et alat eos in fame.

Or: Mk 10:45

The Son of Man has come
to give his life as a ransom for many.

Vel:

Filius hominis venit,
ut daret animam suam
   redemptionem pro multis.

Prayer after Communion

Grant, O Lord, we pray,
that, benefiting from participation
   in heavenly things,
we may be helped by what you give
   in this present age
and prepared for the gifts
   that are eternal.
Through Christ our Lord.

Post communionem

Fac nos, quæsumus, Domine,
cælestium rerum
   frequentatione proficere,
ut et temporalibus
   beneficiis adiuvemur,
et erudiamur æternis.
Per Christum Dominum nostrum.

29 October

THIRTIETH SUNDAY IN ORDINARY TIME

Entrance Antiphon Cf. Ps 104:3-4

LET the hearts that seek
the Lord rejoice;
turn to the Lord and his strength;
constantly seek his face.

Ant. ad introitum

LÆTETUR cor
quærentium Dominum.
Quærite Dominum et confirmamini,
quærite faciem eius semper.

Collect

Almighty ever-living God,
increase our faith, hope and charity,
and make us love
    what you command,
so that we may merit
    what you promise.
Through our Lord Jesus Christ,
    your Son,
who lives and reigns with you
    in the unity of the Holy Spirit,
God, for ever and ever.

Collecta

Omnipotens sempiterne Deus,
da nobis fidei,
    spei et caritatis augmentum,
et, ut mereamur assequi
    quod promittis,
fac nos amare quod præcipis.
Per Dominum nostrum Iesum
    Christum Filium tuum,
qui tecum vivit et regnat
    in unitate Spiritus Sancti,
Deus, per omnia sæcula sæculorum.

FIRST READING

A reading from the book of Exodus   22:20-26

If you are harsh with the widow, the orphan, my anger will flare against you.

The Lord said to Moses, 'Tell the sons of Israel this, "You must not molest
the stranger or oppress him, for you lived as strangers in the land of Egypt.
You must not be harsh with the widow, or with the orphan; if you are
harsh with them, they will surely cry out to me, and be sure I shall hear
their cry; my anger will flare and I shall kill you with the sword, your own
wives will be widows, your own children orphans.

"If you lend money to any of my people, to any poor man among you, you
must not play the usurer with him: you must not demand interest from him.

"If you take another's cloak as a pledge, you must give it back to him before
sunset. It is all the covering he has; it is the cloak he wraps his body in; what
else would he sleep in? If he cries to me, I will listen, for I am full of pity."'

The word of the Lord.

Responsorial Psalm   Ps 17:2-4,47,51. R. v.2

R. **I love you, Lord, my strength.**
    I love you, Lord, my strength,
    my rock, my fortress, my saviour.

My God is the rock where I take refuge;
my shield, my mighty help, my stronghold.
The Lord is worthy of all praise:
when I call I am saved from my foes. R.

Long life to the Lord, my rock!
Praised be the God who saves me.
He has given great victories to his king
and shown his love for his anointed. R.

SECOND READING

A reading from the first letter of St Paul to the Thessalonians   1:5-10
You broke with idolatry and became servants of God; you are now waiting for his Son.

You observed the sort of life we lived when we were with you, which was
for your instruction, and you were led to become imitators of us, and
of the Lord; and it was with the joy of the Holy Spirit that you took to
the gospel, in spite of the great opposition all round you. This has made
you the great example to all believers in Macedonia and Achaia since it
was from you that the word of the Lord started to spread – and not only
throughout Macedonia and Achaia, for the news of your faith in God has
spread everywhere. We do not need to tell other people about it: other
people tell us how we started the work among you, how you broke with
idolatry when you were converted to God and became servants of the real,
living God; and how you are now waiting for Jesus, his Son, whom he
raised from the dead, to come from heaven to save us from the retribution
which is coming.

The word of the Lord.

Gospel Acclamation   Cf. Ac 16:14
R. **Alleluia, alleluia!**
Open our heart, O Lord,
to accept the words of your Son.
R. **Alleluia!**
Or: Jn 14:23
R. **Alleluia, alleluia!**
If anyone loves me he will keep my word,
and my Father will love him,
and we shall come to him.
R. **Alleluia!**

GOSPEL

A reading from the holy Gospel according to Matthew   22:34-40
You must love the Lord your God and your neighbour as yourself.

When the Pharisees heard that Jesus had silenced the Sadducees they got together and, to disconcert him, one of them put a question, 'Master, which is the greatest commandment of the Law?' Jesus said, 'You must love the Lord your God with all your heart, with all your soul, and with all your mind. This is the greatest and the first commandment. The second resembles it: you must love your neighbour as yourself. On these two commandments hang the whole Law, and the Prophets also.'

The Gospel of the Lord.

Prayer over the Offerings	Super oblata
Look, we pray, O Lord, on the offerings we make to your majesty, that whatever is done by us in your service may be directed above all to your glory. Through Christ our Lord.	Respice, quæsumus, Domine, munera quæ tuæ offerimus maiestati, ut, quod nostro servitio geritur, ad tuam gloriam potius dirigatur. Per Christum Dominum nostrum.

Preface of Sundays in Ordinary Time I-VIII, pp.60-67.

Communion Antiphon Cf. Ps 19:6	Ant. ad communionem
We will ring out our joy at your saving help and exult in the name of our God.	Lætabimur in salutari tuo, et in nomine Dei nostri magnificabimur.
Or: Ep 5:2	Vel:
Christ loved us and gave himself up for us, as a fragrant offering to God.	Christus dilexit nos, et tradidit semetipsum pro nobis, oblationem Deo in odorem suavitatis.

Prayer after Communion	Post communionem
May your Sacraments, O Lord, we pray, perfect in us what lies within them, that what we now celebrate in signs we may one day possess in truth. Through Christ our Lord.	Perficiant in nobis, Domine, quæsumus, tua sacramenta quod continent, ut, quæ nunc specie gerimus, rerum veritate capiamus. Per Christum Dominum nostrum.

1 November

ALL SAINTS

Beatitude, holiness, is not a life plan made up only of effort and renunciation, but is above all the joyful discovery of being God's beloved children. And this fills you with joy. It is not a human achievement, it is a gift we receive: we are holy because God, who is the Holy One, comes to dwell in our lives. It is he who gives holiness to us. This is why we are blessed! The joy of the Christian, then, is not a fleeting emotion or a simple human optimism, but the certainty of being able to face every situation under God's loving gaze, with the courage and strength that come from him. Even in the midst of many tribulations, the saints experienced this joy and bore witness to it.

(Pope Francis)

Solemnity

Entrance Antiphon

LET us all rejoice in the Lord,
as we celebrate the feast day
in honour of all the Saints,
at whose festival the Angels rejoice
and praise the Son of God.

Ant. ad introitum

GAUDEAMUS omnes in Domino,
diem festum celebrantes
sub honore Sanctorum omnium,
de quorum sollemnitate
gaudent Angeli,
et collaudant Filium Dei.

The Gloria in excelsis (Glory to God in the highest) is said.

Collect

Almighty ever-living God,
by whose gift we venerate
in one celebration
the merits of all the Saints,
bestow on us, we pray,
through the prayers of so
many intercessors,
an abundance of the reconciliation
with you
for which we earnestly long.
Through our Lord Jesus Christ,
your Son,
who lives and reigns with you in
the unity of the Holy Spirit,
God, for ever and ever.

Collecta

Omnipotens sempiterne Deus,
qui nos omnium Sanctorum
tuorum merita
sub una tribuisti celebritate
venerari, quæsumus,
ut desideratam nobis tuæ
propitiationis abundantiam,
multiplicatis intercessoribus,
largiaris.

Per Dominum nostrum Iesum
Christum Filium tuum,
qui tecum vivit et regnat
in unitate Spiritus Sancti,
Deus, per omnia sæcula sæculorum.

FIRST READING

A reading from the book of the Apocalypse   7:2-4,9-14

I saw a huge number, impossible to count, of people from every nation, race, tribe and language.

I, John, saw another angel rising where the sun rises, carrying the seal of the living God; he called in a powerful voice to the four angels whose duty was to devastate land and sea, 'Wait before you do any damage on land or at sea or to the trees, until we have put the seal on the foreheads of the servants of our God.' Then I heard how many were sealed: a hundred and forty-four thousand, out of all the tribes of Israel.

After that I saw a huge number, impossible to count, of people from every nation, race, tribe and language; they were standing in front of the throne and in front of the Lamb, dressed in white robes and holding palms in their hands. They shouted aloud, 'Victory to our God, who sits on the throne, and to the Lamb!' And all the angels who were standing in a circle round the throne, surrounding the elders and the four animals, prostrated themselves before the throne, and touched the ground with their foreheads, worshipping God with these words: 'Amen. Praise and glory and wisdom and thanksgiving and honour and power and strength to our God for ever and ever. Amen.'

One of the elders then spoke, and asked me, 'Do you know who these people are, dressed in white robes, and where they have come from?' I answered him, 'You can tell me, my Lord.' Then he said, 'These are the people who have been through the great persecution, and they have washed their robes white again in the blood of the Lamb.'

The word of the Lord.

Responsorial Psalm   Ps 23:1-6. R. Cf. v.6

R. **Such are the men who seek your face, O Lord.**

The Lord's is the earth and its fullness,
the world and all its peoples.
It is he who set it on the seas;
on the waters he made it firm. R.

Who shall climb the mountain of the Lord?
Who shall stand in his holy place?
The man with clean hands and pure heart,
who desires not worthless things. R.

He shall receive blessings from the Lord
and reward from the God who saves him.

Such are the men who seek him,
seek the face of the God of Jacob. R.

SECOND READING

A reading from the first letter of St John   3:1-3

We shall see God as he really is.

Think of the love that the Father has lavished on us,
by letting us be called God's children;
and that is what we are.
Because the world refused to acknowledge him,
therefore it does not acknowledge us.
My dear people, we are already the children of God
but what we are to be in the future has not yet been revealed,
all we know is, that when it is revealed
we shall be like him
because we shall see him as he really is.
Surely everyone who entertains this hope
must purify himself, must try to be as pure as Christ.

The word of the Lord.

Gospel Acclamation   Mt 11:28

R. **Alleluia, alleluia!**
Come to me, all of you who labour
    and are overburdened,
and I will give you rest, says the Lord.
R. **Alleluia!**

GOSPEL

A reading from the holy Gospel according to Matthew   5:1-12

Rejoice and be glad, for your reward will be great in heaven.

Seeing the crowds, Jesus went up the hill. There he sat down and was joined
by his disciples. Then he began to speak. This is what he taught them:

'How happy are the poor in spirit;
theirs is the kingdom of heaven.
Happy the gentle:
they shall have the earth for their heritage.
Happy those who mourn:
they shall be comforted.
Happy those who hunger and thirst for what is right:
they shall be satisfied.
Happy the merciful:
they shall have mercy shown them.

Happy the pure in heart:
they shall see God.
Happy the peacemakers:
they shall be called sons of God.
Happy those who are persecuted in the cause of right:
theirs is the kingdom of heaven.

'Happy are you when people abuse you and persecute you and speak all kinds of calumny against you on my account. Rejoice and be glad, for your reward will be great in heaven.'

The Gospel of the Lord.

The Creed is said.

Prayer over the Offerings

May these offerings we bring
  in honour of all the Saints
be pleasing to you, O Lord,
and grant that, just as we believe
  the Saints
to be already assured of immortality,
so we may experience their concern
  for our salvation.
Through Christ our Lord.

Super oblata

Grata tibi sint, Domine, munera,
quæ pro cunctorum offerimus
  honore Sanctorum,
et concede,
ut, quos iam credimus de sua
  immortalitate securos,
sentiamus de nostra salute sollicitos.
Per Christum Dominum nostrum.

Preface: The glory of Jerusalem, our mother.

It is truly right and just,
  our duty and our salvation,
always and everywhere
  to give you thanks,
Lord, holy Father,
  almighty and eternal God.

For today by your gift we celebrate
  our mother,
the festival of your city,
the heavenly Jerusalem,
  where the great array
  of our brothers and sisters
already gives you eternal praise.

Præfatio: De gloria matris nostræ Ierusalem.

Vere dignum et iustum est,
  æquum et salutare,
nos tibi semper et ubique
  gratias agere:
Domine, sancte Pater,
  omnipotens æterne Deus:

Nobis enim hodie civitatem tuam
  quæ mater nostra est,
tribuis celebrare,
cælestique Ierusalem,
ubi iam te in æternum fratrum
  nostrorum corona collaudat.

Towards her, we eagerly hasten
  as pilgrims advancing by faith,
rejoicing in the glory bestowed
    upon those exalted members
    of the Church
through whom you give us,
    in our frailty, both strength
    and good example.

And so, we glorify you with the
    multitude of Saints and Angels,
as with one voice of praise
    we acclaim:

Holy, Holy, Holy Lord God of hosts...

Ad quam peregrini,
    per fidem accedentes,
alacriter festinamus,
    congaudentes de Ecclesiæ
sublimium glorificatione
    membrorum,
qua simul fragilitati nostræ
    adiumenta et exempla concedis.

Et ideo, cum ipsorum
    Angelorumque frequentia,
una te magnificamus,
    laudis voce clamantes:

Sanctus, Sanctus, Sanctus. . .

Communion Antiphon Mt 5:8-10

Blessed are the clean of heart,
  for they shall see God.
Blessed are the peacemakers,
for they shall be called
    children of God.
Blessed are they who are persecuted
    for the sake of righteousness,
for theirs is the Kingdom of Heaven.

Ant. ad communionem

Beati mundo corde, quoniam ipsi
    Deum videbunt;
beati pacifici, quoniam filii
    Dei vocabuntur;
beati qui persecutionem patiuntur
    propter iustitiam,
quoniam ipsorum
    est regnum cælorum.

Prayer after Communion

As we adore you, O God, who alone
    are holy
and wonderful in all your Saints,
we implore your grace,
so that, coming to perfect holiness
    in the fullness of your love,
we may pass from this pilgrim table
    to the banquet
    of our heavenly homeland.
Through Christ our Lord.

Post communionem

Mirabilem te, Deus,
et unum Sanctum in omnibus
    Sanctis tuis adorantes,
tuam gratiam imploramus,
qua, sanctificationem
in tui amoris plenitudine
    consummantes,
ex hac mensa peregrinantium
ad cælestis patriæ
    convivium transeamus.
Per Christum Dominum nostrum.

A formula of Solemn Blessing, pp.146-149, may be used.

2 November

THE COMMEMORATION OF ALL THE FAITHFUL DEPARTED

(ALL SOULS' DAY)

The Lord confirms this, this hope that does not disappoint. The Lord who welcomes us there, where the anchor lies. Life in hope is to live like this: grasping, with the rope in hand, strong, knowing that the anchor is below. And this anchor does not disappoint; it does not disappoint. Today, in the thoughts of many brothers and sisters who have passed on, it will do us good to look at the cemeteries and to look heavenward. And to repeat, like Job: "I know that my Redeemer lives, and I myself will see him. My eyes shall behold him, and not another". And this is the strength that hope gives us, this freely given gift that is the virtue of hope. May the Lord give it to all of us.   (Pope Francis)

The Masses that follow may be used at the discretion of the celebrant.

1

Entrance Antiphon Cf. 1 Th 4:14; 1 Co 15:22	Ant. ad introitum
Just as Jesus died and has risen again, so through Jesus God will bring with him those who have fallen asleep; and as in Adam all die, so also in Christ will all be brought to life.	Sicut Iesus mortuus est et resurrexit, ita et Deus eos qui dormierunt per Iesum adducet cum eo. Et sicut in Adam omnes moriuntur, ita et in Christo omnes vivificabuntur.

The Gloria in excelsis (Glory to God in the highest) is omitted.

Collect	Collecta
Listen kindly to our prayers, O Lord, and, as our faith in your Son, raised from the dead, is deepened, so may our hope of resurrection for your departed servants also find new strength. Through our Lord Jesus Christ, your Son, who lives and reigns with you in the unity of the Holy Spirit, God, for ever and ever.	Preces nostras, quæsumus, Domine, benignus exaudi, ut, dum attollitur nostra fides in Filio tuo a mortuis suscitato, in famulorum tuorum præstolanda resurrectione spes quoque nostra firmetur. Per Dominum nostrum Iesum Christum Filium tuum, qui tecum vivit et regnat in unitate Spiritus Sancti, Deus, per omnia sæcula sæculorum.

Readings, pp.619-622.

Prayer over the Offerings

Look favourably on our offerings,
    O Lord,
so that your departed servants
may be taken up into glory
    with your Son,
in whose great mystery of love
    we are all united.
Who lives and reigns
    for ever and ever.

Preface for the Dead, pp.74-79.

Super oblata

Nostris, Domine,
    propitiare muneribus,
ut famuli tui defuncti assumantur
    in gloriam cum Filio tuo,
cuius magno pietatis
    iungimur sacramento.
Qui vivit et regnat
    in sæcula sæculorum.

Communion Antiphon Cf. Jn 11:25-26

I am the Resurrection and the Life,
    says the Lord.
Whoever believes in me, even
    though he dies, will live,
and everyone who lives and believes
    in me will not die for ever.

Ant. ad communionem

Ego sum resurrectio et vita, dicit
    Dominus.
Qui credit in me, etiam si mortuus
    fuerit, vivet;
et omnis, qui vivit et credit in me,
    non morietur in æternum.

Prayer after Communion

Grant we pray, O Lord, that your
    departed servants,
for whom we have celebrated this
    paschal Sacrament,
may pass over to a dwelling place of
    light and peace.
Through Christ our Lord.

Post communionem

Præsta, quæsumus, Domine,
ut famuli tui defuncti
in mansionem lucis transeant
    et pacis,
pro quibus paschale celebravimus
    sacramentum.
Per Christum Dominum nostrum.

A formula of Solemn Blessing, pp.148-151, may be used.

2

Entrance Antiphon Cf. 4 Esdr 2:34-35

Eternal rest grant unto them, O Lord,
and let perpetual light shine
    upon them.

Ant. ad introitum

Requiem æternam dona eis, Domine,
et lux perpetua luceat eis.

Collect

O God, glory of the faithful and
   life of the just,
by the Death and Resurrection
   of whose Son
we have been redeemed,
look mercifully on your departed
   servants,
that, just as they professed the
   mystery of our resurrection,
so they may merit to receive the
   joys of eternal happiness.
Through our Lord Jesus Christ,
   your Son,
who lives and reigns with you
   in the unity of the Holy Spirit,
God, for ever and ever.

Readings, pp.619-622.

Collecta

Deus, gloria fidelium
   et vita iustorum,
cuius Filii morte et resurrectione
   redempti sumus,
propitiare famulis tuis defunctis,
ut, qui resurrectionis nostræ
   mysterium agnoverunt,
æternæ beatitudinis gaudia
   percipere mereantur.
Per Dominum nostrum Iesum
   Christum Filium tuum,
qui tecum vivit et regnat
   in unitate Spiritus Sancti,
Deus, per omnia sæcula sæculorum.

Prayer over the Offerings

Almighty and merciful God,
by means of these
   sacrificial offerings
wash away, we pray,
   in the Blood of Christ,
the sins of your departed servants,
for you purify unceasingly by your
   merciful forgiveness
those you once cleansed in the
   waters of Baptism.
Through Christ our Lord.

Preface for the Dead, pp.74-79.

Super oblata

Omnipotens et misericors Deus,
his sacrificiis ablue, quæsumus,
   famulos tuos defunctos
a peccatis eorum
   in sanguine Christi,
ut, quos mundasti
   aqua baptismatis,
indesinenter purifices
   indulgentia pietatis.
Per Christum Dominum nostrum.

Communion Antiphon Cf. 4 Esdr 2:35,34

Let perpetual light shine upon
   them, O Lord,
with your Saints for ever,
   for you are merciful.

Ant. ad communionem

Lux æterna luceat eis, Domine,
cum Sanctis tuis in æternum,
   quia pius es.

Prayer after Communion

Having received the Sacrament of
  your Only Begotten Son,
who was sacrificed for us
  and rose in glory,
we humbly implore you, O Lord,
for your departed servants,
that, cleansed by
  the paschal mysteries,
they may glory in the gift of the
  resurrection to come.
Through Christ our Lord.

A formula of Solemn Blessing, pp.148-151, may be used.

Post communionem

Sumpto sacramento Unigeniti tui,
qui pro nobis immolatus
  resurrexit in gloria,
te, Domine, suppliciter exoramus
  pro famulis tuis defunctis,
ut, paschalibus mysteriis mundati,
futuræ resurrectionis
  munere glorientur.
Per Christum Dominum nostrum.

3

Entrance Antiphon Cf. Rm 8:11

God, who raised Jesus from the dead,
will give life also to your
  mortal bodies,
through his Spirit that dwells in you.

Ant. ad introitum

Deus, qui suscitavit Iesum a mortuis,
vivificabit et mortalia corpora nostra,
propter inhabitantem Spiritum
  eius in nobis.

Collect

O God, who willed that your Only
  Begotten Son,
having conquered death,
should pass over into the realm
  of heaven,
grant, we pray,
  to your departed servants
that, with the mortality
  of this life overcome,
they may gaze eternally on you,
their Creator and Redeemer.
Through our Lord Jesus Christ,
  your Son,
who lives and reigns with you in
  the unity of the Holy Spirit,
God, for ever and ever.

Readings, pp.619-622.

Collecta

Deus, qui Unigenitum tuum,
  devicta morte,
ad cælestia transire fecisti,
concede famulis tuis defunctis,
ut, huius vitæ mortalitate devicta,
te conditorem et redemptorem
possint perpetuo contemplari.

Per Dominum nostrum Iesum
  Christum Filium tuum,
qui tecum vivit et regnat
  in unitate Spiritus Sancti,
Deus, per omnia sæcula sæculorum.

Prayer over the Offerings

Receive, Lord, in your kindness,
the sacrificial offering we make
for all your servants who sleep
    in Christ,
that, set free from the bonds
    of death
by this singular sacrifice,
they may merit eternal life.
Through Christ our Lord.

Preface for the Dead, pp.74-79.

Super oblata

Pro omnibus famulis tuis in Christo
    dormientibus
hostiam, Domine, suscipe
    benignus oblatam,
ut, per hoc sacrificium singulare
    vinculis mortis exuti,
vitam mereantur æternam.
Per Christum Dominum nostrum.

Communion Antiphon Cf. Ph 3:20-21

We await a saviour,
    the Lord Jesus Christ,
who will change our mortal bodies,
to conform with his glorified body.

Ant. ad communionem

Salvatorem exspectamus
    Dominum Iesum Christum,
qui reformabit corpus
    humilitatis nostræ,
configuratum corpori claritatis suæ.

Prayer after Communion

Through these sacrificial gifts
which we have received, O Lord,
bestow on your departed servants
    your great mercy
and, to those you have endowed
    with the grace of Baptism,
grant also the fullness of
    eternal joy.
Through Christ our Lord.

Post communionem

Multiplica, Domine,
    his sacrificiis susceptis,
super famulos tuos defunctos
    misericordiam tuam,
et, quibus donasti
    baptismi gratiam,
da eis æternorum
    plenitudinem gaudiorum.
Per Christum Dominum nostrum.

A formula of Solemn Blessing, pp.148-151, may be used.

FIRST READING

The readings below may be used for all the Masses of 2 November. Alternative
readings may be taken from the Masses of the Dead.

A reading from the prophet Isaiah 25:6-9
The Lord will destroy Death for ever.

On this mountain,
the Lord of hosts will prepare for all peoples
a banquet of rich food.

On this mountain he will remove
the mourning veil covering all peoples,
and the shroud enwrapping all nations,
he will destroy Death for ever.
The Lord will wipe away
the tears from every cheek;
he will take away his people's shame
everywhere on earth,
for the Lord has said so.
That day, it will be said: See, this is our God
in whom we hoped for salvation;
the Lord is the one in whom we hoped.
We exult and we rejoice
that he has saved us.

The word of the Lord.

Responsorial Psalm
Ps 26:1,4,7-9,13-14. R. v.1. Alt. R. v.13

R. **The Lord is my light and my help.**

Or: **I am sure I shall see the Lord's goodness
in the land of the living.**

The Lord is my light and my help;
whom shall I fear?
The Lord is the stronghold of my life;
before whom shall I shrink? R.

There is one thing I ask of the Lord,
for this I long,
to live in the house of the Lord,
all the days of my life,
to savour the sweetness of the Lord,
to behold his temple. R.

O Lord, hear my voice when I call;
have mercy and answer.
It is your face, O Lord, that I seek;
hide not your face. R.

I am sure I shall see the Lord's goodness
in the land of the living.
Hope in him, hold firm and take heart.
Hope in the Lord! R.

SECOND READING

A reading from the letter of St Paul to the Romans   5:5-11

Having died to make us righteous, is it likely that he would now fail to save us from God's anger?

Hope is not deceptive, because the love of God has been poured into our hearts by the Holy Spirit which has been given us. We were still helpless when at his appointed moment Christ died for sinful men. It is not easy to die even for a good man – though of course for someone really worthy, a man might be prepared to die – but what proves that God loves us is that Christ died for us while we were still sinners. Having died to make us righteous, is it likely that he would now fail to save us from God's anger? When we were reconciled to God by the death of his Son, we were still enemies; now that we have been reconciled, surely we may count on being saved by the life of his Son? Not merely because we have been reconciled but because we are filled with joyful trust in God, through our Lord Jesus Christ, through whom we have already gained our reconciliation.

The word of the Lord.

Gospel Acclamation   Jn 6:39

R. **Alleluia, alleluia!**

It is my Father's will, says the Lord,
that I should lose nothing
of all that he has given to me,
and that I should raise it up on the last day.

R. **Alleluia!**

GOSPEL

A reading from the holy Gospel according to Matthew   11:25-30

You have hidden these things from the learned and have revealed them to mere children.

Jesus exclaimed, 'I bless you, Father, Lord of heaven and of earth, for hiding these things from the learned and the clever and revealing them to mere children. Yes, Father, for that is what it pleased you to do. Everything has been entrusted to me by my Father; and no one knows the Son except the Father, just as no one knows the Father except the Son and those to whom the Son chooses to reveal him.

'Come to me, all you who labour and are over burdened, and I will give you rest. Shoulder my yoke and learn from me, for I am gentle and humble in heart, and you will find rest for your souls. Yes, my yoke is easy and my burden light.'

The Gospel of the Lord.

5 November

THIRTY-FIRST SUNDAY IN ORDINARY TIME

Entrance Antiphon Cf. Ps 37:22-23

FORSAKE me not, O Lord,
my God;
be not far from me!
Make haste and come to my help,
O Lord, my strong salvation!

Ant. ad introitum

NE derelinquas me,
Domine Deus meus,
ne discedas a me;
    intende in adiutorium meum,
Domine, virtus salutis meæ.

Collect

Almighty and merciful God,
by whose gift your faithful offer you
right and praiseworthy service,
grant, we pray,
that we may hasten
    without stumbling
to receive the things you
    have promised.
Through our Lord Jesus Christ,
    your Son,
who lives and reigns with you
    in the unity of the Holy Spirit,
God, for ever and ever.

Collecta

Omnipotens et misericors Deus,
    de cuius munere venit,
ut tibi a fidelibus tuis digne
    et laudabiliter serviatur,
tribue, quæsumus, nobis,
ut ad promissiones tuas
    sine offensione curramus.
Per Dominum nostrum Iesum
    Christum Filium tuum,
qui tecum vivit et regnat
    in unitate Spiritus Sancti,
Deus, per omnia sæcula sæculorum.

FIRST READING

A reading from the prophet Malachi   1:14-2:2,8-10

You have strayed from the way; you have caused many to stumble by your teaching.

I am a great king, says the Lord of hosts, and my name is feared throughout
the nations. And now, priests, this warning is for you. If you do not listen,
if you do not find it in your heart to glorify my name, says the Lord of
hosts, I will send the curse on you and curse your very blessing. You have
strayed from the way; you have caused many to stumble by your teaching.
You have destroyed the covenant of Levi, says the Lord of hosts. And so I
in my turn have made you contemptible and vile in the eyes of the whole
people in repayment for the way you have not kept to my paths but have
shown partiality in your administration.

Have we not all one Father? Did not one God create us? Why, then, do
we break faith with one another, profaning the covenant of our ancestors?

The word of the Lord.

Responsorial Psalm   Ps 130

R. **Keep my soul in peace before you, O Lord.**

O Lord, my heart is not proud
nor haughty my eyes.
I have not gone after things too great
nor marvels beyond me. R.

Truly I have set my soul
in silence and peace.
A weaned child on its mother's breast,
even so is my soul. R.

O Israel, hope in the Lord
both now and for ever. R.

SECOND READING

A reading from the first letter of St Paul to the Thessalonians   2:7-9,13

We were eager to hand over to you not only the Good News but our whole lives as well.

Like a mother feeding and looking after her own children, we felt so
devoted and protective towards you, and had come to love you so much,
that we were eager to hand over to you not only the Good News but our
whole lives as well. Let me remind you, brothers, how hard we used to
work, slaving night and day so as not to be a burden on any one of you
while we were proclaiming God's Good News to you.

Another reason why we constantly thank God for you is that as soon
as you heard the message that we brought you as God's message, you
accepted it for what it really is, God's message and not some human
thinking; and it is still a living power among you who believe it.

The word of the Lord.

Gospel Acclamation   1 S 3:9; Jn 6:68

R. **Alleluia, alleluia!**
Speak, Lord, your servant is listening:
you have the message of eternal life.
R. **Alleluia!**

Or: Mt 23:9,10

R. **Alleluia, alleluia!**
You have only one Father, and he is in heaven;
you have only one Teacher, the Christ!
R. **Alleluia!**

GOSPEL

A reading from the holy Gospel according to Matthew 23:1-12

They do not practise what they preach.

Addressing the people and his disciples Jesus said, 'The scribes and the Pharisees occupy the chair of Moses. You must therefore do what they tell you and listen to what they say; but do not be guided by what they do: since they do not practise what they preach. They tie up heavy burdens and lay them on men's shoulders, but will they lift a finger to move them? Not they! Everything they do is done to attract attention, like wearing broader phylacteries and longer tassels, like wanting to take the place of honour at banquets and the front seats in the synagogues, being greeted obsequiously in the market squares and having people call them Rabbi.

'You, however, must not allow yourselves to be called Rabbi, since you have only one Master, and you are all brothers. You must call no one on earth your father, since you have only one Father, and he is in heaven. Nor must you allow yourselves to be called teachers, for you have only one Teacher, the Christ. The greatest among you must be your servant. Anyone who exalts himself will be humbled, and anyone who humbles himself will be exalted.'

The Gospel of the Lord.

Prayer over the Offerings	Super oblata
May these sacrificial offerings, O Lord, become for you a pure oblation, and for us a holy outpouring of your mercy. Through Christ our Lord.	Fiat hoc sacrificium, Domine, oblatio tibi munda, et nobis misericordiæ tuæ sancta largitio. Per Christum Dominum nostrum.

Preface of Sundays in Ordinary Time I-VIII, pp.60-67.

Communion Antiphon Cf. Ps 15:11	Ant. ad communionem
You will show me the path of life, the fullness of joy in your presence, O Lord.	Notas mihi fecisti vias vitæ, adimplebis me lætitia cum vultu tuo, Domine.
Or: Jn 6:58	Vel:
Just as the living Father sent me and I have life because of the Father, so whoever feeds on me shall have life because of me, says the Lord.	Sicut misit me vivens Pater, et ego vivo propter Patrem, et qui manducat me, et ipse vivet propter me, dicit Dominus.

Prayer after Communion

May the working of your power,
　O Lord,
increase in us, we pray,
so that, renewed by these
　heavenly Sacraments,
we may be prepared by your gift
for receiving what they promise.
Through Christ our Lord.

Post communionem

Augeatur in nobis,
　quæsumus, Domine,
tuæ virtutis operatio,
ut, refecti cælestibus sacramentis,
ad eorum promissa capienda tuo
　munere præparemur.
Per Christum Dominum nostrum.

12 November

THIRTY-SECOND SUNDAY IN ORDINARY TIME

Entrance Antiphon　　Cf. Ps 87:3

LET my prayer come
into your presence.
Incline your ear to my cry for help,
　O Lord.

Ant. ad introitum

INTRET oratio mea
in conspectu tuo;
inclina aurem tuam ad
　precem meam, Domine.

Collect

Almighty and merciful God,
graciously keep from us all adversity,
so that, unhindered in mind
　and body alike,
we may pursue in freedom of heart
the things that are yours.
Through our Lord Jesus Christ,
　your Son,
who lives and reigns with you
　in the unity of the Holy Spirit,
God, for ever and ever.

Collecta

Omnipotens et misericors Deus,
universa nobis adversantia
　propitiatus exclude,
ut, mente et corpore pariter expediti,
quæ tua sunt liberis
　mentibus exsequamur.
Per Dominum nostrum Iesum
　Christum Filium tuum,
qui tecum vivit et regnat
　in unitate Spiritus Sancti,
Deus, per omnia sæcula sæculorum.

FIRST READING

A reading from the book of Wisdom　　6:12-16

Wisdom is found by those who look for her.

Wisdom is bright, and does not grow dim.
By those who love her she is readily seen,
and found by those who look for her.
Quick to anticipate those who desire her, she makes herself known to them.
Watch for her early and you will have no trouble;
you will find her sitting at your gates.

Even to think about her is understanding fully grown;
be on the alert for her and anxiety will quickly leave you.
She herself walks about looking for those who are worthy of her
and graciously shows herself to them as they go,
in every thought of theirs coming to meet them.

The word of the Lord.

Responsorial Psalm   Ps 62:2-8. R. v.2

R. **For you my soul is thirsting, O God, my God.**

O God, you are my God, for you I long;
for you my soul is thirsting.
My body pines for you
like a dry, weary land without water. R.

So I gaze on you in the sanctuary
to see your strength and your glory.
For your love is better than life,
my lips will speak your praise. R.

So I will bless you all my life,
in your name I will lift up my hands.
My soul shall be filled as with a banquet,
my mouth shall praise you with joy. R.

On my bed I remember you.
On you I muse through the night
for you have been my help;
in the shadow of your wings I rejoice. R.

SECOND READING

A reading from the first letter of St Paul to the Thessalonians   4:13-18
God will bring with him those who have died in Jesus.

[We want you to be quite certain, brothers, about those who have died, to
make sure that you do not grieve about them, like the other people who
have no hope. We believe that Jesus died and rose again, and that it will be
the same for those who have died in Jesus: God will bring them with him.]
We can tell you this from the Lord's own teaching, that any of us who are
left alive until the Lord's coming will not have any advantage over those
who have died. At the trumpet of God, the voice of the archangel will call
out the command and the Lord himself will come down from heaven;
those who have died in Christ will be the first to rise, and then those of us
who are still alive will be taken up in the clouds, together with them, to

meet the Lord in the air. So we shall stay with the Lord for ever. With such thoughts as these you should comfort one another.

[The word of the Lord.]

Shorter Form, verses 13-14. Read between [ ]

Gospel Acclamation   Mt 24:42,44

R. **Alleluia, alleluia!**
Stay awake and stand ready,
because you do not know the hour
when the Son of Man is coming.
R. **Alleluia!**

GOSPEL

A reading from the holy Gospel according to Matthew   25:1-13

The bridegroom is here! Go out and meet him.

Jesus told this parable to his disciples: 'The kingdom of heaven will be like this: Ten bridesmaids took their lamps and went to meet the bridegroom. Five of them were foolish and five were sensible: the foolish ones did take their lamps, but they brought no oil, whereas the sensible ones took flasks of oil as well as their lamps. The bridegroom was late, and they all grew drowsy and fell asleep. But at midnight there was a cry, "The bridegroom is here! Go out and meet him." At this, all those bridesmaids woke up and trimmed their lamps, and the foolish ones said to the sensible ones, "Give us some of your oil: our lamps are going out." But they replied, "There may not be enough for us and for you; you had better go to those who sell it and buy some for yourselves." They had gone off to buy it when the bridegroom arrived. Those who were ready went in with him to the wedding hall and the door was closed. The other bridesmaids arrived later. "Lord, Lord," they said "open the door for us." But he replied, "I tell you solemnly, I do not know you." So stay awake, because you do not know either the day or the hour.'

The Gospel of the Lord.

Prayer over the Offerings	Super oblata
Look with favour, we pray, O Lord, upon the sacrificial gifts offered here, that, celebrating in mystery the Passion of your Son, we may honour it with loving devotion. Through Christ our Lord.	Sacrificiis præsentibus, Domine, quæsumus, intende placatus, ut, quod passionis Filii tui mysterio gerimus, pio consequamur affectu. Per Christum Dominum nostrum.

Preface of Sundays in Ordinary Time I-VIII, pp.60-67.

Communion Antiphon Cf. Ps 22:1-2

The Lord is my shepherd;
  there is nothing I shall want.
Fresh and green are the pastures
  where he gives me repose,
near restful waters he leads me.

Or: Cf. Lk 24:35

The disciples recognised the Lord
  Jesus in the breaking of bread.

Prayer after Communion

Nourished by this sacred gift,
  O Lord,
we give you thanks and beseech
  your mercy,
that, by the pouring forth
  of your Spirit,
the grace of integrity may endure
in those your heavenly power
  has entered.
Through Christ our Lord.

Ant. ad communionem

Dominus regit me,
  et nihil mihi deerit;
in loco pascuæ ibi me collocavit,
super aquam refectionis
  educavit me.

Vel:

Cognoverunt discipuli Dominum
  Iesum in fractione panis.

Post communionem

Gratias tibi, Domine, referimus
  sacro munere vegetati,
tuam clementiam implorantes,
ut, per infusionem Spiritus tui,
in quibus cælestis virtus introivit,
sinceritatis gratia perseveret.
Per Christum Dominum nostrum.

19 November

THIRTY-THIRD SUNDAY IN ORDINARY TIME

Entrance Antiphon Jr 29:11,12,14

THE Lord said: I think thoughts
  of peace and not of affliction.
You will call upon me,
  and I will answer you,
and I will lead back your captives
  from every place.

Ant. ad introitum

DICIT Dominus:
  Ego cogito cogitationes pacis
  et non afflictionis;
invocabitis me, et ego exaudiam vos,
et reducam captivitatem vestram
  de cunctis locis.

Collect

Grant us, we pray, O Lord our God,
the constant gladness of being
    devoted to you,
for it is full and lasting happiness
to serve with constancy
the author of all that is good.
Through our Lord Jesus Christ,
    your Son,
who lives and reigns with you
    in the unity of the Holy Spirit,
God, for ever and ever.

Collecta

Da nobis, quæsumus,
    Domine Deus noster,
in tua semper devotione gaudere,
quia perpetua est et plena felicitas,
si bonorum omnium iugiter
    serviamus auctori.
Per Dominum nostrum Iesum
    Christum Filium tuum,
qui tecum vivit et regnat
    in unitate Spiritus Sancti,
Deus, per omnia sæcula sæculorum.

FIRST READING

A reading from the book of Proverbs   31:10-13,19-20,30-31

A perfect wife - who can find her?

A perfect wife – who can find her?
She is far beyond the price of pearls.
Her husband's heart has confidence in her,
from her he will derive no little profit.
Advantage and not hurt she brings him
all the days of her life.
She is always busy with wool and with flax,
she does her work with eager hands.
She sets her hands to the distaff,
her fingers grasp the spindle.
She holds out her hands to the poor,
she opens her arms to the needy.
Charm is deceitful, and beauty empty;
the woman who is wise is the one to praise.
Give her a share in what her hands have worked for,
and let her works tell her praises at the city gates.

    The word of the Lord.

Responsorial Psalm   Ps 127:1-5. R. v.1

R. **O blessed are those who fear the Lord.**

O blessed are those who fear the Lord
and walk in his ways!
By the labour of your hands you shall eat.
You will be happy and prosper. R.

Your wife like a fruitful vine
in the heart of your house;
your children like shoots of the olive,
around your table. R.

Indeed thus shall be blessed
the man who fears the Lord.
May the Lord bless you from Sion
in a happy Jerusalem
all the days of your life. R.

SECOND READING

A reading from the first letter of St Paul to the Thessalonians   5:1-6

Let not the Day of the Lord overtake you like a thief.

You will not be expecting us to write anything to you, brothers, about
'times and seasons', since you know very well that the Day of the Lord is
going to come like a thief in the night. It is when people are saying, 'How
quiet and peaceful it is' that the worst suddenly happens, as suddenly as
labour pains come on a pregnant woman; and there will be no way for
anybody to evade it.

But it is not as if you live in the dark, my brothers, for that Day to
overtake you like a thief. No, you are all sons of light and sons of the day:
we do not belong to the night or to darkness, so we should not go on
sleeping, as everyone else does, but stay wide awake and sober.

The word of the Lord.

Gospel Acclamation   Rv 2:10

R. **Alleluia, alleluia!**
Even if you have to die, says the Lord,
keep faithful, and I will give you
the crown of life.
R. **Alleluia!**

Or: Jn 15:4,5

R. **Alleluia, alleluia!**
Make your home in me, as I make mine in you,
says the Lord.
Whoever remains in me bears fruit in plenty.
R. **Alleluia!**

GOSPEL

A reading from the holy Gospel according to Matthew   25:14-30

You have been faithful in small things; come and join in your master's happiness.

[Jesus spoke this parable to his disciples: 'The kingdom of heaven is like
a man on his way abroad who summoned his servants and entrusted his
property to them. To one he gave five talents, to another two, to a third
one; each in proportion to his ability. Then he set out.] The man who had
received the five talents promptly went and traded with them and made five
more. The man who had received two made two more in the same way. But
the man who had received one went off and dug a hole in the ground and
hid his master's money. [Now a long time after, the master of those servants
came back and went through his accounts with them. The man who had
received the five talents came forward bringing five more. "Sir," he said "you
entrusted me with five talents; here are five more that I have made."] His
master said to him, "Well done, good and faithful servant; you have shown
you can be faithful in small things, I will trust you with greater; come and
join in your master's happiness." Next the man with the two talents came
forward. "Sir," he said "you entrusted me with two talents; here are two more
that I have made." His master said to him, "Well done, good and faithful
servant; you have shown you can be faithful in small things, I will trust you
with greater; come and join in your master's happiness." Last came forward
the man who had the one talent. "Sir," said he "I had heard you were a hard
man, reaping where you have not sown and gathering where you have not
scattered; so I was afraid, and I went off and hid your talent in the ground.
Here it is; it was yours, you have it back." But his master answered him, "You
wicked and lazy servant! So you knew that I reap where I have not sown and

gather where I have not scattered? Well then, you should have deposited
my money with the bankers, and on my return I would have recovered my
capital with interest. So now, take the talent from him and give it to the man
who has the five talents. For to everyone who has will be given more, and he
will have more than enough; but from the man who has not, even what he
has will be taken away. As for this good-for-nothing servant, throw him out
into the dark, where there will be weeping and grinding of teeth.'"

| [The Gospel of the Lord.]

Shorter Form, verses 14-15, 19-20. Read between [ ]

Prayer over the Offerings

Grant, O Lord, we pray,
that what we offer in the sight
   of your majesty
may obtain for us the grace
   of being devoted to you
and gain us the prize
   of everlasting happiness.
Through Christ our Lord.

Super oblata

Concede, quæsumus, Domine,
ut oculis tuæ maiestatis
   munus oblatum
et gratiam nobis
   devotionis obtineat,
et effectum beatæ
   perennitatis acquirat.
Per Christum Dominum nostrum.

Preface of Sundays in Ordinary Time I-VIII, pp.60-67.

Communion Antiphon   Ps 72:28

To be near God is my happiness,
to place my hope in God the Lord.
Or: Mk 11:23-24
Amen, I say to you:
   Whatever you ask in prayer,
believe that you will receive,
and it shall be given to you,
   says the Lord.

Ant. ad communionem

Mihi autem adhærere Deo bonum est,
ponere in Domino Deo spem meam.
Vel:
Amen dico vobis,
   quidquid orantes petitis,
credite quia accipietis, et fiet vobis,
   dicit Dominus.

Prayer after Communion

We have partaken of the gifts
   of this sacred mystery,
humbly imploring, O Lord,
that what your Son commanded
   us to do
in memory of him
may bring us growth in charity.
Through Christ our Lord.

Post communionem

Sumpsimus, Domine,
   sacri dona mysterii,
humiliter deprecantes,
ut, quæ in sui commemorationem
nos Filius tuus facere præcepit,
in nostræ proficiant
   caritatis augmentum.
Per Christum Dominum nostrum.

26 November

OUR LORD JESUS CHRIST, KING OF THE UNIVERSE

Solemnity

Entrance Antiphon Rv 5:12; 1:6	Ant. ad introitum

Entrance Antiphon   Rv 5:12; 1:6

HOW worthy is the Lamb
who was slain,
to receive power and divinity,
and wisdom and strength
   and honour.
To him belong glory and power
   for ever and ever.

Ant. ad introitum

DIGNUS est Agnus,
qui occisus est,
accipere virtutem et divinitatem
et sapientiam et fortitudinem
   et honorem.
Ipsi gloria et imperium
   in sæcula sæculorum.

The Gloria in excelsis (Glory to God in the highest) is said.

Collect

Almighty ever-living God,
whose will is to restore all things
in your beloved Son,
   the King of the universe,
grant, we pray,
that the whole creation,
   set free from slavery,
may render your majesty service
and ceaselessly proclaim
   your praise.
Through our Lord Jesus Christ,
   your Son,
who lives and reigns with you
   in the unity of the Holy Spirit,
God, for ever and ever.

Collecta

Omnipotens sempiterne Deus,
qui in dilecto Filio tuo,
   universorum Rege,
omnia instaurare voluisti,
concede propitius,
ut tota creatura,
   a servitute liberata,
tuæ maiestati deserviat ac te sine
   fine collaudet.
Per Dominum nostrum Iesum
   Christum Filium tuum,
qui tecum vivit et regnat in unitate
   Spiritus Sancti,
Deus, per omnia sæcula sæculorum.

FIRST READING

A reading from the prophet Ezekiel   34:11-12,15-17

As for you, my sheep, I will judge between sheep and sheep.

The Lord says this: I am going to look after my flock myself and keep all of it in view. As a shepherd keeps all his flock in view when he stands up in the middle of his scattered sheep, so shall I keep my sheep in view. I shall rescue them from wherever they have been scattered during the mist and darkness. I myself will pasture my sheep, I myself will show them where to rest – it is the Lord who speaks. I shall look for the lost one, bring back the stray, bandage the wounded and make the weak strong. I shall watch over the fat and healthy. I shall be a true shepherd to them.

As for you, my sheep, the Lord says this: I will judge between sheep and sheep, between rams and he-goats.

The word of the Lord.

Responsorial Psalm   Ps 22:1-3,5-6. R. v.1

R. **The Lord is my shepherd;**
there is nothing I shall want.

The Lord is my shepherd;
there is nothing I shall want.
Fresh and green are the pastures
where he gives me repose. R.

Near restful waters he leads me,
to revive my drooping spirit.
He guides me along the right path;
he is true to his name. R.

You have prepared a banquet for me
in the sight of my foes.
My head you have anointed with oil;
my cup is overflowing. R.

Surely goodness and kindness shall follow
me all the days of my life.
In the Lord's own house shall I dwell
for ever and ever. R.

SECOND READING

A reading from the first letter of St Paul to the Corinthians   15:20-26,28

He will hand over the kingdom to God the Father; so that God may be all in all.

Christ has been raised from the dead, the first-fruits of all who have fallen asleep. Death came through one man and in the same way the resurrection of the dead has come through one man. Just as all men die in Adam, so all men will be brought to life in Christ; but all of them in their proper order: Christ as the first-fruits and then, after the coming of Christ, those who belong to him. After that will come the end, when he hands over the kingdom to God the Father, having done away with every sovereignty, authority and power. For he must be king until he has put all his enemies under his feet and the last of the enemies to be destroyed is death. And when everything is subjected to him, then the Son himself will be subject in his turn to the One who subjected all things to him, so that God may be all in all.

The word of the Lord.

Gospel Acclamation   Mk 11:10

R. **Alleluia, alleluia!**

Blessings on him who comes in the name of the Lord!
Blessings on the coming kingdom of our father David!

R. **Alleluia!**

GOSPEL

A reading from the holy Gospel according to Matthew   25:31-46

He will take his seat on his throne of glory, and he will separate men one from another.

Jesus said to his disciples: 'When the Son of Man comes in his glory, escorted by all the angels, then he will take his seat on his throne of glory. All the nations will be assembled before him and he will separate men one from another as the shepherd separates sheep from goats. He will place the sheep on his right hand and the goats on his left. Then the King will say to those on his right hand, "Come, you whom my Father has blessed, take for your heritage the kingdom prepared for you since the foundation of the world. For I was hungry and you gave me food; I was thirsty and you gave me drink; I was a stranger and you made me welcome; naked and you clothed me, sick and you visited me, in prison and you came to see me." Then the virtuous will say to him in reply, "Lord, when did we see you hungry and feed you; or thirsty and give you drink? When did we see you a stranger and make you welcome; naked and clothe you; sick or in prison and go to see you?" And the King will answer, "I tell you solemnly, in so far as you did this to one of the least of these brothers of mine, you did it to me." Next he will say to those on his left hand, "Go away from me, with your curse upon you, to the eternal fire prepared for the devil and his angels. For I was hungry and you never gave me food; I was thirsty and you never gave me anything to drink; I was a stranger and you never made me welcome, naked and you never clothed me, sick and in prison and you never visited me." Then it will be their turn to ask, "Lord, when did we see you hungry or thirsty, a stranger or naked, sick or in prison, and did not come to your help?" Then he will answer, "I tell you solemnly, in so far as you neglected to do this to one of the least of these, you neglected to do it to me." And they will go away to eternal punishment, and the virtuous to eternal life.'

The Gospel of the Lord.

The Creed is said.

Prayer over the Offerings

As we offer you, O Lord,
  the sacrifice
by which the human race
  is reconciled to you,
we humbly pray
that your Son himself may bestow
  on all nations
the gifts of unity and peace.
Through Christ our Lord.

Super oblata

Hostiam tibi, Domine,
humanæ reconciliationis
  offerentes, suppliciter deprecamur,
ut ipse Filius tuus cunctis gentibus
unitatis et pacis dona concedat.
Qui vivit et regnat
  in sæcula sæculorum.

Preface: Christ, King of the Universe.

It is truly right and just,
  our duty and our salvation,
always and everywhere
  to give you thanks,
Lord, holy Father,
  almighty and eternal God.

For you anointed your Only
  Begotten Son,
our Lord Jesus Christ,
  with the oil of gladness
as eternal Priest and King
  of all creation,

Præfatio: De Christo universorum Rege.

Vere dignum et iustum est,
  æquum et salutare,
nos tibi semper
  et ubique gratias agere:
Domine, sancte Pater,
  omnipotens æterne Deus:

Qui Unigenitum Filium tuum,
Dominum nostrum
  Iesum Christum,
Sacerdotem æternum
  et universorum Regem,
oleo exsultationis unxisti:

so that, by offering himself
   on the altar of the Cross
as a spotless sacrifice
   to bring us peace,
he might accomplish the mysteries
   of human redemption
and, making all created things
   subject to his rule,
he might present to the immensity
   of your majesty
an eternal and universal kingdom,
a kingdom of truth and life,
a kingdom of holiness and grace,
a kingdom of justice, love and peace.

And so, with Angels and Archangels,
with Thrones and Dominions,
and with all the hosts and Powers
   of heaven,
we sing the hymn of your glory,
as without end we acclaim:

Holy, Holy, Holy Lord God of hosts...

ut, seipsum in ara crucis
hostiam immaculatam
   et pacificam offerens,
redemptionis humanæ
   sacramenta perageret:
et, suo subiectis imperio
   omnibus creaturis,
æternum et universale regnum
immensæ tuæ traderet maiestati:
regnum veritatis et vitæ;
regnum sanctitatis et gratiæ;
regnum iustitiæ,
   amoris et pacis.

Et ideo cum Angelis et Archangelis,
cum Thronis et Dominationibus,
cumque omni
   militia cælestis exercitus,
hymnum gloriæ tuæ canimus,
sine fine dicentes:

Sanctus, Sanctus, Sanctus . . .

Communion Antiphon Ps 28:10-11

The Lord sits as King for ever.
The Lord will bless his people
   with peace.

Ant. ad communionem

Sedebit Dominus Rex in æternum;
Dominus benedicet populo suo
   in pace.

Prayer after Communion

Having received the food
   of immortality,
we ask, O Lord,
that, glorying in obedience
to the commands of Christ,
   the King of the universe,
we may live with him eternally
   in his heavenly Kingdom.
Who lives and reigns
   for ever and ever.

Post communionem

Immortalitatis alimoniam consecuti,
quæsumus, Domine,
ut, qui Christi Regis universorum
gloriamur obœdire mandatis,
cum ipso in cælesti regno sine fine
   vivere valeamus.
Qui vivit et regnat
   in sæcula sæculorum.

RITE OF EUCHARISTIC EXPOSITION AND BENEDICTION

The service of Benediction developed during the Middle Ages during the Corpus Christi processions in which the Blessed Sacrament was held up for veneration. The service was subsequently used at other times throughout the year as an opportunity to give thanks for the Mass and adore Christ present under the form of bread.

Today, the Church encourages this rite to be celebrated in the context of a longer period of reading, prayer and reflection.

Exposition

First of all, the minister exposes the Blessed Sacrament while a hymn is sung, during which he incenses the Sacrament. The following or another hymn may be chosen.

O saving Victim, opening wide The gate of heav'n to man below: Our foes press on from every side: Thine aid supply, thy strength bestow.	O salutaris hostia, Quæ cæli pandis ostium; Bella premunt hostilia, Da robur, fer auxilium.
To thy great name be endless praise, Immortal Godhead, One in Three: O grant us endless length of days In our true native land with thee. Amen.	Uni Trinoque Domino Sit sempiterna gloria, Qui vitam sine termino Nobis donet in patria. Amen.

Adoration

A time for silent prayer, readings from Scripture, litanies or other prayers and hymns may be used. On some occasions, the Prayer of the Church might be said or sung.

Of the Glorious Body Telling	Pange Lingua
Of the glorious Body telling, O my tongue, its mysteries sing, And the Blood, all price excelling, Which the world's eternal King, In a noble womb once dwelling Shed for the world's ransoming.	Pange lingua gloriosi Corporis mysterium, Sanguinisque pretiosi, Quem in mundi pretium Fructus ventris generosi, Rex effudit gentium.

Given for us, for us descending,
Of a Virgin to proceed,
Man with man in
   converse blending,
Scattered he the Gospel seed,
Till his sojourn drew to ending,
Which he closed in wondrous deed.

At the last great Supper lying
Circled by his brethren's band,
Meekly with the law complying,
First he finished its command
Then, immortal Food supplying,
Gave himself with his own hand.

Word made Flesh,
   by word he maketh
Very bread his Flesh to be;
Man in wine Christ's Blood
   partaketh,
And if senses fail to see,
Faith alone the true heart waketh
To behold the mystery.

Nobis datus, nobis natus
Ex intacta Virgine,
Et in mundo conversatus,
Sparso verbi semine,
Sui moras incolatus
Miro clausit ordine.

In supremae nocte cœnæ
Recumbens cum fratribus,
Observata lege plene
Cibis in legalibus,
Cibum turbæ duodenæ
Se dat suis manibus.

Verbum caro, panem verum
Verbo carnem efficit,
Fitque sanguis Christi merum,
Et, si sensus deficit,
Ad firmandum cor sincerum
Sola fides sufficit.

Sweet Sacrament Divine

Sweet Sacrament divine,
Hid in thine earthly home;
Lo! round thy lowly shrine,
With suppliant hearts we come;
Jesus, to thee our voice we raise
In songs of love and heartfelt praise:
Sweet Sacrament divine. (repeat)

Sweet Sacrament of peace,
Dear home of every heart,
Where restless yearnings cease
And sorrows all depart;
There in thine ear, all trustfully
We tell our tale of misery;
Sweet Sacrament of peace. (repeat)

Sweet Sacrament of rest,
Ark from the ocean's roar,
Within thy shelter blest
Soon may we reach the shore;
Save us, for still the tempest raves,
Save, lest we sink beneath the waves:
Sweet Sacrament of rest. (repeat)

Sweet Sacrament divine,
Earth's light and jubilee,
In thy far depths doth shine
Thy Godhead's majesty;
Sweet light, so shine on us, we pray,
That earthly joys may fade away:
Sweet Sacrament divine. (repeat)

(Francis Stanfield)

Benediction

Towards the end of the exposition, the priest or deacon goes to the altar, genuflects and kneels. Then this hymn or a suitable alternative is sung, during which the minister incenses the sacrament.

Therefore we, before him bending	Tantum ergo Sacramentum
This great Sacrament revere	Veneremur cernui,
Types and shadows have their ending,	Et antiquum documentum Novo cedat ritui;
For the newer rite is here	Præstet fides supplementum
Faith, our outward sense befriending,	Sensuum defectui.
Makes the inward vision clear.	
Glory let us give, and blessing	Genitori, Genitoque
To the Father and the Son;	Laus et iubilatio.
Honour, might, and praise addressing,	Salus, honor, virtus quoque
While eternal ages run;	Sit et benedictio;
Ever too his love confessing,	Procedenti ab utroque
Who, from both, with both is one.	Compar sit laudatio.
Amen.	Amen.

The minister then says the following prayer (or a suitable alternative)

Let us pray.	Oremus.
Lord Jesus Christ,	Deus, qui nobis sub
you gave us the eucharist	sacramento mirabili
as the memorial of your suffering and death.	passionis tuæ memoriam reliquisti: tribue, quæsumus,
May our worship of this sacrament of your body and blood	ita nos Corporis et Sanguinis tui sacra mysteria venerari,
help us to experience the salvation you won for us	ut redemptionis tuæ fructum in nobis
and the peace of the kingdom	iugiter sentiamus.
where you live with the Father and the Holy Spirit,	Qui vivis et regnas in sæcula sæculorum.
God, for ever and ever.	℟. Amen.
℟. **Amen.**	

The Priest or Deacon now puts on the humeral veil and blesses the congregation with the Blessed Sacrament.

The Divine Praises formerly said at this point may more properly be included within the period of adoration.

The Divine Praises

Blessed be God.
Blessed be his holy Name.
Blessed be Jesus Christ, true God and true Man.
Blessed be the name of Jesus.
Blessed be his most Sacred Heart.
Blessed be his most Precious Blood.
Blessed be Jesus in the most holy Sacrament of the Altar.
Blessed be the Holy Spirit, the Paraclete.
Blessed be the great Mother of God, Mary, most holy.
Blessed be her holy and Immaculate Conception.
Blessed be her glorious Assumption.
Blessed be the name of Mary, Virgin and Mother.
Blessed be St Joseph, her spouse most chaste.
Blessed be God in his Angels and in his Saints.

Reposition

Immediately after the Blessed Sacrament is reposed in the tabernacle, the following may be sung:

Ant. Let us adore for ever
    the most holy Sacrament.

Ps. O praise the Lord,
    all you nations,
Acclaim him, all you peoples!
For his mercy is confirmed upon us
and the truth of the Lord
    remains for ever.

Glory be to the Father,
    and to the Son
and to the Holy Spirit.
As it was in the beginning, is now
and ever shall be,
    world without end. Amen.

Ant. Let us adore for ever the most
    holy Sacrament.

Ant. Adoremus in æternum
    sanctissimum Sacramentum.

Ps. Laudate Dominum,
    omnes gentes:
laudate eum, omnes populi:
Quoniam confirmata est super
    nos misericordia eius:
et veritas Domini manet
    in æternum.

Gloria Patri, et Filio,
    et Spiritui Sancto.
Sicut erat in principio,
    et nunc, et semper,
et in sæcula sæculorum. Amen.

Ant. Adoremus in æternum
    sanctissimum Sacramentum.

An alternative acclamation:

O Sacrament most holy,
    O Sacrament divine!
All praise, and all thanksgiving,
Be every moment thine!